GREAT READINGS IN CLINICAL SCIENCE

ESSENTIAL SELECTIONS FOR MENTAL HEALTH PROFESSIONALS

GREAT READINGS IN CLINICAL SCIENCE

ESSENTIAL SELECTIONS FOR MENTAL HEALTH PROFESSIONALS

Scott O. Lilienfeld
Emory University

William T. O'Donohue
University of Nevada, Reno

Boston   Columbus   Indianapolis   New York   San Francisco   Upper Saddle River
Amsterdam   Cape Town   Dubai   London   Madrid   Milan Munich   Paris   Montreal   Toronto
Delhi   Mexico City   Sao Paulo   Sydney   Hong Kong   Seoul   Singapore   Taipei   Tokyo

Editor-in-Chief: Jessica Mosher
Acquisitions Editor: Susan Hartman
Editorial Assistant: Alexandra Mitton
Executive Marketing Manager: Nicole Kunzmann
Marketing Assistant: Jessica Warren
Production Manager: Kathy Sleys
Production Project Manager: Maggie Brobeck
Editorial Production and Composition Service: Hemalatha/Integra Software Services
Creative Director: Jayne Conte
Cover Designer: Bruce Kenselaar

Credits and acknowledgments borrowed from other sources and reproduced, with permission, in this textbook appear on the appropriate page within the text.

Many of the designations by manufacturers and seller to distinguish their products are claimed as trademarks. Where those designations appear in this book, and the publisher was aware of a trademark claim, the designations have been printed in initial caps or all caps.

Library of Congress Cataloging-in-Publication Data
Great readings in clinical science : essential selections for mental health professionals /
[edited by] Scott O. Lilienfeld, William T. O'Donohue.
    p. cm.
Includes bibliographical references.
ISBN-13: 978-0-205-69803-5 (alk. paper)
ISBN-10: 0-205-69803-4 (alk. paper)
1. Clinical psychology.   I. Lilienfeld, Scott O.,   II. O'Donohue, William T.
[DNLM: 1. Psychology, Clinical—Collected Works.   2. Psychological Theory—
Collected Works. WM 105]
RC467.G697 2012
616.89—dc23

2011017884

10 9 8 7 6 5 4 3 2 1—EB—15 14 13 12 11

ISBN-10:   0-205-69803-4
ISBN-13: 978-0-205-69803-5

CONTENTS

PREFACE

The past several decades have witnessed a continuing divide between researchers and clinicians in the diverse fields of mental health: clinical psychology, counseling psychology, social work, psychiatry, and psychiatric nursing. This schism is marked by a striking disparity between scientific evidence and everyday clinical practice. Much of this "scientist–practitioner gap" reflects a seeming absence of consensus regarding what kinds of evidence should "count" when evaluating claims. Some people—whom psychiatrist Paul McHugh calls "empiricists"—believe that evidence derived from carefully controlled studies should be the major arbiter of questions regarding the causes, assessment, diagnosis, treatment, and prevention of mental disorder. In contrast, others—whom McHugh calls "romantics"—believe that subjective and informal data from clinical impressions should be the major arbiter of such questions. In fact, both empiricism and romanticism have crucial roles to play in clinical practice and research, but many beginning students are confused about what these roles should be.

Much of the problem stems from the fact that undergraduate and graduate programs typically do a solid job of teaching students about the scientific evidence bearing on mental illness, but they rarely explain *why* a scientific approach is essential, or what implementing such an approach actually entails. More broadly, these programs rarely provide students with the thinking skills needed to scientifically evaluate claims about the assessment, diagnosis, causes, and treatment of mental disorders. As a consequence, students often know *what* to think, but not *how* to think, about clinical psychology and allied fields.

Moreover, many undergraduates and beginning graduate students are understandably resistant to a scientific approach to clinical psychology, because this approach is often portrayed as a series of pronouncements from established authorities ("Researchers have found that . . ."; "Treatment X has been found to be empirically supported") rather than as an evolving and self-correcting process of acquiring and evaluating practical knowledge that can be used to help real people with real problems. A scientific approach consists of a set of systematic safeguards against human error, and a willingness to acknowledge that we might be wrong. In essence, a scientific approach to clinical psychology is a prescription for *modesty*—modesty in our beliefs and claims. Such modesty is an essential attitude and is highlighted in what's often thought of as the Hippocratic oath. "First, do no harm." Yet a scientific approach is rarely taught or described this way; to the contrary, students in training who express skepticism regarding a scientific approach to clinical psychology may be met with condescension, even derision. Moreover, teachers often portray a scientific approach to clinical psychology as dry, static, and dull rather than what it is in practice—exciting, dynamic, and fun.

Along with the marked disunity within our field, the training of students in clinical psychology, counseling psychology, social work, and allied areas has become increasingly fragmented over the past several decades. Any two students graduating from PhD or PsyD programs accredited by the American Psychological Association (APA) can have surprisingly little shared knowledge concerning the core principles of clinical science. Moreover, many students emerge from their programs with few skills for evaluating claims scientifically, even though the capacity to operate as an informed consumer of research evidence is an avowed goal of both "scientist-practitioner" and "clinical science" programs (most of which award the PhD) and "scholar-professional" programs (most of which award the PsyD). Even many students who administer scientifically based treatments may do so largely because they've been told to do so (sometimes jokingly called "eminence-based practice"), not because they grasp the body of research evidence and theory that underpins these treatments (evidence-based practice).

Understandably, many students in clinical psychology and allied domains leave their programs confused about the state of their discipline. Some may assume that scientific research is largely or entirely irrelevant to their clinical work, and others may even take this bewildering state of affairs as an implicit license to "do almost anything" in their practice. On the research front, the increasing "hyper-specialization" of graduate training has made the broad-minded clinical scientist a rarity in many university settings. With the relatively recent deaths of Paul Meehl, Robyn Dawes, Donald Campbell, Lee J. Cronbach, David Lykken, Jane Loevinger, Michael Mahoney, Brendan Maher, and several other giants, precious few "big picture" thinkers in our field remain.

This edited book of readings, *Great Readings in Clinical Science: Essential Selections for Mental Health Professionals*, is an attempt to remedy the current state of affairs. The 23 readings we've selected for inclusion are diverse in scope and content, but they all have one thing in common: They're designed to help psychology students and other mental health professionals in training to think scientifically about their subject matter. These readings are appropriate for undergraduates, graduate students, mental health practitioners, researchers, and instructors. These readings explain what science is, why science is essential to clinical psychology, and how science can help them to minimize—although not eliminate—their risk for errors in clinical practice and research. They show how a scientific approach to clinical psychology can profitably be applied to the understanding and alleviation of psychological suffering, and how such an approach is more effective and humane than one that doesn't rely on science. At the same time, these readings demonstrate to students that their informal clinical impressions have an invaluable place in practice and research, but that these impressions must ultimately be subjected to rigorous scientific testing.

The readings in this text derive from a variety of sources, including some that are not readily accessible using most computer databases. They span over a half century of the best thinking in clinical psychology, psychiatry, social work, and related domains, and come from some of the great minds of our field, including Paul Meehl, Richard McFall, Robyn Dawes, Lee Sechrest, Brendan Maher, Hal Arkes, David Faust, and Kenneth Kendler. We've tried to mix more formal academic readings with less formal, even occasionally humorous, selections. The book is divided into five broad parts: (1) The Scientific Attitude: An Introduction; (2) Clinical Psychology: Why a Scientific Approach Matters; (3) Clinical Science as a Safeguard Against Human Error; (4) Interpreting Evidence in Clinical Psychology; and (5) Thinking Scientifically About Assessment and Psychotherapy. Each of these parts is preceded by an introduction by the editors that (a) sets the stage for that part by exposing readers to core principles, concepts, and terms and (b) previews and summarizes each of the readings in that part.

We are deeply grateful to a number of individuals who were essential to the preparation of this book. In particular, we thank our editor at Pearson, Susan Hartman, for her invaluable advice, support, and encouragement throughout the project. As always, Susan was a pleasure to work with. We also thank Alexandra Mitton at Pearson for her terrific—and patient—assistance with organizing the readings, sorting through permissions, and finalizing the product. Finally, we thank Linda Goddard at the Cumming Foundation for her outstanding help with securing permissions, and Hemalatha and Ashwin Krishnan at Integra for their helpful editorial assistance.

We very much hope that you will find *Great Readings in Clinical Science: Essential Selections for Mental Health Professionals* to be not only an indispensible guide to thinking critically about mental health practice and research, but also an enjoyable and enlightening reading experience. We welcome your comments and feedback on the readings for future editions, and look forward to hearing from you.

Scott O. Lilienfeld, PhD
Emory University
slilien@emory.edu

William T. O'Donohue, PhD
University of Nevada, Reno
wto@unr.edu

GREAT READINGS IN CLINICAL SCIENCE

ESSENTIAL SELECTIONS FOR MENTAL HEALTH PROFESSIONALS

PART ONE

The Scientific Attitude: An Introduction

Why, readers might ask, should we use science to attempt to answer the central questions of clinical psychology, such as, "What causes this psychological problem?"; "How can we best measure this problem?"; "What's the most effective treatment for this problem?"; and "How can we prevent this problem from occurring?" Our answer is twofold.

First, science is the most effective problem-solving strategy that we humans have devised (Lilienfeld & O'Donohue, 2007). Despite its imperfections, in the last three centuries it has resulted in an unprecedented growth of knowledge and an unprecedented development of technologies that have helped to solve real-world problems. Thus, as clinical psychologists, we should adopt a scientific posture, not because it's flawless (it isn't) because it's worked so well in the past. Our clients desperately need us to possess knowledge that works—and science has proven itself again and again to be the best means of acquiring this knowledge. Science results in slow but steady progress by eliminating errors in our web of beliefs, and such progress means better outcomes for our clients. Thus, the "best bet" to providing answers to the key questions of clinical psychology is scientific inquiry (O'Donohue & Lilienfeld, 2007).

Second, there's no other viable candidate. There's no "plan b" or good alternative to science, as no other strategy even comes close to science with respect to problem-solving effectiveness. Our field at times seems to be confused about this issue. The ethics code of the American Psychological Association (APA, 2002) refers to "scientific and professional knowledge," but it never explicates what "professional knowledge" is. Nevertheless, if we trace back how some problem was solved, such as why children tantrum (see Patterson, 1995), we know the answer—intermittent reinforcement by parents and others—because others have conducted scientific inquiries before us. It may be tempting to take another path—such as forming beliefs based on reading the writings of an authority figure or on several anecdotes overheard at a weekend workshop—perhaps because doing so is easier or because others do it. But the past problem-solving effectiveness of these strategies pales compared to that of science.

Science, simply put, is the best corrective to human fallibility in belief formation. It's human to err, as the old saying reminds us. In our beliefs, we as clinical psychologists and other mental health professionals have erred in the past and surely will continue to err in the future. But it's our duty as professionals to possess expertise—specialized knowledge—because our clients are relying on this knowledge to reduce their suffering.

Yet the fields of clinical psychology and mental health practice at large have often been too slow and sporadic in their acceptance of a scientific attitude (Dawes, 1994; Lilienfeld, Lynn, & Lohr, 2003). Too often, practitioners prescribe a therapy based largely on anecdote or subjective impressions, while ignoring replicated evidence from randomized controlled trials. Practitioners may administer an assessment device simply

Sagan, C. (1995). Wonder and skepticism. *Skeptical Inquirer*, *19*(1), 24–30.

Feynman, R. (1974, June). Cargo cult science. *Engineering and Science*, *37*(7), 10–13.

Shermer, M. (1994). How thinking goes wrong: Twenty-five fallacies that can lead us to believe weird things. *Skeptic*, *2*(3), 42–49.
    Schafersman, S. D. (1994). An introduction to science: Scientific thinking and the scientific method. *Free Inquiry Website*.

Hempel, C. (1966). The case of Dr. Semmelweis. In *Philosophy of natural science*. Englewood Cliffs, NJ: Prentice Hall.

because it's named "Harvard Self-Esteem Inventory" without examining psychometric data on whether it's assessing what it claims to measure.

It's not entirely clear why the field of clinical psychology seems to sort itself into those who value and use science and those who don't. Almost surely, there are deep-seated philosophical differences between the camps, such as the belief on some people's part that there are legitimate paths to knowledge other than science. For others, resistance to science may stem from other reasons: After all, science takes hard work (such as a lot of careful reading); science can require painful change (science tells us that we sometimes need to revise our beliefs); and science can involve long and extensive training (such as learning complex evidence-based therapy protocols). Science can also be tough on our self-esteem, as it means that we're not infallible and must subject our egos to data.

THE READINGS IN PART 1

The five readings in Part 1 reflect on the power of science, on its corrective to ever-present human error, and on its unprecedented ability to improve the human condition. In this way, we hope to persuade readers to adopt a scientific attitude toward clinical psychology and related fields.

In his essay "Wonder and Skepticism," the well-known popularizer of astronomy Carl Sagan provides an instructive and engaging primer of the landscape of science. The scientific quest can begin with curiosity about a simple question encountered in everyday life or the news media that we can express in plain language, such as, "What is a star?" (or, closer to our concerns, "What leads people to think they've been abducted by aliens?"; see Clancy, 2005). Then, we can ask what answers to these questions exist and whether they hold up to critical scrutiny, especially if they're widely accepted. Such inquiry may lead us to call conventional wisdom into question. After all, for much of human history, many people "knew" that the earth is flat. We can ask whether we can construct a better answer and then test it in a systematic study, perhaps by pitting it against commonly accepted answers. If I'm open-minded, I'll be persuaded by the data from these studies, not by my prior beliefs. We need science, Sagan reminds us, because we're all fallible: Some of our past and current beliefs are wrong. Sagan raises other fascinating questions: Who controls science? Are we becoming scientifically illiterate to the extent that we can't properly exert counter-control over those who claim authority regarding science and technology? What role do the scientist's personal imperfections play in the process of science? Sagan rightly argues that there is no genuine alternative to the instrumental power of science and its resultant technology.

In his 1974 commencement address to the California Institute of Technology, Nobel Prize–winning physicist Richard Feynman next delineates the key distinctions between science and nonscience, and argues convincingly that the essence of the former is the incessant drive to avoid fooling oneself and others. Feynman contends that in science, we should bend over backward to try to prove ourselves wrong. Only by adopting this approach to inquiry can we increase the odds that we're right, because in this way we're more likely to root out errors in our belief systems. The same principle, it's worth adding, applies to the science of clinical practice: We're most likely to arrive at correct inferences about our clients if we subject our beliefs to scrutiny, continually asking ourselves whether we might be mistaken. Feynman also likens pseudosciences to the "cargo cults" of the Pacific Islands, which emulated the practices of the U.S. Air Force during World War II in a desperate effort to lure back the planes that brought bountiful resources. The cargo cults constructed simulated runways, air traffic control towers, and headphones, but as Feynman observed, it was all in vain: "the planes don't land." Pseudosciences, Feynman points out, simulate the superficial trappings of science, but lack its substance—and like cargo cults, they don't deliver the goods (also see the article by Lilienfeld in Part 2).

In the next reading, Michael Shermer explores the fallibility of human belief by providing engaging responses to the question of what pathways lead to errors in our belief formation. Shermer first emphasizes the ideal of rational belief formation expressed by eighteenth-century Scottish philosopher David Hume: "A wise person proportions his belief to strength of the evidence." He outlines four major categories that can lead us away from Hume's maxim: (1) problems in scientific thinking (e.g., the fact that our observations can be influenced by our theories); (2) problems in pseudoscientific thinking (e.g., neither anecdotes nor scientific language is sufficient to make something scientific); (3) logical problems in thinking (e.g., overreliance on established authorities); and (4) psychological problems in thinking (e.g., psychological needs for certainty, control, and simplicity). Shermer points out that these fallacies occur in the belief formation of those who reject science, but that scientists themselves are prone to them too, because error is part and parcel of being human. Yet scientific methods can help researchers and practitioners to keep these problems under control.

Steven Schafersman then provides a brief but instructive overview of scientific thinking and of the scientific method. He outlines three central components to the scientific method: (1) the use of empirical evidence (*empiricism*—evidence gathered through sense experience); (2) logical reasoning (*rationalism*); and (3) a skeptical attitude (*skepticism*). Such philosophers of science as Karl Popper (1957) and Carl Hempel (1970) pointed out that science relies on deductive logic, that is, deducing hypotheses (specific predictions) from broader theories. Popper argued that the scientific method relies on the rule known as *modus tollens*. Modus tollens takes the following form:

1. If A, then B
2. *Not B*
3. Therefore: Not A

This is a valid logical law. As applied to science, this valid logical inference has the following content:

1. If this Theory is true, then this Observation will be seen
2. *But the Observation was not seen*
3. Therefore, The Theory is False.

Thus, Popper argued that deduction plays an essential role in science. It provides the valid inference structure for scientists to reason from observations to the falseness (error) of their beliefs.

Schafersman's third component of the scientific method is careful observation. We may observe swans if we're attempting to test the proposition, "All swans are white," or results from intelligence tests if we're testing the proposition that "Depression is associated with a decrease in intelligence." In either case, the point is that science necessarily involves "reading the book of the world," to use Galileo's famous phrase.

In the final essay in Part 1, philosopher of science Carl Hempel describes the process by which physician Ignaz Semmelweis solved a profoundly important medical problem in a mid-nineteenth-century Vienna hospital.

This case underscores the point that our problem-solving effectiveness can be a matter of life and death for our patients. Semmelweis was faced with the fact that women who'd just given birth were dying at two different rates. In one ward, about 2 percent of women were dying; in the other ward, nearly 10 percent were dying. Semmelweis wanted to find out why this differential mortality was occurring. He first criticized existing conjectures, such as toxic atmospheres in the district and overcrowding on both wards; however, these hypotheses didn't square with the data. So he began to intervene systematically by modifying one variable at a time and determining if any change in death rates followed. He tested the hypothesis that the death rates were due to different body positions at birth by changing the body positions in one ward to match that of the other, but rejected this hypothesis because he observed no reduction in mortality. Then, by sheer chance he noted that women in the ward with higher death rates were examined by physicians who'd conducted autopsies immediately beforehand and hadn't washed their hands. He hypothesized that this difference could explain the different death rates and tested it by having physicians thoroughly wash their hands with a specific chemical after the autopsy. The death rate then plummeted to that of the other ward. This example illustrates science at its best: the systematic ruling out of rival hypotheses by careful reasoning, which yielded the happy outcome of saving many lives.

Wonder and Skepticism

Carl Sagan

I was a child in a time of hope. I grew up when the expectations for science were very high: in the thirties and forties. I went to college in the early fifties, got my Ph.D. in 1960. There was a sense of optimism about science and the future. I dreamt of being able to do science. I grew up in Brooklyn, New York, and I was a street kid. I came from a nice nuclear family, but I spent a lot of time in the streets, as kids did then. I knew every bush and hedge, streetlight and stoop and theater wall for playing Chinese handball. But there was one aspect of that environment that, for some reason, struck me as different, and that was the stars.

Even with an early bedtime in winter you could see the stars. What were they? They weren't like hedges or even streetlights; they were different. So I asked my friends what they were. They said, "They're lights in the sky, kid." I could tell they were lights in the sky, but that wasn't an explanation. I mean, what were they? Little electric bulbs on long black wires, so you couldn't see what they were held up by? What were they?

Not only could nobody tell me, but nobody even had the sense that it was an interesting question. They looked at me funny. I asked my parents; I asked my parents' friends; I asked other adults. None of them knew. My mother said to me, "Look, we've just got you a library card. Take it, get on the streetcar, go to the New Utrecht branch of the New York Public Library, get out a book and find the answer."

That seemed to me a fantastically clever idea. I made the journey. I asked the librarian for a book on stars. (I was very small; I can still remember looking up at her, and she was sitting down.) She was gone a few minutes, brought one back, and gave it to me. Eagerly I sat down and opened the pages. But it was about Jean Harlow and Clark Gable, I think, a terrible disappointment. And so I went back to her, explained (it wasn't easy for me to do) that that wasn't what I had in mind at all, that what I wanted was a book about real stars. She thought this was funny, which embarrassed me further. But anyway, she went and got another book, the right kind of book. I took it and opened it and slowly turned the pages, until I came to the answer.

It was in there. It was stunning. The answer was that the Sun was a star, except very far away. The stars were suns; if you were close to them, they would look just like our sun. I tried to imagine how far away from the Sun you'd have to be for it to be as dim as a star. Of course I didn't know the inverse-square law of light propagation; I hadn't a ghost of a chance of figuring it out. But it was clear to me that you'd have to be very far away. Farther away, probably, than New Jersey. The dazzling idea of a universe vast beyond imagining swept over me. It has stayed with me ever since.

I sensed awe. And later on (it took me several years to find this), I realized that we were on a planet—a little, nonself-luminous world going around our star. And so all those other stars might have planets going around them. If planets, then life, intelligence, other Brooklyns—who knew? The diversity of those possible worlds struck me. They didn't have to be exactly like ours, I was sure of it.

It seemed the most exciting thing to study. I didn't realize that you could be a professional scientist; I had the idea that I'd have to be, I don't know, a salesman (my father said that was better than the manufacturing end of things), and do science on weekends and evenings. It wasn't until my sophomore year in high school that my biology teacher revealed to me that there was such a thing as a professional scientist, who got paid to do it; so you could spend all your time learning about the universe. It was a glorious day.

It's been my enormous good luck—I was born at just the right time—to have had, to some extent, those childhood ambitions satisfied. I've been involved in the exploration of the solar system, in the most amazing parallel to the science fiction of my childhood. We actually send spacecraft to other worlds. We fly by them; we orbit them; we land on them. We design and control the robots: Tell it to dig, and it digs. Tell it to determine the chemistry of a soil sample, and it determines the chemistry. For me the continuum from childhood wonder and early science fiction to professional reality has been almost seamless. It's never been, "Oh, gee, this is nothing like what I had imagined." Just the opposite: It's exactly like what I imagined. And so I feel enormously fortunate.

Science is still one of my chief joys. The popularization of science that Isaac Asimov did so well—the communication not just of the findings but of the methods of science—seems to me as natural as breathing. After all, when you're in love, you want to tell the world. The idea that scientists shouldn't talk about their science to the public seems to me bizarre.

There's another reason I think popularizing science is important, why I try to do it. It's a foreboding I have—maybe ill-placed—of an America in my children's generation, or my grandchildren's generation, when all the manufacturing industries have slipped away to other countries; when we're a service and information-processing economy; when awesome technological powers are in the hands of a very few, and no one representing the public interest even grasps the issues; when the people (by "the people" I mean the broad population in a democracy) have lost the ability to set their own agendas, or even to knowledgeably question those who do set the agendas; when there is no practice in questioning those in authority; when, clutching our crystals and religiously consulting our horoscopes, our critical faculties in steep decline, unable to distinguish between what's true and what feels good, we slide, almost without noticing, into superstition and darkness. CSICOP [Committee for the Scientific Investigation of Claims of the Paranormal, now the Committee for Skeptical Inquiry] plays a sometimes lonely but still—and in this case the word may be right—heroic role in trying to counter some of those trends.

We have a civilization based on science and technology, and we've cleverly arranged things so that almost nobody understands science and technology. That is as clear a prescription for disaster as you can imagine. While we might get away with this combustible mixture of ignorance and power for a while, sooner or later it's going to blow up in our faces. The powers of modern technology are so formidable that it's insufficient just to say, "Well, those in charge, I'm sure, are doing a good job." This is a democracy, and for us to make sure that the powers of science and technology are used properly and prudently, we ourselves must understand science and technology. We must be involved in the decision-making process.

The predictive powers of some areas, at least, of science are phenomenal. They are the clearest counterargument I can imagine to those who say, "Oh, science is situational; science is just the current fashion; science is the promotion of the self-interests of those in power." Surely there is some of that. Surely if there's any powerful tool, those in power will try to use it, or even monopolize it. Surely scientists, being people, grow up in a society and reflect the prejudices of that society. How could it be otherwise? Some scientists have been nationalists; some have been racists; some have been sexists. But that doesn't undermine the validity of science. It's just a consequence of being human.

So, imagine—there are so many areas we could think of—imagine you want to know the sex of your unborn child. There are several approaches. You could, for example, do what the late film star who Annie [my wife] and I admire greatly—Cary Grant—did before he was an actor. In a carnival or fair or consulting room, you suspend a watch or a plumb bob above the abdomen of the expectant mother; if it swings left-right it's a boy, and if it swings forward-back it's a girl. The method works one time in two. Of course he was out of there before the baby was born, so he never heard from customers who complained he got it wrong. Being right one chance in two—that's not so bad. It's better than, say, Kremlinologists used to do. But if you really want to know, then you go to amniocentesis, or to sonograms; and there your chance of being right is 99 out of 100. It's not perfect, but it's a whole lot better than one out of two. If you really want to know, you go to science.

Or suppose you wanted to know when the next eclipse of the Sun is. Science does something really astonishing: It can tell you a century in advance where the eclipse is going to be on Earth and when, say, totality will be, to the second. Think of the predictive power this implies. Think of how much you must understand to be able to say when and where there's going to be an eclipse so far in the future.

Or (the same physics exactly) imagine launching a spacecraft from Earth, like the *Voyager* spacecraft in 1977; 12 years later *Voyager 1* arrives at Neptune within 100 kilometers or something of where it was supposed to be—not having to use some of the mid-course corrections that were available; 12 years, 5 billion kilometers, on target!

So if you want to really be able to predict the future—not in everything, but in some areas—there's only one regime of human scholarship, of human claims to knowledge, that really delivers the goods, and that's science. Religions would give their eyeteeth to be able to predict anything like that well. Think of how much mileage they would make if they ever could do predictions comparably unambiguous and precise.

Now how does it work? Why is it so successful?

Science has built-in error-correcting mechanisms—because science recognizes that scientists, like everybody else, are fallible, that we make mistakes, that we're driven by the same prejudices as everybody else. There are no forbidden questions. Arguments from authority are worthless. Claims must be demonstrated. Ad hominem arguments—arguments about the personality of somebody who disagrees with you—are irrelevant; they can be sleazeballs and be right, and you can be a pillar of the community and be wrong.

If you take a look at science in its everyday function, of course you find that scientists run the gamut of human emotions and personalities and character and so on. But there's one thing that is really striking to the outsider, and that is the gauntlet of criticism that is considered acceptable or even desirable. The poor graduate student at his or her Ph.D. oral exam is subjected to a withering crossfire of questions that sometimes seem hostile or contemptuous; this from the professors who have the candidate's future in their grasp. The students naturally are nervous; who wouldn't be? True, they've prepared for it for years. But they understand that at that critical moment they really have to be able to answer questions. So in preparing to defend their theses, they must anticipate questions; they have to think, "Where in my thesis is there a weakness that someone else might find—because I sure better find it before they do, because if they find it and I'm not prepared, I'm in deep trouble."

You take a look at contentious scientific meetings. You find university colloquia in which the speaker has hardly gotten 30 seconds into presenting what she or he is saying, and suddenly there are interruptions, maybe withering questions, from the audience. You take a look at the publication conventions in which you submit a scientific paper to a journal, and it goes out to anonymous referees whose job it is to think, Did you do anything stupid? If you didn't do anything stupid, is there anything in here that is sufficiently interesting to be published? What are the deficiencies of this paper? Has it been done by anybody else? Is the argument adequate, or should you resubmit the paper after you've actually demonstrated what you're speculating on? And so on. And it's anonymous: You don't know who your critics are. You have to rely on the editor to send it out to real experts who are not overtly malicious. This is the everyday expectation in the scientific community. And those who don't expect it—even good scientists who just can't hold up under criticism—have difficult careers.

Why do we put up with it? Do we like to be criticized? No, no scientist likes to be criticized. Every scientist feels an affection for his or her ideas and scientific results. You feel protective of them. But you don't reply to critics: "Wait a minute, wait a minute; this is a really good idea. I'm very fond of it. It's done you no harm. Please don't attack it." That's not the way it goes. The hard but just rule is that if the ideas don't work, you must throw them away. Don't waste any neurons on what doesn't work. Devote those neurons to new ideas that better explain the data. Valid criticism is doing you a favor.

There is a reward structure in science that is very interesting: Our highest honors go to those who disprove the findings of the most revered among us. So Einstein is revered not just because he made so many fundamental contributions to science, but because he found an imperfection in the fundamental contribution of Isaac Newton. (Isaac Newton was surely the greatest physicist before Albert Einstein.)

Now think of what other areas of human society have such a reward structure, in which we revere those who prove that the fundamental doctrines that we have adopted are wrong. Think of it in politics, or in economics, or in religion; think of it in how we organize our society. Often, it's exactly the opposite: There we reward those who reassure us that what we've been told is right, that we need not concern ourselves about it. This difference, I believe, is at least a basic reason why we've made so much progress in science, and so little in some other areas.

We are fallible. We cannot expect to foist our wishes on the universe. So another key aspect of science is experiment. Scientists do not trust what is intuitively obvious, because intuitively obvious gets you nowhere. That the Earth is flat was once obvious. I mean, really obvious; obvious! Go out in a flat field and take a look: Is it round or flat? Don't listen to me; go prove it to yourself. That heavier bodies fall faster than light ones was once obvious. That blood-sucking leeches cure disease was once obvious. That some people are naturally and by divine right slaves was once obvious. That the Earth is at the center of the universe was once obvious. You're skeptical? Go out, take a look: stars rise in the East, set in the West; here we are, stationary (do you feel the Earth whirling?); we see them going around us. We are at the center; they go around us.

The truth may be puzzling. It may take some work to grapple with. It may be counterintuitive. It may contradict deeply held prejudices. It may not be consonant with what we desperately want to be true. But our preferences do not determine what's true. We have a method, and that method helps us to reach not absolute truth, only asymptotic approaches to the truth—never there, just closer and closer, always finding vast new oceans of undiscovered possibilities. Cleverly designed experiments are the key.

In the 1920s, there was a dinner at which the physicist Robert W. Wood was asked to respond to a toast. This was a time when people stood up, made a toast, and then selected someone to respond. Nobody knew what toast they'd be asked to reply to, so it was a challenge for the quick-witted. In this case the toast was: "To physics and metaphysics." Now by metaphysics was meant something like philosophy—truths that you could get to just by thinking about them. Wood took a second, glanced about him, and answered along these lines: The physicist has an idea, he said. The more he thinks it through, the more sense it makes to him. He goes to the scientific literature, and the more he reads, the more promising the idea seems. Thus prepared, he devises an experiment to test the idea. The experiment is painstaking. Many possibilities are eliminated or taken into account; the accuracy of the measurement is refined. At the end of all this work, the experiment is completed and . . . the idea is shown to be worthless. The physicist then discards the idea, frees his mind (as I was saying a moment ago) from the clutter of error, and moves on to something else.

The difference between physics and metaphysics, Wood concluded, is that the metaphysicist has no laboratory.

Why is it so important to have widely distributed understanding of science and technology? For one thing, it's the golden road out of poverty for developing nations. And developing nations understand that, because you have only to look at modern American graduate schools—in mathematics, in engineering, in physics—to find, in case after case, that more than half the students are from other countries. This is something America is doing for the world. But it conveys a clear sense that the developing nations understand what is essential for their future. What worries me is that Americans may not be equally clear on the subject.

Let me touch on the dangers of technology. Almost every astronaut who has visited Earth orbit has made this point: I was up there, they say, and I looked toward the horizon, and there was this thin, blue band that's the Earth's atmosphere. I had been told we live in an ocean of air. But there it was, so fragile, such a delicate blue: I was worried for it.

In fact, the thickness of the Earth's atmosphere, compared with the size of the Earth, is in about the same ratio as the thickness of a coat of shellac on a schoolroom globe is to the diameter of the globe. That's the air that nurtures us and almost all other life on Earth, that protects us from deadly ultraviolet light from the Sun, that through the greenhouse effect brings the surface temperature above the freezing point. (Without the greenhouse effect, the entire Earth would plunge below the freezing point of water and we'd all be dead.) Now that atmosphere, so thin and fragile, is under assault by our technology. We are pumping all kinds of stuff into it. You know about the concern that chlorofluorocarbons are depleting the ozone layer; and that carbon dioxide and methane and other greenhouse gases are producing global warming, a steady trend amidst fluctuations produced by volcanic eruptions and other sources. Who knows what other challenges we are posing to this vulnerable layer of air that we haven't been wise enough to foresee?

The inadvertent side effects of technology can challenge the environment on which our very lives depend. That means that we must understand science and technology; we must anticipate long-term consequences in a very clever way—not just the bottom line on the profit-and-loss column for the corporation for this year, but the consequences for the nation and the species 10, 20, 50, 100 years in the future. If we absolutely stop all chlorofluorocarbon and allied chemical production right now (as we're in fact doing), the ozonosphere will heal itself in about a hundred years. Therefore our children, our grandchildren, our great-grandchildren must suffer through the mistakes that we've made. That's a second reason for science education: the dangers of technology. We must understand them better.

A third reason: origins. Every human culture has devoted some of its intellectual, moral, and material resources to trying to understand where everything comes from—our nation, our species, our planet, our star, our galaxy, our universe. Stop someone on the street and ask about it. You will not find many people who never thought about it, who are incurious about their ultimate origins.

I hold there's a kind of Gresham's Law that applies in the confrontation of science and pseudoscience: In the popular imagination, at least, the bad science drives out the good. What I mean is this: If you are awash in lost continents and channeling and UFOs and all the long litany of claims so well exposed in *Skeptical Inquirer*, you may not have intellectual room for the findings of science. You're sated with wonder. Our culture in one way produces the fantastic findings of science, and then in another way cuts them off before they reach the average person. So people who are curious, intelligent, dedicated to understanding the world, may nevertheless be (in our view) enmired in superstition and pseudoscience. You could say, Well, they ought to know better, they ought to be more critical, and so on; but that's too harsh. It's not very much their fault, I say. It's the fault of a society that preferentially propagates the baloney and holds back the ambrosia.

The least effective way for skeptics to get the attention of these bright, curious, interested people is to belittle, or condescend, or show arrogance toward their beliefs. They may be credulous, but they're not stupid. If we bear in mind human frailty and fallibility, we will understand their plight.

For example: I've lately been thinking about alien abductions, and false claims of childhood sexual abuse, and stories of satanic ritual abuse in the context of recovered memories. There are interesting similarities among those classes of cases. I think if we are to understand any of them, we must understand all of them. But there's a maddening tendency of the skeptics, when addressing invented stories of childhood sexual abuse, to forget that real and appalling abuse happens. It is not true that all these claims of childhood sexual abuse are silly and pumped up by unethical therapists. Yesterday's paper reported that a survey of 13 states found that one-sixth of all the rape victims reported to police are under the age of 12. And this is a category of rape that is preferentially under-reported to police, for obvious reasons. Of these girls, one-fifth were raped by their fathers. That's a lot of people, and a lot of betrayal. We must bear that in mind when we consider patients who, say, because they have an eating disorder, have suppressed childhood sexual abuse diagnosed by their psychiatrists.

People are not stupid. They believe things for reasons. Let us not dismiss pseudoscience or even superstition with contempt.

In the nineteenth century it was mediums: You'd go to the stance, and you'd be put in touch with dead relatives. These days it's a little different; it's called channeling. What both are basically about is the human fear of dying. I don't know about you; I find the idea of dying unpleasant. If I had a choice, at least for a while, I would just as soon not die. Twice in my life I came very close to doing so. (I did not have a near-death experience, I'm sorry to say.) I can understand anxiety about dying.

About 14 years ago both my parents died. We had a very good relationship. I was very close to them. I still miss them terribly. I wouldn't ask much: I would like five minutes a year with them; to tell them how their kids and their grandchildren are doing, and how Annie and I are doing. I know it sounds stupid, but I'd like to ask them, "Is everything all right with you?" Just a little contact. So I don't guffaw at women who go to their husbands' tombstones and chat them up every now and then. That's not hard to understand. And if we have difficulties on the ontological status of who it is they're talking to, that's all right. That's not what this is about. This is humans being human.

In the alien-abduction context, I've been trying to understand the fact that humans hallucinate—that it's a human commonplace—yes, under conditions of sensory deprivation or drugs or deprival of REM sleep, but also just in the ordinary course of existence. I have, maybe a dozen times since my parents died, heard one of them say my name: just the single word, "Carl." I miss them; they called me by my first name so much during the time they were alive; I was in the practice of responding instantly when I was called; it has deep psychic roots. So my brain plays it back every now and then. This doesn't surprise me at all; I sort of like it. But it's a hallucination. If I were a little less skeptical, though, I could see how easy it would be to say, "They're around somewhere. I can hear them."

Raymond Moody, who is an M.D., I think, an author who writes innumerable books on life after death, actually quoted me in the first chapter of his latest book, saying that I heard my parents calling me Carl, and so, look, even he believes in life after death. This badly misses my point. If this is one of the arguments from Chapter 1 of the latest book of a principal exponent of life after death, I suspect that despite our most fervent wishes, the case is weak.

But still, suppose I wasn't steeped in the virtues of scientific skepticism and felt as I do about my parents, and along comes someone who says, "I can put you in touch with them." Suppose he's clever, and found out something about my parents in the past, and is good at faking voices, and so on—a darkened room and incense and all of that. I could see being swept away emotionally.

Would you think less of me if I fell for it? Imagine I was never educated about skepticism, had no idea that it's a virtue, but instead believed that it was grumpy and negative and rejecting of everything that's humane. Couldn't you understand my openness to being conned by a medium or a channeler?

The chief deficiency I see in the skeptical movement is its polarization: Us vs. Them—the sense that we have a monopoly on the truth; that those other people who believe in all these stupid doctrines are morons; that if you're sensible, you'll listen to us; and if not, to hell with you. This is nonconstructive. It does not get our message across. It condemns us to permanent minority status. Whereas, an approach that from the beginning acknowledges the human roots of pseudoscience and superstition, that recognizes that the society has arranged things so that skepticism is not well taught, might be much more widely accepted.[1]

If we understand this, then of course we have compassion for the abductees and those who come upon crop circles and believe they're supernatural, or at least of extraterrestrial manufacture. This is key to making science and the scientific method more attractive, especially to the young, because it's a battle for the future.

Science involves a seemingly self-contradictory mix of attitudes: On the one hand, it requires an almost complete openness to all ideas, no matter how bizarre and weird they sound, a propensity to wonder. As I walk along, my time slows down; I shrink in the direction of motion, and I get more massive. That's crazy! On the scale of the very small, the molecule can be in this position, in that position, but it is prohibited from being in any intermediate position. That's wild! But the first is a statement of special relativity, and the second is a consequence of quantum mechanics. Like it or not, that's the way the world is. If you insist that it's ridiculous, you will be forever closed to the major findings of science. But at the same time, science requires the most vigorous and uncompromising skepticism, because the vast majority of ideas are simply wrong, and the only way you can distinguish the right from the wrong, the wheat from the chaff, is by critical experiment and analysis.

Too much openness and you accept every notion, idea, and hypothesis—which is tantamount to knowing nothing. Too much skepticism—especially rejection of new ideas before they are adequately tested—and you're not only unpleasantly grumpy, but also closed to the advance of science. A judicious mix is what we need.

It's no fun, as I said at the beginning, to be on the receiving end of skeptical questioning. But it's the affordable price we pay for having the benefits of so powerful a tool as science.

Notes

1. If skeptical habits of thought are widely distributed and prized, then who is the skepticism going to be mainly applied to? To those in power. Those in power, therefore, do not have a vested interest in everybody being able to ask searching questions.

2

Cargo Cult Science

RICHARD P. FEYNMAN

Some remarks on science, pseudoscience, and learning how to not fool yourself. Caltech's 1974 commencement address.

During the Middle Ages there were all kinds of crazy ideas, such as that a piece of rhinoceros horn would increase potency. (Another crazy idea of the Middle Ages is these hats we have on today—which is too loose in my case.) Then a method was discovered for separating the ideas—which was to try one to see if it worked, and if it didn't work, to eliminate it. This method became organized, of course, into science. And it developed very well, so that we are now in the scientific age. It is such a scientific age, in fact, that we have difficulty in understanding how witch doctors could *ever* have existed, when nothing that they proposed ever really worked—or very little of it did.

But even today I meet lots of people who sooner or later get me into a conversation about UFOs, or astrology, or some form of mysticism, expanded consciousness, new types of awareness, ESP, and so forth. And I've concluded that it's *not* a scientific world.

Most people believe so many wonderful things that I decided to investigate why they did. And what has been referred to as my curiosity for investigation has landed me in a difficulty where I found so much junk to talk about that I can't do it in this talk. I'm overwhelmed. First I started out by investigating various ideas of mysticism, and mystic experiences. I went into isolation tanks (they're dark and quiet and you float in Epsom salts) and got many hours of hallucinations, so I know something about that. Then I went to Esalen, which is a hotbed of this kind of thought (it's a wonderful place; you should go visit there). Then I became overwhelmed. I didn't realize how *much* there was.

I was sitting, for example, in a hot bath and there's another guy and a girl in the bath. He says to the girl, "I'm learning massage and I wonder if I could practice on you?" She says OK, so she gets up on a table and he starts off on her foot—working on her big toe and pushing it around. Then he turns to what is apparently his instructor, and says, "I feel a kind of dent. Is that the pituitary?" And she says, "No, that's not the way it feels." I say, "You're a hell of a long way from the pituitary, man." And they both looked at me—I had blown my cover, you see—and she said, "It's reflexology." So I closed my eyes and appeared to be meditating.

That's just an example of the kind of things that overwhelm me. I also looked into extrasensory perception and PSI phenomena, and the latest craze there was Uri Geller, a man who is supposed to be able to bend keys by rubbing them with his finger. So I went to his hotel room, on his invitation, to see a demonstration of both mind reading and bending keys. He didn't do any mind reading that succeeded; nobody can read my mind, I guess. And my boy held a key and Geller rubbed it, and nothing happened. Then he told us it works better under water, and so you can picture all of us standing in the bathroom with the water turned on and the key under it, and him rubbing the key with his finger. Nothing happened. So I was unable to investigate that phenomenon.

But then I began to think, what else is there that we believe? (And I thought then about the witch doctors, and how easy it would have been to check on them by noticing that nothing really worked.) So I found things that even *more* people believe, such as that we have some knowledge of how to educate. There are big schools of reading methods and mathematics methods, and so forth, but if you notice, you'll see the reading scores keep going down—or hardly going up—in spite of the fact that we continually use these same people to improve the methods. *There's* a witch doctor remedy that doesn't work. It ought to be looked into; how do they know that their method should work? Another example is how to treat criminals. We obviously have made no progress—lots of theory, but no progress—in decreasing the amount of crime by the method that we use to handle criminals.

Yet these things are said to be scientific. We study them. And I think ordinary people with commonsense ideas are intimidated by this pseudoscience. A teacher who has some good idea of how to teach her children to read is forced by the school system to do it some other way—or is even fooled by the school system into thinking that her method is not necessarily a good one. Or a parent of bad boys, after disciplining them in one way or another, feels guilty for the rest of her life because she didn't do "the right thing," according to the experts.

So we really ought to look into theories that don't work, and science that isn't science.

I tried to find a principle for discovering more of these kinds of things, and came up with the following system. Any time you find yourself in a conversation at a cocktail party in which you do not feel uncomfortable that the hostess might come around and say, "Why are you fellows talking shop?" or that your wife will come around and say, "Why are you flirting again?"—then you can be sure you are talking about something about which nobody knows anything.

Using this method, 1 discovered a few more topics that I had forgotten—among them the efficacy of various forms of psychotherapy. So 1 began to investigate through the library, and so on, and I have so much to tell you that I can't do it at all. I will have to limit myself to just a few little things. I'll concentrate on the things more people believe in. Maybe I will give a series of speeches next year on all these subjects. It will take a long time.

I think the educational and psychological studies I mentioned are examples of what I would like to call Cargo Cult Science. In the South Seas there is a Cargo Cult of people. During the war they saw airplanes land with lots of good materials, and they want the same thing to happen now. So they've arranged to make things like runways, to put fires along the sides of the runways, to make a wooden hut for a man to sit in, with two wooden pieces on his head like headphones and bars of bamboo sticking out like antennas—he's the controller—and they wait for the airplanes to land. They're doing everything right. The form is perfect. It looks exactly the way it looked before. But it doesn't work. No airplanes land. So I call these things Cargo Cult Science, because they follow all the apparent precepts and forms of scientific investigation, but they're missing something essential, because the planes don't land.

Now it behooves me, of course, to tell you what they're missing. But it would be just about as difficult to explain to the South Sea Islanders how they have to arrange things so that they get some wealth in their system. It is not something simple like telling them how to improve the shapes of the earphones. But there is *one* feature I notice that is generally missing in Cargo Cult Science. That is the idea that we all hope you have learned in studying science in school—we never explicitly say what this *is*, but just hope that you catch on by all the examples of scientific investigation. It is interesting, therefore, to bring it out now and speak of it explicitly. It's a kind of scientific integrity, a principle of scientific thought that corresponds to a kind of utter honesty—a kind of leaning over backwards. For example, if you're doing an experiment, you should report everything that you think might make it invalid—not only what you think is right about it: other causes that could possibly

explain your results; and things you thought of that you've eliminated by some other experiment, and how they worked—to make sure the other fellow can tell they have been eliminated.

Details that could throw doubt on your interpretation must be given, if you know them. You must do the best you can—if you know anything at all wrong, or possibly wrong—to explain it. If you make a theory, for example, and advertise it, or put it out, then you must also put down all the facts that disagree with it, as well as those that agree with it. There is also a more subtle problem. When you have put a lot of ideas together to make an elaborate theory, you want to make sure, when explaining what it fits, that those things it fits are not just the things that gave you the idea for the theory; but that the finished theory makes something else come out right, in addition.

In summary, the idea is to try to give *all* of the information to help others to judge the value of your contribution; not just the information that leads to judgment in one particular direction or another.

The easiest way to explain this idea is to contrast it, for example, with advertising. Last night I heard that Wesson Oil doesn't soak through food. Well, that's true. It's not dishonest; but the thing I'm talking about is not just a matter of not being dishonest, it's a matter of scientific integrity, which is another level. The fact that should be added to that advertising statement is that *no* oils soak through food, if operated at a certain temperature. If operated at another temperature, they *all* will—including Wesson Oil. So it's the implication which has been conveyed, not the fact, which is true, and the difference is what we have to deal with.

We've learned from experience that the truth will out. Other experimenters will repeat your experiment and find out whether you were wrong or right. Nature's phenomena will agree or they'll disagree with your theory. And, although you may gain some temporary fame and excitement, you will not gain a good reputation as a scientist if you haven't tried to be very careful in this kind of work. And it's this type of integrity, this kind of care not to fool yourself, that is missing to a large extent in much of the research in Cargo Cult Science.

A great deal of their difficulty is, of course, the difficulty of the subject and the inapplicability of the scientific method to the subject. Nevertheless, it should be remarked that this is not the only difficulty. That's *why* the planes don't land—but they don't land.

We have learned a lot from experience about how to handle some of the ways we fool ourselves. One example: Millikan measured the charge on an electron by an experiment with falling oil drops and got an answer which we now know not to be quite right. It's a little bit off, because he had the incorrect value for the viscosity of air. It's interesting to look at the history of measurements of the charge of the electron, after Millikan. If you plot them as a function of time, you find that one is a little bigger than Millikan's, and the next one's a little bit bigger than that, and the next one's a little bit bigger than that, until finally they settle down to a number which is higher.

Why didn't they discover that the new number was higher right away? It's a thing that scientists are ashamed of—this history—because it's apparent that people did things like this: When they got a number that was too high above Millikan's, they thought something must be wrong—and they would look for and find a reason why something might be wrong. When they got a number closer to Millikan's value they didn't look so hard. And so they eliminated the numbers that were too far off, and did other things like that. We've learned those tricks nowadays, and now we don't have that kind of a disease.

But this long history of learning how to not fool ourselves—of having utter scientific integrity—is, I'm sorry to say, something that we haven't specifically included in any particular course that I know of. We just hope you've caught on by osmosis.

The first principle is that you must not fool yourself—and you are the easiest person to fool. So you have to be very careful about that. After you've not fooled yourself, it's easy not to fool other scientists. You just have to be honest in a conventional way after that.

I would like to add something that's not essential to the science, but something I kind of believe, which is that you should not fool the layman when you're talking as a scientist. I am not trying to tell you what to do about cheating on your wife, or fooling your girl friend, or something like that, when you're not trying to be a scientist, but just trying to be an ordinary human being. We'll leave those problems up to you and your rabbi. I'm talking about a specific, extra type of integrity that is not lying, but bending over backwards to show how you're maybe wrong, that you ought to do when acting as a scientist. And this is our responsibility as scientists, certainly to other scientists, and I think to laymen.

For example, I was a little surprised when I was talking to a friend who was going to go on the radio. He does work on cosmology and astronomy, and he wondered how he would explain what the applications of this work were. "Well," I said, "there aren't any." He said, "Yes, but then we won't get support for more research of this kind." *I* think that's kind of dishonest. If you're representing yourself as a scientist, then you should explain to the layman what you're doing—and if they don't want to support you under those circumstances, then that's their decision.

One example of the principle is this: If you've made up your mind to test a theory, or you want to explain some idea, you should always decide to publish it whichever way it comes out. If we only publish results of a certain kind, we can make the argument look good. We must publish *both* kinds of result. For example—let's take advertising again—suppose some particular cigarette has some particular property, like low nicotine. It's published widely by the company that this means it is good for you—they don't say, for instance, that the tars are a different proportion, or that something else is the matter with the cigarette. In other words, publication probability depends upon the answer. That should not be done.

I say that's also important in giving certain types of government advice. Supposing a senator asked you for advice about whether drilling a hole should be done in his state; and you decide it would be better in some other state. If you don't publish such a result, it seems to me you're not giving scientific advice. You're being used. If your answer happens to come out in the direction the government or the politicians like, they can use it as an argument in their favor; if it comes out the other way, they don't publish it at all. That's not giving scientific advice.

Other kinds of errors are more characteristic of poor science. When I was at Cornell, I often talked to the people in the psychology department. One of the students told me she wanted to do an experiment that went something like this—I don't remember it in detail, but it had been found by others that under certain circumstances, X, rats did something, A. She was curious as to whether, if she changed the circumstances to Y, they would still do A. So her proposal was to do the experiment under circumstances Y and see if they still did A.

I explained to her that it was necessary first to repeat in her laboratory the experiment of the other person—to do it under condition X to see if she could also get result A—and then change to Y and see if A changed. Then she would know that the real difference was the thing she thought she had under control.

She was very delighted with this new idea, and went to her professor. And his reply was, no, you cannot do that, because the experiment has already been done and you would be wasting time. This was in about 1935 or so, and it seems to have been the general policy then to not try to repeat psychological experiments, but only to change the conditions and see what happens.

Nowadays there's a certain danger of the same thing happening, even in the famous field of physics. I was shocked to hear of an experiment done at the big acceleration at the National Accelerator Laboratory, where a person used deuterium. In order to compare his heavy hydrogen results to what might happen with light hydrogen he had to use data from someone else's experiment on light hydrogen, which was done on different apparatus. When asked why, he said it was because he couldn't get time on the program (because there's so little time and it's such expensive apparatus) to do the experiment with light hydrogen on this apparatus because there wouldn't be any new result. And so the men in charge of programs at NAL are so anxious for new results, in order to get more money to keep the thing going for public relations purposes, they are destroying—possibly—the value of the experiments themselves, which is the whole purpose of the thing. It is often hard for the experimenters there to complete their work as their scientific integrity demands.

All experiments in psychology are not of this type, however. For example, there have been many experiments running rats through all kinds of mazes, and so on—with little clear result. But in 1937 a man named Young did a very interesting one. He had a long corridor with doors all along one side where the rats came in, and doors along the other side where the food was. He wanted to see if he could train the rats to go in at the third door down from wherever he started them off. No. The rats went immediately to the door where the food had been the time before.

The question was, how did the rats know, because the corridor was so beautifully built and so uniform, that this was the same door as before? Obviously there was something about the door that was different from the other doors. So he painted the doors very carefully, arranging the textures on the faces of the doors exactly the same. Still the rats could tell. Then he thought maybe the rats were smelling the food, so he used chemicals to change the smell after each run. Still the rats could tell. Then he realized the rats might be able to tell by seeing the lights and the arrangement in the laboratory like any commonsense person. So he covered the corridor, and still the rats could tell.

He finally found that they could tell by the way the floor sounded when they ran over it. And he could only fix that by putting his corridor in sand. So he covered one after another of all possible clues and finally was able to fool the rats so that they had to learn to go in the third door. If he relaxed any of his conditions, the rats could tell.

Now, from a scientific standpoint, that is an A-Number-1 experiment. That is the experiment that makes rat-running experiments sensible, because it uncovers the clues that the rat is really using—not what you think it's using. And that is the experiment that tells exactly what conditions you have to use in order to be careful and control everything in an experiment with rat-running.

I looked into the subsequent history of this research. The next experiment, and the one after that, never referred to Mr. Young. They never used any of his criteria of putting the corridor on sand, or being very careful. They just went right on running rats in the same old way, and paid no attention to the great discoveries of Mr. Young, and his papers are not referred to, because he didn't discover anything about the rats. In fact, he discovered *all* the things you have to do to discover something about rats. But not paying attention to experiments like that is a characteristic of Cargo Cult Science.

Another example is the ESP experiments of Mr. Rhine, and other people. As various people have made criticisms—and they themselves have made criticisms of their own experiments—they improve the techniques so that the effects are smaller, and smaller, and smaller until they gradually disappear. All the parapsychologists are looking for some experiment that can be repeated—that you can do again and get the same effect—statistically, even. They run a million rats—no, it's people this time—they do a lot of things and get a certain statistical effect. Next time they try it they don't get it any more. And now you find a man saying that it is an irrelevant demand to expect a repeatable experiment. This is *science*?

This man also speaks about a new institution, in a talk in which he was resigning as Director of the Institute of Parapsychology. And, in telling people what to do next, he says that one of the things they have to do is be sure they only train students who have shown their ability to get PSI results to an acceptable extent—not to waste their time on those ambitious and interested students who get only chance results. It is very dangerous to have such a policy in teaching—to teach students only how to get certain results, rather than how to do an experiment with scientific integrity.

So I wish to you—I have no more time, so I have just one wish for you—the good luck to be somewhere where you are free to maintain the kind of integrity I have described, and where you do not feel forced by a need to maintain your position in the organization, or financial support, or so on, to lose your integrity. May you have that freedom.

3

How Thinking Goes Wrong
Twenty-five Fallacies That Lead Us to Believe Weird Things

MICHAEL SHERMER

In 1994 NBC began airing a New Age program called *The Other Side* that explored claims of the paranormal, various mysteries and miracles, and assorted "weird" things. I appeared numerous times as the token skeptic—the "other side" of *The Other Side*, if you will. On most talk shows, a "balanced" program is a half-dozen to a dozen believers and one lone skeptic as the voice of reason or opposition. *The Other Side* was no different, even though the executive producer, many of the program producers, and even the host were skeptical of most of the beliefs they were covering. I did one program on werewolves for which they flew in a fellow from England. He actually looked a little like what you see in werewolf movies—big bushy sideburns and rather pointy ears—but when I talked to him, I found that he did not actually remember becoming a werewolf. He recalled the experience under hypnosis. In my opinion, his was a case of false memory, either planted by the hypnotist or fantasized by the man.

Another program was on astrology. The producers brought in a serious, professional astrologer from India who explained how it worked using charts and maps with all the jargon. But, because he was so serious, they ended up featuring a Hollywood astrologer who made all sorts of predictions about the lives of movie stars. He also did some readings for members of the audience. One young lady was told that she was having problems staying in long-term relationships with men. During the break, she told me that she was fourteen years old and was there with her high-school class to see how television programs were produced.

In my opinion, most believers in miracles, monsters, and mysteries are not hoaxers, flimflam artists, or lunatics. Most are normal people whose normal thinking has gone wrong in some way. In Chapters 4, 5, and 6, I will discuss in detail psychic power, altered states of consciousness, and alien abductions, but I would like to round out part I of the book by looking at twenty-five fallacies of thinking that can lead anyone to believe weird things. I have grouped them in four categories, listing specific fallacies and problems in each. But as an affirmation that thinking can go right, I begin with what I call Hume's Maxim and close with what I call Spinoza's Dictum.

HUME'S MAXIM

Skeptics owe a lot to the Scottish philosopher David Hume (1711–1776), whose *An Enquiry Concerning Human Understanding* is a classic in skeptical analysis. The work was first published anonymously in London in 1739 as *A Treatise of Human Nature*. In Hume's words, it "fell dead-born from the press, without reaching such distinction as even to excite a murmur among the zealots." Hume blamed his own writing style and reworked the manuscript into *An Abstract of a Treatise of Human Nature*, published in 1740, and then into *Philosophical Essays Concerning the Human Understanding*, published in 1748. The work still garnered no recognition, so in 1758 he brought out the final version, under the title *An Enquiry Concerning Human Understanding*, which today we regard as his greatest philosophical work.

Hume distinguished between "antecedent skepticism," such as René Descartes' method of doubting everything that has no "antecedent" infallible criterion for belief; and "consequent skepticism," the method Hume employed, which recognizes the "consequences" of our fallible senses but corrects them through reason: "A wise man proportions his belief to the evidence." Better words could not be found for a skeptical motto.

Even more important is Hume's foolproof, when-all-else-fails analysis of miraculous claims. For when one is confronted by a true believer whose apparently supernatural or paranormal claim has no immediately apparent natural explanation, Hume provides an argument that he thought so important that he placed his own words in quotes and called them a maxim:

> The plain consequence is (and it is a general maxim worthy of our attention), "That no testimony is sufficient to establish a miracle, unless the testimony be of such a kind, that its falsehood would be more miraculous than the fact which it endeavors to establish."
>
> When anyone tells me that he saw a dead man restored to life, I immediately consider with myself whether it be more probable, that this person should either deceive or be deceived, or that the fact, which he relates, should really have happened. I weigh the one miracle against the other, and according to the superiority, which I discover, I pronounce my decision, and always reject the greater miracle. If the falsehood of his testimony would be more miraculous than the event which he relates; then, and not till then, can he pretend to command my belief or opinion. ([1758] 1952, p. 491)

PROBLEMS IN SCIENTIFIC THINKING

1. Theory Influences Observations

About the human quest to understand the physical world, physicist and Nobel laureate Werner Heisenberg concluded, "What we observe is not nature itself but nature exposed to our method of questioning." In quantum mechanics, this notion has been formalized as the "Copenhagen interpretation" of quantum action: "a probability function does not prescribe a certain event but describes a continuum of possible events until a measurement interferes with the isolation of the system and a single event is actualized" (in Weaver 1987, p. 412). The Copenhagen interpretation eliminates the one-to-one correlation between theory and reality. The theory in part *constructs* the reality. Reality exists independent of the observer, of course, but our perceptions of reality are influenced by the theories framing our examination of it. Thus, philosophers call science theory laden.

That theory shapes perceptions of reality is true not only for quantum physics but also for all observations of the world. When Columbus arrived in the New World, he had a theory that he was in Asia and proceeded to perceive the New World as such. Cinnamon was a valuable Asian spice, and the first New World shrub that smelled like cinnamon was declared to *be* it. When he encountered the aromatic gumbo-limbo tree of the West Indies, Columbus concluded it was an Asian species similar to the mastic tree of the Mediterranean. A New World nut was matched with Marco Polo's description of a coconut. Columbus's surgeon even declared, based on some Caribbean roots his men uncovered, that he had found Chinese rhubarb. A theory of Asia produced observations of Asia, even though Columbus was half a world away. Such is the power of theory.

2. The Observer Changes the Observed

Physicist John Archibald Wheeler "Even to observe so minuscule an object as an electron, [a physicist] must shatter the glass. He must reach in. He must install his chosen measuring equipment. . . . Moreover, the measurement changes the state of the electron. The universe will never afterward be the same" (in Weaver 1987, p. 427). In other words, the act of studying an event can change it. Social scientists often encounter this phenomenon. Anthropologists know that when they study a tribe, the behavior of the members may be altered by the fact they are being observed by an outsider. Subjects in a psychology experiment may alter their behavior if they know what experimental hypotheses are being tested. This is why psychologists use blind and double-blind controls. Lack of such controls is often found in tests of paranormal powers and is one of the classic ways that thinking goes wrong in the pseudosciences. Science tries to minimize and acknowledge the effects of the observation on the behavior of the observed; pseudoscience does not.

3. Equipment Constructs Results

The equipment used in an experiment often determines the results. The size of our telescopes, for example, has shaped and reshaped our theories about the size of the universe. In the twentieth century, Edwin Hubble's 60- and 100-inch telescopes on Mt. Wilson in southern California for the first time provided enough seeing power for astronomers to distinguish individual stars in other galaxies, thus proving that those fuzzy objects called nebulas that we thought were in our own galaxy were actually separate galaxies. In the nineteenth century, craniometry defined intelligence as brain size and instruments were designed that measured it as such; today intelligence is defined by facility with certain developmental tasks and is measured by another instrument, the IQ test. Sir Arthur Stanley Eddington illustrated the problem with this clever analogy:

> Let us suppose that an ichthyologist is exploring the life of the ocean. He casts a net into the water and brings up a fishy assortment. Surveying his catch, he proceeds in the usual manner of a scientist to systematize what it reveals. He arrives at two generalizations:
>
> **1.** No sea-creature is less than two inches long.
> **2.** All sea-creatures have gills.
>
> In applying this analogy, the catch stands for the body of knowledge which constitutes physical science, and the net for the sensory and intellectual equipment which we use in obtaining it. The casting of the net corresponds to observations.
>
> An onlooker may object that the first generalization is wrong. "There are plenty of sea-creatures under two inches long, only your net is not adapted to catch them." The ichthyologist dismisses this objection contemptuously. "Anything uncatchable by my net is *ipso facto* outside the

scope of ichthyological knowledge, and is not part of the kingdom of fishes which has been defined as the theme of ichthyological knowledge. In short, what my net can't catch isn't fish." (1958, p. 16)

Likewise, what my telescope can't see isn't there, and what my test can't measure isn't intelligence. Obviously, galaxies and intelligence exist, but how we measure and understand them is highly influenced by our equipment.

PROBLEMS IN PSEUDOSCIENTIFIC THINKING

4. Anecdotes Do Not Make a Science

Anecdotes—stories recounted in support of a claim—do not make a science. Without corroborative evidence from other sources, or physical proof of some sort, ten anecdotes are no better than one, and a hundred anecdotes are no better than ten. Anecdotes are told by fallible human storytellers. Farmer Bob in Puckerbrush, Kansas, may be an honest, church-going, family man not obviously subject to delusions, but we need physical evidence of an alien spacecraft or alien bodies, not just a story about landings and abductions at 3:00 A.M. on a deserted country road. Likewise with many medical claims. Stories about how your Aunt Mary's cancer was cured by watching Marx Brothers movies or taking a liver extract from castrated chickens are meaningless. The cancer might have gone into remission on its own, which some cancers do; or it might have been misdiagnosed; or, or, or. . . . What we need are controlled experiments, not anecdotes. We need 100 subjects with cancer, all properly diagnosed and matched. Then we need 25 of the subjects to watch Marx Brothers movies, 25 to watch Alfred Hitchcock movies, 25 to watch the news, and 25 to watch nothing. Then we need to deduct the average rate of remission for this type of cancer and then analyze the data for statistically significant differences between the groups. If there are statistically significant differences, we better get confirmation from other scientists who have conducted their own experiments separate from ours before we hold a press conference to announce the cure for cancer.

5. Scientific Language Does Not Make a Science

Dressing up a belief system in the trappings of science by using scientific language and jargon, as in "creation-science," means nothing without evidence, experimental testing, and corroboration. Because science has such a powerful mystique in our society, those who wish to gain respectability but do not have evidence try to do an end run around the missing evidence by looking and sounding "scientific." Here is a classic example from a New Age column in the Santa Monica News: "This planet has been slumbering for eons and with the inception of higher energy frequencies is about to awaken in terms of consciousness and spirituality. Masters of limitation and masters of divination use the same creative force to manifest their realities, however, one moves in a downward spiral and the latter moves in an upward spiral, each increasing the

resonant vibration inherent in them." How's that again? I have no idea what this means, but it has the language components of a physics experiment: "higher energy frequencies," "downward and upward spirals," and "resonant vibration." Yet these phrases mean nothing because they have no precise and operational definitions. How do you measure a planet's higher energy frequencies or the resonant vibration of masters of divination? For that matter, what *is* a master of divination?

6. Bold Statements Do Not Make Claims True

Something is probably pseudoscientific if enormous claims are made for its power and veracity but supportive evidence is scarce as hen's teeth. L. Ron Hubbard, for example, opens his *Dianetics: The Modern Science of Mental Health*, with this statement: "The creation of Dianetics is a milestone for man comparable to his discovery of fire and superior to his invention of the wheel and arch" (in Gardner 1952, p. 263). Sexual energy guru Wilhelm Reich called his theory of Orgonomy "a revolution in biology and psychology comparable to the Copernican Revolution" (in Gardner 1952, p. 259). I have a thick file of papers and letters from obscure authors filled with such outlandish claims (I call it the "Theories of Everything" file). Scientists sometimes make this mistake, too, as we saw at 1:00 P.M., on March 23, 1989, when Stanley Pons and Martin Fleischmann held a press conference to announce to the world that they had made cold nuclear fusion work. Gary Taubes's excellent book about the cold fusion debacle, appropriately named *Bad Science* (1993), thoroughly examines the implications of this incident. Maybe fifty years of physics will be proved wrong by one experiment, but don't throw out your furnace until that experiment has been replicated. The moral is that the more extraordinary the claim, the more extraordinarily well-tested the evidence must be.

7. Heresy Does Not Equal Correctness

They laughed at Copernicus. They laughed at the Wright brothers. Yes, well, they laughed at the Marx brothers. Being laughed at does not mean you are right. Wilhelm Reich compared himself to Peer Gynt, the unconventional genius out of step with society, and misunderstood and ridiculed as a heretic until proven right: "Whatever you have done to me or will do to me in the future, whether you glorify me as a genius or put me in a mental institution, whether you adore me as your savior or hang me as a spy, sooner or later necessity will force you to comprehend that I have discovered the laws of the living" (in Gardner 1952, p. 259). Reprinted in the January-February 1996 issue of the *Journal of Historical Review*, the organ of Holocaust denial, is a famous quote from the nineteenth-century German philosopher Arthur Schopenhauer, which is quoted often by those on the margins: "All truth passes through three stages. First, it is ridiculed. Second, it is violently opposed. Third, it is accepted as self-evident." But "all truth" does not pass through these stages. Lots of true ideas are accepted without ridicule or opposition, violent or otherwise. Einstein's theory of relativity was largely ignored until 1919, when experimental evidence proved him right. He was not ridiculed, and no one violently opposed his ideas. The Schopenhauer quote is just a rationalization, a fancy way for those who are ridiculed or violently opposed to say, "See, I must be right." Not so.

History is replete with tales of the lone scientist working in spite of his peers and flying in the face of the doctrines of his or her own field of study. Most of them turned out to be wrong and we do not remember their names. For every Galileo shown the instruments of torture for advocating a scientific truth, there are a thousand (or ten thousand) unknowns whose "truths" never pass muster with other scientists. The scientific community cannot be expected to test every fantastic claim that comes along, especially when so many are logically inconsistent. If you want to do science, you have to learn to play the game of science. This involves getting to know the scientists in your field, exchanging data and ideas with colleagues informally, and formally presenting results in conference papers, peer-reviewed journals, books, and the like.

8. Burden of Proof

Who has to prove what to whom? The person making the extraordinary claim has the burden of proving to the experts and to the community at large that his or her belief has more validity than the one almost everyone else accepts. You have to lobby for your opinion to be heard. Then you have to marshal experts on your side so you can convince the majority to support your claim over the one that they have always supported. Finally, when you are in the majority, the burden of proof switches to the outsider who wants to challenge you with his or her unusual claim. Evolutionists had the burden of proof for half a century after Darwin, but now the burden of proof is on creationists. It is up to creationists to show why the theory of evolution is wrong and why creationism is right, and it is not up to evolutionists to defend evolution. The burden of proof is on the Holocaust deniers to prove the Holocaust did not happen, not on Holocaust historians to prove that it did. The rationale for this is that mountains of evidence prove that both evolution and the Holocaust are facts. In other words, it is not enough to have evidence. You must convince others of the validity of your evidence. And when you are an outsider this is the price you pay, regardless of whether you are right or wrong.

9. Rumors Do Not Equal Reality

Rumors begin with "I read somewhere that . . ." or "I heard from someone that. . . ." Before long the rumor becomes reality, as "I know that . . ." passes from person to person. Rumors may be true, of course, but usually they are not. They do make for great tales, however. There is the "true story" of the escaped maniac with a prosthetic hook who haunts the lover's lanes of America. There is the legend of "The Vanishing Hitchhiker," in which a driver picks up a hitchhiker who vanishes from his car along with his jacket; locals then tell the driver that his hitchhiking woman had died that same day the year before, and eventually he discovers his jacket on her grave. Such stories spread fast and never die.

Caltech historian of science Dan Kevles once told a story he suspected was apocryphal at a dinner party. Two students did not get back from a ski trip in time to take their final exam because the activities of the previous day had extended well into the night. They told their professor that they had gotten a flat tire, so he gave them a makeup final the next day. Placing the students in separate rooms, he asked them just two questions: (1) "For 5 points, what is the chemical formula for water?" (2) "For 95 points, which tire?" Two of the dinner guests had heard a vaguely similar story. The next day I repeated the story to my students and before I got to the punch line, three of them simultaneously blurted out, "Which tire?" Urban legends and persistent rumors are ubiquitous. Here are a few:

- The secret ingredient in Dr. Pepper is prune juice.
- A woman accidentally killed her poodle by drying it in a microwave oven.
- Paul McCartney died and was replaced by a look-alike.
- Giant alligators live in the sewers of New York City.
- The moon landing was faked and filmed in a Hollywood studio.
- George Washington had wooden teeth.
- The number of stars inside the "P" on Playboy magazine's cover indicates how many times publisher Hugh Hefner had sex with the centerfold.
- A flying saucer crashed in New Mexico and the bodies of the extraterrestrials are being kept by the Air Force in a secret warehouse.

How many have you heard . . . and believed? None of them are true.

10. Unexplained Is Not Inexplicable

Many people are overconfident enough to think that if *they* cannot explain something, it must be inexplicable and therefore a true mystery of the paranormal. An amateur archeologist declares that because he cannot figure out how the pyramids were built, they must have been constructed by space aliens. Even those who are more reasonable at least think that if the experts cannot explain something, it must be inexplicable. Feats such as the bending of spoons, firewalking, or mental telepathy are often thought to be of a paranormal or mystical nature because most people cannot explain them. When they are explained, most people respond, "Yes, of course" or "That's obvious once you see it." Firewalking is a case in point. People speculate endlessly about supernatural powers over pain and heat, or mysterious brain chemicals that block the pain and prevent burning. The simple explanation is that the capacity of light and fluffy coals to contain heat is very low, and the conductivity of heat from the light and fluffy coals to your feet is very poor. As long as you don't stand around on the coals, you will not get burned. (Think of a cake in a 450°F oven. The air, the cake, and the pan are all at 450°F, but only the metal pan will burn your hand. It has a high heat capacity and high conductivity, while air and cake are light and fluffy and have a low heat capacity and low conductivity.) This is why magicians do not tell their secrets. Most of their tricks are extremely simple and knowing the secret takes the magic out of the trick.

There are many genuine unsolved mysteries in the universe and it is okay to say, "We do not yet know but someday perhaps we will." The problem is that most of us find it more comforting to have certainty, even if it is premature, than to live with unsolved or unexplained mysteries.

11. Failures Are Rationalized

In science, the value of negative findings—failures—cannot be overemphasized. Usually they are not wanted, and often they are not published. But most of the time failures are how we get closer to truth. Honest scientists will readily admit their errors, but all scientists are kept in line by the fact that their fellow scientists will publicize any attempt to fudge. Not pseudoscientists. They ignore or rationalize failures, especially when exposed. If they are actually caught cheating—not a frequent occurrence—they claim that their powers usually work but not always, so when pressured to perform on television or in a laboratory, they sometimes resort to cheating. If they simply fail to perform, they have ready any number of creative explanations: too many controls in an experiment cause negative results; the powers do not work in the presence of skeptics; the powers do not work in the presence of electrical equipment; the powers come and go, and this is one of those times they went. Finally, they claim that if skeptics cannot explain everything, then there must be something paranormal; they fall back on the unexplained is not inexplicable fallacy.

12. After-the-Fact Reasoning

Also known as "*post hoc, ergo propter hoc,*" literally "after this, therefore because of this." At its basest level, it is a form of superstition. The baseball player does not shave and hits two home runs. The gambler wears his lucky shoes because he has won wearing them in the past. More subtly, scientific studies can fall prey to this fallacy. In 1993 a study found that breast-fed children have higher IQ scores. There was much clamor over what ingredient in mother's milk increased intelligence. Mothers who bottle-fed their babies were made to feel guilty. But soon researchers began to wonder whether breast-fed babies are attended to differently. Maybe nursing mothers spend more time with their babies and motherly vigilance was the cause behind the differences in IQ. As Hume taught us, the fact that two events follow each other in sequence does not mean they are connected causally. Correlation does not mean causation.

13. Coincidence

In the paranormal world, coincidences are often seen as deeply significant. "Synchronicity" is invoked, as if some mysterious force were at work behind the scenes. But I see synchronicity as nothing more than a type of contingency—a conjuncture of two or more events without apparent design. When the connection is made in a manner that seems impossible according to our intuition of the laws of probability, we have a tendency to think something mysterious is at work.

But most people have a very poor understanding of the laws of probability. A gambler will win six in a row and then think he is either "on a hot streak" or "due to lose." Two people in a room of thirty people discover that they have the same birthday and conclude that something mysterious is at work. You go to the phone to call your friend Bob. The phone rings and it is Bob. You think, "Wow, what are the chances; This could not have been a mere coincidence. Maybe Bob and I are communicating telepathically." In fact, none of these coincidences are coincidences under the rules of probability. The gambler has predicted both possible outcomes, a fairly safe bet! The probability that two people in a room of thirty people will have the same birthday is 71 percent. And you have forgotten how many times Bob did not call under such circumstances, or someone else called, or Bob called but you were not thinking of him, and so on. As the behavioral psychologist B. F. Skinner proved in the laboratory, the human mind seeks relationships between events and often finds them even when they are not present. Slot-machines are based on Skinnerian principles of intermittent reinforcement. The dumb human, like the dumb rat, only needs an occasional payoff to keep pulling the handle. The mind will do the rest.

14. Representativeness

As Aristotle said, "The sum of the coincidences equals certainty." We forget most of the insignificant coincidences and remember the meaningful ones. Our tendency to remember hits and ignore misses is the bread and butter of the psychics, prophets, and soothsayers who make hundreds of predictions each January 1. First they increase the probability of a hit by predicting mostly generalized sure bets like "There will be a major earthquake in southern California" or "I see trouble for the Royal Family." Then, next January, they publish their hits and ignore the misses, and hope no one bothers to keep track.

We must always remember the larger context in which a seemingly unusual event occurs, and we must always analyze unusual events for their representativeness of their class of phenomena. In the case of the "Bermuda Triangle," an area of the Atlantic Ocean where ships and planes "mysteriously" disappear, there is the assumption that something strange or alien is at work. But we must consider how representative such events are in that area. Far more shipping lanes run through the Bermuda Triangle than its surrounding areas, so accidents and mishaps and disappearances are more likely to happen in the area. As it turns out, the accident rate is actually lower in the Bermuda Triangle than in surrounding areas. Perhaps this area should be called the "Non-Bermuda Triangle." (See Kusche 1975 for a full explanation of this solved mystery.) Similarly, in investigating haunted houses, we must have a baseline measurement of noises, creaks, and other events before we can say that an occurrence is unusual (and therefore mysterious). I used to hear rapping sounds in the walls of my house. Ghosts? Nope. Bad plumbing. I occasionally hear scratching sounds in my basement. Poltergeists? Nope. Rats. One would be well-advised to first thoroughly understand the probable worldly explanation before turning to otherworldly ones.

LOGICAL PROBLEMS IN THINKING

15. Emotive Words and False Analogies

Emotive words are used to provoke emotion and sometimes to obscure rationality. They can be positive emotive words—*motherhood, America, integrity, honesty.* Or they can be negative—*rape, cancer, evil, communist.* Likewise, metaphors and analogies can cloud thinking with emotion or steer us onto a side path. A pundit talks about inflation as "the cancer of society" or industry "raping the environment." In his 1992 Democratic nomination speech, Al Gore constructed an elaborate analogy between the story of his sick son and America as a sick country. Just as his son, hovering on the brink of death, was nursed back to health by his father and family, America, hovering on the brink of death after twelve years of Reagan and Bush, was to be nurtured back to health under the new administration. Like anecdotes, analogies and metaphors do not constitute proof. They are merely tools of rhetoric.

16. *Ad Ignorantiam*

This is an appeal to ignorance of lack of knowledge and is related to the *burden of proof* and *unexplained is not inexplicable* fallacies, where someone argues that if you cannot disprove a claim it must be true. For example, if you cannot prove that there isn't any psychic power, then there must be. The absurdity of this argument comes into focus if one argues that if you cannot prove that Santa Claus does not exist, then he must exist. You can argue the opposite in a similar manner. If you cannot prove Santa Claus exists, then he must not exist. In science, belief should come from positive evidence in support of a claim, not lack of evidence for or against a claim.

17. *Ad Hominem* and *Tu Quoque*

Literally "to the man" and "you also," these fallacies redirect the focus from thinking about the idea to thinking about the person holding the idea. The goal of an *ad hominem* attack is to discredit the claimant in hopes that it will discredit the claim. Calling someone an atheist, a communist, a child abuser, or a neo-Nazi does not in any way disprove that person's statement. It might be helpful to know whether someone is of a particular religion or holds a particular ideology, in case this has in some way biased the research, but refuting claims must be done directly, not indirectly. If Holocaust deniers, for example, are neo-Nazis or anti-Semites, this would certainly guide their choice of which historical events to emphasize or ignore. But if they are making the claim, for example, that Hitler did not have a master plan for the extermination of European Jewry, the response "Oh, he is saying that because he is a neo-Nazi" does not refute the argument. Whether Hitler had a master plan or not is a question that can be settled historically. Similarly for *tu quoque.* If someone accuses you of cheating on your taxes, the answer "Well, so do you" is no proof one way or the other.

18. Hasty Generalization

In logic, the hasty generalization is a form of improper induction. In life, it is called prejudice. In either case, conclusions are drawn before the facts warrant it. Perhaps because our brains evolved to be constantly on the lookout for connections between events and causes, this fallacy is one of the most common of all. A couple of bad teachers mean a bad school. A few bad cars mean that brand of automobile is unreliable. A handful of members of a group are used to judge the entire group. In science, we must carefully gather as much information as possible before announcing our conclusions.

19. Overreliance on Authorities

We tend to rely heavily on authorities in our culture, especially if the authority is considered to be highly intelligent. The IQ score has acquired nearly mystical proportions in the last half century, but I have noticed that belief in the paranormal is not uncommon among Mensa members (the high-IQ club for those in the top 2 percent of the population); some even argue that their "Psi-Q" is also superior. Magician James Randi is fond of lampooning authorities with Ph.D.s—once they are granted the degree, he says, they find it almost impossible to say two things: "I don't know" and "I was wrong." Authorities, by virtue of their expertise in a field, may have a better chance of being right in that field, but correctness is certainly not guaranteed, and their expertise does not necessarily qualify them to draw conclusions in other areas.

In other words, *who* is making the claim makes a difference. If it is a Nobel laureate, we take note because he or she has been right in a big way before. If it is a discredited scam artist, we give a loud guffaw because he or she has been wrong in a big way before. While expertise is useful for separating the wheat from the chaff, it is dangerous in that we might either (1) accept a wrong idea just because it was supported by someone we respect (false positive) or (2) reject a right idea just because it was supported by someone we disrespect (false negative). How do you avoid such errors? Examine the evidence.

20. Either-Or

Also known as the *fallacy of negation* or the *false dilemma,* this is the tendency to dichotomize the world so that if you discredit one position, the observer is forced to accept the other. This is a favorite tactic of creationists, who claim that life either was divinely created or evolved. Then they spend the majority of their time discrediting the theory of evolution so that they can argue that since evolution is wrong, creationism must be right. But it is not enough to point out weaknesses in a theory. If your theory is indeed superior, it must explain both the "normal" data explained by the old theory and the "anomalous" data not explained by the old theory. A new theory needs evidence in favor of it, not just against the opposition.

21. Circular Reasoning

Also known as the *fallacy of redundancy, begging the question,* or *tautology,* this is when the conclusion or claim is merely a restatement of one of the premises. Christian apologetics is filled with tautologies: *Is there a God? Yes. How do you know? Because the Bible says so. How do you know the Bible is correct? Because it was inspired by God.* In other words, God is because God is. Science also has its share of redundancies: *What is gravity? The tendency for objects to be attracted to one another: Why are objects attracted to one another? Gravity*. In other words, gravity is because gravity is. (In fact, some of Newton's contemporaries rejected his theory of gravity as being an unscientific throwback to medieval occult thinking.) Obviously, a tautological operational definition can still be useful. Yet, difficult as it is, we must try to construct operational definitions that can be tested, falsified, and refuted.

22. *Reductio ad Absurdum* and the Slippery Slope

Reductio ad absurdum is the refutation of an argument by carrying the argument to its logical end and so reducing it to an absurd conclusion. Surely, if an argument's consequences are absurd, it must be false. This is not necessarily so, though sometimes pushing an argument to its limits is a useful exercise in critical thinking; often this is a way to discover whether a claim has validity, especially if an experiment testing the actual reduction can be run. Similarly, the slippery slope fallacy involves constructing a scenario in which one thing leads ultimately to an end so extreme that the first step should never be taken. For example: *Eating Ben & Jerry's ice cream will cause you to put on weight. Putting on weight will make you overweight. Soon you will weigh 350 pounds and die of heart disease. Eating Ben & Jerry's ice cream leads to death. Don't even try it*. Certainly eating a scoop of Ben & Jerry's ice cream may contribute to obesity, which could possibly, in very rare cases, cause death. But the consequence does not necessarily follow from the premise.

PSYCHOLOGICAL PROBLEMS IN THINKING

23. Effort Inadequacies and the Need for Certainty, Control, and Simplicity

Most of us, most of the time, want certainty, want to control our environment, and want nice, neat simple explanations. All this may have some evolutionary basis, but in a multifarious society with complex problems, these characteristics can radically oversimplify reality and interfere with critical thinking and problem solving. For example, I believe that paranormal beliefs and pseudoscientific claims flourish in market economies in part because of the uncertainty of the marketplace. According to James Randi, after communism collapsed in Russia there was a significant increase in such belief. Not only are the people now freer to try to swindle each other with scams and rackets but many truly believe they have discovered something concrete and significant about the nature of the world. Capitalism is a lot less stable a social structure than communism. Such uncertainties lead the mind to look for explanations for the vagaries and contingencies of the market (and life in general), and the mind often takes a turn toward the supernatural and paranormal.

Scientific and critical thinking does not come naturally. It takes training, experience, and effort, as Alfred Mander explained in his *Logic for the Millions*: "Thinking is skilled work. It is not true that we are naturally endowed with the ability to think clearly and logically—without learning how, or without practicing. People with untrained minds should no more expect to think clearly and logically than people who have never learned and never practiced can expect to find themselves good carpenters, golfers, bridge players, or pianists" (1947, p. vii). We must always work to suppress our need to be absolutely certain and in total control and our tendency to seek the simple and effortless solution to a problem. Now and then the solutions may be simple, but usually they are not.

24. Problem-Solving Inadequacies

All critical and scientific thinking is, in a fashion, problem solving. There are numerous psychological disruptions that cause inadequacies in problem solving. Psychologist Barry Singer has demonstrated that when given the task of selecting the right answer to a problem after being told whether particular guesses are right or wrong, people:

A. Immediately form a hypothesis and look only for examples to confirm it.

B. Do not seek evidence to disprove the hypothesis.

C. Are very slow to change the hypothesis even when it is obviously wrong.

D. If the information is too complex, adopt overly-simple hypotheses or strategies for solutions.

E. If there is no solution, if the problem is a trick and "right" and "wrong" is given at random, form hypotheses about coincidental relationships they observed. Causality is always found. (Singer and Abell 1981, p. 18)

If this is the case with humans in general, then we all must make the effort to overcome these inadequacies in solving the problems of science and of life.

25. Ideological Immunity, or the Planck Problem

In day-to-day life, as in science, we all resist fundamental paradigm change. Social scientist Jay Stuart Snelson calls this resistance an *ideological immune system*: "educated, intelligent, and successful adults rarely change their most fundamental presuppositions" (1993, p. 54). According to Snelson, the more knowledge individuals have accumulated, and the more well-founded their theories have become (and remember, we all tend to look for and remember confirmatory evidence, not counterevidence), the greater the confidence in their ideologies. The consequence of this, however, is that we build up an "immunity" against new ideas that do not corroborate previous ones. Historians of science call this the *Planck Problem*, after physicist Max Planck, who made this observation on what must happen for innovation to occur in science: "An important scientific innovation rarely makes its way by gradually winning over and converting its opponents: it rarely happens that Saul becomes Paul. What does happen is that its opponents gradually die out and that the growing generation is familiarized with the idea from the beginning" (1936, p. 97).

Psychologist David Perkins conducted an interesting correlational study in which he found a strong positive correlation between intelligence (measured by a standard IQ test) and the ability to give reasons for taking a point of view and defending that position; he also found a strong negative correlation between intelligence and the ability to consider other alternatives. That is, the higher the IQ, the greater the potential for ideological immunity. Ideological immunity is built into the scientific enterprise, where it functions as a filter against potentially overwhelming novelty. As historian of science I. B. Cohen explained, "New and revolutionary systems of science tend to be resisted rather than welcomed with open arms, because every successful scientist has a vested intellectual, social, and even financial interest in maintaining the status quo. If every revolutionary new idea were welcomed with open arms, utter chaos would be the result" (1985, p. 35).

In the end, history rewards those who are "right" (at least provisionally). Change does occur. In astronomy, the Ptolemaic geocentric universe was slowly displaced by Copernicus's heliocentric system. In geology, George Cuvier's catastrophism was gradually wedged out by the more soundly supported uniformitarianism of James Hutton and Charles Lyell. In biology, Darwin's evolution theory superseded creationist belief in the immutability of species. In Earth history, Alfred Wegener's idea of continental drift took nearly a half century to overcome the received dogma of fixed and stable continents. Ideological immunity can be overcome in science and in daily life, but it takes time and corroboration.

SPINOZA'S DICTUM

Skeptics have the very human tendency to relish debunking what we already believe to be nonsense. It is fun to recognize other people's fallacious reasoning, but that's not the whole point. As skeptics and critical thinkers, we must move beyond our emotional responses because by understanding how others have gone wrong and how science is subject to social control and cultural influences, we can improve our understanding of how the world works. It is for this reason that it is so important for us to understand the history of both science and pseudoscience. If we see the larger picture of how these movements evolve and figure out how their thinking went wrong, we won't make the same mistakes. The seventeenth-century Dutch philosopher Baruch Spinoza said it best: "I have made a ceaseless effort not to ridicule, not to bewail, not to scorn human actions, but to understand them."

4

An Introduction to Science
Scientific Thinking and the Scientific Method

STEVEN D. SCHAFERSMAN

INTRODUCTION

To succeed in this science course and, more specifically, to answer some of the questions on the first exam, you should be familiar with a few of the concepts regarding the definition of science, scientific thinking, and the methods of science. Most textbooks do an inadequate job of this task, so this essay provides that information. This information in its present form is not in your textbook, so please read it carefully here, and pay close attention to the words in boldface and the definitions in italics.

THE DEFINITION OF SCIENCE

Science is not merely a collection of facts, concepts, and useful ideas about nature, or even the systematic investigation of nature, although both are common definitions of science. *Science is a method of investigating nature—a way of knowing about nature—that discovers reliable knowledge about it.* In other words, science is a **method** of discovering **reliable knowledge** about nature. There are other methods of discovering and learning knowledge about nature (these other knowledge methods or systems will be discussed below in contradistinction to science), but science is the *only* method that results in the acquisition of reliable knowledge.

Reliable knowledge is knowledge that has a high probablility of being true because its veracity has been justified by a reliable method. Reliable knowledge is sometimes called **justified true belief,** to distinguish reliable knowledge from belief that is false and unjustified or even true but unjustified. (Please note that I do not, as some do, make a distinction between belief and knowledge; I think that what one believes is one's knowledge. The important distinction that should be made is whether one's knowledge or beliefs are true and, if true, are justifiably true.) Every person has knowledge or beliefs, but not all of each person's knowledge is reliably true and justified. In fact, most individuals believe in things that are untrue or unjustified or both: most people possess a lot of unreliable knowledge and, what's worse, they act on that knowledge! Other ways of knowing, and there are many in addition to science, are *not reliable* because their discovered knowledge is *not justified.* Science is a method that allows a person to possess, with the highest degree of certainty possible, reliable knowledge (justified true belief) about nature. The method used to justify scientific knowledge, and thus make it reliable, is called the **scientific method.** I will explain the formal procedures of the scientific method later in this essay, but first let's describe the more general practice of **scientific or critical thinking.**

SCIENTIFIC AND CRITICAL THINKING

When one uses the scientific method to study or investigate nature or the universe, one is practicing scientific thinking. All scientists practice scientific thinking, of course, since they are actively studying nature and investigating the universe by using the scientific method. But scientific thinking is not reserved solely for scientists. Anyone can "think like a scientist" who learns the scientific method and, most importantly, applies its precepts, whether he or she is investigating nature or not. When one uses the methods and principles of scientific thinking in everyday life—such as when studying history or literature, investigating societies or governments, seeking solutions to problems of economics or philosophy, or just trying to answer personal questions about oneself or the meaning of existence—one is said to be practicing **critical thinking.** *Critical thinking is thinking correctly for oneself that successfully leads to the most reliable answers to questions and solutions to problems.* In other words, critical thinking gives you reliable knowledge about all aspects of your life and society, and is not restricted to the formal study of nature. Scientific thinking is identical in theory and practice, but the term would be used to describe the method that gives you reliable knowledge about the natural world. Clearly, scientific and critical thinking are the same thing, but where one (scientific thinking) is always practiced by scientists, the other (critical thinking) is sometimes used by humans and sometimes not. Scientific and critical thinking was not discovered and developed by scientists (that honor must go to ancient Hellenistic philosophers, such as Aristotle, who also are sometimes considered the first scientists), but scientists were the ones to bring the practice of critical thinking to the attention and use of modern society (in the 17th and 18th centuries), and they are the most explicit, rigorous, and successful practitioners of critical thinking today. Some professionals in the humanities, social sciences, jurisprudence, business, and journalism practice critical thinking as well as any scientist, but many, alas, do not. Scientists *must* practice critical thinking to be successful, but the qualifications for success in other professions do not necessarily require the use of critical thinking, a fact that is the source of much confusion, discord, and unhappiness in our sociey.

The scientific method has proven to be the most reliable and successful method of thinking in human history, and it is quite possible to use scientific thinking in other human endeavors. For this reason, critical thinking—the application of scientific thinking to all areas of study and topics of investigation—is being taught in schools throughout the United States, and its teaching is being encouraged as a universal ideal. You may perhaps have been exposed to critical thinking skills and exercises earlier in your education. The important point is this: critical thinking is perhaps the most important skill a student can learn in school and college, since if you master its skills, you know how to think successfully and reach reliable conclusions, and such ability will prove valuable in any human endeavor, including the humanities, social sciences, commerce, law, journalism, and government, as well as in scholarly and scientific pursuits. Since critical thinking and scientific thinking are, as I claim, the same thing, only applied for different purposes, it is therefore reasonable to believe that if one learns scientific thinking in a science class, one learns, at the same time, the most important skill a student can possess—critical thinking. This, to my mind, is perhaps the foremost reason for college students to study science, no matter what one's eventual major, interest, or profession.

THE THREE CENTRAL COMPONENTS OF SCIENTIFIC AND CRITICAL THINKING

What is scientific thinking? At this point, it is customary to discuss questions, observations, data, hypotheses, testing, and theories, which are the formal parts of the scientific method, but these are NOT the most important components of the scientific method. The scientific method is practiced within a context of scientific thinking, and scientific (and critical) thinking is based on three things: using **empirical evidence (empiricism),** practicing **logical reasonsing (rationalism),** and possessing a **skeptical attitude (skepticism)** about presumed knowledge that leads to self-questioning, holding tentative conclusions, and being undogmatic (willingness to change one's beliefs). These three ideas or principles are universal throughout science; without them, there would be no scientific or critical thinking. Let's examine each in turn.

1. Empiricism: The Use of Empirical Evidence

Empirical evidence is evidence that one can see, hear, touch, taste, or smell; it is evidence that is susceptible to one's senses. Empirical evidence is important because it is evidence that others besides yourself can experience, and it is repeatable, so empirical evidence can be checked by yourself and others after knowledge claims are made by an individual. Empirical evidence is the *only* type of evidence that possesses these attributes and is therefore the only type used by scientists and critical thinkers to make vital decisions and reach sound conclusions.

We can contrast empirical evidence with other types of evidence to understand its value. Hearsay evidence is what someone says they heard another say; it is not reliable because you cannot check its source. Better is testimonial evidence, which, unlike hearsay evidence, is allowed in courts of law. But even testimonial evidence is notoriously unreliable, as numerous studies have shown. Courts also allow circumstantial evidence (e.g., means, motive, and opportunity), but this is obviously not reliable. Revelatory evidence or revelation is what someone says was revealed to them by some deity or supernatural power; it is not reliable because it cannot be checked by others and is not repeatable. Spectral evidence is evidence supposedly manifested by ghosts, spirits, and other paranormal or supernatural entities; spectral evidence was once used, for example, to convict and hang a number of innocent women on charges of witchcraft in Salem, Massachusetts, in the seventeenth century, before the colonial governor banned the use of such evidence, and the witchcraft trials ended. Emotional evidence is evidence derived from one's subjective feelings; such evidence is often repeatable, but only for one person, so it is unreliable.

The most common alternative to empirical evidence, authoritarian evidence, is what authorities (people, books, billboards, television commercials, etc.) tell you to believe. Sometimes, if the authority is reliable, authoritarian evidence is reliable evidence, but many authorities are not reliable, so you must check the reliability of each authority before you accept its evidence. In the end, you must be your own authority and rely on your own powers of critical thinking to know if what you believe is reliably true.(Transmitting knowledge by authority is, however, the most common method among humans for three reasons: first, we are all conditioned from birth by our parents through the use of positive and negative reinforcement to listen to, believe, and obey authorities; second, it is believed that human societies that relied on a few experienced or trained authorities for decisions that affected all had a higher survival value than those that didn't, and thus the behavioral trait of susceptibility to authority was strengthened and passed along to future generations by natural selection; third, authoritarian instruction is the quickest and most efficient method for transmitting information we know about. But remember: some authoritarian evidence and knowledge should be validated by empirical evidence, logical reasoning, and critical thinking before you should consider it reliable, and, in most cases, only you can do this for yourself.

It is, of course, impossible to receive an adequate education today without relying almost entirely upon authoritarian evidence. Teachers, instructors, and professors are generally considered to be reliable and trustworthy authorities, but even they should be questioned on occasion. The use of authoritarian evidence in education is so pervasive, that its use has been questioned as antithetical to the true spirit of scholarly and scientific inquiry, and attempts have been made in education at all levels in recent years to correct this bias by implementing discovery and inquiry methodologies and curricula in classrooms and laboratories. The recently revised geology laboratory course at Miami University, GLG 115.L, is one such attempt, as are the Natural Systems courses in the Western College Program at Miami. It is easier to utilize such programs in humanities and social sciences, in which different yet equally valid conclusions can be reached by critical thinking, rather than in the natural sciences, in which the objective reality of nature serves as a constant judge and corrective mechanism.

Another name for empirical evidence is natural evidence: the evidence found in nature. Naturalism is the philosophy that says that "Reality and existence (i.e. the universe, cosmos, or nature) can be described and explained solely in terms of natural evidence, natural processes, and natural laws." This is exactly what science tries to do. Another popular definition of naturalism is that "The universe exists as science says it does." This definition emphasizes the strong link between science and natural evidence and law, and it reveals that our best understanding of material reality and existence is ultimately based on philosophy. This is not bad, however, for, whether naturalism is ultimately true or not, science and naturalism reject the concept of ultimate or absolute truth in favor of a concept of proximate reliable truth that is far more successful and intellectually satisfying than the alternative, the philosophy of supernaturalism. The supernatural, if it exists, cannot be examined or tested by science, so it is irrelevant to science. It is impossible to possess reliable knowledge about the supernatural by the use of scientific and critical thinking. Individuals who claim to have knowledge about the supernatural do not possess this knowledge by the use of critical thinking, but by other methods of knowing.

Science has unquestionably been the most successful human endeavor in the history of civilization, because it is the only method that successfully discovers and formulates reliable knowledge. The evidence for this statement is so overwhelming that many individuals overlook exactly how modern civilization came to be (our modern civilization is based, from top to bottom, on the discoveries of science and their application, known as technology, to human purposes). Philosophies that claim to possess absolute or ultimate truth invariably find that they have to justify their beliefs by faith in dogma, authority, revelation, or philosophical speculation, since it is impossible to use finite human logic or natural evidence to demonstrate the existence of the absolute or ultimate in either the natural or supernatural worlds. Scientific and critical thinking require that one reject blind faith, authority, revelation, and subjective human feelings as a basis for reliable belief and knowledge. These human cognitive methods have their place in human life, but not as the foundation for reliable knowledge.

2. Rationalism: The Practice of Logical Reasoning

Scientists and critical thinkers always use logical reasoning. Logic allows us to reason correctly, but it is a complex topic and not easily learned; many books are devoted to explaining how to reason correctly, and we can not go into the details here. However, I must point out that most individuals do not reason logically, because they have never learned how to do so. Logic is not an ability that humans are born with or one that will gradually develop and improve on its own, but is a skill or discipline that must be learned within a formal educational environment. Emotional thinking, hopeful thinking, and wishful thinking are much more common than logical thinking, because they are far easier and more congenial to human nature. Most individuals would rather believe something is true because they feel it is true, hope it is true, or wish it were true, rather than deny their emotions and accept that their beliefs are false.

Often the use of logical reasoning requires a struggle with the will, because logic sometimes forces one to deny one's emotions and face reality, and this is often painful. But remember this: emotions are not evidence, feelings are not facts, and subjective beliefs are not substantive beliefs. Every successful scientist and critical thinker spent years learning how to think logically, almost always in a formal educational context. Some people can learn logical thinking by trial and error, but this method wastes time, is inefficient, is sometimes unsuccessful, and is often painful.

The best way to learn to think logically is to study logic and reasoning in a philosophy class, take mathematics and science courses that force you to use logic, read great literature and study history, and write frequently. Reading, writing, and math are the traditional methods that young people learned to think logically (i.e. correctly), but today science is a fourth method. Perhaps the best way is to do a lot of writing that is then reviewed by someone who has critical thinking skills. Most people never learn to think logically; many illogical arguments and statements are accepted and unchallenged in modern society—often leading to results that are counterproductive to the good of society or even tragic—because so many people don't recognize them for what they are.

3. Skepticism: Possessing a Skeptical Attitude

The final key idea in science and critical thinking is skepticism, the constant questioning of your beliefs and conclusions. Good scientists and critical thinkers constantly examine the evidence, arguments, and reasons for their beliefs. Self-deception and deception of yourself by others are two of the most common human failings. Self-deception often goes unrecognized because most people deceive themselves. The only way to escape both deception by others and the far more common trait of self-deception is to repeatedly and rigorously examine your basis for holding your beliefs. You must question the truth and reliability of both the knowledge claims of others and the knowledge you already possess. One way to do this is to test your beliefs against objective reality by predicting the consequences or logical outcomes of your beliefs and the actions that follow from your beliefs. If the logical consequences of your beliefs match objective reality—as measured by empirical evidence—you can conclude that your beliefs are reliable knowledge (that is, your beliefs have a high probability of being true).

Many people believe that skeptics are closed-minded and, once possessing reliable knowledge, resist changing their minds—but just the opposite is true. A skeptic holds beliefs tentatively, and is open to new evidence and rational arguments about those beliefs. Skeptics are undogmatic, i.e., they are willing to change their minds, but only in the face of new reliable evidence or sound reasons that compel one to do so. Skeptics have open minds, but not so open that their brains fall out: they resist believing something in the first place without adequate evidence or reason, and this attribute is worthy of emulation. Science treats new ideas with the same skepticism: extraordinary claims require extraordinary evidence to justify one's credulity. We are faced every day with fantastic, bizarre, and outrageous claims about the natural world; if we don't wish to believe every pseudoscientific allegation or claim of the paranormal, we must have some method of deciding what to believe or not, and that method is the scientific method which uses critical thinking.

THE SCIENTIFIC METHOD IN PRACTICE

Now, we are ready to put the scientific method into action. Many books have been written about the scientific method, and it is a long and complex topic. Here I will only treat it briefly and superficially. The scientific method, as used in both scientific thinking and critical thinking, follows a number of steps.

1. One must ask a meaningful question or identify a significant problem, and one should be able to state the problem or question in a way that it is conceivably possible to answer it. Any attempt to gain knowledge must start here. Here is where emotions and outside influences come in. For example, all scientists are very curious about nature, and they have to possess this emotional characteristic to sustain the motivation and energy necessary to perform the hard and often tedious work of science. Other emotions that can enter are excitement, ambition, anger, a sense of unfairness, happiness, and so forth. Note that scientists have emotions, some in high degree; however, they don't let their emotions give false validity to their conclusions, and, in fact, the scientific method prevents them from trying to do this even if they wished.

Many outside factors can come into play here. Scientists must choose which problems to work on, they decide how much time to devote to different problems, and they are often influenced by cultural, social, political, and economic factors. Scientists live and work within a culture that often shapes their approach to problems; they work within theories that often shape their current understanding of nature; they work within a society that often decides what scientific topics will be financially supported and which will not; and they work within a political system that often determines which topics are permitted and financially rewarded and which are not.

Also, at this point, normally nonscientific emotional factors can lead to divergent pathways. Scientists could be angry at polluters and choose to investigate the effects of pollutants; other scientists could investigate the results of smoking cigarettes on humans because they can earn a living doing this by working for tobacco companies; intuition can be used to suggest different approaches to problems; even dreams can suggest creative solutions to problems. I wish to emphasize, however, that the existence of these frankly widespread nonscientific emotional and cultural influences does *not* compromize the ultimate reliability and objectivity of scientific results, because subsequent steps in the scientific method serve to eliminate these outside factors and allow science to reach reliable and objective conclusions (admittedly it may take some time for subjective and unreliable scientific results to be eliminated). There exists a school of thought today in the humanities (philosophy, history, and sociology) called post-modernism or scientific constructivism, that claims that science is a social and cultural construct, that scientific knowledge inevitably changes as societies and cultures change, and that science has no inherently valid foundation on which to base its knowledge claims of objectivity and reliability. In brief, post-modernists believe that the modern, scientific world of Enlightenment rationality and objectivity must now give way to a post-modern world of relativism, social constructivism, and equality of belief. Almost all scientists who are aware of this school of thought reject it, as do I; postmodernism is considered irrelevant by scientists and has had no impact on the practice of science at all. We will have to leave this interesting topic for a later time, unfortunately, but you may be exposed to these ideas in a humanities class. If you are, remember to think critically!

2. One must next gather relevant information to attempt to answer the question or solve the problem by making observations. The first observations could be data obtained from the library or information from your own experience. Another souce of observations could be from trial experiments or past experiments. These observations, and all that follow, must be empirical in nature—that is, they must be sensible, measurable, and repeatable, so that others can make the same observations. Great ingenuity and hard work on the part of the scientist is often necessary to make scientific observations. Furthermore, a great deal of training is necessary in order to learn the methods and techniques of gathering scientific data.

3. Now one can propose a solution or answer to the problem or question. In science, this suggested solution or answer is called a **scientific hypothesis,** and this is one of the most important steps a scientist can perform, because the proposed hypothesis must be stated in such a way that it is testable. *A scientific hypothesis is an informed, testable, and predictive solution to a scientific problem that explains a natural phenomenon, process, or event.* In critical thinking, as in science, your proposed answer or solution must be testable, otherwise it is essentially useless for further investigation. Most individuals—noncritical thinkers all—stop here, and are satisfied with their first answer or solution, but this lack of skepticism is a major roadblock to gaining reliable knowledge. While some of these early proposed answers may be true, most will be false, and further investigation will almost always be necessary to determine their validity.

4. Next, one must **test** the hypothesis before it is corroborated and given any real validity. There are *two* ways to do this. First, one can conduct an *experiment*. This is often presented in science textbooks as the only way to test hypotheses in science, but a little reflection will show that many natural problems are not amenable to experimentation, such as questions about stars, galaxies, mountain formation, the formation of the solar system, ancient evolutionary events, and so forth.

The second way to test a hypothesis is to *make further observations.* Every hypothesis has consequences and makes certain predictions about the phenomenon or process under investigation. Using logic and empirical evidence, one can test the hypothesis by examining how successful the predictions are, that is, how well the predictions and consequences agree with new data, further insights, new patterns, and perhaps with models. The testability or predictiveness of a hypothesis is its most important characteristic. Only hypotheses involving natural processes, natural events, and natural laws can be tested; the supernatural cannot be tested, so it lies outside of science and its existence or nonexistence is irrelevant to science.

5. If the hypothesis fails the test, it must be rejected and either abandoned or modified. Most hypotheses are modified by scientists who don't like to simply throw out an idea they think is correct and in which they have already invested a great deal of time or effort. Nevertheless, a modified hypothesis must be tested again. If the hypothesis passes the further tests, it is considered to be a **corroborated hypothesis,** and can now be published. *A corroborated hypothesis is one that has passed its tests, i.e., one whose predictions have been verified.* Now other scientists test the hypothesis. If further corroborated by subsequent tests, it becomes highly corroborated and is now considered to be reliable knowledge. By the way, the technical name for this part of the scientific method is the "hypotheticco-deductive method," so named because one deduces the results of the predictions of the hypothesis and tests these deductions. Inductive reasoning, the alternative to deductive reasoning, was used earlier to help formulate the hypothesis. Both of these types of reasoning are therefore used in science, and both must be used logically.

Scientists never claim that a hypothesis is "proved" in a strict sense (but sometimes this is quite legitimately claimed when using popular language), because proof is something found only in mathematics and logic, disciplines in which all logical parameters or constraints can be defined, and something that is not true in the natural world. Scientists prefer to use the word "corroborated" rather than "proved," but the meaning is essentially the same. A highly corroborated hypothesis becomes something else in addition to reliable knowledge—it becomes a **scientific fact.** *A scientific fact is a highly corroborated hypothesis that has been so repeatedly tested and for which so much reliable evidence exists, that it would be perverse or irrational to deny it.* This type of reliable knowledge is the closest that humans can come to the "truth" about the universe (I put the word"truth" in quotation marks because

there are many different kinds of truth, such as logical truth, emotional truth, religious truth, legal truth, philosophical truth, etc.; it should be clear that this essay deals with scientific truth, which, while certainly not the sole truth, is nevertheless the best truth humans can possess about the natural world).

There are many such scientific facts: the existence of gravity as a property of all matter, the past and present evolution of all living organisms, the presence of nucleic acids in all life, the motion of continents and giant tectonic plates on Earth, the expansion of the universe following a giant explosion, and so forth. Many scientific facts violate common sense and the beliefs of ancient philosophies and religions, so many people persist in denying them, but they thereby indulge in irrationality and perversity. Many other areas of human thought and philosophy, and many other knowledge systems (methods of gaining knowledge), exist that claim to have factual knowledge about the world. Some even claim that their facts are absolutely or ultimately true, something science would never claim. But their "facts" are not reliable knowledge, because—while they might fortuitously be true—they have not been justified by a reliable method. If such unreliable "facts" are true—and I certainly don't maintain that all such knowledge claims are false—we can never be *sure* that they are true, as we can with scientific facts.

6. The final step of the scientific method is to construct, support, or cast doubt on a **scientific theory.** A theory in science is not a guess, speculation, or suggestion, which is the popular definition of the word "theory." *A scientific theory is a unifying and self-consistent explanation of fundamental natural processes or phenomena that is totally constructed of corroborated hypotheses.* A theory, therefore, is built of reliable knowledge—built of scientific facts—and its purpose is to explain major natural processes or phenomena. Scientific theories explain nature by unifying many once-unrelated facts or corroborated hypotheses; they are the strongest and most truthful explanations of how the universe, nature, and life came to be, how they work, what they are made of, and what will become of them. Since humans are living organisms and are part of the universe, science explains all of these things about ourselves.

These scientific theories—such as the theories of relativity, quantum mechanics, thermodynamics, evolution, genetics, plate tectonics, and big bang cosmology—are the most reliable, most rigorous, and most comprehensive form of knowledge that humans possess. Thus, it is important for every educated person to understand where scientific knowledge comes from, and how to emulate this method of gaining knowledge. Scientific knowledge comes from the practice of scientific thinking-using the scientific method—and this mode of discovering and validating knowledge can be duplicated and achieved by anyone who practices critical thinking.

5

The Case of Dr. Semmelweis

CARL HEMPEL

As a simple illustration of some important aspects of scientific inquiry let us consider Semmelweis' work on childbed fever. Ignaz Semmelweis [1818–1865], a physician of Hungarian birth, did this work during the years from 1844 to 1848 at the Vienna General Hospital. As a member of the medical staff of the First Maternity Division in the hospital, Semmelweis was distressed to find that a large proportion of the women who were delivered of their babies in that division contracted a serious and often fatal illness known as puerperal fever or childbed fever. In 1844, as many as 260 out of 3,157 mothers in the First Division, or 8.2 per cent, died of the disease; for 1845, the death rate was 6.8 per cent, and for 1846, it was 11.4 per cent. These figures were all the more alarming because in the adjacent Second Maternity Division of the same hospital, which accommodated almost as many women as the First, the death toll from childbed fever was much lower: 2.3, 2.0, and 2.7 per cent for the same years. In a book that he wrote later on the causation and the prevention of childbed fever, Semmelweis describes his efforts to resolve the dreadful puzzle.

He began by considering various explanations that were current at the time; some of these he rejected out of hand as incompatible with well-established facts; others he subjected to specific tests. One widely accepted view attributed the ravages of puerperal fever to "epidemic influences", which were vaguely described as "atmospheric-cosmic-telluric changes" spreading over whole districts and causing childbed fever in women in confinement. But how, Semmelweis reasons, could such influences have plagued the First Division for years and yet spared the Second? And how could this view be reconciled with the fact that while the fever was raging in the hospital, hardly a case occurred in the city of Vienna or in its surroundings: a genuine epidemic, such as cholera, would not be so selective. Finally, Semmelweis notes that some of the women admitted to the First Division, living far from the hospital, had been overcome by labor on their way and had given birth in the street: yet despite these adverse conditions, the death rate from childbed fever among these cases of "street birth" was lower than the average for the First Division.

On another view, overcrowding was a cause of mortality in the First Division. But Semmelweis points out that in fact the crowding was heavier in the Second Division, partly as a result of the desperate efforts of patients to avoid assignment to the notorious First Division. He also rejects two similar conjectures that were current, by noting that there were no differences between the two Divisions in regard to diet or general care of the patients. In 1846, a commission that had been appointed to investigate the matter attributed the prevalence of illness in the First Division to injuries resulting from rough examination by the medical students, all of whom received their obstetrical training in the First Division. Semmelweis notes in refutation of this view that (a) the injuries resulting naturally from the process of birth are much more extensive than those that might be caused by rough examination; (b) the midwives who received their training in the Second Division examined their patients in much the same manner but without the same ill effects; (c) when, in response to the commission's report, the number of medical students was halved and their examinations of the women were reduced to a minimum, the mortality, after a brief decline, rose to higher levels than ever before.

Various psychological explanations were attempted. One of them noted that the First Division was so arranged that a priest bearing the last sacrament to a dying woman had to pass through five wards before reaching the sickroom beyond: the appearance of the priest, preceded by an attendant ringing a bell, was held to have a terrifying and debilitating effect upon the patients in the wards and thus to make them more likely victims of childbed fever. In the Second Division, this adverse factor was absent, since the priest had direct access to the sickroom. Semmelweis decided to test this conjecture. He persuaded the priest to come by a roundabout route and without ringing of the bell, in order to reach the sick chamber silently and unobserved. But the mortality in the First Division did not decrease. A new idea was suggested to Semmelweis by the observation that in the First Division the women were delivered lying on their backs; in the Second Division, on their sides. Though he thought it unlikely, he decided "like a drowning man clutching at a straw, to test whether this difference in procedure was significant. He introduced the use of the lateral position in the First Division, but again, the mortality remained unaffected.

At last, early in 1847, an accident gave Semmelweis the decisive clue for his solution of the problem. A colleague of his, Kolletschka, received a puncture wound in the finger, from the scalpel of a student with whom he was performing an autopsy, and died after an agonizing illness during which he displayed the same symptoms that Semmelweis had observed in the victims of childbed fever. Although the role of microorganisms in such infections had not yet been recognized at the time, Semmelweis realized that "cadaveric matter" which the student's scalpel had introduced into Kolletschka's blood stream had caused his colleague's fatal illness. And the similarities between the course of Kolletschka's disease and that of the women in his clinic led Semmelweis to the conclusion that his patients had died of the same kind of blood poisoning: he, his colleagues, and the medical students had been the carriers of the infectious material, for he and his associates used to come to the wards directly from performing dissections in the autopsy room, and examine the women in labor after only superficially washing their hands, which often retained a characteristic foul odor.

Again, Semmelweis put his idea to a test. He reasoned that if he were right, then childbed fever could be prevented by chemically destroying the infectious material adhering to the hands. He therefore issued an order requiring all medical students to wash their hands in a solution of chlorinated lime before making an examination. The mortality from childbed fever promptly began to decrease, and for the year 1848 it fell to 1.27 per cent in the First Division, compared to 1.33 in the Second. In further support of his idea, or of his *hypothesis*, as we will also say, Semmelweis notes that it accounts for the fact that the mortality in the Second Division consistently was so much lower: the patients there were attended by midwives, whose training did not include anatomical instruction by dissection of cadavers. The hypothesis also explained the lower mortality among "street births": women who arrived with babies in arms were rarely examined after admission and thus had a better chance of escaping infection. Similarly, the hypothesis accounted for the fact that the victims of childbed fever among the newborn babies were all among those whose mothers had contracted the disease during labor; for then the infection could be transmitted to the baby before birth, through the common bloodstream of mother and child, whereas this was impossible when the mother remained healthy.

Further clinical experiences soon led Semmelweis to broaden his hypothesis. On one occasion, for example, he and his associates, having carefully disinfected their hands, examined first a woman in labor who was suffering from a festering cervical cancer; then they proceeded to examine twelve other women in the same room, after only routine washing without renewed disinfection. Eleven of the twelve patients died of puerperal fever. Semmelweis concluded that childbed fever can be caused not only by cadaveric material, but also by "putrid matter derived from living organisms."

We have seen how, in his search for the cause of childbed fever, Semmelweis examined various hypotheses that had been suggested as possible answers. How such hypotheses are arrived at in the first place is an intriguing question which we will consider later. First, however, let us examine how a hypothesis, once proposed, is tested. Sometimes, the procedure is quite direct. Consider the conjectures that differences in crowding, or in diet, or in general care account for the difference in mortality between the two divisions. As Semmelweis points out, these conflict with readily observable facts. There are no such differences between the divisions; the hypotheses are therefore rejected as false. But usually the test will be less simple and straightforward. Take the hypothesis attributing the high mortality in the First Division to the dread evoked by the appearance of the priest with his attendant. The intensity of that dread, and especially its effect upon childbed fever, are not as directly ascertainable as are differences in crowding or in diet, and Semmelweis uses an indirect method of testing. He asks himself: Are there any readily observable effects that should occur if the hypothesis were true? And he reasons: *If* the hypothesis were true, *then* an appropriate change in the priest's procedure should be followed by a decline in fatalities. He checks this implication by a simple experiment and finds it false, and he therefore rejects the hypothesis.

Similarly, to test his conjecture about the position of the women during delivery, he reasons: *If* this conjecture should be true, *then* adoption of the lateral position in the First Division will reduce the mortality. Again, the implication is shown false by his experiment, and the conjecture is discarded. In the last two cases, the test is based on an argument to the effect that if the contemplated hypothesis, say *H*, is true, then certain observable events (e.g., decline in mortality) should occur under specified circumstances (e.g., if the priest refrains from walking through the wards, or if the women are delivered in lateral position); or briefly, if H is true, then so is *I*, where *I* is a statement describing the observable occurrences to be expected. For convenience, let us say that *I* is inferred from, or implied by, *H;* and let us call *I* a *test implication of the hypothesis H*. In our last two examples, experiments show the test implication to be false, and the hypothesis is accordingly rejected. The reasoning that leads to the rejection may be schematized as follows:

If *H* is true, then so is *I*.

2a, But (as the evidence shows) *I* is not true.

H is not true.

Any argument of this form . . . is deductively valid; that is, if its premises (the sentences above the horizontal line) are true, then its conclusion (the sentence below the horizontal line) is unfailingly true as well. Hence, if the premises of (2a) are properly established, the hypothesis *H* that is being tested must indeed be rejected.

Next, let us consider the case where observation or experiment bears out the test implication *I*. From his hypothesis that childbed fever is blood poisoning produced by cadaveric matter, Semmelweis infers that suitable antiseptic measures will reduce fatalities from the disease. This time, experiment shows the test implication to be true. But this favorable outcome does not conclusively prove the hypothesis true, for the underlying argument would have the form

If H is true, then so is I.

2b, (As the evidence shows) I is true.

H is true.

And this mode of reasoning, which is referred to as *the fallacy of affirming the consequent*, is deductively invalid, that is, its conclusion may be false even if its premises are true. This is in fact illustrated by Semmelweis' own experience. The initial version of his account of childbed fever as a form of blood poisoning presented infection with cadaveric matter essentially as the one and only source of the disease; and he was right in reasoning that if this hypothesis should be true, then destruction of cadaveric particles by antiseptic washing should reduce the mortality. Furthermore, his experiment did show the test implication to be true. Hence, in this case, the premises of *(2b)* were both true. Yet, his hypothesis was false, for as he later discovered, putrid material from living organisms, too, could produce childbed fever.

Thus, the favorable outcome of a test, i.e., the fact that a test implication inferred from a hypothesis is found to be true, does not prove the hypothesis to be true. Even if many implications of a hypothesis have been borne out by careful tests, the hypothesis may still be false. The following argument still commits the fallacy of affirming the consequent:

If H is true, then so are $I, I, \ldots . I$

2c (As the evidence shows) $I, I, \ldots . I$ are all true.

H is true.

This, too, can be illustrated by reference to Semmelweis' final hypothesis in its first version. As we noted earlier, his hypothesis also yields the test implications that among cases of street births admitted to the First Division, mortality from puerperal fever should be below the average for the Division, and that infants of mothers who escape the illness do not contract childbed fever; and these implications, too, were borne out by the evidence—even though the first version of the final hypothesis was false. But the observation that a favorable outcome of however many tests does not afford conclusive proof for a hypothesis should not lead us to think that if we have subjected a hypothesis to a number of tests and all of them have had a favorable outcome, we are no better off than if we had not tested the hypothesis at all. For each of our tests might conceivably have had an unfavorable outcome and might have led to the rejection of the hypothesis. A set of favorable results obtained by testing different test implications, $I, I, \ldots . I$, of a hypothesis, shows that as far as these particular implications are concerned, the hypothesis has been borne out; and while this result does not afford a complete proof of the hypothesis,

it provides at least some support, some partial corroboration or confirmation for it. The extent of this support will depend on various aspects of the hypothesis and of the test data.

We have considered [a] scientific [investigation] in which a problem was tackled by proposing tentative answers in the form of hypotheses that were then tested by deriving from them suitable test implications and checking these by observation or experiment. But how are suitable hypotheses arrived at in the first place? It is sometimes held that they are inferred from antecedently collected data by means of a procedure called *inductive inference* . . . . The idea that in scientific inquiry, inductive inference from antecedently collected data leads to appropriate general principles is clearly embodied in the following account of how a scientist would ideally proceed:

If we try to imagine how a mind of superhuman power and reach, but normal so far as the logical processes of its thought are concerned, . . . would use the scientific method, the process would be as follows: First, all facts would be observed and recorded, *without selection* or a *priori* guess as to their relative importance. Second, the observed and recorded facts would he analyzed, compared, and classified, *without hypothesis* or *postulates* other than those necessarily involved in the logic of thought. Third, from this analysis of the facts generalizations would be inductively drawn as to the relations, classificatory or causal, between them. Fourth, further research would be deductive as well as inductive, employing inferences from previously established generalizations.

This passage distinguishes four stages in an ideal scientific inquiry: (1) observation and recording of all facts, (2) analysis and classification of these facts, (3) inductive derivation of generalizations from them, and (4) further testing of the generalizations. The first two of these stages are specifically assumed not to make use of any guesses or hypotheses as to how the observed facts might be interconnected; this restriction seems to have been imposed in the belief that such preconceived ideas would introduce a bias and would jeopardize the scientific objectivity of the investigation. But the view expressed in the quoted passage—I will call it the *narrow inductivist conception of scientific inquiry*—is untenable, for several reasons. A brief survey of these can serve to amplify and to supplement our earlier remarks on scientific procedure.

First, a scientific investigation as here envisaged could never get off the ground. Even its first phase could never be carried out, for a collection of *all* the facts would have to await the end of the world, so to speak; and even all the facts *up to now* cannot be collected, since there are an infinite number and variety of them. Are we to examine, for example, all the grains of sand in all the deserts and on all the beaches, and are we to record their shapes, their weights, their chemical composition, their distances from each other, their constantly changing temperature, and their equally changing distance from the center of the moon? Are we to record the floating thoughts that cross our minds in the tedious process? The shapes of the clouds overhead, the changing color of the sky? The construction and the trade name of our writing equipment? Our own life histories and those of our fellow investigators? All these, and untold other things, are, after all, among "all the facts up to now". Perhaps, then, all that should be required in the first phase is that all the *relevant* facts be collected. But relevant to what? Though the author does not mention this, let us suppose that the inquiry is concerned with a specified problem. Should we not then begin by collecting all the facts—or better, all available data—relevant to that problem? This notion still makes no clear sense. Semmelweis sought to solve one specific problem, yet he collected quite different kinds of data at different stages of his inquiry. And rightly so; for what particular sorts of data it is reasonable to collect is not determined by the problem under study, but by a tentative answer to it that the investigator entertains in the form of a conjecture or hypothesis. Given the conjecture that mortality from childbed fever was increased by the terrifying appearance of the priest and his attendant with the death hell, it was relevant to collect data on the consequences of having the priest change his routine; but it would have been totally irrelevant to check what would happen if doctors and students disinfected their hands before examining their patients. With respect to Semmelweis' eventual contamination hypothesis, data of the latter kind were clearly relevant, and those of the former kind totally irrelevant. Empirical "facts" or findings, therefore, can be qualified as logically relevant or irrelevant only in reference to a given hypothesis, but not in reference to a given problem.

In sum, the maxim that data should be gathered without guidance by antecedent hypotheses about the connections among the facts under study is self-defeating, and it is certainly not followed in scientific inquiry. On the contrary, tentative hypotheses are needed to give direction to a scientific investigation. Such hypotheses determine, among other things, what data should be collected at a given point in a scientific investigation. It is of interest to note that social scientists trying to check a hypothesis by reference to the vast store of facts recorded by the U.S. Bureau of the Census, or by other data-gathering organizations, sometimes find to their disappointment that the values of some variable that plays a central role in the hypothesis have nowhere been systematically recorded. This remark is not, of course, intended as a criticism of data gathering: those engaged in the process no doubt try to select facts that might prove relevant to future hypotheses; the observation is simply meant to illustrate the impossibility of collecting "all the relevant data" without knowledge of the hypotheses to which the data are to have relevance.

The second stage envisaged in our quoted passage is open to similar criticism. A set of empirical "facts" can be analyzed and classified in many different ways, most of which will be unilluminating for the purposes of a given inquiry. Semmelweis could have classified the women in the maternity wards according to criteria such as age, place of residence, marital status, dietary habits, and so forth; but information on these would have provided no clue to a patient's prospects of becoming a victim of childbed fever. What Semmelweis sought were criteria that would be significantly connected with those prospects; and for this purpose, as he eventually found, it was illuminating to single out those women who were attended by medical personnel with contaminated hands; for it was with this characteristic, or with the corresponding class of patients, that high mortality from childbed fever was associated. Thus, if a particular way of analyzing and classifying empirical findings is to lead to an explanation of the phenomena concerned, then it must be based on hypotheses about how those phenomena are connected; without such hypotheses, analysis and classification are blind.

Our critical reflections on the first two stages of inquiry as envisaged in the quoted passage also undercut the notion that hypotheses are introduced only in the third stage, by inductive inference from antecedently collected data. . . . . . . There are . . . no generally applicable "rules of induction", by which hypotheses or theories can be mechanically derived or inferred from empirical data. The transition from data to theory requires creative imagination. Scientific hypotheses and theories are not *derived* from observed facts, but *invented* in order to account for them. They constitute guesses at the connections that might obtain between the phenomena under study, at uniformities and patterns that might underlie their occurrence. "Happy guesses" of this kind require great ingenuity, especially if they involve a radical departure from current modes of scientific thinking, as did, for example, the theory of relativity and quantum theory. The inventive effort required in scientific research will benefit from a thorough familiarity with current knowledge in the field. A complete novice will hardly make an important scientific discovery, for the ideas that may occur to him are likely to duplicate what has been tried before or to run afoul of well-established facts or theories of which he is not aware.

Nevertheless, the ways in which fruitful scientific guesses are arrived at are very different from any process of systematic inference. The chemist Kekulé, for example, tells us that he had long been trying unsuccessfully to devise a structural formula for the benzene molecule when, one evening in 1865, he found a solution to his problem while he was dozing in front of his fireplace. Gazing into the flames, he seemed to see atoms dancing in snakelike arrays. Suddenly, one of the snakes formed a ring by seizing hold of its own tail and then whirled mockingly before him. Kekulé awoke in a flash: he had hit upon the now famous and familiar idea of representing the molecular structure of benzene by a hexagonal ring. He spent the rest of the night working out the consequences of this hypothesis. This last remark contains an important reminder concerning the objectivity of science. In his endeavor to find a solution to his problem, the scientist may give free rein to his imagination, and the course of his creative thinking may be influenced even by scientifically questionable notions. Kepler's study of planetary motion, for example, was inspired by his interest in a mystical doctrine about numbers and a passion to demonstrate the music of the spheres. Yet, scientific objectivity is safeguarded by the principle that while hypotheses and theories may be freely invented and *proposed* in science, they can be *accepted* into the body of scientific knowledge only if they pass critical scrutiny, which includes in particular the checking of suitable test implications by careful observation or experiment.

Scientific knowledge, as we have seen, is not arrived at by applying some inductive inference procedure to antecedently collected data, but rather by what is often called "the method of hypothesis", i.e. by inventing hypotheses as tentative answers to a problem under study, and then subjecting these to empirical test. It will be part of such test to see whether the hypothesis is borne out by whatever relevant findings may have been gathered before its formulation; an acceptable hypothesis will have to fit the available relevant data. Another part of the test will consist in deriving new test implications from the hypothesis and checking these by suitable observations or experiments. As we noted earlier, even extensive testing with entirely favorable results does not establish a hypothesis conclusively, but provides only more or less strong support for it. Hence . . . . . . any "rules of induction" will have to be conceived . . . as canons of validation rather than of discovery.

PART TWO

Clinical Psychology:
Why a Scientific Approach Matters

The past several decades have witnessed much wringing of hands and grinding of teeth about the deep divide between scientific psychology and clinical practice. In the eyes of many observers, it's troubling that clinical psychology continues to debate the question of whether science is essential to practice. The field of medicine largely resolved this issue nearly a century ago. In contrast, clinical psychology is still bogged down in seemingly endless debates about fundamentals (e.g., Should we trust scientific evidence over clinical intuition? Can we evaluate psychotherapy outcome objectively?). Still, the good news is that the field is moving gradually in a more scientific direction.

The historian of science Thomas Kuhn (2009) might have suggested that debates over fundamentals make clinical psychology pre-paradigmatic—that is, we've yet to adopt a coherent *paradigm*, or theoretical framework, for understanding nature, in our case, human nature. Nevertheless, the recent movement to establish criteria and lists for *empirically supported therapies*—treatments supported by well-controlled evidence (Chambless & Hollon, 1998)—suggests that our field possesses exemplars of effective problem solving, which according to Kuhn define paradigmatic science. For instance, the application of learning principles to clinical problems—a key component of behavior therapy—has resulted in solutions to problems ranging from child management difficulties to anxiety disorders (Spiegler & Guevremont, 2009). Perhaps there are two worlds in clinical psychology: one that's settled on a scientific paradigm and one that's still haggling over fundamentals.

Many stakeholders pay a dear price for nonscientific and pseudoscientific practices within mental health. We know that errors that health professionals commit can harm, even kill, people. The Institute of Medicine report, *Crossing the Quality Chasm* (Institute of Medicine, 2001), suggests that 90,000 Americans die each year as a consequence of medical errors. In addition, pain and disability can increase as patients fail to improve. Such absence of improvement can stem from what economists term *opportunity costs*: the time, energy, effort, and money expended in seeking out and obtaining ineffective treatments can deprive clients of the resources needed to seek out and obtain effective treatments.

The ever-decreasing incomes of mental health professionals may be due to what economists call "the lemon problem" (O'Donohue, Ammirati, & Lilienfeld, 2011). This problem describes how duds in the marketplace reduce price. If we're willing to pay $5 a gallon for milk that's consistently of sound quality, what would we be willing to pay for a gallon of milk that has only a 50 percent chance of being of sound quality? The price of $2.50 produces an equivalency (we still on average pay $5 for a good gallon of milk). But note

---

McFall, R. M. (1991). Manifesto for a science of clinical psychology. *Clinical Psychologist*, *44*(6), 75–88.

O'Donohue, W. T. (1989). The (even) bolder model: The clinical psychologist as metaphysician-scientist-practitioner. *American Psychologist*, *44*, 1460–1468.

O'Donohue, W. T., & Henderson, D. (1999). Epistemic and ethical duties in clinical decision-making. *Behaviour Change*, *16*, 10–19.

Gambrill, E., & Dawes, R. M. (2003). Ethics, science, and the helping professions: A conversation with Robyn Dawes. *Journal of Social Work Education*, *39*, 27–40.

Lilienfeld, S. O. (1998). Pseudoscience in contemporary clinical psychology: What it is and what we can do about it. *The Clinical Psychologist*, *51*, 3–9.

how the presence of lemons drove down the price dramatically. If half of the psychotherapy delivered is a lemon, we can see how this state of affairs can exert a depressing effect on the price of therapy.

THE READINGS IN PART 2

The five articles in Part 2 highlight arguments for a scientific approach to clinical psychology and explore the substance of this approach. While raising many fascinating questions, these readings paint a clear overall picture: Scientific scrutiny is essential to progress and to helping our clients.

If there is *one* classic article on the essential role of science in clinical psychology, it is the first in Part 2: Richard McFall's "Manifesto for a Science of Clinical Psychology." McFall distinguishes what he argues is the only legitimate approach to clinical psychology—a scientific approach—from a pseudoscientific approach. His manifesto consists of one cardinal principle, namely, that "Scientific Clinical Psychology is the only Legitimate and Acceptable Form of Clinical Psychology," and two corollaries. The first corollary is that "Psychological services should not be administered to the public (except under strict experimental control) until they have satisfied these four minimal criteria: (1) The exact nature of the service must be described clearly; (2) The claimed benefits of the service must be stated explicitly; (3) These claimed benefits must be validated scientifically; and (4) Possible negative side effects that might outweigh any benefits must be ruled out empirically." McFall's second corollary is that "The primary and overriding objective of doctoral training programs in clinical psychology must be to produce the most competent clinical scientists possible." McFall also discusses the critically important relationship between science and quality improvement technology, namely, techniques designed to enhance the effectiveness of clinical practice by learning from one's mistakes (see O'Donohue et al., 2011). This is an inspiring article that forthrightly lays out the rationale for the scientific nature of clinical psychology, its implications for practice, and the costs of failing to do so. We heartily endorse McFall's proposals and suggest that all clinical psychologists strive to deliver therapies that meet his four criteria.

In the next article, William O'Donohue discusses the role of philosophical beliefs in clinical science and clinical practice. The philosopher Wilfred Van Orman Quine (e.g., Quine & Ullian, 1978) argued that scientists don't test beliefs one by one (i.e., only one specific hypothesis) when they conduct a study. Instead, they put their entire "web of belief" to the test. Quine states that "[O]ur statements about the external world face the tribunal of sense experience not individually but only as a corporate body" (p. 265). A key implication of Quine's view is that our beliefs are interconnected; although some are more central and connected to many other beliefs, our beliefs cannot be separated from each other as easily as we might assume. Thus, a variety of philosophical commitments in our web of belief, such as ethical beliefs, political beliefs, fundamental beliefs about the nature of the world, and aesthetic beliefs, can all influence our research and clinical practice. O'Donohue shows how these diverse beliefs can play a role in defining research problems, in research design, in experimental observations, and in modifying our belief systems in light of failures in our predictions. Finally, he shows how our philosophical beliefs influence problem definition in therapy, therapy design, and observations in clinical practice.

O'Donohue and Deborah Henderson next contend that clinical psychologists, by virtue of their professional expert status, possess *epistemic duties*, that is, obligations to acquire specialized knowledge and skills. Our clients are willing to pay many times the minimum wage because psychotherapy involves their assumption that the knowledge and skills that we apply to their problems surpass those of the ordinary individual. When clinicians just make up therapy as they go along (what the authors call "the jazz approach") or administer assessment devices that exhibit problematic validity for relevant clinical inferences, they are behaving unethically, because they are not fulfilling their epistemic duties to clients. The authors acknowledge that fulfilling these duties isn't always easy, because a therapy case may involve several different kinds of information: causal information (e.g., What causes the problem to improve); empirical information (e.g., How often has the client said she wants to kill herself?); ethical information (e.g., Is this treatment goal ethically appropriate?); and even economic information (e.g., What's the cost-benefit ratio of this treatment plan?). The duty to master such knowledge and skills, the authors insist, can be found only in the scientific method.

In the penultimate reading in Part 2, social worker Eileen Gambrill interviews clinical psychologist Robyn Dawes. Dawes argues that clinical psychologists should know the fundamentals of basic psychology, such as the principles of learning, as these principles set boundaries for what we can accomplish in psychotherapy. For example, understanding the reconstructive nature of memory puts us in a better position to evaluate claims about allegedly accurate "flashback" memories in the recovered memory movement (see Loftus, 1993). Dawes contends that scientific evidence often suggests a need for humility and caution in evaluating the efficacy of our treatments, because it implies that people can often recover on their own. In other cases, scientific evidence informs us that we have no specialized knowledge for how to predict behaviors or treat a problem effectively. Dawes also offers several cogent criticisms of problematic graduate training that can contribute to suboptimal clinical practices.

In the final reading in Part 2, Scott Lilienfeld argues that a significant amount of *pseudoscience*—roughly defined as a discipline that possesses the appearance of science without its substance—has entered the field in many guises: unvalidated treatments for posttraumatic stress disorder (e.g., Thought Field Therapy), autism (e.g., facilitated communication), and many other conditions; the continued use of unvalidated assessment devices (e.g., human figure drawings); the use of herbal remedies of unknown effectiveness for depression and anxiety; and untested self-help books. He provides evidence that pseudoscientific techniques often spark more popular interest than their scientific competitors, as the former techniques yield far more Web hits than the latter. Lilienfeld follows the lead of philosopher of science Mario Bunge (1984), who proposes that pseudoscience often has the following properties: (1) overuse of *ad hoc hypotheses* (escape hatches or loopholes) to escape refutation; (2) emphasis on confirmation rather than refutation; (3) absence of self-correction; (4) reversed burden of proof (placing the onus of proof on skeptics rather than proponents of claims); (5) overreliance on testimonials and anecdotal evidence; (6) use of obscurantist language; and (7) absence of "connectivity" with other disciplines. Lilienfeld proposes a number of steps that could improve the scientific status of psychology. For example, he recommends that (1) the American Psychological Association (APA) and other professional organizations play more active roles in identifying and "outing" pseudoscience; (2) the APA adopt professional standards for evaluating self-help materials; (3) all clinical psychology graduate programs implement a core curriculum focusing on biases and heuristics (see also Part 3: Clinical Science as a Safeguard Against Human Error), the fallible nature of memory, statistical prediction, and criteria for distinguishing science from pseudoscience; and (4) psychologists enter into the marketplace of ideas to promote and popularize good science and to stigmatize and marginalize pseudoscience.

6

Manifesto for a Science of Clinical Psychology

RICHARD M. MCFALL

ABSTRACT

The future of clinical psychology hinges on our ability to integrate science and practice. Pointing to quality-control problems in the field, the author proposes that clinical psychologists adopt a Manifesto, consisting of one Cardinal Principle and two corollaries, aimed at advancing clinical psychology as an applied science. The rationale behind the proposed Manifesto, and the implications of the Manifesto for practice and training in clinical psychology are presented.

Traditionally, this Presidential Address has been devoted to a discussion of the speaker's personal research interests. I am deviating from that tradition, focusing instead on a topic of more general concern: the future of clinical psychology, Section III's mission in shaping that future, and an agenda for pursuing that mission into the 1990s.

The full, official name of Section III was carefully chosen by our founders: Section for the Development of Clinical Psychology as an Experimental/Behavioral Science. With this ungainly name, the founders ensured that there would be no confusion about the group's aims and values.[1] In this respect, the Section is unlike most other organizations in psychology, which tend to reflect narrower content interests or theoretical preferences. Section III was founded for the sole purpose of building a science of clinical psychology, with no allegiances to any particular population, content, or theory.

What does Section III actually do to help develop clinical psychology as an experimental/behavioral science? Among other things, we send a representative to the Division 12 Council, hold annual elections, collect a modest amount of dues, conduct periodic membership drives, publish a quarterly newsletter, publish directories of internships and training programs, organize programs for the annual APA convention, give annual awards to a Distinguished Scientist and to the author of an outstanding published dissertation, and hold a business meeting at the annual APA convention. The rest of the time, our executive committee keeps an eye on unfolding events in clinical psychology and responds appropriately to whatever opportunities or threats may arise.

It would be fair, I think, to characterize Section III as an organization that has preferred to promote science primarily by setting an example. Membership in Section III has been more a declaration of one's values than a commitment to any activities. Over the years, the Section's membership roster has read like the "Who's Who" of empirically-oriented clinical psychologists, with representatives from a variety of content areas and scientific perspectives. But our members would rather do science than talk about it or get involved in political struggles over it. Section III members have tended to be too busy advancing scientific knowledge through their own research on specific problems to spend much time on general causes and crusades.

Perhaps the time has come, however, for Section III members to take a more active role in building a science of clinical psychology. Specifically, I believe that we must make a greater effort to differentiate between scientific and pseudoscientific clinical psychology and to hasten the day when the former replaces the latter. Section III could encourage and channel such activism among its members—and among clinical psychologists generally—by developing and publishing a "Manifesto," which would spell out clearly, succinctly, and forcefully what is meant by "a science of clinical psychology," and outline the implications of such a science for clinical practice and training.

---

[1] In the Spring of 1991, Section III voted to change its name to "Society for a Science of Clinical Psychology." This action represented no change in organizational philosophy but simply was an effort to state the organization's purpose more succinctly.

What follows is my draft proposal of such a Manifesto for a Science of Clinical Psychology. On its face, it is deceptively simple, consisting of only one Cardinal Principle and two Corollaries, but its implications for practice and training in clinical psychology are profound. I am not so foolish as to expect that everyone will agree with my analysis of the situation or with all of my proposal. If I focus attention on Section III's mission and stimulate constructive discussion of how best to achieve this mission, however, then I will have served a worthwhile purpose.[2]

Cardinal Principle: Scientific Clinical Psychology Is the Only Legitimate and Acceptable Form of Clinical Psychology

This first principle seems clear and straightforward to me—at least as an ideal to be pursued without compromise. After all, what is the alternative? *Unscientific* clinical psychology? Would anyone openly argue that unscientific clinical psychology is a desirable goal that should be considered seriously as an alternative to scientific clinical psychology?

Probably the closest thing to a counterargument to this proposed Cardinal Principle is the commonly offered rationalization that science doesn't have all the answers yet, and until it does, we must do the best we can to muddle along, relying on our clinical experience, judgment, creativity, and intuition (cf. Matarazzo, 1990). Of course, this argument reflects the mistaken notion that science is a set of answers, rather than a set of processes or methods by which to arrive at answers. Where there are lots of unknowns—and clinical psychology certainly has more than its share—it is all the more imperative to adhere as strictly as possible to the scientific approach. Does anyone seriously believe that a reliance on intuition and other unscientific methods is going to hasten advances in knowledge? The systematic procedures of science represent the best methods yet devised for exploring the unknown. There are no close competitors. This is the rationale behind the Cardinal Principle of my proposed Manifesto.

So the alternative to scientific clinical psychology probably is not unscientific clinical psychology. Are there any other alternatives or contrasts? The most frequently mentioned is Clinical Practice. The dichotomy between science and practice is the classic one—the one codified in the Boulder Model of clinical training with its hyphenated characterization of clinical psychologists as "scientist-practitioners." The implication commonly attributed to the hyphenated Boulder Model is that there are two legitimate types of clinical psychology: clinical science and clinical practice.

This is the dichotomy one hears, for example, from undergraduates who are applying to graduate training programs in clinical psychology and are struggling with making what they perceive to be the difficult, but necessary, career choice between science and practice. When I counsel these undergraduates, I try to persuade them that they are not framing the issue correctly—that there really is no choice between science and practice. I tell them that all clinical psychologists must be scientists first, regardless of the particular jobs they fill after they earn their degrees; that becoming a clinical scientist does not mean that they are committed to working in a laboratory or university; and that choosing not to receive the best scientific training possible, by purposely opting for a training program that does not emphasize scientific training, means that they will not be prepared to do any form of psychological activity as well. What I am saying to them, of course, is that all forms of legitimate activity in clinical psychology must be grounded in science, that all competent clinical psychologists must be scientists first and foremost, and that clinicians must ensure that their practice is scientifically valid.

Regrettably, many students dismiss my advice. They are convinced by the official pronouncements of psychological organizations, the characterizations of clinical psychology put forward by prominent textbooks, and the depictions of clinical psychology promulgated by other psychologists with whom they consult that the conventional distinction between scientists and practitioners is the correct one and that my counsel is completely out of touch with reality. My advice scares them, I suspect. Their futures are on the line, after all, and they are not about to lose out by following the advice of someone who seems so at odds with the dominant view.

It would go beyond the scope of this presentation to trace the history of clinical psychology's split personality, as manifested in the Boulder Model, but psychologists committed to science somehow have allowed the perspective they represent to be characterized as just one of the acceptable alternatives within clinical psychology, with no greater claim to legitimacy or primacy than any other. Look at the status of Section III within APA's Division of Clinical Psychology, for instance. Section III is just one of six sections within the Division, the others being special interest groups focusing on Clinical Child Psychology (1); Clinical Psychology of Women (IV); Pediatric Psychology (V); Racial/Ethnic and Cultural Issues (VI); and Theory, Practice, and Research in Group Psychotherapy (VII). I don't mean to imply any criticism of these other sections, but it strikes me as peculiar that the advocates for a science of clinical psychology have been relegated on the organizational chart to the level of a special interest group.

The development of clinical psychology as a science should be the central mission of Division 12, not merely one of its many competing interests. Some might argue, at this point, that Division 12 does regard the promotion of scientific clinical psychology as its foremost mission. I am skeptical, however. If Division 12 adequately represented the scientific interests of clinical psychology, then Section III would be redundant and would disappear. Let me cite just one example of why we are not redundant: it was largely through the alertness and lobbying efforts of Lynn Rehm, Section III's 1989 Chair, that the Division of Clinical Psychology was included as a cosponsor of "Science Weekend" at the 1990 APA convention.

---

[2] Reviewers of an earlier draft of this manuscript made a number of helpful suggestions and raised several questions. In the spirit of encouraging a dialogue about the proposed Manifesto, yet hoping to avoid digressions that might obscure the thread of my original argument, I have summarized the reviewers' questions in footnotes and have offered replies.

Speaking of Science Weekend, doesn't the idea behind this event strike you as a bit odd? The annual convention of the American Psychological Association meets over a 5-day period, Friday through Tuesday. Two of those 5 days are set aside for Science Weekend, with its special focus on scientific psychology. What does that suggest? That three fifths of the convention will be devoted to unscientific or extrascientific matters? Look at the rest of the APA program and judge for yourself how much weight is given to psychology as a science, as opposed to extrascientific issues. Fortunately, Karen Calhoun and Lynn Rehm, the 1989 and 1991 Chairs of Section III, respectively, are Division 12's program chairs for the 1990 and 1991 APA conventions, thus helping to encourage a strong representation of scientific clinical psychology on the program. I would argue, however, that scientific merit should be the primary selection criterion for all APA program entries, not just the entries scheduled for a special Science Weekend. If this were the case, then it would be meaningless to designate a special weekend for the coverage of science.

The tendency to regard science as only one of the many interests of APA is reflected in an Opinion column in the July 1990 of The APA Monitor by APA President Stanley Graham. Taking what he must have considered to be a conciliatory stance toward the scientists in APA, he said,

> There are many groups that represent some special aspect of psychology, but APA is still the organization that represents all of psychology. APA has more scientists, publishes more learned journals, and does more to support psychological research than any psychological organization in the world. As a person largely identified with practice, I am pleased that my presidential year has had, among its major accomplishments, the establishment of an Education Directorate and the enhancement of the Science Directorate. (p. 3)

Reflected in this brief depiction of psychology is the implicit idea that there are several coequal and legitimate constituencies within psychology, scientific psychology being only one—on the same organizational level as psychologists concerned with educational issues or with practice issues. Elsewhere in the same column, Graham's wording seems to suggest that scientific psychologists, research psychologists, and academic psychologists are one and the same—and distinguishable from practitioners. If this is how an APA President divides the world of psychology, is it any wonder that undergraduates applying to graduate schools equate scientific clinical psychology with academia and laboratory research, as contrasted with clinical practice? No wonder these students feel that they must choose between science and practice.

Can you imagine a similar state of affairs in any other scientific discipline? Imagine, for instance, an undergraduate chemistry major discussing her choice of graduate schools with her advisor. The student announces that she has decided to apply only to those doctoral programs in chemistry that will require the least amount of scientific training; after all,

she explains, she plans to do applied chemical work, rather than basic research, after she completes her degree. Or imagine another student applying to medical school. Because he is interested in applied medicine, he is considering only those schools that require the fewest science courses. These examples are ludicrous; yet academic advisors in psychology regularly hear such views expressed by prospective graduate students in clinical psychology. What makes this situation even more disturbing is that some advisors have come to accept such views of clinical psychology as reasonable and legitimate.

The time has come for Section III—whose mission it is to promote a science of clinical psychology—to declare unequivocally that there is only one legitimate form of clinical psychology: grounded in science, practiced by scientists, and held accountable to the rigorous standards of scientific evidence. Anything less is pseudoscience. It is time to declare publicly that much of what goes on under the banner of clinical psychology today simply is not scientifically valid, appropriate, or acceptable. When Section III members encounter invalid practices in clinical psychology, they should "blow the whistle," announce that "the emperor is not wearing any clothes," and insist on discriminating between scientific and pseudoscientific practices.

Understandably, the prospect of publicly exposing the questionable practices of fellow psychologists makes most of us feel uncomfortable. Controversy never is pleasant. Public challenges to colleagues' activities certainly will anger those members of the clinical psychology guild who are more concerned with image, profit, and power than with scientific validity. However, if clinical psychology ever is to establish itself as a legitimate science, then the highest standards must be set and adhered to without compromise. We simply cannot afford to purchase superficial tranquility at the expense of integrity.

Some might argue: "But who is to say what is good science and what is not? If we cannot agree on what is scientific, then how can we judge the scientific merit of specific clinical practices?" This is a specious argument. Most of us have become accustomed to giving dispassionate, objective, critical evaluations of the scientific merits of journal manuscripts and grant applications; now we must apply the same kind of critical evaluation to the full spectrum of activities in clinical psychology. Although judgments of scientific merit may be open to occasional error, the system tends to be self-correcting. Besides, this system of critical evaluation is far better than the alternatives: authoritarianism, market-driven decisions (caveat emptor), or an "anything goes" approach with no evaluations at all. It is our ethical and professional obligation to ensure the quality of the products and services offered to the public by clinical psychology. We cannot escape this responsibility by arguing that because no system of quality assurance is 100% perfect, we should not even try to provide any quality assurance at all.

This need for quality assurance is the focus of the First Corollary of the Cardinal Principle in my proposed Manifesto for a Science of clinical Psychology:

First Corollary: Psychological services should not be administered to the public (except under strict experimental control) until they have satisfied these four minimal criteria:

1. The exact nature of the service must be described clearly.
2. The claimed benefits of the service must be stated explicitly.
3. These claimed benefits must be validated scientifically.
4. Possible negative side effects that might outweigh any benefits must be ruled out empirically.

This Corollary may look familiar. It is adapted from recommendations made by Julian B. Rotter in the Spring 1971 issue of *The Clinical Psychologist*. Unfortunately, Rotter's proposal never received the serious consideration it deserved. If it had, we would be much closer to the goal of a scientific clinical psychology. Explicit standards of practice, such as I am recommending here, are a direct implication of the proposed Cardinal Principle. Adopting such standards is a prerequisite to moving clinical psychology out of the dark ages. Rotter offered this analogy:

> Most clinical psychologists I know would be outraged to discover that the Food and Drug Administration allowed a new drug on the market without sufficient testing, not only of its efficacy to cure or relieve symptoms, but also of its short term side effects and the long term effects of continued use. Many of these same psychologists, however, do not see anything unethical about offering services to the public—whether billed as a growth experience or as a therapeutic one—which could not conceivably meet these same criteria. (p. 1)

"Excellence," "accountability," "competence," "quality"—these are key concepts nowadays in education, government, business, and health care. It is ironic that psychologists, with their expertise in measurement and evaluation, have played a major role in promoting such concepts in other areas of society while ignoring them in their own backyard. One is reminded of the old saying: "The cobbler's children always need new shoes." The failure to assure the quality of services in clinical psychology—whatever its causes—cannot continue. Rotter (1971) sounded this warning in his concluding paragraph:

> If psychologists are not more active and more explicit in their evaluation of techniques of intervention, they will find themselves restrained from the outside (as are drug companies by the FDA) as a result of their own failure to do what ethical and scientific considerations require. (p. 2)

External regulation, whether by government bureaucracies or the courts, is not the only threat. The experiences of U.S. business and industry over the past 45 years might teach clinical psychology something about other dire consequences of ignoring quality control. The story is familiar to everyone by now: U.S. manufacturers, thriving in the boom economy of the postwar period, saw little need to be concerned about the quality of their products, which were selling well the way they were. Meanwhile, the Japanese, struggling to rebuild their economy after the war, took the longer view and decided to build their industrial future on a foundation of quality. They became obsessed with quality. As a result, the Japanese now dominate the world markets in autos, electronics, cameras, and numerous other industries.

Ironically, it was an American, W. Edwards Deming, who taught the Japanese the quality control system that helped them achieve their remarkable industrial superiority (Walton, 1986). Deming's ideas about quality were ignored in the U.S. throughout those postwar years. Only recently—when it was almost too late—has American industry come to realize, as the Ford commercial proclaims, that "Quality is job 1." A recent turn-around in quality at Ford Motor Company is due, in large part, to their better late than never adoption of the same Deming Management Method that had helped the Japanese build higher quality cars than Ford (Walton, 1986).

What is this remarkable Deming Management Method that spawned the Quality Revolution? Stripped of its outer shell, its engine is basically the scientific method, with its requirement for objective specification; quantification and measurement; systematic analysis and problem solving; hypothesis testing; and a commitment to persistent, programmatic, evolutionary development, as opposed to quick fixes, flashy fads, and short-term gains.

What possible relevance does all this have for modern clinical psychology I see direct parallels. In clinical psychology, "validity" is another word for "quality." Clinical services are some of our most important products. An insistence on establishing the validity of clinical services, through the application of the scientific method, is our system of quality control. To the extent that clinical psychologists offer services to the public that research has shown to be invalid, or for which there is no dear empirical support, we have failed as a discipline to exercise appropriate quality control (cf. Dawes, Faust, & Meehl, 1989; Faust & Ziskin, 1988a, 1988b; Fowler & Matarazzo, 1988; Matarazzo, 1990). No matter how many research contributions a particular clinical psychologist may have made, or how knowledgeable that individual may be about research literature or methodological issues, if that individual fails to meet the basic standards of scientific validity in clinical practice, then that individual cannot claim to be practicing as a scientist. Furthermore, to the extent that colleagues allow an individual's unscientific practices to go unchallenged, the scientific status of the profession is diminished accordingly.

Another parallel between the struggles for quality control in industry and in clinical psychology is noteworthy: Psychologists tend to raise many of the same objections to the imposition of scientific standards on clinical psychology as were raised by U.S. companies to the ideals of consumer-oriented design and zero defect production. For example, one objection sure to be raised to the four criteria for quality control proposed in my First Corollary is: "They are unrealistic and unachievable." This objection represents a self-fulfilling prophesy; if accepted as true, it never will be proved wrong, even if it is wrong. One of the biggest obstacles to effective quality control in industry was the deep-seated conviction that significant improvements in product quality were impossible (Walton, 1986). Advocates for increased quality were faced with a barrage of reasons why it couldn't be done, anecdotes about past failures, and rationalizations about inherent flaws in human character. Deming and the Japanese simply ignored such arguments, set out to improve quality, and left the doubters in the dust. We need to do likewise in clinical psychology. Another argument against implementing scientific standards of practice in psychology is: "Although standards certainly are desirable and might be feasible someday, they simply are too costly and impractical to implement at this time." The CEOs of U.S. industries offered similar resistance to immediate change, blaming such short-term pressures as the need to show stockholders a quarterly profit (Walton, 1986). As clinical psychologists, we should recognize such excuses for avoiding change as the impostors that they are. There never seems to be a convenient moment for fundamental change. But viewed in retrospect, feared dislocations seldom are as bad as anticipated, and the resulting improvements usually prove to be worth the price.

I have had personal, real-world experience with the very kind of quality standards for psychological services that I am advocating here. I am a member of the Board of Directors of my local Community Mental Health Center, where I chair the Program Planning and Evaluation Committee. In 1990, we proposed to the full Board that it incorporate into the Center's mission statement and adopt as official Center policy a fundamental commitment to quality assurance: specifically, the Center would provide only those services that have been shown to be effective, according to the best scientific evidence available. I was pleasantly surprised by the positive reception this proposal received from the Board, the Center's administration, and many of the staff. It was adopted by the Board.

Of course, it is one thing to adopt an abstract policy, another thing to make it work. Our Center needed to develop and implement new procedures for the systematic review and evaluation of the scientific validity of all treatments. But the new policy required more than new procedures; it also required increased resolve and courage. The Center's commitment to the new policy was put to a difficult test almost immediately. Based on recent reviews of the research literature on treatment programs for sexual offenders (e.g., Furby, Weinrott, & Blackshaw, 1989) which raised serious questions about the effectiveness of these clinical services, the clinical staff in the Center's treatment program for sex offenders initiated a full review of their program under the Center's new policy. Understandably, there was a strong negative community reaction to the possible discontinuation of the program. The courts, for example, were distressed by the prospect of losing the program as a sentencing option for offenders. I am pleased to report that so far the Center has stuck to its policy, is proceeding with its reevaluation of treatment programs (including the sex offenders program), and has begun to consider alternative approaches to handling various patient problems. In the long run, the Center will serve the community best by devoting its limited resources to the delivery of only the most valid programs.

One of the problems facing clinical psychology is that it has oversold itself. As a consequence, the public is not likely to respond charitably when told to adjust its expectations downward. We cannot blame consumers for wishing that psychologists could solve all of their problems. Nor should we be surprised if consumers become upset when told the truth about what psychologists can and cannot do. We should expect that some consumers simply will not accept the truth, and will keep searching until they find someone else who promises to give them what they want. However, the fact that some consumers are ready and willing to be deceived is no justification for false or misleading claims; the vulnerability of our consumers makes it all the more imperative that clinical psychologists practice ethically and responsibly.

Clinical psychologists cannot justify marketing unproven or invalid services simply by pointing to the obvious need and demand for such services, any more than they could justify selling snake oil remedies by pointing to the prevalence of diseases and consumer demand for cures. Some clinicians may ask: "But what will happen to our patients if we limit ourselves to the few services that have been proven effective by scientific evidence?" Snake oil merchants probably asked a similar question. The answer, of course, is that there is no reason to assume that patients will be harmed if we withhold unvalidated services. In fact, in the absence of evidence to the contrary, it is just as reasonable to assume that some unvalidated remedies actually are detrimental to patients and that the withholding of these will benefit patients.

If the practices of clinical psychologists were constrained, as proposed in my First Corollary, where would that leave us? That is, what valid contributions, if any, might psychologists make to the assessment, prediction, and treatment of Clinical problems? This question highlights the major reason why scientific training must be the sine qua non of graduate education in clinical psychology. Faced with uncertainty about the validity of assessments, predictions, and interventions, clinicians would be required by the First Corollary to reduce that uncertainty through empirical evidence before proceeding to offer such services.[3] The Corollary explicitly states that clinical scientists may administer unproven psychological services to the public, but only under controlled experimental conditions. While

---

[3] Q. How adequately can conventional research methods, with their reliance on quantitative analyses and group results, answer clinical questions about how best to approach the unique problems of a specific client? A: This question raises the classic debate concerning "idiographic vs. nomothetic" approaches to clinical prediction, where "prediction" incudes the task of choosing, based on estimated results, the most promising treatment for a particular client with a particular set of problems. Despite the intuitive appeal of the idiographic approach, both the empirical evidence and the force of logical analysis unequivocally support the superior validity of the nomothetic approach (e.g., Dawes, Faust, & Meehl, 1989). The specifics of the evidence and arguments on this issue go far beyond the bounds of the immediate presentation. Helping students work through this issue, in fact, is one of the central aims of graduate training in scientific clinical psychology, taking several years and requiring a mastery of demanding material ranging from the concepts of base rates and cutting scores to the accuracy of clinical and actuarial predictions. Contrary to popular opinion, the scientific method, with its quantitative and nomothetic emphasis, consistently does the best job of predicting the optimal treatments for individual cases. Dubious readers are encouraged to start by retreading Meehl's (1973) collected papers.

untested services represent the future hope of clinical psychology and thus deserve to be tested, they also represent potential risks to patients and must be tested cautiously and systematically. Until scientific evidence convincingly establishes their validity, such services must be labeled dearly as "experimental."[4] Only those psychologists with scientific training and expertise will be in a position to participate in this critical evaluation of clinical services.

It should be added that clinicians-in-training are unproven commodities, as well, even when they are administering services that have been proven to be effective in the hands of experienced clinicians. Therefore, the validity of the services offered by these apprentice clinicians must be evaluated systematically before each individual therapist—an integral component of the clinical service—is moved from the "experimental status" to the "approved" list. Even "approved" and "senior" clinicians must be cognizant of the limits to their personal validities and take an experimental approach to validating changes in their cal roles.

In short, the First Corollary requires that clinicians practice as scientists. This brings us to the Second, and final, Corollary of my proposed Manifesto for a Science of Clinical Psychology:

> *Second Corollary: The primary and overriding objective of doctoral training programs in clinical psychology must be to produce the most competent clinical scientists possible.*

This point follows logically, I believe, from all that has been presented thus far. It also should require little elaboration. In a practical sense, however, it is not entirely dear what the most effective methods are for training clinical psychologists to be scientists. Everyone seems to have opinions about what makes for effective scientific training, but such views seldom are backed by sound empirical evidence. Even where evidence exists, it may exert little influence on the design of clinical training programs. It ought to be otherwise, of course; those who train scientists should be reflexive, taking a scientific approach themselves toward the design and evaluation of their training programs. Unfortunately, the structure and goals of graduate training in clinical psychology tend to be highly resistant to change. Institutional, departmental, and personal traditions, alliances, and empires are at stake, and these tend to make the system unresponsive to logical, empirical, or ethical appeals. These limits notwithstanding, let me sketch four of the more important issues raised by this Second Corollary.

First, the Boulder Model, with its stated goal of training, "scientist-practitioners," is confusing and misleading. On the one hand, if the scientist and practitioner are synonymous, then the hyphenated term is redundant. On the other hand, if the scientist and the practitioner represent two distinct goals, either as competing alternatives or as separate but complementary components, then this two-headed view of clinical psychologists is inconsistent with the kind of unified scientific training being advocated in the present Manifesto. Therefore, the Boulder Model's dualistic, hyphenated goal should be replaced by one that stresses the unified and overriding goal of training clinical scientists.

Second, scientific training should not be concerned with preparing students for any particular job placements. Graduate programs should not be trade schools. Scientists are not necessarily academics, and persons working in applied settings are not necessarily nonscientists. Well-trained clinical scientists might function in any number of contexts—from the laboratory, to the clinic, to the administrator's office. What is important is not the setting, but how the individual functions within the setting. Training program faculty members need to break out of the old stereotypic dichotomous thinking represented by the Boulder Model. They need to stop worrying about the particular jobs their students will take and focus instead on training all students to think and function as scientists in every aspect and setting of their professional lives.

Third, some hallmarks of good scientific training are rigor, independence, scholarship, flexibility in critical thinking, and success in problem solving. It is unlikely that these attributes will be assured by a checklist approach to required content areas within the curriculum. Increasingly, however, there has been a tendency—prompted largely by the need to ensure that the criteria for state licensing and certification will survive legal challenges—toward taking a checklist approach to the accreditation of graduate training programs in clinical psychology. Too much emphasis has been placed on the acquisition of facts and the demonstration of competency in specific professional—techniques, and too little emphasis has been placed on the mastery of scientific principles; the demonstration of critical thinking; and the flexible and independent application of knowledge, principles, and methods to the solution of new problems. There is too much concern with structure and form, too little with function and results.

Ideally, we would have been taking a scientific approach to answering the question of how best to train clinical psychologists; unfortunately, this has not been done. For the present, then, there simply is no valid basis for deciding what is the "best" way to train clinical scientists in these desired attributes. The political move to homogenize the structure and content of clinical training programs not only is inappropriately premature, but it also is likely to retard progress toward the goal of developing truly effective training programs. The state of knowledge in our field is primitive and rapidly changing; therefore, efforts to establish a required core curriculum for clinical training, based on such uncertain knowledge, would result in "training for obsolescence." Similarly, efforts to standardize prematurely on training program structures and methods simply win perpetuate the status quo, discourage

---

[4] Q. Won't this emphasis on employing only well-documented interventions tend to stifle creativity in the search for even better interventions? A: If "creativity" is equated with "winging it" in therapy, then the emphasis should, indeed, curtail such unwarranted freelance activity. But if "creativity" refers to the systematic development of ever-improving treatment methods, then the recommendations presented here should enhance, rather than stifle, such creativity. Without documented treatment standards against which to compare the effects of novel interventions, how would it ever be possible to tell if the new (creative) approaches are any better than the established approaches? The requirement that new approaches beat the current standards before they can be accepted ensures that clinical psychology will show genuine advancement, rather than merely chasing after fads and fashions.

experimentation, and inhibit evolutionary growth. Until we have good evidence that one method of training is superior to any others, how can we possibly decide (except on political or other arbitrary grounds) that all training programs should cover a fixed body of content and technique, follow a set curriculum, or adopt a common structure? Recently, for example, there has been a move to require that accredited clinical training programs provide first-year students with practicum training. This proposed requirement has received considerable support, despite the complete lack of any clear evidence that it would lead to increased scientific or clinical competence in students.

Until we have a valid basis for choosing among the various options, our policy should be to encourage diversity—to "let a thousand flowers grow."[5] Out of such diversity, we might learn something valuable about effective training methods. Of course, diversity by itself is uninformative; it must be accompanied by systematic assessment and evaluation. The ultimate criterion for evaluating a program's effectiveness is how well its graduates actually perform as independent clinical scientists. Thus, program evaluations should focus on the quality of a program's products—the graduates—rather than on whether the program conforms to lists of courses, methods, or training experiences. How a program's graduates perform becomes the dependent variable; program characteristics serve as independent variables. If the aim of our graduate programs is to train clinical scientists, then every program's faculty ought to model scientific decision making when designing and evaluating its program.

Richard Feynman (1985), the Nobel Prize-winning physicist, used the term "Cargo Cult Science" to characterize "sciences" that are not sciences. He drew an analogy with the "cargo cult" people of the South Seas [see also Reading 2, this volume]:

> During the war (the cargo cult people) saw airplanes land with lots of good materials, and they want the same thing to happen now. So they've arranged to make things like runways, to put fires

along the sides of the runways, to make a wooden hut for a man to sit in, with two wooden pieces on his head like headphones and bars of bamboo sticking out like antennas—he's the controller and they wait for the airplanes to land. They're doing everything right. The form is perfect. It looks exactly the way it looked before. But it doesn't work. No airplanes land. (p. 311)

Much of the debate over how best to train scientists in clinical psychology smacks of Cargo Cult Science—preoccupation with superficial details of form, but a failure to comprehend the essence. Many clinical training programs scrupulously follow rituals that they believe to be associated with the successful production of scientists. They design curricula, assign readings, hold discussions, emphasize statistics and research methodology, give tests, require theses and dissertations, arrange for practica and internships, and hold formal rites of passage. But something essential is missing. Scientists don't emerge. Airplanes don't land.

Like the South Sea Islanders, the faculties of clinical training programs cling to the belief that if only they could arrange things properly—improve the shapes of the headphones, improve the sequence of courses—their systems at last would produce results. But their preoccupation with arranging details is like rearranging the deck chairs on the Titanic. When something essential is missing, no amount of tinkering with form will make things work properly.

According to Feynman (1985), one of the essential missing ingredients in Cargo cult Science is "scientific integrity, a principle of scientific thought that corresponds to a kind of utter honesty—a kind of leaning over backwards."

> If you make a theory, for example, and advertise it, or put it out, then you must also put down all the facts that disagree with it, as well as those that agree with it. There is also a more subtle problem. When you have put a lot of ideas together to make an elaborate theory, you want to make sure, when explaining what it fits, that those things it fits are not just the things that gave you the idea for the theory; but that the finished theory makes something else come out right, in addition. . . . The idea is to try to give all of theinformation to help others to judge the value of your contribution; not just the information that leads to judgment in one particular direction or another. (pp. 311–312)

This suggests a good place to focus our attention when thinking about how we might improve the quality of graduate training in clinical psychology. As a field, if we fail to display such scientific integrity, how can we hope to be successful in training scientists. No amount of formal classwork will replace the integrity lost by a failure, for example, to challenge exaggerated clients concerning the value of a clinical service. We can give students lectures about professional ethics, but if the lecturers fail to model utter honesty by leaning over backwards to provide a full, fair, critical discussion of psychological

---

[5] Isn't there a logical inconsistency here between recommending diversity in clinical training, on the one hand, and recommending that only "the best" therapy be used for a given clinical problem, on the other hand? A: No. In training and therapy alike, when valid evidence indicates that one approach is better than another, we are obligated to choose the "best" approach. (There are exceptions, of course, such as when the costs of the best approach are prohibitive, or when controlled experimental trials are being conducted in an effort to surpass the current best.) Where there is no evidence of a best approach, there are two possibilities: (a) The evidence indicates that doing something is better than doing nothing, in which case choosing any of the comparable options is justified, or (b) the evidence does not indicate that doing something is better than doing nothing, in which case it is not appropriate to proceed. Thus, because we can demonstrate positive gains in the graduates of scientific training programs in clinical psychology (but not necessarily in the area of increased clinical sensitivity, according to Berman & Norton, 1985), it is appropriate that clinical programs continue to offer scientific training, with a diversity of training approaches being tolerated until valid grounds for a preference are found. In clinical practice, there are some problems for which an obligatory best approach has been identified. There are other problems, however, for which no approach has shown incremental validity, making "no intervention" the appropriate choice (except under controlled experimental conditions).

theories, research, and clinical practice, then few students will emerge as scientists, few planes will land.

Fourth and finally, for clinical psychology to have integrity, scientific training must be integrated across settings and tasks. Currently, many graduate students are taught to think rigorously in the laboratory and classroom, while being encouraged—implicitly or explicitly—to check their critical skills at the door when entering the practicum or internship setting. Such contradictions in training cannot be tolerated any longer. Training programs in clinical psychology must achieve a scientific integration of research, theory, and practice. The faculties of clinical training programs must assume the responsibility for ensuring that students' practical experiences are integrated with their scholarly, conceptual, and research experiences. Until that happens, there can be no unified scientific training in clinical psychology.

THE MANIFESTO AS A CALL TO ACTION

Different camps within clinical psychology have maintained an uneasy truce over the years, partly out of necessity (in the early days they were allies against the threats of psychiatry) and partly out of convenience, custom, and economic self-interest. But events such as the unsuccessful effort to reorganize APA, the subsequent creation of competitive organizations such as The American Psychological Society (APS) from the Association for Psychological, and recent challenges to APA's sole authority to accredit graduate training programs in psychology are examples of the tension, distrust, and conflict that have surfaced among the various camps over the past decade. Change is in the wind; nothing is likely to be quite the same in the future.

Today's clinical psychologists face a situation somewhat like that of the bicyclists in the Tour de France race. We have been riding along at a comfortable pace, all bunched together, warily eyeing one another, worrying that someone might try to get a jump on us and break away from the pack. It has been like an unspoken conspiracy. As long as no one gets too ambitious and tries to raise the standards, we all can lay back and continue at this pace indefinitely. Labor unions have a name for the wise guys who won't go along with the pack: They're called "rate busters." In my more cynical moments, I sometimes suspect that many psychologists view serious proposals for scientific standards in practice and training as a betrayal, rate busting, or breaking away from the pack.

Inevitably, a breakaway will come. Some groups of clinical psychologists will become obsessed with quality, dedicated to achieving it. These psychologists will adopt as their manifesto something similar to the one I have outlined here. When this happens, the rest of clinical psychology—all those who said that it couldn't be done, that it was not the right time—will be left behind in the dust.

The Manifesto I have outlined here is a serious proposal; I was not trying to be provocative. The time is long overdue for a breakaway, for taking seriously the idea of building a science of clinical psychology. I would like to believe that Section III members will be well represented among the group of psychologists that successfully makes the break, when it comes. In fact, I dare to wish that Section III might promote such a break by formally adopting my proposed Manifesto, or one like it, hoisting it high as a banner around which all those who are committed to building a science of clinical psychology might rally.

References

Berman, J.S., & Norton, N.C (1985). Does professional training make a therapist more effective? Psychological Bulletin, 98, 401–407.

Dawes, R.M., Faust, D., & Meehl, P.E. (1989). Clinical versus actuarial judgment. Science, 243, 1668–1674.

Faust, D., & Ziskin, J. (1988a). The expert witness in psychology and psychiatry. Science, 241, 31–35.

Faust, D., & Ziskin, J. (1988b). Response to Fowler and Matarazzo. Science, 241, 1143–1144.

Feynman, R.P. (1985). Surely you're joking, Mr. Feynman! New York: W. W. Norton.

Furby, L., Weinrott, M.R., & Blackshaw, L. (1989). Sex offender recidivism: A review. Psychological Bulletin, 105, 3–30.

Fowler, R.D., & Matarazzo, J.D. (1988). Psychologists and psychiatrists as expert witnesses. Science, 241, 1143.

Graham, S. (1990). APA supports psychology in both science and academe. The APA Monitor, 21, 3.

Matarazzo, J.D. (1990). Psychological assessment versus psychological testing: Validation from Binet to the school, clinic, and courtroom. American Psychologist, 45, 999–1017.

Meehl, P.E. (1973). Psychodiagnosis: Selected papers. Minneapolis: University of Minnesota Press.

Rotter, J.B. (1971). On the evaluation of methods of intervening in other people's lives. The Clinical Psychologist, 24, 1–2.

Walton, M. (1986). The Deming Management Method. New York: Perigee.

7

The (Even) Bolder Model
The Clinical Psychologist as Metaphysician–Scientist–Practitioner

WILLIAM O'DONOHUE

ABSTRACT

Is the clinical psychologist best characterized as a scientist-practitioner? Or does the practice of science and psychotherapy involve metaphysics to such an extent that the clinical psychologist ought to be considered a metaphysician-scientist-practitioner? To answer these questions, the roles, if any, of metaphysics in science and psychotherapy are examined. This article investigates this question by examining the views of the logical positivists, Karl Popper and Imre Lakatos, and concludes that the practice of science and psychotherapy involves metaphysics in (a) problem choice, (b) research and therapy design, (c) observation statements, (d) resolving the Duhemian problem, and (e) modifying hypotheses to encompass anomalous results.

The following problem is addressed in this article: What are the roles, if any, of metaphysics in clinical psychology? Because clinical psychologists are prescribed by the so called Boulder Model to be trained as scientist-practitioners (Derner, 1965), there are actually two questions: What are the roles of metaphysics in research, especially clinical research, and what are the roles of metaphysics in clinical practice?

The issue of the roles of metaphysics in clinical research and practice is important for several reasons. First, if psychologists want to understand the exact nature of clinical research and practice, then psychologists need to understand the roles of metaphysics in these areas. Some have argued that both facts and values (claims about the good and the bad) play essential roles in psychotherapy (Krasner & Houts, 1984; O'Donohue, Fisher, & Krasner, 1987). However, does a tripartite distinction—facts, values and metaphysics—better capture all the kinds of claims involved in clinical research and practice? Second, if we want to understand the possible continuities with and implications of other fields (e.g., philosophy, religion, and literature), then we need to address this question. Third, if metaphysics does indeed have significant roles in clinical research and practice, then perhaps we need a new training model that explicitly recognizes this and seeks to train the clinical psychologist in relevant metaphysical matters. Fourth, this problem has implications for how we write the history of clinical psychology: Is its history to be traced merely as a function of the elimination of metaphysics? Finally, this problem has direct implications on how we appraise scientific research programs and therapy programs in clinical psychology. If we find nonfactual, extrascientific content in a research or therapy program, is this sufficient grounds for condemnation?

WHAT IS METAPHYSICS?

These questions can be made clearer by a more precise understanding of what is meant by *metaphysics*. Metaphysics has had various uses in the history of philosophy, from purely ontological concerns (i.e., the study of what there is and how to property categorize all there is) to a priori speculation regarding that which putatively transcends sense preception, (e.g., God, platonic forms, or the Kantian noumenal world). Here we shall characterize a metaphysical sentence as a sentence that has a particular kind of relation to experience.

To understand this, we must first realize that sentences differ as to the extent that experience is relevant to determining their truth or falsity. Experience is entirely irrelevant to the determination of the truth value of certain kinds of sentences because these sentences are neither true nor false. Imperatives, interrogatives, exclamations, and syntactically or semantically incorrect sentences (e.g., "Green ideas sleep furiously.") all fail to assert and therefore fail to have truth values.

Next, there are sentences commonly called analytic or logically true or logically false sentences that, unlike the previous kind of sentences, are either true or false but to which experience still is not directly relevant to the determination of their truth value. For what empirical observations would be required before one could reasonably decide whether it is the case that "Psychology is not psychology"?

On the other hand, there are sentences such as "John cried during the intake interview" and "Males are more aggressive than females" that obviously require empirical observation before one can determine whether they are true or false. Directly or indirectly, the truth value of these sentences is a function of a "situation that is inter-subjectively observable, that is, it will be the sort of situation to which multiple witnesses, could, if present, attest. Further it will be a situation that the witnesses can witness one another's witnessing of" (Quine & Ullian, 1978, p. 25).

Among sentences for which experience is relevant in ascertaining their truth value, there are sentences that are not tested directly against experience, but for which experience has some evidentiary value in determining their truth or falsity. Examples of these sentences include "Human behavior as well as physiology has been shaped by natural selection" and "The future will be like the past in all respects in which natural laws are taken to operate." Sentences such as these are not tested directly in any experiment, but empirical results are not irrelevant to the determination of their truth values. In this article, such sentences will be considered metaphysical. Historically, metaphysical sentences also have been regarded, at least by their utterers, as important; that is, they give a world view, or are relevant to the important questions in life, such as the following: What is there? What is the fundamental nature of things? What is the meaning of life? What is human nature? Metaphysical sentences may be further characterized, then, as sentences that are highly connected to other beliefs by being deeply entrenched in our web of belief. Metaphysical sentences would appear in the center of the web. That is, they would depend on the truth of few beliefs, but the truth or plausibility of many other beliefs would directly or indirectly depend on them.

To gain a proper understanding of this latter critical point and to set this discussion in its proper historical context so as to show the development of the dialectic, I will now examine the development of views on this issue in 20th century philosophy of science.

Logical Positivism: Metaphysics as Cognitively Meaningless

Philosophers have debated the truth of sentences such as "A property (e.g., redness) exists independently of its exemplifications (e.g., a ruby)," "There exist unknowable, imperceptible things-in-themselves," and "Things exist by virtue of being ideas in the mind of God." The logical positivists claimed, however, that these sentences were neither true nor false and that the consideration of the determination of their truth value as a substantive problem was based on a linguistic misunderstanding—or to use Wittgenstein's (1958)

colorful phrase by "the bewitchment of our intelligence by means of language" (p. 47).

On the face of it, these sentences look all right: After all, they seem syntactically well formed. However, the logical positivists claimed that because it was in principle impossible to cite empirical evidence that would count for or against these claims, the sentences were neither true nor false, but meaningless. To arrive at this conclusion, the logical positivists were relying on the verification criterion of meaning. Although the positivists never were able to develop a version of this criterion that was free of logical and philosophical difficulties (see Ashby, 1967; Nakhnikian, 1981), the criterion asserted, roughly, that the meaning of any indicative sentence consists in the actual or possible confirming sense data relevant to it. Thus, if a sentence met the verification criterion (if, as logical positivists sometimes put it, it made a difference to experience), it was considered meaningful.

If the sentence failed to meet the criterion, it still had another chance to be considered meaningful because the positivists considered analytic sentences to be meaningful. Metaphorically, a sentence is analytic if the predicate "unpacks" what is contained either implicitly or explicitly in the subject, such as, "A square has four sides" (see Nakhnikian, 1981, pp. 179–184 for a more rigorous definition). However, if the sentence was neither verifiable nor analytic, then it was considered to be meaningless.

Many later positivists drew another distinction. Sentences that failed the verification criterion and were not analytic were considered to be *cognitively* meaningless, but were considered as possessing *emotive* meaning, that is, as expressing or evoking emotions and attitudes. Metaphysical sentences, then, were to be distinguished from mere random strings of words because metaphysical sentences express or evoke emotions. The function of a metaphysical sentence such as "God is everywhere" was to express the speaker's approval, joy, respect, love, and so on concerning, for example, his or her life and perhaps to attempt to induce similar attitudes in the listener. The sentences of poetry and ethics were considered by the logical positivists as possessing only emotive meaning: Poetry fixes attitudes to experience, whereas ethics fixes attitudes to conduct. However, it is also important to note that although the logical positivists made a place for emotive meaning, they had a very low opinion of it. Carnap, a prominent logical positivist was reputed to have stated, "Metaphysicians are musicians without musical ability" (Malcolm, 1967, p. 334).

Thus, for the positivists, science consisted of verified sentences and analytic sentences (see Figure 1). As Koertge (1979) maintained, the logical positivist view of science has a certain *prima facie* plausibility. Guesses and hypotheses can be found in many fields of discourse, but what we want from science is not more speculation but rather verified, true propositions, that is, knowledge.

Popper: Metaphysics as a Psychological Aid

In *The Logic of Scientific Discovery*, Popper (1961) argued that there were a number of difficulties with the positivists' claim that

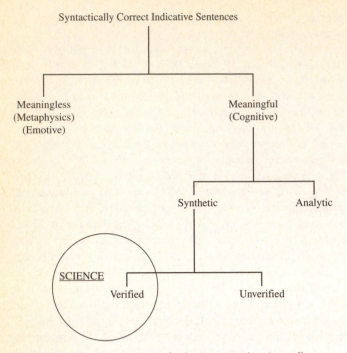

FIGURE 1 The Science–Metaphysics Demarcation According to the Logical Positivists

science consists of verified sentences and analytic sentences. A principal difficulty was that scientific laws (e.g., "All copper conducts electricity") are not capable of complete verification because it always remains logically possible that some as-yet-unexamined piece of copper will not conduct electricity. Thus, the verification criterion has the unwanted consequence of excluding universal generalizations, and therefore scientific laws, from science. The problem is that because there can be no logic that can infallibly increase content, no conjunction of factual sentences is sufficient to inductively prove a universal generalization. (For other views and work on the problem of induction, see Salmon, 1979.)

Second, Popper claimed that the verification criterion failed to distinguish proper science such as modern physics from (alleged) pseudosciences such as astrology, psychoanalysis, and Marxist historiography. Devotees of these areas can easily recount verifications of their claims—and therein lies the rub. Theories that can assimilate any state of affairs are inadequate precisely because they can do so.

Popper (1963) told a story of his experiences with Alfred Adler that illustrates this point:

> As for Adler, I was much impressed by a personal experience. Once, in 1919, I reported to him a case which to me did not seem particularly Adlerian, but which he found no difficulty in analyzing in terms of his theory of inferiority feelings, although he had not even seen the child. Slightly shocked, I asked him how he could be so sure. "Because of my thousand-fold experience," he replied; whereupon I could not help saying: "And with this new case, I suppose, your experience has become thousand-and-one-fold." (p. 35)

Popper would insist that Adler clearly state the observable states of affairs that his theory excludes. In order for a theory to serve as an explanation of some state of affairs, it must rule out some others.

Popper claimed it is not verifiability that distinguishes science from nonscience, and good science from bad, but rather falsifiability. In order to be falsifiable, the theory or hypothesis must exclude some observable possibilities. Theories and hypotheses that are not refutable were regarded by Popper as "metaphysical." In Popper's view, a metaphysical sentence is a sentence that is not falsifiable; that is, it excludes no observable possibilities. Although Popper (1961) asserted that metaphysical sentences are external to science, he claimed that metaphysics could still be useful to science.

> I do not even go so far as to assert that metaphysics has no value for empirical science. For it cannot be denied that along with metaphysical ideas which have obstructed the advance of science there have been others—such as speculative atomism—which have aided it. And looking at the matter from the psychological angle, I am inclined to think that scientific discovery is impossible without faith in ideas which are of a purely speculative kind, and sometimes even quite hazy; a faith which is completely unwarranted from the point of view of science, and which, to that extent is "metaphysical." (p. 38)

Unlike the logical positivists, Popper counted as internal to science sentences that passed his criterion (i.e., that were falsifiable) but were not yet tested (see Figure 2). Remember that the logical positivists counted within science among verifiable sentences only those that were actually verified. Popper argued that the inclusion of untested sentences within science allows the development of science to be understood from an internal perspective. For Popper, ideas that are "of a purely speculative kind and sometimes even quite hazy" can

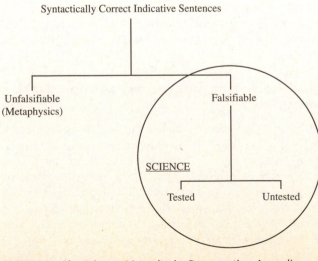

FIGURE 2 The Science–Metaphysics Demarcation According to Popper

play two important roles in the development of science: (a) They can influence the choice of experiment, and (b) they can play a role in the importance attached to an experimental outcome (Koertge, 1979).

I first will examine the way in which untested hypotheses influence the choice of experiment. Why did Watson and Raynor (1920) conduct their classic experiment in which a loud noise followed a young child's approach to a white rat? Were they simply cataloging the child's every reaction to every stimulus? This is not plausible. Rather it is likely that an untested, speculative belief that all fears are learned guided their choice of experiment. Moreover, philosophers of science (e.g., Agassi, 1975) have argued that scientists choose experiments and theories that are relevant to their metaphysics. For example, this experiment may be interpreted as shedding some light on speculative background beliefs regarding to what extent and how people change, the nature of fear and other emotions, and even what kind of entities there are and which are relevant to understanding humans.

Let us now examine an instance (first discussed by Koertge, 1979) in which untested claims played a role in the determination of the significance of an experimental result. In the 1930s, learning researchers were studying what would today be called schedules of reinforcement. They found that learning takes place not only in schedules of continuous reinforcement (i.e., every response results in a reinforcer) but also in schedules of intermittent reinforcement, in which only some responses (say, every third response) are followed by a reinforcer. The following question then arose: Which response would extinguish more easily, the one learned on a continuous reinforcement schedule or the one learned on an intermittent reinforcement schedule?

Of course, today all are familiar with the results of such an experiment: The response learned on the continuous schedule extinguishes more easily. When researchers were first confronted with this result, however, they called it "Humphrey's paradox" (after Lloyd Humphreys, 1939, the individual who first demonstrated this experimentally) and made much of it. Why was it considered a "paradox"? It is reasonable to infer that researchers were surprised by this result because of their speculative background views of learning. For example, researchers might have held physiological notions that learning consisted of the stamping in of neuronal connections, with continuous reinforcement schedules stamping more firmly or more purely. Again, untested speculative beliefs that were in the conceptual background appear to have played an important role not only in the formulation of the conjecture-hypothesis but also in determining the significance of the results of an experiment.

Popper also differed with the logical positivists regarding the unity of the sciences. The logical positivists maintained that the sciences could be unified because there was nothing in the subject matter of the diverse disciplines that was inherently refractory to study using the experimental methods and language of physics. Various sciences might have their own concepts and methods, but ultimately these could be reduced to the language and methods of physics. However, Popper argued that although the method of severe testing of highly falsifiable conjectures was a proper characterization of the "hard" sciences, it was not a proper description of the *Geisteswissenshaften*, roughly, the social sciences.

In *The Open Society and Its Enemies*, Popper (1945) gave metaphysics a central role in economics and psychology when he argued that a metaphysical statement, the *rationality principle*, is at the core of these sciences. Popper argued that human actions are to be explained in part by an appeal to the individual's perception of his or her problem situation. The description of the individual's perception of the problem situation corresponds to the initial and boundary conditions in explanations found in the natural sciences. The rationality principle states that individuals always act appropriately to their situation. It functions as the nomological premise in Hempel's (1966) deductive nomological type of scientific explanation. Popper apparently envisioned psychological explanations to have the following form:

1. *Description of the agent's situation*. Agent A was in a situation of type C.
2. *Analysis of the situation*. In a situation of type C, the agent believes the appropriate thing to do is X.
3. *Rationality principle*. Agents always act according to what they think is appropriate to their situations.
4. *Explanandum*. Therefore, A did X.

In the case of a prediction failure, Popper advised psychologists never to abandon the rationality principle, but rather to revise their models of the agent's situation. An implication of adopting this stratagem is that the rationality principle never is tested: Prediction failures do not count against it, but rather against the truth of the description of the agent's situation, or the truth of the analysis of the situation.

Thus, Popper thought that metaphysical statements were external to the natural sciences, which consisted of severe testing of highly falsifiable conjectures, that is, the strenuous search for the observable possibilities that the theory excludes. Metaphysical statements still could function as an important source for the formation of these conjectures. On the other hand, in the social sciences, metaphysical statements such as the rationality principle were essential to psychological explanation and prediction. These were never to be tested, but in some sense, vindicated by their usefulness.

Lakatos: Metaphysical Statements in the Hard Core and Positive Heuristic

Lakatos (1970), a student of Popper's, agreed with Popper's claim that metaphysical statements were a part of the social sciences. Lakatos argued that metaphysical sentences were internal to all the sciences. Popper's characterization of the special case of the social sciences came to be Lakatos's normative paradigm for all science. Lakatos argued for the dissolution of the metaphysical-scientific demarcation because of two principal considerations: (a) the theory-ladenness of "fact" and (b) the Duhemian problem, which involves the question of what is actually refuted by a prediction failure.

First, Lakatos (1970) argued that there is no natural demarcation between observational and theoretical sentences. "Immaculate perception" is a myth because perception is influenced by expectations and biases. Social and cognitive psychologists have, of course, studied these phenomena rather extensively. Perception is thought to be influenced by "top-down processes" in which sensations are unconsciously interpreted in light of previous experience to arrive at the percept (Rock, 1983). For example, Warren (1970) presented audiotaped spoken sentences that had one brief speech sound excised and replaced with a nonspeech sound such as a cough. Listeners claimed to hear not only the cough but also the speech sound. Moreover, Bruner and Potter (1964) created a series of slides in which the images were blurred. Some subjects initially saw very blurred slides and some did not. When given a much more focused slide of the same object, the subjects who had seen the very blurred slides had a much harder time recognizing what they were seeing. Why should early exposure to a greater degree of blurring retard the recognition of the slide? Subjects were asked to express their thoughts aloud when looking at the slides. Subjects tended to develop hypotheses and to become locked into these (often wrong) interpretations.

Beyond biases that operate in unaided perception, Lakatos maintained that observation in science is theory laden because scientists often observe with instruments and these instruments produce data that are interpretable only in reference to the theories concerning how the instruments work. Lakatos (1970) stated that

> Galileo claimed that he could "observe" mountains on the moon and spots on the sun and that these "observations" refuted the time-honoured theory that celestial bodies are faultless crystal balls. But his "observations" were not "observational" in the sense of being observed by the—unaided—senses: Their reliability depended on the reliability of his telescope—and of the optical theory of the telescope—which was violently questioned by his contemporaries. It was not Galileo's—pure, untheoretical—*observations* that confronted Aristotelian *theory* but rather Galileo's "observations" in the light of his optical theory that confronted the Aristotelians' "observations" in the light of their theory of the heavens. This gave us two inconsistent theories, prima facie on a par. (p. 98)

Second, Lakatos was led to his position regarding the role of metaphysics in science by the Duhemian problem, named after the French philosopher and physicist Pierre Duhem (1962). The Duhemian problem relates to the question of what a prediction failure actually refutes. If theories (T) by themselves entailed particular observation statements (O), then by *modus tollens* a refutation of the observation statement would entail a refutation of the theory. An example of the inference rule of *modus tollens* is as follows: Given the premises "If it is raining, then the streets are wet" and "The streets are not wet," one can infer by *modus tollens* that "therefore, it is not raining."

According to the falsificationists, the logic of testing theories or hypotheses also depends on *modus tollens*, as Popper pointed out:

1. If T, then 0
2. not 0

Therefore: not T.

Unfortunately, as Duhem (1962) and Quine (1961) have argued, in general, theories do not entail observable consequences by themselves: A variety of auxiliary hypotheses (H) pertaining to factors such as the ways in which theoretical terms are operationalized, the degree to which the test is isolated from extraneous factors, and the validity of certain measures are usually needed to obtain particular observational statements. We then have:

1. If (T and H1 and H2 . . . Hn), then 0
2. not 0

Therefore: not (T and H1 and H2 . . . Hn)
Therefore: not T or not H1 or not H2 . . . or not Hn.

In these cases logic does not tell us how to assign blame for the prediction failure. It could be that T is false, or that H1, H2, or Hn is false, or some combination of these.

Logic no longer dictates which sentence is false. If our deductions have been valid, then logic tells us only that we hold at least one set of contradictory beliefs. However, it fails to tell us which beliefs are involved in the contradiction. Indeed, we are logically free to apportion blame to any belief in our belief system. Because the logic of testing does not decisively indicate that a particular belief is false, and therefore we are logically free to blame any belief, our belief system as a whole rather than an individual sentence faces the test of experience.

However, sentences differ as to how remote they are from experience. Some sentences (e.g., "The cat is on the mat") are at the edge of our web of belief where it makes contact with experience. However, an implication of the Duhemian problem is that experience is not decisive even in the determination of the truth value of observational sentences: We can point the arrows of modus tollens either to or away from these sentences by deciding whether there was some error in our observations.

In response to these considerations, Lakatos (1970) recommended that we appraise a series of theories rather than a single theory. We are interested in what sort of change occurs in a theory in light of new, anomalous findings. Lakatos's basic unit of analysis is a series of theories, T1, T2, T3, and so on, in which each subsequent theory is a revision of the previous theory in that auxiliary clauses have been added to accommodate some anomaly. A series of theories is to be considered scientific and progressive if subsequent theories in the series have excess empirical content (i.e., they predict some novel facts) *and* if some of these new facts are corroborated. If either of these criteria is not met, then Lakatos suggested that the series of theories be considered to be degenerating.

According to Lakatos, research programs consist of a negative heuristic, a positive heuristic, and a hard core. The negative heuristic forbids directing the arrows of *modus tollens* at the hard core. Instead, the scientist invents or proposes auxiliary hypotheses that are to take the force of anomalous findings. The negative heuristic and the auxiliary hypotheses form a protective belt around the hard core. For example, in Newton's research program, the negative heuristic directs the arrows of *modus tollens* away from Newton's laws of dynamics and gravitation (i.e., his hard core) and to auxiliary hypotheses.

The hard core is made to be irrefutable by a (perhaps implicit) methodological decision of its proponents. Anomalous results lead to changes in the protective belt of auxiliary hypotheses, observational hypotheses, or initial conditions. Lakatos maintained that this is rational as long as the corroborated empirical content of the protective belt increases as these changes are made.

The research plan is set out in the positive heuristic of the research program. The positive heuristic consists of a semi-articulated set of suggestions on how to change and develop the hard core and how to modify the refutable protective belt. The positive heuristic also contains metaphysical statements in that it is a metaphysical heuristic for scientific hypothesizing. For example, in Newton's research program part of the positive heuristic might be given as "the planets are essentially of roughly spherical shape."

Here I will quickly and roughly illustrate Lakatos's ideas with an example from behavioral clinical psychology. The law of effect, among other conditioning principles, is contained in the hard core of the behavioral research program. The negative heuristic directs the arrows of *modus tollens* away from the law of effect to auxiliary hypotheses or to initial conditions. The positive heuristic might be given as follows: "Events that are contingent on certain behavior influence the probability of subsequent behavior."

To be more specific, suppose a behavioral clinical psychologist, after collecting baseline information, changes the extant contingencies of reinforcement in an attempt to increase the amount of homework a child client completes. Now, whenever the child completes a page of homework, the child receives a cookie. Suppose further, however, that the rate of completed homework pages does not increase. Does this state of affairs, then, falsify the law of effect? No, the arrows of *modus tollens* can be directed by the negative heuristic to auxiliary hypotheses. For example, it can be held that cookies are not reinforcers for this child at this time, or that cookies are reinforcers but that they were not delivered appropriately (e.g., not quickly enough), or that there were other sources of higher magnitude reinforcers maintaining competing behavior, and so on. The positive heuristic would suggest that perhaps the researcher could modify the relevant theory along certain lines—probably along the lines of experimental learning or cognitive psychology—if the researcher becomes inclined to do so.

Thus, for Lakatos, unlike the logical positivists and Popper, metaphysical sentences are internal to all the sciences in that they are contained in the hard core and the positive heuristic of a scientific research program. Therefore, there can be no rigid demarcation of science and metaphysics. I now will review the roles of metaphysics in

science, while illustrating these with examples relevant to clinical research.

METAPHYSICS AND PROBLEM CHOICE IN CLINICAL RESEARCH

Metaphysics influences problem choice in research in several ways. First, problems presuppose an ontology in that the problem statement makes reference to certain kinds of entities (Gods, witches, ESP, cosmic unconsciousness, mental entities, physical objects, etc.). Different metaphysics result in the framing of different kinds of problems: "What sin or demonic possession caused this speaking in tongues, and what penance or prayer can remedy it?" versus "What physiological problem caused this delirium and what physical–chemical intervention can remedy it?"

Second, even if two metaphysical systems agree as to what kind of entities there are, they still can differ as to the particular ways these entities are related to one another. Beliefs that have the requisite remoteness from experience, here characterized as metaphysical, can result in the framing of questions making the same ontic commitments but differing as to the relationships between the entities. For example, consider the following:

Metaphysical belief: Blacks and Whites are by nature equal in intelligence.

Problem: What is wrong with the testing situation (culturally biased tests, tester-subject interaction) that causes Whites to score higher on the WAIS-R?

Metaphysical belief: Blacks and Whites by nature differ in intelligence.

Problem: How do brain structures/mechanisms differ between Blacks and Whites?

Finally, as illustrated earlier, one's choice of what problems are significant, among a host of possible problems, is influenced by the relevance the problems have to our metaphysical beliefs. Agassi (1975) has suggested that many scientific theories are designed to be tentative, partial answers to metaphysical questions. Problems occur when they have implications for beliefs that are directly or indirectly connected to many other beliefs in our web. The problem of nature versus nurture is important because of its manifold relations to beliefs that themselves are fairly central. The problem of what causes some individuals to chew gum is much less important because it is not central and because it has few implications for central beliefs. As Koertge (1980) maintained,

> Scientific problems arise when our expectations are violated, when what we consider to be regularities call for a deeper explanation, when two previously disparate fields look as if they could be unified, or when a good scientific theory clashes with our familiar metaphysical framework. In each instance the scientist's background experience and preferred world view enters into her or his assessment of what is problematic and deserving of investigation. (p. 347)

Metaphysics and Research Design

Once a problem has been selected and characterized, metaphysics influences the design of the relevant experiments. First, in research design the choice of the hypothesis we test is influenced by our metaphysics. Metaphysics bestows antecedent plausibility on an as-yet-untested conjecture. We believe that the hypothesis under test is plausible because we believe other related sentences to be true, many of which are not observational.

Second, the major goal of research design is to structure experience so that a certain inference can be made with maximal validity. To do this, plausible rival hypotheses must be ruled out, but what counts as a *plausible* rival hypothesis is again influenced by our metaphysics because metaphysics determines what can be taken as serious possibilities. Psychologists do not typically attempt to rule out hypotheses that have to do with astrological factors or the subject's history of sin because our metaphysics does not bestow the mantle of "plausible rival hypothesis" on sentences containing these kinds of entities.

Metaphysics and Observation Statements

At the point at which we actually start making observations, metaphysics is the least influential. Because scientists attempt to make observation statements as inter-subjective as possible, observation statements are least vulnerable to influence by metaphysics. Still, as cognitive psychologists have found, observations can be influenced by our expectations, schemata, and so on. The interpretation of observations from scientific instruments is based on the acceptance of certain background beliefs, and the Duhemian problem can be, and sometimes is, resolved by the rejection of observation statements.

To illustrate how expectations can influence what is observed, consider the following problem. What number comes next in this sequence: 8, 5, 4, 9, 1, 7, 6?

Perceiving these as mathematical entities instead of semantical ones makes one unlikely to notice that these numerals are in alphabetical order and that the next one, therefore, is 3.

Metaphysics and the Duhemian Problem

In the case of a prediction failure, logic does not dictate which statement is false. An auxiliary hypothesis or the hypothesis under test, or both, might be false. For example, in the face of the lack of symptom substitution in behavioral outcome studies, psychoanalysts can respond by searching for symptoms that are more subtle or diffuse, or that take longer to manifest themselves. The logic of the situation allows what Lakatos suggested: that in the case of prediction failures we can protect certain central beliefs—our metaphysical hard core—by directing the arrows of *modus tollens* to auxiliary hypotheses.

Metaphysics and the Modification of Refitted Hypotheses

However, if some anomaly or some number of prediction failures seem to weigh heavily on our central beliefs and we decide to consider them false, then we can modify these beliefs while still retaining much of their central content. In Lakatos's terms, our metaphysical positive heuristic would suggest variants that retain the essence of the core notions: The new hypothesis comes from the same metaphysical research program. For example, a behavioral researcher initially committed to understanding phobias as being classically conditioned might, given many prediction failures, try to understand phobias using an operant analysis. It would be much more unlikely for the researcher to begin to investigate hypotheses involving anxiety over surfacing id impulses.

METAPHYSICS AND PSYCHOTHERAPY

I now will turn to an examination of the roles of metaphysics in the practice of psychotherapy. First, I must make the general point that if one accepts the foregoing conclusions regarding the roles of metaphysics in clinical research and if this research influences clinical practice, then metaphysics influences clinical practice through its influence on clinical research. Beyond this general point, though, there are other more specific roles that metaphysics plays in clinical practice.

Therapy Programs

The diverse approaches to psychotherapy (e.g., behavior therapy, Freudian analysis, or client-centered psychotherapy) are structured and function analogously to Lakatos's scientific research programs. Here I shall consider these approaches to psychotherapy as therapy programs and describe their close analogies with Lakatosian research programs.

First, notice that the same epistemic considerations hold for psychotherapy: There is no clear demarcation between observational statements and theoretical statements, and the Duhemian problem is still relevant. I shall discuss these points in the context of understanding the structure of therapy programs.

A therapy program, like a scientific research program, contains a hard core, a negative heuristic, and a positive heuristic. The hard core contains central beliefs that are not falsifiable, again because of an implicit methodological decision. For example, the hard core of behavior therapy contains sentences such as, "Undesirable behavior itself, rather than some presumed underlying cause, is the focus of change"; "Undesirable behavior is learned through the same processes by which other behavior is learned"; and "Undesirable behavior can be modified by using psychological principles, especially conditioning principles." The statements in the hard core are again considered to be metaphysical in that although experience is relevant to their truth value, they are sheltered from refutation.

The negative heuristic of a therapy program directs the arrows of *modus tollens* away from the hard core. Therapists do not abandon their central beliefs when faced with a treatment failure. The logic of psychotherapy is essentially as follows:

If the therapy applied is appropriate, then there is change.

There is no change.

Therefore, the therapy was not appropriate.

But again, the actual logic of the situation is more complex:

> If the therapy applied was appropriate and H1 . . . Hn, then there is change.
>
> <u>There is no change.</u>
>
> Therefore: not (therapy and H1 . . . Hn).
>
> Therefore: not therapy or not H1 . . . or not Hn.

Again, there is such commitment to the hard core of the therapy program that other beliefs will be considered suspect in the case of a treatment failure. "The client was insufficiently motivated or compliant" (which is essentially a statement of a boundary condition) seems to be a particular favorite, or, "Therapy was not long enough or was not properly administered" and so on.

The positive heuristic gives a general pattern for new variants. In behavioral clinical psychology, the positive heuristic might be given as "Human behavior is learned," and thus when new learning paradigms come along, or traditional paradigms are modified, these can be used to suggest alterations in the therapy program. This perhaps has been done, to some extent, in the so-called "cognitive revolution," in that symbolic learning and other findings in cognitive psychology have altered behavior modification. In Freudian analysis, the positive heuristic might be given as "Observable behavior is a result of intrapsychic processes involving basic motivational forces," and the variants might be seen in the various neo-Freudian theories.

Metaphysics and Clinical Problems

In the main, psychotherapy is an attempt to remediate some cognitive, affective, or behavioral disorder as defined by the patient, significant others, or society. Such problem statements involve an ontological commitment, in that if one accepts them as true sentences one becomes committed to the existence of certain kinds of entities. Therapy programs influence the problem statement and thereby ontic commitment. Whether a given problem is described in terms of medical/disease entities, behavioral excesses or deficits, unconscious conflicts, or existential problems in living is determined by the therapy program. Second, that psychologists view a certain state of affairs as problematic is influenced by our metaphysical views concerning such issues as what constitutes the good life, human nature, and morality (O'Donohue et al., 1987). That we provide treatment seems, at least, to be involved with our notions of the plasticity of human behavior and the belief that the current state of affairs is (relatively) undesirable.

Metaphysics and Therapy Design

The metaphysical hard core of the therapy program influences the choice of what therapy techniques will be used. Our map of the causal structure of the world, or indeed whether it has a causal structure, is partly given by our metaphysics. Moreover, some therapy techniques are blatantly concerned with the client's own metaphysics. Their aim is to achieve "cognitive restructuring," which often involves a change in metaphysical beliefs.

We also need to realize that there is much empirical information that is missing in psychotherapy. We have not researched all the questions that are involved in psychotherapy (e.g., What is the best way to introduce oneself to a client, or this particular kind of client? What influence does a therapist's style of dress have on particular kinds of clients?). When we lack research information about a particular question we must rely on our shared "clinical experience." This is metaphysically influenced. For example, Chapman and Chapman (1969) found that there was a high degree of consensus among clinicians that certain Rorschach responses (e.g., buttocks, feminine clothing) were indicative of male homosexuality, despite the fact that these turn out not to be valid signs. Perhaps the clinicians here were relying on their world pictures (which have a considerable degree of overlap because these clinicians have similar backgrounds) to fill in missing in formation regarding diagnostic signs. Given that research supplies only a small fraction of the information needed to completely understand the psychotherapeutic process, we are often compelled to rely on our tacit, background metaphysical notions.

Metaphysics and Observation Statements

As in the case of research, expectations and previous experience will influence what is observed in psychotherapy. Observation is selective; what is considered clinically significant will to a large degree be determined by the therapy program. This is particularly obvious in the taking of a clinical case history. The therapist is not interested in every event in the client's life, but rather only those that are significant—with "significant" being at least partially determined by metaphysical considerations. Just as Popper (1957) has suggested, interpretive frameworks are used to select and structure what is contained in a history.

Finally, like physical scientists, psychologists observe through their instruments. These instruments can be founded and justified on metaphysical grounds. For example, in a concurrent validity study of the WAIS-R, what are the implications of the fact that groups such as Blacks and Whites or men and women attain significantly different full-scale IQs? The question seems to depend on one's criteria of validity, which in turn depend on one's metaphysics. In one world picture, where groups can differ on such traits and where Whites and men happen to have more of one trait—intelligence (after all, look at their achievements)—this would be a result supporting the test's validity. In another metaphysical belief system where all groups are created equal in intelligence (but are subjected to either conducive or deleterious environments), a different conclusion is reached. The general point is that the so-called "criterion problem" in test construction forces us to make some prior assumptions, and these assumptions are influenced by our metaphysics. Thus, debate over the validity of the WAIS-R may be as much a debate over metaphysical beliefs as a debate over the narrower issue of the psychometrics of the test.

Metaphysics and the Duhemian Problem

As alluded to earlier, when faced with a treatment failure, the psychotherapist is logically free to choose any belief involved in the prediction of success to bear the blame for the failure. This allows certain cherished beliefs in the metaphysical hard core of the therapy program to avoid the arrows of *modus tollens*. The therapist may choose to consider as false any one of many auxiliary hypotheses. Furthermore, as with a scientific research program, even when the therapist decides to modify a central belief, he or she may do so while retaining the spirit of the previous belief by modifying it along the lines suggested by the metaphysical positive heuristic. For example, consider the behaviorist who has increased the frequency of putative response-contingent positive reinforcement in an effort to improve a client's depression. If the client shows little response, the behaviorist is logically free to point the arrows of *modus tollens* at an auxiliary hypothesis, for example, by claiming that the reinforcers used were not mood-related reinforcers for this client.

Modifying Hypotheses to Encompass Anomalous Results

Moreover, if the behavioral therapist should abandon this view of the client's depression, he or she is more likely to adopt another behavioral view (what is relevant is the amount of punishers in the client's life) or perhaps a cognitive view (the client's attributional style is problematic), rather than an alternative from a more dissimilar metaphysical framework.

CONCLUSION

In sum, if the considerations given earlier are correct, then metaphysics has a significant role in clinical research and practice. Through the influence of metaphysics on clinical research, problem definition, therapy design, the informal beliefs used in therapy, observations (especially test-based observations), attempts to resolve the Duhemian problem, and efforts to modify hypotheses to encompass anomalous results, one must conclude that scientific psychotherapy rests on an infrastructure of metaphysics. The picture of rational inquiry presented here is one in which programs of metaphysical and empirical propositions compete with other programs of metaphysical and empirical propositions in their ability to resolve conceptual and empirical problems. This should not be cause for any great despair. After all, not only is this the epistemic situation everyone is in, but if clinical research and psychotherapy are to be truly meaningful, then they need to be relevant to central beliefs. Psychologists' research and therapy efforts do not involve merely a circumscribed set of isolated beliefs concerning "clinical psychology." No firm barrier separates our beliefs qua clinical psychologists from all our other beliefs. The results of our efforts to understand and help other human beings are a function of our entire web of belief. This web, and especially beliefs central to it, need at times to be considered open questions—indeed open metaphysical questions—and to be subjected to the best criticism we psychologists can muster.

References

Agassi, J. (1975). *Science in flux: Boston studies in the philosophy of science* (Vol. 28). Dordrecht, The Netherlands: Reidel.

Ashby, R. W. (1967). Verifiability principle. In P. Edwards (Ed.), *The encyclopedia of philosophy* (pp. 240–247). New York: MacMillan.

Bruner, J. S., & Potter, M. C. (1964). Interference in visual recognition. *Science, 144*, 424–425.

Chapman, L. J., & Chapman, J. P. (1969). Illusory correlation as an obstacle to the use of valid psychodiagnostic signs. *Journal of Abnormal Psychology, 74*, 271–287.

Derner, G. F. (1965). Graduate education in clinical psychology. In B. B. Wolman (Ed.), *Handbook of clinical psychology*. New York: McGraw-Hill.

Duhem, P. (1962). *The aim and structure of physical theory* (P. P. Weiner, Trans.). New York: Atheneum.

Hempel, C. G. (1966). *Aspects of scientific explanation*. New York: Free Press.

Humphreys, L. G. (1939). The effect of random alternation of reinforcement on the acquisition and extinction of conditioned eyelid reactions. *Journal of Experimental Psychology, 25*, 141–148.

Koertge, N. (1979). *Braucht die Sozialwissenschaft wirklich metaphysik?* [Do the social sciences really need metaphysics?] In H. Albert & K. H. Stapf (Eds.), *Theorie und Erfahrung*. Klett-Cotta.

Koertge, N. (1980). Methodology, ideology, and feminist critiques of science. *Philosophy of Science Association, 2*, 346–259.

Krasner, L., & Houts, A. C. (1984). A study of the "value" systems of behavioral scientists. *American Psychologist, 39*, 840–850.

Lakatos, I. (1970). Falsification and the methodology of scientific research programmes. In I. Lakatos & A. Musgrave (Eds.), *Criticism and the growth of knowledge* (pp. 91–196). Cambridge, England: Cambridge University Press.

Malcolm, N. (1967). Wittgenstein. In P. Edwards (Ed.), *The encyclopedia of philosophy* (pp. 327–34). New York: Macmillan.

Nakhnikian, G. (1981). *An introduction to philosophy*. Bloomington, IN: Publications Press.

O'Donohue, W., Fisher, J. E., & Krasner, L. (1987). Ethics and psychotherapy with the elderly, In L. Carstensen & B. Edelstein (Eds.), *Handbook of clinical gerontology* (pp. 387–400). New York: Pergamon.

Popper, K. R. (1945). *The open society and its enemies*. London: Routledge & Kegan Paul.

Popper, K. R. (1957). *The poverty of historicism*. London: Routledge & Kegan Paul.

Popper, K. R. (1961). *The logic of scientific discovery*. New York: Basic Books.

Popper, K. R. (1963). *Conjectures and refutations: The growth of scientific knowledge*. New York: Harper & Row.

Quine, W. V. O. (1961). Two dogmas of empiricism. In W. Quine (Ed.), *From a logical point of view* (pp. 20–46). New York: Harper & Row.

Quine, W. V. Q., & Ullian, J. S. (1978). *The web of belief*. New York: Random House.

Rock, I. (1983). *The logic of perception*. Cambridge, MA: The MIT Press.

Salmon, W. C. (1979). *The foundation of scientific inference*. Pittsburgh: University of Pittsburgh Press.

Warren, V. (1970). Perceptual restoration of missing speech sounds. *Science, 67*, 392–393.

Watson, J. B., & Rayner, R. (1920). Conditioning emotional responses. *Journal of Experimental Psychology, 3*, 1–14.

Wittgenstein, L. (1958). Philosophical investigations (G. E. M. Anscombe, Trans.). New York: Macmillan.

8

Epistemic and Ethical Duties in Clinical Decision-making

WILLIAM O'DONOHUE AND DEBORAH HENDERSON

In the course of psychotherapy, psychologists need to make important clinical decisions regarding treatment goal selection, measurement procedures, and treatment methods. These decisions can be made without regard to the epistemic and ethical responsibilities that accompany professional status. Epistemic duties are obligations to obtain and have knowledge, while ethical duties are obligations to apply this knowledge accurately. We argue that these epistemic and ethical responsibilities are invoked and can be adequately addressed in the informed consent process. When the informed consent process is violated or done poorly, our epistemic and ethical responsibilities are not met and the client may be harmed. We argue that what the public assumes it is buying from us (and what we purport to sell) are specialised knowledge and skills; when psychologists are not meeting their epistemic duties, what our clients are receiving instead is intuition and performance art. We discuss errors that occur in the course of psychotherapy, as well as how we as professionals must seek to reduce or eliminate them.

Psychotherapists need to make complex decisions during the course of psychotherapy. They must make decisions regarding three main issues: (a) What are the *goals* of treatment?, (b) What are the *measuring procedures* to be used in this case?, and (c) What *treatment methods* are to be used? The quality of the decisions that are made at these choice points determine both the ethical quality of therapy and the practical quality of therapy, that is, the degree of success that will be achieved in therapy.

For instance, goal formation is a complex matter. Therapy is directional: it involves something-to-be-changed. Explicit goal setting allows progress toward the goal to be assessed. One needs to know where one wants to go in order to assess the extent to which one is getting closer. Explicit goal setting also identifies when the end of therapy has been reached. Goals, too, can be evaluated with respect to their quality. When a violent sex offender is court-ordered to be in therapy and the sole goal of therapy becomes helping the offender with the stress of dealing with his conviction, then this goal is problematic. The goal of therapy in this case should be to reduce the client's future probability of offending. It should not be to allow the client to vent about his disappointments concerning the judicial system. Below, we will deal with some of the complexities of proper goal formation.

Measurement is probably the most fundamental process in psychotherapy because, for any descriptive statement to be made, a measurement (i.e., detection) process must occur. "The client is crying" involves the valid discrimination of crying versus non-crying. "The client is depressed" involves additional and more complex measurements involving such matters as dysphoric mood, sleep, appetite, sexual interest, and suicidal ideation. The accuracy of these measurements can all, of course, vary considerably. The psychologist can form and believe false descriptive statements. He or she can believe, for example, that the client has not contemplated suicide in the past two weeks, when in fact the client has thought for hours about jumping off a building.

Choosing treatment methods involves knowing and instantiating causal relations. The treatment methods are the means to the ends (i.e., the treatment goals). They bring the client from their status at the beginning of therapy to the desired status at the end of therapy. Decisions regarding treatment goals can also vary in their quality. Bad decisions would involve treatment methods that have not been shown to be causes of the effects desired, methods that are not in fact causally related to the desired ends, or methods that bring about undesired side effects (iatrogenesis). Bad decisions could also involve methods that are not the most cost-effective causes of the goals desired. O'Donohue (1991, pp. 70–71) has argued that these decisions can be formally explicated as follows:

Goal Selection

Argument 1A: Client-driven model

1. Client C wants to achieve state of affairs S.
2. C is informed about alternatives and the costs and benefits associated with achieving S.
3. S is a morally permissible state of affairs.
4. S is a practically feasible state of affairs.
5. S is not inconsistent with any overriding states of affairs that C wants to, or should, obtain.
6. Variables influencing S, or S itself, are psychological entities.
7. If 1, 2, 3, 4, 5, 6, and *ceteris paribus*, then S is an appropriate treatment goal.
8. *Ceteris paribus* (i.e., all things being equal).

Therefore: S is an appropriate treatment goal.

Argument 1B: Other-driven models of goal selection

1. Significant other O wants individual I to be in state of affairs S.
2. I does not want to be in S.
3. There is some factor that legitimately overrides I's desire not to be in S.
4. O is informed concerning alternatives and the costs and benefits associated with achieving S.
5. S is a morally permissible state of affairs.
6. S is a practically feasible end state.
7. S is not inconsistent with any overriding state of affairs that I should obtain.
8. Variables influencing S or S itself are psychological entities.
9. If 1, 2, 3, 4, 5, 6, 8, and *ceteris paribus*, then S is an appropriate treatment goal.
10. *Ceteris paribus*.

Therefore: S is an appropriate treatment goal.

Assessment Method Selection

Argument 2: What assessment methods will be used in this case?

1. Therapist T wants information I1 . . . In.
2. Information I1 . . . In is potentially relevant to the treatment of client C.
3. Gathering information I1 . . . In is morally permissible.
4. Gathering information I1 . . . In is practically feasible.
5. Information I1 . . . In is sufficiently complete and comprehensive information about the principal dimensions of the case.
6. Assessment methods A1 . . . An are reliable and valid methods for gathering information I1 . . . In.
7. Assessment methods A1 . . . An are cost-effective methods for gathering information I1 . . . In.
8. C is fully informed regarding alternatives to gathering this information and these assessment methods, but consents to the gathering of this information by the use of these methods.
9. If 1, 2, 3, 4, 5, 6, 8 and *ceteris paribus*, then assessment methods A1 . . . An are the proper assessment methods to use in this case.
10. *Ceteris paribus*.

Therefore: Assessment methods A1 . . . An are the proper assessment methods to use in this case.

Treatment Method Selection

Argument 3: What treatment methods should be used in this case?

1. Treatment goal G entails the realisation of states of affairs S1 . . . Sn.
2. F1 . . . Fn are all factors that are known or hypothesised to be causally relevant to S1 . . . Sn.
3. F1 . . . Fn are cost-efficient methods to obtain S1 . . . Sn.
4. F1 . . . Fn-m are the least restrictive methods to obtain S1 . . . Sn.
5. Client C is fully informed concerning alternative methods and the costs and benefits of these methods, and consents to the use of F1 . . . Fn-m.
6. If 1, 2, 3, 4, 5 and *ceteris paribus*, then F1 . . . Fn-m are the proper treatment methods to use in this case.
7. *Ceteris paribus*.

Therefore: F1 . . . Fn-m, where Fn-m indicates that some subset of all potential factors will be manipulated, are the proper treatment methods to use in this case.

The argument outlined above demonstrates that clinical decision-making necessitates the consideration of many different kinds of information. It is the clinician's duty to gather particular facts with regard to each of these kinds of information for every client in order to make true assertions that can serve as premises in the above models. The type of information that needs to be considered assumes that values are inherent in psychotherapy, and includes (a) *empirical information* concerning particular facts, such as the client's goals; (b) *moral and ethical considerations*, such as the appropriateness of treatment goals; (c) *economic information* with regard to costs of treatment alternatives; (d) *causal information* in order to determine which variables to manipulate in order to achieve desired ends; (e) *pragmatic considerations*, that is, what is practically possible for the client with regard to treatment options; and (f) *metaphysical information* that assists us in forming plausible alternative hypotheses (O'Donohue, 1991). These information requirements constitute the substance of a clinician's epistemic duties.

INFORMED CONSENT

The ethical principle that the client should give informed consent in therapy is, in our view, one of the most fundamental ethical safeguards. It is also our view that it is one of the most violated safeguards; few would want any of our clients to be quizzed at any point in therapy regarding the costs and benefits of treatment alternatives. It is violated fairly regularly for at least two reasons. The first reason is that the ethical codes binding psychologists function much more as rhetorical devices designed to have certain effects on our consumers, potential consumers, and potential overseers than as our actual commitments whose seriousness is at least partially shown by the policing and punishments associated with transgressions (O'Donohue & Mangold, 1996). The second reason is that allowing the client to be in the position of giving informed consent is admittedly a difficult process: How much information about each option should be given? How is this information to be presented fairly and objectively (e.g., how are design flaws in outcome studies to be communicated?). Are there external forces on the client (e.g., wife, boss, judge) that preclude the client's "consent" actually being given?

It is the central thesis of this paper that the mental health professional has epistemic duties (obligations to have knowledge) by virtue of his or her role as a professional and, in particular, these epistemic duties are invoked in the informed consent process. Psychologists have fiduciary duties toward their clients. Fiduciary means "trust or reliance" (Simpson & Weiner, 1989). The professional role is such that clients can expect to trust their therapist, and to rely on their therapist to have the requisite knowledge and competencies. Thus, in order for the psychologist to be truthful, honest, beneficent, and non-harming, they must honour their epistemic duties. In short, the psychologist must know what should be measured by which assessment methods, and what treatment methods are the most cost-effective means to properly derived treatment goals. These are not easy matters, but such knowledge must be obtained and implemented if the psychologist is to properly fulfil his or her representation as a professional and actually help people while minimally harming them.

EPISTEMIC DUTIES AND THE ETHICAL CODE

The *Ethical Principles of Psychologists and Code of Conduct* (Ethics Code; American Psychological Association (APA), 1992) for psychologists is not terribly effective at synthesising the professional's epistemic and ethical responsibilities. As a result, it is entirely possible for a licensed psychologist to comply with the Ethics Code and yet at the same time fail in his or her epistemic duties. In order to better understand how this might be the case, let us take a look at the Ethics Code. It is "intended to provide standards of professional conduct that can be applied by the APA and by other bodies that choose to adopt them" (p. 1598). Principle A reads, in part, "Psychologists . . . provide only those services and use only those techniques for which they are qualified by education, training, or experience . . . They maintain knowledge of relevant scientific and professional information related to the services they render" (p. 1599). Standard 1.05 of this code reads, in part, "Psychologists . . . maintain a reasonable level of awareness of current scientific and professional information . . . and undertake ongoing efforts to maintain competence in the skills they use" (p. 1600), while Standard 1.06 states that "psychologists rely on scientifically and professionally derived knowledge when making scientific or professional judgments or when engaging in scholarly or professional endeavors" (p. 1600).

At first reading, these statements seem perfectly adequate. Even a cursory second reading, however, will make it obvious that these statements say nothing about what *types* of education, training, or experience will qualify a psychologist for the services they provide; *what* scientific or professional information is to be considered relevant; *how* psychologists are to maintain a reasonable level of awareness (and what may be considered reasonable) of current information; or *how* to go about maintaining competence in the skills they use. Nowhere in the Ethics Code does it state that the skills psychologists should be competent in must be those that are considered scientifically valid. In stating that psychologists should *rely on* scientifically and professionally derived knowledge, the Ethics Code leaves open the door for psychologists to use literally any method at their discretion. A reliance on scientific or professional knowledge does not necessarily imply the use of such knowledge in any direct way. Even assuming that it did, the particular way that this standard is phrased would still allow for the use of techniques that have not been validated by scientific means—whether or not the client is judged to require such services. In such a way, behaviour that is consistent with the Ethics Code may not be consistent with professional behaviour.

PSYCHOLOGISTS AS KNOWLEDGE EXPERTS

It can be instructive to ask why psychologists should have special status. The fact that they do have special status is clear. They are called *Doctor*, an honorific; they earn many times the minimum wage; and legally in many states they are empowered to initiate involuntary commitment to institutions—a significant exception to the general doctrine that such freedom is infringed on only after due process with numerous safeguards.

Psychologists enjoy this special status because they are viewed as having (and represent themselves as actually possessing) important, specialised knowledge. They (purportedly) know how to solve important problems such as threats posed by sex offenders and wife batterers. They can help individuals afraid of coming out of their houses because of their fear of panic attacks to be able to leave their houses and live normal lives. They can help depressed individuals feel happier. They know how to measure intelligence to better understand or predict a child's school performance. They can help retarded individuals learn important skills to aid in leading more normal lives. They can conduct assessments that provide information to courts to help decide child custody in divorces. They can help embarrassed 10-year-old children stop wetting their beds. They can develop prevention programs to decrease the incidence of smoking or date rape. These certainly are important problems, and those having knowledge of how to solve them certainly deserve respect. Life is full of hard, sometimes very intractable and sometimes very painful, problems. Szasz (1961, 1971) has very wisely said that the normal state is problem filled.

A general point needs to be made regarding how individuals use experts. Experts are not used to solve problems that the individual has knowledge and skills to solve themselves. We do not go to a veterinarian to solve the problem of a dog whimpering due to hunger pains; we simply open a can of dog food. We do visit the veterinarian when we see the dog whimpering and limping, after we have exhausted our folk knowledge of possible solutions (e.g., looking to see if there is a thorn in its paw). We do this because we believe that the veterinarian has special assessment, diagnostic, and treatment skills that exceed our own. Thus, we are willing to assume the expense and inconvenience of consulting with an expert when we believe there is an important problem that is beyond our knowledge to solve but which we believe the professional has special skills and knowledge to solve. We believe the same is true with individuals consulting mental health professionals. They seek their help because they believe the mental health professional has specialised knowledge and skills that exceed their folk knowledge and skills to solve what they see as non-trivial problems.

O'Donohue, Fisher, Plaud, and Link (1989) asked clients what they thought was a good treatment decision. Clients stated that they expected their therapist to use research findings to make clinical decisions; additionally, they expected their therapist to have experience with the methods decided upon. We will call this the *specialised knowledge and skills criterion*. We argue that the specialised knowledge and skills criterion is also accepted by the mental health professional by virtue of his or her acceptance of the privileges associated with their specialised role. Charging and accepting in excess of one hundred dollars per hour implies a high value regarding what is delivered. Telling others that you should be addressed as doctor is another. And, most importantly, meddling in someone else's life is the ultimate demonstration of this acceptance.

So there is an acceptance of this criterion on the part of both the mental health professional and the consumer of these services (note: sometimes these are third parties). It is important to recognise five implications of the acceptance of the specialised knowledge and skills criterion:

1. Consumers can make false *knowledge assumptions* regarding what a particular mental health professional or the profession as a whole actually has.
2. Mental health professionals can make false representations or passively accept false client assumptions regarding their knowledge of the knowledge state of the field.
3. When either 1 or 2 obtains, then the therapist is behaving unethically with regard to their epistemic duties.
4. When there are no false therapist representations or client assumptions, then the therapist is behaving ethically on this dimension. The therapist may or may not be unethical for other reasons (e.g., the therapist may be engaging in a sexual relationship with the client).
5. The information phase of the informed consent process is a process that can, when properly conducted, ensure that 4 obtains.

There is no basis to believe that clients are coming to us for reasons other than epistemic ones (e.g., because of the alleged quality of our intuitions). This is good, because there is no reason to believe that we should represent that our intuitions are better than those of other individuals. Moreover, there is no course on intuitions in the curricula of any of the mental health professions. Thus, clients should not enter into professional relationships with us to trust or rely on our intuitions. There is no reason to believe that a fair price for our intuitions is in the order of one hundred dollars per hour. Our intuitions regarding child placement in custody evaluations, in predictions of violence, in the assessment of suicide risk, in what treatments will bring about a less depressed person, and so on do not faithfully fulfil the contract.

The most basic condition of consulting an expert—a professional—is a differential knowledge condition. There is no basis to believe that clients are coming to mental health professionals for their "superior" aesthetic judgments. Mental health professionals have no aesthetic enhancement courses in their graduate training curricula. We have not demonstrated superiority (whatever this may be) on this dimension.

Furthermore, there is no basis to believe that clients are simply buying our a-epistemic emotional warmth, caring, and friendship. Psychotherapy has been criticised as the "purchase of a friend", but this is not the contract we are purporting to sell. Our graduate training curricula is not focused on friendship skills but on how to measure and treat behaviour. Certainly, all our skills can and should be practiced in a warm, friendly, and caring manner—this is certainly part of what clients are buying (i.e., a good bedside manner)—but not solely this. If they were solely buying this, they could certainly get it cheaper elsewhere and we certainly should redesign our training programs.

There is no basis to believe that clients are buying a jazz performance. That is, they are not buying our creative improvisations—our unique speculative jumps (unlike any other therapist and even significantly unlike any of our previous performances). Unfortunately, we fear that this is often happening in psychotherapy: that clients believe they are purchasing specialised knowledge and skills but therapists are delivering intuitions, aesthetics judgments, emotions, and jazz performances. This point is consistent with one made by Sechrest (1992), in his discussion of development in clinical psychology. Sechrest notes that the claims made by professional psychologists are far more ambitious than the actual contributions.

THE COSTS OF VIOLATING EPISTEMIC AND ETHICAL DUTIES IN CLINICAL DECISION-MAKING

As a profession, we must take seriously the costs to our clients that can (and unfortunately, very often do) occur when we fail to meet our epistemic and ethical duties with regard to clinical decision-making. Epistemic errors in clinical practice can cause serious harm. When we make a descriptive claim about a client that is not true, for example, we can miss something that actually required treatment, and thus we can prolong the client's suffering. On the other hand, overdiagnosis can stigmatise a client and cause them to have negative beliefs about themselves that are not true. Practicing therapies that we erroneously believe cause change, when they do not, wastes everyone's resources. Treating a client with therapy A, when therapy B is more effective, needlessly prolongs the client's suffering and results in an inefficient expenditure of resources. Economists state that all activities have opportunity costs: engaging in one has the cost of forcing the actor to forgo engaging in another. All ineffective therapies have opportunity costs in that they displace the opportunity to engage in other, more productive options. Let us not mince words here. Our epistemic mistakes can cause a lot of harm. Children can be abused again and severely injured or killed. Suicides can be committed. Wives can be beaten. Overdoses can be taken. Marriages can end. Arrests can occur. Illnesses can be exacerbated. As clinical psychologists, we can be meddling with situations in which the stakes are very high.

Costs are not limited to the client. As a profession, we also incur costs as a result of not meeting our professional duties. Among these costs are the development of professional standards, the establishment of more empirically supported treatments, the respect of other relevant professions such as the medical and legal professions, and perhaps even progress in the field of psychology as a whole.

EPISTEMIC AND ETHICAL DUTIES
AND INFORMED CONSENT

If we proceed on the assumption that informed consent is critical to obtain if we are to behave ethically with our clients, we must then ask what it means that a client is giving informed consent. In this paper, we are focusing on the *informed* component of the informed consent process. For interesting explications of the thorny issues regarding autonomy and cognitive competence in the process, the reader is referred to Ringen (1993).

In order for a client to give informed consent for treatment, he or she must be made aware of (a) how the therapist has conceptualised his or her problem, (b) the best alternatives for treating this particular problem, (c) the risks and benefits associated with each of these treatment alternatives, and (d) who is the best person to provide the treatments (an issue that should include a discussion of the therapist's own training and experience in treating similar problems). Once a client is familiar with this information, he or she is then in a position to be able to make a decision with regard to which treatment to pursue (if any), and with which professional. To the extent that a client does not have this information, then his or her consent to participate in psychotherapy cannot be said to be informed. It stands to reason, then, that the therapist providing the client with this information should in fact know these things. It is this knowledge, after all, that is supposed to separate laypersons from professionals.

We argue that, in order for mental health professionals to provide this information to clients, at least four responsibilities must be met by the therapist:

1. Mental health professionals must be current with regard to the knowledge state of the field as it pertains to the problems he or she is treating.
2. Mental health professionals must make accurate, relevant judgments regarding this knowledge with respect to the particular client at hand.
3. Mental health professionals must be aware of their own limitations with regard to training and experience.
4. Mental health professionals must accurately and effectively communicate this knowledge to the client. By

accurately, we mean faithfully. By effectively, we mean in a way that the client understands.

FALLIBILISM

What is the substance of relying on scientific information in making clinical decisions, and why is it a good thing to behave in this manner? The Popperians have suggested that science begins with fallibilism, that is, the notion that our current beliefs, despite the fact that they are "ours" and despite all the attractions that they hold for us, may still be wrong. Fallibilism also applies to the previously stated belief; see Bartley (1984) for his comprehensive critical rationalism.

That our set of beliefs may not have optimal verisimilitude can be quickly discerned from a few considerations. First, we frequently encounter refutations of our beliefs in our daily life: teams that we are sure to win, lose; people who we are sure will behave in one way, don't; the short cut, isn't. Another way we can see that we may be wrong is that people disagree with us. The logical principle of noncontradiction entails that, when we assert A and someone else asserts not-A, one side is wrong.

Science is concerned with error and ways of eliminating error. A vigorous scientific attitude toward clinical decision-making involves a desire to detect error in one's beliefs and to attempt to replace these beliefs with those of greater accuracy. Science involves belief change, that is, learning. (It is ironic that those committed to a thoroughgoing scientific approach are often called "dogmatic" as they are dedicated to the very process of belief change. It is those outside the purview of science that are in the most important sense dogmatic; they far less frequently experience the corrective potential of science.)

An assumption of psychometrics, for example, is that all measurement contains error. Statistical inference is concerned with errors or falsely rejecting the null hypotheses. Experimentation is concerned with valid (not invalid) causal inference, and so on. This is as it should be: we need to be worried that our confirmation biases and other heuristic errors may be influencing us to believe something we ought not (Siegert, 1996, this issue).

When we are conducting psychotherapy, we can make the following kinds of errors:

1. *False descriptive statements.* We can claim, for example, that our client never thought of suicide in the preceding week, when in fact she thought of it four times.
2. *False causal statements.* We can believe that our client's erectile dysfunction is caused by performance anxiety, when in fact it is caused by a neurological problem.
3. *False ontic statements.* We can believe that things exist when in fact they do not. We may believe that there is something such as an inner child, when there is not.
4. *False relational claims.* We can believe that therapy x produces more change than therapy y, when this is not the case.
5. *False predictions.* We can believe that therapy x in certain situations will result in the greatest change for this client, when it does not.

6. *False professional ethical claims.* We can believe that it is ethically permissible to have a certain kind of extra-therapeutic relationship with our client, when it is actually ethically impermissible.

Next, one must realise that all professional behaviour is based upon knowledge claims. That is, when I recommend that my client take test T to measure his depression, this act is based on a knowledge claim, to wit, that in this situation test T is the most accurate, cost-efficient, and so on, manner for my client's depression to be measured. Furthermore, this act is based on the knowledge claim that I know that it is a priority to measure my client's depression in this situation. When I start treating my client with psychotherapy P, the knowledge claim is that my client has the kind of problem that therapy P should be given for and that therapy P is the most cost-effective way to treat this problem.

Next, one must realise that all knowledge claims need to be evaluated with respect to the quality of the epistemic procedures used to form these. If I claim that I know that tomorrow you will experience a serious stressor because I have read your horoscope, then one must evaluate horoscopes as a means of reliably attaining such knowledge.

Importantly, the decision regarding what epistemic methods we should use has been made for us. Our profession, through its training model and through its Ethical Code, has explicitly stated that the way we seek to gain knowledge is through science. This is a wise decision because the application of science to problems has caused a historically unprecedented growth of knowledge. The problem is not that our profession is committed to a problematic epistemology. The problem is that too many clinical psychologists' commitment to this epistemology has been too superficial, sporadic, and rhetorical.

To behave scientifically is to behave in an explicitly critical manner, particularly in a self-critical manner. That is, one acknowledges that one's beliefs may be in error and one seeks to rigorously criticise one's beliefs to see if they are in error and thus in need of revision. Why is this a good thing? Because we are often wrong and because criticism allows error to be eliminated and knowledge to grow.

The characterisation of science that we are giving here is a neo-Popperian one. In this view, science is simply an epistemology—a way of knowing. The view is that we all start out with a "web of belief". For example, a clinical psychologist may hold beliefs such as "If I do therapy x with this client she will improve", "Multiple personality is caused by child sexual abuse", and "I can accurately measure someone's sexual preferences by a clinical interview". Science begins when one realises that one's current beliefs—no matter how "commonsensical", no matter how well they seem to cohere with other beliefs, no matter how much they are generally accepted by others, and no matter how many times they have appeared to be confirmed by one's experience—may still be false. Science begins with the epistemologically humble attitude of "I may be wrong".

The next step is exposing beliefs to criticism to see how well they withstand criticism. This step involves designing tests of the belief to see how they stand up to these tests. Sometimes testing beliefs is easy. If I believe my wife is on the phone,

I simply need to pick up the extension. Because we have only one line, if I hear a dial tone then I have falsified my belief. In another example, if I believe that all depressives make internal, stable, global attributions, then a reasonable form of criticism is to gather a decent sample of depressives and accurately measure their attributions and see if this experience contradicts the prior belief. If I believe some proposition that is expressed more tentatively, such as "More people who are depressed make global stable attributions than people who are not depressed", I essentially do the same thing. I just need to get a little more mathematically sophisticated because I need to look at correlations or conditional probabilities.

However, the distinction we want to make here is between the details of criticism and the general commitment to criticism. The details (research design) can get complicated as one attempts to investigate subtle or complicated criticisms. However, the general process remains the same: one is testing some claim by allowing it to be exposed to criticism, and one is not being critical for the sake of being critical. Rather, criticism is the means to detect error and thus a way of experiencing a growth of knowledge, and thus a way of basing your professional acts upon less error.

Note that this general characterisation nicely captures what is learned in research methodology. Research methodology is essentially a codification of some standard criticisms.

Why do we seek a representative sample to begin our research? Because we are not vulnerable to the criticism that our sample was biased and therefore the results are skewed. Why do we seek random assignment to groups? Because we do not want to be vulnerable to the criticism that observed differences at the end of the experiment were due to initial differences. Why do we worry about manipulating one variable at a time? Because if we want to say that differences were due to one variable, then in order to make the criticism that some other variable also changed we need to make sure we only manipulate one at a time. Why do we make sure our conclusions are worded so that they cover only the domains that we studied? Because we do not want to be vulnerable to the criticism that we are generalising to facets not directly studied—and so on. As Code (1987) wrote:

> Intellectually virtuous persons value knowing and understanding how things really are. They resist the temptation to live with partial explanations where fuller ones are attainable; they resist the temptation to live in fantasy or in a world of dream or illusion, considering it better to know, despite the tempting comfort and complacency a life of fantasy or illusion (or one well tinged with fantasy or illusion) can offer. (p. 37)

An individual who is motivated by something other than truth when forming a belief will be epistemically irresponsible and cowardly insofar as he or she will consider only the evidence that supports his or her prematurely formed conclusion. For instance, suppose a therapist holds the belief that facilitated communication is the most effective treatment for the problems of autistic children, and his or her motivation for holding that belief is to enjoy the popularity with parents that a quick cure provides, to enjoy the financial rewards, as well as to avoid the hard work of an intensive, long-term, behaviour-analytic treatment program. Moreover, the therapist refuses to read journals that provide critiques of facilitated communication and refuses to read or receive training in a behaviour-analytic approach. This selective consumption of information allows the therapist to feel confident that what he or she is prescribing is sound. Although the individual's holding such a belief may enable him or her to derive a number of positive personal outcomes, maintaining that belief is epistemically reprehensible because he or she is motivated by her own happiness rather than an earnest desire for truth. The therapist is failing in his or her epistemic duties as an expert in this field.

Thus, we must have at least a competent grasp of the scientific knowledge contained in our profession. It is our duty to actually know what is known in our field to justify the public and our customers treating us as experts. It is our duty to master this knowledge so as to maximise our beneficial effect on our clients. We must meet our epistemic duties in order to minimise the harm we do (unintentionally) to the people who are affected by our actions. We must meet our epistemic duties to honestly meet the reasonable expectations of our consumers regarding what we as professionals know. Knowledge-based action is what we are supposed to being selling. But this, of course, depends on the question "Do we actually know what we think we know?"

Our last major contention is that the only way we can meet our epistemic duties as clinical psychologists is to have a firm grasp of the state of scientific evidence for our actions and to honestly convey this evidence to our publics, and to seek to participate in the growth of knowledge of our profession. To do this is to actively exemplify what has been previously discussed in this article: we must acknowledge that our beliefs may be in error. We must rely on beliefs in our clinical practice that have best survived past criticism (or, roughly, have been vindicated by past scientific research; see McFall, 1991). We must realise that even these beliefs may still contain error and seek to expose these beliefs to further criticism to advance knowledge. We must do all of this to deserve our expert status and to minimise harm we do to people who trust us and pay us their hard-won resources. Thus, practically, we must:

1. Accept the general attitude that we may be wrong.
2. Seek to see if our beliefs are beliefs most consistent with the scientific literature (i.e., where these beliefs and their competitors have been evaluated).
3. Seek criticism from our peers, particularly peers that have greater relevant scientific expertise. Ask an objector group what criticism they may have of our beliefs/actions.
4. Conduct clinical practice in a way in which we can gain critical feedback regarding our beliefs. Conduct single-subject experimental designs (Barlow, Hayes, & Nelson, 1984). Conduct client satisfaction surveys. Seek to do program evaluation. Seek to engage in long-term follow-up to see relapse rates. Compare these to those in literature.
5. Give criticism to others. We believe that this field has for too long tolerated psychologists not meeting their epistemic duties. We have, out of some misguided sense of professional courtesy, bitten our tongues when colleagues use assessment devices that have no psychometric data or therapies that have no outcome research. This must stop. We propose that another duty we have to the public is to explicitly criticize these practices.
6. Impress on our students that when they accept expert status that they are concomitantly accepting the attendant epistemic duties and that to meet these duties they must have at least a competent knowledge of epistemologically sound knowledge claims, and this involves a knowledge of the scientific literature.

References

American Psychological Association. (1992). Ethical principles of psychologists and code of conduct. *American Psychologist, 47,* 1597–1612.

Barlow, D.H., Hayes, S.C., Nelson, R.O. (1984). *The scientist practitioner: Research and accountability in clinical and educational settings.* New York: Pergamon.

Bartley, W.W. (1984). *The retreat to commitment.* La Salle, IL: Open Court.

Code, L. (1987). *Epistemic responsibility.* Hanover: University Press of New England.

McFall, R.M. (1991). Construct validity of two heterosocial perception skill measures for assessing rape proclivity. *Violence and Victims, 6 (1),* 17–30.

O'Donohue, W.T. (1991). Normative models of clinical decisions. *Behavior Therapist, 14,* 70–72.

O'Donohue, W.T., Fisher, J.E., Plaud, J.J., & Link, W. (1989). What is a good treatment decision? The client's perspective. *Professional Psychology Research and Practice, 20,* 404–407.

O'Donohue, W.T., & Mangold, R. (1996). A critical examination of the *Ethical Principles of Psychologists and Code of Conduct.* In W.T. O'Donohue & R.F. Kitchener (Eds.), *The philosophy of psychology* (pp. 371–380). London, UK: Sage.

Ringen, J. (1993). Dennett's intentions and Darwin's legacy. *Behavioral and Brain Sciences, 16,* 386–390.

Sechrest, L. (1992). The past future of clinical psychology: A reflection on Woodworth (1937). *Journal of Consulting and Clinical Psychology, 60,* 18–23.

Siegert, R.J. (1999). Some thoughts about reasoning in clinical neuropsychology. *Behaviour Change, 16,* 37–48.

Simpson, J.A., & Weiner, E.S.C. (Eds.). (1989). *The Oxford English dictionary* (2nd ed., Vols. 1–20). New York: Oxford University Press.

Szasz, T.S. (1961). *The myth of mental illness: Foundations of a theory of personal conduct.* New York: Hoeber-Harper.

Szasz, T.S. (1971). *The manufacture of madness.* New York: Dell.

9

Ethics, Science, and the Helping Professions: A Conversation with Robyn Dawes

Eileen Gambrill

The integration of practice and research is an ongoing issue in the helping professions. This interview with Robyn Dawes reflects some of the related issues in this quest. Robyn Dawes is well known for his contributions to the literature on decision making. Recent books include Rational Choice in an Uncertain World: The Psychology of Judgement and Decision Making *(Hastie & Dawes, 2001) and* Everyday Irrationality: How Pseudo-scientists, Lunatics, and the Rest of Us Systematically Fail to Think Rationally *(Dawes, 2001). His areas of research interest include intuitive expertise, human cooperation, irrationality, and methodology. He is well known for* House of Cards: Psychology and Psychotherapy Built on Myth *(Dawes, 1994) in which he reviews the psychotherapy literature and concludes that it reflects a similarity in effects achieved by professionals and nonprofessionals.*

EG: What would you say is the basic role of science in professional practice?

RD: When people practice professionally, they claim—and sometimes it's true—that there is some scientific basis to what they are doing. People say "Oh, but science doesn't tell me exactly what to do." It does in a way—it frames what you can do. That is, science says: "Here are principles if you want to practice ethically and scientifically, you should be aware of these principles and work within them." There is a continuum ranging from one side, with "protocol therapies" related to principles of behavior and social learning which are applied pretty uniformly and self-consciously, to the other side where you have "relationship therapy" where there is an alliance with the client and you can't say "Do this, do that" based on guidance from scientific inquiry. Still, the science that we know, or what we think we know, should bound what it is we do, and certain things are out of bounds.

For example, memory is reconstructive. We don't have a videotape in our head that replays what our life was like when we are trying to recall something. We are right here and now and we are trying to look for traces of what occurred. We are filling in gaps. We are trying to make sense of what happened; that's a common memory process and, as far as we know, common to all memory. People come along and say "Ah, but there is a special sort of memory which is a repressed memory and this is something different. This just appears and you suddenly recall everything; you recall it perfectly accurately." That conflicts with everything we know about memory so if you want to work with a client on a memory, what you should do is say: "OK, now we've got to understand that all memory is reconstructive, even flashback memory that appears as if it were on videotape, and I should advise you to know that" and the therapist should know that and operate within that principle. Consider another example. If you want to make predictions about people, doing it systematically is more accurate. This is the clinical versus statistical prediction controversy. You are more likely to be accurate if you try to figure out what variables predict and then, looking across many people, say "OK, here's a variable that predicts, here's a variable that doesn't predict" rather than trying to Intuit about a single individual without searching for that sort of generality.

For example if you follow a statistical prediction rule you might find that past behavior predicts some future behavior such as criminal behavior or successful behavior in an academic institution. Being swayed by how much you remind me of somebody does not predict much, and, in fact, predicts very little except insofar as it is related to these general predictive rules, and professionals should be aware of that. You should not say "You're different. In general, people are going to do well if they did well in the past and if they do well on these tests specifically tailored to predict how well they will do. But I can tell you are different." It is what psychologists commonly call the "counterinductive generalization," and I and other people have studied this. When people make these sorts of exceptions, they do badly.

EG: How would you define science?

RD: I would define it as testing hypotheses through the systematic collection and analysis of observation of data whether via what are called "randomized trials experiments," where we randomly assign people to be given a vaccine or not or to a placebo group, all the way to informal observation. There are really two essences of science. You have to be able to address the question of "show me." That is, why do I believe this? Someone would say, "I believe it because I have had five years of experience with these types of people over ten years." This is not science. The second point is that a scientific, rational judgement is always comparative. You always ask: "Compared to what?" For example, you don't say, "Well, I had the experience with child abuse and I sort of associate nightmares with childhood abuse" or something like this because you've got to also ask "What about children who aren't abused? Do they have nightmares?" These are two important characteristics of science. It must respond to the "show me" challenge and it's got to be comparative. That's much different from the way most people apparently have behaved throughout most of the ages where you accept authority. Whether it is the church or government and you are told: "You should believe this because the authority does." "You should believe this because Freud says it is true." Or, "You should believe this because I've just figured out that when I give this person Prozac, right away the person gets better"— even though Prozac doesn't act right away. Science entails skepticism. You ask "Compared to what?" and you say "Show me your evidence."

EG: Thinking about professional training programs today, for example, psychology and social work—would you say they do a good job of encouraging scientific boundaries on professional practice?

RD: My impression is no. In the programs I've been involved with we try, but in general people are encouraged to "go out and do it" and believe in themselves. It's nice to believe in yourself. They are not trained in this sort of critical thinking—Is this hypothesis correct? "Is it this or that?" And we are not usually trained in keeping multiple hypotheses in mind at the same time.

Now compare this to medicine. Medicine is not perfect, but you ask: "What could have led to these symptoms?" And, you have a number of hypotheses, and then you ask "Well is it A or B?" You try to have some test and you might rule out B and say it could be A but it might be C. You are always comparing A with B, A with C, B with C and unfortunately, in a lot of professional training programs, this kind of comparison is not done. So, I think that ethical practice is one which recognizes what science there is. It often doesn't tell you exactly what to do, but recognizes what science there is and asks for critically testing ideas. You want to test your ideas and always ask "Compared to what?" If I believe this, what would follow? What would I have to check out?

Statisticians talk about basing a hypothesis on testing. You have ideas about what might be going on and then you try to compare and test them. That's one thing science in general does—to compare ideas. For example, you have various hypotheses about the orbits of the planets; Are they elliptical or are they circular? Where are they located? Then you check it out. You say "This observation is consistent with an elliptical type of an orbit and this other observation is not consistent with a circular orbit." The point is that social science is really no different. Psychology is really no different. There is a tendency to say "Oh, but this is all intuition; this is all just a feeling." Some of it will be your feeling. But it has to be disciplined. It has to take account of what is going on, what could be going on. We should question, compare hypotheses, be skeptical. All too often we are not. Let me give you an example.

I was trained in Freudian psychology in my first two years in graduate school and you are not supposed to question it. You don't say, "Hey, wait a minute, could this be something else? Could this be related to environmental factors? Maybe this person doesn't have this hang-up? How will I test it?" These sort of questions were not emphasized at all. Anecdotes are easy. Let me give you one of my favorites. A patient was seen who was considered "obviously psychotic" because he thought he was growing breasts and one parent had committed suicide earlier that week. No one said "Maybe he is growing breasts; let's look." It turned out he was. This was discovered only after six weeks in a locked hospital ward because it was "just so obvious that this man was psychotic," right? And, it had been assumed that his "delusion" was related to the suicide of a parent. We all know that, right? No one said, "Wait a minute, let's test this out." And, when they did test it out, they found a metabolic problem.

EG: What do you think could be done differently and how much hope is there for changing professional training programs?

RD: It's very hard because I believe what has happened (and now I'm going to act like a sociologist), is that the profession has so far out-distanced what it is we know, in the sense of having influenced society to believe this, that it is very hard to draw back and ask, "Do I really know this?" You turn on your television set and you find experts about everything—gurus. You should do this. You shouldn't do that. You find drug ads, "Are you anxious? Take Paxil." But few ask: "Wait a minute, are we really sure that people are better off taking these drugs?" It's the comparative question again. Are we sure that it's better to be immediately relaxed after watching a horrible thing like 9–11? There are studies, one done in England, indicating that the attempt to make people immediately relaxed after trauma, such as a traffic accident, has bad long-term effects. But I remember after 9–11, you could call up a number given out on CNN and the American Psychological Association would tell you who to talk to avoid post-traumatic stress syndrome. Post-traumatic stress syndrome is something that is real, but it occurs in only a small percentage of cases and you can only diagnose it apparently on the basis that people can't forget things, so how can I tell you right away that you are going to have it? There it was, right after 9–11, almost every hour. Call this number to avoid post-traumatic stress and you look at the evidence and ask: "Wait a minute. Where is the evidence that this is doing any good?"

EG: So would you say that professional organizations themselves are on the forefront of forwarding inflated claims of knowledge?

RD: Yes, and often there is a later retraction of sorts. I read Silver's article from the American Psychological Association published almost a year after 9–11. The gist of the article was; "You know, maybe people are better off dealing with it on their own. We've got to have more respect for what people can do on their own." But that sort of wisdom—as opposed to "you need professional help"—was almost a year too late. A kind of retraction about needing such help that I found fascinating was from a former colleague. He described a survey about people getting over addictions: "You know you can't get over it without external professional help." Most people who get over addictions get over it on their own after a series of failed attempts. So the inference is, that because you tried on your own and failed the last time [then] you need me, is not a valid inference.

EG: Doesn't it seem odd that rather than being in the forefront of trying to convey accurate information and the state of ignorance, what occurs is almost the opposite?

RD: Yes. The actual findings may be in the opposite direction. When we obtain accurate information and compare what we were told with what is accurate, we become skeptical. "Why should I pay you $150 an hour when I can get better myself?" Acting as if you are an expert airplane builder, who knows all about the laws of aerodynamics when you don't, is a problem. The theories we have don't predict as well as we might like. Let me give you an example. I've worked in the clinical versus statistical prediction area. You have

predictions about how well people will do on parole. Consider John Carroll's study with eight hundred and some Pennsylvania parolees. Parole interviewers recommend parole. These interviewers have access to background information such as how young the person was when he was first arrested, bow many crimes he has been convicted of, how many prison violations he has had, and the parole interviewer makes a judgment. In the study, the parole interviewer also made an estimate of whether the person would come back: How likely is it that this person will fail on parole? How likely is this person to engage in violent behavior? Predictions based on three variables that the parole interviewer knows about, yield a correlation of about .22. This is impressive when you consider a prediction based on the parole interviewer's judgment is .07. The correlation between smoking and lung cancer is .22. One in ten people who smoke in general develop lung cancer. One in 200 who don't smoke develop lung cancer. This correlation of .22 is the basis for the most extensive public health program in this country ever. But people say .22—that's nothing, forget it. I know I can do better. However, there are a lot of places where you can't, so you say: "I'll throw away the science. I'll throw away the predictability and just use my 'intuition'" and then you do worse, like the parole interviewers. Their prediction whether a person would be violent or not was much worse than the single variable prediction about whether the person used cocaine or heroin or hard drugs.

In the Second World War, Bloom and Brundage studied how well people in the armed forces did in military elementary school, which refers to school prior to specialized training. Personnel officers either knew about a person's high school record, about the person's aptitude test scores, or knew both and made judgements. Their judgements were worse than the two sources of information taken alone. Why would that be? Well, because a high school record represents the combined opinion of many, many professors or teachers. The tests were set up specifically to test certain types of aptitudes. This is not the case with intuition. Experience does not provide systematic feedback. It does not provide controlled comparisons.

EG: Taking advantage of this kind of information clearly seems to facilitate clinical decision making yet professional training programs do not seem to take advantage of it. Do you think this is the case?

RD: Yes, they unfortunately do not.

EG: Do you have much hope that they will?

RD: Well, no. I was at the University of Oregon. I was the department head. Our graduate students got the highest scores on the intellectual part of the state licensing exam of all clinical programs. Why?—Because we insisted they know something about psychology. Most clinical psychology students don't know the principles of learning. Often they don't even know Freudian principles.

EG: What should a student do who would like a good education regarding scientific findings related to clinical practice?

RD: I think the student would be on his or her own. You'd have to go talk to professors and say: "Are you sure my course in learning or neuropsychology is relevant to what I want to do?" You would have to say: "I don't care if you can't tell me exactly where it is directly relevant. I want to know about neuropsychology. I want to know about principles of learning." The student would have to take a much more active role and many do. And of course there is pressure to get through, get out, and make money. It is the same thing with clients. You have to take an active role to try to figure out whether you're getting good treatment or not.

EG: What would you suggest to help clients do that? Do you see any bright spots on the horizon toward helping clients be more informed consumers?

RD: I wish I did. Let me give you an example. There are what are called regression effects. If I toss a coin five times it comes up five heads, the next time I toss it five times it's likely to be two and a half heads in general— two or three. It could come up five heads again or it could come up five tails. But the point is that it will be closer to the average in general—an expectation of two and a half in the first five tosses. Clients come to a therapist when they are distressed and they are likely to be less distressed later anyway without help. So clinicians should know that. But you run into physicians and psychologists who don't know that.

   I have a friend, Joe Strayhorn, who is a psychiatrist. He has a problem with the places he works because they want to start treatment right away. He says: "I don't want to confuse regression effects with treatment so if I'm going to treat anybody here, you are going to have this person here about a week on no treatment so I can have some idea of how clients are affected going from probably a tough environment into a hospital." They say: "Six days without treatment, are you crazy?" And he says: "I just can't do it." Without such a time you don't know what's going on. It gets back to the scientific idea that you have to have comparisons. It's very hard to know what would happen if you didn't give the drug right away. That's why we have randomized clinical trials—people who are randomly given the drug and randomly not given the drug and given a placebo and you say "Since I have randomly done this I can treat these people as interchangeable." Now no one likes that but they are, and because there is no specific bias in whether I assigned a person to the experimental or control group, I can estimate what would have happened to this experimental subject if the subject had been in the control group. We have a comparison and that's what's called a hypothetical

counter-factual. Without that comparison, who knows? This is why, if we are ethically and scientifically guided in our practice, we have to say on occasion: "I don't feel this is true, but I know from the general science that it is true."

EG: And you think the clinician is obligated to share this with clients?

RD: Right. I just read an interesting article in Harper's which I quote from in my latest book (Dawes, 2001). A physician is talking about clinical trials. He says "It is so hard to ignore my personal experience." This is an example of *availability bias*. We have to examine the clinical trial results—that's the only fair way to treat patients. This is a real problem because sometimes you have to set aside your intuition and say "I know my intuitions aren't valid, even though I believe them strongly." Other times you say: "I have to use my intuition, but it's got to be within the bounds that I know."

EG: Are you saying that there is an ethical obligation to be a critical, skeptical inquirer, asking: "Is there any science related to the professional decisions I have to make"?

RD: That's correct. There is an obligation to do that and to find out what it is. This is another problem—dismal ignorance. This goes back to my example of the graduate student who says "I want to know about neuropsychology. I want to know about principles of learning even though I'm not sure how to use them next year or two years after I get out of my clinical internship because this provides the basis of knowing what to look for." If you don't know, you don't know what to look for.

EG: It seems that drugs are taking the place of psychotherapy in many areas. Advertisements are common. Could you comment on this?

RD: This is again big business. When you look at the sales of these psychoactive drugs, especially the selective serotonin reuptake Inhibitors (SSRIs), you find that this is multi, multi-big bucks and they advertise directly to clients and potential clients. They say "If you feel a little depressed or anxious, take this." How can you say you are not—come on, who is perfectly happy and mellow all the time? And, there are no *exclusion criteria* (e.g., "compared to what?"). There are no criteria that say "Maybe this is just an ordinary part of life. Maybe I'm learning something." Some things should make you anxious. Just because I woke up last night and didn't sleep for an hour or something should I be depressed and seek help? Medicine does not work perfectly, but an MD can say to you: "No, you may think you have diabetes but you don't." Certainly people make errors. It's not perfect. But there are exclusion criteria. Often, there are no exclusion criteria regarding alleged psychological problems.

Many psychologists have been anxious (and social workers will follow I'm sure) to obtain drug prescription privileges. They now have such privileges in New Mexico. Those of us who are skeptical, such as myself, have been yelled at: "You are unethical for not letting us do what we feel like doing," or, an argument that really irritates me, "They don't know what they are doing either so let us do it." There is a promiscuous use of psychoactive drugs creating brain changes. At least with tobacco, cocaine, and alcohol, we know their long term effects. We know it is probabilistic—most people do not become addicted, some do.

Again, most people get over most things themselves. Most marijuana smokers don't go on to hard drugs and even people who do often stop. Consider young American men going to Vietnam and using heroin and coming back and stopping (Cohen et al., 1989). People have said to me: "How can you be so cruel?" Most people get over most things on their own. That does not mean that some people don't get over them. Problems with professionalism are highlighted by responses to an article by Rind et al. (1998). These authors reviewed the literature regarding people who said they had been sexually abused at some point in their lives. Most reported that "That happened and I got over it." The authors were accused of trying to normalize sexual abuse. Their accusers started lobbying and the American Psychological Association folded. They said, "Maybe the meta-analysis wasn't that good." They asked the American Association for the Advancement of Science to get an independent panel to review the article 2 years after it was published. This association said "No way, we are not in the business of looking over your shoulder." Then Congress went off on this emotional winging and condemned the study unanimously in the House and in their condemnations claimed that "Nobody ever gets over childhood sexual abuse," in fact, claiming that sexually abused children are *"unable"* (their term) to develop healthy, affectionate relationships later in life (H.R. 107, 1999). This is nonsense. Now again, that doesn't mean that some people don't suffer from long-term effects. But the idea that everybody does or that everyone who watched that horror of the twin towers will be shaken up for the rest of their lives is not true.

Paul Meehl describes the spun glass model of the human psyche in a wonderful essay—the idea that the psyche is so fragile that any little thing will result in it falling apart and you need me to keep you from falling apart. Not true.

EG: Is that his chapter, "Why I Do Not Attend Case Conferences," where he described a variety of fallacies?

RD: That's right. And his example involved a hard-core delinquent who they were hoping was getting better. And they were going to present him to the staff and have him answer questions and the therapist said: "Oh, you can't have him in here because the furniture is in a different configuration. It will upset him too much." The science suggests that a small proportion of people are going to suffer from these things and that most people get over most things on their own.

EG: How can clinicians take maximal advantage of their experience?

RD: That's a tough one. I would advise them to seek feedback as far as possible. I've been a department head for 12 years. You make predictions in your administrative work. You put them in a desk drawer and don't get back to them for 2 or 3 years at least and then you look and review, "How good was my judgment?" Who's going to accept the job? Who's going to work out? Who isn't? This sort of thing. It was fifty-fifty. That's at least some feedback. It is confounded with what you do. It's not like a clinical trial where there is nothing about the person that says that the person will get a drug or a placebo.

EG: But you write it down?

RD: You write it down, put it in a desk drawer and then look later and avoid the problem—manipulation of the feedback without realizing it to make sense of whatever you did or to please yourself. I've heard this crazy stuff: "My client committed suicide but I kept my client alive for a number of years; he wouldn't have been alive otherwise." Well, how do you know that?

EG: Do you mean that we take responsibility for a suicide when we couldn't have prevented it?

RD: Right. We don't know what we can prevent or can't. This is tough stuff and I again get back to the nature of science as probabilistic. It's like those .22 correlations which everyone sneezes at but they are sure better than nothing.

EG: Let me take you back to your experience as head of the department of psychology. Could you be more specific about what you would include (or what you did include in your program) that you think offers a good educational program for professionals? What exact courses?

RD: We wanted to have statistical methodology courses, courses in physiological psychology and learning theory. Then students can go on to the practicum—hands-on experience. They should know what basic psychology is all about. You get people who have never heard of principles of reinforcement. They say: "I don't have to know that." What about regression effects? "I took statistics and I got a 'C' and I don't like that stuff." You want to be sure that people have a basic understanding of key content areas. Unfortunately, people get out who don't and then they sometimes have great trouble, especially in psychology where if you don't know what's going on, you try to compensate by not behaving very well.

EG: So questioning yourself is an ethical requirement?

RD: Yes. It is an ethical requirement. It is a tough one because it would be nice to be absolutely selfish or believe that whatever you do is absolutely correct.

EG: It seems some students have little sense of curiosity—they seem to assume they are right. What do you think?

RD: I'm curious about what the world is going to be like and I think there is a certain joy in not knowing. I don't know all the answers. Some people who now appear to be doing very badly are going to do well and vice versa. That's interesting. But what you want to avoid is saying "I wasn't able to predict that before but now I could have predicted it because I now know the outcomes." The kind of storytelling which Adolph Grünbaum (who once was the chair of the philosophy of science unit at the University of Pittsburgh) called the "Tally Theory" is common—I make up a story about you and it sort of tallies with what you do and then I say "Is that true?" and you say "Yeah." Freud did this all the time. And Freud had a very interesting tally criterion that was, in effect, "I know I'm right if you agree with me." That was extreme defensiveness. Freud actually proposed that psychoanalysts shouldn't present their analysis of a case history until an analysis is completed (see Spince, 1982). There is no way of knowing if your analysis is accurate because all you do is fit your analysis to whatever happened.

EG: One topic you discuss in *House of Cards* (Dawes, 1994) concerns the comparison of non-professionals and professionals in terms of outcome and this seems to be an important area of inquiry. Is this still the case?

RD: Yes. When I talked about how much therapy should be influenced by science people say "Science doesn't tell me what to do." In so-called "protocol therapies" you have a fairly specific idea of what to do. But in most therapy you don't have much of an idea. You are on your own. Some emphasize the alliance of the client with the therapist. How do you decide if you have a good alliance? How do you decide if you have a good relationship? We should really study what it is about the relationship. Instead, we have a massive denial campaign going on that says "You know these other studies? I don't like them. They show that it doesn't matter if you have a PhD or an MD or something like this or years of experience." You support the myth instead of trying to find out what it is that is really working. Leonard Bickman (1999) had a fascinating article in the *American Psychologist* about what he called the "myths of psychology." One of the myths is that there is a lot of evidence that having a degree or a certain number of years of experience makes you a better therapist. It doesn't. We can check that. We can do randomized trials where we assign some clients to people with credentials and others to people without credentials. We find out—no difference in outcomes.

EG: These data seem to be ignored in social work. Are they ignored in psychology?

RD: They are ignored very much in psychology because I think (again, I'm acting like a sociologist), status is very important in psychology—in social work too. When I was first doing psychological work, psychologists were under the thumb of psychiatrists. Later psychologists said: "How wonderful—we can do psychotherapy now; we are not just testers." Psychiatrists moved on to use drugs almost exclusively. Now the psychologists want to use drugs. This began in the absence of really skeptical analysis about what is going on.

Moreover, the therapy result is very clear. Except for protocol therapies, pretty much all types of therapy and all types of therapists do equally well. This result is referred to as the dodo bird result. The dodo bird says, "How would we dry off? We are going to have a race and when we run around in a circle we'll all dry off." This is *Alice in Wonderland* and the race is over and Alice asks: "Who won?" The dodo bird replied: "Everybody won and everyone must have prizes."

Janet Landman and I (1982) re-analyzed a large database of psychotherapy studies reviewed by Smith and Glass in their famous 1977 meta-analysis (Smith & Glass, 1977) where they combined different studies. We noted that they took the abstracts awfully seriously. We examined every fifth study and really studied them and we discovered some interesting things. One was that, despite the arguments in the abstract that these involved random assignment, about 35% of them did not, so they have little significance.

For example, in one study about 40% of the kids stopped going to the groups. When they compared the people assigned to group therapy and the control group, there was no difference. But, you can't have group therapy for people who don't have group therapy. So they just looked at the 60% who went and the results seemed pretty good. Again we get back to comparison. We don't know which 60% of the people in the control group would have gone if they had been assigned to the experimental group, so you can't look at the whole control group as a comparison with the 60% of the experimental group who did go.

EG: If a professional organization wanted to pursue the integration of science and practice, what could it do?

RD: There are two things it could do. It can specify that there is a core knowledge in psychology with which students should be familiar, not just anything a student wants to take. The other thing is that it has to bite the bullet and say there are certain behaviors or certain types of therapy, certain types of procedures, that are out of bounds; you cannot use them (e.g., give people ink blot tests to make decisions in custody disputes) because it is not fair to the people.

EG: So there would be prohibitions?

RD: Yes. There would be training and prohibitions. Now, people don't like prohibitions. Wouldn't it be wonderful if we just tried to encourage you to be good, OK? The medical people have a system of prohibitions. They say "You cannot use worthless or harmful treatment." If it is shown that you are doing something worthless or harmful you're sanctioned and you may be out. In a case in Oregon it was found that a physician was ordering urine tests for all his male patients. He hypothesized that about 96% had some sort of urinary infection. That can't be true. An investigative committee found out that he had a financial interest in the laboratory doing the tests. He was out because this is a worthless procedure. Obviously it is not true that 90-some percent of male clients have a urinary infection. You've got to protect the client.

EG: So what would you do about people who are teaching in professional education programs who don't pay attention to this?

RD: I don't know what I'd do. There's a real problem because we're all interested in autonomy in our educational programs. I teach what I want. An eminent colleague who will remain nameless got up recently in a seminar on academic freedom and said: "The way I see academic freedom is I should be paid to do whatever I feel like doing and teach whatever I feel like teaching." I don't quite feel that way. I mean if I'm going to teach statistics I'm going to teach valid principles of statistics. If I'm going to teach behavioral decision making, I'm going to teach valid principles of behavioral decision making and if I get up and tell people nonsense, somebody's gotta say: "Wait, that person should not be influencing students."

EG: Doesn't it seem that medical schools are ahead of us in this way? I mean if someone actually got up and said totally incorrect things, they wouldn't just say "It is academic freedom."

RD: Right. This goes back to around 1910–1920. Apparently medical schools were not very good at that time.

EG: You're referring to the Flexner report?

RD: Yes. Abraham Flexner came along and things started getting good. I had hoped when I wrote *House of Cards* that this would be picked up by the general public and people would say "Wait a minute; we've got to insist on better standards." Not just standards of training, but standards of actual behavior. We seem to have this belief: "As the tree is bent, so grows the tree." We say, "We'll just train the students for a few years then forget it." You can't do that because we are influenced by what our peers do. You can't just say, "I'm going to give you good education and then I'm going to send you to a clinic where all clients are assumed to be recovering from repressed memories or being given Prozac and expect them to say "I was well educated. I'm not going to do this."

EG: Don't some people suggest that continuing education requirements make up for that?

RD: We figured out that in Minnesota you could get all your continuing education credits for 10 years by taking courses in how to give children ink blot tests. Before I was president of the Oregon Psychological Association, there was a severe problem which involved a lawsuit; the people who were the leaders of this association lost and the association had significant legal bills. This small professional association was suddenly burdened with over $20,000 in debt, which in 1973 was no small sum. Someone came up with the idea to give workshops on the beautiful Oregon coast for continuing education credit. By the time I was president of the Oregon Psychological Association we made more money on those continuing education workshops than we did from dues. Splitting the profits with workshop leaders had a pernicious effect of encouraging presenters to give the most popular, crazy stuff.

At one meeting of the American Psychological Association, Elizabeth Loftus (an eminent researcher on memory) was giving a talk describing how people can be convinced that they have done things they never did or say they saw things they never saw. Upstairs people were in crowded rooms listening to advice about how to regress clients to recover memories. Attendees at both workshops were awarded continuing education credits. It has been the position of the American Psychological Association for years that "We sponsor organizations; we don't exert any quality control over what is offered." We've had conversations about this—emails back and forth. Imagine the American Medical Association saying: "We're not in the business of monitoring what people say, what people with adult onset diabetes should do, or what people with hypertension should do. Whatever the Oregon Medical Association says is OK."

EG: Wouldn't some people argue that it's a different kettle of fish in psychology and social work?

RD: There may be some situations that involve a different kettle of fish but the question about evaluating whether this is working, whether this is doing any good, these are questions that require making comparisons, questions about testing ideas.

EG: Isn't there an ethical issue here?

RD: Yes, if I present myself as an expert in a field because of my scientific training but don't have it or ignore it, that's basically fraud. (My point of view has been called "consumerism" by people who didn't like it.)

EG: Would you consider this to be false advertising; advertising yourself to be one thing when you're not?

RD: Yes.

EG: It doesn't seem like you think there's many positive bright lights out there. Is this correct?

RD: Well, I don't know. My experience in Pittsburgh as a child may be relevant. I grew up in Pittsburgh during the Second World War. Before, during, and after it was a mess. There was so much smog. You couldn't see the tops of the buildings. People were not that concerned during the Second World War even though there were some rules in force such as shifting from a steam locomotive to an electrical locomotive once you hit the city limits. This pollution situation went on for years and suddenly there was a huge smog event in Donora, a suburb, with people dropping dead. I'm afraid that is often what it takes. I think we're seeing this now—abuses of great power in large corporations. It sometimes takes dramatic events—something people focus on, saying "God, what's going on?" We must pursue change at this point. And then of course you can change, but it is sad. We are not great at anticipating and acting on our anticipation. I think it is going to collapse but it will probably take a horrific event. This is the way the world works.

EG: What do you think will make it collapse?

RD: My guess is getting into the drug business. My guess is that what's going to happen is somebody is going to have a brain tumor or something like this and a psychologist is going to give her drugs and then the family is going to say: "She could have survived. It was an operable one. Why is the psychologist giving drugs?" It might be that a psychiatrist would have done just as badly, but the concern about the "not a real doctor" will remain.

I don't think giving junk advice over the television about how to deal with life is ever going to stop. I believe in free speech but I don't believe in charging insurance companies or the government $150 an hour when there is no control over what I tell you. I could just say anything. You are paying me because presumably I'm basing what I say on something solid, and again, it's not anywhere near a correlation of 1.0. It's often small. That .22 regarding lung cancer and smoking is one of the extremes. That's why I'm paying you and you have an ethical obligation to tell me why you're doing what you're doing, which is basing what you say on some science, or at the least if you are operating in the dark, you are not violating what we know.

EG: Otherwise is it a house of cards?

RD: Yes, it is.

References

Bickman, L. (1999). Leonard Bickman: Award for distinguished contributions to research in public policy. *American Psychologist, 54*, 963–978.

Bloom, R. F., & Brundage, E. G. (1947). Predictions of success in elementary school for enlisted personnel. In D. B. Stuit (Ed.), *Personnel research and test development in the naval bureau of personnel* (pp. 233–261). Princeton, NJ: Princeton University Press.

Carroll, J.S., Winer, R.L., Coates, D., Galegher, J., & Alibrio, J. J. (1988). Evaluation, diagnosis, and prediction in parole decision making. *Law and Society Review, 17*, 199–228.

Cohen, S., Lichtenstein, E., Prochaska, J. O., Rossi, J. S., Gritz, E. R., Carr, C. R., et al. (1989). Debunking myths about self-quitting. *American Psychologist, 44*, 1355–1365.

Dawes, R. M. (1994). *House of cards: Psychology and psychotherapy built on myth.* New York: Free Press.

Dawes, R. M. (2001). *Everyday irrationality: How pseudo-scientists, lunatics, and the rest of us systematically fail to think rationally.* Boulder, CO: Westview Press.

Flexner, A. (1925), *Medical education: A comparative study.* New York: Macmillan.

Flexner, A. (1910). *Medical education in the United States and Canada: A report to the Carnegie Foundation for the Advancement of Teaching.* New York: The Carnegie Foundation.

Hastie, R., & Dawes, R. M. (2001). *Rational choice in an uncertain world: The psychology of judgement and decision making.* Thousand Oaks, CA: Sage.

H.R. 107, 106 Cong., (1999).

Landman, L. T., & Dawes, R. M. (1982). Psychotherapy outcome: Smith & Glass's conclusions stand up under scrutiny. *American Psychologist, 377*, 504–516.

Meehl, P. E. (1973). Why I do not attend case conferences, *Psychodiagnosis: Selected papers* (pp. 228–302). Minneapolis, MN: University of Minnesota Press.

Rind, B., Tromovitch, P., & Bauserman, R. (1998). A meta-analytic examination of assumed properties of child sexual abuse using college samples. *Psychological Bulletin, 124*, 22–53.

Silver, R. C., Holman, E. A., Mclntosh, D. N., Poulin, M., & Gil-Rivas, V. (2002). Nationwide longitudinal study of psychological responses to September 11. *Journal of the American Medical Association, 288*, 1235–1244.

Smith, M. L., & Glass, G. V. (1977). Meta-analysis of psychotherapy outcome studies. *American Psychologist, 32*, 752–760.

Spence, D. (1982). *Narrative truth and historical truth: Meaning and interpretation in psychoanalysis.* New York: Norton.

10

Pseudoscience in Contemporary Clinical Psychology: What it is and what we can do about it

Scott O. Lilienfeld

This article is Dr. Scott O. Lilienfeld's acceptance speech of the 1998 David Shakow Award for early career contributions to clinical psychology. This award was presented at the American Psychological Association Convention in San Francisco.

I'm deeply honored to have received the David Shakow award for early career contributions to clinical psychology, and I'm very grateful to the Division 12 awards committee for inviting me to speak with you today. In struggling with what I wanted to present today, I ultimately decided that I would do something a bit unorthodox. Specifically, I decided that rather than talk about my research, I would speak about an issue that has become something of a hobby-horse of mine—the ever-present and increasingly troubling problem of pseudoscience in contemporary clinical psychology.

I suspect that little, if anything, I will say today will be perceived as novel. And with good reason: the problem of pseudoscience has been with us for centuries and is in reality nothing terribly new. What is largely new, I will argue, is that pseudoscience poses an increasingly major threat to both the welfare of the general public and the integrity and reputation of our profession.

In further pondering what to talk about today, I struggled with finding something that I thought might best honor the memory of David Shakow, whose legacy the award I have received today commemorates. Shakow emphasized that the scientist-practitioner, or what he liked to call the scientist-professional, was first and foremost a clinical scientist—a critical thinker who places a high premium on healthy skepticism. In a 1976 article in American Psychologist, Shakow argued that the ideal scientist-professional embraces what Jacob Bronowski called the "habit of truth." As Shakow noted, "this habit is manifested in the constant effort to guide one's actions through inquiry into what is fact and verifiable, rather than to act on the basis of faith, wish, or precipateness" – in other words, to base one's beliefs on critical rather than wishful thinking.

PSEUDOSCIENTIFIC PRACTICES IN MODERN CLINICAL PSYCHOLOGY

Yet if we look at the psychotherapeutic and assessment practices of many of our clinical brethren in the sprawling world outside of the academy, we find precisely this propensity toward uncritical acceptance of claims that Shakow so presciently warned us about over two decades ago. Moreover, as a field, we in clinical psychology seem to have shown surprisingly little interest in doing much about the problem of pseudoscience that has been festering in our own backyards. As Paul Meehl (1993) recently noted:

> It is absurd, as well as arrogant, to pretend that acquiring a PhD somehow immunizes me from the errors of sampling, perception, recording, retention, retrieval, and inference to which the human mind is subject. In earlier times, all introductory psychology courses devoted a lecture or two to the classic studies in the psychology of testimony, and one mark of a psychologist was hard-nosed skepticism about folk beliefs. It seems that quite a few clinical psychologists never got exposed to this basic feature of critical thinking. My teachers at Minnesota . . . shared what Bertrand Russell called the dominant passion of the true scientist—the passion not to be fooled and not to fool anybody else . . . all of them asked the two searching questions of positivism: "What do you mean?" "How do you know?" If we clinicians lose that passion and forget those questions, we are little more than bedoc-tored, well-paid soothsayers. I see disturbing signs that this is happening and I predict that, if we do not clean up our clinical act and provide our students with role models of scientific thinking, outsiders will do it for us (pp. 728–729).

As clinical psychologists in turn-of-the-century America, we are confronted with the specter of pseudoscience in many guises. The past decade alone has witnessed (a) an explosion of largely unvalidated and in some cases bizarre treatments for trauma (e.g., thought field therapy, emotional freedom techniques), (b) a proliferation of demonstrably ineffective treatments for infantile autism and related disorders (e.g., facilitated communication), (c) the continued use of inadequately validated assessment instruments (e.g., human figure drawing tests and several other questionable projective techniques), (d) the widespread use of herbal remedies for depression and anxiety whose efficacy has often yet to be tested, let alone demonstrated (e.g., kava, ginkgo), (e) the marketing of subliminal self-help tapes that have repeatedly been found to be of no value in the treatment of psychopathology, (f) a burgeoning industry of self-help books, many or most of which make unsubstantiated claims, and the (g) use of highly suggestive therapeutic techniques to unearth memories of child abuse (including satanic ritual abuse) and the purported "alter" personalities of dissociative identity disorder (multiple personality disorder). And this, of course, is only a partial list. As Martin Gardner (1957) noted in his classic book *Fads and Fallacies in the Name of Science*, the field of psychology has long had an intimate acquaintance with questionable scientific practices (see also Leahey & Leahey, 1983). But the modern information age, ushered in by the popular media and Internet, has allowed these practices to flourish with unprecedented intensity and vigor.

I don't want to imply that all of these practices are necessarily harmful or devoid of value. It is possible, for example, that some of the new and controversial therapies for trauma will ultimately turn out to possess some efficacy. It is also possible that a subset of recovered memories of abuse will turn out to be genuine—and Jonathan Schooler (1996) has some suggestive but still preliminary data consistent with this possibility. But what is disconcerting about the claims of these practices' most vocal proponents is that they are often made without an adequate appreciation for either the importance of controlled research evidence or for the human mind's propensity to draw premature conclusions in the absence of convincing data.

So let me be clear: the bone I am picking is not primarily with the validity of the claims I've discussed, as some of these claims (e.g., the efficacy of herbal remedies) have yet to be subjected to adequate tests. As scientists, we should of course keep an open mind to all largely untested assertions. Instead, the bone I am picking is with the ways in which these claims have been marketed and promoted.

My central thesis is that clinical psychology, more than ever, has become a world divided. Carol Tavris (1998) has recently written eloquently about the widening split between the world of academic clinical psychology and the world of the couch, and of the disconcerting discrepancy between what we have learned about the psychology of memory, suggestibility, hypnosis, clinical judgment, and psychopathology, on the one hand, and the practices of many clinicians in the real world, on the other. We see a similarly widening gulf between academic and popular psychology, between the world of research as we understand it and the world of mental health as understood by the general public. The problem is not that all of popular psychology is necessarily pseudoscientific. To the contrary, I'll argue later that as academic clinical psychologists we have not done enough to popularize our findings and to communicate the scientific side of our discipline to the general public. Instead, the problem is that we have done little to assist the public with distinguishing those practices within popular psychology that are scientific from those that are not.

SCIENCE VERSUS PSEUDOSCIENCE

Before proceeding, it is first necessary to say a bit about the distinction between science and pseudoscience. In reality, this distinction is almost certainly one of degree rather than kind. Both science and pseudoscience are probably best viewed as Roschian concepts, which are characterized by indefinite boundaries and an absence of singly necessary and jointly sufficient features (see Rosch, 1973). But this absence of clear-cut boundaries does not imply, as some of the more radical deconstructivists might have us believe, that the distinction between science and pseudoscience is meaningless, or that a line of demarcation cannot be drawn between these two concepts for practical purposes. As the psychophysicist S.S. Stevens noted, there may be no qualitative difference between day and night, but that does not preclude us from making a distinction between day and night for pragmatic reasons.

As most of us know, many philosophers of science would probably concur with Karl Popper (1959) that falsifiability is an important, if not central, characteristic of the scientific enterprise, and that what distinguishes scientific from metaphysical questions (e.g., the existence of the soul) is their susceptibility to refutation. In contrast, pseudosciences, as Lakatos (1978) and others have noted, are disciplines whose advocates have effectively immunized their claims from falsification. Pseudoscientific claims are unfalsifiable not in principle—like metaphysical claims—but rather in practice, because their proponents have found innumerable escape hatches with which to protect their cherished beliefs from refutation.

Pseudoscientific disciplines are characterized by a variety of characteristics. These characteristics are probably best viewed as stochastic rather than strictly nomological, but they can be thought of as useful warning signs for the scientific consumer. The more such features a given discipline exhibits, the more it begins to cross the fuzzy but nonetheless pragmatically useful boundary that demarcates science from pseudoscience (see Table 1).

First, pseudosciences tend to be characterized by an overuse of ad hoc hypotheses to escape refutation. As Lakatos noted, ad hoc hypotheses are sometimes defensible in science, but only when they are content-increasing and enhance a theory's capacity to generate successful predictions. In the case of most pseudosciences, neither of these conditions is met. Second, pseudosciences tend to place primary emphasis on confirmation, rather than refutation. If the physicist Richard Feynman was correct that the hallmark of science is bending over backwards to prove oneself wrong, most pseudosciences seem to bend over backwards in precisely the

(from Bunge, 1984)

TABLE 1   Common Characteristics of Pseudosciences

(1) Overuse of ad hoc hypotheses to escape refutation

(2) Emphasis on confirmation rather than refutation

(3) Absence of self-correction

(4) Reversed burden of proof

(5) Overreliance on testimonials and anecdotal evidence

(6) Use of obscurantist language

(7) Absence of "connectivity" with other disciplines

opposite direction. Third, in contrast to sciences, which tend to be self-correcting over the long haul, pseudosciences typically pursue a confirmation-based strategy until the bitter end, and rarely engage in self-correction. Fourth, proponents of pseudosciences typically place the onus of proof on critics, rather than on themselves. For example, they may insist that critics demonstrate conclusively that a novel treatment technique is ineffective. Fifth, pseudosciences tend to overrely on testimonials and anecdotal evidence—including informal clinical experience—as a means of testing hypotheses. As a consequence, they confuse Reichenbach's (1938) context of discovery with the context of justification or, in somewhat different terms, the wellspring of hypothesis generation with the crucible of hypothesis testing. Sixth, pseudosciences often utilize obscurantist language, much of which is sprinkled liberally with scientific-sounding terms intended to provide these disciplines with the veneer of scientific rigor and respectability. Seventh and finally, as Mario Bunge (1984) pointed out, many pseudosciences are characterized by an absence of "connectivity" with other disciplines. In other words, they often purport to construct entirely new paradigms in the absence of compelling evidence, and do not build on extant scientific knowledge.

ACADEMIC AND POPULAR PSYCHOLOGY: THE WIDENING GAP

I mentioned earlier that the divide between academic and popular psychology is enormous, and that it may be growing. To provide us with a sense of the magnitude of this gap, let me present some revealing comparisons from a Web search

I recently performed in the comfort of my own office using a widely available Internet search engine. If one accepts the face valid premise that the Internet provides a least a rough indicator of the pulse of public interest, these results may tell us something about what's on the mind of the general public as opposed to what's on the mind of those of us within the halls of the academy. The methodology I've used is admittedly somewhat crude and could surely be called into question. For example, not all Web sites dealing with questionable or pseudoscientific topics deal with these topics in an uncritical fashion, although it is clear from my inspection of these sites that the overwhelming majority provide little or no critical commentary. Moreover, the exact numbers I'll present would of course change if a different search engine were used, although I can assure you that the overall pattern of results would remain very much the same.

In the next two tables, I've presented some findings that should perhaps give pause to those of us in academic clinical psychology (see Table 2). Following each topic is the number of Web Hits I obtained. In parentheses following this number is the number of PsychLit citations for each topic. These two numbers are not directly comparable, of course, because PsychLit uses different criteria for identifying sources than Web search engines. On the right is what is probably a more meaningful statistic for comparing across topics: the ratio of Web hits to PsychLit citations in each case. This ratio provides a rough index of the amount of popular attention received by a topic relative to the amount of research attention it has received. As you can see in this Table, I've plugged in a number of standard terms for widely researched treatment and assessment techniques. As you can see from the ratios on the right, there are far fewer Web hits than PsychLit citations in each case, with ratios ranging from .07 to .22. Nothing terribly surprising here.

As one can see in the next Table (see Table 3), in contrast, I've plugged in a number of terms reflecting treatment and assessment techniques that are either demonstrably invalid—such as subliminal self-help tapes—or inadequately researched—such as St. John's Wort. Here the results are remarkably different—with ratios of Web hits to PsychLit citations ranging from 34 for Thought Field Therapy to infinity for rebirthing. Those of you engaged in psychological assessment research might be interested to know that Enneagrams received 1408 Web hits, which means that it beats out the MMPI by over 200 Web hits.

TABLE 2   Comparions of Web Hits and PsychLit Citations for Several Widely Researched Treatment and Assessment Techniques (PsychLit Citations in Parentheses)

Topic	Web Hits	Ratio
Systematic desensitization	272 (2144)	.13
Token economy	182 (845)	.22
Minnesota Multiphasic Personality Inventory / MMPI	1187 (7371)	.16
California Psychological Inventory / CPI	62 (847)	.07
Beck Depression Inventory	306 (3472)	.09

TABLE 3   Comparisons of Web Hits and PsychLit Citations for Several Treatment and Assessment Techniques in Popular Psychology (PsychLit Citations in Parentheses)

Topic	Web Hits	Ratio
Past life regression	1328 (6)	221.3
St. John's Wort (Hypericum)	5867 (13)	451.3
Kava	5844 (17)	343.8
Thought field therapy	102 (3)	34.0
Rebirthing	933 (0)	∞
Inner Child/Inner Child Therapy	2737 (44)	62.2
Facilitated communication	9652 (50)	193.0
Subliminal self-help tapes	406 (2)	203.0
Enneagrams	1408 (10)	140.8

THE SELF-HELP INDUSTRY

Another indication of the ever-widening gap between academic and popular psychology is the burgeoning popularity of the self-help industry. One widely quoted estimate has it that self-help books are appearing at a rate of approximately 2000 books per year (see Rosen, 1993). My informal survey of large commercial bookstores in Atlanta revealed that self-help and recovery books outnumber traditional psychology books by a factor of at least 3 to 1. Moreover, this ratio is almost surely an underestimate, because a number of books in the psychology sections of these bookstores are in fact of the self-help variety, whereas the converse is not true. There is also a growing industry peddling unvalidated self-help audiotapes and videotapes for almost every imaginable psychological malady. Moreover, there is some evidence that self-help programs are receiving less, rather than more, research attention over time. In literature reviews conducted by Glasgow and Rosen (1979, 1982), the ratio of studies conducted on self-help books to self-help books themselves decreased over a two year period from .86 to .59—and there is scant indication that this downward trend is changing.

On the positive side, research on self-help programs shows that some of them, particularly those grounded on well-established psychological principles, can be helpful (Kutzweil, Scogin, & Rosen, 1996). But we also know from the literature reviews of Rosen and his colleagues (e.g., Glasgow & Rosen, 1979; Rosen, 1987) that self-help materials can be harmful in some cases. Moreover, even seemingly minor changes in an effective self-help treatment program have been found to reduce or even eliminate that program's efficacy. To address these problems, an APA Task Force headed up by Gerald Rosen in the 1980's offered a number of quite modest and reasonable suggestions for curbing the excesses of the self-help industry—such as developing guidelines for the development and evaluation of self-help materials comparable to those for psychological tests, and involving APA and other organizations in endorsing self-help books based on sound psychological principles and adequate research—but these suggestions have heretofore gone unheeded.

WHY SHOULD WE CARE?

So it is clear that there is a huge other world out there, one that most of us in research settings are blissfully unaware of and have been reluctant to peer into, let alone do anything about. But why should we care? If the general public wants to believe in the efficacy of subliminal self-help tapes and herbal remedies, why should we lose sleep over it? One major reason, of course, is that many of these techniques may prove to be harmful to the general public. The recent fiasco regarding facilitated communication for infantile autism serves as a much-need reminder of the serious damage that can result when novel psychological treatments are disseminated without adequate critical scrutiny—and, on the positive side, of how the research and writings of academics can play a crucial role in falsifying dangerous and pseudoscientific claims (see Jacobson, Mulick, & Schwartz, 1995). Moreover, even those techniques that prove to be innocuous can lead consumers to spend money and waste time on useless interventions that could better be spent seeking and obtaining adequate care. And, not least of all, the damage to the reputation and integrity of our profession is difficult to estimate.

But why is it our job or even our business to police these problems? It is both our job and our business, I would argue, because we, as clinical psychologists, are in a unique position. If there is one thing that sets our field apart from allied disciplines, it is our capacity to conduct and interpret research, and to impart this understanding to the general public. Yet with some notable exceptions, this has been a responsibility that our field has been reluctant to shoulder.

HAS THE APA HELPED?

In fact, some critics might contend that as a field we have actually nurtured or even provided support for questionable psychological practices. When the APA purchased Psychology Today in 1983, it did so in conjunction with a companion Psychology Today Tape Series, featuring a large number of self-help audiotapes that had never been subjected to empirical tests. These audiotapes included weight loss, mental imagery, and body image improvement programs of unknown efficacy, and were accompanied by the following statement: "Backed by the expert resources of the 87,000 members of the American Psychological Association, The Psychology Today Tape Program provides a vital link between psychology and you" (Rosen, 1993).

Moreover, even a casual perusal of recent editions of the APA Monitor reveals that the APA has been accepting advertisements for a plethora of unvalidated treatments, including Thought Field Therapy and Imago Relationship Therapy, two techniques for which no published controlled research exists. In addition, among the recent workshops for which the APA has provided continuing education credit are courses in Thought Field Therapy, calligraphy therapy, Jungian sandplay therapy, and the use of psychological theatre to "catalyze critical consciousness." Although the APA might maintain that advertisements of products or workshops do not constitute endorsements, this practice inevitably tarnishes the reputation of APA and fosters the impression of an organization unable or unwilling to police its own membership.

WHAT CAN WE DO DIFFERENTLY?

Thus far, my talk has probably sounded very much like a Jeremiad. Up to this point I have said little, if anything, about recommendations for dealing with this problem. So let me try to end on a constructive and hopefully more positive note. Assuming that we care about the burgeoning problem of pseudoscience in our field—and I hope that I've convinced at least some of you that we should—what can we do differently?

First, I would suggest that APA become more actively involved in the evaluation and even debunking of pseudoscientific techniques. One possibility might be for APA to set up a watchdog group or division to critically investigate claims in popular psychology. Like the Committee for the Scientific Investigation of Claims of the Paranormal, the organization that publishes one of my favorite journals, the *Skeptical Inquirer*, this watchdog group would keep an open mind to any and all claims, but subject them to careful scrutiny and communicate its findings to the general public. Debunking is sometimes viewed as a purely negative activity, one that entails harsh criticism and little else. But as Stephen Jay Gould has pointed out, debunking has an unappreciated positive side, because in debunking one claim one is necessarily affirming others.

Second, I would suggest that the APA and other professional organizations assist with setting up explicit guidelines for the evaluation of self-help materials. As noted earlier, this might include developing standards similar to those for psychological tests. In his 1969 Presidential Address to the APA, George Miller argued for "giving psychology away" to the general public. By this he meant providing the public with the fruits of psychological science so that they could better learn to help themselves. Unless we do a better job of assisting the public with distinguishing legitimate from illegitimate self-help methods, Miller's dream of giving psychology away is almost certain to remain unfulfilled.

My third suggestion—and perhaps the one most likely to be controversial—concerns what those of us in clinical psychology programs can do to tend to the problems within our own house. Although it might be tempting to dismiss the pseudoscience problem as not of our own making, clinical psychologists have not been immune from making unsubstantiated claims. In the pages of this newsletter several years ago, Richard McFall (1991) argued that we should encourage clinical graduate programs to develop their own creative ways of meeting APA accreditation requirements. I agree. But diversity in training can go too far, and I fear that it has. In granting clinical programs considerable flexibility in finding ways to meet APA curriculum requirements, we may have neglected to ensure that certain critical issues receive the coverage they deserve. I find it disconcerting to see bright and intellectually curious students graduating with PhDs and PsyDs from APA-accredited clinical programs knowing little or nothing about the limitations of clinical judgment and clinical prediction, the effect of base rates on clinical decision-making, the fallibility of human memory, and fundamental issues in the philosophy of science. APA should encourage creativity in meeting basic curriculum requirements, while also insisting on a core set of knowledge to ensure that the clinical psychologists of the next generation emerge with a modicum of critical thinking skills.

Fourth and finally, I would maintain that as clinical psychologists we have not done enough to popularize our findings and methods to the general public, and to convey to outsiders both the excitement of our scientific enterprise and the successful applications that have been derived from it. Popular psychology need not be a nonscientific psychology. There is precious little encouragement for those of us in academia to communicate our science to the public in the way that the late Carl Sagan, for example, did so effectively for astronomy and related disciplines. To the contrary, on several occasions I've actually seen academic psychologists who have attempted to follow Sagan's lead maligned as "popularizers" by their colleagues. We in academia need to find ways of rewarding, rather than punishing, our colleagues who take the time to popularize the findings of their profession and who are talented at it. I consider myself fortunate to have had as my graduate mentor a psychologist—David Lykken—who not only conducted active research on the polygraph or so-called "lie detector" test, but also spent a good deal of his career educating lawyers, legislators, and the public about its misuses and dangers. Lykken was a valuable role model for me, and we need more role models that like in academia.

In closing, I would like to conclude with a quotation from Mario Bunge (1984) that I believe underscores the dilemma that we are presently confronting as clinical psychologists:

> Scientists and philosophers tend to treat superstition, pseudoscience, and antiscience as harmless rubbish, or even as proper for mass consumption; they are far too busy with their own research to bother about such nonsense. This attitude is most unfortunate . . . superstition, pseudoscience, and antiscience are not rubbish that can be recycled into something useful; they are intellectual viruses that can attack anybody, layman or scientist, to the point of sickening an entire culture and turning it against scientific research (p. 46).

Only if we heed Bunge's warnings can we as a profession hope to safeguard the integrity and reputation that we have fought so long and hard to attain. Thank you.

References

Bunge, M. (1984, Fall). What is pseudoscience? *Skeptical Inquirer, 9*, 36–46.

Gardner, M. (1957). *Fads and fallacies in the name of science*. New York: Dover.

Glasgow, R.E., & Rosen, G.M. (1978). Behavioral bibliotherapy: A review of self-help behavior therapy manuals. *Psychological Bulletin, 85*, 1–23.

Glasgow, R.E., & Rosen, G.M. (1982). Self-help therapy manuals: Recent developments and clinical usage. *Clinical Behavior Therapy Review, 1*, 3–20.

Jacobson, J.W., Mulick, J.A., & Schwartz, A.A. (1995). A history of Facilitated Communication: Science, pseudoscience, and anti-science. *American Psychologist, 50*, 750–765.

Kurtzweil, P.L., Scogin, F., & Rosen, G.M. (1996). A test of the fail-safe N for self-help programs. *Professional Psychology: Science and Practice, 27*, 629–630.

Lakatos, I. (1978). *Philosophical papers (Vol. 1): The methodology of scientific research programmes* (J. Worrall & G. Currie, Eds). New York: Cambridge University Press.

Leahey, T.H., & Leahey, G.E. (1996). *Psychology's occult doubles: Psychology and the problem of pseudoscience*. Chicago: Nelson-Hall.

McFall, R.M. (1991). Manifesto for a science of clinical psychology. *The Clinical Psychologist, 44*, 75–88.

Meehl, P.E. (1993). Philosophy of science: Help or hindrance? *Psychological Reports, 72*, 707–733.

Miller, G.A. (1969). Psychology as a means of promoting human welfare. *American Psychologist, 24*, 1063–1075.

Popper, K.R. (1959). *The logic of scientific discovery*. New York: Basic Books.

Reichenbach, H. (1938). *Experience and prediction*. Chicago, Ill.: University of Illinois Press.

Rosch, E. (1973). Natural categories. *Cognitive Psychology, 4*, 328–350.

Rosen, G.M. (1987). Self-help treatment books and the commercialization of psychotherapy. *American Psychologist, 42*, 46–51.

Rosen, G.M. (1993). Self-help or hype? Comments on psychology's failure to advance self-care. *Professional Psychology: Research and Practice, 24*, 340–345.

Schooler, J.W. (1996). Seeking the core: The issues and evidence surrounding accounts of sexual trauma. In K. Pezdek & W.P. Banks (Eds.), *The recovered memory/false memory debate* (pp. 279–296). San Diego, CA: Academic Press.

Shakow, D. (1976). What is clinical psychology? *American Psychologist, 31*, 553–560.

Tavris, C. (1998). A widening gulf splits lab and couch. *New York Times*, June 21.

PART THREE

Clinical Science as a Safeguard Against Human Error

Science, as we've discovered, is not a body of knowledge. Nor it is a straightforward "truth generating machine" that automatically spits out correct answers whenever we ask it questions. Instead, science, including clinical science, is a systematic set of tools that researchers have developed to minimize error (Lilienfeld, 2010; O'Donohue & Lilienfeld, 2007). Phrasing it a bit differently, science is a toolbox of safeguards designed to protect investigators from fooling themselves and others. As Robert Pirsig (1974) put it in his book, *Zen and the Art of Motorcycle Maintenance*, "The real purpose of the scientific method is to make sure that Nature hasn't misled you into thinking something you know something you don't actually know" (p. 107).

Science is also an approach to seeking out and acknowledging errors in our web of beliefs, and to subjecting our most cherished assumptions to rigorous scrutiny (Bartley, 1984; Popper, 1959). It requires both a sense of humility (McFall, 1996; O'Donohue & Lilienfeld, 2007) and a thick skin, because admitting that we might be wrong can be bruising to our egos. But this intellectual nondefensiveness is essential to good clinical research and practice. "Okay, Nature, that's the end of the nice guy" (p. 111), wrote Pirsig (1974) in his apt depiction of science as a means of ruthlessly rooting out our mistakes.

In clinical psychology, all research designs, whatever their superficial differences, are intended to eliminate errors in our observations, interpretations of data, or both. Correlational designs prevent us from perceiving *illusory correlations* (Chapman & Chapman, 1967), that is, statistical associations that don't exist. For example, many individuals believe that the administration of certain vaccines (especially those containing thimerosal, a mercury-bearing preservative) is correlated with the incidence of autism, although numerous well-designed correlational studies disconfirm this claim, suggesting that it reflects an illusory correlation (Lilienfeld, Lynn, Ruscio, & Beyerstein, 2010). Double-blind designs, which shield both investigators and participants from knowing who's in the experimental group and who's in the control group, minimize the impact of *confirmation bias* (Nickerson, 1998), that is, the tendency of people—including scientists—to seek out evidence that supports their favored hypotheses, but to deny, dismiss, or distort evidence that doesn't. The same holds for all other research designs in psychology: Each is designed to eliminate one or more sources of error. A confound, for example, is a possible error that our research design has neglected to rule out.

But just how necessary is science as a safeguard against our fallibility? Can't we just rely on our intuitions to tell us when we're wrong? The past several decades of psychological research have yielded an unambiguous answer. There's no longer any question that all of us, including researchers and practitioners, are susceptible to certain predictable errors (Garb, 1998; Myers, 2002). Moreover, we're often woefully ignorant of when we're committing these mistakes, so we can't always rely on our hunches to detect them.

Arkes, H. R. (1981). Impediments to accurate clinical judgment and possible ways to minimize their impact. Journal of Consulting and Clinical Psychology, 49, 323–330.

Crumlish, N., & Kelly, B. D. (2009). How psychiatrists think. Advances in Psychiatric Treatment, 15, 72–79.

Dawes, R. M., Faust, D., & Meehl, P. E. (1989). Clinical versus actuarial judgment. Science, 243, 1668–1674.

Meehl, P. E. (1973). Why I do not attend case conferences. In P. E. Meehl (Ed.), Psychodiagnosis: Selected papers (pp. 225–302). Minneapolis, MN: University of Minnesota Press. (Excerpt)

As we'll discover in Part 3, we're all prone to relying too heavily on *heuristics*—mental shortcuts and "rules of thumb." Heuristics are helpful in most everyday circumstances, but they can lead us badly astray in some others (Tversky & Kahneman, 1974). For example, the *representativeness* heuristic, which operates by the guideline of "like goes with like," can lead us to conclude mistakenly that a therapy client who vaguely reminds us of a psychopathic client we treated last year ("I can't put my finger on it, but he just seems a bit like that client I saw") must himself be a psychopath. We're also vulnerable to a plethora of *biases*, that is, systematic errors in judgment. For example, *hindsight bias*, which is the "I knew it all along" effect, can lead us to conclude erroneously that a client who has low self-esteem must have been neglected or mistreated by her parents in childhood. And confirmation bias can induce tunnel vision, causing us to ask our clients leading questions. For example, if we suspect that a client might have been sexually abused in childhood, we may ask her questions that strongly suggest a history of abuse (e.g., "In my experience, most people with problems like yours have been sexually abused. Do you think it's possible you've been abused too?"). As a consequence, we may end up concluding mistakenly that she was abused even if she wasn't. By learning to think scientifically, clinical researchers and practitioners can avoid falling prey to these and other widespread errors in judgment. To do so, however, they need to become aware of their strengths and weaknesses as information processors.

Minimizing errors matters not only because we should strive to establish a web of beliefs that has as much verisimilitude (literally meaning "truth-likeness") as possible, but also because errors can harm our clients. In the helping professions, we act on our beliefs. If we believe that a certain assessment device measures a construct with minimal error, we may administer it and then act on the results. If we believe that a certain therapy is safe and the most effective for a problem a client is experiencing, we may deliver this therapy. But what if we're mistaken? What if the assessment technique contains huge amounts of measurement error and our inferences are incorrect? What if the therapy isn't as effective as we believe or is much less effective than an alternative therapy? Our clients who've trusted us to possess specialized knowledge may be needlessly harmed.

Regrettably, as a profession we've been rather lax in this regard. Too many mental health professionals practice a therapy they "like," largely independent of the evidence for its efficacy or of comparison studies on the efficacy of alternative therapies (Baker, McFall, & Shoham, 2009; Mischel, 2009). And too many therapists administer assessment devices that they learned in graduate school or that are widely accepted in the profession despite feeble evidence for their validity (Hunsley, Lee, & Wood, 2003). If we could wave a magic wand and change our profession in one way, it would be for our profession

to be more critical about its accepted practices and to care more about scientific evidence.

THE READINGS IN PART 3

The four readings in Part 3 focus on the challenges faced by practitioners in clinical judgment and prediction, as well as commonplace errors in thinking that are especially relevant to clinical scientists inside and outside the therapy room.

In an article that is three decades old but every bit as timely today, Hal Arkes examines five crucial sources of error in the clinical setting, including overconfidence and hindsight bias. Just as importantly, Arkes discusses several ways of "debiasing" practitioners against these errors, including actively considering alternative hypotheses and attending to neglected data. The key point here is that forewarned is forearmed. Clinicians who are cognizant of their propensity toward bias can often find ways of compensating for it. In this way, they may be able to engage in more effective practices.

In their breezy and helpful tour of "how psychiatrists think," Niall Crumlish and Brendan Kelly outline a host of heuristics that streamline information processing in practice settings. As they note, the intelligent use of heuristics is essential to mature clinical decision making. At the same time, Crumlish and Kelly observe, the thoughtless use of heuristics can lead to numerous avoidable errors in clinical settings. As a consequence, we must be prepared to override these heuristics in certain situations. Although framed as an article on the cognitive processes of psychiatrists, their piece is equally relevant to clinical psychologists, counseling psychologists, social workers, and all mental health professionals who are confronted with the task of making complex decisions under considerable time pressure.

Robyn Dawes and his colleagues next compare two alternative methods of combining data to generate clinical judgments and predictions, such as whether a client will attempt suicide or benefit from a specific type of psychotherapy. In the more widely used "clinical" approach, practitioners subjectively combine different sources of data, such as biographical information, scores on psychological tests, and interview impressions, in their heads. In contrast, in the "statistical" or "actuarial" approach, practitioners combine such data using well-established statistical formulas derived from real-world data. As Dawes and his coauthors note, a large body of literature stretching across several decades shows conclusively that the far cheaper and more efficient statistical approach tends to do just as well as, and often better than, the clinical approach. Yet, for a host of reasons the authors delineate, the statistical approach remains massively underutilized. The quality of clinical decisions—and patient care—often suffers as a consequence.

In a classic chapter—large portions of which we've excerpted here—Paul Meehl, often considered the most prominent clinical psychologist of the last half of the twentieth century, humorously vents his frustration at the typical (low) level of critical thinking at many clinical case conferences. Along the way, he manages to skewer a host of errors in logic that are often on vivid display at such conferences. Among them are the "spun glass theory of the mind," which proposes that most of us humans are delicate creatures who will fall apart at the slightest provocation; "Uncle George's Pancake Fallacy," the mistake of concluding that because someone we know well (e.g., good old Uncle George) engages in a bizarre behavior, it must be normal; and the "Multiple Napoleon's Fallacy," the error of assuming that if a belief (e.g., that the government is persecuting us) is "real" to the patient, it is doesn't matter whether or not it's objectively genuine. Meehl's memorable chapter is a much needed reminder that sloppy thinking can be one step along the slippery slope to suboptimal clinical practice.

11

Impediments to Accurate Clinical Judgment and Possible Ways to Minimize Their Impact

HAL R. ARKES

Recent research in cognitive psychology has begun to uncover some of the factors that make clinical judgment a difficult task. Five impediments to accurate judgment were discussed: inability to assess covariation, influence of preconceived notions, lack of awareness of one's judgmental processes, overconfidence, and the hindsight bias. To minimize the impact of these impediments, three strategies were suggested: active consideration of alternative outcomes, increased attention to certain types of usually ignored data, and minimization of the role of memory.

The investigation of clinical judgment began in earnest in the 1950s due in large part to the "statistical versus clinical" controversy engendered by Meehl's 1954 book. The controversy was fueled by several studies which suggested that the reliability of clinicians' judgments was low (e.g., Goldberg & Werts, 1966; Little & Schneidman, 1959; Phelan, 1964; Wallach & Schooff, 1965). The purpose of this article is not to enter into that controversy but instead to analyze clinical judgment from the perspective of a cognitive psychologist. I have two goals in attempting this analysis: first, to point out several factors that make diagnosis such a difficult task, and second, to suggest ways in which improved diagnostic accuracy might be achieved.

IMPEDIMENTS

Covariation Misestimation

The first impediment to high diagnostic accuracy is the inability to assess covariation accurately. Figure 1 depicts a prototypical situation. A clinician notes that some people have Symptom S while others do not. The clinician then attempts to determine if the presence of the symptom is diagnostic of some future outcome (e.g., psychotic episode). Research by Arkes and Harkness (Note 1), Nisbett and Ross (1980), and Smedslund (1963) suggests that people base their assessment of covariation largely on the number of instances in Cell A. For example, Arkes, Harkness, and Biber (Note 2) showed subjects 12 pieces of evidence from Cell A, 6 from B, 6 from C, and 3 from D. Subjects estimated the relation between the row factor and column factor to be 54 on a 0–100 scale of contingency (0 = no relation, 100 = complete relation). However, the actual relation is zero, since the outcome is twice as likely to occur whether or not the symptom is present. It is the large magnitude of Cell A that apparently causes the badly biased estimate of contingency.

Consideration of information in the bottom row of Figure 1 is mandatory in order for a diagnostician to determine whether a symptom and disease are related. Yet, Arkes, Harkness, and Biber (Note 2) have shown that in the typical covariation estimation situation, such information is ignored. Augmenting the salience of instances in Cell B helped reduce the

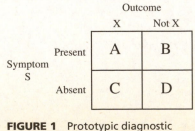

FIGURE 1 Prototypic diagnostic situation.

contingency to a more accurate level; increasing the salience of the information in Cell C had no effect, even though information in Cell C mathematically lowers the true contingency as much as the information in Cell B does. We believe that subjects perceived the information in Cell C to be completely irrelevant to contingency estimates (Meehl & Rosen, 1955).

Placing oneself in the role of a diagnostician may heighten the appreciation of how unimportant Cells C and D appear to be. Assume that you suspect that a certain MMPI (Minnesota Multiphasic Personality Inventory) profile is diagnostic of an impending psychotic break. To check this suspicion, you keep track of how many people with this profile do or do not have a subsequent psychotic episode. Would you also consider keeping track of those without that profile in order to test the hypothesis? Since the hypothesis deals only with people having a certain profile, disregarding those without it appears sensible. Yet those instances need to be recorded to test the hypothesis adequately. Therefore, increasing the utilization of such information will be one way to improve diagnostic accuracy. A way to accomplish this will be discussed later.

Preconceived Notions

The second major impediment to accurate clinical judgment is the influence of preconceived notions or expectancies. The classic study in this area (Chapman & Chapman, 1967) is so famous that only a brief overview is needed. When drawings were randomly paired with personality traits presumably characteristic of the person who did the drawings, subjects fabricated illusory correlations between drawing features and personality traits. For example, drawings containing large eyes were said by subjects to be frequently done by people who were said to be suspicious. Chapman and Chapman (1967) suggested that these false relations were due to a prior association between eyes and suspicion. This prior association warped the perception of incoming data so much that a positive correlation was seen even when the true relation between a drawing feature and a trait was negative.

Prior associations do not merely warp the perception of correlation; at a more basic level, they impede the accurate processing of an individual datum. Perhaps the most powerful example is by Shweder (1977), who reanalyzed data collected by Newcomb (1929). Newcomb had asked camp counselors to monitor and record the behavior of each camper every day. At the end of the 24-day camping session, the counselors were asked to recall the behaviors performed by each camper. The correlation between the initial recording of the behaviors and subsequent memory for the behaviors was −.27. In an attempt to explain this abysmal correlation in the 1929 data, Shweder asked undergraduates (almost a half century later) to fill out a simple questionnaire. Each question was of the form, "Assume that a boy is aggressive. How likely is it that he is also friendly?" Subjects were to answer on a 0–100 scale. By looking at answers to numerous questions such as this one, Shweder was able to tap the general "implicit personality theory" (Bruner & Tagiuri, 1954). Most people probably think that aggressive people are not likely to be friendly or charitable but

are likely to be cold and self-centered. Shweder found that the various correlations between such traits were very highly related to the counselors' memories of the campers' behaviors. Shweder suggests that when a counselor tried to recall the behavior of camper Joey, the counselor might have recalled an incident such as Joey's inverting the oatmeal bowl over his friend's head. Recall of this behavior triggered the inference that Joey was also aggressive, cold, and self-centered but not friendly or charitable. The implicit personality theory thus guided the counselor's recall of Joey's behavior. This preconceived matrix of assumptions simply overwhelmed whatever the data might actually have been. This explains the enormous correlation of .84 between the implicit personality theory matrix of behavior and remembered camper behavior.

The influence of such preconceived ideas also influences the perception of current as opposed to remembered data. Lord, Ross, and Lepper (1979) found that proponents and opponents of capital punishment found arguments supporting their own viewpoints to be more convincing and probative than arguments against. Mahoney (1977) found the same type of bias among journal referees reviewing articles consistent with or opposed to their own theoretical persuasion. This research gains added importance when one realizes that clinicians' Q-sorts of clients stabilize after only two to four sessions (Meehl, 1960). It is quite likely that all subsequent data gleaned from the client will be biased by whatever opinions have been formed during this brief initial period. Data consistent with the tentative diagnosis will be given added credence; data inconsistent with the hypothesis will be disregarded. The fact that the initial hypothesis or diagnosis is merely tentative does not decrease its biasing influence (Ross, Lepper, Strack, & Steinmetz, 1977).

Lack of Awareness

No matter what bias a diagnostician demonstrates, attempts to eliminate it would be fostered by awareness of one's own clinical judgment process. Research by Brehmer, Kuylenstierna, and Liljergren (1974), Oskamp (1967), and Summers, Taliaferro, and Fletcher (1969) suggests that we have negligible awareness of the factors that influence our judgment. For example, Summers et al. (1969) presented subjects with four economic indicators for each of several countries. Subjects were asked to use these cues to predict the future economic growth of each country. At the conclusion of the task, subjects were asked to report how much they used each of the four economic indicators in making their predictions. These self-reports of cue usage were not closely related to the actual extent of cue usage. In short, subjects were unaware of the impact each symptom had on their diagnosis (see also Nisbett & Wilson, 1977).

A study by Gauron and Dickinson (1966) makes the same point using a clinical judgment task. Clinicians asked for information previously collected from a client. As each category of information was received, the clinician announced a tentative diagnosis and the confidence level with which that diagnosis was held. Gauron and Dickinson deemed a piece of information to be important if that information either caused the clinician to switch to the final diagnosis or if it increased the confidence in the diagnosis that proved to be the final one. This measure of importance was not significantly related to the clinicians' own estimates of the importance of each piece of information. In other words, the clinicians had minimal awareness of which factors actually influenced their judgment.

Overconfidence

Another factor that impedes the improvement of clinical judgment is the serious overconfidence that diagnosticians have in their diagnoses. Oskamp (1965) has shown that providing a judge with more information increases his or her confidence in the decision without necessarily increasing the accuracy of the decision. Worse yet, Holsopple and Phelan (1954) have shown that the most confident diagnosticians tend to be the least accurate.

Numerous factors undoubtedly contribute to this overconfidence. Einhorn and Hogarth (1978) demonstrated that treatment effects are one such factor. To use one of their examples, suppose a granting agency wishes to check the validity of their own granting procedures. It checks the quantity and quality of the research it has funded. If the proportion of satisfactory research projects among those funded is high, the agency might conclude that the judgmental procedures used to decide among the grant applicants were excellent. However, funding of a grant request enables a researcher to buy equipment, hire assistants, and do other things that enable him or her to perform successful research. Even if the agency's judgment procedures were woefully inadequate, most of its funded applicants might have successful research programs due to the benefits derived from receiving the grant. This high proportion of successes might be interpreted by the agency as a validation of their procedures, thereby instilling overconfidence in those procedures. Note that a similar problem can occur whenever there is a placebo effect. As long as a group or individual improves in performance for any reason, the therapist or experimenter administering the treatment may attribute the improvement to the treatment. This Hawthorne effect scenario, probably relatively common in psychological situations, would lead to overconfidence in the treatment.

Snyder (1981) has demonstrated that people selectively seek evidence that confirms the hypothesis currently under consideration. Such biased information gathering will lend support to the hypothesis. For example, when testing the hypothesis that a person is an introvert, questions such as "What factors make it hard for you to really open up to people?" are asked. When testing the hypothesis that a person is an extravert, questions like "In what situations are you most talkative?" are more probable. Those questions generate answers that will in turn lead to overconfidence in the current hypothesis. Similarly, Koriat, Lichtenstein, and Fisch-hoff (1980) presented evidence that people disregard evidence that contradicts their current judgment. Given selective seeking of confirmatory evidence and selective censoring of disconfirmatory evidence, a hypothesis simply cannot fail to be well substantiated. Such a hypothesis is very unlikely to be modified or discarded.

Hindsight Bias

There is always enough evidence in a rich source of data to nurture all but the most outlandish diagnosis. This impediment to optimal judgment is manifested in the hindsight bias, which

was systematically investigated first by Fischhoff (1975). Fischhoff asked one group of subjects, the foresight group, to read psychotherapy case histories and then judge the likelihood of four possible circumstances that may have followed therapy. One hindsight group was shown the case history and then was told that a certain outcome, A, occurred. The group was then asked whether they would have been able to predict the occurrence of A had they been asked to do so. These hindsight subjects assigned probabilities to Event A that were 49% higher than the probability assigned to A by the foresight group. Thus, the occurrence of A was obvious only in hindsight. Other hindsight subjects were told that Event B actually occurred. These subjects claimed that B would have been relatively easy for them to predict. Of course, the foresight group, not having outcome knowledge, did not consider B to be a likely outcome. Arkes, Wortmann, Saville, and Harkness (in press) have found this same effect in the area of medical diagnosis. The foresight group was shown an actual case history and was asked to assign probabilities to four possible diagnoses. Each of four hindsight groups was told that a different one of the four diagnoses was true. The hindsight groups then assigned probabilities to each of the four diagnoses. Even in the area of medical diagnosis, presumably where the symptom-disease relation is more exact than in psychology, the hindsight bias emerged. Given enough data, many diagnoses can appear obvious.

Possible Debiasing Techniques

One technique that has proven to be absolutely worthless is telling people what a particular bias is and then telling them not to be influenced by it (Fischhoff, 1977: Kurtz & Garfield, 1978; Wood, 1978). If people truly do have limited awareness of the factors that influence their judgments, exhortations to increase or decrease the impact of these factors may be doomed to ineffectiveness.

Chapman and Chapman (1967) attempted to reduce the illusory correlations reported by their subjects by creating a negative correlation between the symptoms and diagnoses that prior subjects had perceived to be positively correlated. This debiasing technique was not very successful: The illusory correlation was reduced but not eliminated. Also, it is not possible to rearrange correlations in the real world to promote the debiasing of diagnosticians; therefore, this debiasing technique is not practical.

Consider Alternatives

A debiasing technique that has shown some success has been demonstrated by Slovic and Fischhoff (1977). In an effort to reduce the hindsight bias, Slovic and Fischhoff asked hindsight subjects to explain why Outcome A might have been expected from the prior events and how alternative Outcome B might be explained had it occurred instead of A. Being forced to consider B reduced (but did not completely eliminate) the hindsight bias toward A. Using a similar technique, Koriat et al. (1980) presented people with two-alternative questions and asked them to list reasons for and against each of the two possible options. Only then could the subjects choose one of the answers and state their confidence in the correctness of their choice. This procedure produced a marked improvement in confidence ratings compared to the ratings given by control subjects.

Research by Ross et al. (1977) helps us to understand the relative effectiveness of the Slovic and Fischhoff (1977) and Koriat et al. (1980) debiasing techniques. Ross et al. showed that given a body of prior events, any purported outcome that a subject is asked to explain is perceived by the subject as more likely to occur. This effect takes place even if the subject knows the outcome to be explained is merely hypothetical. Thus, when Slovic and Fischhoff (1977) asked a subject to concoct a scenario for both purported Outcome A and hypothetical Outcome B, the authors were really using the Ross et al. bias on B to offset the hindsight bias on A. As a result, the hindsight bias was reduced. Similarly, when Koriat et al. (1980) asked their subjects to list reasons against the option that was eventually not chosen, overconfidence was largely eliminated.

Considering alternatives may be an effective means of reducing unwarranted over-confidence in a number of contexts divorced from the hindsight situation. Problem solvers from Benjamin Franklin to Wayne Wickelgren (1974) have suggested that decision making is improved if one ensures that all alternatives are given substantial consideration. Consistent with this, Elstein, Shul-man, and Sprafka (1978) have found that the most accurate diagnosticians tend to arrive at their final diagnosis later than do less accurate diagnosticians. Premature closure results in the biased processing of subsequent data. Perhaps the most dramatic example of this may be found in a series of studies by Dailey (1952). Subjects were first asked to read an autobiography of a person and then were asked to predict how that person would have answered each item on a personality inventory. The criterion was how the writer of the autobiography actually did respond to each inventory item. Dailey had some subjects make some predictions after reading half of the autobiography and the rest of the predictions at the end. A second group made all of their predictions at the end. Dailey found that the latter group performed significantly better on the questions both groups answered at the end. Presumably, asking some subjects to predict in the middle forced the formulation of premature hypotheses. The final half of the data were then biased by these hypotheses based on inadequate data. This interpretation is supported by the results of a second experiment. Merely having subjects pause halfway through the autobiography to think about the data resulted in inferior performance on the final predictions. From data such as these, it would appear that one way to improve accuracy and reduce bias would be to entertain alternative hypotheses for a long period of time. As Slovic and Fischhoff (1977) have shown, active consideration of such hypotheses may be particularly beneficial in combating bias.

Think Bayesian

To improve judgment by increasing the impact of usually ignored information, some researchers (e.g., Galen & Gambino, 1975; Lusted, 1968; Schwartz, Gorry, Kassirer, & Essig, 1973) have presented what amounts to a tutorial in Bayesian statistics.

This example, taken from Schwartz et al., demonstrates diagnosticians' need for some statistical guidance:

> A total of 290 subjects were asked to assume that a test for cancer was available that has the following characteristics: (1) The test is positive in 95 of 100 patients with cancer. (2) The test is negative in 95 of 100 patients without cancer. They were also asked to assume that, on the average, 5 people in a population of 1,000 have previously undetected cancer.
>
> The problem posed was as follows: if the test described is given to a randomly selected patient from this population and the test is positive, what is the probability that the patient actually has cancer? (1973, p. 467)

The great majority of the subjects (medical students and physicians) answered with values of 50% or greater. The correct answer is 9%. A Bayesian analysis will help us discover why this typical diagnostic problem is so difficult.

Bayes's theorem enables one to examine the impact of information on a hypothesis or diagnosis. The prior odds are expressed as a ratio of the likelihood of the hypothesis being true divided by the likelihood of the hypothesis being not true, or $p(\mathrm{H})/p(\bar{\mathrm{H}})$. If a piece of information is now obtained (e.g., a test score), these prior odds must be modified in light of this information. The prior odds are multiplied by the likelihood ratio. This ratio is simply the probability of obtaining that piece of datum if the hypothesis were true divided by the probability of obtaining the datum if the hypothesis were false, or $p(\mathrm{DIH})/p(\mathrm{DI\bar{H}})$. When the prior odds are multiplied by the likelihood ratio, we obtain the posterior odds. This final product is the probability that the hypothesis is true given this piece of information divided by the probability that the hypothesis is not true given this piece of information, or $p(\mathrm{HID})/p(\bar{\mathrm{H}}\mathrm{ID})$. The whole formula is

$$\frac{p(\mathrm{HID})}{p(\bar{\mathrm{H}}\mathrm{ID})} = \frac{p(\mathrm{DIH})}{p(\mathrm{DI\bar{H}})} \times \frac{p(\mathrm{H})}{p(\bar{\mathrm{H}})}.$$

Let us examine the example presented by Schwartz et al. The prior odds of having cancer are

$$\frac{p(\mathrm{H_c})}{p(\bar{\mathrm{H}}_c)} = \frac{5}{995},$$

since 5 out of every 1,000 people have the disease. These are the odds before any test information is obtained. The likelihood ratio is

$$\frac{p(\mathrm{DIH_c})}{p(\mathrm{DI\bar{H}_c})} = \frac{95}{5},$$

since a positive test result is obtained 95% of the time when cancer is present and 5% of the time when cancer is absent, The posterior odds are

$$\frac{p(\mathrm{H_cID})}{p(\bar{\mathrm{H}}_c\mathrm{ID})} = \frac{95}{5} \times \frac{5}{995} = \frac{475}{4975}.$$

Since this fraction is an expression of odds, it means that out of every 5,450 positive tests results, 475 will be from a patient with cancer, and 4,975 will be from a patient without cancer. The probability that a positive test is from a patient with cancer is

$$\frac{475}{475 + 4975} = 9\%.$$

The physicians who grossly overestimated the probability of cancer were probably impressed by the wonderfully high diagnosticity of the test for cancer: Fully 95% of those who tested positively had the disease. Diagnosticity is reflected in the likelihood ratio of 95/5. The gross overestimation by the physicians ignores the prior odds, which are a reflection of the base rate, the proportion of the population having cancer. Abundant evidence in the judgment (Kahneman & Tversky, 1973) and social psychology (Nisbett & Borgida, 1975) literatures indicates that base rates are grievously underutilized in many instances. If there were some way to get diagnosticians to attend more to the prior odds, immense improvement in diagnostic accuracy would be achieved. One way to achieve this is by asking diagnosticians to pit the prior odds and likelihood ratio against each other. An example will illustrate this technique.

Following the reported diagnosis of a patient at a mental institution as a multiple personality, I asked a class of graduate students what the probability would be of a true multiple personality at that institution. The class settled on 1 out of 100,000. The prior odds are thus:

$$\frac{p(\text{Hmp})}{p(\bar{\text{H}}\text{mp})} = \frac{1}{99,999}.$$

I then asked the class to imagine the type of testing and interviewing that had gone on at the institution in the diagnostic process. I told them to imagine the type of responses a person with multiple personalities might have made. Finally, I instructed the class to divide the probability that a multiple personality would provide those data by the probability that a nonmultiple personality would provide those data. The class settled on 100 to 1. The likelihood ratio is thus:

$$\frac{p(\text{DIHmp})}{p(\text{DI}\bar{\text{H}}\text{mp})} = \frac{100}{1}.$$

Thus, the posterior odds are

$$\frac{p(\text{HmpID})}{p(\bar{\text{H}}\text{mpID})} = \frac{100}{1} \times \frac{1}{99,999} = \frac{100}{99,999}.$$

The probability that the diagnosis of multiple personality was correct was a paltry .1%. In order for the probability of being correct to have exceeded 50%, the likelihood ratio would have to have exceeded 99,999/1. There are two crucial rules to be gleaned from this. First, if the prior odds are x/y, the likelihood ratio must be larger than y/x in order for the hypothesis to be correct more than 50% of the time. Since no student was

convinced that any group of psychological tests could have provided data that overwhelming, all students agreed that the diagnosis of multiple personality was probably not correct.

The second rule to be learned from this example is that the more unlikely the hypothesis, that is, the lower the prior odds are, the greater the likelihood ratio must be to justify that hypothesis. For example, if the prior odds are 1/2, a likelihood ratio of 4/1 makes the hypothesis likely ($p = .67$). If the prior odds are 1/100, the same likelihood ratio still leaves the hypothesis in the long-shot category ($p = .04$).

As long as the posterior odds are viewed as a contest between the prior odds and the likelihood ratio, the base rate cannot be ignored. This will lead to much more accurate assessment of covariation. Note also that this technique requires that attention be paid to p (DI$\bar{\text{H}}$), the denominator of the likelihood ratio. This is precisely the data that Arkes et al. (Note 2) found were disregarded by their subjects, leading to poor judgmental performance.

Decrease Reliance on Memory

A final strategy to increase judgmental accuracy is predicated on the fallibility of recall: Try to decrease reliance on memory. Arkes and Harkness (1980) found that un-presented symptoms consistent with a diagnosis tended to be remembered as having been presented. Under some circumstances, previously presented symptoms inconsistent with the diagnosis were not remembered as having been presented. Both types of memory errors would lead to overconfidence in the diagnosis. Without access to a list of those symptoms that actually did and did not occur, one tends to remember the facts supportive of the hypothesis under consideration and to forget the facts inconsistent with the hypothesis.

Another cost of relying on memory rather than records is discussed by Ward and Jenkins (1965). Estimates of covariation were grossly incorrect when the individual pieces of datum were presented one at a time. When box-score summaries were presented based on the four categories of Figure 1, the estimates were much more accurate. The box scores impose no memory load, since all past instances are represented in the summary (Shaklee & Mims, Note 3).

A third way in which excessive reliance on memory may lead to poorer clinical judgment was recently discovered by Lueger and Petzel (1979). Using the Chapman and Chapman (1967) task, Lueger and Petzel found that the illusory correlation became more pronounced when greater amounts of information had to be processed by the subjects. It is important to note that in all three of these examples, memory losses did not merely result in less information with which to make a judgment. Memory loss resulted in more biased judgment. Hopefully a more humble view of one's own memory will result in less of a need to be humble about the accuracy of one's judgment.

Reference Notes

1. Arkes, H. R., & Harkness, A. R. *Factors influencing estimates of contingency*. Manuscript submitted for publication, 1980.
2. Arkes, H. R., Harkness, A. R., & Bibcr, D. *Salience and the judgment of contingency*. Paper presented at the annual meeting of the Midwestern Psychological Association, St. Louis, Missouri, May 1980.
3. Shaklee, H., & Mims, M. *Sources of error in judging event covariations: Effects of memory demands*. Manuscript submitted for publication, 1980.

References

Arkes, H. R., & Harkness, A. R. The effect of making a diagnosis on subsequent recognition of symptoms. *Journal of Experimental Psychology: Human Learning and Memory*, 1980, *6*, 568–575.

Arkes, H. R., Wortmann, R. L., Saville, R. D., & Harkness, A. R. The hindsight bias among physicians weighing the likelihood of a diagnosis. *Journal of Applied Psychology*, in press.

Brehmer, B., Kuylenstierna, J., & Liljergren, J. Effects of function form and cue validity on the subjects' hypotheses in probabilistic inference tasks. *Organizational Behavior and Human Performance*, 1974, *11*, 338–354.

Bruner, J. S., & Tagiuri, R. The perception of people. In G. Lindzey (Ed.), *Handbook of social psychology*. Reading, Mass.: Addison-Wesley, 1954.

Chapman, L., & Chapman, J. Genesis of popular but erroneous psycho-diagnostic observations. *Journal of Abnormal Psychology*, 1967, *72*, 193–204.

Dailey, C. A. The effects of premature conclusions upon the acquisition of understanding of a person. *Journal of Psychology*, 1952, *33*, 133–152.

Einhorn, H. J., & Hogarth, R. M. Confidence in judgment: Persistence in the illusion of validity. *Psychological Review*, 1978, *85*, 395–416.

Elstein, A. S., Shulman, A. S., & Sprafka, S. A. *Medical problem solving: An analysis of clinical reasoning*. Cambridge, Mass.: Harvard University Press, 1978.

Fischhoff, B. Hindsight ≠ foresight: The effect of outcome knowledge on judgment under uncertainty. *Journal of Experimental Psychology: Human Perception and Performance*, 1975, *1*, 288–299.

Fischhoff, B. Perceived informativeness of facts. *Journal of Experimental Psychology: Human Perception and Performance*, 1977, *3*, 349–358.

Galen, R. S., & Gambino, S. R. *Beyond normality: The predictive value and efficiency of medical diagnoses*. New York: Wiley, 1975.

Gauron, E. G., & Dickinson, J. K. Diagnostic decision-making in psychiatry: 1. Information usage. *Archives of General Psychiatry*, 1966, *14*, 225–232.

Goldberg, L. R., & Werts, C. E. The reliability of clinicians' judgments: A multitrait-multimethod approach. *Journal of Consulting Psychology*, 1966, *30*, 199–206.

Holsopple, J. G., & Phelan, J. G. The skills of clinicians in analysis of projective tests. *Journal of Clinical Psychology*, 1954, *10*, 307–320.

Kahneman, D., & Tversky, A. On the psychology of prediction. *Psychological Review*, 1973, *80*, 237–251.

Koriat, A., Lichtenstein, S., & Fischhoff, B. Reasons for confidence. *Journal of Experimental Psychology: Human Learning and Memory*, 1980, *6*, 107–118.

Kurtz, R. M., & Garfield, S. L. Illusory correlation: A further exploration of Chapman's paradigm. *Journal of Consulting and Clinical Psychology*, 1978, *46*, 1009–1015.

Little, K. B., & Schneidman, E. S. Congruences among interpretations of psychological test and anamnestic data. *Psychological Monographs*, 1959, *73* (6, Whole No. 476).

Lord, C. G., Ross, L., & Lepper, M. R. Biased assimilation and attitude polarization: The effects of prior theories on subsequently considered evidence. *Journal of Personality and Social Psychology*, 1979, *37*, 2098–2109.

Lueger, R. J., & Petzel, T. P. Illusory correlation in clinical judgment: Effects of amount of information to be processed. *Journal of Consulting and Clinical Psychology*, 1979, *47*, 1120–1121.

Lusted, L. B. *Introduction to medical decision making*. Springfield, Ill.: Charles C Thomas, 1968.

Mahoney, M. J. Publication prejudices: An experimental study of confirmatory bias in the peer review system. *Cognitive Therapy and Research*, 1977, *1*, 161–175.

Meehl, P. E. *Clinical versus statistical prediction*. Minneapolis: University of Minnesota Press, 1954.

Meehl, P. E. The cognitive activity of the clinician. *American Psychologist*, 1960, *15*, 19–27.

Meehl, P. E., & Rosen, A. Antecedent probability and the efficiency of psychometric signs, patterns, or cutting scores. *Psychological Bulletin*, 1955, *52*, 194–216.

Newcomb, T. M. *The consistency of certain extrovert-introvert behavior patterns in 51 problem boys*. New York: Teachers College, 1929.

Nisbett, R. E., & Borgida, E. Attribution and the psychology of prediction. *Journal of Personality and Social Psychology*, 1975, *32*, 932–945.

Nisbett, R. E., & Ross, L. *Human inference: Strategies and shortcomings of social judgment*. Englewood Cliffs, N.J.: Prentice-Hall, 1980.

Nisbett, R. E., & Wilson, T. D. Telling more than we can know: Verbal reports on mental processes. *Psychological Review*, 1977, *84*, 231–259.

Oskamp, S. Overconfidence in case-study judgments. *Journal of Consulting Psychology*, 1965, *29*, 261–265.

Oskamp, S. Clinical judgment from the MMPI: Simple or complex. *Journal of Clinical Psychology*, 1967, *23*, 411–415.

Phelan, J. G. Rationale employed by clinical psychologists in diagnostic judgment. *Journal of Clinical Psychology*, 1964, *20*, 454–458.

Ross, L., Lepper, M. R., Strack, F., & Steinmetz, J. Social explanation and social expectation: Effects of real and hypothetical explanations on subjective likelihood. *Journal of Personality and Social Psychology*, 1977, 35, 817–829.

Schwartz, W. B., Gorry, G. A., Kassirer, J. P., & Essig, A. Decision analysis and clinical judgment. *American Journal of Medicine*, 1973, *55*, 459–472.

Shweder, R. A. Likeness and likelihood in everyday thought: Magical thinking in judgments about personality. *Current Anthropology*, 1977, *18*, 637–648.

Slovic, P., & Fischhoff, B. On the psychology of experimental surprises. *Journal of Experimental Psychology: Human Perception and Performance*, 1977, *3*, 544–551.

Smedslund, J. The concept of correlation in adults. *Scandinavian Journal of Psychology*, 1963, *4*, 165–173.

Snyder, M. "Seek and ye shall find . . ." In E. T. Higgins, C. P. Herman, & M. P. Zanna (Eds.), *Social cognition: The Ontario symposium on personality and social psychology*. Hillsdale, N.J.: Erlbaum, 1981.

Summers, D. A., Taliaferro, D. J., & Fletcher, D. J. Subjective vs. objective description of judgment policy. *Psychonomic Science*, 1969, *18*, 249–250.

Wallach, M. S., & Schooff, K. Reliability of degree of disturbance rating. *Journal of Clinical Psychology*, 1965, *21*, 273–275.

Ward, W. C., & Jenkins, H. M. The display of information and the judgment of contingency. *Canadian Journal of Psychology*, 1965, *19*, 231–241.

Wickelgren, W. A. *How to solve problems: Elements of a theory of problems and problem solving*. San Francisco: Freeman, 1974.

Wood, G. The knew-it-all-along effect. *Journal of Experimental Psychology: Human Perception and Performance*, 1978, *4*, 345–353.

12

How Psychiatrists Think

NIALL CRUMLISH AND
BRENDAN D. KELLY

SUMMARY

Over the past decade, the study of error in medicine has expanded to incorporate new insights from cognitive psychology, generating increased research and clinical interest in cognitive errors and clinical decision-making. The study of cognitive error focuses on predictable errors in thinking that result from the use of cognitive shortcuts or 'heuristics'. Heuristics reduce the time, resources and cognitive effort required for clinical decision-making and are a feature of mature clinical thinking. Heuristics can also lead to bias and must be used with an awareness of their weaknesses. In this article, we describe heuristics commonly used in clinical decision-making and discuss how failure of heuristics results in cognitive error. We apply research findings on decision-making in medicine to decision-making in psychiatry and suggest directions for training and future research into cognitive error in psychiatry.

To err is human, and medicine is no exception (Horton 1999). In the USA, Kohn and colleagues (1999) reported that at least 44000 deaths a year resulted from medical error; this statistic generated alarm not only among patients and the clinical community, but also in the Clinton White House (Pear 1999). As a result, subsequent years have seen substantially increased interest in medical error in both scientific (Leape 2005) and popular literature (Gawande 2002). Indeed, the field has grown to the point that sub-specialties in medical error research have opened up, including medication error, diagnostic error and cognitive error.

In *How Doctors Think*, Professor Jerome Groopman, a Harvard haematologist and writer with the *New Yorker*, has defined cognitive errors in medicine simply, as 'errors in thinking that physicians can make' (Groopman 2007: p. 23). He argues that errors in thinking, rather than errors of technique, form the majority of mistakes in modern medicine, i.e. there is a 'cascade of cognitive errors' that results in a clinical error (p. 260). Groopman catalogues common cognitive errors in medical practice and outlines practical strategies for acknowledging and correcting them. *How Doctors Think* generated many enthusiastic reviews (Crichton 2007), of which few drew attention to the footnote on page 7: 'I quickly realised', wrote Groopman, 'that trying to assess how psychiatrists think was beyond my abilities'.

The omission of psychiatry from *How Doctors Think*, and for this reason, was arguably unnecessary: the cognitive style of psychiatrists is surely not so esoteric as to be un-understandable. We suspect that Professor Groopman would have found psychiatrists to be like any other doctors, had he applied the literature on cognitive error to psychiatry. In this article, we do just that.

COGNITIVE ERROR AND HEURISTICS

The study of cognitive error in medicine finds its roots in the literature on cognitive psychology from the past four decades (Redelmeier 2001). The key point of departure was the work of Amos Tversky and Daniel Kahneman, two psychologists whose studies of decision-making under conditions of uncertainty won the Nobel Prize for Economics in 2002. In a seminal paper for the journal *Science*, they discussed reliance on heuristics in decision-making (Tversky 1974). Heuristics are cognitive shortcuts that allow decisions to be reached in conditions of uncertainty. Many individual heuristics are identifiable (Table 1), but what they have in common is that they reduce the time, resources and cognitive effort required to

TABLE 1   Ten Heuristics, with Strengths and Weaknesses of Each

Heuristic	Strength	Weakness
Representativeness	Quick diagnosis, action through pattern recognition	Non-prototypical variants may be missed
Availability	Events that come to mind easily are common and should therefore be considered	Events that do not come quickly to mind are not considered
Anchoring	First impressions often give valuable information	It is difficult to move from incorrect first impressions
Confirmation bias	None	Can compound the failure to adjust from initial impressions (anchoring)
Search satisfying	Saves the time and effort of a search for comorbidity, as often none exists	Comorbidity, which is particularly common in psychiatry, is missed
Diagnosis momentum	None	Inaccurate diagnostic labels persist, potentially resulting in incorrect treatment and stigma
Commission bias	Avoids omission bias; optimal information is not always available in the real world	Adverse effects of unjustified treatment may violate the ethic of *primo non nocere*
Affective heuristic	Clinicians should be sympathetic towards patients	Unpleasant diagnoses or interventions may not be adequately considered
Playing the odds	Assumption of benign diagnosis or positive outcome is usually correct	Negative diagnoses or outcome may not be adequately considered
Fundamental attribution error	Not applicable	Patients may be inappropriately blamed and judged, to the detriment of their care

make a decision (Croskerry 2002). The use of heuristics can be contrasted with the hypothetico-deductive method of decision-making, in which all necessary evidence for and against any potential course of action is carefully examined and weighed. The latter assumes no bias on the part of the decision maker, and optimal time and resources.

Heuristics are useful, particularly when time and information are limited. Indeed, Groopman (2007: p. 36) argues that heuristics are 'the foundation of all mature medical thinking'. However, they are prone to bias. Decisions based on heuristics are more likely to be wrong than decisions made using hypothetico-deductive methods (Croskerry 2003). Tversky & Kahneman noted that reliance on heuristics leads to cognitive bias and 'severe and systematic errors' (Tversky 1974). Heuristics that result in error are called 'failed heuristics' (Croskerry 2002). In this article, we refer to error resulting from failed heuristics as cognitive error.

WHY SHOULD MEDICAL PRACTITIONERS BE PRONE TO COGNITIVE ERROR?

Heuristics are likely to be used in situations of high complexity or uncertainty (Tversky 1974), when there is a high cognitive load or a high density of decision-making (Croskerry 2002) and when time for individual decisions is short (Groopman 2007). These conditions are most obviously met in emergency medicine (Croskerry 2002), but in any branch of medicine, time is inadequate (Davidoff 1997) and cognitive effort is high (Schwarz 2005), while decisions are complex and must be made despite inherent uncertainty (uncertainty that is rarely acknowledged; Coles 2006).

Examples of Cognitive Error in Medicine

The list of potential cognitive errors is long, with 30 failed heuristics described in an influential paper on error in emergency medicine (Croskerry 2002). Here we discuss cognitive errors in medicine that may arise from the ten heuristics listed in Table 1. They include those discussed by Groopman (2007), with others that recur in the literature (Tversky 1974; Redelmeier 2001; Croskerry 2002, 2003).

Representativeness

Representativeness occurs when thinking is guided by a prototype, so that an event is not considered probable unless the presentation is prototypical of it. (In medicine, the event is often a diagnosis.) The representativeness heuristic may be useful when the doctor is confronted with a prototypical presentation: pulmonary embolism can be diagnosed almost without cognitive effort in a patient who presents with pleuritic chest pain of acute onset with dyspnoea following a deep venous thrombosis. A representativeness error may occur when the absence of prototypical features leads to atypical variants being missed: for example, if pulmonary embolism is not considered in the absence of severe pleuritic chest pain. In fact, only 60% of patients over 65 years old who have a pulmonary embolism present with chest pain (Timmons 2003).

Availability

The availability heuristic is seen when a doctor's assessment of the probability of an event is determined by the ease with which an example comes to mind; a doctor reviewing a patient with headache may overestimate the probability of subarachnoid haemorrhage if they have recently seen such a case. Often, availability is a useful heuristic, as events come easily to mind either because they are common or, if occurring more rarely, serious enough always to be considered as a possibility (e.g. meningitis). An availability error occurs when the probability of an event is overestimated because it comes easily to mind, or underestimated because it does not. In the above example, the doctor's recent encounter with subarachnoid haemorrhage has no bearing on the likelihood that the current presentation is that of tension headache, migraine or a rarer, potentially serious condition such as temporal arteritis.

Anchoring

Anchoring is the tendency to focus on prominent features of a presentation too early in the decision-making process, to arrive at an early hypothesis and to fail to adjust it in the light of later information. First impressions are often accurate, particularly among clinicians with highly developed pattern recognition skills, but they may be wrong. Tversky & Kahneman demonstrated that adjustments from first impressions are 'typically insufficient . . . payoffs for accuracy did not reduce the anchoring effect' (Tversky 1974); that is, first impressions have lasting power, even when they are wrong and when correcting them in the light of contradictory information is rewarded.

Confirmation Bias

Confirmation bias is the tendency to seek only information that will support rather than refute an initial hypothesis, or to selectively interpret information acquired after the hypothesis is formed in a way that supports it. The bias here is evident: a hypothesis that is true can withstand attempts to disprove it and should be subjected to such attempts. Confirmation bias is always an error, as it aims simply to avoid the cognitive effort that would be required to revise an initial impression, regardless of whether or not the hypothesis is correct.

Search Satisfying

Search satisfying may follow on from anchoring and confirmation bias. Search satisfying is the tendency to stop the diagnostic process once one diagnosis has been made. Even in the event that the first diagnosis is correct, search satisfying may be an error, as comorbid conditions are not considered. Examples are the second fracture in an X-ray or co-ingestants in poisoning (Croskerry 2003).

Diagnosis Momentum

Diagnosis momentum occurs when a diagnostic label applied to a patient sticks, whether or not subsequent events confirm the diagnosis. A working diagnosis may become a final diagnosis without any new diagnostic information having been acquired.

Commission Bias

Commission bias is the tendency to action rather than inaction, even when the correct course of action is unclear and inaction may be more appropriate. A doctor exhibiting commission bias may decide to institute treatment without adequate information to guide it, believing that it is better to do something than nothing.

The Affective Heuristic

Affective error occurs when the clinician's judgements are biased by their emotions or hopes: judgements of likelihood may be based on what the clinician would like to be the case rather than what actually is. A doctor may allow positive feelings towards a patient to influence their clinical judgement: because the doctor wishes the patient well, a symptom may be interpreted benignly when a more ominous interpretation is valid.

Playing the Odds

Affective error may combine with the heuristic of playing the odds. The latter is the tendency in ambiguous situations to opt for a benign interpretation, on the basis that benign causes and outcomes are more common than more ominous ones (tension headaches are more common than temporal arteritis). Playing the odds fails when a rare and serious disease similar in presentation to a common benign disease is missed.

Fundamental Attribution Error

The fundamental attribution error is the tendency to attribute someone's behaviour to their dis-positional qualities rather than to environmental or situational factors (Ross 1977). However, people systematically underestimate the extent to which other people's behaviour is influenced by external factors (Fiske 1991). In medicine, the fundamental attribution error is the tendency to be judgemental and blame patients inappropriately for their illnesses. Classically, it occurs when patients present with symptoms that are in some way precipitated or perpetuated by their own behaviour, for example smokers who present with exacerbations of pulmonary disease or intravenous drug users who present with skin abscesses after injecting. This may have implications for the level of care received, as it may be felt that patients with illnesses that are not of their own making are more deserving of care.

ERROR IN PSYCHIATRY

Mistakes in psychiatry can have serious consequences for patients, clinical teams and the wider community (Kapur 2000). However, the literature on error in psychiatry is small (Grasso 2003) and narrow, with most studies focusing on medication. Little has been written on diagnostic error, which was just briefly touched on in the most thorough review of error in psychiatric practice (Nath 2006). Some work has been done on error in predicting forensic risk (Freedman 2001). Other than a novel technical paper on cognition in emergency psychiatry (Cohen 2006), there has been no systematic study of cognitive error in psychiatry. There are, however, reasons why the practice of psychiatry might be prone to error of this type.

WHY SHOULD PSYCHIATRISTS BE PRONE TO COGNITIVE ERROR?

As noted above, heuristics are likely to be used, with their attendant risk of cognitive error, when there is a high cognitive load and limited time to make decisions, and in situations of complexity and uncertainty. On the face of it, psychiatry would appear to proceed at a more leisurely pace than emergency medicine. However, general adult psychiatrists frequently make decisions about risk (Holloway 1997). Moreover, psychiatric practice is practically defined by its complexity and uncertainty.

Error in Diagnosis

Among the uncertainties of psychiatry are diagnostic and symptomatic uncertainty. It has been argued that psychiatric diagnoses have limited reliability and validity (Read 2004). Psychiatrists have long strived to improve reliability, and DSM–III (American Psychiatric Association 1997) was developed largely for this purpose. Nevertheless, as recently as 2005, Robert Spitzer, who led the development of DSM–III, said that 'the reliability problem' was still not solved (Spiegel 2005). Validity in part depends on reliability, and the validity of schizophrenia in particular has been questioned. The observation that two people with no symptoms in common can both be diagnosed with schizophrenia has raised doubts about the validity of schizophrenia as a discernible disease entity (Read 2004).

Diagnosis in part depends on the reliability of individual symptoms. The reliability of symptoms in psychiatry may be limited for reasons such as subjectivity on the part of the diagnostician, with excessive scope for interpretation of symptoms or signs; underreporting of symptoms by patients, with no reliable objective method of identifying unreported psychopathology; and overreporting of symptoms, again, without the possibility of objectively verifying them. Diagnostic reliability also depends on agreement about the degree of severity of symptoms necessary for a clinical disorder to be diagnosed, when symptoms occur on a continuum (e.g. situational anxiety symptoms v. persistent panic, or intermittent ideas of reference v. paranoid delusions). The decision to diagnose a DSM–IV–TR mental disorder, when symptoms are clearly elicited, depends on the psychiatrist's judgement as to what constitutes 'clinically significant distress or impairment in social, occupational, or other areas of functioning' (American Psychiatric Association 2000). Clearly, the degree of impairment judged to be 'clinically significant' may vary from psychiatrist to psychiatrist. The psychosocial dimension of diagnosis distinguishes psychiatry from other disciplines and adds to diagnostic complexity; to take a medical example, the diagnosis of hypothyroidism depends on the results of a thyroid function test, not the degree of functional impairment the hypothyroidism appears to cause.

Error in Risk Assessment

In addition to diagnosis, there is a high degree of subjectivity and uncertainty in psychiatric decision-making regarding risk: for example, in the frequently taken decision of whether or not to detain a patient under the Mental Health Act after an episode of self-harm. The subjectivity may reside in whether or not ambiguous symptoms are held to be psychotic, or depressive, or neither; whether or not the patient is underreporting symptoms in the hope of being discharged, perhaps to self-harm again; and whether or not the patient will adhere to a commitment to engage with follow-up. The decision-making process may be further complicated by the attitudes and preferences of carers. Discharge may increase the risk of suicide, violence towards others or deterioration of mental state, affecting the patient, carers and community; unnecessary admission may inappropriately stigmatise a patient and family, may signal that self-harm and admission to hospital is an appropriate response to a crisis, and may result in the use of an in-patient bed that will then not be available to another patient. This decision must be made despite research demonstrating that risk prediction is difficult and imprecise (Kapur 2000).

Examples of Cognitive Error in Psychiatry

The ten heuristics discussed can give rise to cognitive error in psychiatry as in medicine.

Representativeness

Representativeness error occurs when atypical variants of a disorder are missed because the clinician is relying on a prototypical presentation. In psychiatry, prototypical presentations may be unreliable for a number of reasons. A given diagnosis can, according to current diagnostic classification, present in various ways. For example, DSM–IV–TR major depressive disorder requires the presence of low mood and/or reduced interest and pleasure, plus three or four of another seven symptoms. Clearly, two people with major depressive disorder can have very dissimilar clinical presentations. Similarly, schizophrenia can be diagnosed even in the absence of delusions or hallucinations, the prototypical symptoms; a patient with negative and disorganised symptoms alone can also be diagnosed with schizophrenia. Additionally, presentations that are prototypical in one population may not be so in another; for example, depressive disorders in later life rarely meet rigorous diagnostic criteria (Beekman 2002). Other disorders with textbook presentations, such as neuroleptic malignant syndrome or Wernicke's encephalopathy, could be vulnerable to representativeness error. In Wernicke's encephalopathy, the classic triad of confusion, ophthalmoplegia and ataxia is present only 16% of the time (Thomson 2008).

Availability

The availability heuristic is in play when an intervention is chosen because it was recently selected for another patient with a similar presentation or was discussed at a recent journal club: this 'availability' precludes a full assessment of need for the patient in question. It has been suggested (Waddington 2000) that referral letters to psychotherapists might lead to availability error, as the diagnostic formulation suggested in a letter would be easily remembered and thus be considered likely.

Anchoring

Referral letters may lead to anchoring as much as to availability. If a colleague writes that a patient has a diagnosis of schizophrenia, it requires a certain amount of cognitive effort and confidence to adjust this diagnosis (and to write back with a dissenting opinion). As might be expected, a strong anchoring effect has been reported in decisions regarding patients with antisocial personality traits (Richards 1990).

Confirmation bias

Confirmation bias may be the most common cognitive error in psychiatry. Confirmation bias depends on the ambiguity of the information used in decision-making, so that the clinician can interpret it to suit a pre-existing hypothesis. In psychiatry, diagnostic information is often so subjective that the same symptom can be interpreted in opposing ways; and unlike most medical symptoms, a psychiatric symptom is not always considered absent simply because a patient says it is. In a woman with progressive weight loss who reports an intake of 3000 calories a day, a diagnosis of anorexia nervosa can be justified as easily as a diagnosis of coeliac disease, the assumption being that the self-report of someone with anorexia nervosa is unreliable (Groopman 2007). Alternatively, the decision whether or not to diagnose psychosis and start the patient on a year or a lifetime of antipsychotic medications may hang on the interviewer's idiosyncratic interpretation of the patient's experiences, or the subjective distinctions between a delusion and an overvalued idea, or between a 'true' and 'pseudo-' hallucination.

Search Satisfying

Once a psychiatric diagnosis that could explain medical symptoms is made, search satisfying may result in the overlooking of medical comorbidity. Similarly, 'psych-out' error occurs when medical conditions (such as delirium, central nervous system infections, metabolic disorders or head injury) are misdiagnosed as purely psychiatric conditions (Croskerry 2003). Consistent with this, it has been shown that mentally ill patients receive unequal access to medically necessary procedures, even after controlling for other confounders (Kisely 2007). One might expect search satisfying to occur especially frequently in psychiatry, as comorbidity between Axis I disorders is common (Kessler 1994) and symptomatic overlap is significant between DSM Axis I and Axis II disorders (Flanagan 2006).

Diagnosis Momentum

Diagnosis momentum may also occur in psychiatry. A decision to commence a trial of antipsychotic medication, after a provisional diagnosis of psychotic disorder has been made from incomplete information, may result in diagnosis momentum. The trial of treatment may subsequently be taken as evidence of a final rather than a provisional diagnosis. At later clinic visits, no further symptoms may have emerged, but the diagnosis may go unquestioned. Confirmation bias may, in fact, lead to the circular conclusion that the lack of symptoms is evidence for antipsychotic effectiveness.

Commission bias

Commission bias occurs when an intervention is undertaken although the correct course of action—whether and how to intervene—is unclear. In psychiatry, when the patient's psychopathology is unknown, treatments may be instigated on the basis of assumptions about their mental state. Indeed, this may be necessary, as in the case of a mute patient with profound psychomotor retardation and reduced fluid intake, who is treated with a trial of electroconvulsive therapy. Treatments may also be instituted, however, without any real reason to expect that they will help the patient. For example, when a patient or family member (or even the psychiatrist) is frustrated with the rate of recovery, the psychiatrist may prematurely increase the dose of an antidepressant, possibly resulting in worsening of adverse effects without therapeutic gain, so as to be seen to be 'doing something'.

The Affective Heuristic

Affective error commonly accompanies confirmation bias in psychiatry: if either of two diagnoses can be made to fit ambiguous symptoms, a sympathetic psychiatrist may opt for the more benign, and this decision may be based more on hope than objective fact. Clearly, this is an error if it results in a serious diagnosis not being considered.

However, a psychiatrist may be aware of all possible diagnoses in a particular case, may be aware of the influence of hope on decision-making, and may still be faced with enduring diagnostic uncertainty. Additionally, cases arise in which the distinction between more benign and more severe diagnoses is not of prime importance when choosing a treatment. In a patient presenting with marked social anxiety and avoidance, it can be difficult to decide whether the diagnosis is a primary anxiety disorder or major depression with mood-congruent paranoid ideation; in either case, an antidepressant and psychological treatment are likely to help. What may not help is disclosing a suspected diagnosis of psychosis to the patient. The consequences of diagnosis with a severe mental illness include an increased risk of self-stigma and low self-esteem (Birchwood 1993), as well as depression and suicidality years later (Crumlish 2005). The psychiatrist might well err on the side of the more benign diagnosis, to avoid the negative psychological consequences of labelling with the more severe disorder.

Playing the Odds

The heuristic of playing the odds—decision-making biased towards a positive outcome, since positive outcomes are statistically more likely than negative outcomes—may be at play whenever a psychiatrist discharges a patient who is at chronic high risk of suicide. Prediction of suicide is exceedingly difficult (Kapur 2000) and the discharging psychiatrist, regardless of their risk assessment skills, has little idea whether the patient will act on suicidal impulses before the next scheduled appointment. It is the rarity of completed suicide—even among high-risk groups—that allows the psychiatrist confidently to discharge such a patient, and the playing the odds heuristic fails when that rare, catastrophic event happens.

Fundamental Attribution Error

Psychiatric patients may be particularly vulnerable to fundamental attribution error (Croskerry 2003), as challenging patients, such as those who recurrently self-harm, may be inappropriately judged or blamed for their behaviour (Nafisi 2007), with inadequate attention paid to the circumstances in which it occurs.

TAKING STEPS TO AVOID COGNITIVE ERROR

The first step in reducing the impact of error is to acknowledge that it exists and is a part of everyday practice. Horton (1999) argued that clinicians should move away from the idea of the 'perfect doctor' and focus on learning from error, when it occurs.

A barrier to addressing cognitive error may be the perception that to admit error in decision-making is to admit weakness as a clinician. In fact, cognitive error results from the use of heuristics, and the use of heuristics is characteristic of doctors with good clinical acumen (Croskerry 2002). Competing strategies, such as always relying on the hypothetico-deductive method for diagnosis or exhaustively investigating patients, are not practical in the real clinical world. Heuristics should not be abandoned, but should be used consciously, with an awareness of their potential pitfalls (Groopman 2007). Croskerry (2003) has gone so far as to suggest that the term 'failed heuristic' should be replaced by the term 'cognitive disposition to respond', so as to remove the stigma of bias or personal failure from discussion of cognitive error.

Another barrier to prevention of error is the perception that all cognitive error is inevitable. In fact, strategies exist for reducing cognitive error—one such is cognitive debiasing (Croskerry 2002)—and individual cognitive errors can be avoided or allowed for, provided that clinicians are aware of them (Table 2). Psychiatrists may have an advantage over other doctors in this regard, as psychiatrists have frequent exposure to the cognitive psychology that underpins cognitive error (Redelmeier 2001). Also, being familiar with transference and countertransference, psychiatrists are intuitively aware of fundamental attribution error and affective error, i.e. that feelings for a patient affect clinical decision-making.

For both trainees in psychiatry and practising psychiatrists, teaching in cognitive psychology could usefully incorporate training on cognitive biases in clinical decision-making. Trainee psychiatrists should be familiarised with the common cognitive biases and teaching should include cognitive forcing strategies such as insisting on a differential diagnosis even when the diagnosis seems obvious—it may seem obvious because of undetected biases (Bradley 2005). Such training should include non-punitive supervision, so that trainees can be corrected on errors and learn from them without damage to team cohesion or careers. Trainers should be willing to accept feedback from junior staff, including critique of their decisions. All doctors should actively seek feedback from patients and carers, and encourage them to ask searching questions about the rationale for diagnoses and interventions (Groopman 2007). Additionally, psychiatry could usefully adapt the tradition of the morbidity and mortality conference common in surgery (Holland 2007).

TABLE 2   Ten Cognitive Errors (Failed Heuristics), with Debiasing Strategies for Reducing Error

Cognitive error	Cognitive debiasing strategies
Representativeness	Be aware of individual variation; always ask 'what else could this be?'; rule out worst-case scenario
Availability	Judge cases on their own merits rather than recent experiences; be aware of the recency effect; routinely question the objective basis for clinical decisions
Anchoring	Avoid early judgements and preconceptions; do not assume that information from referrers is accurate
Confirmation bias	Try to disconfirm initial hypotheses; ensure that alternatives are considered; routinely consider, and argue the case for and against, several diagnoses or treatments
Search satisfying	Always consider comorbidity; be aware of points of similarity and difference between comorbidities
Diagnosis momentum	Question previously documented diagnoses; review criteria for diagnoses to ensure agreement
Commission bias	Review evidence for any intervention; identify dangers associated with action; set clear, timed goals for any intervention, if instituted under conditions of uncertainty; be prepared to stop an intervention if targets are not achieved
Affective error	Be aware of the influence of emotion on decision-making; recognise liking for a patient and be conscious of hopes for the patient as distinct from objective facts
Playing the odds	Be aware of the risk of a negative outcome; if there is doubt about the outcome, review the evidence carefully and err on the side of caution until more information is available
Fundamental attribution error	Recognise and try to understand dislike for a patient; avoid value judgements; recognise that patients' lives and behaviours are complex and that judgemental treatment oversimplifies those complexities; imagine a friend or relative in the patient's position

Adapted from Redelmeier 2001; Croskerry 2002, 2003.

CONCLUSIONS

The study of cognitive error in psychiatry is at an early stage. We have noted reasons why psychiatrists might be prone to cognitive error, but this is largely speculation on our part. There are no data on the prevalence or consequences of cognitive error among psychiatrists, and research in the area would be welcome. Individual cognitive errors are targets for research in psychiatry, just as psychologists and psychotherapists have studied anchoring (Richards 1990), availability (Waddington 2000) and fundamental attribution errors (Nafisi 2007). Equally, empirical evidence to support the effectiveness of cognitive debiasing strategies is still minimal (Bradley 2005), and further work is needed to develop rigorous, evidence-based programmes for teaching and supervision. Indeed, given the ubiquity of cognitive error and bias in medical practice, it is particularly appropriate that strategies for minimising error should be carefully evaluated—if only to avoid bias.

References

American Psychiatric Association (1997) *Diagnostic and Statistical Manual of Mental Disorders (3rd edn) (DSM–III)*. APA.

American Psychiatric Association (2000) *Diagnostic and Statistical Manual of Mental Disorders (4th edn, revised) (DSM–IV–TR)*. APA.

Beekman ATF, Geerlings SW, Deeg DJH, et al (2002) The natural history of late-life depression. A 6-year prospective study in the community. *Archives of General Psychiatry*; 59: 605–11.

Birchwood M, Mason R, MacMillan F, et al (1993) Depression, demoralization and control over psychotic illness: a comparison of depressed and non-depressed patients with a chronic psychosis. *Psychological Medicine*; 23: 387–95.

Bradley CP (2005) Can we avoid bias? *BMJ*; 330: 784.

Cohen T, Blatter B, Almeida C, et al (2006) A cognitive blueprint of collaboration in context: distributed cognition in the psychiatric emergency department. *Artifcial Intelligence in Medicine*; 37: 73–83.

Coles C (2006) Uncertainty in a world of regulation. *Advances in Psychiatric Treatment*; 12: 397–401.

Crichton M (2007) Where does it hurt? *New York Times;* April 1 (www.nytimes. com/2007/04/01/books/review/Crichton.t.html).

Croskerry P (2002) Achieving quality in clinical decision making: cognitive strategies and detection of bias. *Academic Emergency Medicine*; 9: 1184–204.

Croskerry P (2003) The importance of cognitive errors in diagnosis and strategies to minimize them. *Academic Medicine*; 78: 775–80.

Crumlish N, Whitty P, Kamali M, et al (2005) Early insight predicts depression and attempted suicide after 4 years in first-episode schizophrenia and schizophreniform disorder. *Acta Psychiatrica Scandinavica*; 112: 449–55.

Davidoff F (1997) Time. *Annals of Internal Medicine*; 127: 483–5.

Fiske ST, Taylor SE (1991) *Social Cognition* (2nd edn). McGraw-Hill.

Flanagan E, Blashfield R (2006) Do clinicians see Axis I and Axis II as different kinds of disorders? *Comprehensive Psychiatry*; 47: 496–502.

Freedman D (2001) False prediction of future dangerousness: error rates and Psychopathy Checklist – Revised. *Journal of the American Academy of Psychiatry and the Law*; 29: 89–95.

Gawande A (2002) *Complications: A Surgeon's Notes on an Imperfect Science*. Metropolitan Books.

Grasso BC, Bates DW (2003) Medication errors in psychiatry: are patients being harmed? *Psychiatric Services*; 54: 599.

Groopman J (2007) *How Doctors Think*. Houghton Mifflin.

Holland J (2007) A role for morbidity and mortality conferences in psychiatry. *Australasian Psychiatry*; 15: 338–42.

Holloway F (1997) The assessment and management of risk in psychiatry: can we do better? *Psychiatric Bulletin*; 21: 283–5.

Horton R (1999) The uses of medical error. *Lancet*; 353: 422–3.

Kapur N (2000) Evaluating risks. *Advances in Psychiatric Treatment*; 6: 399– 406.

Kessler RC, McGonagle KA, Zhao S, et al (1994) Lifetime and 12-month prevalence of DSM–III–R psychiatric disorders in the United States. Results from the National Comorbidity Survey. *Archives of General Psychiatry*; 51: 8–19.

Kisely S, Smith M, Lawrence D, et al (2007) Inequitable access for mentally ill patients to some medically necessary procedures. *Canadian Medical Association Journal*; 176: 779–84.

Kohn KT, Corrigan JM, Donaldson MS (1999) *To Err Is Human: Building a Safer Health System*. National Academy Press.

Leape LL, Berwick DM (2005) Five years after To Err Is Human: what have we learned? *JAMA*; 293: 2384–90.

Nafisi N, Stanley B (2007) Developing and maintaining the therapeutic alliance with self-injuring patients. *Journal of Clinical Psychology*; 63: 1069–79.

Nath SB, Marcus SC (2006) Medical errors in psychiatry. *Harvard Review of Psychiatry*; 14: 204–11.

Pear R (1999) A Clinton order seeks to reduce medical errors. *New York Times*; 7 December: 1.

Read J (2004) Does schizophrenia exist? Reliability and validity. In *Models of Madness. Psychological, Social and Biological Approaches to Schizophrenia* (eds J Read, LR Mosher, R Bentall): 43–56. Brunner-Routledge.

Redelmeier DA, Ferris LE, Tu JV, et al (2001) Problems for clinical judgement: introducing cognitive psychology as one more basic science. *Canadian Medical Association Journal*; 164: 358–60.

Richards MS, Wierzbicki M (1990) Anchoring errors in clinical-like judgements. *Journal of Clinical Psychology*; 46: 358–65.

Ross LD (1977) The intuitive psychologist and his shortcomings: distortions in the attribution process. In *Advances in Experimental Social Psychology* (ed L Berkowitz): 173–220. Academic Press.

Schwarz N (2005) When thinking feels difficult: meta-cognitive experiences in judgement and decision making. *Medical Decision Making*; 25: 105–12.

Spiegel A (2005) The dictionary of disorder. *New Yorker*; 5 January: 56–63.

Thomson AD, Cook CC, Guerrini I, et al (2008) Wernicke's encephalopathy: 'plus ca change, plus c'est la meme chose'. *Alcohol and Alcoholism*; 43: 180– 6.

Timmons S, Kingston M, Hussain M, et al (2003) Pulmonary embolism: differences in presentation between older and younger patients. *Age and Ageing*; 32: 601–5.

Tversky A, Kahneman D (1974) Judgement under uncertainty: heuristics and biases. *Science*; 185: 1124–31.

Waddington L, Morley S (2000) Availability bias in clinical formulation: the first idea that comes to mind. *British Journal of Medical Psychology*; 73: 117–27.

13

Clinical Versus Actuarial Judgment

ROBYN M. DAWES, DAVID FAUST,
AND PAUL E. MEEHL

Professionals are frequently consulted to diagnose and predict human behavior; optimal treatment and planning often hinge on the consultant's judgmental accuracy. The consultant may rely on one of two contrasting approaches to decision-making—the clinical and actuarial methods. Research comparing these two approaches shows the actuarial method to be superior. Factors underlying the greater accuracy of actuarial methods, sources of resistance to the scientific findings, and the benefits of increased reliance on actuarial approaches are discussed.

A PSYCHIATRIC PATIENT DISPLAYS AMBIGUOUS SYMPTOMS. Is this a condition best treated by psychotherapy alone or might it also require an antipsychotic medication with occasionally dangerous side effects? An elderly patient complains of memory loss but neurologic examination and diagnostic studies are equivocal. The neuropsychologist is asked to administer tests to help rule out progressive brain disease. A medical work-up confirms a patient's worst fears: he has terminal cancer. He asks the doctor how long he has to put his life in order.

These three brief scenarios illustrate a few of the many situations in which experts are consulted to diagnose conditions or to predict human outcomes. Optimal planning and care often hinge on the consultant's judgmental accuracy. Whether as physicians, psychiatrists, or psychologists, consultants perform two basic functions in decision-making: they collect and interpret data. Our interest here is in the interpretive function, specifically the relative merits of clinical versus actuarial methods.

METHODS OF JUDGMENT AND MEANS OF COMPARISON

In the clinical method the decision-maker combines or processes information in his or her head. In the actuarial or statistical method the human judge is eliminated and conclusions rest solely on empirically established relations between data and the condition or event of interest. A life insurance agent uses the clinical method if data on risk factors are combined through personal judgment. The agent uses the actuarial method if data are entered into a formula, or tables and charts that contain empirical information relating these background data to life expectancy.

Clinical judgment should not be equated with a clinical setting or a clinical practitioner. A clinician in psychiatry or medicine may use the clinical or actuarial method. Conversely, the actuarial method should not be equated with automated decision rules alone. For example, computers can automate clinical judgments. The computer can be programmed to yield the description "dependency traits," just as the clinical judge would, whenever a certain response appears on a psychological test. To be truly actuarial, interpretations must be both automatic (that is, prespecified or routinized) and based on empirically established relations.

Virtually any type of data is amenable to actuarial interpretation. For example, interview observations can be coded quantitatively (patient appears withdrawn: [1] yes, [2] no). It is thereby possible to incorporate qualitative observations and quantitative data into the predictive mix. Actuarial output statements, or conclusions, can address virtually any type of diagnosis, description, or prediction of human interest.

The combination of clinical and actuarial methods offers a third potential judgment strategy, one for which certain viable approaches have been proposed. However, most proposals for clinical-actuarial combination presume that the two judgment methods work together harmoniously and overlook the many situations that require dichotomous choices, for example, whether or not to use an antipsychotic medication, grant parole, or hospitalize. If clinical and actuarial interpretations agree, there is no need to combine them. If they disagree, one must choose one or the other. If clinical interpretation suggests brain damage but the actuarial method indicates otherwise, one does not conclude that the patient is and is not brain damaged.

Although some research appeared on clinical and actuarial judgment before the mid-fifties, Meehl (1) introduced the issue to a broad range of social scientists in 1954 and stimulated a flurry of studies. Meehl specified conditions for a fair comparison of the two methods.

First, both methods should base judgments on the same data. This condition does not require that clinical judge and statistical method, before comparison, use the same data to derive decision strategies or rules. The clinician's development of interpretive strategies depends on prior experience and knowledge. The development of actuarial methods requires cases with known outcome. The clinical and actuarial strategies may thus be derived from separate or overlapping data bases, and one or the other may be based on more or fewer cases or more or less outcome information. For example, the clinician may have interpreted 1000 intelligence tests for indications of brain dysfunction and may know the outcome for some of these cases based on radiologic examination. The actuarial method may have been developed on the subset of these 1000 cases for which outcome is known.

Second, one must avoid conditions that can artificially inflate the accuracy of actuarial methods. For example, the mathematical procedures (such as regression analysis or discriminant analysis) used to develop statistical actuarial decision rules may capitalize on chance (nonrepeating) relations among variables. Thus, derivation typically should be followed by cross-validation, that is, application of the decision rule to new or fresh cases, or by a standard statistical estimate of the probable outcome of cross-validation. Cross-validation counters artificial inflation in accuracy rates and allows one to determine, realistically, how the method performs. Such application is essential because a procedure should be shown to work where it is needed, that is, in cases in which outcome is unknown. If the method is only intended for local use or in the setting in which it was developed, the investigator may partition a representative sample from that setting into derivation and cross-validation groups. If broader application is intended, then new cases should be representative of the potential settings and populations of interest.

RESULTS OF COMPARATIVE STUDIES

The three initial scenarios provide examples of comparative studies. Goldberg studied the distinction between neurosis and psychosis based on the Minnesota Multiphasic Personality Inventory (MMPI), a personality test commonly used for such purposes (2, 3). This differential diagnosis is of practical importance. For example, the diagnosis of psychosis may lead to needed but riskier treatments or to denial of future insurance applications. Goldberg derived various decision rules through statistical analysis of scores on 11 MMPI scales and psychiatric patients' discharge diagnoses. The single most effective rule for distinguishing the two conditions was quite simple: add scores from three scales and then subtract scores

from two other scales. If the sum falls below 45, the patient is diagnosed neurotic; if it equals or exceeds 45, the patient is diagnosed psychotic. This has come to be known as the "Goldberg Rule."

Goldberg next obtained a total of 861 new MMPIs from seven different settings, including inpatient and outpatient services from either medical school, private, or Veterans Administration hospital systems in California, Minnesota, and Ohio. The accuracy of the decision rules when applied to these new cases was compared with that of 29 judges who analyzed the same material and attempted the same distinction. Some of the judges had little or no prior experience with the MMPI and others were Ph.D. psychologists with extensive MMPI experience.

Across the seven settings, the judges achieved mean validity coefficients ranging from $r = 0.15$ to 0.43, with a total figure of 0.28 for all cases, or 62% correct decisions. The single best judge achieved an overall coefficient of 0.39, or 67% correct decisions. In each of the seven settings, various decision rules exceeded the judges' mean accuracy level. The Goldberg Rule performed similarly to the judges in three of the settings and demonstrated a modest to substantial advantage in four of the settings (where the rule's validity coefficient exceeded that of the judges by 0.16 to 0.31). For the total sample, the Goldberg Rule achieved a validity coefficient of 0.45, or 70% correct decisions, thereby exceeding both the mean accuracy of the 29 judges and that of the single best judge.

Rorer and Goldberg then examined whether additional practice might alter results. Judges were given MMPI training packets consisting of 300 new MMPI profiles with the criterion diagnosis on the back, thus providing immediate and concrete feedback on judgmental accuracy. However, even after repeated sessions with these training protocols culminating in 4000 practice judgments, none of the judges equaled the Goldberg Rule's 70% accuracy rate with these test cases. Rorer and Goldberg finally tried giving a subset of judges, including all of the experts, the outcome of the Goldberg Rule for each MMPI. The judges were free to use the rule when they wished and knew its overall effectiveness. Judges generally made modest gains in performance but none could match the rule's accuracy; every judge would have done better by always following the rule.

In another study using the same 861 MMPI protocols, Goldberg constructed mathematical (linear) models of each of the 29 judges that reproduced their decisions as closely as possible (4). Modeling judges' decisions requires no access to outcome information. Rather, one analyzes relations between the information available to the judge and the judge's decisions. In principle, if a judge weights variables with perfect consistency or reliability (that is, the same data always lead to the same decision), the model will always reproduce that judge's decisions. In practice, human decision-makers are not perfectly reliable and thus judge and model will sometimes disagree. Goldberg found that in cases of disagreement, the models were more often correct than the very judges on whom they were based. The perfect reliability of the models likely explains their superior performance in this and related studies (5).

Leli and Filskov studied the diagnosis of progressive brain dysfunction based on intellectual testing (6). A decision rule derived from one set of cases and then applied to a new sample correctly identified 83% of the new cases. Groups of inexperienced and experienced clinicians working from the same data correctly identified 63% and 58% of the new cases, respectively. In another condition, clinicians were also given the results of the actuarial analysis. Both the inexperienced and experienced clinicians showed improvement (68% and 75% correct identifications, respectively), but neither group matched the decision rule's 83% accuracy. The clinicians' improvement appeared to depend on the extent to which they used the rule.

Einhorn (7) studied the prediction of survival time following the initial diagnosis of Hodgkin's disease as established by biopsy. At the time of the study, survival time was negatively correlated with disease severity (Hodgkin's is now controllable). All of the 193 patients in the study subsequently died, thus tragically providing objective outcome information.

Three pathologists, one an internationally recognized authority, rated the patients' initial biopsy slides along nine histological dimensions they identified as relevant in determining disease severity and also provided a global rating of severity. Actuarial formulas were developed by examining relations between the pathologists' ratings and actual survival time on the first 100 cases, with the remaining 93 cases used for cross-validation and comparison. The pathologists' own judgments showed virtually no relation to survival time; cross-validated actuarial formulas achieved modest but significant relations. The study revealed more than an actuarial advantage. It also showed that the pathologists' ratings produced potentially useful information but that only the actuarial method, which was based on these ratings, tapped their predictive value.

Additional research. These three studies illustrate key features of a much larger literature on clinical versus actuarial judgment. First, the studies, like many others, met the previously specified conditions for a fair comparison.

Second, the three studies are representative of research outcomes. Eliminating research that did not protect sufficiently against inflated results for actuarial methods, there remain nearly 100 comparative studies in the social sciences. In virtually every one of these studies, the actuarial method has equaled or surpassed the clinical method, sometimes slightly and sometimes substantially (8–10). For example, in Watley and Vance's study on the prediction of college grades the methods tied (11); in Carroll *et al.*'s study on the prediction of parole violation, the actuarial method showed a slight to modest advantage (12); and in Wittman's study on the prediction of response to electroshock therapy, the actuarial method was correct almost twice as often as the clinical method (13).

The earlier comparative studies were often met with doubts about validity and generalization. It was claimed, for example, that the studies misrepresented the clinical method either by denying judges access to crucial data sources such as interviews, by using artificial tasks that failed to tap their areas of expertise, or by including clinicians of questionable experience or expertise.

The evidence that has accumulated over the years meets these challenges. First, numerous studies have examined judgments that are not artificial but common to everyday practice and for which special expertise is claimed. Examples include the three studies described above, which involved the differential between less serious and major psychiatric disorder, the detection of brain damage, and the prediction of survival time. Other studies have examined the diagnosis of medical versus psychiatric disorder (14); the description or characterization of personality (15); and the prediction of treatment outcome (16), length of psychiatric hospitalization (17), and violent behavior (18). These are decisions that general practitioners or specialists often address, and in a number of studies investigators did not introduce judgment tasks that clinicians then performed, but rather examined decisions already made in the course of everyday practice.

Other studies have provided clinicians or judges with access to preferred sources of information. Even in 1966, Sawyer was able to locate 17 comparisons between actuarial and clinical judgment based on the results of psychological testing and interview (8). Other investigators have allowed judges to collect whatever data they preferred in whatever manner they preferred. In Carroll *et al.*'s naturalistic study on the prediction of parolees' behavior after release, the parole board did not alter the data collection procedures (12). In Dawes's study on the prediction of graduate student performance, the admissions committee relied on the same data normally used to reach decisions (19). None of the 17 comparisons reviewed by Sawyer and neither the study by Carroll *et al.* nor Dawes favored clinical over actuarial judgment.

Nor has the outcome varied within or across studies involving judges at various levels of experience or expertise. In Goldberg's study novice and experienced MMPI interpreters performed similarly when using the clinical method and neither group surpassed the actuarial method, results parallel to those of Leli and Filskov in their study on the detection of brain damage (2, 6). Other studies on the detection and localization of brain damage have yielded similar results (20, 21). For example, Wedding found that neither clinicians with extensive experience interpreting the tests under study nor a nationally prominent neuropsychologist surpassed the overall accuracy of actuarial methods in determining the presence, location, and cause of brain damage (20).

The comparative studies often do not permit general conclusions about the superiority of one or another specific actuarial decision rule. Some studies, such as Goldberg's, do show application across settings, but much of the research has involved restricted samples. Investigators have been less interested in a specific procedure's range of application than in performing an additional test of the two methods and thereby extending the range of comparative studies.

The various studies can thus be viewed as repeated sampling from a universe of judgment tasks involving the diagnosis and prediction of human behavior. Lacking complete knowledge of the elements that constitute this universe, representativeness cannot be determined precisely. However, with a sample of about 100 studies and the same outcome obtained in almost every case, it is reasonable to conclude that the actuarial advantage is not exceptional but general and likely encompasses many of the unstudied judgment tasks.

Stated differently, if one poses the query: "Would an actuarial procedure developed for a particular judgment task (say, predicting academic success at my institution) equal or exceed the clinical method?", the available research places the odds solidly in favor of an affirmative reply. "There is no controversy in social science that shows such a large body of qualitatively diverse studies coming out so uniformly . . . as this one" (9, p. 373).

Possible exceptions. If fair comparisons consistently favor the actuarial method, one may then reverse the impetus of inquiry and ask whether there are certain circumstances in which the clinical judge might beat the actuary. Might the clinician attain superiority if given an informational edge? For example, suppose the clinician lacks an actuarial formula for interpreting certain interview results and must choose between an impression based on both interview and test scores and a contrary actuarial interpretation based on only the test scores. The research addressing this question has yielded consistent results (8, 10, 22). Even when given an information edge, the clinical judge still fails to surpass the actuarial method; in fact, access to additional information often does nothing to close the gap between the two methods.

It is not difficult to hypothesize other circumstances in which the clinical judge might improve on the actuarial method: (i) judgments mediated by theories and hence difficult or impossible to duplicate by statistical frequencies alone, (ii) select reversal of actuarial conclusions based on the consideration of rare events or utility functions that are not incorporated into statistical methods, and (iii) complex configural relations between predictive variables and outcome (23–25).

The potential superiority of theory-mediated judgments over conclusions reached solely on the basis of empirical frequencies may seem obvious to those in the "hard" sciences. Prediction mediated by theory is successful when the scientist has access to the major causal influences, possesses accurate measuring instruments to assess them, and uses a well-corroborated theory to make the transition from theory to fact (that is, when the expert has access to a specific model). Thus, although most comparative research in medicine favors the actuarial method overall, the studies that suggest a slight clinical advantage seem to involve circumstances in which judgments rest on firm theoretical grounds (26).

The typical theory that underlies prediction in the social sciences, however, satisfies none of the needed conditions. Prediction of treatment response or violent behavior may rest on psychodynamic theory that permits directly contradictory conclusions and lacks formal measurement techniques. Theory-mediated judgments may eventually provide an advantage within psychology and other social sciences, but the conditions needed to realize this possibility are currently but a distant prospect or hope.

Clinicians might be able to gain an advantage by recognizing rare events that are not included in the actuarial formula (due to their infrequency) and that countervail the actuarial conclusion. This possibility represents a variation of the clinical-actuarial approach, in which one considers the outcome of both methods and decides when to supersede the actuarial conclusion. In psychology this circumstance has come to be known as the "broken leg" problem, on the basis of an illustration in which an actuarial formula is highly successful in predicting an individual's weekly attendance at a movie but should be discarded upon discovering that the subject is in a cast with a fractured femur (1, 25). The clinician may beat the actuarial method if able to detect the rare fact and decide accordingly. In theory, actuarial methods can accommodate rare occurrences, but the practical obstacles are daunting. For example, the possible range of intervening events is infinite.

The broken leg possibility is easily studied by providing clinicians with both the available data and the actuarial conclusion and allowing them to use or countervail the latter at their discretion. The limited research examining this possibility, however, all shows that greater overall accuracy is achieved when clinicians rely uniformly on actuarial conclusions and avoid discretionary judgments (3, 8). When operating freely, clinicians apparently identify too many "exceptions," that is, the actuarial conclusions correctly modified are outnumbered by those incorrectly modified. If clinicians were more conservative in overriding actuarial conclusions they might gain an advantage, but this conjecture remains to be studied adequately.

Consideration of utilities raises a related possibility. Depending on the task, certain judgment errors may be more serious than others. For example, failure to detect a condition that usually remits spontaneously may be of less consequence than false identification of a condition for which risky treatment is prescribed. The adjustment of decision rules or cutting scores to reduce either false-negative or false-positive errors can decrease the procedure's overall accuracy but may still be justified if the consequences of these opposing forms of error are unequal. As such, if the clinician's counter-actuarial judgments, although less likely than the actuarial to be correct, were shown empirically to lower the probability of the rule's deliverances being correct (say, from 0.8 to 0.6), then in some contexts consideration of the joint probability-utility function might rationally reverse the action suggested by reliance on the formula alone. This procedure is formally equivalent to putting the clinician's judgment (as a new variable) into the actuarial equation, and more evidence on this process is needed to adequately appraise its impact. Here again, one cannot assume that the clinician's input helps. The available research suggests that formal inclusion of the clinician's input does not enhance the accuracy, nor necessarily the utility, of the actuarial formula and that informal or subjective attempts at adjustment can easily do more harm than good (8).

The clinician's potential capacity to capitalize on configural patterns or relations among predictive cues raises two related but separable issues that we will examine in order: the capacity to recognize configural relations and the capacity to use these observations to diagnose and predict. Certain forms of human pattern recognition still cannot be duplicated or equaled by artificial means. The recognition of visual patterns has challenged a generation of researchers in the field of artificial intelligence. Humans maintain a distinct advantage, for example, in the recognition of facial expressions. Human superiority also exists for language translation and for the invention of complex, deep-structure theories. Thus, for example, only the human observer may recognize a particular facial expression or mannerism (the float-like walk of certain schizophrenic patients) that has true predictive value. These observational abilities provide the potential for gathering useful (predictive) information that would otherwise be missed.

The possession of unique observational capacities clearly implies that human input or interaction is often needed to achieve maximal predictive accuracy (or to uncover potentially useful variables) but tempts us to draw an additional, dubious inference. A unique capacity to observe is not the same as a unique capacity to predict on the basis of integration of observations. As noted earlier, virtually any observation can be coded quantitatively and thus subjected to actuarial analysis. As Einhorn's study with pathologists and other research shows, greater accuracy may be achieved if the skilled observer performs this function and then steps aside, leaving the interpretation of observational and other data to the actuarial method (7).

FACTORS UNDERLYING THE SUPERIORITY OF ACTUARIAL METHODS

Contrasts between the properties of actuarial procedures and clinical judgment help to explain their differing success (27). First, actuarial procedures, unlike the human judge, always lead to the same conclusion for a given data set. In one study rheumatologists's and radiologists's reappraisals of cases they themselves had evaluated previously often resulted in different opinions (28). Such factors as fatigue, recent experience, or seemingly minor changes in the ordering of information or in the conceptualization of the case or task can produce random fluctuations in judgment (29). Random fluctuation decreases judgmental reliability and hence accuracy. For example, if the same data lead to the correct decision in one case but to a different, incorrect decision in the second case, overall accuracy will obviously suffer.

Perhaps more importantly, when properly derived, the mathematical features of actuarial methods ensure that variables contribute to conclusions based on their actual predictive power and relation to the criterion of interest. For example, decision rules based on multiple regression techniques include only the predictive variables and eliminate the nonpredictive ones, and they weight variables in accordance with their independent contribution to accurate conclusions. These achievements are essentially automatic with actuarial prediction but present formidable obstacles for human judges.

Research shows that individuals have considerable difficulty distinguishing valid and invalid variables and commonly develop false beliefs in associations between variables (30). In psychology and psychiatry, clinicians often obtain little or no information about the accuracy of their diagnoses and predictions. Consultants asked to predict violence may never learn whether their predictions were correct. Furthermore, clinicians rarely receive immediate feedback about criterion judgments (for example, diagnoses) of comparable validity to that physicians obtain when the pathologist reports at the end of a clinicopathological conference (31). Lacking sufficient or clear information about judgmental accuracy, it is problematic to determine the actual validity, if any, of the variables on which one relies. The same problem may occur if actuarial methods are applied blindly to new situations or settings without any performance checks.

In other circumstances, clinical judgments produce "self-fulfilling prophecies." Prediction of an outcome often leads to decisions that influence or bias that outcome (32). An anecdote illustrates this problem. A psychiatrist in a murder trial predicted future dangerousness, and the defendant was sentenced to death. While on death row the defendant acted violently, which appeared to support the psychiatrist's predictive powers. However, once sentenced to death this individual had little to lose; he may have acted differently had the psychiatrist's appraisal, and in turn the sentence, been different.

Additionally, known outcomes seem more predictable than they are in advance (33), and past predictions are mistakenly recalled as overly consistent with actual outcomes (34, 35). For example, Arkes et al. presented the same case materials to groups of physicians and asked them to assign probabilities to alternate diagnoses. When probabilities were assigned in foresight, each diagnosis was considered about equally likely. However, when the physicians were informed that one or another diagnosis had been established previously and they were then asked to state what initial diagnosis they likely would have made, they assigned the highest probability to whatever diagnosis they were told had been established (36). If one's view or recall of initial judgments is inadvertently shaped to fit whatever happens to occur, outcome information will have little or no corrective value.

The clinician is also exposed to a skewed sample of humanity and, short of exposure to truly representative samples, it may be difficult, if not impossible, to determine relations among variables. For example, suppose that about half of the adolescents appraised for a history of juvenile delinquency show subtle electroencephalographic (EEG) abnormalities. Based on these co-occurrences, the clinician may come to consider EEG abnormality a sign of delinquency or may conclude that delinquency is associated with brain dysfunction. In fact, clinicians have often postulated these relations (37).

One cannot determine, however, whether a relation exists unless one also knows whether the sign occurs more frequently among those with, versus those without, the condition. For example, to determine whether EEG abnormality is associated with delinquency, one must also know the frequency with which delinquents do not obtain EEG abnormalities and the frequencies with which nondelinquents do and do not obtain EEG abnormalities. Further, even should a valid relation exist, one cannot determine the sign's actual utility unless one knows: (i) how much more frequently it occurs when the condition is present than when it is absent and (ii) the frequency of the condition. For example, a sign that is slightly more common among those with the condition may be of little diagnostic utility. If the condition is infrequent, then positive identifications based on the sign's presence can even be wrong in most cases, for most individuals who display the sign will not have the condition. If 10% of brain-damaged individuals make a particular response on a psychological test and only 5% of normals, but nine of ten clinic patients are not brain-damaged, most patients who show the feature will not be brain-damaged.

In practice, the clinician is far more likely to evaluate individuals with significant problems than those without them, and this skewed exposure hinders attempts to make all of the needed comparisons. In fact, empirical study shows that EEG "abnormalities" are common among normal children and further suggests that the incidence of delinquency is no greater among those with than without neurological disorder (37, 38). The formation of such false beliefs is further compounded by a decided human tendency to overattend to information consistent with one's hypotheses and to underattend to contradictory information (39). The result is that mistaken beliefs or conclusions, once formed, resist counterevidence. Error is also fostered by a tendency to disregard frequency data and instead to form diagnostic judgments based on the perceived match between one or more of the presenting symptoms (for example, EEG abnormality) and some prototype or instance of the diagnostic category (delinquency) stored in memory (40, 41).

The same factors that hinder the discovery of valid relations also promote overconfidence in clinical judgment. When the clinician misinterprets contrary evidence as indicative of judgmental accuracy, confidence will obviously be inflated. Research shows that judges are typically more confident than their accuracy warrants (42). In one study demonstrating the upper range of misappraisal, most clinicians were quite confident in their diagnosis although not one was correct (43).

The difficulty in separating valid and invalid variables on the basis of clinical experience or judgment is demonstrated in many studies examining diagnostic or predictive accuracy (44). Research shows that clinical judgments based on interviews achieve, at best, negligible accuracy or validity (12). Other studies show that clinical judgments based on psychological test results may be of low absolute validity (6, 18, 20, 21). Although clinical interviews or psychological tests can produce useful information, the clinical judge often cannot distinguish what is useful from what is useless. In all studies cited immediately above, statistical analysis of the same data uncovered useful variables or enhanced predictive accuracy.

The optimal weighting of variables is a less important advantage of the statistical method than is commonly assumed. In fact, unit (equal) weights yield predictions that correlate highly with those derived from optimally weighted composites, the only provisos being that the direction in which each predictor is related to the criterion can be specified beforehand and the predictors not be negatively correlated with each other (5, 45–47). Further, optimal weights are specific to the population in which they were derived, and any advantage gained in one setting may be lost when the same method is applied in another setting. However, when optimal weighting adds meaningfully to predictive accuracy, the human judge is at a decided disadvantage. As Meehl (9, p. 372) has stated:

> Surely we all know that the human brain is poor at weighting and computing. When you check out at a supermarket, you don't eyeball the heap of purchases and say to the clerk, "Well it looks to me as if it's about $17.00 worth; what do you think?" The clerk adds it up. There are no strong arguments . . . from empirical studies . . . for believing that

human beings can assign optimal weights in equations subjectively or that they apply their own weights consistently.

It might be objected that this analogy, offered not probatively but pedagogically, presupposes an additive model that a proponent of configural judgment will not accept. Suppose instead that the supermarket pricing rule were, "Whenever both beef and fresh vegetables are involved, multiply the logarithm of 0.78 of the meat price by the square root of twice the vegetable price"; would the clerk and customer eyeball that any better? Worse, almost certainly. When human judges perform poorly at estimating and applying the parameters of a simple or component mathematical function, they should not be expected to do better when required to weight a complex composite of these variables.

LACK OF IMPACT AND SOURCES OF RESISTANCE

Research on clinical versus statistical judgment has had little impact on everyday decision making, particularly within its field of origin, clinical psychology. Guilmette et al.'s survey showed that most psychologists specializing in brain damage assessment prefer procedures for which actuarial methods are lacking over those for which actuarial formulas are available (48). The interview remains the sine qua non of entrance into mental health training programs and is required in most states to obtain a license to practice (49). Despite the studies that show that clinical interpretation of interviews may have little or no predictive utility, actuarial interpretation of interviews is rarely if ever used, although it is of demonstrated value.

Lack of impact is sometimes due to lack of familiarity with the scientific evidence. Some clinicians are unaware of the comparative research and do not even realize an issue exists. Others still refer to earlier studies and claim that the clinician was handicapped, unaware of the subsequent research that has rendered these arguments counterfactual.

Others who know the evidence may still dismiss it based on tendentiousness or misconception. Mental health professionals' education, training, theoretical orientations and identifications, and personal values may dictate against recognition of the actuarial advantage. Some psychologists, for example, believe that the use of a predictive equation dehumanizes their clients. The position overlooks the human costs of increased error that may result.

A common anti-actuarial argument, or misconception, is that group statistics do not apply to single individuals or events. The argument abuses basic principles of probability. Although individuals and events may exhibit unique features, they typically share common features with other persons or events that permit tallied observations or generalizations to achieve predictive power. An advocate of this anti-actuarial position would have to maintain, for the sake of logical consistency, that if one is forced to play Russian roulette a single time and is allowed to select a gun with one or five bullets in the chamber, the uniqueness of the event makes the choice arbitrary.

Finally, subjective appraisal may lead to inflated confidence in the accuracy of clinical judgment and the false impression that the actuarial method is inferior. Derivation and cross-validation of an actuarial method yields objective information on how well it does and does not perform (*50*). When the clinician reviews research that shows, for example, that the Goldberg Rule for the MMPI achieved 70% accuracy in a comparable setting and exceeded the performance of all 29 judges in the study, this may still seem to compare unfavorably to self-perceived judgmental powers. The immediacy and salience of clinical experience fosters the misappraisal. The clinician may recall dramatic instances in which his interpretations proved correct or in which he avoided error by countervailing an actuarial conclusion, failing to recognize or correctly tally counter instances.

Ultimately, then, clinicians must choose between their own observations or impressions and the scientific evidence on the relative efficacy of the clinical and actuarial methods. The factors that create difficulty in self-appraisal of judgmental accuracy are exactly those that scientific procedures, such as unbiased sampling, experimental manipulation of variables, and blind assessment of outcome, are designed to counter. Failure to accept a large and consistent body of scientific evidence over unvalidated personal observation may be described as a normal human failing or, in the case of professionals who identify themselves as scientific, plainly irrational.

APPLICATION OF ACTUARIAL METHODS: LIMITS, BENEFITS, AND IMPLICATIONS

The research reviewed in this article indicates that a properly developed and applied actuarial method is likely to help in diagnosing and predicting human behavior as well or better than the clinical method, even when the clinical judge has access to equal or greater amounts of information. Research demonstrating the general superiority of actuarial approaches, however, should be tempered by an awareness of limitations and needed quality controls.

First, although surpassing clinical methods, actuarial procedures are far from infallible, sometimes achieving only modest results. Second, even a specific procedure that proves successful in one setting should be periodically reevaluated within that setting and should not be applied to new settings mindlessly. Although theory and research suggest that the choice of predictive variables is often more important than their weighting, statistical techniques can be used to yield weights that optimize a procedure's accuracy when it is applied to new cases drawn from the same population. Moreover, accuracy can be easily monitored as predictions are made, and methods modified or improved to meet changes in settings and populations. Finally, efforts can be made to test whether new variables enhance accuracy.

When developed and used appropriately, actuarial procedures can provide various benefits. Even when actuarial methods merely equal the accuracy of clinical methods, they may save considerable time and expense. For example, each year millions of dollars and many hours of clinicians' valuable time are spent attempting to predict violent behavior. Actuarial prediction of violence is far less expensive and would free time for more productive activities, such as meeting unfulfilled therapeutic needs. When actuarial methods are not used as the sole basis for decisions, they can still serve to screen out candidates or options that would never be chosen after more prolonged consideration.

When actuarial methods prove more accurate than clinical judgment the benefits to individuals and society are apparent. Much would be gained, for example, by increased accuracy in the prediction of violent behavior and parole violation, the diagnosis of disorder, and the identification of effective treatment. Additionally, more objective determination of limits in knowledge or predictive power can prevent inadvertent harm. Should a confident but incorrect clinical diagnosis of Alzheimer's disease be replaced by a far more cautious statement, or even better by the correct conclusion, we would avoid much unnecessary human misery.

Actuarial methods are explicit, in contrast to clinical judgment, which rests on mental processes that are often difficult to specify. Explicit procedures facilitate informed criticism and are freely available to other members of the scientific community who might wish to replicate or extend research.

Finally, actuarial methods—at least within the domains discussed in this article—reveal the upper bounds in our current capacities to predict human behavior. An awareness of the modest results that are often achieved by even the best available methods can help to counter unrealistic faith in our predictive powers and our understanding of human behavior. It may well be worth exchanging inflated beliefs for an unsettling sobriety, if the result is an openness to new approaches and variables that ultimately increase our explanatory and predictive powers.

The argument that actuarial procedures are not available for many important clinical decisions does not explain failure to use existent methods and overlooks the ease with which such procedures can be developed for use in special settings. Even lacking any outcome information, it is possible to construct models of judges that will likely surpass their accuracy (*4, 5*). What is needed is the development of actuarial methods and a measurement assurance program that maintains control over both judgment strategies so that their operating characteristics in the field are known and an informed choice of procedure is possible. Dismissing the scientific evidence or lamenting the lack of available methods will prove much less productive than taking on the needed work.

References and Notes

1. P. E. Meehl, *Clinical Versus Statistical Prediction* (Univ. of Minnesota Press, Minneapolis, MN, 1954).
2. L. R. Goldberg, *Psychol. Monogr.*, 79 (no. 9) (1965).
3. ———, *Am. Psychol.* 23, 483 (1968).
4. ———, *Psychol. Bull.* 73, 422 (1970).
5. R. M. Dawes and B. Corrigan, *ibid.* 81, 95 (1974).
6. D. A. Leli and S. B. Filskov, *J. Clin. Psychol.* 40, 1435 (1984).
7. H. J. Einhorn, *Organ. Behav. Human Perform.* 7, 86 (1972).

8. J. Sawyer, *Psychol. Bull.* 66, 178 (1966).

9. P. E. Meehl, *J. Personal. Assess.* 50, 370 (1986).

10. W. M. Grove, who is conducting the first formal meta-analysis of studies in the social sciences and medicine (and a few other areas) that compared clinical and actuarial judgement, has reported a preliminary analysis in simple "box score" terms (paper presented at the Annual Meeting of the Minnesota Psychological Association, Minneapolis, 8 May 1986). The clinical method showed an advantage in only 6 of 117 studies. These exceptions mainly involved the medical field. The clinical advantage was generally slight and the rarity of this outcome across so many comparisons raises the possibility that some or most of these exceptions were statistical artifacts.

11. D. J. Watley and F. L. Vance, U.S. Office of Education Cooperative Research Project No. 2022 (University of Minnesota, Minneapolis, MN 1974).

12. J. S. Carroll *et al.*, *Law Society Rev.* 17, 199 (1982).

13. M. P. Wittman, *Elgin Pap.* 4, 20 (1941).

14. S. Oskamp, *Psychol. Monogr.* 76 (no. 28) (1962).

15. C. C. Halbower, thesis, University of Minnesota, Minneapolis, MN (1955).

16. F. Barron, *J. Consult. Clin. Psychol.* 17, 233 (1953).

17. H. W. Dunham and B. M. Meltzer, *Am. J. Sociology* 52, 123 (1946).

18. P. D. Werner, T. L. Rose, J. A. Yesavage, *J. Consult. Clin. Psychol.* 51, 815 (1983).

19. R. M. Dawes, *Am. Psychol.* 26, 180 (1971).

20. D. Wedding, *Clin. Neuropsychol.* V, 49 (1983).

21. D. A. Leli and S. B. Filskov, *J. Clin. Psychol.* 37, 623 (1981).

22. J. S. Wiggins, *Clin. Psychol. Rev.* 1, 3 (1981).

23. P. E. Meehl, *J. Counseling Psychol.* 6, 102 (1959).

24. ———, *Problems in Human Assessment*, D. N. Jackson and S. Messick, Eds. (McGraw-Hill, New York, 1976), pp. 594–599.

25. ———, *J. Counseling Psychol.* 4, 268 (1957).

26. W. B. Martin, P. C. Apostolakos, H. Roazen, *Am J. Med. Sci.* 240, 571 (1960).

27. L. R. Goldberg, in preparation.

28. J. F. Fries *et al., Arthritis Rheum.* 29, 1 (1986).

29. D. Kahneman and A. Tversky, *Am. Psychol.* 39, 341 (1984); K. R. Hammond and D. A. Summers, *Psychol. Rev.* 72, 215 (1965).

30. L. J. Chapman and J. P. Chapman, *J. Abnorm. Psychol.* 72 193 (1967); *ibid.* 74, 271 (1969).

31. P. E. Meehl, *Psychodiagnosis: Selected Papers* (Univ. of Minnesota Press, Minneapolis, MN 1973).

32. H. J. Einhorn and R. M. Hogarth, *Psychol. Rev.* 85, 395 (1978).

33. B. Fischhoff, *J. Exper. Psychol. Human Percep. Perform.* 1, 288 (1975).

34. ———, *New Directions for Methodology of Social and Behavioral Science*, R. A. Schweder and D. W. Fiske, Eds. (Jossey-Bass, San Francisco, CA, 1980), pp. 79–93.

35. B. Fischhoff and R. Beyth-Marom, *Organ. Behav. Human Perform.* 13, 1 (1975).

36. H. R. Arkes *et al.*, *J. Appl. Psychol.* 66, 252 (1981).

37. O. Spreen, *J. Nerv. Ment. Dis.* 169, 791 (1981).

38. A. J. Capute, E. F. L. Neidermeyer, F. Richardson, *Pediatrics* 41, 1104 (1968).

39. A. G. Greenwald, A. R. Pratkanis, M. R. Leippe, M. H. Baumgardner, *Psychol. Rev.* 93, 216(1986).

40. A. Tversky and D. Kahneman, *Cognit. Psychol.* 5, 207 (1973).

41. R. M. Dawes, *Clin. Psychol. Rev.* 6, 425 (1986).

42. B. Fischhoff, in *Judgment Under Uncertainty*, D. Kahneman, P. Slovic, A. Tversky, Eds. (Cambridge Univ. Press, New York, 1982), pp. 424–444.

43. D. Faust, K. Hart, T. J. Guiimctte, *J. Consul. Clin. Psychol.* 56, 578 (1988).

44. D. Faust, *The Limits of Scientific Reasoning* (Univ. of Minnesota Press, Minneapolis MN, 1984).

45. H. J. Einhorn and R. M. Hogarth, *Organ. Behav. Human Perform.* 13, 171 (1975).

46. H. Wainer, *Psychol. Bull.* 85, 267 (1978).

47. S. S. Wilks, *Psychometrika* 8, 23 (1938).

48. T. J. Guilmette, D. Faust, K. Hart, H. R. Arkes, *Arch. Clin. Neuropsychol.*, in press.

49. *Handbook of Licensing and Certification Requirements for Psychologists in North American* (American Association of State Psychology Boards, Washington, DC, August 1987).

50. R. M. Dawes, *Am. Psychol.* 34, 571 (1979).

51. We would like to thank S. Fienberg, B. Fischhoff, L. Furby, L. Goldberg W Grove, J. Kadane, and L. Yonce for their helpful comments and suggestions.

14

Why I Do Not Attend Case Conferences (Excerpt)

P. E. MEEHL

I HAVE FOR MANY YEARS been accustomed to the social fact that colleagues and students find some of my beliefs and attitudes paradoxical (some would, perhaps, use the stronger word *contradictory*). I flatter myself that this paradoxicality arises primarily because my views (like the world) are complex and cannot be neatly subsumed under some simple-minded undergraduate rubric (e.g., behavioristic, Freudian, actuarial, positivist, hereditarian). I find, for example, that psychologists who visit Minneapolis for the first time and drop in for a chat with me generally show clinical signs of mild psychic shock when they find a couch in my office and a picture of Sigmund Freud on the wall. Apparently one is not supposed to think or practice psychoanalytically if he understands something about philosophy of science, thinks that genes are important for psychology, knows how to take a partial derivative, enjoys and esteems Albert Ellis, or is interested in optimizing the prediction of behavior by the use of actuarial methods! I maintain that there is no unresolvable conflict between these things, but do not propose to argue that position here.

On the local scene, one manifestation of this puzzlement has come frequently to my attention and, given its nature, I think it likely that for each time I hear the question there are numerous other occasions when it is raised. In substance, the puzzle—sometimes complaint—among our graduate students goes like this: "Dr. Meehl sees patients on the campus and at the Nicollet Clinic, averaging, so we are told, around a dozen hours a week of psychotherapy. With the exception of a short period when he was APA president, he has been continuously engaged in the practice of psychotherapy for almost thirty years. It is well known that he not only thinks it important for a psychologist to work as a responsible professional with real-life clinical problems but, further, considers the purely 'theoretical' personality research of academic psychologists to be usually naive and unrealistic when the researcher is not a seasoned, practicing clinician. When he taught the introductory assessment course, the lectures were about evenly divided between rather abstract theoretical and methodological content (such as 'What is the nature of a phenotypic trait, considered as a class of related dispositions?' 'What precisely do we mean by the phrase *disease entity*?' 'What is *specific etiology*?') and practical, down-to-earth material (such as 'How do you handle a patient's questions about yourself?' 'What do you do with the patient who in the initial interview sits passively expecting you to cross-examine him?' 'How do you assess the severity of a depression, especially with respect to suicidal potential?' 'How do you tell the difference between an acting-out neurotic and a true psychopath?'). He took the trouble to become a (non-grandfathered) diplomate of ABPP although in his academic position this had little advantage either of economics or of status. When he was chairman of the Psychology Department he had a policy of not hiring faculty to teach courses in the clinical and personality area unless they were practitioners and either had the ABPP diploma or intended to get it. He has been an (unsuccessful) advocate of a special doctorate in clinical psychology, the Ps.D., which would dispense with some of the medieval academic requirements for the Ph.D. degree and would permit a much more intensive and diversified clinical training for persons aiming at full-time work as practitioners in the profession. Meehl lists himself in the Yellow Section of the phone book and is a member of such outfits as the American Academy of Psychotherapists, the American Academy of Psychoanalysis, and the Institute for Advanced Study in Rational Psychotherapy. On all these counts, it seems evident that Meehl is 'clinically oriented,' that his expressed views about the importance of professional practice are sincere rather than pro forma. It is therefore puzzling to us students, and disappointing to us after having been stimulated by him as a lecturer, to find that he almost never shows up in the clinical settings where we take our clerkship and internship. We never see Dr. Meehl at a case conference. Why is this?"

This understandable puzzlement was the precipitating cause of my writing the present paper, partly because it becomes tiresome to explain this mystery repeatedly to baffled, well-meaning students, but also because responding to the puzzlement provides an occasion for some catharsis and, I hope, for making a constructive contribution to the field. Accordingly the first portion of the paper will be highly critical and aggressively polemic. (If you want to shake people up, you have to raise a little hell.) The second part, while not claiming grandiosely to offer a definitive solution to the problem, proposes some directions of thinking and "experimenting" that might lead to a significant improvement over current conditions.

The main reason I rarely show up at case conferences is easily stated: The intellectual level is so low that I find them boring, sometimes even offensive. Why the level of a psychiatric case conference is usually so mediocre, by contrast with conferences in internal medicine or neurology—both of which I have usually found stimulating and illuminating—is not known, and it is a topic worthy of research. I do not believe my attitude is as unusual as it may seem. I think I am merely more honest than most clinical psychologists about admitting my reaction. Witness the fact that the staff conferences in the Medical School where I work are typically attended by only a minority of the faculty—usually those who *must* be there as part of their paid responsibility, or who have some other special reason (such as invitation) for attending a particular one. If the professional faculty found them worthwhile, they wouldn't be so reluctant to spend their time that way. Pending adequate research on "What's the matter with the typical case conference," I present herewith some clinical impressions by way of explanation, and some constructive suggestions for improvement. My impressionistic list of explanations constitutes the "destructive criticism" portion of this paper.

WHAT'S WRONG?

1. *Buddy-buddy syndrome.* In one respect the clinical case conference is no different from other academic group phenomena such as committee meetings, in that many intelligent, educated, sane, rational persons seem to undergo a kind of intellectual deterioration when they gather around a table in one room. The cognitive degradation and feckless vocalization characteristic of committees are too well known to require comment. Somehow the group situation brings out the worst in many people, and results in an intellectual functioning that is at the lowest common denominator, which in clinical psychology and psychiatry is likely to be pretty low.

2. *"All evidence is equally good."* This absurd idea perhaps arises from the "groupy," affiliative tendency of behavioral scientists in "soft" fields like clinical, counseling, personality, and social psychology. It seems that there are many professionals for whom committee work and conferences represent part of their social, intellectual, and erotic life. If you take that "groupy" attitude, you tend to have a sort of mush-headed approach which says that everybody in the room has something to contribute (absurd on the face of it, since most persons don't usually have anything worthwhile to contribute about anything, especially if it's the least bit complicated). In order to maintain the fiction that everybody's ideas are worthwhile, it is necessary to lower the standards for what is evidential. As a result, a casual anecdote about one's

senile uncle as remembered from childhood is given the same group interest and intellectual respect that is accorded to the citation of a high-quality experimental or field-actuarial study. Or a casual impression found in the nurses' notes is given the same weight as the patient's MMPI code. Nobody would be prepared to defend this rationally in a seminar on research methods, but we put up with it in our psychiatric case conferences.

3. *Reward everything—gold and garbage alike.* The tradition of exaggerated tenderness in psychiatry and psychology reflects our "therapeutic attitude" and contrasts with that of scholars in fields like philosophy or law, where a dumb argument is *called* a dumb argument, and he who makes a dumb argument can expect to be slapped down by his peers. Nobody ever gives anybody negative reinforcement in a psychiatric case conference. (Try it once—you will be heard with horror and disbelief.) The most inane remark is received with joy and open arms as part of the groupthink process. Consequently the educational function, for either staff or students, is prevented from getting off the ground. Any psychologist should know that part of the process of training or educating is to administer differential reinforcement for good versus bad, effective versus ineffective, correct versus incorrect behaviors. If *all* behavior is rewarded by friendly attention and nobody is ever nonreinforced (let alone punished!) for talking foolishly, it is unlikely that significant educational growth will take place.

A corollary of the "reward everything" policy with respect to evidence and arguments is a substantive absurdity, namely, everyone is right—or at least, nobody is *wrong*. The group impulse toward a radical democratization of qualifications and opinions leads almost to denying the Law of Noncontradiction. A nice quotation from the statistician M. G. Kendall is apposite: "A friend of mine once remarked to me that if some people asserted that the earth rotated from East to West and others that it rotated from West to East, there would always be a few well-meaning citizens to suggest that perhaps there was something to be said for both sides and that maybe it did a little of one and a little of the other; or that the truth probably lay between the extremes and perhaps it did not rotate at all" (Kendall, 1949, p. 115) .

4. *Tolerance of feeble inferences (e.g., irrelevancies).* The ordinary rules of scientific inference, and reliance upon general principles of human development, which everybody takes for granted in a neurology staff conference, are somehow forgotten in a psychiatric case conference. This is perhaps due to the fact that the psychiatrist has had to learn to live with the sorry state of his specialty after having had training in the more scientific branches of medicine, with the result that once having learned to live this way, he assumes that the whole set of rules about how to think straight have to be junked, so that logic, statistics, experiments, scientific evidence, and so on don't apply. I have heard professionals say things in a psychiatric staff conference which I am certain they would never have said about a comparable problem in a conference room one floor below (neurology service). Example: In a case conference involving a differential diagnosis between schizophrenia and anxiety reaction in a pan-anxious patient that any well-read clinician would easily recognize as a classical case of the Hoch-Polatin "pseudoneurotic schizophrenia" syndrome (Hoch and Polatin, 1949; Meehl, 1964) the psychiatrist presiding at the conference argued that the patient was probably latently or manifestly schizophrenic. He argued thus partly because—in addition to her schizophrenic MMPI profile—she had a vivid and sustained hallucinatory experience immediately preceding her entry into the hospital. She saw a Ku Klux Klansman standing in the living room, in full regalia, eyeing her malignantly and making threatening gestures with a knife, this hallucination lasting for several minutes. Since hallucinations of this sort are textbook symptoms of a psychotic break in ego function (reality testing), it seemed pretty clear to the presiding psychiatrist (and myself) that this would have to be considered evidence—not dispositive, but pretty strong—for our schizophrenic diagnosis as against the anxiety-neurosis alternative. At this point one of the nurses said, "I don't see why Dr. Koutsky and Dr. Meehl are laying emphasis upon this Ku Klux Klansman. After all, I remember having an imaginary companion when I was a little girl." Now suppose that this well-meaning nurse, whose remark was greeted with the usual respectful attention to "a contribution," had been attending a case conference on the neurology service. And suppose that in attempting a differential diagnosis of spinal cord tumor the presiding neurologist had offered in evidence the fact that the patient was incontinent of urine. It would never occur to this nurse to advance, as a counterargument, the fact that she used to wet her pants when she was a little girl. (If she did advance such a stupid argument on neurology, my colleague Dr. A. B. Baker—who has "standards"—would tromp on her with his hobnail boots, and she would never make *that* mistake again.) But somehow when she gets into a psychiatric case conference she undergoes a twenty-point decrement in functional IQ score, so as to forget how to distinguish between different degrees of pathology or between phenomena occurring at different developmental levels. Equating a childhood imaginary companion with an adult's experiencing a clear and persisting visual hallucination of a Ku Klux Klansman is of course just silly—but in a psychiatry case conference no one would be so tactless as to point this out.

5. *Failure to distinguish between an inclusion test and an exclusion test*: In a differential diagnosis between schizophrenia and manic-depressive psychosis, a psychology trainee argues against schizophrenia on the ground that the patient does not have delusions or hallucinations with clear sensorium. Of course this is just plain uninformed, because delusions and hallucinations are among Bleuler's "accessory" symptoms, present in some schizophrenics but not all, and they are *not* part of the indicator family that "defines" the disease (Bleuler, 1911 as reprinted 1950). Some American clinicians (not I) would hold that delusions and hallucinations with clear sensorium are so rare in uncomplicated manic depression that when *present* they could be used as a quasi-exclusion test against that diagnosis. But since many schizophrenics—not only borderline cases of "pseudoneurotic schizophrenia" but those cases known in the present nomenclature as "schizophrenia, chronic undifferentiated" and "schizophrenia, acute episode" and "schizophrenia, simple type"—are without these particular accessory symptoms, the trainee's argument is without merit. Psychodynamically,

delusions and hallucinations are among the so-called restitutional symptoms of the disorder, as contrasted with the regressive ones. Depending upon the form and stage of the disease, restitutional symptoms may or may not be in evidence. That delusions and hallucinations with unclouded sensorium are absent in many schizophrenics is not an idiosyncratic clinical opinion of mine. It is a theory found in all of the textbooks, it is in the standard nomenclature, it is in Kraepelin and Bleuler, who defined the entity "schizophrenia." There is no justification for utilizing the *absence* of these accessory symptoms as an exclusion test. Neither semantic nor empirical grounds exist for this practice. But when I point this out forcefully, the trainee looks at me as if I were a mean ogre.

6. *Failure to distinguish between mere consistency of a sign and differential weight of a sign.* Once the differential diagnosis has been narrowed to two or three nosological possibilities, it is inappropriate to cite in evidence signs or symptoms which are nondifferentiating as between them. This is so obvious a mistake that one thinks it would never happen; but some clinicians do it regularly. In distinguishing *between* a sociopathic personality, an acting-out neurotic delinquent, and a garden-variety "sociological" criminal, it is fallacious to argue that the patient was a marked underachiever or a high school dropout, in spite of high IQ, as grounds for a diagnosis of sociopathic personality, because, whereas this sign is a correlate of the sociopathic diagnosis, we have now narrowed the nosological range to three possibilities, each of which is a correlate of academic underachievement, so that this sign has lost its diagnostic relevancy at this stage of the investigation. This illustrates one of the generic features of case conferences in psychiatry, namely, the tendency to mention things that don't make any difference one way or the other. The idea seems to be that as long as something is true, or is believed to be true, or is possibly true, it is worth mentioning! In other medical specialties in order to be worth mentioning the statement must not only be true but be *differentially* relevant, i.e., it must argue for one diagnosis, outlook, or treatment, rather than another.

7. *Shift in the evidential standard, depending upon whose ox is being gored.* A favorite tactic of case conference gamesmanship is to use a "double standard of morals" on the weight of the evidence. When you are putting your own diagnostic case, you permit indirect inferences (mediated by weak theoretical constructions and psychodynamic conclusions); then when the other fellow is making his case for a different diagnosis, you become superscientific and behavioristic, making comments like "Well, of course, all we actually know is the *behavior.*" You *don't really* know "the behavior" in the sense it is usually discussed in the staff conference, since even phenotypic characterizations are almost invariably summary-type statements with a large component of sampling inference at least involved. Further, to this sampling inference we usually conjoin theory-mediated inferences, relying on extrapolations from other contexts as justification for weighting some sources of data more heavily than others. As a result this superbehaviorism is not even intellectually honest.

The opposite of this ("simpleminded") error is, of course, the failure to connect theoretical constructs with behavioral data, actual or *possible*. This is the error of the "muddleheaded."

Projective tests lend themselves particularly well to this, since trends, forces, and structures that are *latent* (a perfectly legitimate metaconcept) cannot be operationally defined, hence offer unusual temptation for a muddlehead to use them without regard for any kind of corroborative evidence, direct or indirect, tight or probabilistic.

8. *Ignorance (or repression) of statistical logic.* A whole class of loosely related errors made in the clinical case conference arises from forgetting (on the part of the psychologist) or never having learned (in the case of the psychiatrist and social worker) certain elementary statistical or psychometric principles. Examples are the following:

a. *Forgetting Bayes' Theorem.* One should always keep in mind that there is a relationship between prior probability (e.g., the base rate P of a certain diagnosis or dynamic configuration in the particular clinic population) and the increment in probability contributed by a certain diagnostic symptom or sign. If the prior probability is extremely low, you don't get very much mileage out of a moderately strong sign or symptom. On the other hand, when the prior probability is extremely high, you get mileage out of an additional fact, but you don't really "need it much," so to speak. The considerations advanced by Meehl and Rosen (1955) apply in a clinical case conference just as strongly as they do in a research design involving psychometrics.

b. *Forgetting about unreliability when interpreting score changes or difference scores* (e.g., on subtests of the WAIS). Despite the mass of adverse research and psychometric theoretical criticism of the practice of overinterpreting small difference scores on unreliable subtests (which are of doubtful validity for the alleged noncognitive traits anyway!), one still hears this kind of "evidence" pressed in case conferences. Who cares whether the patient "did well on the Block Design subtest but seemed to enjoy it less than Picture Arrangement"?

c. *Reliance upon inadequate behavior samples for trait attribution.* Sometimes the inadequacy is *qualitative*, in the sense that the context in which the behavior was sampled is in some way unusual or atypical for the population or for this particular individual; more commonly, the error is simply one of believing that you can estimate the proportion of white marbles in an urn after sampling only a couple of marbles. This error is particularly serious because in addition to the numerical smallness of the samples of behavior adduced as the basis for trait attribution, we have almost no control over the conscious or unconscious selection factor that has determined which behavior chunk was noticed, was remembered, and is now reproduced for tendentious purposes. It is obvious that over a period of several hours or days of unsystematic observation, practically any human being is likely to emit at least a few behaviors which can be subsumed under almost any trait in the phenotypic or genotypic lexicon.

d. *Inadequate consideration of whether and when the (fact → fact) linkage is stronger or weaker than the (multiple-fact → diagnosis → fact) linkage.* It seems there are some cases in which the best way to infer to a certain fact, whether postdictive or predictive, is by relying upon its correlation with certain other relatively atomistic facts with which, from previous experience or research, the inferred fact is known to be correlated. In other cases it appears that a set of facts which qualitatively does not seem related to the fact of interest is related to it rather strongly because this first set of facts known to us converges powerfully upon a taxonomic decision (whether formal diagnosis, environmental mold, personality "type," or dynamic configuration). When that taxonomic decision has been made with high confidence, certain other individual atomistic facts or dispositions may follow with reasonably high confidence. It is a mistake to assume, without looking into the matter, that one or the other of these approaches is "obviously" the way to proceed most powerfully. (Cf. Meehl, 1960)

e. *Failing to understand probability logic as applied to the single case.* This disability is apparently endemic to the psychiatric profession and strangely enough is also found among clinical psychologists in spite of their academic training in statistical reasoning. There are still tough, unsolved philosophical problems connected with the application of frequencies to individual cases. But we cannot come to grips with those problems, or arrive at a pragmatic decision policy in staff conferences, unless we have gotten beyond the blunders characteristically enunciated by clinicians who are not familiar with the literature on this subject from Lundberg (1941) and Sarbin (1942) through Meehl (1945a, 1954a, 1956a, 1956b, 1956c, 1957, 1959a, 1959b, 1960, Meehl and Dahlstrom, 1960) to recent contributors like Goldberg (1968, 1970), Sawyer (1966), Kleinmuntz (1968, 1969), Einhorn (1970, 1972), Pankoff and Roberts (1968), Marks and Sines (1969), Alker and Hermann (1971), Mirabile, Houck, and Glueck (1971); see also footnote 4 in Livermore, Malmquist, and Meehl, 1968 (at page 76), and footnotes 8 and 9 in Meehl, 1970b (at pp. 8–9), and references cited thereat. The vulgar error is the cliché that "We aren't dealing with groups, we are dealing with this individual case." It is doubtful that one can profitably debate this cliché in a case conference, since anyone who puts it quite this way is not educable in ten minutes. He who wishes to reform the thinking in case conferences must constantly reiterate the elementary truth that if you depart in your clinical decision making from a well-established or even moderately well-supported empirical frequency—whether it is based upon psychometrics, life-history material, rating scales or whatever—your departure may save a particular case from being misclassified predictively or therapeutically; but that such departures are, prima facie, counterinductive, so that a decision *policy* of this kind is almost certain to have a cost that exceeds its benefits. The research evidence strongly suggests that a policy of making such departures, except very sparingly, will result in the misclassifying of other cases that would have been correctly classified had such nonactuarial departures been forbidden; it also suggests that more of this second kind of misclassification will occur than will be compensated for by the improvement in the first kind (Meehl, 1957). That there are occasions when you should use your head instead of the formula is perfectly clear. But which occasions they are is most emphatically *not* clear. What *is* clear on the available empirical data is that these occasions are much rarer than most clinicians suppose.

9. *Inappropriate task specification.* Nobody seems very clear about which kinds of tasks are well performed in the case

conference context and which would be better performed in other ways. There are some cognitive jobs for which it seems doubtful that the case conference is suitable. I myself think that the commonest form of this mistake is the spinning out of complicated psychodynamics which are explained in terms of the life history and which in turn are used to explain the present aberrant behavior, on evidence which is neither quantitatively nor qualitatively adequate to carry out such an ambitious enterprise (assuming, as I believe, that the enterprise is sometimes feasible in the present state of psychology). Any psychologist who has practiced long-term, intensive, "uncovering" psychotherapy knows that there are psychodynamic puzzles and paradoxes which remain in his mind after listening to fifty or a hundred hours of the patient's productions. Yet this same psychotherapist may undergo a strange metamorphosis when he enters the case conference context, finding himself pronouncing (sometimes rather dogmatically) about the psychodynamics of the presented patient, on the basis of ten minutes' exposure to the patient during the conference, plus some shoddy, scanty "material" presented by the resident and social worker (based in turn upon a relatively small total time of contact with the patient and interviewing that *on the psychotherapist's own usual criteria* would be considered "superficial").

Part of the difficulty here lies in American psychiatry's emphasis upon psychodynamics at the expense of nosology. A case conference *can* be, under some circumstances, an appropriate place to clarify the nosological or taxonomic issue provided that the participants have bothered to learn some nosology, and that the clinicians mainly concerned with the patient have obtained the relevant clinical data. But since diagnosis is devalued, the prestigious thing to do is to contribute psychodynamic ideas to the conference, so we try to do that, whether or not the quality and quantity of the material available to us is adequate to such an enterprise, which it usually isn't.

10. *Asking pointless questions.* Participants in a case conference frequently ask questions the answers to which make no conceivable difference, or only the most negligible difference, to the handling of the case. I have often thought that the clinician in charge of the case conference should emulate a professor of law from whom I took a course in equitable remedies, David Bryden. When a law student advanced a stupid argument about the case being discussed, he would respond with a blank stare and the question "And therefore?" This would usually elicit some further response from the student (attempting to present the next link in an argumentative chain), but this shoring-up job would in turn be greeted by the same blank stare, the same inquisitorial "And therefore?" I daresay Professor Bryden made the law students nervous; but he also forced them to *think*. I suspect that one who persisted in asking the question "And therefore?" every time somebody made a half-baked contribution to the case conference would wreak havoc, but it might be an educational experience for all concerned.

11. *Ambiguity of professional roles.* When the conference is not confined to one of the three professions in the team, there may arise a sticky problem about roles. For example, in mixed-group conferences I note a tendency to assume that the psychologist's job should be to present the psychometrics and that he is only very gingerly and tentatively to talk about

anything else. I think this attitude is ridiculous. I can conduct a diagnostic interview or take a history as well as most psychiatrists, and nonpsychometric data are just as much part of my subject matter as they are of the psychiatrist's. Similarly, if a physician has developed clinical competence in interpreting Rorschachs or MMPI profiles or practicing behavior modification, I listen to what he says without regard to trade-union considerations. By the same token, if I discern that a patient walks with the "schizophrenic float" or exhibits paranoid hypervigility or sociopathic insouciance, I feel free to offer this clinical observation in evidence.

12. *Some common fallacies.* Not all of these fallacies are clearly visible in case conferences, and none of them is confined to the case conference, being part of the general collection of sloppy thinking habits with which much American psychiatry is infected. I have given some of them special "catchy" names, admittedly for propaganda purposes but also as an aid to memory.

a. *Barnum effect.* Saying trivial things that are true of practically all psychiatric patients, or sometimes of practically all human beings—this is the Barnum effect. It is not illuminating to be told that a mental patient has intrapsychic conflicts, ambivalent object relations, sexual inhibitions, or a damaged self-image! (Cf. Meehl, 1956c; Sundberg, 1955; Tallent, 1958; Forer, 1949; Ulrich, Stachnik, and Stainton, 1963; and Paterson in Blum and Balinsky, 1951, p. 47, and Dunnette, 1957, p. 223.)

b. *Sick-sick fallacy* ("pathological set"). There is a widespread tendency for people in the mental health field to identify their personal ideology of adjustment, health, and social role, and even to some extent their religious and political beliefs and values, with freedom from disease or aberration. Therefore if we find somebody very unlike us in these respects we see him as being sick. The psychiatric establishment officially makes a point of never doing this and then proceeds to do it routinely. Thus, for example, many family psychiatrists have a stereotype of what the healthy family ought to be; and if anybody's family life does not meet these criteria, this is taken as a sign of pathology. Other stereotypes may exist in connection with the "genital character," the person who "fulfills his potential," and so on. Don't let this one pass by, saying that we already know about it! We *do* know about it "officially," but the point is that many people in the mental health field are not very clear about the question in their own thinking. Example: Despite the Kinsey research, some psychiatrists of sexually conservative tastes are likely to overinterpret forms of sexual behavior such as cunnilingus or fellatio as symptomatic of psychopathology, even though the data indicate that mouth-genital contacts have occurred in the *majority* of members of Kinsey's "sophisticated" classes. In my opinion it is almost impossible to say anything clinically significant about a patient on the basis of a history of cunnilingus or fellatio unless one knows a good deal about the motivations. That is to say, it is the motivational basis and not the act which is clinically relevant.

c. *"Me too"* fallacy (the unconsidered allegation that "anyone would do that"). This is the opposite of the overpathologizing "sick-sick" fallacy, and one might therefore suppose that clinicians fond of committing the "sick-sick" fallacy would be unlikely to commit the "me too" fallacy. I have no quantitative data on this, but my impression is that the same clinicians have a tendency to commit both. Perhaps the common property is not conservatism or liberalism in diagnosing pathology but mere sloppy-headedness. The sloppy-headed clinician unconsciously selects, in terms of his personal biases and values, which things he is going to look upon as "terribly sick" and which things he is going to look upon as "perfectly okay" (normal). The example I gave earlier of the nurse who tried to mitigate the diagnostic significance of a patient's visual hallucination by telling us that as a child she had imaginary companions is an example of the "me too" fallacy, although it is compounded with various other errors, such as false analogy and the failure to take developmental stages into account.

I was first forcibly struck with the significance and seductiveness of the "me too" fallacy when I was a graduate student in clinical training. One of my first diagnostic workups was with a girl in late adolescence (a classic Cleckley psychopath: Cleckley, 1964) who was brought in for evaluation on a district court order. She had a considerable history of minor acting out in the form of truancy, impulsive behavior, and running away from home; but the problem which brought her in was that she had "in a fit of pique" hit her foster mother over the head with a lamp base, as a result of which the foster mother sustained a fracture and concussion. One important thing to assess, from the standpoint of the court's inquiry, was the extent to which the patient could exert behavioral control over her impulses. In the 1940's, the patients on our psychiatric service did not have continuous access to their cigarettes but could only smoke at certain times. One of the times when everybody was allowed to come to the nurses' cage to get a cigarette was, let us say, at 3:00 P.M. This particular patient came to the cage around a half hour early and said she wanted her cigarette. The charge nurse told her kindly but firmly that it wasn't quite time yet. The patient insisted that she wanted a cigarette right now and that she didn't want to wait a half hour. The nurse repeated that it wasn't time yet but that she could have a cigarette at 3 P.M. Whereupon the patient began pounding with her fists on the nurse's cage and then flung herself on the floor where she kicked and screamed like a small child having a tantrum. When this episode was discussed in the weekly conference with the junior medical students, the student physician told Dr. Hathaway, the clinical psychologist presiding at the conference, that he didn't see any point in "making a lot out of this tantrum" because, "after all, anybody might act the same way under the circumstances." The dialogue continued thus:

DR. HATHAWAY: "How do you mean 'under the circumstances'?"

MEDICAL STUDENT: "Well, she wanted a cigarette and it's kind of a silly rule."

DR. HATHAWAY: "Let's assume it's a silly rule, but it is a rule which she knows about, and she knows that the tantrum is probably going to deprive her of some privileges on the station. Would you act this way under the circumstances?"

MEDICAL STUDENT: "Sure I would."

DR. HATHAWAY: "Now, think a moment; *would* you, really?"

MEDICAL STUDENT: "Well, perhaps I wouldn't, actually." (thoughtful)

And of course he wouldn't. Point: If you find yourself minimizing a recognized sign or symptom of pathology by thinking, "Anybody would do this," think again. *Would* just anybody do it? Behavioristically speaking, what is the actual objective probability of a mentally healthy person behaving just this way? Or, from the introspective point of view, would you *really* do or say what the patient did? Obviously it is *not* the same to say that you might feel an impulse or have a momentary thought similar to that of the patient. The question is, in the case of cognitive distortions, whether you would seriously entertain or believe the thought; or, in the case of overt acting-out conduct, whether you would act out the impulse, having experienced it. You will find that many times, when your initial tendency is to mitigate the symptom's significance in this way, a closer look will convince you that the behavior or belief is actually a serious aberration in reality testing or normal impulse control.

d. *Uncle George's pancakes fallacy.* This is a variant of the "me too" fallacy, once removed; rather than referring to what anybody would do or what you yourself would do, you call to mind a friend or relative who exhibited a sign or symptom similar to that of the patient. For example, a patient does not like to throw away leftover pancakes and he stores them in the attic. A mitigating clinician says, "Why, there is nothing so terrible about that—I remember good ole Uncle George from my childhood, *he* used to store uneaten pancakes in the attic." The proper conclusion from such a personal recollection is, of course, not that the patient is mentally well but that good ole Uncle George—whatever may have been his other delightful qualities—was mentally aberrated. The underlying premise in this kind of fallacious argument seems to be the notion that none of one's personal friends or family could have been a psychiatric case, partly because the individual in question was not hospitalized or officially diagnosed and partly because (whereas other people may have crazy friends and relatives) *I* obviously have never known or been related to such persons in my private life. Once this premise is made explicit, the fallacy is obvious.

e. *Multiple Napoleons fallacy* (the Doctrine of Unreal Realities). This is the mush-headed objection that "Well, it may not be 'real' to us, but it's 'real' to him." (This arises partly from the relativism cultivated by American education or, at a more sophisticated level, from extreme instrumentalism in one's philosophy of science.) It is unnecessary to resolve the deep technical questions of realism and instrumentalism before one can recognize a distinction between reality and delusion as clinical categories. So far as I am aware, even Dewey, Vaihinger, and Heidegger would allow that a man who believes he is Napoleon or has invented a perpetual-motion machine is crazy. If I think the moon is made of green cheese and you think it's a piece of rock, one of us must be wrong. To point out that the aberrated cognitions of a delusional patient "seem real to him" is a complete waste of time. Furthermore, there is some research evidence and considerable clinical experience to suggest that the reality feeling of delusions and hallucinations does differ at least quantitatively, and some investigators allege even qualitatively, from the reality feeling of normal people or from that of the patient regarding familiar nondistorted objects. Thus the statement "It is reality to him," which is philosophically either trivial or false, is also clinically misleading. Nevertheless I have actually heard clinicians in conference invoke this kind of notion on quasi-philosophical grounds, as if to suggest that since nobody knows for certain what reality is, we have no justification for invoking the distinction between the real and the imaginary in assessing a patient.

    f. *Crummy criterion fallacy.* It is remarkable that eighteen years after the publication of Cronbach and Meehl's "Construct Validity in Psychological Tests" (1955) and fourteen years after the beautiful methodological development by Campbell and Fiske (1959) and a philosophical treatment by Meehl which has been widely reprinted (1959b; see also Loevinger, 1957), many clinical psychology trainees (and some full professors) persist in a naive undergraduate view of psychometric validity. (I mention "contemporary" writers—the point about construct validity was made clearly enough by several authors cited in the Cronbach-Meehl paper, and by the great Spearman, whom we unaccountably failed to mention. It reflects on the shoddy state of psychology that a *graduate* student recently asked me, "Who is this Spearman?") Repeatedly in a clinical case conference one finds psychologists seeing their task as "explaining away" the psychometrics rather than "explaining them" in the sense of genuinely integrating them with the interview, life-history, and ward-behavior material on the patient. It rarely occurs to anyone to feel that he must explain away the intelligence test: the psychiatrist has come to recognize that a successful "bootstraps operation" (Cronbach and Meehl, 1955—see p. 11 above) has been achieved in the measurement of intellect. We do not ordinarily say, "The social worker thought Johnny was dumb, but he has a WISC IQ of 160; isn't it a shame that the test missed again!" But if an MMPI profile indicates strongly that the patient is profoundly depressed or has a schizoid makeup, this psychometric finding is supposed to agree with the global impression of a first-year psychiatric resident, and if it doesn't the psychologist typically adopts a posture of psychometric apology. Now this is silly. Even from the armchair, we start with the fact that an MMPI profile represents the statistical distillation of 550 verbal responses which is considerably in excess of what the clinician has elicited from the patient in most instances, even assuming that the clinician knows how to combine the information he does elicit in an optimal fashion—a proposition at least arguable. Surely there are cases where the psychometrics disagree with the interviewer's clinical impression and yet are at least as likely to be correct as the interviewer, particularly if he is a relatively fresh practitioner in the early stages of his clinical training.

    The methodological point is so obvious that it is almost embarrassing to explain it, but I gather it is still necessary. Point: If a psychometric device has been empirically constructed and cross-validated in reliance upon the average statistical correctness of a series of clinical judgments, including judgments by well-trained clinicians as well as ill-trained ones, there is a pretty good probability that the score pattern reflects

the patient's personality structure and dynamics better than does the clinical judgment of an individual contributor to the case conference—even if he is a seasoned practitioner, and a fortiori if he is a clinical fledgling. The old-fashioned concept of the "criterion," which applies literally in *forecasting* contexts (such as predicting how much life insurance a person will sell from the insurance salesman key of the SVIB), is not the only appropriate model for the clinical case conference except when we are explicitly engaged in pragmatic forecasting tasks (e.g., predicting whether the patient will be a continuer or a dropout in outpatient psychotherapy, predicting whether he will respond favorably to Stelazine or EST). It is necessary to be clear about the clinical *task*. Sometimes the clinical task is comparable to the task of the industrial or military psychologist or the educational psychologist trying to select applicants for engineering school who will not flunk out. Most of the time, however, the (alleged) purpose of the clinical case conference is to attain a psychodynamic, nosological, and etiological understanding of the individual patient. I do not enter here into the controversy whether this is an achievable or socially defensible goal, which it may or may not be. The point is that it is the tacitly understood function of much (not all!) of the discussion that goes on in the case conference; given that, it is inappropriate to treat the psychometrics in the same way that we treat them when we have a problem of pure concurrent or predictive validity in the traditional sense.

    An MMPI profile is a behavior sample which has been analyzed and summarized in quasi-rigorous fashion on the basis of very extensive clinical experience. This extensive clinical experience has operated first in the construction of the item pool, then in construction and cross-validation of the scales, and then in the development of the various actuarial interpretative cookbook systems. If a patient was diagnosed "reactive depression" by the resident, appears mainly depressed when he is interviewed in the case conference, but has a clearly schizophrenic MMPI supported by some bad schizophrenic F– responses, contamination, and the like on the Rorschach, I cannot imagine why a psychologist would take the simplistic position that his "psychological Wassermann" has failed. If the aim of psychometrics is to help us infer the psychodynamic equivalent of pathology in organic medicine—and that is surely one of its main aims when it is used in a sophisticated way—what the analogy suggests is that there will be, from time to time, discrepancies between what we are prone to infer from the brief interview contact and what Omniscient Jones knows about the psychological innards of the patient.

    I don't mean to suggest that we accept the psychometrics as criterion in the old-fashioned sense, which would equally be a mistake. The point *is* that there is no criterion in the traditional sense, and it is preposterous that one still has to explain this to full professors. We do not know the psychological states and processes from which the various kinds of clinical behavior arise. We *infer* them from a variety of lines of evidence. Our problem is that of the detective (or theory builder!) who is trying to put together different kinds of data to form a more or less coherent picture of unknown latent and historical situations to which he does not have direct operational access. That being so, the task of explaining an apparent discrepancy between the resident's opinion or the impression we get in a case conference and what the MMPI or Rorschach tells us is a much more complicated intellectual job than it seems generally thought to be. As I pointed out in "Some Ruminations on the Validation of Clinical Procedures" (Meehl, 1959b), giving a Rorschach or an MMPI in order to predict the verbal behavior of the psychiatrist (dynamically or diagnostically) is pointless. It's a waste of the patient's time and the taxpayer's money. If all I want to do is forecast what the psychiatrist will say about the patient's diagnosis or dynamics, it is obvious that the easiest way to do that is to walk down the hall and ask him! A psychometric instrument is not a parlor trick in which, for some strange (union-card?) reason, you keep yourself from having access to easily available information about a patient for the fun of seeing whether you can guess it instead of getting it directly. The psychologist who doesn't understand this point is not even in the ball park of clinical sophistication. To "validate" a test, in any but the crudest sense of initial investigation to determine whether the test has anything going for it at all, a sophisticated thinker realizes that one must use a criterion that is qualitatively and quantitatively superior to what is regularly available in a clinical workup. We validate the Wassermann against the pathologist's and bacteriologist's findings, *not* against the general practitioner's impression after a ten-minute hearing of the presenting complaints. Validation studies that take as the criterion the nosological label or the psychodynamic assessment which one gets on the basis of a couple of interviews are at most always a waste of time. The statements we infer about the patient from psychometrics ought to have attached to them a probability that arises from qualitatively and quantitatively *better* data than we routinely have from the nonpsychometric sources in the ordinary clinical workup. If we don't have that, it is doubtful how much point there is in giving the test in the first place. If a patient has a schizophrenic MMPI and Rorschach but does not appear schizophrenic when interviewed in staff, the *proper* questions are: "What are some of the things we might have looked for more skillfully to elicit data on the schizoid disposition that the psychometrics indicate are almost certainly present?" "What can be inferred about the psychological defense system of a patient who manages to look like a case of simple depression when he is actually a latent schizophrenic?" "What speculations would we have about discrepancies of this kind?" "What kinds of research might we carry out in order to check these speculations?" "Are there identifiable subclasses of psychometric/interview discrepancies for which the psychometrics are likely to be correct, and others for which the reverse obtains?" I do not assert that one *never* hears these important metaquestions asked in the case conference; but you can attend a hundred conferences without hearing them raised a dozen times.

g. "*Understanding it makes it normal*" (and, if legal or ethical issues are involved, "acceptable"). This is a psychiatric variant of the ethical notion that understanding behavior makes that behavior ethically permissible or "excusable." I once heard a clinical psychologist say that it was "unimportant" whether a defendant for whom I testified was legally insane, since his homicide was "dynamically understandable" in either case. (The defendant and both counsel, benighted nonpsychologists they, felt it *was* important whether a man is called a murderer

and he is put in prison for twenty years or whether he is considered insane and is discharged from the state security hospital after his psychosis lifts.) As for T. Eugene Thompson, the St. Paul lawyer who cold-bloodedly murdered his wife to get a million dollars from life insurance, this psychologist argued that "I suppose if I knew enough about T. Eugene Thompson, like the way his wife sometimes talked to him at breakfast, I would understand why he did it." I gather that this psychologist (a Ph.D.!!) believes that if T. Eugene Thompson's wife was sometimes grumpy in the morning, he was entitled to kill her.

h. *Assumption that content and dynamics explain why this person is abnormal.* Of all the methodological errors committed in the name of dynamic psychiatry, this one is probably the most widespread, unquestioned, and seductive. The "reasoning" involved is simple. We find ourselves in possession of two sorts of facts about a person. The first kind of fact, present by virtue of his being a patient, is that he has mental or physical symptoms, or characterological traits, that are pathological in some accepted sense of that term.

This is not the place rigorously to define "pathological," for a beautiful discussion of which see the wise treatment by my colleague William Schofield (1964). For present purposes, it will suffice to say that behavior pathology is roughly defined by some (subjectively) weighted combination of marked statistical deviations from biological and cultural norms, on dimensions and in directions involving (1) subjective distress (anxiety, depression, rage, inadequacy feeling, dissatisfaction, boredom, and the like), (2) medical complaints, symptoms, or concerns, (3) impairment of educational, economic, sexual, or "social" performance, and (4) distorted appreciation of reality, external or internal. It will not usually be the case that any of these aberrations taken alone suffices to define pathology, although there are exceptions involving extreme degrees. For example, no matter how well adjusted socially, economically self-sufficient, and subjectively comfortable a person may be, if he is firmly convinced that he is Napoleon he is pathological ipso facto. It is regrettable, from the standpoint of philosophical cleanness, but the semantic situation must be honestly faced: our conception of psychopathology almost always involves some *mixture* of statistical deviation, "health" or "adjustment" evaluations, and notions of adequate ego function (reality testing and executive competence).

The point is that the individual under study in a clinical case conference comes to be there, unless there has been some sort of mistake (e.g., wrong party in a marriage is the "patient"), because he is psychologically aberrated, i.e., he has psychiatric or medical symptoms, gross social incompetence (delinquency, economic dependency), or extreme deviations in characterological structure. It does not seem useful to define "psychopathology" in solely statistical terms (is absolute pitch, an IQ = 160, or long-sustained sexual performance pathological?). Yet statistical deviations on selected dimensions considered relevant to "health," "social adaptation," "gratification," "effectiveness," and "reality appraisal" seem somehow involved. A down-playing of statistical rarity, in contrast to the work of Schofield cited above, can be found in Fine (1971, pp. 2–6; see also footnote 11 in Livermore, Malmquist, and Meehl, 1968, and citations therein).

The second kind of fact about the person is not true of him by virtue of his being a "patient," but is true of him simply because he is a human being—namely, he has conflicts and frustrations; there are areas of life in which he is less than optimally satisfied, aspects of reality he tends to distort, and performance domains in which he is less than maximally effective. There is nobody who can honestly and insightfully say that he is always efficient in his work, that he likes everyone he knows ("lie" item on MMPI L scale!), that everybody finds him a fascinating person, that he is idyllically happy in his marriage and his job, that he always finds life interesting rather than boring, that he never gets discouraged or has doubts about "whether it's all worth the trouble," and the like. If you examine the contents of a mental patient's mind, he will, by and large, have pretty much the same things on his mind as the rest of us do. If asked whether there is something that bothers him a lot, he will not emphasize his dissatisfaction with the weather. The seductive fallacy consists in *assuming*, in the absence of a respectable showing of causal connection, that this first set of facts, i.e., the medical, psychological, or social aberrations that define him as a patient, *flows from* the second set, i.e., his conflicts, failures, frustrations, dissatisfactions, and other facts which characterize him as a fallible human being, subject like the rest of us to the human condition. Example: A patient has paranoid delusions that people do not appreciate his merits. He had a father who favored his older brother. One (nonclassical) psychodynamic conclusion is that his present aberrations are mainly attributable to this bit of childhood family dynamics. I do not mean to say that this cannot happen or to deny that sometimes it does. It may be, for all I know, that this inference is true more often than not. By and large, the research literature on retrospective data for persons who have become mentally ill shows only rather weak (and frequently inconsistent) statistical relations between purportedly pathogenic background factors and mental illness (e.g., Schofield and Balian, 1959; Frank, 1965; Gottesman and Shields, 1972). Even those antecedent conditions which do show some association are ambiguous concerning causal interpretation because one does not have any scientific way of determining to what extent the life-history datum—almost always a perception by or of the patient in some interpersonal relation— was itself a reflection of personality aberrations in the "pre-patient" which led siblings, parents, teachers, or peer group to behave differently toward him at an early age. (See, for example, the fascinating study comparing mothers' attitudes toward normal, schizophrenic, and brain-damaged offspring by Klebanoff, 1959.) I do not object to speculating whether a certain event in the patient's past or a certain kind of current mental conflict *may* have played an important role in producing his present pathological behavior or phenomenology. I merely point out that most of the time these are little more than speculations, whereas the tradition is to take almost any kind of unpleasant fact about the person's concerns or deprivations, present or historical, as *of course* playing an etiological role.

It is worthwhile to distinguish two forms of the mistake in connection with current psychological conflicts or frustrations. The grosser error is to attribute a causal role to an intrapsychic or situational evil when, in the eyes of Omniscient Jones, it has no connection whatever with the presented psychopathology. Thus, for example, a paranoid patient has been out of work for some time due to fluctuations in the economic cycle, and while the development of his paranoid mentation has proceeded quite independently of this unemployment, we assign a causal role to his being out of a job. Sometimes this is done even if the paranoid content itself bears no clear relationship to the alleged situational stressor. But even when it does, the inference remains highly problematic. If I feel put upon by my social environment, I will naturally look around for the most plausible cognitive content in harmony with this feeling; and the fact that I was fired from my job recently is a suitable candidate.

The other form of the mistake is less serious because, philosophically speaking, the alleged factor is really a factor, but its quantitative role is not assigned in a sophisticated manner. These are cases in which a certain factor *does* enter the causal chain eventuating in the pathological symptom which makes the individual classifiable as a mental patient, but it is a factor shared by a very large number—let us say the vast majority—of "normal" persons; and it does not exist in a greater quantitative degree in the patient than it does in the rest of us. The question then arises, why is this particular individual a patient when the rest of us are not? Most often the clarification of such situations lies in the distinction between a genetic or early-acquired disposition and a psychological (environmental) event or condition that appears in the logician's formula as the antecedent term of that disposition. (See Meehl, 1972c.) Strictly speaking, a *disposition* and *the event that constitutes the realization of its antecedent* count equally as causes. The person can be said to actualize the consequent of the disposition *because* his environment actualizes the antecedent and *because* he had the disposition [antecedent → consequent] to begin with, owing to his biological heredity or childhood history. However, when we ask, in a medical or social setting, "What is the matter with this individual?" we do not usually intend to ask, "What is the complete, detailed causal analysis of all the causal chains that converge upon his diagnosably aberrated state as we now see it?" That would be a legitimate question, of course. But it is *not* what we are ordinarily asking when we ask the etiological question "Why?" What we ordinarily have in mind by our etiological "Why?" is "What does this person have, or what befell him, that makes him different from those who have not developed clinical psychopathology?" That means we are looking for the *differentiating* causal agent, the thing which is true of him and not of the others who have remained "healthy." Whether that differentiating agent, picked out of the total causal confluence by our clinical interests, should more properly be the disposition or the realized antecedent term of the disposition depends primarily upon the relative frequencies of the two in the population. If many, perhaps most, persons experience the realization of the antecedent term of the disposition but do not become aberrated because they do not have the disposition to begin with, then the disposition is what is specifically abnormal in this person and should usually be the focus of our clinical and theoretical interest.

The clearest examples of the distinction between the two cases (that is, between a rare disposition whose antecedent is so commonly realized that the antecedent is considered normal and a rarely realized antecedent of a disposition so common that the disposition is called normal) are from medical genetics. In order for a child to develop the PKU syndrome, it is not sufficient that he have a mutated gene at a particular locus, and it is not sufficient that his diet contain phenylalanine. However, the conjunction [mutated gene + dietary phenylalanine] is, given the set of "normal developmental conditions" necessary for the organism to survive at all, jointly necessary and sufficient for PKU (clinical) disease. Why then do we consider this disease hereditary? Obviously, because normal children have considerable phenylalanine in their diet, and the reason they do not develop PKU is that they do not have the mutated gene, i.e., they do not have the disposition. Since the phenylalanine dietary intake is common, PKU is extremely rare, and the reason for its rarity lies in the extreme rarity of the disposition [phenylalanine intake → PKU disease], we use the common-language term "cause" to designate the genetic mutation, i.e., the source of the rare disposition. Comparable examples are diabetes (normal dietary intake of sugar), gout (normal dietary intake of certain nitrogenous foodstuffs), allergies (e.g., normal dietary intake of buckwheat), and the like. And on the other side, the "cause" of lead poisoning or scurvy is taken to be an anomalous dietary intake (excess of lead or deficiency of ascorbic acid), but these are realizations of dispositions that constitute the norm.

There are some circumstances in which, population frequency aside, our choice between the disposition and the realized antecedent as the culprit depends on other contextual parameters, notably therapeutic interest. It may be useful to concentrate our attention upon that which can be changed, irrespective of its rarity. But it is worth noting that in the case of PKU, although we cannot change the child's genes and we can manipulate his diet, any knowledgeable person would unhesitatingly answer the question "Is PKU a genetic disease?" affirmatively. The only basis I can see for this preferential assignment of causality—since a disposition and its actualized antecedent are equally causal in the philosophical sense—is the matter of frequency, i.e., what is the statistically aberrant condition? Expressed in nomic notation, with a genetic (or other constitutional or early-acquired disposition) as 'D,' the antecedent activation condition of the disposition as 'C,' and the resulting disease outcome of the combination as 'R,' the disposition may be written:

$$D = [C \rightarrow R]$$

In our ordinary medical and sociological usage of the term *cause*, with rare exceptions, what we consider is the set of population probabilities $p(D)$, $p(C)$, and $p(R)$. If the relation among these probabilities is

$$p(C) \gg p(D) > p(R)$$

we identify the (rare) disposition as the cause; whereas if

$$p(D) \gg p(C) > p(R)$$

we instead identify the (rare) actualized antecedent of the disposition as the cause. There is no harm in this selective use of *cause* on the basis of rarity, so long as we are philosophically clear about the situation as thus spelled out. The research tasks in medicine, psychology, criminology, etc., are often profitably put in terms of directing our interest and identification of the cause in this sense of statistical rarity, since one of the first things we want to know is what it is specifically that is the matter with these individuals, i.e., in what respect do they differ from others who have not fallen ill, have not become delinquent or economically marginal, or whatever.

i. *Hidden decisions.* In practical decision making about patients, it is undesirable to deceive ourselves about those "hidden decisions" that we might challenge were they made explicit, especially that important class of decisions forced upon us by a variety of economic and social factors not presently within our institutional or professional control. An unforced hidden decision is exemplified by the research showing that lower class patients are more likely to receive pills, shock, or supportive therapy than are middle and upper class patients, who are more likely to receive intensive, uncovering, long-term psychotherapy—the latter being, by and large, more congenial to the interests and self-concepts of most practitioners. While this was anecdotally apparent to many of us before it was well documented by Hollingshead and Redlich (1958; see also Myers and Schaffer, 1954), some had supposed that the decision to treat proletarians in a different way hinged almost wholly upon economic considerations. We now know that other factors are also operative, since the social-class correlations persist when economics is substantially eliminated (as at Veterans Administration or other free clinics, graduated-fee community clinics, and the like). These other factors, which should have been obvious to any middle class WASP psychotherapist by introspection, include social-class "cultural compatibility," verbal fluency, conceptual intelligence, the tendency to think psychologically, lesser reliance on somatization (with epinosic gains), less preference for acting-out extrapunitive mechanisms over intropunitive guilt-laden mechanisms, a reality situation that provides some gratification and is modifiable in the nongratifying domains, and the like. Schofield (1964) has described the modal psychotherapist's "ideal patient" as the YAVIS syndrome (young, attractive, verbal, intelligent, and successful).

These YAVIS preferences aside, no practitioner, with or without systematic quantitative research on the sociology of the mental health professions, could be unaware that whether a patient receives a certain kind of treatment—never mind its merits—may hinge negligibly on his objective psychological appropriateness for it, depending instead upon factors of income, geography, available personnel, and the like. It is important in thinking administratively (one may often say also *ethically*) about the selection of patients for psychotherapy and the assignment of personnel, to face squarely the social fact that even in the affluent society our situation with respect to hours available of professionally skilled time really does present a different situation from that prevailing in other branches of the healing arts. I do not wish to defend the current status of delivery of *non*-mental health care in the United States, which is generally perceived as unsatisfactory. But there are some important quantitative differences between the situation pertaining to psychology and that pertaining to organic disease.

Admittedly an indigent patient with a brain tumor may have a significantly lower probability of diagnosis partly because he does not wish to spend money to see a physician about early symptoms, partly because of "social incompetence" traits that show up in caring for one's health (as in all other areas—a social fact that one is not supposed to mention, but is documented by statistical data from prepaid group health care plans). Furthermore, anyone who has gone through (anonymously, not as the "professor" or "doctor" he is) the outpatient department of a charity hospital (something that should be annually required of hospital administrators!) can attest that the underprivileged patient is kept waiting a longer time, is treated with less courtesy and sympathy by paramedical professionals (sometimes scandalously so), is often dealt with rather more high-handedly by the physician, and the like. But despite these conditions, for which there is no excuse, it remains true that the indigent patient, once diagnosed, will not go untreated for his operable brain tumor just because he is poor or because he lives a hundred miles away from the nearest competent neurosurgeon; whereas it is a statistical fact, *not* changeable by some sort of ethical decision or act of will on our part, that the majority of psychiatric patients will not get intensive, long-term psychotherapy (assuming that were the ideal method of treatment for them), money or no money, socially conscious clinic administrator or not, because there are just not enough psychotherapists around.

I have noted in discussion with fellow professionals, and very much in the classroom, that those predictive and prognostic problems that press upon us the clinical-actuarial issue (Meehl, 1954a; Sawyer, 1966) are sometimes rejected with considerable moral indignation, on the plausible-sounding ground that we should not be predicting (fallibly!) who will respond favorably to psychotherapy, since everybody has alright to it; that we ought to provide it for all comers, even if it happens that their actuarial odds are sometimes rather low for significant improvement. Unfortunately for the clientele but fortunately for the argument, we need not debate the merits of that ethical position—with which I personally have considerable sympathy—because it is a literal, physical impossibility to satisfy this demand, even if all clinical, counseling, and school psychologists, psychiatrists, social workers, clergymen, marriage counselors, and other "mental healers" avoided all teaching and research, and could manage to go without any sleep, recreation, or family life. The situation in psychotherapy is not like the brain tumor, appendicitis, or pernicious anemia situation; it is, regrettably, closer to the situation of a shortage of surgeons or blood plasma in a military field hospital (where overpressed surgeons may literally have to make the decision who shall live and who shall die) or to that of a public health official who runs into a shortage of plague serum during an epidemic of plague. It is not a question of unethically deciding to withhold maximum-intensity psychological treatment from some in favor of others. That decision is already made for us by the sheer logistics of the situation. The point is that we are, willy-nilly, going to withhold intensive psychotherapy from the great majority of persons who come in for some sort of medical or psychological help. Consequently the *character* of our ethical dilemma is fixed. We are not confronted with the problem *whether* to treat some patients intensively and not others. Our present ethical dilemma is whether to assign treatment and nontreatment (or kinds of treatments) in a random fashion or by some selection procedure which improves the average long-term outcome. I cannot think that anyone with a clear head would argue for random assignment (except for research purposes), but I have come across all sorts of strange arguments in this world. In any case, whatever ethical considerations we may raise about the utilization of skilled professional personnel in the foreseeable future, and whatever conclusion we may reach (or agree to disagree on), at least we should keep in mind the fact of hidden decisions.

j. *The spun-glass theory of the mind.* Every great intellectual and social movement seems to carry some "bad" correlates that may not, strictly speaking, follow *logically* from society's acceptance of the "good" components of the movement but that *psychologically* have a tendency to flow there from. One undesirable side effect of the mental hygiene movement and the over-all tradition of dynamic psychiatry has been the development among educated persons (and here I do not refer only to professionals but to many persons who get an undergraduate degree in a variety of majors) of what I call the "spun-glass theory of the mind." This is the doctrine that the human organism, adult or child (particularly the latter), is constituted of such frail material, is of such exquisite psychological delicacy, that rather minor, garden-variety frustrations, deprivations, criticisms, rejections, or failure experiences are likely to play the causative role of major traumas. It is well known among psychotherapists that part of the chronic, free-floating guilt feelings of the educated American woman is her fear that she is not a perfect mother because she is not always 100 percent loving, giving, stimulating, and accepting toward her children. (There is more than a mild suspicion in my mind that some child therapists are ideological "parent haters," drawn to the field by their own parent-surrogate hang-ups.) Some psychotherapists—myself included—actually find it necessary to *undo* the educational and social impact of the mental hygiene movement in women of this sort.

I would do myself a disservice as a clinical practitioner to let these toughminded comments go unqualified. I have a clock on my desk which makes it unnecessary to glance surreptitiously at my wristwatch—one need not hold the spun-glass theory of the mind to notice that checking how close one is to the end of the hour can sometimes have a distinctly adverse effect on patients (particularly schizotypes who, more often than not, react to it as a rejection experience). I offer this minor clinical example to show that I do not here defend a clumsy, insensitive, bull-in-a-china-shop approach to the human psyche. After all, part of the reason people come to psychotherapists is that we offer tact, sensitivity, and empathy beyond that provided by the patient's nurturing environment and by his present family and work group.

Nevertheless, even in one's relations with the patient, it is possible to have a countertherapeutic effect because of subscribing to the spun-glass theory of the mind. The concept of extreme psychic fragility is likely to be truer for the schizotype than for most other kinds of patient, for example. Yet a therapist's *super*-delicacy, flowing from the spun-glass theory of the mind, can boomerang in working with some schizotypes. If, for instance, the therapist is so frightened by the concept "schizophrenia" that he regards it as a kind of psychic cancer, and therefore tends to react skittishly to some of its major symptoms (e.g., confused thinking, body-image aberrations, reality distortion), he may find himself trying to humor the patient, as "lunatics" are handled in the funny papers, even though all the books and lectures have taught him that this humoring maneuver cannot be successfully carried out. The schizotypic patient, with his hyper-acute perception of others' thoughts and motives—especially when aversive to himself—perceives this therapeutic double-talk as a form of insincerity and feels that the therapist is fooling him while pretending to be honest with him, as, in the patient's view, other people have done in the past. Such an experience confirms the schizotype's deep-seated mistrust, as well as aggravating his cognitive confusions about "what reality is."

The most preposterous example of the spun-glass theory of the mind that has come to my attention illustrates it so beautifully that I can close this portion of my discussion with it. Thirty years ago, when I was an advanced graduate student in Dr. Hathaway's therapy seminar, live-mike interviews were piped in so the staff and students in the class could discuss the therapeutic technique demonstrated. One day we were scheduled to hear an interview by a social worker who (as I had already inferred from other facts) was thoroughly imbued with the spun-glass theory of the mind. The interviewee was a preadolescent male with a prostitute mother and a violent, drunken father, living in marginal economic circumstances in a high-delinquency neighborhood, the child having been rejected by his parents, his peer group, and the teachers in his school. His acting-out tendencies and morbid fantasies were such that he was seen on the inpatient child psychiatry service; this session was to be his last interview before discharge, although the social worker planned to continue seeing him with lower density on an outpatient basis. The therapy was considered a success. Shortly before the seminar was scheduled to be held, the social worker informed Dr. Hathaway that she really could not go ahead with the interview as planned, having just learned that the microphone (concealed in a lamp base) was in a different room from the office in which the child was accustomed to being interviewed. She felt that to interview him in this "strange situation" (= different office) might have a traumatic effect and undo the successful achievements of the therapy. This is the spun-glass theory of the mind with a vengeance. Here is this poor little urchin about to be returned to his multiply pathogenic environment, presumably with his psyche properly refurbished by the interviews so that he will be able to maintain himself in the harsh outside world; yet, despite the "successful" psychotherapy, he is still so fragile that these therapeutic achievements could be liquidated by having an interview in a different office! I submit that the best way to describe that combination of views is that it is just plain silly.

k. *Identifying the softhearted with the softheaded.* While there is surely no logical connection between having a sincere concern for the suffering of the individual patient (roughly, being "softhearted") and a tendency to commit logical or empirical mistakes in diagnosis, prognosis, treatment choice,

and the like (roughly, being "softheaded"), one observes clinicians who betray a tendency to conflate the two. Because of my own longtime interest in the clinical-actuarial issue, this is the domain of clinical decision making where the tendency to think and act in terms of the unspoken equation [softhearted = softheaded] has come forcibly to my attention. Given space limitations, its somewhat peripheral relevance, and a firm intention to revise my 1954 monograph (Meehl, 1954a) on the clinical-statistical issue, I shall not reiterate the old arguments—to which, I may say, there have been remarkably few amendments or rebuttals—in the discussion here. But two arguments commonly heard in case conferences bring out the point so beautifully that I cannot resist the impulse to discuss them briefly. One is the old argument that rejects even a strong actuarial prediction concerning the instant patient on the ground that we are concerned not with groups but with this particular individual. Now all predictions about the consequences of clinical action (including inaction, "waiting to see what happens"—often the physician's tactic in accordance with the ancient medical maxim *primum non nocere*) are inherently probabilistic in nature. For one who explicitly recognizes this inherently probabilistic character (even when, as rarely, $p = .99$) of *all* our clinical inferences, the advice to defy our formalized actuarial experience in decision making about the single patient before us amounts to saying that the unformalized inductive inferences of the clinician should be trusted in preference to the formalized probability inferences of a regression equation or an actuarial table. I said in 1954, and have repeated in subsequent publications (Meehl, 1954b, 1956b, 1957, 1959a, 1960, 1965c, 1967b, 1970c, 1972b), that there are individual instances in which this counteractuarial choice is correct. But I have also pointed out, and have as yet seen no persuasive rebuttal, that it is very rarely the preferred action and that a policy that permits it frequently is indefensible. Permitting a weak or moderately strong clinical inference to countervail a well-supported actuarial backlog of data on patients resembling the immediate case in a researched set of predictively powerful respects will lead, in the long run, to an increase in erroneous clinical decisions. Some clinicians still do not see that this question is itself one of the questions that is answered, "in the average sense," by the now numerous (over seventy-five) empirical investigations of the clinical-actuarial controversy.

What befalls the softheaded clinician in his admirable desire to be softhearted (i.e., to be most helpful to this particular patient) is that he fears the very real possibility—which the actuarial data themselves express in terms of the error rate—that he will treat the patient nonoptimally through reliance on actuarial experience. I empathize intensely with his existential predicament; I have often felt it acutely myself as a practitioner. But I must insist that he is wrong. In thinking thus, he fails to take two considerations into account. The first is that by departing from the recorded actuarial expectations in reliance upon lower validity informal clinical inferences, he is probably *not* doing the best thing for the immediate case. He thinks (or feels) that he is—but he is probably not. Secondly, should it turn out that by this counteractuarial departure he *has* in fact done the best thing for the particular patient, he will have achieved this individually desirable result by applying a decision policy that (according to the studies) will lead him to mispredict for other patients, who are also individual human beings with presumably as much claim upon his ethical concerns as the one currently before him. In the absence of some showing that we have a kind of superordinate method—whether actuarial or clinical in nature—for discriminating before the fact which are the cases that will be better handled by counteractuarial decisions and which should be left where the table puts them, such a policy is not ethically defensible, regardless of how good it makes us feel.

As to the stock argument that we are not concerned with probabilities, frequencies, or group trends but with the unique individual before us, I do not really know how to add to what I have said, with others before and since, on this vexed issue. There are admittedly some profound unresolved problems, still in dispute among statisticians and logicians, concerning the logical reconstruction of "rational decision" under these circumstances (see, for example, the excellent discussion by Hacking, 1965). But, so far as I am aware, the technical debates among the experts concern the logical reconstruction of the matter, rather than being disputes concerning what a reasonable man would be well advised to do. In teaching our first-year clinical assessment class—where one invariably hears students who offer this "single case" objection to actuarial decision methods in the clinic—I have found it helpful to consider the following hypothetical example (I like this example because it really puts the student on the "existential knife-edge," where he himself is the "patient," and the issue is one of life or death): Suppose I place before you two revolvers. I show you that one of them is loaded with five live shells, having a single empty chamber; the other has five empty chambers and a single live shell. I am, let us say, a sadistic decision-theorist in charge of a concentration camp in which you are an inmate, and I tell you that you are forced to play a single game of Russian roulette with one of these two revolvers. You are not going to have to repeat it. In your ordinary life you are not in the habit of playing Russian roulette. You have never done so before, and you are firmly determined never to do it again. If you avoid blowing your brains out, I promise to release you from the camp. In the other eventuality, we leave the probable outcome to your theology. Which revolver would you choose under these circumstances? Whatever may be the detailed, rigorous, logical reconstruction of your reasoning processes, can you honestly say that you would let me pick the gun or that you would flip a coin to decide between them?

I have asked quite a few persons this question, and I have not yet encountered anybody who alleged that he would just as soon play his single game of Russian roulette with the five-shell weapon. *But why not?* Suppose I am told, by a "soft-headed" clinician, "Well, but you are only going to do it once, it is a *unique event*, we are not talking about groups or classes or frequencies—we are talking about whether *you*, Regents' Professor Paul Everett Meehl, that unique human individual, live or die in the next couple of minutes. What do you *care* about probabilities and such, since this choice will never be presented to you again?" I have not found anybody willing to apply such nonactuarial reasoning to the Russian roulette case. Point: We should apply to the unique patient before us the same

kind of rational decision rule that we would insist upon applying if our own life were hanging in the balance.

Despite what I take to be the irrefutability of this two-revolver argument, I can sometimes work myself into the frame of mind of a soft-headed clinician by putting his favorite query, "Do *you* want to be treated as a mere tally mark in an actuarial table?" No, I do not want to be "treated as a *mere* tally mark." But I put it to you, dear reader, that the seductiveness of this appeal lies in a confusion between thinking about my physician's personal concern for my welfare—which I value as highly as anybody else—and trusting him to "bet on the best horse" in my behalf. As a matter of fact, one thing I happen to like about my physician is his tendency (noted appreciatively by other faculty patients of his who are not in the statistics business) to cite statistics when considering whether a certain painful or expensive diagnostic procedure or a certain therapeutic regime is worth trying. I cannot convince myself that it would be a charitable act on my physician's part to think fuzzily about my diagnosis or treatment as a result of his "feeling sympathetic" toward me. Hence I do not think I have a "double standard of morals" that depends upon whether I am considering myself as clinical decision maker or as patient. Whether my physician decides for me, or, as is usually more appropriate—and I would say this also for the psychiatric patient—helps me to decide, I prefer that he act on the principle of Thomas Aquinas that charity is not a state of the emotions but a state of the rationally informed will, i.e., that charity consists of willing the other person's good. On this philosophic basis, it is a *pseudocharitable* act, given the presently available evidence, for a psychiatrist to withhold EST from a patient with classical psychotic depression on the ground that there is something about deliberately inducing a cerebral storm by pushing that button which offends his human sensibility (a feeling I share). By the same token, the psychoanalytic therapist must learn to dissolve resistances rather than timidly playing along with them; an RET practitioner must be able to point out to a proud, educated, intellectualizing patient that he is operating irrationally on a postulate which is unrealistic and self-defeating (tactless though such a confrontation would be in most ordinary human relationships); a behavior modifier must be able to stick to a reinforcement schedule; and the surgeon must not be afraid to shed blood.

It should not require mentioning, but to forestall any possibility of misunderstanding I shall state explicitly, that all of the foregoing discussion is predicated upon the assumption that a clinical case conference sometimes eventuates in decisions "for" or "about" the patient. Consider the clearly psychotic patient who constitutes a danger to himself or others and whose ego function is so grossly impaired that his relatives (acting through the agency of the state) have placed certain decisions in our hands. One can raise fundamental philosophical questions about such a patient's autonomy in considering the justification of civil commitment (see Livermore, Malmquist, and Meehl, 1968) and if one concludes against current practice, he may have an ethical obligation to refuse to participate in some case conferences, at least in their decision-making aspects. But aside from the involuntary commitment issue, if we do not believe it is a legitimate professional function to decide anything, or even (by advice or by the presentation of relevant information to the patient or his relatives) to help decide anything, then most of the discussion above concerning *how* to decide becomes pointless.

l. *Neglect of overlap.* This one is so trite and has become so much a part of standard elementary instruction in applied statistics that I would have little justification in mentioning it were it not for the almost incredible fact that respectable journals in clinical psychology and psychiatry still persist in publishing articles on the validity of clinical instruments which give no indication that either the author or the journal editor ever heard of the overlap problem. Partly as a result of this "academic" perpetuation of error, case conferences—which usually operate several notches lower in the hierarchy of scholarliness than scientific journals—continue to make the mistake. I suppose the statistics professors are right in their opinion that the primary villainous influence was the unfortunate semantic choice (by whom?) decades ago of the term "significant" in referring to an obtained group difference that cannot plausibly be attributed to random-sampling fluctuations. I am not concerned here with *theoretical* (causal-structure) inferences, commonly made from refutations of the null hypothesis, for a discussion of which see the excellent collection by Morrison and Henkel (1970). The question before us here is the *pragmatic application* of a statistically significant difference, taken for present purposes as being nonproblematic from the statistician's standpoint. The point is that various psychological tests, rating scales, symptom checklists, and the like are unashamedly proposed for clinical use on the basis of "statistical significance" with little or no attention paid to the overlap of the clinical populations it is desired to discriminate (assuming that we were to treat the sample statistics not only as establishing a "significant difference" but as infallible estimators). I have repeatedly observed that reminders to faculty and students of the truism that statistical significance does not mean practical importance fail of effect when presented *in abstracto*. At the risk of seeming utterly trivial I shall therefore present a single, simplified numerical example that I hope will carry more pedagogical punch. Suppose I have devised the Midwestern Multiplastic Tennis-Ball Projection Test which I allege to be clinically useful in discriminating schizophrenics from anxiety-neurotics. I set aside the terrible complexities of assessing construct validity for this type of problem, assuming for simplicity that we treat the construct validity as approximately equivalent to a concurrent validity (Cronbach and Meehl, 1955) when the latter has been established on two groups of patients in whose formal diagnoses we are entitled to have much more confidence than we would have on the basis of routine clinical workup (see point f above, "crummy criterion fallacy"). Despite the Fisherian emphasis upon small samples, given our aim to obtain reasonably solid conclusions about the psychometric characteristics of these populations for future use, we would probably be somewhat uncomfortable (if not, we should be!) with sample sizes barely large enough to squeak out a respectable power in refuting the null hypothesis with a *t* test. So let us suppose that we have run the Midwestern Multiplastic Tennis-Ball Projection Test on a carefully diagnosed sample of 100 schizophrenics and 100 anxiety-neurotics.

And let us suppose we succeed in achieving a "statistically significant difference" between the two groups at the $p = .01$ level (about par for the course in most journal articles of this sort). To make the computations easy, I shall assume the standard deviations to be equal, and, as indicated above, I shall treat the obtained values as if they were parameters. A little arithmetic applied to these assumptions shows that the ratio of the mean difference $\bar{d}$ to each patient group's standard deviation is approximately .37 which, assuming equal base rates in the clinical population, locates the "hitmax cut" (Meehl, 1973) midway between the two means, i.e., about .18 sigma units above the mean of the lower frequency distribution and .18 sigma units below the mean of the upper distribution. Entering normal curve tables we find that clinical application of this optimal cutting score to the dichotomous diagnosis would yield around 57 percent "hits," i.e., a measly 7 percent improvement over what we could achieve by flipping pennies. From my perusal of the current clinical literature I think it not an unfair exaggeration to say that a considerable number—perhaps the majority—of all psychometric differentiators urged upon us for clinical use are close to worthless. A scientific cost accounting of their role in the decision-making process would usually not justify the expense to the patient (or the taxpayer) in the use of skilled clinical time required to administer and score the instrument and to present it in evidence at the case conference.

The conclusion is obvious. We ought to stop doing this sort of silly business, and we should constantly reiterate this elementary point when we note that it has been forgotten by clinicians in the case conference. Also it would be salutary—and would cut down on the garbage found in clinical periodicals—if editors *insisted* that several standard overlap measures be included in every manuscript submitted for publication in which a clinical instrument is purportedly validated or seriously proposed as a device worthy of further exploration. These might be Tilton's overlap, statements of percentages of valid positives attainable by cutting at certain standard percentiles or sigma points on the other distribution (e.g., the median, the 75th percentile, the 90th percentile, the 99th percentile), and, for most clinical problems worth arguing about, an indication of how much employing the hitmax cut on the proposed instrument would be better than "playing the base rate" (Meehl and Rosen, 1955) for various base-rate values.

m. *Ad hoc fallacy.* On this I shall say little at this point because my constructive suggestions for improving the quality of clinical case conferences in Part II below are devoted heavily to this problem. Like the preceding statistical mistake, the ad hoc fallacy is one that everybody "officially" knows about and recognizes as a source of error, but we find it so tempting that we frequently commit it anyway. The ingenuity of the human mind in "explaining" things, the looseness of the theoretical network available to us in the present stage of clinical psychology, and the absence of a quasi-definitive criterion (comparable to the pathologist's report in internal medicine) of what the truth about the patient really is, all combine to make it easy for us to cook up plausible-sounding explanations, after the available relevant evidence is in, of why the patient is the way he is. The only solution to this problem that is likely to be successful, because it will go beyond mere exhortation and provide quasi-objective differential reinforcement to the verbal behavior of the clinical conferees, is some method that introduces a *predictive* (epistemologically speaking, hence including *postdictive*) element that is now largely lacking. The possibilities that occur to me as reasonably toughminded, not unduly artificial in the pragmatic clinical context, feasible in terms of time and money, and sufficiently enjoyable so that staff can be induced to bear their share of the increased burden, are developed in Part II below.

n. "*Doing it the hard way.*" By this I mean employing some clinical instrument or procedure, such as a time-consuming projective test, to ascertain something that documents in the patient's social record or an informant could tell one in a few minutes. I have witnessed tedious and tenuous discussions aimed at making inferences concerning, say, why the patient is an academic underachiever, when nobody had taken the trouble to get in touch with the school and find out how the staff viewed the disparity between his measured intelligence and his academic performance, how the peer group accepted him, what temporal trends showed up in his cumulative record (e.g., teacher ratings), whether he ever was seen by the school counselor, and so on. There are some types of cases in which such failure to look at the record may be especially misleading, such as the clever and ingratiating psychopath who can sometimes fool even a moderately experienced clinician and can completely bamboozle a beginner. Clinicians prone to the [softhearted = softheaded] equation described above, reason, in effect, "Why, this friendly, tousle-headed thirty-five-year-old lad is very cooperative and forms a good relationship with me; I am sure he couldn't have been sticking switchblades into old ladies." In the differential diagnosis between an "unlucky" normal, an acting-out neurotic, a hard-core psychopath, and a solid-gold professional con man, the Rorschach, TAT, and MMPI (or, for that matter, even a short Mental Status interview) may be less illuminating than the school record, a social agency's file, or the police blotter. (See, in this connection, Meehl, 1970a, pp. 10–13.)

In considering psychometrics on their validity, we should try to think clearly about the *role* of our tests in the particular clinical situation. For what purpose are the tests being given? (Of course in thinking about this question, a psychologist who is not clear about the distinctions between content, concurrent, predictive, and construct validity is not up to the task's demands.) You have to make up your mind *why* you are bothering to give an intelligence test or an MMPI or a TAT. I cannot myself imagine doing so for the purpose of postdicting delinquency, social withdrawal, economic dependency, over-drinking, and the like; but many clinicians seem to view that pointless guessing game as their psychometric task. Just as treating a personality test as a means of predicting some other professional's impressionistic opinion from non-psychometric data is "doing it the hard way," so postdicting a relatively objective fact about the patient's life history is a wasteful exercise in psychometric muscle flexing.

o. *Social scientist's anti-biology bias.* Associated with the spun-glass theory of the mind (as one of the undesirable side effects of the mental hygiene and dynamic psychiatry movements in this country) is a deep, pervasive, and recalcitrant prejudice among psychologists, sociologists, and psychiatrists against biological factors in abnormality. This bias often correlates with a diffuse and fact-blind rejection of biologically oriented treatment procedures. Thus many clinical psychologists are anti-drug, anti-genetic, and anti-EST in their attitudes. Articles and books on psychopathology have been written by eminent and brilliant men (e.g., Thomas Szasz) which not only fail to *refute* the considerable (and rapidly growing) data on genetic determiners of human and animal behavior, including the major psychoses, but—as in the case of Dr. Szasz—do not so much as *mention* in a footnote the existence of such data (see, for example, Erlenmeyer-Kimling, 1972; Gottesman and Shields, 1972; Heston, 1972; Manosevitz, Lindzey, and Thiessen, 1969; and Rosenthal, 1970). One wonders, in reading his writings, whether he is literally unaware of the research on the genetics of schizophrenia; or, if he is aware of it, why he considers it acceptable scholarship to leave the nonprofessional reader in complete darkness about the fact that a scientific controversy exists. For many psychotherapists, everything that is wrong with anybody is attributable either to having a battle-ax mother, being raised on the wrong side of the tracks, or having married the wrong mate. It is dangerous to be the parent or spouse of a mentally ill person because you will almost certainly get blamed for it, even if he was patently abnormal before you met him and his family tree abounds with food faddists, recluses, perpetual-motion inventors, suicides, and residents of mental hospitals. Part of this attitude springs from the two related ideas that if it were the case that genes had something to do with aberrated behavior, then (1) psychotherapy could not "work," and (2) the psycho-dynamics we think we understand about mental patients would have to be abandoned. For what I hope is a clear refutation of that undergraduate mistake, see Meehl, 1972c. There simply isn't any contradiction, or even any "friction," between saying in a case conference, "This patient is a schizotype, the specific etiology of which I hypothesize is a dominant gene that produces a specific kind of integrative neural deficit (see Meehl, 1962)" and saying, "This patient's paranoid delusions are restitutional symptoms, forms of miscarried repair the dynamic meaning of which is the patient's effort to reinvest cathexis in social objects." If a clinician thinks that these two statements are incompatible, it merely shows that he is a muddleheaded thinker and needs to take an undergraduate course in genetics plus, perhaps, a little philosophy of science to get clear about dispositions and actualization of their antecedents. Reading Freud will help too.

p. *Double standard of evidential morals.* One common way in which the anti-biological prejudices of the preceding subsection are maintained against contrary evidence is by shifting the standards of evidential rigor depending upon whose ox is being gored. Having been drawn into psychology as a teenager by my reading of Menninger, Adler, and Freud, and preferring psychoanalytic therapy (when the patient is appropriate) because it is more theoretically interesting and gives me what I believe to be a deeper causal understanding of the individual, I cannot perceive myself as being a hardnosed, super-rigorous, compulsively operational type of psychologist—although I am aware that the impact of some of my writings on the special problem of prediction has been that other psychologists often view me in this stereotyped way. As mentioned in the introductory section, I have found myself in a strange position vis-à-vis my colleagues: the typical (non-Minnesota) cliniker perceives me as excessively critical and objective, whereas my local psychonomic brethren find it odd that I should be seriously interested in the interpretation of dreams. This is not the place to develop that paradox at length, but in discussing the double standard of evidential morals I must say something about it. I think that one big error committed by psychologists who insist upon sorting other psychologists into boxes like "humanistic" and "scientific" or "dynamic" and "behaviorist" is the failure to distinguish between two sorts of statements.

The first sort of statement is the kind that you might be willing to bet money on, act upon in your personal affairs, rely upon in making decisions concerning a patient—questions on where you place your bets when forced, even though you may be acutely conscious of the fact that you cannot develop the evidence for your choice (when on the existential knife-edge) in a rigorous fashion. The writings on personalistic probability exemplify this (Savage, 1954; Hacking, 1965; Levi, 1967; Raiffa, 1968). There is a difference—but not an inconsistency—between saying, "Lacking coercive evidence, I am prepared, until further notice, to bet that Gallumpher will place in the third," and saying, "It can be shown by rigorous mathematical analysis that the prediction of Gallumpher's placing in the third is the best decision." Consider, for example, psychoanalytic theory. I classify myself as a "60 percent Freudian." I consider that the two men who have contributed most to our understanding of behavior in the first half of the twentieth century are Sigmund Freud and B. Frederic Skinner. I find it a little hard to imagine a conversation between these two geniuses, although I would love to have heard one. But the point is that I can decide, on the existential knifeedge—*required* by the pragmatic context to make decisions willy-nilly—to play it Freudian or Skinnerian, without supposing I can make a rigorous scientific case that my decision is the right one. There is a distinction between what we believe (on the best evidence available, and given the social fact that we *must* decide) and what we would think as pure scientists, which might very well cause us to abstain from any decision until more and better evidence becomes available.

I have no objection if professionals choose to be extremely rigorous about their standards of evidence, but they should recognize that if they adopt that policy, many of the assertions made in a case conference ought not to be uttered because they cannot meet such a tough standard. Neither do I have any objection to freewheeling speculation; I am quite willing to engage in it myself (e.g., I have published some highly speculative views concerning the nature of schizophrenia: Meehl, 1962, 1964, 1972c). You can play it tight, or you can play it loose. What I find objectionable in staff conferences is a tendency to shift the criterion of tightness so that the evidence offered is upgraded or downgraded in the service of polemical interests. Example: A psychologist tells me that he is perfectly confident that psychotherapy benefits psychotic depressions (a question open on available data), his reason being that his

personal experience shows this. But this same psychologist tells me that he has never seen a single patient helped by shock therapy. (Such a statement, that he has never seen a *single patient* helped by shock therapy, can only be attributed to some sort of perceptual or memory defect on his part.) When challenged with the published evidence indicating that shock is a near specific for classical depression, he says that those experiments are not perfect, and further adds, "You can prove anything by experiments." (Believe it or not, these are quotations!) I confess I am at a loss to know how I can profitably pursue a conversation conducted on these ground rules. He is willing (1) to rely upon *his* casual impressions that psychotherapy helps patients, (2) to deny *my* casual impression that shock treatment helps patients, but (3) to reject the controlled research on the subject of electroshock—which meets considerably tighter standards evidentially than *either* his clinical impressions or mine—on the grounds that it is not perfectly trustworthy. It is not intellectually honest or, I would argue, clinically responsible thus to vary your tightness-looseness parameter when evaluating conflicting evidence on the same issue.

I am well aware of a respectable counterargument to these construct-validity considerations, the substance of which is the following: Whatever may be the philosophical or mathematical reconstruction for the idea of construct validity (and the rebuttal is sometimes offered by psychologists who are sophisticated about construct validity as a *theoretical* metanotion), in the pragmatic context whatever we say in the case conference must ultimately come down to some practical decision of a predictive nature. It can even be argued that postdictive, content, and concurrent validity interests—and, a fortiori, construct-validity interests—are defensible in this setting only in reliance upon some relation they have to predictive validity, because the aim of the conference is to decide what to *do* for the patient; this "do" of course includes proposing treatment alternatives to him, making prognostic statements to a referring social institution (court, school), advising the family about the odds on a regime requiring major financial outlay, and the like. In substance, the argument is that whatever the theoretical merits of other kinds of validity, or their technological value over the long run (e.g., improving psychometric instruments through better insight about the construct), in the context of clinical case conferences the *only* kind of validity that counts is predictive validity. There is much to be said for this line of thought, and no reader familiar with my writings on the actuarial prediction problem would expect me to be unsympathetic to it. And I want to reiterate that there are numerous specific decision-making tasks that do have this pure predictive validity form. Example: A court puts to the professional staff a list of specific forecasting questions, for example, "If the defendant stands trial, will he be able to function well enough cognitively so that his counsel can provide him with an adequate defense?" "This hitherto law-abiding person committed an act of violence under unusual circumstances; if, following your presentence investigation, the court releases him on probation, is he likely to commit acts dangerous to himself or others?" The test of any construct's value in such situations is obviously its predictive power.

Nevertheless, I cannot accept the anti-construct-validity argument when presented in its extreme (hyperoperational) form. My first reservation arises from the social fact that decision making on behalf of the patient or a social institution is not typically the sole function of a clinical case conference. I think it would be generally agreed that the conference is also intended to serve an educational function for the faculty and students attending it. We are supposedly trying to improve our decision-making skills as helpers and societal advisers, and to clarify our thoughts as teachers and researchers.

In that connection, the display—especially by prestigeful faculty figures—of inefficient decisional procedures must be viewed as countereducational as well as countertherapeutic for the patient. It is not, therefore, even a partial excuse for committing some of the methodological errors I am criticizing to say, "Well, Meehl, you are talking as though the only reason we meet in a clinical case conference is to make decisions about the patient. But we also meet for educational purposes." To the extent that the content of the discussants' contributions is predictive content, fallacies and nonoptimalities in that content, when allowed to go unchallenged or, worse, positively reinforced by group approval, presumably have the effect of indoctrinating our student clinicians with undesirable decision-making habits of mind. Hence the same features that make inefficient decision-making procedures undesirable from the standpoint of helping the individual patient make them undesirable as an educational practice.

The main point I wish to make concerning the educational functions of the conference is that while clinical comments advocating inefficient predictive methods cannot be justified on educational grounds, we are endeavoring to teach the students (and one another) several things in addition to how best to reach concrete clinical decisions about patients for treatment and social forecasting purposes. Admittedly the items in this list of nonpredictive pedagogical aims will differ somewhat from one teacher-professional to another, and I have no wish to impose my hierarchy of personal preferences upon others. I shall merely mention some of the main items that would surely be found in *some* competent persons' lists, without claiming completeness or attempting to argue the merits of the items fully. First, I take it that psychiatrists and clinical psychologists are typically interested in understanding the human person, despite the fact that this understanding does not always lead in any straightforward way to a specific practical decision concerning treatment. I know that this is true for me, and it seems pretty clearly true for many of my colleagues and students. Psychological curiosity is unquestionably among the motives inducing some able minds to enter the profession, and the gratification of *n Cognizance* is for many professionals among the important rewards that keep them going in the face of what is often a somewhat discouraging level of satisfaction of our *n Nurturance*. While some clinicians come fairly close to being pure behavioral engineers, others are more like psychological physicists, the vast majority of us being somewhere in between, characterized by a mixture—sometimes leading to uncomfortable role conflicts—of the wish to *heal*, the wish to *control*, and the wish to *understand*.

I have heard it argued, by extreme representatives of the "tough-minded" end of the tough-tender continuum, that even from the purely theoretical standpoint (setting aside practical relevance in treating the immediate case) this aim to understand cannot be distinguished from the predictive one, since "the purpose of scientific theories is to predict and control." Aside from an element of dogmatism displayed in imposing such a pure instrumentalist view of theoretical science, with which it is possible for a rational man to disagree philosophically, I would emphasize that *some* pragmatically useless inferences may serve epistemologically as corroborators and refuters of nomothetic psychological theories (or their explanatory application to the idiographic material). Such "useless" inferences, when sound, can contribute to the satisfaction of psychological curiosity without contributing to our role as helpers of patients and social forecasters.

Several kinds of concurrent and postdictive validity illustrate this point. I may, for instance, formulate a construction about the patient's personality by integrating, in the course of the conference discussion, a couple of subtle signs (manifested by the patient when presented in staff conference) with certain aspects of the psychometrics. Relying on this tentative psychodynamic construction, I am led to a probabilistic prediction concerning his ward behavior, which the participant nursing staff then confirms. Assuming that I have not committed any of the methodological errors herein discussed, and that the base rate of my ward-behavior "prediction" (actually postdictive or concurrent validation) is low enough so that its correctness—given the small evidential "prior" p in Bayes' Formula—counts as a strong corroborator; then I have probably learned (and taught) something about this patient's mind and, indirectly, about the verisimilitude of the nomothetic network mediating my inference. But the specificity of treatment in our field is not such that corroborating (in a moderate degree) a particular inference (e.g., this patient has rigid reaction formations against his oral-dependent impulses) must lead directly to a concrete prescription for treatment. The same is, of course, often true for construct-validity-mediated inferences susceptible of confirmation by the patient's psychotherapist.

Again, consider a postdiction which would be, I suppose, largely useless for our helping aim. Suppose I am interested in the theory of depression and entertain the speculation, based partly upon my clinical experience and partly upon quantitative research, that there are at least four, and possibly as many as seven, kinds of depression. Deciding among these for the immediate case *may* have treatment implications; e.g., neurotic depressions and depressions secondary to schizoid anhedonia do not react favorably to EST. But among some of my other speculative depression types, I am not aware of any therapeutic indications. Thus, for example, I believe there is such a state as "rage-depression," and that it even has characteristic somatic complaint aspects not found as frequently in the other varieties, such as the patient's presenting complaint that his head feels as if it had a pressure on it or in it, or as if it were about to explode. These patients also, I believe, are more likely to manifest bruxism. I would contrast this syndrome with object-loss depression, and would distinguish both from the very common reactive depressions attributable (as Skinner pointed out in 1938) to a prolonged extinction schedule. I speculate that childhood (even adolescent?) object loss predisposes genetically vulnerable persons to subsequent object-loss depression, and the reason it does not show up consistently but only as a statistically significant trend in retrospective studies of depression-prone individuals is that it characterizes only this subgroup (Malmquist, 1970; Beck, Sethi, and Tuthill, 1963; Beck, 1967, Chapter 14). I am not concerned here with arguing the merits of these speculations. The point is that on the basis of the evidence presented in conference, I might be interested in a (quite useless!) postdiction of childhood object loss, whereas in another depressed patient, I might be moved by the way the patient describes his head as feeling as if it were about to explode, together with some violent Rorschach content and some "aggressive" MMPI signs, to inquire whether, according to the patient's wife, he had a tendency to grind his teeth when asleep.

These examples serve also to illustrate the research-stimulus function of the case conference. From the standpoint of research strategy, it may be rational for a research-oriented clinician to find in bits and pieces of concurrent and postdictive validity encouragement to embark upon a research project, although their probabilistic linkage to pragmatically important dispositions of the patient might be too weak to justify reliance upon them in handling the immediate case.

Finally, there is a simple point about construct validity (whether the construct involved is nosological, dynamic, or "historical") that is easy to overlook when our mental set as clinicians emphasizes the importance of predictive statements. A narrowly operational view of the relations between behavioral dispositions (phenotypic, with a minimum of theoretical construction) demands that we have direct evidential support for what would turn out to be an unmanageably huge collection of pair-wise dispositional statistical linkages. If one were to list, in a huge catalog, all of the first-order descriptive traits, signs, symptoms, psychometric patterns, and life-history facts dealt with in psychiatry, it is hardly conceivable that such a list would contain fewer than several hundred elements. Even if we were to prune the list mercilessly—eliminating all elements having (1) marginal reliability, (2) base rates very close to zero or one, or (3) too highly correlated with others having nearly identical "content," and then finally (4) throwing out anything that we had little or no clinical or research basis for believing was appreciably correlated with anything else we cared about—I find it hard to suppose that such a list would contain fewer than, say, 100 variables. First-order predictions among all these pair wise, if based upon directly researched empirical linkages, would therefore require investigation of 10,000 correlations. But suppose that one investigator finds that bruxism, complaint of exploding headache, and certain MMPI and Rorschach signs cluster as a syndrome which, while "loose," is good enough to provide construct validity for the dynamic nosological entity "rage-depression." And suppose that another investigator, also interested in rage-depression but not familiar with these indicators, reports that patients he and a colleague independently classified as rage-depression (from Mental Status plus psychotherapy evidence plus precipitating situation) respond especially well to a particular antidepressant drug but do badly on Dexamyl. Then, pending the monster study of 10,000 pairwise correlations between everything and everything, clinicians who read these two articles can begin

prescribing that specific antidepressant for patients showing the syndrome of bruxism, aggressive psychometrics, and exploding headache.

The same line of reasoning applies to the teaching of diagnostic, dynamic, and etiological factors. Presumably one justification for having case conferences instead of just sending all of the residents and psychology trainees to the library is our belief that certain things can be best taught with dramatic punch in the real-life clinical situation. I do not know whether that generally accepted pedagogic principle has been quantitatively researched in medicine, but the psychiatric and clinical psychology conference has accepted the tradition from other branches of medicine, and I am willing here to presuppose it. You can "tell" a resident or psychology trainee that many schizophrenic patients are baffling and frustrating to the therapist, and elicit adverse countertransference reactions not because the therapist has been technically mishandling the case—although he may now begin to do so!—but because the schizotype is prone to "testing" operations on persons he would like to trust but dare not. You can also state in a lecture that some schizophrenic patients have a special way of walking (I will not try to describe it verbally here) which I refer to as the "schizophrenic float." A fledgeling therapist, mistreating a pseudoneurotic schizophrenic as a "good healthy neurotic," comes into the conference hurt and puzzled by the patient's ambivalent testing operations. The schizophrenic float is called to the therapist's attention by his conference neighbor (who spots it as the patient walks in), and the student therapist has a chance to observe it as the patient leaves the conference room. This resident or psychology trainee will have formed a vivid connection in his clinical thinking that it is likely he will never forget. However, such a linkage need not be formed on the same patient, although it's better that way. If the senior staff succeed in convincing the resident in this week's conference that the reason for his countertransference troubles lay in the patient's being a pseudoneurotic schizophrenic, and next week he sees some other student's patient showing the schizophrenic float as he walks into the room, that pair of experiences will perhaps do almost as well.

13. *Antinosological bias.* It is common knowledge that American psychiatry and clinical psychology, the former under psychodynamic influence and the latter under both psychodynamic and learning theory influence, have an animus against formal "diagnosis." The status of formal nosological diagnosis in American theory and practice warrants detailed treatment, and I am preparing such a discussion of theory and research literature for presentation elsewhere. I shall therefore confine myself here to a mere listing of some of the current clichés, with brief critical comments upon each but without attempting an adequate exposition of the argument or—when decent empirical data exist—detailed survey of the research findings. There are, of course, good reasons for being skeptical about diagnostic rubrics, and even more skeptical about their current application in a psychiatric tradition that deemphasizes training in diagnostic skills. But it is regrettable to find that the majority of beginning graduate students in clinical psychology "know" that "mere diagnostic labels" have no reliability or validity, no theoretical significance, no prognostic importance, and no relevance to treatment choice. They "know" these things because they were told them dogmatically in undergraduate abnormal psychology classes. They typically react with amazement, disbelief, and resentment to find a psychologist who bluntly challenges these ideas. If you want to be a diagnostic nihilist, you should be one in an intellectually responsible way, for scientific reasons rather than from bobbysoxer antidiagnostic propaganda. On the current scene, antidiagnostic prejudices of the familiar kinds (four of which I consider here) have recently been bolstered by a new ideological factor, to wit, the tendency of many students to *politicize everything*. A professor can (perhaps) discuss the helium nucleus or the sun's temperature without finding himself shortly involved in a debate on women's liberation, police brutality, Indochina, "establishment" bourgeois values, or the black ghetto. But psychiatric diagnosis is one of those topics that are reflexly politicized by many of our students.

Herewith, then, a brief summary of the usual antidiagnostic arguments, and my objections to each:

a. "Formal diagnoses are extremely unreliable." If it were empirically shown that formal diagnoses are extremely unreliable, it would remain an open question whether they are unreliable because (1) the diagnostic constructs do not refer to anything that really exists (i.e., there *is* no typology or taxonomy of behavior aberration that "carves nature at its joints,"), or (2) differential diagnosis of behavior disorders is unusually difficult, or (3) it is not unusually difficult but many clinicians perform it carelessly and uninformedly. One ought not, after all, be astounded to find that American psychiatrists and psychologists, educated in an antinosological tradition in which they have been taught that diagnosis is of no importance (and consequently never exposed to the classic nosological writings in the European tradition), have been presented with professional models of senior staff who do not take diagnosis seriously, and have not been differentially reinforced for good and poor diagnostic behavior, are unable to do it well!

It is not true that formal nosological diagnosis in psychiatry is as unreliable as the usual statements suggest. If we confine ourselves to major diagnostic categories (e.g., schizophrenia versus nonschizophrenia, organic brain syndrome versus functional disorder, and the like), if we require adequate clinical exposure to the patient (why would anyone in his right mind conduct a study of diagnostic rubrics based upon brief outpatient contact?), and if we study well-trained clinicians who take the diagnostic process seriously, then it is not clear that interclinician diagnostic agreement in psychiatry is worse than in other branches of medicine. (A colleague responds with "That's true, but medical diagnoses are completely unreliable also." I am curious what leads this colleague, given his "official" classroom beliefs, to consult a physician when he is ill? Presumably such an enterprise is pointless, and taking your sick child to a pediatrician is wasted time and money. Do any of my readers *really* believe this?) For instance, as to the diagnostic dichotomy schizophrenia versus nonschizophrenia, one study—based upon a very large *N*—shows the interjudge reliability to equal that of a good individual intelligence test (Schmidt and Fonda, 1956). I do not mean to suggest that the various interjudge reliability studies are consistent,

which they are not (see, for example, Rosen, Fox, and Gregory, 1972, Table 3–1, p. 46); nor do I assert that the evidence on this question is adequate at present. I merely point out that the majority of psychologists and psychiatrists in this country persist in reflexly repeating the dogma "Diagnosis is very unreliable" without paying due attention to the diagnostic circumstances and personnel involved in various studies, or telling us how unreliable something has to be before it is "very unreliable." The spectacle of a clinical psychologist spitting on formal psychiatric diagnostic labels on grounds of unreliability, meanwhile asking us to make clinical decisions on the basis of Rorschach interpretations, can only be described as ludicrous. For an excellent survey and sophisticated criticism of the empirical research on diagnostic interjudge reliability, plus some impressive new data on the subject, see Gottesman and Shields (1972, Chapter 2). I need hardly add that the errors criticized in this paper are presumably a major source of diagnostic unreliability, so that their reduction would yield an improvement (I predict a big improvement) over typical reported coefficients.

b. "We should be interested in understanding the patient rather than labeling him." This muddleheaded comment may be given additional controversial power by describing a taxonomic rubric as a "pigeonhole," whereby a clinician who diagnoses his patients or clients is adjudged guilty of "putting people into pigeonholes"—a manifestly wicked practice, the wickedness being immediately apparent from the very words, so no further argument is required. *Res ipsa loquitur!*

It should not be necessary to explain to sophisticated minds that whether "labeling" in the nosological sense is *part* of "understanding" the patient cannot be decided by fiat, but hinges upon the etiological content of the label. If the nosological label is a completely arbitrary classification corresponding to nothing in nature, then it is admittedly not contributory to our understanding the patient we are trying to help. And of course if that is its status, it is not contributory to anything (even epidemiological statistics) and shouldn't be engaged in. Anyone who uses formal nosological categories responsibly should, in consistency, believe that the rubrics mean something. (He need not, obviously, believe that they *all* mean something.) A diagnostic label means something about genetics or salient conflicts or schizophrenogenic mothers or social-class factors or unconscious fantasies or preferred mechanisms of defense or aberrated neurochemistry or whatever; and these kinds of entities are aspects—frequently clinically relevant aspects—of an adequate "causal understanding." It is important to see that which *class* of theoretical entities is implied by the nosologic term still remains open after a methodological decision to permit nosological labels is made. To conflate the two questions—"Are there taxonomic entities in psychiatry?" and "Is aberrated behavior sometimes caused by germs, genes, or structural CNS conditions?"—is just dumb, but the conflation is well nigh universal in American clinical thinking. See, in this connection, Meehl, 1972c; also footnote 19 (at p. 80) of Livermore, Malmquist, and Meehl, 1968; and footnote 10 (at p. 12) of Meehl, 1970b. The widespread habit of mentioning the "medical model" without having bothered to think through what it is (causally, statistically, and epistemologically) prevents an intellectually responsible consideration of complex taxonomic questions. An "organic" causal factor (e.g., vitamin deficiency) may be taxonomic or not; so also for a genetic causal factor (e.g., PKU mental deficiency is taxonomic, but garden-variety hereditary stupidity is not). On the other hand, a "nonorganic, nongenetic," purely social-learning etiology, while perhaps *usually* non-taxonomic, may sometimes be taxonomic. The schizophrenogenic mother has been so conceived by some. Suppose that Freud had been correct in his (pre-1900) opinion about the respective etiologies of hysteria and the obsessional neurosis. He held, on the basis of his early psychoanalytic treatment of these two groups of patients, and before his shattering discovery that much of his psychoanalytic reconstruction of their early childhood was fantasy, that the specific life-history etiology of hysteria consisted of prepubescent sexual (specifically *genital*-stimulation) experience in which the future patient was passive and in which fear or disgust predominated over pleasure. Whereas he thought that the obsessional neurosis had its specific life-history origin in prepubescent sexual experience in which the subsequent patient played an active (aggressive) role and in which pleasure predominated over the negative affects. Had this specific life-history etiology been corroborated by subsequent investigation, the diagnostic labels "hysteria" and "obsessional neurosis" would have carried a heavy freight of causal understanding, and would have been truly taxonomic. It makes no difference what *kind* of etiology we focus on (social, genetic, biochemical, or whatever), so long as the label points to it.

The notion that subsuming an individual under a category or rubric somehow prevents us from understanding the causal structure of his situation is one which has been repeatedly criticized but with negligible effect. The methodological level at which such discussions are typically carried on in the American tradition is pathetic in its superficiality. So far as I can discern, most clinicians who talk about the subject in this way have never even asked themselves what they *mean* by saying that "There are no disease entities in functional psychiatry." To make such a negative statement significantly, one ought presumably to have some idea about what would be the case if there *were* "entities" in functional psychiatry. One cannot deal with complicated questions of this sort by a few burblings to the effect that schizophrenia is not the same kind of thing as measles. What kinds of causal structures (and resultant phenotypic correlations and clusterings) may conveniently be labeled as "real entities" is a metaquestion of extraordinary complexity. To think about it in an intellectually responsible way requires philosophical, mathematical, and substantive competence at a level possessed by very few psychiatrists or clinical psychologists. Much of what we have to think clearly about in connection with the nosology-dynamics problem is tied up with the genetic factors problem in psychodynamics (cf. Meehl, 1972c).

c. "Formal diagnoses are prognostically worthless." This statement is just plain false as a matter of empirical fact. No one familiar with the published statistics, and for that matter no one who has kept his eyes and ears open around a mental hospital for a while, can deny—unless he has been brainwashed into a rabid antidiagnostic prejudice that paranoid schizophrenia has a very different outlook from a nice clean hypomanic attack in a cyclothymic personality, or that a "reactive depression" (precipitated, say, by failing one's Ph.D. prelims) will run a shorter course (with or without psychotherapy or chemotherapy) than a textbook compulsion neurosis, or that a hard-core Cleckley psychopath (Cleckley, 1964) is likely to continue getting into trouble until he becomes old enough to "simmer down" or "burn out," or that a case of hypochondriasis has a very poor outlook. I find it strange that psychologists urge us to rely upon psychological tests (especially the low-validity projective methods) for predictive purposes when, so far as the record shows, they do not have as much prognostic power as does formal diagnosis *even when made sloppily as in this country*.

Consider such a life-or-death prognostic problem as suicide risk in patients suffering from psychotic depression. Despite Bayes' Formula, and the arguments advanced by my doctoral student and co-author Albert Rosen in his paper on suicide (Rosen, 1954; see also Meehl and Rosen, 1955), in cases of psychotic depression the suicide risk figure is large enough to take into serious account. The usual estimates are that, before the introduction of EST and the antidepressant psychotropic drugs, roughly *one psychotic depression in six managed to kill himself.* (This figure cannot, of course, be easily calculated from the usual epidemiologic "rate" value.) More recently, follow-up studies of psychotically depressed patients who had made a "clinical recovery" sufficient to be discharged from the hospital found that another 3–5 percent will commit suicide in the ensuing two or three years after discharge. Point: Suicide probability among patients with psychotic depression is approximately equivalent to death risk in playing Russian roulette. If the responsible clinician does not recognize a psychotically depressed patient as such, and (therefore) fails to treat him as having a suicide risk of this magnitude, what he is in effect doing is handing the patient a revolver with one live shell and five empty chambers. Considering the irreversibility of death as an event, and the disutility attached to it in our society's value system, I assume my readers will agree that a Russian roulette probability figure is nothing to treat cavalierly. *Any psychiatrist or psychologist who does not make a thorough effort to ascertain whether his patient has a psychotic depression rather than a "depressive mood"* (the most common single psychiatric symptom, found in a wide variety of disorders), *in order to determine whether the patient requires treatment as a suicide risk of this magnitude, is behaving incompetently and irresponsibly.*

I will add some punch to this statistical argument by relating an anecdote (it comes to me directly from the student clinician to whom it happened). I report it in the form of a dialogue between myself and the student. This student therapist (a "psychiatric assistant") is an extremely bright, highly motivated, and very conscientious Arts College senior with three majors (one of which is psychology) and an HPR = 3.80. I mention these facts as evidence that the student's ignorance arises *not* from stupidity, lack of curiosity, poor motivation, or irresponsibility. It arises from the antinosological bias (more generally, the antiscientific, anti-intellectual attitudes) of his teachers and supervisors. The exchange goes as follows:

MEEHL: "You look kind of low today."

STUDENT: "Well, I should be—one of my therapy cases blew his brains out over the weekend."

MEEHL: "Oh, I'm sorry to hear that—that is a bad experience for any helper. Do you want to talk about it?"

STUDENT: "Yes. I have been thinking over whether I did wrong, and trying to figure out what happened. I have been his therapist and I thought we were making quite a bit of progress; we had a good relationship. But then he went home on a weekend pass and shot himself."

MEEHL: "Had the patient talked to you about suicide before?"

STUDENT: "Oh, yes, quite a number of times. He had even tried to do it once before, although that was before I began to see him."

MEEHL: "What was the diagnosis?"

STUDENT: "I don't know."

MEEHL: "You mean you didn't read the chart to see what the formal diagnosis was on this man?"

STUDENT: "Well, maybe I read it, but it doesn't come to my mind right now. Do you think diagnosis is all that important?"

MEEHL: "Well, I would be curious to know what it says in the chart."

STUDENT: "I am not sure there is an actual diagnosis in the chart."

MEEHL: "There *has* to be a formal diagnosis in the chart, by the regulations of any hospital or medical clinic, in conformity with the statistical standards of the World Health Organization, for insurance purposes, and so on. Even somebody who doesn't believe in diagnosis and wouldn't bother to put it in a staff note must record a formal diagnosis on the face sheet somewhere. He has to put something that is codeable in terms of the WHO *Manual of the International Statistical Classification of Diseases, Injuries, and Causes of Death.*"

STUDENT: "Oh, really? I never knew that."

MEEHL: "Did you see this man when he first came into the hospital?"

STUDENT: "Yes, I saw him within the first week after he was admitted."

MEEHL: "How depressed did he look then?"

STUDENT: "Oh, he was pretty depressed all right. He was very depressed at that time."

MEEHL: "Well, was he psychotically depressed?"

STUDENT: "I don't know how depressed 'psychotically depressed' is. How do you tell a psychotic depression?"

MEEHL: "Hasn't anybody ever given you a list of differential diagnostic signs for psychotic depression?"

STUDENT: "No."

MEEHL: "Tell me some of the ways you thought he was 'very depressed' at the time he came into the hospital."

STUDENT: "Well, he was mute, for one thing."

MEEHL: "*Mute?*"

STUDENT: "Yes, he was mute."

MEEHL: "You mean he was not very talkative, or do you mean that he wouldn't talk at all?"

STUDENT: "I mean he wouldn't talk at all—he was mute, literally mute."

MEEHL: "And you don't know whether that tells you the diagnosis—is that right?"

STUDENT: "No, but I suppose that means he was pretty depressed."

MEEHL: "If he was literally mute, meaning that he wouldn't answer simple questions like what his name is, or where he lives, or what he does for a living, then you have the diagnosis right away. If the man is not a catatonic schizophrenia, and if you know from all the available evidence that he is some kind of depression, you now know that he is a psychotic depression. There is no such thing as a neurotic depression with muteness."

STUDENT: "I guess I didn't know that."

MEEHL: "Why was he sent out on pass?"

STUDENT: "Well, we felt that he had formed a good group relationship and that his depression was lifting considerably."

MEEHL: "Did you say his depression was *lifting*?"

STUDENT: "Yes, I mean he was less depressed than when he came in—although he was still pretty depressed."

MEEHL: "When does a patient with a psychotic depression have the greatest risk of suicide?"

STUDENT: "I don't know."

MEEHL: "Well, what do the textbooks of psychiatry and abnormal psychology *say* about the time of greatest suicide risk for a patient with psychotic depression?"

STUDENT: "I don't know."

MEEHL: "You mean you have never read, or heard in a lecture, or been told by your supervisors, that the time when a psychotically depressed patient is most likely to kill himself is when his depression is 'lifting'?"

STUDENT: "No, I never heard of that."

MEEHL: "Well you have heard of it now. You better read a couple of old books, and maybe next time you will be able to save somebody's life."

The obvious educational question is, how does it happen that this bright, conscientious, well-motivated, social-service-oriented premed psychology major with a 3.80 average *doesn't know the most elementary things about psychotic depression*, such as its diagnostic indicators, its statistical suicide risk, or the time phase in the natural history of the illness which presents the greatest risk of suicide? The answer, brethren, is very simple: Some of those who are "teaching" and "supervising" him either don't know these things themselves or don't think it is important for him to know them. This hapless student is at the educational mercy of a crew that is so unscholarly, antiscientific, "groupy-groupy," and "touchy-feely" that they have almost no concern for facts, statistics, diagnostic assessment, or the work of the intellect generally.

d. "Diagnosis does not help with treatment." This is, of course, not a valid criterion for determining whether formal diagnoses have factual meaning, empirical validity, or interjudge reliability; that it is even thought to be so reflects the shoddy mental habits of our profession. But its conceptual implications aside, how much truth is there in the assertion, given the baselines of accuracy in treatment choice we generally have to live with in clinical psychology? I would be interested to learn that any psychological, test, or any psychodynamic inference, has a treatment selection validity as high as the nosological distinction between the affective psychoses and other disorders with regard to the efficacy of one of the few near-specifics we have in psychiatry, to wit, EST. Even a much less specific treatment indication, the phenothiazines for schizophrenia, has, as I read the record, as good a batting average as psychometrics or psychodynamic inference (see, for example, Meltzoff and Kornreich, 1970; Bergin and Strupp, 1972).

As elsewhere in this paper, I have here the occasion to point out the problem of a "double standard of methodological morals." If somebody is superskeptical and superscientific and requires reliability coefficients regularly better than .90 before he will use a proposed category or dimension in clinical decision making, then he will have a hard time justifying formal psychiatric diagnosis even when it is made by well-trained diagnosticians. (He will also have to advocate that physicians abandon their pernicious habit of taking blood pressures!) But such a superskeptic ought not, in consistency, waste his or our time in a case conference gassing about the patient's family dynamics or his unconscious mechanisms or his Rorschach or TAT or MMPI—*because none of these, singly or collectively, can measure up to his strict methodological demands either.* The decrying of diagnosis by psychiatrists and psychologists in favor of psychodynamic understanding or psychologist's test interpretation would require a showing that these competing methods of prediction and treatment choice are superior to psychiatric diagnosis when each is being done respectably. So far as I have been able to make out, there is no such showing. . . .

ADDENDUM

As this volume was going to press, my psychiatric colleague Dr. Leonard L. Heston commented, on reading the manuscript that an alternative to the somewhat complicated construct-validity approach proposed herein as surrogate for clinicopathological conference criteria would be the use of the follow-up. I am at a loss to understand my omitting this important alternative, except for the fact that my mental set was so strongly oriented toward solving the problem *of providing fairly quick differential reinforcement*, of the kind that the internist receives at the end of each clinicopathological conference when the pathologist presents his quasi-criterial report on what the tissue showed. But, as Dr. Heston reminds me, we

ought to be prepared to do some special things in psychiatry and clinical psychology, in trying to make up for the absence of the pathologist's report as a quasi-criterion of diagnosis. Dr. Heston points out that the clinician participating in a psychiatric case conference could be, so to speak, on record (we could even tape-record the conference—which might in itself tend to reduce some of the garbage generated!), and one's differential reinforcements would be forthcoming days, weeks, months (sometimes even years) later. Actually, there would be quite a few patients whose response to therapeutic intervention (e.g., phenothiazines in schizophrenia, electroplexy in psychotic depression, lithium carbonate in hypomania, valium in relatively uncomplicated anxiety states, RET in the "philosophical neurosis") would be ascertainable fairly soon after the case conference. Special provisions, including what might be a considerable financial outlay, would be necessary in order to achieve feedback on longer term forecasts. But I think that Dr. Heston's alternative suggestion is extremely important, and my discussion of the problem would be seriously defective without mention of it.

Of course, he and I agree that these are not really "competing alternatives," since both could be implemented, except insofar as we face the usual problem of opportunity costs. I have little doubt that the impact of some kinds of dramatic follow-up findings, their "convincing power," would be greater than the best souped-up, construct-valid, at-the-time quasi-criterion that could be devised with present methods. Two examples may be given.

Several years ago I had a two-hour diagnostic interview with a theology student from another city who presented with complaints of depression, anxiety, and "loss of interest," but who showed no clinical evidence of textbook schizophrenic thought disorder or markedly inappropriate affect. His flatness was no more severe on Mental Status appraisal than that which we find in many obsessional neurotics or other overintellectualizing, character-armored types. I dare say many of my American colleagues, and the majority of European clinicians, would say that my interview-based diagnosis, "Schizotype, early stages of decompensation, marginal Hoch-Polatin syndrome," was an example of Meehl indulging his schizotypal hobby again. Nor would most such skeptics have been convinced—although they might have been somewhat influenced—by the (post-interview) scoring of the patient's MMPI profile, which yielded not merely the "gullwing curve" suggestive of pseudoneurotic schizophrenia but had a grossly psychotic (schizophrenic) configuration. As it happened, I subsequently found this patient to have shown up in a Canadian mental hospital with more obvious symptoms of schizophrenia; and then a year or so later, he again showed up (at the Minneapolis Veterans Administration Hospital) with symptoms of schizophrenia so unmistakable that even a very conservative diagnostician, such as Dr. Eliot Slater, would, I am sure, agree with the schizophrenic diagnosis there made.

A quicker but equally dramatic differential reinforcement for the diagnosticians I recall from my graduate school days, at a psychiatric grand rounds conducted by the late J. C. McKinley, M.D., co-author with Dr. Hathaway of the Minnesota Multiphasic Personality Inventory and then head of the

Department of Neuropsychiatry. The patient seen in rounds that Saturday morning had presented with complaints of depression and anxiety, plus (as I recall it) rather vague nondelusional feelings that things seemed "not quite solid or real." He had a suspicious Rorschach with some rather bad 0^- responses [that is, original, but low quality responses] but nothing so gross as confabulation or contamination, and with a marginal over-all form level; his MMPI was also borderline, although somewhat more in the psychotic than the neurotic direction by the then available "eyeballed" profile criteria. On interview a certain flatness, as in the preceding example, was clinically in evidence; but it was not gross and one could not really speak properly of Kraepelinian "inappropriate affect." After the interview was concluded and the patient had left the conference room a spirited debate took place among staff and students about whether the patient was an early schizophrenia or a neurotic with mixed anxiety, depression, and obsessional features. While we were still engaged in this debate (giving arguments pro and con from the history, the resident's Mental Status interview report, the interview that we had just observed, and the MMPI/Rorschach combination) the intern and charge nurse came back to inform us that the patient, after having left the conference to be taken back to his room, had suddenly become mute and immobile, and was now standing in the corridor in a classical catatonic condition! This kind of quick and unmistakable feedback is of course unusual, but I don't think anybody who was present at that conference will ever forget the experience.

Allowing for the fact, as Jevons put it, that "Men mark where they hit and not when they miss," a series of such

follow-up findings would either (a) show my colleagues that when I say somebody is a schizotype, I usually know what I am talking about or (b) convince me that I am erring in the direction of schizotypal overdiagnosis. On the other hand, I cannot close this necessarily brief discussion of Dr. Heston's proposed emphasis on follow-up as an alternative criterion without emphasizing that follow-up is unfortunately an asymmetrical affair, in the sense that certain *positive* subsequent developments are capable of strongly supporting some diagnoses as against others; but the theoretical and clinical positions with regard to "open-concept" entities like schizoidia, subclinical manic depression, and the like are such that the *failure* subsequently to develop unmistakable clinical phenomena pointing to diagnosis Dl and away from diagnosis D2 cannot, as is recognized by all sophisticated persons, be argued very strongly in the negative. (Cf. the diagnostic situation involving a patient at risk for Huntington's Disease, in a family strain with late onset, who shows irritability but no positive neurology at age 40, and dies of coronary disease two years later. Did he carry the Huntington gene? We will never know.) I regret that the limitations of space (in this already too long chapter) prevent my giving Dr. Heston's suggestion the full consideration that it merits.

I take this opportunity to add that since my scholarly psychiatric colleagues Drs. Leonard Heston and Neil Yorkston are now running a new weekly clinical case conference which is being inched up steadily to clinically and scientifically respectable standards, the title of this essay has become out-of-date for its author, since I am attending their conference regularly, with enjoyment and profit.

References

Alker, H. A., & H. G. Hermann. Are Bayesian decisions artificially intelligent? *Journal of Personality and Social Psychology*, 1971, 19, 31–41.

Beck, A. T. *Depression: Clinical, experimental and theoretical aspects.* New York: Harper and Row, 1967.

Beck, A. T., B. B. Sethi, & R. W. Tuthill. Childhood bereavement and adult depression. *Archives of General Psychiatry*, 1963, 9, 295–302.

Bergin, A., & H. Strupp. *Changing frontiers in the science of psychotherapy.* Chicago: Aldine, 1972.

Bleuler, E. *Dementia praecox; or, the group of schizophrenias* (1911), tr. Joseph Zinkin. New York: International Universities Press, 1950.

Burks, B. S., D. W. Jensen, & L. M. Terman. *Genetic studies of genius, 111: The promise of youth.* Stanford, Calif.: Stanford University Press, 1930.

Campbell, D. P. The vocational interests of American Psychological Association presidents. *American Psychologist*, 1965, 20, 636–644.

Campbell, D. P. *Handbook for the Strong Vocational Interest Blank.* Stanford Calif.: Stanford University Press, 17.

Campbell, D. P., & D. W. Fiske. Convergent and discriminant validation by the multitrait-multimethod matrix. *Psychological Bulletin*, 1959, 56, 81–105. Reprinted in E. Megargee, ed. *Research in clinical assessment.* New York: Harper and Row, 1966. Pp. 89–111. Also reprinted in W. Mehrens and R. L. Ebel, eds. *Principles of educational and psychological measurement*, Chicago: Rand McNally, 1967. Pp. 273–302. Also reprinted in D. N. Jackson and S. Messick, eds. *Problems in human assessment.* New York: McGraw-Hill, 1967. Pp. 124–132.

Castleman, B., & J. Burke. *Surgical clinicopathological conferences of the Massachusetts General Hospital.* Boston: Little, Brown, 1964.

Castleman, B., & H. R. Dudley, Jr. *Clinicopathological conferences of the Massachusetts General Hospital: Selected medical cases.* Boston: Little, Brown, 1960.

Castleman, B., & J. M. McNeill. *Bone and joint clinicopathological conferences of the Massachusetts General Hospital.* Boston: Little, Brown, 1967.

Castleman, B., & E. P. Richardson. *Neurologic clinicopathological conferences of the Massachusetts General Hospital.* Boston: Little, Brown, 1969.

Clark, K. E. *America's psychologists: A survey of a growing profession*, Washington, D.C.: American Psychological Association, 1957.

Cleckley, H. *The mask of sanity.* (4th ed.) St. Louis: C. V. Mosby, 1964.

Cronbach, L. J., & P. E. Meehl. Construct validity in psychological tests. *Psychological Bulletin*, 1955, 52, 281–302. Also available in the Bobbs-Merrill Reprint Series in the Social Sciences, no. P–82.

Dahlstrom, W. G., G. S. Welsh, & L. E. Dahlstrom. *An MMPI handbook, I: Clinical interpretation.* Minneapolis: University of Minnesota Press, 1972.

Dellas, M., & E. L. Gaier. Identification of creativity: The individual. *Psychological Bulletin*, 1970, 73, 55–73.

Dunnette, M. D. Use of the sugar pill by industrial psychologists. *American Psychologist*, 1957, 12, 223–225.

Einhorn, H. J. The use of nonlinear noncompensatory models in decision making. *Psychological Bulletin*, 1970, 73, 221–230.

Einhorn, H. J. Expert measurement and mechanical combination. *Organizational behavior and human performance*, 1972, 7, 86–106.

Erlenmeyer-Kimling, L., ed. Genetics and mental disorders. *International Journal of Mental Health*, 1972, 1, 1–230.

Fine, R. *The healing of the mind: The technique of psychoanalytic psychotherapy.* New York: McKay, 1971.

Forer, B. R. The fallacy of personal validation: A classroom demonstration of gullibility. *Journal of Abnormal and Social Psychology*, 1949, 44, 118–123.

Frank, G. H. The role of the family in the development of psychopathology. *Psychological Bulletin*, 1965, 64, 191–205.

Freud, S. A reply to criticisms on the anxiety-neurosis (1895). In *Collected papers*, I. London: Hogarth Press, 1950. Pp. 107–127. Also in J. Strachey, ed. *Standard edition of the complete psychological works of Sigmund Freud*, III. London: Hogarth Press, 1962. Pp. 119–139.

Gilberstadt, H. Comprehensive MMPI codebook for males. IB 11–5. Washington, D.C.: Veterans Administration, 1970.

Gilberstadt, H. *Supplementary MMPI codebook for VA male medical consultation.* IB 11–5, Supplement 1. Washington, D.C.: Veterans Administration. 1972.

Gilberstadt, H., & J. Duker. *A handbook for clinical and actuarial MMPI interpretation.* Philadelphia: W. B. Saunders, 1965.

Glueck, B. C., Jr., P. E. Meehl, W. Schofield, & D. J. Clyde. *Minnesota-Hartford Personality Assay*: *Doctor's sub-set.* Hartford, Conn.: Institute of Living, n.d.

Glueck, B. C., Jr., P. E. Meehl, W. Schofield, & D. J. Clyde. *Minnesota- Hartford Personality Assay*: *Forty factors.* Hartford, Conn.: Institute of Living, n.d.

Glueck, B. C., Jr., P. E. Meehl, W. Schofield, & D. J. Clyde. The quantitative assessment of personality. *Comprehensive Psychiatry*, 1964, 5, 15–23.

Glueck, B. C., Jr., & C. F. Stroebel. The computer and the clinical decision process, 11. *American Journal of Psychiatry*, Supplement, 1969, 125, 2–7.

Goldberg, L. R. Simple models or simple processes? Some research on clinical judgments. *American Psychologist*, 1968, 23, 483–496.

Goldberg, L. R. Man versus model of man: A rationale, plus some evidence, for a method on improving on clinical inferences. *Psychological Bulletin*, 1970, 73, 422–432.

Goldsmith, S. R. and A. 1. Mandell. The psychodynamic formulation: A critique of a psychiatric ritual. *American Journal of Psychiatry*, 1969, 125, 1738–1743.

Gottesman, I. 1., & J. Shields. *Schizophrenia and genetics*: A twin study vantage point. New York: Academic Press, 1972.

Goulett, H. M. *The insanity defense in criminal trials.* St. Paul, Minn.: West Publishing Company, 1965.

Hacking, I. *Logic of statistical inference.* Cambridge: Cambridge University Press, 1965.

Hedberg, D. L., J. H. Houck, & B. C. Glueck, Jr. Tranylcypromine-trifluoperazine combination in the treatment of schizophrenia. *American Journal of Psychiatry*, 1971, 127, 1141–1146.

Heston, L. Genes and schizophrenia. In J. Mendels, ed. *Textbook of biological psychiatry.* New York: Wiley-Interscience, 1973 (in press).

Hoch, P., & P. Polatin. Pseudoneurotic forms of schizophrenia. *Psychiatric Quarterly*, 1949, 3, 248–276.

Hollingshead, A. B., & F. C. Redlich. *Social class and mental illness: A community study.* New York: Wiley, 1958.

Hollingworth, L. S. *Gifted children.* New York: Macmillan, 1926.

Kendall, M. G. On the reconciliation of theories of probability. *Biometrika*, 1949, 36, 101–116.

Klebanoff, L. B. Parental attitudes of mothers Sf schizophrenic, brain-injured and retarded, and normal children. *American Journal of Orthopsychiatry*, 1959, 29, 445–454.

Kleinmuntz, B. *Clinical information processing by computer.* New York: Holt Rinehart, and Winston, 1969.

Kleinmuntz. B., ed. *Formal representation of human judgment.* New York: Wiley, 1968.

Levi, I. *Gambling with truth: An essay on induction and the aims of science.* New York: Knopf, 1967.

Livermore, J. M., C. P. Malmquist, and P. E. Meehl. On the justifications for civil commitment. *University of Pennsylvania Law Review*, 1968, 117, 75–96.

Loevinger, J. Objective tests as instruments of psychological theory. *Psychological Reports*, Monograph Supplement 9, 1957, 3, 635–694. Reprinted in D. N. Jackson and S. Messick, eds. *Problems in human assessment.* New York: McGraw-Hill, 1967.

Lundberg, G. A. Case-studies vs. statistical method—an issue based on misunderstanding. *Sociometry*, 1941, 4, 379–383.

McNemar, Q. Lost: Our intelligence? why? *American Psychologist*, 1964, 19, 87 1–882.

Malmquist, C. P. Depression and object loss in acute psychiatric admissions. *American Journal of Psychiatry*, 1970, 126, 1782–1787.

Manning, H. M. Programmed interpretation of the MMPI. *Journal of Personality Assessment*, 1971, 35, 162–176.

Manosevitz, M., G. Lindzey, and D. D. Thiessen. *Behavioral genetics: Method and research.* New York: Appleton-Century-Crofts, 1969.

Marks, P. A., and W. Seeman. *The actuarial description of abnormal personality.* Baltimore: Williams and Wilkins, 1963.

Marks, P. A., and J. O. Sines. Methodological problems of cookbook construction. In J. Butcher, ed. *MMPI: Research developments and clinical applications.* New York: McGraw-Hill, 1969. Pp. 71–96.

Meehl, P. E. An examination of the treatment of stimulus patterning in Professor Hull's Principles of behavior. *Psychological Review*, 1945, 52, 324–332. (a)

Meehl, P. E. *Clinical versus statistical prediction: A theoretical analysis and a review of the evidence.* Minneapolis: University of Minnesota Press, 1954. (a).

Meehl, P. E. Clinical versus actuarial prediction. *Proceedings of the 1955 Invitational Conference on Testing Problems.* Princeton, N.J.: Educational Testing Service, 1956. Pp. 136–141. (a)

Meehl, P. E. Symposium on clinical and statistical prediction. *Journal of Counseling Psychology*, 1956, 3, 163–173. (b)

Meehl, P. E. Wanted—a good cookbook. *American Psychologist*, 1956, 11, 263–272. (c)

Meehl, P. E. When shall we use our heads instead of the formula? *Journal of Counseling Psychology*, 1957 4, 268–273.

Meehl, P. E. A comparison of clinicians with five statistical methods of identifying psychotic MMPI profiles. *Journal of Counseling Psychology*, 1959, 6, 102–109. (a)

Meehl, P. E. Some ruminations on the validation of clinical procedures. *Canadian Journal of Psychology*, 1959, 13, 102–128. Also available in the Bobbs-Merrill Reprint Series in the Social Sciences, no. 517. (b)

Meehl, P. E. The cognitive activity of the clinician. *American Psychologist*, 1960, 15, 19–27. Also available in the Bobbs-Merrill Reprint Series in the Social Sciences, no. P-518.

Meehl, P. E. Schizotaxia, schizotypy, schizophrenia, *American Psychologist*, 1962, 17, 827–838. Also available in the Bobbs-Merrill Reprint Series in the Social Sciences, no. P-516.

Meehl, P. E. *Manual for use with checklist of schizotypic signs.* Minneapolis: Psychiatric Research Unit, University of Minnesota Medical School, 1964.

Meehl, P. E. Seer over sign: The first good example. *Journal of Experimental Research in Personality*, 1965, 1, 27–32. (c)

Meehl, P. E. What can the clinician do well? In D. N. Jackson and S. Messick, eds. Problems in human assessment. New York: McGraw-Hill, 1967. Pp. 594–599. (b)

Meehl, P. E. Nuisance variables and the ex post facto design. *Reports from the Research Laboratories of the Department of Psychiatry, University of Minnesota*. Report no. PR-69–4. Minneapolis: University of Minnesota, April 15, 1969. (b)

Meehl, P. E. Nuisance variables and the ex post facto design. In M. Radner and S. Winokur, eds. *Minnesota studies in the philosophy of science*, IV. Minneapolis: University of Minnesota Press, 1970. (Expanded version of Meehl, 1969b.) Pp. 373–402. (a)

Meehl, P. E. Psychology and the criminal law. *University of Richmond Law Review*, 1970, 5, 1–30. (b)

Meehl, P. E. Some methodological reflections on the difficulties of psychoanalytic research. In M. Radner and S. Winokur, eds. *Minnesota studies in the philosophy of science*, IV. Minneapolis: University of Minnesota Press, 1970. Pp. 403–416. (c)

Meehl, P. E. Reactions, reflections, projections. In J. Butcher, ed. *Objective personality assessment: Changing perspectives*. New York: Academic Press, 1972. Pp. 131–189. (b)

Meehl, P. E. Specific genetic etiology, psychodynamics and therapeutic nihilism. *International Journal of Mental Health*, 1972, 1, 10–27. (c)

Meehl, P. E. MAXCOV-HITMAX: A taxonomic search method for loose genetic syndromes. 1973.

Meehl, P. E. The concept 'specific etiology': Some quantitative meanings. To appear.

Meehl, P. E., and W. G. Dahlstrom. Objective configural rules for discriminating psychotic from neurotic MMPI profiles. *Journal of Consulting Psychology*, 1960, 24, 375–387.

Meehl, P. E., D. T. Lykken, W. Schofield, and A. Tellegen. Recaptured-item technique (RIT): A method for reducing somewhat the subjective element in factor-naming. *Journal of Experimental Research in Personality*, 1971, 5, 171–190.

Meehl, P. E., and A. Rosen. Antecedent probability and the efficiency of psychometric signs, patterns, or cutting scores. *Psychological Bulletin*, 1955, 52, 194–216. Also available in the Bobbs-Merrill Reprint Series in the Social Sciences, no. P-514.

Meehl, P. E., W. Schofield, B. C. Glueck, Jr., W. B. Studdiford, D. W. Hastings, S. R. Hathaway, and D. J. Clyde. *Minnesota-Ford pool of phenotypic personality items*. (August 1962 ed.) Minneapolis: University of Minnesota, 1962.

Melrose, J. P., C. F. Stroebel, and B. C. Glueck, Jr. Diagnosis of psychopathology using stepwise multiple discriminant analysis, I. *Comprehensive Psychiatry*, 1970, 11, 43–50.

Meltzoff, J., and M. Kornreich. *Research in psychotherapy*. New York: Atherton Press, 1970.

Mirabile, C. S., J. H. Houck, and B- C- Glueck, Jr. Computer prediction of treatment success. *Comprehensive Psychiatry*, 1971, 12, 48–53.

Morrison, D. E., and R. E. Henkel, eds. *The significance test controversy*. Chicago: Aldine, 1970.

Myers, J. K., and L. Schaffer. Social stratification and psychiatric practice. *American Sociological Review*, 1954, 19, 307–310.

Nash, L. K. *The atomic-molecular theory*. Cambridge, Mass.: Harvard University Press, 1950.

Pankoff, L. D., and H. B. Roberts. Bayesian synthesis of clinical and statistical prediction. *Psychological Bulletin*, 1968, 70, 762–773.

Paterson, D. G. Character reading at sight of Mr. X according to the system of Mr. P. T. Barnum. Unpublished, mimeographed. First printed in M. L. Blum and B. Balinsky. *Counseling and psychology*. New York: Prentice-Hall, 1951. P. 47. Reprinted in M. D. Dunnette. Use of the sugar pill by industrial psychologists. *American Psychologist*, 1957, 12, 223.

Raiffa, H. *Decision analysis: Introductory lectures on choices under uncertainty*. Reading, Mass.: Addison-Wesley, 1968.

Rosen, A. Detection of suicidal patients: An example of some limitations in the prediction of infrequent events. *Journal of Consulting Psychology*, 1954, 18, 397–403.

Rosen, E., R. E. Fox, and I. Gregory. *Abnormal psychology*. (2nd ed.) Philadelphia: W. B. Saunders, 1972.

Rosenberg, M., B. C. Glueck, Jr., and C. F. Stroebel. The computer and the clinical decision process. *American Journal of Psychiatry*, 1967, 124, 595–599.

Rosenthal, D. *Genetic theory and abnormal behavior*. New York: McGraw-Hill, 1970.

Sarbin, T. R. A contribution to the study of actuarial and individual methods of prediction. *American Journal of Sociology*, 1942, 48, 593–602.

Savage, L. J. *The foundations of statistics*. New York: Wiley, 1954.

Sawyer, J. Measurement and prediction, clinical and statistical. *Psychological Bulletin*, 1966, 66, 178–200.

Schmidt, H. O. and C. P. Fonda. The reliability of psychiatric diagnosis: A new look. *Journal of Abnormal and Social Psychology*, 1956, 52 262–267.

Schofield, W. *Psychotherapy: The purchase of friendship*. Englewood Cliffs, N.J.: Prentice-Hall, 1964.

Schofield, W., and L. Balian. A comparative study of the personal histories of schizophrenic and nonpsychiatric patients. *Journal of Abnormal and Social Psychology*, 1959, 59, 216–225.

Shaffer, L. F. Of whose reality I cannot doubt. *American Psychologist*, 1953, 8, 608–623.

Strong, E. K., Jr. *Vocational interests of men and women*. Stanford, Calif.: Stanford University Press, 1943.

Sundberg, N. D. The acceptability of "fake" Versus "bona fide" personality test interpretations. *Journal of Abnormal and Social Psychology*, 1955, 50, 145–1 17.

Tallent, N. On individualizing the psychologist's clinical evaluation. *Journal of Clinical Psychology*, 1958, 14, 243–244.

Terman, L. M. *Genetic studies of genius, 1: Mental and physical traits of a thousand gifted children*. Stanford, Calif., Stanford University Press, 1925.

Terman, L. M., and M. H. Oden. *Genetic studies of genius, IV: The gifted child grows up*. Stanford, Calif.: Stanford University Press, 1947.

Terman, L. M., and M. H. Oden. *Genetic studies of genius, V: The gifted group at mid-life*. Stanford, Calif.: Stanford University Press, 1959.

Thorndike, R. L. The psychological value systems of psychologists. *American Psychologist*, 1954, 9, 787–789.

Thorndike, R. L. The structure of preferences for psychological activities among psychologists. *American Psychologist*, 1955, 10, 205–207.

Ulrich, R. E., T. J. Stachnik, and N. R. Stainton. Student acceptance of generalized personality interpretations. *Psychological Reports*, 1963, 13, 831–834.

PART FOUR

Interpreting Evidence in Clinical Psychology

Becoming a competent clinical psychologist requires us to be a thoughtful consumer of the research literature. Among other things, accomplishing this goal means perpetually trying to avoid confirmation bias by not imposing our theoretical views on data. Unless we're eternally vigilant, our theoretical orientations, whether they be psychoanalytic, behavioral, cognitive, humanistic, or something else, can blind us more than guide us, predisposing us to interpret ambiguous data in accord with our preexisting views (Mahoney, 1977; Ruscio, 2006). This error, in turn, can cause us to overlook important findings that are inconsistent with our hypotheses. In clinical practice, this mistake can lead us to fail to seek out crucial evidence that could *disconfirm* our initial hunches about our clients.

For example, a devout psychoanalyst might interpret a woman's fear of romantic intimacy as definitive evidence of early sexual abuse; in contrast, a devout behaviorist might interpret the same case as definitive evidence of a disturbed learning history. Although there may well be some truth to both possibilities, either or both could be wrong. Alternatively, both could be providing us with one small part of a complex picture.

To interpret evidence properly in clinical psychology, we also must be careful to avoid several errors that often arise when we consider the etiology (a fancy word for causation) of mental disorders. For example, many beginning students are tempted to ask the question, "What is *the* cause of Disorder X?" Such questions almost always lend themselves to misleading answers, because virtually all (in fact, we might even safely say "all") mental disorders are *multiply determined*, that is, produced by many causal factors (Ghaemi, 2009; Meehl, 1977). So we should be skeptical of theoretical explanations that attempt to account for complex clinical phenomena, like fear of romantic intimacy, depression, or anxiety, in terms of only a single variable. In clinical practice, this "one size fits all" approach can lead us to overlook important variables, like recent life stressors, job conflicts, or medical problems, that are contributing to our client's difficulties.

Many beginning students are also tempted to interpret the causes of mental disorders at only one level of explanation, such as the biological level, the psychological level, or the cultural level. But this approach too is overly simplistic, because each level of explanation contributes unique information that is not accounted for fully by other levels (Lilienfeld, 2007; McNally, 2010). For example, knowing that psychopathic personality—a condition marked by callousness, lack of guilt and empathy, dishonesty, and superficial charm—is associated with underactivity of the amygdala, a brain structure intimately involved in the processing of fear (Blair, Mitchell, & Blair, 2005), helps us to better understand the neurophysiology of this complex disorder. But this finding doesn't tell us *why* psychopaths possess fear deficits. To that, we may need to turn to the psychological level of explanation, which informs us that children who are callous tend to lack deep social emotions and do not develop adequate classically conditioned reactions to aversive stimuli (Frick & White, 2008; Lykken, 1995). Again, each level affords new insights into the disorder not provided by other levels.

Finally, being a thoughtful consumer of the clinical psychology literature requires us to acquire at least a modicum of statistical literacy. By statistical literacy, we mean the capacity to understand what statistics can and can't

Ayllon, T., Haughton, E., & Hughes, H. B. (1965). Interpretation of symptoms: Fact or fiction? *Behaviour Research and Therapy, 3*, 1–7.

Maher, B. A. (1978). A reader's, writer's, and reviewer's guide to assessing research reports in clinical psychology. *Journal of Consulting and Clinical Psychology, 46*, 835–838.

Kendler, K. S. (2005). Toward a philosophical structure for psychiatry. *American Journal of Psychiatry, 162*, 433–440.

Gigerenzer, G., et al. (2009, April). Knowing your chances: What health stats really mean. *Scientific American Mind*, 44–51.

tell us—and to avoid being seduced by superficially compelling but deceptive numbers. Humorist Mark Twain said famously that "there are three kinds of lies: lies, damned lies, and statistics." Of course, not all statistics are lies. Yet Twain's wry remark reminds us that statistics, although often immensely useful, can fool us unless we're trained to interpret them properly (Paulos, 1989; Seife, 2010).

Take the familiar statistic that 50 percent of all American marriages end in divorce. It derived largely from studies showing that there are about twice as many marriages (in one recent survey, 7.5 out of 1000 people) as divorces (in the same survey, 3.8 out of 1000 people) in the United States (Hurley, 2005). Yet, interpreting these data to mean that half of all marriages end in divorce is misleading, because the people who are getting divorced aren't the same as those who were getting married. In fact, the divorce rate in the United States is probably closer to between 30 and 40 percent—still high, but not as high as typically believed.

As we'll discover in Part 4, statistical literacy also requires us to evaluate health statistics with a skeptical eye. For example, many people confuse relative risk ratios with absolute risk ratios. A relative risk ratio tells us the *proportion* by which a variable increases one's risk for a disorder. If the recent death of a parent doubles one's chances of developing clinical depression, the relative risk ratio of this event is 200 percent. An absolute risk ratio, in contrast, tells us the actual percentage by which a given factor increases one's risk for a disorder. If the recent death of a parent increases one's chances of developing clinical depression from 1 percent to 3 percent, the absolute risk ratio is a measly 2 percent—even though the relative risk ratio is 300 percent! The news media routinely report relative risk ratios, probably because they often make for eye-popping headlines ("Drinking coffee quadruples your odds of cancer!"). Yet such ratios can be misleading, especially when what psychologists call the *base rate*—a fancy term for how common something is—is low.

Let's take an example. Research shows that having a grandparent or cousin with schizophrenia increases one's risk of developing schizophrenia about fivefold (Gottesman, 1991). That statistic sounds scary. Yet it becomes far less frightening when we realize that the base rate of schizophrenia in the general population is about 1 percent, so the increase is only from 1 to 5 percent—and the absolute risk ratio is only 4 percent. Moreover, 95 percent of people who have a grandparent or cousin with schizophrenia will never develop the disorder. The distinction between relative and absolute risk ratios is merely one example of why basic statistical literacy should be a requirement for all clinical practitioners and researchers.

THE READINGS IN PART 4

The four readings in Part 4 are diverse in content. Nevertheless, they share an emphasis on assisting readers to become more discerning consumers of the literature in clinical psychology and allied fields.

In a brief but incisive piece, Theodore Allyon and his colleagues highlight the dangers of confirmation bias, or what we might call "theoretical tunnel vision." They describe the case study of a 54-year-old female inpatient with schizophrenia who displayed a bizarre symptom—compulsive carrying of a broom around the unit—and discuss how two psychiatrists managed to interpret the symptom from a psychoanalytic (Freudian) perspective. The authors demonstrate how they managed to bring the symptom under control using straightforward operant conditioning principles derived from learning theory. As Allyon and his coauthors note, learning theory offers a far more plausible explanation for the patient's symptom than does psychoanalytic theory. Yet the two psychiatrists in this case "saw" their preferred theoretical explanation as the most likely.

Next, Brendan Maher provides a straightforward and user-friendly blueprint for evaluating research articles in clinical psychology and related fields. He offers helpful checklist guidelines to readers, reviewers, and authors for what information to include in such articles. Students will find Maher's article valuable in interpreting articles on the assessment, causes, and treatment of mental disorders.

Kenneth Kendler then presents a philosophical framework for conceptualizing the etiology of mental disorders. Although Kendler's article focuses on psychiatry, it is equally pertinent to clinical psychology and allied fields concerned with the causes and treatment of psychopathology. In this respect, it is an invaluable guide to navigating the complex research and theoretical literature on mental illness. Kendler reminds us that mental disorders are multiply determined, and that the search for a single cause (like a single gene or infectious agent) for schizophrenia, bipolar disorder, or other mental disorders is almost surely destined to fail. He also underscores the dangers of *explanatory reductionism*, that is, the effort to reduce the causes of mental disorders to only a single level of explanation, such as the biological level. As Kendler observes, *explanatory pluralism*, an approach that values multiple perspectives on psychopathology, including the biochemical, brain-based, psychological, and cultural levels, is most likely to yield fruit in the long run.

Finally, Gerd Gigerenzer and his coauthors tackle the issues of statistical literacy and illiteracy, especially as applied to the interpretation of health statistics. Although their article focuses on physical health statistics, it is equally relevant to statistics concerning psychological health. The authors offer vivid examples of common errors in interpreting health statistics—including differences between relative and absolute risk ratios—and equip readers with critical thinking skills for how to avoid such errors. They also show how surprisingly simple approaches, such as presenting data in terms of natural frequencies (9 out of 10 women) rather than percentages (90 percent of women), can help practitioners to better gauge clients' risks for negative outcomes.

15

Interpretation of Symptoms: Fact or Fiction?

T. AYLLON, E. HAUGHTON, AND H. B. HUGHES

SUMMARY

Psychotic patients frequently display bizarre behaviour patterns, usually considered to be symptomatic of the psychiatric disturbance. The present study is an illustration of how such symptoms can be measured in terms of frequency of occurrence. A bizarre symptom (compulsive broom-carrying) was developed, and maintained, by making reinforcement contingent on its occurrence. The reinforcement consisted of cigarettes or tokens which could be exchanged for cigarettes. The severity of the symptom, in terms of amount of time during which it was displayed, was shown to be a function of the temporal intervals between rewards. When reinforcement was withdrawn, the bizarre behaviour pattern disappeared.

Every culture, be it large or small, has developed a set of norms for the behaviour of its members. Deviations from the common patterns are only tolerated within certain limits, and societies usually develop effective systems of reward and punishment in order to produce socially adaptive behaviour (LeVine, 1963).

Whether or not deviations are tolerated within a given culture seems to be a function of the amount of time the individual spends displaying the odd behaviour. A productive scientist who paces the floor occasionally, gesticulating and talking to himself, elicits no more than an indulgent smile from his fellow men; but the person who spends the major part of his waking day pacing back and forth in a seemingly purposeless fashion is rushed to a psychiatric institution where efforts are made to uncover the underlying personality disturbance responsible for the symptom, i.e. compulsive pacing. Thus, symptoms lead to interpretations which overlook the observable behaviour. For example, Freud (1918) stated that compulsive acts are expressive rather than instrumental and arise out of inner needs. The object of the "compulsion to repeat" seemingly purposeless acts, or the reliving of traumatic experiences in dreams and delusions is to reduce anxiety aroused by the original event (Freud, 1920). To Jung (1917) symptoms or symbolic gestures are an attempt to represent archetypal memories by analogy through actions.

Colourful as these interpretations may be, they explain symptomatic or maladaptive behaviour patterns in a way which resembles fiction rather than fact. A more realistic approach toward the understanding of symptoms has been proposed by Eysenck (1959, 1960) and Wolpe (1958; Wolpe *et al.,* 1964), who regard symptoms as behaviour, the acquisition, maintenance, and elimination of which follows the principles of learning described by such men as Hull, Spence, Dollard and Miller, Mowrer, and Skinner (Hilgard, 1956). Skinner's work has been particularly influential in suggesting alternative ways of understanding persistent behaviour or behaviour which occurs at high frequencies. Within his methodological framework, commonly referred to as operant conditioning, investigators found that a single pairing of a reinforcement (food) with a specific response increases the probability of the reoccurrence of that response (Skinner, 1938). The persistence or maintenance of a response was found to be a function of the frequency with which reinforcement is programmed (Ferster and Skinner, 1957).

Lindsley (1956) has pioneered the extension of operant techniques to the study of human behaviour with special attention to psychotic behaviour. His data indicate that psychotic behaviour is lawful and amenable to analysis by established techniques (Lindsley, 1960, 1963). The implications of Lindsley's findings for the understanding and treatment of abnormal behaviour have been demonstrated in recent laboratory and field investigations.

In laboratory studies, for example, a variety of symptoms such as hysterical blindness (Brady and Lind. 1961), thumbsucking (Baer, 1962), tics (Barrett, 1962), and stuttering (Flanagan *el al.,* 1958) have been modified by programming special consequences to follow the presence or absence of the symptoms. Not only did the methodology derived from conditioning prove useful in the reduction of undesirable "symptoms", but the same techniques were also found to be effective in initiating and maintaining desirable responses. Ferster and DeMeyer (1961) were able to initiate discriminative judgement in autistic children, and Lovaas *et al.* (1964) found that severely withdrawn children learned to make social approaches if the response was followed by the termination of unpleasant stimuli.

In field applications, certain modifications may have to be considered in terms of reduced automation, albeit without abandoning precise definition of the behaviour and its consequences. Ayllon and his associates demonstrated that drastic alterations in the behaviour of adult chronic schizophrenic patients were possible within a hospital ward setting through the manipulation of specific environmental consequences. Symptoms like hoarding, violence, refusal to eat, and psychotic verbalizations were substantially modified or eliminated (Ayllon and Michael. 1959; Ayllon and Haughton, 1962; Ayllon. 1963). Wolf *et al.* (1964), also working in a hospital setting, successfully altered the frequency of tantrums. sleeping and eating problems, as well as appropriate social and verbal behaviour in one autistic child. Finally, Russo (1964) reported that maladaptive behaviour in children could be modified by the parents when conditioning techniques were explained and demonstrated to them. The successful alteration from maladaptive to more acceptable behaviour, described by Russo, indicates that conditioning techniques can be effective even in situations of minimal experimental control.

Despite the wealth of experimental evidence to the effect that a wide range of behaviour can be altered, it is still difficult to determine how maladaptive responses are acquired and maintained in many instances. The present study may serve as an illustration of the process involved in the development of one of the many so-called psychotic symptoms. Since the "symptom" was experimentally induced, deliberately maintained, and finally eliminated, the etiology is pretty straightforward, and inferences can be drawn about the origin of similar bizarre behaviour patterns.

The particular "symptom" reported in this case consisted of a patient's compulsively carrying a broom while pacing the floor or standing around. Since the patient never used the broom in order to sweep, her behaviour can be described as "purely expressive and without purpose" (Freud, 1918). The clinical picture and the authenticity of the "symptom" were verified by descriptions obtained from two board-certified psychiatrists who were asked to observe the patient through a one-way window facing the day room of the hospital ward where the patient resided.

Dr. X described the patient as follows:

"The broom represents to this patient some essential perceptual element in her field of consciousness . . . it is certainly a stereotyped form of behaviour such as is commonly seen in rather regressed schizophrenics and is rather analogous to the way small children or infants refuse to be parted from some favourite toy, piece of rag, etc."

Dr. Y made these comments about the same patient:

"Her constant and compulsive pacing, holding a broom in the manner she does, could be seen as a ritualistic procedure, a magical action. . . . Her broom would be then: (1) a child that gives her love and she gives him in return her devotion, (2) a phallic symbol, (3) the sceptre of an omnipotent queen . . . this is a magical procedure in which the patient carries out her wishes, expressed in a way that is far beyond our solid, rational and conventional way of thinking and acting."

Neither psychiatrist, of course, was aware of the experimental origin of the behaviour, and their descriptions indicate that the woman with her broom represented a typical, chronic, female patient who exhibited a specific symptom. The following sections of this paper contain a description of the actual etiology of that symptom.

METHOD

The Experimental Setting

The investigation was conducted in a psychiatric hospital ward set aside for the experimental study of operant techniques and their application to psychiatric problems. The patient population consisted of 40 female, chronic schizophrenics. Only authorized personnel had access to the ward. The ward staff, consisting of attendants and nurses,* made and recorded behavioural observations under strict instructions and direct supervision. During the present experiment, a time-sample technique of observation was utilized. Attendants checked the patient every 30 min from 7.00 a.m. to 10.30 p.m. without interacting with the patient and recorded the location, position, and activity of the patient on specially prepared forms. These represented the raw data from which the behavioural analysis was made.

Additional observations obtained every 15 min at different times during the investigation paralleled the 30 min samples and suggest that the time-sample technique employed gives a satisfactory measurement of a stable behaviour pattern.

In order to minimize observer's bias, attendants took turns observing different patients according to a pre-arranged schedule. Hence, observations on any one patient were collected by numerous, different attendants. The attendants, furthermore, had no access to the compiled data, thus minimizing contamination of results through knowledge of the procedures. None of the attendants was versed in conditioning theory.

Subject

The subject was a 54-year-old, female patient, classified as schizophrenic reaction, chronic undifferentiated type, who had been hospitalized for 23 years. She received no medication during this investigation. According to the ward reports, the patient stayed in bed or lay on a couch most of the time. She

---

*In this paper, the terms "nurse" and "attendant" are used synonymously.

was described as an idle patient who simply refused to do anything on the ward except smoke numerous cigarettes. This idleness had persisted for 13 years.

Procedure

A baseline of the patient's behaviour was obtained by means of the 30 min time-sample observations. According to these, the patient spent 60 per cent of her waking time lying in bed. Approximately 20 per cent of her time was spent in sitting and walking. The rest of the time was accounted for by behaviour associated with meals, grooming, and elimination.

During this pre-experimental period the patient's smoking was restricted to one cigarette at each meal in order to induce deprivation.

A response was selected, the topography of which closely resembled the typical symptoms displayed by some chronic schizophrenic patients, and which would allow easy observation. The response that met these characteristics was defined for the ward staff as "the patient must be in an upright position and hold a broom".

During the period of baseline observations (25 days), the response (carrying a broom) was never observed. The bizarre behaviour was initiated, using the method of successive approximation (Keller and Schoenfeld, 1950). This technique consisted of having one attendant give the patient a broom, and while the broom was being held by the patient, another attendant gave her a cigarette. After the second day of shaping, the patient picked up the broom herself.

Once the response had been initiated, it was maintained on an intermittent schedule of reinforcement (Ferster and Skinner, 1957). On the average the patient received a cigarette every 15 min if she was holding the broom. The intervals between reinforcements varied from 5 to 25 min. Each attendant was given a schedule specifying the exact times at which the patient was to be reinforced with a cigarette, provided she was carrying the broom.

The effectiveness of a conditioned or secondary reinforcer (a token) was explored also. After 75 days of using cigarettes as reinforcers, tokens were introduced. To facilitate the switch from cigarette to token reinforcement, the patient received verbal instructions, and for the first few times was permitted to exchange her token immediately for a cigarette. Later on, the exchange (token for cigarette) took place whenever the next reinforcement was scheduled, i.e. the patient received a token if she was carrying the broom at the scheduled time, kept that token until the next reinforcement was scheduled, and if she again carried the broom at that time, she exchanged the token received earlier for a cigarette. The tokens acquired conditioned (secondary) reinforcing properties in a similar fashion to that described by an early worker in the area of secondary reinforcement (Wolfe, 1936). In order to explore the limits within which the behaviour could be maintained, the average length of the intervals between reinforcements was increased. After 95 days the mean interval was set at 30 min, on the 220th day at 60 min, and finally on the 225th day at 480 min. Extinction was started on the 295th day of the experiment.

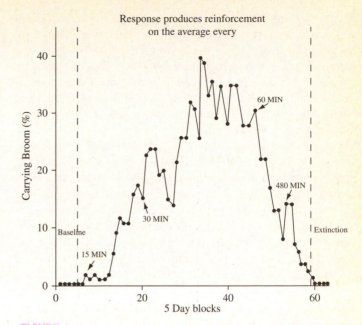

FIGURE 1   Percentage of time during which the patient displayed the response "carrying broom". The percentage is obtained by dividing the number of observed responses by the total number of 160 observations collected in a 5 day period.

RESULTS

Figure 1 shows that holding and carrying a broom for long periods can be brought under experimental control. The bizarre behaviour was developed from an original level of no response prior to the introduction of reinforcement to a maximum level of responding where the behaviour was displayed during 40 per cent of the patient's waking time.

The substitution of token reinforcement for cigarettes had no adverse effect upon the development of the "symptom" (75th day of the experiment: 15th 5-day block on Fig. 1). The tokens maintained the behaviour effectively.

Complete withdrawal of reinforcement (extinction) led to a disappearance of the "symptom".

DISCUSSION

The present study illustrates how the acquisition and persistence of an essentially meaningless and bizarre behaviour pattern can be brought under environmental control. The response (carrying a broom) was quickly initiated simply by pairing a reinforcement (cigarette or token) with the occurrence of the response. The study further shows that once the behaviour has been established, it can be maintained over long periods of time (in this instance approximately one year) through intermittent or occasional reinforcement. It should be noted that the patient continued to display the symptom even when she received no more than one reinforcement on the average of every eight hours, and only stopped when reinforcement was completely withdrawn.

Another interesting aspect of symptomatic behaviour is the fact that its occurrence frequently prevents the display of other more constructive behaviour. Implicit in the present study is the finding that as the frequency of carrying a broom increased, a decrease in the frequency of lying in bed took place. Conversely, when the "symptom" was displayed less often, the patient spent more time lying in bed as measured by the time-sample technique. From a rehabilitative standpoint, it seems worth considering not only the elimination of symptomatic behaviour, but a simultaneous strengthening or shaping of constructive, socially adaptive responses.

The persistent display of a bizarre and purposeless behaviour pattern over long periods of time is frequently the only reason for hospitalization of individuals. Relatives, neighbours, or friends do not initiate commitment procedures to a psychiatric institution because a person fails to resolve his Oedipus Complex. Institutionalization becomes necessary only when the patient engages in a socially deviant behaviour and spends a sufficiently large amount of time at it to disrupt normal functioning.

The etiology of many so-called psychotic symptoms exhibited by hospitalized patients or those in need of hospitalization does not have to be sought in the obscure dynamics of a psychiatric disturbance. Symptoms may be the result of an accidental pairing of the peculiar behaviour with some form of reinforcement meted out by the unsuspecting environment. The "superstitious behaviour" observed in pigeons in the experimental laboratory (Skinner, 1948; Morse and Skinner, 1957) demonstrates how a single reinforcement accidentally paired with a certain response will increase the probability of that response occurring again in the future. The animal behaves as if the response had produced the reward.

It seems plausible that symptoms like the one developed in the present study might have been initiated without intent on the part of anyone. Peculiar behaviour patterns which originally may occur infrequently and in a random fashion, occupying a relatively small amount of the person's total waking time, meet with such social or other environmental reaction as to alter their future frequency. For example, the elderly woman who refuses to be parted from her rag doll may indeed exhibit a symptom of underlying guilt feelings in regard to some child she either never had or rejected if she did have it. However, such an interpretation becomes superfluous when one considers that the act of carrying the rag doll is bound to elicit occasional attention from attendants in the patient's environment in the form of pleasant remarks about her "baby". In fact, the behaviour is maintained by these intermittent reinforcements given by the hospital staff, rather than by guilt or other feelings, the existence of which is questionable at best.

Learning principles deduced in psychological laboratories may well represent the foundation upon which effective therapeutic procedures will be built. Certainly, the number of recent books devoted to the application of conditioning principles to behavioural problems would appear to indicate a trend among clinicians to move away from fiction in the direction of facts consonant with laboratory findings (Bachrach, 1962; Bandura and Walters, 1963; Eysenck, 1960, 1961; Franks, 1964; Lundin, 1961; Wolpe et al., 1964).

References

Ayllon T. (1963) Intensive treatment of psychotic behaviour by stimulus satiation and food reinforcement. *Behav. Res. Ther.* 1, 53–61.

Ayllon T. and Haughton E. (1962) The control of behaviour of schizophrenic patients by food. *J. exp. anal. Behav.* 5, 343–352.

Ayllon T. and Michael J. (1959) The psychiatric nurse as a behavioural engineer. *J. exp. anal. Behav.* 2, 323–334.

Bachrach A. J. (Ed.) (1962) *Experimental Foundations of Clinical Psychology.* Basic Books, New York.

Baer D. M. (1962) Laboratory control of thumbsucking by withdrawal and re-presentation of reinforcement. *J. exp. anal. Behav.* 5, 525–528.

Bandura A. and Walters R. H. (1963) *Social learning and personality development.* Holt, Rinehart & Winston, New York.

Barrett Beatrice H. (1962) Reduction in rate of multiple tics by free operant conditioning methods. *J. nerv. ment. Dis.* 135, 187–195.

Brady J. P. and Lind D. L. (1961) Experimental analysis of hysterical blindness. *Arch. gen. Psychiat.* 4, 331–339.

Eysenck H. J. (1959) Learning theory and behaviour therapy. *J. ment. Sci.* 105, 61–75.

Eysenck H. J. (1960) *Behaviour Therapy and the Neuroses.* Pergamon Press, New York.

Eysenck H. J. (Ed.) (1961) *Handbook of Abnormal Psychology.* Basic Books, New York.

Ferster C. B. and DeMeyer M. K. (1961) The development of performances in autistic children in an automatically controlled environment. *J. chron. Dis.* 13, 312–345.

Ferster C. B. and Skinner B. F. (1957) *Schedules of Reinforcement.* Appleton-Century-Crofts, New York.

Flanagan B., Goldiamond I. and Azrin N. H. (1958) Operant stuttering: the control of stuttering behaviour through response contingent consequences. *J. exp. anal. Behav.* 1, 173–177.

Franks, C. M. (Ed.) (1964) *Conditioning Techniques in Clinical Practice and Research.* Springer, New York.

Freud S. (1918) Totem and taboo, in *The Complete Psychological Works* (transl. J. Strachey, 1955). Hogarth, London.

Freud S. (1920) Beyond the pleasure principle, in *The Complete Psychological Works* (transl. J. Strachey, 1955). Hogarth, London.

Hilgard E. R. (1956) *Theories of Learning.* Appleton-Century-Crofts, New York.

Jung C. G. (1917) *Collected Papers on Analytical Psychology.* Moffat, Yard, New York.

Keller F. S. and Schoeneeld W. N. (1950) *Principles of Psychology.* Appleton-Century-Crofts, New York.

LeVine R. A. (1963) Behaviorism in psychological anthropology, in *Concepts of Personality.* (Eds. J. M. Wepman and R. W. Heine). Aldine, Chicago.

Lindsley O. R. (1956) Operant conditioning methods applied to research in chronic schizophrenia. *Psychiat. Res. Repts.* 5, 118 139.

Lindsley O. R. (1960) Characteristics of the behavior of chronic psychotics as revealed by free-operant conditioning methods. *Diseases of the Nervous System Monogr. Suppl.,* Vol. XXI, No. 2.

Lindsley O. R. (1963) Direct measurement and functional definition of vocal hallucinatory symptoms. *J. nerv. went. Dis.* 136, 293–297.

Lovaas I., Freitag; G., Kinder M., Rubenstein B., Schaeffer B. and Simmons J. (1964) Developing social behaviors in autistic children using electric shock. Unpublished paper presented at the American Psychological Association, Los Angeles.

Lundin R. W. (1961) *Personality: An Experimental Approach.* Macmillan, New York.

Morse W. H. and Skinner B. F. (1957) A second type of "superstition" in the pigeon. *Amer: J. Psychol.* 70, 308–311.

Russo S. (1964) Adaptations in behavioral therapy with children. *Behav. Res. Ther.* 2, 43–47.

Skinner B. F. (1938) *The Behavior of Organisms.* Appleton-Century-Crofts, New York.

Skinner B. F. (1948) "Superstition" in the pigeon. *J. exp. Psychol.* 38, 168–172.

Wolf M., Risley T. and Mees H. (1964) Application of operant conditioning procedures to the behaviour problems of an autistic child. *Behav. Res. Ther.* 1, 305–312.

Wolff, J. B. (1936) Effectiveness of token-rewards for chimpanzees. *Comp. Psychol. Monogr.* 12, No. 60.

Wolpe J. (1958) *Psychotherapy by Reciprocal Inhibition.* Stanford University Press, Stanford.

Wolpe J., Salter A. and Reyna L. J. (1964) *Conditioning Therapies: the Challenge in Psychotherapy.* Holt, Rinehart, & Winston, New York.

16

A Reader's, Writer's, and Reviewer's Guide to Assessing Research Reports in Clinical Psychology

BRENDAN A. MAHER

The Editors of the Journal of Consulting and Clinical Psychology *who served between 1974 and 1978 have seen some 3,500 manuscripts in the area of consulting and clinical psychology. Working with this number of manuscripts has made it possible to formulate a set of general guidelines that may be helpful in the assessment of research reports. Originally developed by and for journal reviewers, the guidelines are necessarily skeletal and summary and omit many methodological concerns. They do, however, address the methodological concerns that have proved to be significant in a substantial number of cases. In response to a number of requests, the guidelines are being made available here.*

TOPIC CONTENT

1. Is the article appropriate to this journal? Does it fall within the boundaries mandated in the masthead description?

STYLE

1. Does the manuscript conform to APA style in its major aspects?

INTRODUCTION

1. Is the introduction as brief as possible given the topic of the article?
2. Are all of the citations correct and necessary, or is there padding? Are important citations missing? Has the author been careful to cite prior reports contrary to the current hypothesis?
3. Is there an explicit hypothesis?
4. Has the *origin* of the hypothesis been made explicit?
5. Was the hypothesis *correctly* derived from the theory that has been cited? Are other, contrary hypotheses compatible with the same theory?
6. Is there an explicit rationale for the selection of measures, and was it derived logically from the hypothesis?

METHOD

1. Is the method so described that replication is possible without further information?
2. **Subjects:** Were they sampled randomly from the population to which the results will be generalized?
3. Under what circumstances was informed consent obtained?
4. Are there probable biases in sampling (e.g., volunteers, high refusal rates, institution population atypical for the country at large, etc.)?
5. What was the "set" given to subjects? Was there deception? Was there control for experimenter influence and expectancy effects?
6. How were subjects debriefed?
7. Were subjects (patients) led to believe that they were receiving "treatment"?

8. Were there special variables affecting the subjects, such as medication, fatigue, and threat that were not part of the experimental manipulation? In clinical samples, was "organicity" measured and/or eliminated?

9. **Controls:** Were there appropriate control groups? What was being controlled for?

10. When more than one measure was used, was the order counterbalanced? If so, were order effects actually analyzed statistically?

11. Was there a control task(s) to confirm specificity of results?

12. **Measures:** For both dependent and independent variable measures—was validity and reliability established and reported? When a measure is tailor-made for a study, this is very important. When validities and reliabilities are already available in the literature, it is less important.

13. Is there adequate description of tasks, materials, apparatus, and so forth?

14. Is there discriminant validity of the measures?

15. Are distributions of scores on measures typical of scores that have been reported for similar samples in previous literature?

16. Are measures free from biases such as
    a. Social desirability?
    b. Yeasaying and naysaying?
    c. Correlations with general responsivity?
    d. Verbal ability, intelligence?

17. If measures are scored by observers using categories or codes, what is the interrater reliability?

18. Was administration and scoring of the measures done blind?

19. If short versions, foreign-language translations, and so forth, of common measures are used, has the validity and reliability of these been established?

20. In correlational designs, do the two measures have theoretical and/or methodological independence?

REPRESENTATIVE DESIGN

1. When the stimulus is a human (e.g., in clinical judgments of clients of differing race, sex, etc.), is there a *sample* of stimuli (e.g., more than one client of each race or each sex)?

2. When only one stimulus or a few human stimuli were used, was an adequate explanation of the failure to sample given?

STATISTICS

1. Were the statistics used with appropriate assumptions fulfilled by the data (e.g., normalcy of distributions for parametric techniques)? Where necessary, have scores been transformed appropriately?

2. Were tests of significance properly used and reported? For example, did the author use the p value of a correlation to justify conclusions when the actual size of the correlation suggests little common variance between two measures?

3. Have statistical significance levels been accompanied by an analysis of practical significance levels?

4. Has the author considered the effects of a limited range of scores, and so forth, in using correlations?

5. Is the basic statistical strategy that of a "fishing expedition"; that is, if many comparisons are made, were the obtained significance levels predicted in advance? Consider the number of significance levels as a function of the total number of comparisons made.

FACTOR ANALYTIC STATISTICS

1. Have the correlation and factor matrices been made available to the reviewers and to the readers through the National Auxiliary Publications Service or other methods?

2. Is it stated what was used for communalities and is the choice appropriate? Ones in the diagonals are especially undesirable when items are correlated as the variables.

3. Is the method of termination of factor extraction stated, and is it appropriate in this case?

4. Is the method of factor rotation stated, and is it appropriate in this case?

5. If items are used as variables, what are the proportions of yes and no responses for each variable?

6. Is the sample size given, and is it adequate?

7. Are there evidences of distortion in the final solution, such as singlet factors, excessively high communalities, obliqueness when an orthogonal solution is used, linearly dependent variables, or too many complex variables?

8. Are artificial factors evident because of inclusion of variables in the analysis that are alternate forms of each other?

FIGURES AND TABLES

1. Are the figures and tables (a) necessary and (b) self-explanatory? Large tables of nonsignificant differences, for example, should be eliminated if the few obtained significances can be reported in a sentence or two in the text. Could several tables be combined into a smaller number?

2. Are the axes of figures identified clearly?

3. Do graphs correspond logically to the textual argument of the article? (E.g., if the text states that a certain technique leads to an *increment* of mental health and the accompanying graph shows a *decline* in symptoms, the point is not as clear to the reader as it would be if the text or the graph were amended to achieve visual and verbal congruence.)

DISCUSSION AND CONCLUSION

1. Is the discussion properly confined to the findings or is it digressive, including new post hoc speculations?
2. Has the author explicitly considered and discussed viable alternative explanations of the findings?
3. Have nonsignificant trends in the data been promoted to "findings"?

4. Are the limits of the generalizations possible from the data made clear? Has the author identified his/her own methodological difficulties in the study?
5. Has the author "accepted" the null hypothesis?
6. Has the author considered the possible methodological bases for discrepancies between the results reported and other findings in the literature?

17

Toward a Philosophical Structure for Psychiatry

Kenneth S. Kendler

This article, which seeks to sketch a coherent conceptual and philosophical framework for psychiatry, confronts two major questions: how do mind and brain interrelate, and how can we integrate the multiple explanatory perspectives of psychiatric illness? Eight propositions are proposed and defended: 1) psychiatry is irrevocably grounded in mental, first-person experiences; 2) Cartesian substance dualism is false; 3) epiphenomenalism is false; 4) both brain→mind and mind→brain causality are real; 5) psychiatric disorders are etiologically complex, and no more "spirochete-like" discoveries will be made that explain their origins in simple terms; 6) explanatory pluralism is preferable to monistic explanatory approaches, especially biological reductionism; 7) psychiatry must move beyond a prescientific "battle of paradigms" to embrace complexity and support empirically rigorous and pluralistic explanatory models; 8) psychiatry should strive for "patchy reductionism" with the goal of "piecemeal integration" in trying to explain complex etiological pathways to illness bit by bit.

(Am J Psychiatry 2005; 162:433–440)

Many a psychiatrist has said that he did not want to burden himself with a philosophy . . . but the exclusion of philosophy would . . . be disastrous for psychiatry.

—K. Jaspers (1, p. 769)

Whether we know it or not, to practice or to do research in the field of mental health requires us to assume certain positions on several philosophical issues, two of which are particularly central. The first such issue is the nature of the interrelationship of the brain and the mind. The second is to understand how the various explanatory approaches that can be taken toward psychiatric disorders can best be interrelated.

Because our field deals with fundamental questions of what it means to be human, psychiatry is particularly susceptible to preconceptions that can strongly color the value we assign to differing methodological perspectives. With the growth of neuroscience and molecular biology, psychiatry is set to inherit rich insights into the basic workings of the human brain. To maximally use this new information, however, will require that we have our conceptual house in order.

This article seeks to sketch a coherent conceptual and philosophical framework for psychiatry that consists of eight major propositions:

1. Psychiatry is irrevocably grounded in mental, first-person experiences.
2. Cartesian substance dualism is false.
3. Epiphenomenalism is false.
4. Both brain→mind and mind→brain causality are real.
5. Psychiatric disorders are etiologically complex, and we can expect no more "spirochete-like" discoveries that will explain their origins in simple terms.
6. Explanatory pluralism is preferable to monistic explanatory approaches, especially biological reductionism.
7. Psychiatry needs to move from a prescientific "battle of paradigms" toward a more mature approach that embraces complexity along with empirically rigorous and pluralistic explanatory models.
8. Finally, we need to accept "patchy reductionism" with the goal of piecemeal integration in trying to explain the complex etiological pathways to psychiatric illness a little bit at a time.

GROUNDING IN THE MENTAL WORLD

Foundational to this framework is the view that the field of psychiatry is deeply and irreversibly wedded to the mental world. The questions that have played such a prominent role in the history of psychology—whether mental processes can or ought to be studied (2)—are simply not relevant for psychiatry. Our central goal as a medical discipline is the alleviation of the human suffering that results from dysfunctional alterations in certain domains of first-person, subjective experience, such as mood, perception, and cognition. Our nosological constructs are largely composed of descriptions of first-person experiences (e.g., sad mood, hallucinations, and irrational fears). The clinical work of psychiatry constantly requires us to assess and interpret the first-person reports of our patients. Many of the target symptoms that we treat can only be evaluated by asking our patients about their subjective experiences. While we want to take advantage of the many advances in the neurosciences and molecular biology, this cannot be done at the expense of abandoning our grounding in the world of human mental suffering.

SHEDDING THE CHAINS OF DESCARTES

An initial task is to confront one large piece of historical baggage. No philosophical concept has been as widely influential in our field or as potentially pernicious in its effects as that of Cartesian dualism. While individual psychiatrists may, for their own personal or religious reasons, continue to advocate mind-body dualism, it is time for the field of psychiatry to declare that Cartesian substance dualism is false. We need to reject definitively the belief that mind and brain reflect two fundamentally different and ultimately incommensurable kinds of "stuff." Rather, in accord with an overwhelming degree of clinical and scientific evidence, we should conclude that the human first-person world of subjective experience emerges from and is entirely dependent upon brain functioning. The mental world does not exist independently of its physical instantiation in the brain. To reject Cartesian dualism (and accept monism, the view that mental and physical processes are both reflections of the same fundamental stuff) means to no longer consider the mental (or functional) to be a fundamentally different thing from the biological (or organic). Rather, the mental and the biological become different ways of viewing and/or different levels of analysis of the mind-brain system.

This rejection of Cartesian dualism requires a significant shift in our way of thinking. Although American psychiatry officially abandoned the functional-organic dichotomy—one of the many echoes of Cartesian dualism— with DSM-IV (3), and the abandonment of dualism has been recently called for by Kandel (4), dualistic thinking and vocabulary remain deeply entrenched in our approach to clinical and research problems. From the ways we organize our clinical presentations to our categorizations of risk factors, we remain deeply imbedded in the Cartesian framework of seeing the mind and brain as reflecting fundamentally different spheres of reality.

One immediate beneficial consequence of a rejection of Cartesian dualism is our confrontation with the misunderstandings that can arise from the claims of what *might* be called weak biological explanation. The rejection of Cartesian dualism logically leads to the conclusion that all psychiatric disorders are biological. Although we should not belittle this claim (that, for example, would eliminate primary spiritual causes of mental illness), the greater danger now is a tendency to exaggerate its significance. By rejecting dualism, we accept that all psychiatric disorders are biological. But so then are all mental processes, pathological or otherwise. The very ubiquity of this claim of weak biology robs it of much of its gravitas. Indeed, if the rejection of Cartesian dualism is correct, then the declaration that a particular psychiatric disorder is biological is a tautology and is as informative as saying, "This circle is round." Nothing new is learned by this claim that was not already evident by the acceptance of a monistic view of mind-brain functioning.

FACING DOWN EPIPHENOMENALISM

Having rejected Cartesian dualism, we are not yet home free philosophically. Another major viewpoint on the mind-body problem would, if true, also have a profound impact on the field of psychiatry. The core assertion of epiphenomenalism is that the mental world is without causal efficacy, our mental life being simply froth on the wave or steam from the engine. Thoughts, feelings, and impulses occur within our subjective experience, but they do nothing. All the causal action occurs at the level of brain function. Whether and how this assertion can be formally disproven is a subject beyond the bounds of this essay. For the present purposes, I wish to simply assert its falsity and argue that thoughts, feelings, and impulses matter not only because they are responsible for huge amounts of human suffering but because they do things.

ACCEPTANCE OF BIDIRECTIONAL MIND→BRAIN AND BRAIN→MIND CAUSALITY

Given our rejection of Cartesian dualism and our acceptance of an integrated mind-brain system, it becomes necessary to accept the concept of brain-to-mind causality. That is, changes in the brain can directly affect mental functioning. In our rejection of epiphenomenalism, we commit ourselves to the concept of mind-to-brain causality. In ways we can observe but not yet fully understand, subjective, first-person mental phenomena have causal efficacy in the world. They affect our brains and our bodies and through them the outside world. (In asserting the causal efficacy of mental phenomena, I am not reintroducing dualism "through the back door." Rather, consistent with several philosophical positions—in particular, nonreductive materialism [5, 6]—I argue that mental processes carry critical causal information about human behavior. For two recent thoughtful treatments of this problem, see references 7 and 8.)

STOP SEARCHING FOR BIG, SIMPLE EXPLANATIONS

Our strongly held desires to find *the* explanation for individual psychiatric disorders are misplaced and counterproductive. Psychiatry has historically seen a few big explanations, most notably the discovery of the spirochete for general paresis. It is highly unlikely that spirochete-like big explanations remain to be discovered for major psychiatric disorders. We have hunted for big, simple neuropathological explanations for psychiatric disorders and have not found them. We have hunted for big, simple neurochemical explanations for psychiatric disorders and have not found them. We have hunted for big, simple genetic explanations for psychiatric disorders and have not found them.

Our current knowledge, although incomplete, strongly suggests that all major psychiatric disorders are complex and multifactoral. What we can best hope for is lots of small explanations, from a variety of explanatory perspectives, each addressing part of the complex etiological processes leading to disorders. It will be particularly challenging to understand how these many different small explanations all fit together.

In grieving for our loss of big explanations, we similarly have to give up our hope for simple, linear explanatory models. It will not be "A→B→C→D." Etiological pathways will be complex and interacting, more like networks than individual linear pathways.

ACCEPTANCE OF EXPLANATORY PLURALISM

Introduction to Levels of Explanation

Multiple explanatory perspectives can be adopted in our attempts to understand most natural phenomena. Furthermore, for any given phenomenon, these perspectives will differ in their informativeness and efficiency. It is possible to study scientific questions from perspectives that are both too basic and too abstract. However, currently, the former is a greater concern and so will be the focus of this discussion. The concept of "levels of explanation" is so central to this argument that I will illustrate it with three scenarios.

Scenario 1

Jackie is a physiologist studying hormonal regulation. She accepts that the large biological molecules she is examining are constituted of atoms that are made up of particles that are in turn made up of subatomic particles. However, in seeking to alter certain aspects of a hormonal system that she is studying, she might consult with a biochemist or pharmacologist but not with a particle physicist. Why? Because the kind of effects she wants to produce—the stimulation of particular hormonal receptors—results from the actions of large biological molecules. Knowing what quarks are doing in these molecules will not help her achieve her desired goal.

Scenario 2

Bill is performing a statistical analysis on his computer and is getting the wrong result because he has made a mistake in his statistical program. Being a down-to-earth kind of guy, Bill decides to take off the back of his computer, pull out the motherboard, and reach for his soldering iron, hoping to find a loose connection to solder, thereby solving his programming problem. Why is this the wrong approach? After all, a computer is really just a bunch of circuits and electrons. Using a soldering iron is a highly inefficient approach because it is an intervention directed at the wrong explanatory level in the complex system. The cause of the dysfunction is at the level of high-order computer code and could not be easily perceived or repaired at the level of circuits on a motherboard.

Scenario 3

Kathy, a young psychiatrist, is asked by a distressed parent to consult with her about her son, Brian, who has decided to leave a career in science to enter the priesthood. The upset parent insists that Kathy order a brain scan to find a way to change his decision. "There must be something the matter with his brain, doctor. How could he throw away such a promising scientific career?" Kathy sees the young man, who appears thoughtful and mature, and he describes the deep satisfaction and inspiration he feels in the Catholic religion. He understands the possible hardships ahead of him but feels he is making the right decision. Kathy tells the parent that she is not going to order a magnetic resonance imaging scan. There is no evidence, she states, that there is anything the matter with his brain, and no interventions that would act directly on his brain are indicated in this situation. She feels that he has reached his decision in a reasonable way, but the mother should feel free, if she wants, to try to argue her son out of his decision.

What is going on in these three scenarios? In each case, we have a higher-order system that is completely constituted from lower-order elements. That is, Jackie's macromolecules are made up of subatomic particles. Bill's computer is made up of circuits and electrons. Brian's mental processes are expressed in the biology of his brain. However, in each of these scenarios, an intervention at the level of the lower-order elements is likely to be, at best, inefficient and, at worst, ineffective and possibly harmful.

The Limits of Biological Reductionism

> *There is no such thing as a psychiatry that is too biological.*
>
> —S.B. GUZE (9)

The last several decades have seen a rise to prominence within psychiatry of a biological reductionist perspective. Advocates of this point of view argue that the only valid approach to understanding psychiatric disorders or, more broadly, psychological functioning is in terms of basic neurobiological processes (10). Multilevel models, especially those including mental and social explanatory perspectives, are typically rejected (sometimes with the epithet of being nonscientific or "soft-headed") or accepted only with the caveat that all the "real" causal effects occur at the level of basic biology.

This position might be seen as a logical consequence of the rejection of Cartesian dualism. After all, if we agree that there are no mental processes that are independent of brain function, then should not all the causes of psychiatric disorders be reduced to brain processes? Although this reductionist perspective is understandable in sociological terms as a reaction to prior radical mentalistic programs within psychiatry (e.g., some forms of dynamic psychiatry) and is appealing because of the ease with which it fits into a medical model, this approach is too narrow to encompass the range of causal processes that are operative in psychiatric disorders.

The limits of biological reductionism are well illustrated by the three scenarios just outlined. Contrary to Guze's assertion, psychiatry can be too biological in the same sense that it would be an error for Jackie to focus on subatomic particles in her physiological research, for Bill to try to fix his problem with statistical analysis by using a soldering iron, or for Kathy to employ psychopharmacology to reverse Brian's career decision. Note that I do not contest that ultimately (in the sense of "weak biology") all psychiatric illness is biological. What is at issue here is the optimal level in the causal processes underlying psychiatric illness at which intervention can be best focused and understanding most easily achieved.

Explanatory Pluralism

In the tradition of other thoughtful commentators (especially Engel [11] and McHugh and Slavney [12]), in place of biological reductionism, I advocate *explanatory pluralism* (13–17) as the approach best suited to understanding the nature of psychiatric illness. Explanatory pluralism hypothesizes multiple mutually informative perspectives with which to approach natural phenomena. Typically, these perspectives differ in their levels of abstraction, use divergent scientific tools, and provide different and complementary kinds of understanding. Explanatory pluralism is especially appropriate for psychiatry because psychiatric disorders are typically influenced by causal processes operating at several levels of abstraction.

A clear example of explanatory pluralism comes from biology, where it is useful to distinguish between "how" questions and "why" questions (18). For example, in examining the large and colorful tail of the male peacock, we could study its developmental biology to clarify physiologically how such a tail develops. Alternatively, we could seek, in the evolutionary history of the peacock, an answer about why the tail develops, presumably through mechanisms of sexual selection. Neither the how/physiological nor the why/evolutionary explanatory perspective can easily replace or invalidate the other. It is simply in the nature of the phenomenon that it can be usefully approached scientifically from two different perspectives.

(The pluralistic explanatory approach outlined in this essay assumes the natural science perspective that Jaspers termed "explanation" [1]. I do not here address another highly relevant question—how does the information acquired from this perspective relate to knowledge obtained, through empathy, from human relationships, through the process termed "understanding" by Jaspers [1]?)

Arguments for Explanatory Pluralism and Against Biological Reductionism

I will now review eight arguments in favor of explanatory pluralism and against biological reductionism or other unimodal perspectives on psychiatric illness (including radical mentalistic accounts). These arguments assume the conclusive demonstration that specific biological processes that are manifest, for example, at the level of genetic risk factors or neurochemical alterations play a significant causal role in all psychiatric disorders.

First, a long clinical tradition and much empirical evidence of increasing methodological rigor point to the importance of first-person mental processes in the etiology of psychiatric disorders. Of the many possible studies, one recent investigation will illustrate this point (19). In a large epidemiological sample of twins, severely stressful life events and onsets of major depression and generalized anxiety were studied. Descriptions of the severely stressful life events were blindly reviewed by trained raters and scored for their level of loss, humiliation, entrapment, and danger. Even though only highly threatening life events were studied, these ratings further predicted the risk of depression and anxiety.

Humiliation and loss are classical, subjective, first-person experiences that humans can recognize in themselves and in others. Although humiliation is ultimately expressed in the brain, this does not mean that the basic neurobiological level is necessarily the most efficient level at which to observe humiliation. Trying to understand humiliation by looking at basic brain biology may be like Bill trying to fix his statistical analyses with his soldering iron. It may be the wrong explanatory level.

Second, a large body of descriptive literature shows convincingly that cultural processes affect psychiatric illness. For example, a recent meta-analysis (20) concluded that rates of bulimia have meaningfully increased in Western countries in recent years. Furthermore, in non-Western countries, the prevalence of bulimia is strongly related to the degree of contact with Western culture (20). One study in Fiji (21) has shown a substantial rise in eating disorder pathology in adolescent girls after the introduction of television and the associated intense exposure to Western ideals about body image. These results suggest that the risk for bulimia is related to cultural models of ideal body size. While culture ultimately exists as belief systems in the brains of individual members of a cultural group, it is unlikely that cultural forces that shape psychopathology can be efficiently understood at the level of basic brain biology.

Third, our first two examples illustrate that, in addition to neurobiological and genetic risk factors, a full etiological understanding of at least some psychiatric disorders will require consideration of psychological and cultural factors. We have, however, been naively assuming a model in which biological, psychological, and cultural factors each independently affect risk. However, the reality is more complex, thereby posing further difficulties for the reductionist biological model. The impact of genetic factors on the risk for psychiatric disorders or drug use can be modified by the rearing environment

(22, 23), stressful life experiences (24, 25), and exposure to cultural forces (26). Recent work in bulimia suggests that this disorder arises given a combination of a biological/ genetic predisposition and cultural factors encouraging slim body ideals. The actions of basic biological risk factors for psychiatric illness are modified by forces acting at higher levels of abstraction.

Furthermore, gene expression is extensively modified by both simple (e.g., light-dark cycle) and complex (e.g., learning tasks, maternal separation) environmental stimuli (27), and even relatively gross aspects of neuronal and brain anatomy can be modified by experience (28). A bottom-up hard reductionist approach to psychiatric illness will be futile if basic neurobiological risk factors are frequently modified by higher-order processes, including environmental, psychological, and cultural experiences.

Fourth, biological reductionists assume that neurobiological risk factors for psychiatric disorders operate through physiological "inside-the-skin" pathways. However, an emerging body of research suggests that this assumption is false. Part of the way in which genetic risk factors influence the liability to psychiatric disorders is through "outside-the-skin" pathways that alter the probability of exposure to high-risk environments. For example, genetic risk factors for major depression increase the probability of interpersonal and marital difficulties, which are known risk factors for depression (29). This is not a theoretical issue. If the impact of genetic risk factors is mediated through environmental processes, this opens up new possible modes of prevention.

Fifth, hard reductive models in science strive for clear "one-to-one" relationships between basic processes and outcome variables. Such simple relationships are not plausible for psychiatric illnesses. For example, individual genetic risk factors probably predispose to a range of different psychiatric disorders, depending on other genetic, developmental, and environmental factors (30), and many different DNA variants probably predispose to one disorder (31). This pattern of many-to-many causal links between basic etiological processes and outcomes is more compatible with pluralistic than with monistic reductive etiological models.

Sixth, a series of important questions in psychiatry are historical in nature and not plausibly subject to reductive biological explanations. Why are humans prone to develop depression when exposed to social adversity? Why do genetic risk factors for schizophrenia persist in human populations? Like the puzzle of the peacock's tail, these questions are best answered at historical/evolutionary and not physiological levels.

Seventh, how, using a hard reductive biological approach toward psychiatry, can we define dysfunction (14)? While certain psychiatric symptoms may be pathological at a basic biological level (e.g., hallucinations), many symptoms are dysfunctional only in certain contexts. At a physiological level, a panic attack during a near-fatal climbing accident in a psychiatrically healthy individual or in a crowded shopping mall in a patient with agoraphobia are probably the same. Since many psychiatric disorders include, by definition, some degree of psychosocial dysfunction (32), explanation at the level of biology alone is unlikely to be sufficient.

Eighth, biological systems generally and mind-body systems more specifically have goals and generate processes to address these goals, such as the maintenance of blood pressure or self-esteem and the acquisition of food, sexual partners, or status. As argued persuasively by Bolton and Hill (7), these information-based systems cannot be reduced to their molecular constituents without a loss of explanatory power. After all, the biology of a neural impulse—the influx and efflux of sodium, potassium, and calcium ions—is essentially the same all over the brain. These impulses have specific causal efficacy only through the particular neuronal system in which they are imbedded. Critical causal processes in the mind-brain system can only be captured through an understanding of the higher organizational levels of these goal-directed systems.

What Kind of Explanatory Pluralism Do We Need?

As outlined in an illuminating chapter by Mitchell et al. (33), explanatory pluralism can come in several "flavors," two of which interest us here. *Compatible pluralism* recognizes the existence of distinct and independently meaningful levels of analysis. However, for scientific and/or sociological reasons, research in these distinct levels occurs largely in isolation. In *integrative pluralism*, by contrast, active efforts are made to incorporate divergent levels of analysis. This approach assumes that, for most problems, single-level analyses will lead to only partial answers. However, rather than building large theoretical structures, integrative pluralism establishes small "local" integrations across levels of analysis.

Our field may be in particular need of integrative pluralism, where scientists, without abandoning conceptual rigor, cross borders between different etiological frameworks or levels of explanation. Such efforts may be unusually scientifically fruitful and work bit by bit toward broader integrative paradigms. Recent examples of integrative pluralism in psychiatric research would include the incorporation by Gutman and Nemeroff (34) of early traumatic events into neurobiological models for depression and the efforts by Caspi and colleagues to include specific genotypes in an epidemiological study examining the development of antisocial behavior (35) and depression (25) after exposure to environmental adversity.

PROBLEMS WITH IMPLEMENTATION OF EXPLANATORY PLURALISM

In mental health research, explanatory orientations are too often adopted for ideological rather than empirical reasons. At its worst, our field consists of mutually antagonistic, noninteracting theoretical camps. One approach to this cacophony of divergent explanatory orientations would be to impose rigidly one methodological perspective, such as biological reductionism. However, this is unfeasible and would be unlikely to succeed even if it could be accomplished.

Rather, our task, the difficulty of which is hard to overestimate, is to establish a methodologically rigorous but conceptually open-minded scientific playing field. Advocating explanatory pluralism for psychiatry should not be construed as a vacuous invitation to treat all methodologies as of equal value. As divergent perspectives compete for resources and students, the deciding factors should not be the orientation of the methods but rather the power of the designs, the replicability of the results, and their relevance to understanding the causal pathways to psychiatric disorders.

Thomas Kuhn (36), the famous philosopher of science who stressed the degree to which science was intrinsically a social activity, would suggest that this agenda may be a fool's quest. He might argue that the competing scientific paradigms within psychiatry are "incommensurable," that their advocates have such widely divergent viewpoints that they effectively inhabit different professional worlds. Furthermore, he would assert that data in our field are heavily theory-laden and deeply intertwined with theoretical assumptions. In such circumstances, effective communication across paradigms and finding a common ground on which the various paradigms might fairly compete would be difficult.

These arguments have force. I recall too many sterile arguments between psychoanalysts, social psychiatrists, and biological psychiatrists in the late 1970s to lightly dismiss Kuhn's contention of the incommensurability of different theoretical perspectives. Furthermore, I remember with surprise the growing realization that in earlier generations, researchers from divergent perspectives had taken the same set of data—evidence that schizophrenia ran in families—and assumed that it proved biological (37) or family-dynamic (38) etiological theories of schizophrenia.

However, Kuhn's perspective may be too pessimistic. Many philosophers of science now disagree with the more radical versions of his claims (39). Getting researchers from different perspectives to agree on broadly similar interpretations of data is not impossible. Within the field of mental health research, we have seen increasing "crossparadigm" discussions and collaborations. The ideological rancor that characterized earlier debates may be lessening, and the optimists among us might ascribe that to a maturation of the field.

Kuhn argues that to be considered a mature science, a field has to agree on a basic scientific paradigm (36). Psychiatry, by this criterion, would be in an immature "preparadigmatic" state. Although vastly underspecified and in need of being "filled in" in different ways for each of the major psychiatric and drug abuse disorders, explanatory pluralism might form the substrate of such a shared paradigm.

ACCEPTANCE OF PATCHY REDUCTIONS LEADING TO PIECEMEAL INTEGRATION

What should be our goals in seeking to understand the extraordinarily complex causal networks within the mind-brain system and its interaction with the psychosocial environment that lead to psychiatric illness? Another assertion of the biological reductionists is that the value of a causal explanation is directly related to how far down it goes on the causal chain—the more basic and biological the better (10). While tempting, this "zeitgeist" should be resisted.

A thought experiment might help. Imagine that there are 15 discrete levels, with the mind-brain system between DNA on one hand and the clinical manifestations of schizophrenia on the other. Researcher 1 is conducting linkage and association studies that attempt to directly relate levels 1 and 15 but would provide no insight into the intervening levels. Researcher 2 is trying to understand, at a basic molecular level, the actions of a putative altered gene transcript, thereby trying to move from level 1 to level 2 or 3. Meanwhile, researcher 3 is seeking to understand the neuropsychological deficits in schizophrenia, trying to clarify the link between levels 13 and 15. Although biological reductionists might declare the work of researcher 2 to be more "scientific" and valuable because it is more basic, I hope that this thought experiment makes it clear that we can make no such judgments a priori. There are many links in the chain, and their ultimate value and scientific fruitfulness are unlikely to bear any strong relationship with where on the causal chain (or, more realistically, network) they sit.

This thought experiment leads to a final point. Although developing the "grand theory" is attractive and may provide a fruitful heuristic framework, we are not close to developing a full causal network for any psychiatric disorder. Nor should this now be our primary goal. Rather, we should settle for what we have called "bit-by-bit" efforts of integrative pluralism. Schaffner (40, p. 282) has expressed a similar idea in what he calls "patchy reductions" in "a structure of overlapping inter-level causal models." Such efforts should, over time, result in clarification of parts of the causal network from which it may be possible to move toward a more complete etiological understanding of the extremely complex mind-brain dysfunctions that it is our task to understand and treat.

INTEGRATION AND CONCLUSIONS

Working in the field of psychiatry inevitably involves us in some of the most important and perplexing questions that humans can face. Two are of paramount importance for our field: how do mind and brain interrelate, and how can we integrate the multiple explanatory perspectives on psychiatric illness? I have tried to pose tentative answers to these questions in the hope that they might contribute toward providing, for psychiatric research, a pragmatic integrated rubric. We need to move from sterile, ideologically driven debates toward critical, creatively conceptualized empirical questions. How much real explanatory power is provided by the many possible etiological perspectives on a given psychiatric disorder? How can we begin to understand how the various explanatory levels interrelate with one another?

Our hope should be for the scientific maturation of psychiatry that will in turn allow us to use and integrate the coming scientific advances. This will require our moving beyond the clumsy and outdated baggage left us by Cartesian dualism. We should not, however, thereby reject our fundamental roots within the mental and psychosocial spheres or succumb to the temptations of simplistic reductionist models. Psychiatric disorders are, by their nature, complex multilevel phenomena. We need to keep our heads clear about their stunning complexity and realize, with humility, that their full understanding will require the rigorous integration of multiple disciplines and perspectives.

References

1. Jaspers K: General Psychopathology. Chicago, University of Chicago Press, 1963.

2. Kendler HH: Historical Foundations of Modern Psychology. Philadelphia, Temple University Press, 1987.

3. Spitzer RL, Williams JB, First M, Kendler KS: A proposal for DSM-IV: solving the "organic/nonorganic" problem (editorial). J Neuropsychiatry Clin Neurosci 1989; 1:126–127.

4. Kandel ER: A new intellectual framework for psychiatry. Am J Psychiatry 1998; 155:457–469.

5. Kendler KS: A psychiatric dialogue on the mind–body problem. Am J Psychiatry 2001; 158:989–1000.

6. Hannan B: Subjectivity and Reduction: An Introduction to the Mind-Body Problem. Boulder, Colo, Westview Press, 1994.

7. Bolton D, Hill J: Mind, Meaning, and Mental Disorder: The Nature of Causal Explanation in Psychology and Psychiatry. Oxford, UK, Oxford University Press, 1996.

8. Edelman GM: The Phenomenal Gift of Consciousness. New Haven, Conn, Yale University Press, 2004.

9. Guze SB: Biological psychiatry: is there any other kind? Psychol Med 1989; 19:315–323.

10. Bickle J: Philosophy and Neuroscience: A Ruthlessly Reductive Account. Boston, Kluwer Academic, 2003.

11. Engel GL: The need for a new medical model: a challenge for biomedicine. Science 1977; 196:129–136.

12. McHugh PR, Slavney PR: The Perspectives of Psychiatry. Baltimore, Johns Hopkins University Press, 1986.

13. Mitchell SD: Biological Complexity and Integrative Pluralism. Cambridge, UK, Cambridge University Press, 2003.

14. Zachar P: Psychological Concepts and Biological Psychiatry: A Philosophical Analysis. Amsterdam, John Benjamins, 2000.

15. Kety SS: A biologist examines the mind and behavior. Science 1960; 132:1861–1867.

16. Cacioppo JT, Berntson GG, Sheridan JF, McClintock MK: Multilevel integrative analyses of human behavior: social neuroscience and the complementing nature of social and biological approaches. Psychol Bull 2000; 126:829–843.

17. Ghaemi N: The Concepts of Psychiatry: A Pluralistic Approach to the Mind and Mental Illness. Baltimore, Johns Hopkins University Press, 2003.

18. Mayr E: The Growth of Biological Thought. Cambridge, Mass, Belknap Press, 2004.

19. Kendler KS, Hettema JM, Butera F, Gardner CO, Prescott CA: Life event dimensions of loss, humiliation, entrapment, and danger in the prediction of onsets of major depression and generalized anxiety. Arch Gen Psychiatry 2003; 60:789–796.

20. Keel PK, Klump KL: Are eating disorders culture-bound syndromes? implications for conceptualizing their etiology. Psychol Bull 2003; 129:747–769.

21. Becker AE, Burwell RA, Gilman SE, Herzog DB, Hamburg P: Eating behaviours and attitudes following prolonged exposure to television among ethnic Fijian adolescent girls. Br J Psychiatry 2002; 180:509–514.

22. Cloninger CR, Bohman M, Sigvardsson S: Inheritance of alcohol abuse: cross-fostering analysis of adopted men. Arch Gen Psychiatry 1981; 38:861–868.

23. Cadoret RJ, Yates WR, Troughton E, Woodworth G, Stewart MA: Gene-environment interaction in genesis of aggressivity and conduct disorders. Arch Gen Psychiatry 1995; 52:916–924.

24. Kendler KS, Kessler RC, Walters EE, MacLean C, Neale MC, Heath AC, Eaves LJ: Stressful life events, genetic liability, and onset of an episode of major depression in women. Am J Psychiatry 1995; 152:833–842.

25. Caspi A, Sugden K, Moffitt TE, Taylor A, Craig IW, Harrington H, McClay J, Mill J, Martin J, Braithwaite A, Poulton R: Influence of life stress on depression: moderation by a polymorphism in the 5-HTT gene. Science 2003; 301:386–389.

26. Kendler KS, Karkowski LM, Pedersen NC: Tobacco consumption in Swedish twins reared-apart and reared-together. Arch Gen Psychiatry 2000; 57:886–892.

27. Gottlieb G: Normally occurring environmental and behavioral influences on gene activity: from central dogma to probabilistic epigenesis. Psychol Rev 1998; 105:792–802.

28. Gaser C, Schlaug G: Brain structures differ between musicians and non-musicians. J Neurosci 2003; 23:9240–9245.

29. Kendler KS, Karkowski-Shuman L: Stressful life events and genetic liability to major depression: genetic control of exposure to the environment? Psychol Med 1997; 27:539–547.

30. Kendler KS, Prescott CA, Myers J, Neale MC: The structure of genetic and environmental risk factors for common psychiatric and substance use disorders in men and women. Arch Gen Psychiatry 2003; 60:929–937.

31. Harrison PJ, Owen MJ: Genes for schizophrenia? recent findings and their pathophysiological implications. Lancet 2003; 361: 417–419.

32. Deep A, Nagy L, Weltzin T, Rao R, Kaye W: Premorbid onset of psychopathology in long-term recovered anorexia nervosa. Int J Eat Disord 1995; 17:291–298.

33. Mitchell SD, Daston L, Gigerenzer G, Sesardic N, Sloep P: The whys and hows of interdisciplinarity, in Human by Nature: Between Biology and the Social Sciences. Edited by Weingart P, Richerson P, Mitchell S, Maasen S. Mahwah, NJ, Lawrence Erlbaum Associates, 1997, pp 103–150.

34. Gutman DA, Nemeroff CB: Persistent central nervous system effects of an adverse early environment: clinical and preclinical studies. Physiol Behav 2003; 79:471–478.

35. Caspi A, McClay J, Moffitt TE, Mill J, Martin J, Craig IW, Taylor A, Poulton R: Role of genotype in the cycle of violence in maltreated children. Science 2002; 297:851–854.

36. Kuhn TS: The Structure of Scientific Revolutions, 3rd ed. Chicago, University of Chicago Press, 1996.

37. Kallmann FJ: The Genetics of Schizophrenia. New York, JS Augustin, 1938.

38. Lidz T, Fleck S, Cornelison AR: Schizophrenia and the Family. Madison, Conn, International Universities Press, 1965.

39. Okasha S: Philosophy of Science: A Very Short Introduction. New York, Oxford University Press, 2002.

40. Schaffner KF: Psychiatry and molecular biology: reductionistic approaches to schizophrenia, in Philosophical Perspectives on Psychiatric Diagnostic Classification. Edited by Sadler JZ, Wiggins OP, Schwartz M. Baltimore, Johns Hopkins University Press, 1994, pp 279–294.

41. Turkheimer E: Heritability and biological explanation. Psychol Rev 1998; 105:782–791.

42. Schaffner KF: Genes, behavior, and developmental emergentism: one process, indivisible? Philos Sci 1998; 65:209–252.

18

Knowing Your Chances
What Health Stats Really Mean

Gerd Gigerenzer, Wolfgang Gaissmaier, Elke Kurz-Milcke, Lisa M. Schwartz, and Steven Woloshin

When might a positive HIV test be wrong? Are your chances of surviving cancer better in the U.S. or in England? Learn how to put aside unjustified fears and hopes and how to weigh your real risk of illness—or likelihood of recovery.

In a 2007 campaign advertisement, former New York City mayor Rudy Giuliani said, "I had prostate cancer, five, six years ago. My chances of surviving prostate cancer—and thank God, I was cured of it—in the United States? Eighty-two percent. My chances of surviving prostate cancer in England? Only 44 percent under socialized medicine." Giuliani used these statistics to argue that he was lucky to be living in New York and not in York. This statement was big news. As we will explain, it was also a big mistake.

In 1938 in *World Brain* (Methuen & Co.), English writer H. G. Wells predicted that for an educated citizenship in a modern democracy, statistical thinking would be as indispensable as reading and writing. At the beginning of the 21st century, nearly everyone living in an industrial society has been taught reading and writing but not statistical thinking—how to understand information about risks and uncertainties in our technological world. That lack of understanding is shared by many physicians, journalists and politicians such as Giuliani who, as a result, spread misconceptions to the public.

Statistical illiteracy is not rooted in inherent intellectual deficits—say, in the lack of a "math gene"—but rather in societal and emotional forces. These influences include the paternalistic nature of the doctor-patient relationship, the illusion of certainty in medicine, and the practice of presenting health information in opaque forms that erroneously suggest big benefits and small harms from interventions. When citizens do not understand the numbers, they are susceptible to political and commercial manipulation of their anxieties and hopes. The result can be serious damage to physical health and emotional well-being.

We show you how to spot three types of statistical manipulation and confusion in medicine, to translate opaque figures into ones that make sense and to use that information to make better medical decisions. To avoid such misunderstandings in the first place, we argue that medical journals, the media and others should communicate risk in more easily understood forms. In addition, we recommend introducing young children to statistical thinking and teaching statistics as a way of solving real-world problems rather than as a purely mathematical discipline.

TRUST YOUR DOCTOR?

Medicine has held a long-standing antagonism toward statistics. For centuries, treatment was based on an ethic of personal trust as opposed to quantitative facts, which were dismissed as impersonal or irrelevant to the individual. Even today many doctors think of themselves as artists, relying more on intuition and faith in their own judgment than on numbers. For their part, many patients prefer to trust their doctors rather than even asking for data to analyze. For example, in a 2008 unpublished survey by one of us (Gigerenzer) and his colleagues, two thirds of more than 100 American economists said they had not weighed any pros and cons of getting a prostate cancer screening test but simply followed their doctor's recommendation.

Moreover, individuals often shy away from statistics because they have an emotional need for certainty—a concept at odds with statistical literacy, which prepares us to make decisions in the face of uncertainty [*see box on opposite page*]. Much of the public harbors illusory certainty about the reliability of tests such as those for cancers and HIV, suggests a survey Gigerenzer conducted in 2006.

Furthermore, statistically unsophisticated patients and their doctors tend to wildly overestimate the benefits of screening tests and are blind to their harms. For example, mammography reduces the risk of a woman in her 50s dying from breast cancer from about five to four in 1,000 over some 13 years, but 60 percent of a random sample of U.S. women believed the benefit to be 80 times as high. Americans are similarly overenthusiastic about total-body computed tomographic scans: in a random sample of 500 Americans, nearly three quarters said they would prefer a free total-body CT scan to $1,000 in cash. Yet no professional medical organization endorses such scans, and several discourage them because screening tests such as this one can result in important harm from a cascade of medical quandries and invasive treatments triggered by ambiguous findings.

A citizen in a modern technological society faces a bewildering array of medical decisions. Should a pregnant woman undergo prenatal screening for chromosomal anomalies at age 35? Should parents send their teenage daughters to be vaccinated against human papillomavirus, to protect them against cervical cancer, despite a few reports that the vaccine (Gardasil) could lead to paralysis? If people want to make informed decisions, they need to understand health statistics. In particular, they need to understand the difference between absolute and relative risks and how to use natural frequencies to infer the true chances of disease from a positive test result. Individuals also should know to trust mortality rates over five-year survival statistics when evaluating screening tests, which look for disease in healthy people. We deal with each of these issues in turn.

ABSOLUTE RISKS

In October 1995 the U. K. Committee on Safety of Medicines warned that third-generation oral contraceptive pills increased the likelihood of potentially life-threatening blood clots in the legs or lungs twofold—that is, by 100 percent. This information was passed on in "Dear Doctor" letters to 190,000 general practitioners, pharmacists and directors of public health and in an emergency announcement to the media. The news caused great anxiety, and women stopped taking the pill, which led to an estimated 13,000 additional abortions in the following year in England and Wales. For every additional abortion, there was also one extra birth, including some 800 more conceptions among girls younger than 16. (Ironically, abortions and pregnancies are associated with an increased risk of thrombosis that exceeds that of the third-generation pill.)

Such panic could have been avoided had the data been reported in a more straightforward manner. The evidence showed that about one in every 7,000 women who took the second-generation pill had a blood clot; this number increased to two in 7,000 among women who took third-generation pills. That is, the *absolute* risk increase was only one in 7,000 even though the *relative* risk increase was indeed 100 percent. Absolute risks are typically small numbers, whereas the corresponding relative changes tend to look big—particularly when the base rate is low.

Reporting relative risks can create unrealistic hopes as well as undue anxiety. Many patients and doctors evaluate a treatment or test more favorably if benefits are expressed in terms of relative risk reduction. In a 2007 review of experimental studies, for example, psychologist Judith Covey of the University of Durham in England found that when the benefit of a drug was presented in the form of relative risk reduction, 91 percent of Danish general practitioners would recommend it to their patients. But when given the absolute risk reduction, only 63 percent would recommend the same drug.

Information brochures, doctors, medical journals and the media continue to inform the public in terms of relative changes, in part because big numbers make better headlines and generate more attention. One leaflet even conflated the two, stating that hormone replacement therapy (HRT) "has

---

Living with Uncertainty

Although people often apply a need for certainty to test results and treatments, no unequivocal answers or absolute cures exist. Risk is unavoidable; it comes with all action or inaction. Here are questions to ask about all risks:

>>1 Risk of what? Understand the outcome to which the risk refers. Is it the risk of dying from a disease, getting the disease or manifesting a symptom?

>>2 What is the time frame? Time frames such as "the next 10 years" are easier to imagine than the widely used "lifetime" risks. They are more informative because risks change over time, and yet such time frames are long enough to enable action.

>>3 How big is the risk? Because there are no zero risks, size is what matters. That number should be expressed in absolute terms—for instance, 13 out of 1,000 50-year-old female smokers die of heart disease within 10 years—or in comparative

terms, relating the risk to other ones. For example, a 50-year-old female smoker has about the same chance of dying of heart disease as of lung cancer within the next decade—and these chances are about seven times higher than her risk of perishing in a car accident.

>>4 Does the risk apply to me? Find out if the risk is based on studies of people like you—individuals of your age or sex or with health problems similar to yours.

>>5 What are the harms of "finding out?" Screening tests may lead to false alarms, prompting unnecessary anxiety. When women participate in a 10-year program of annual mammography, every other woman without cancer can expect one or more false-positive test results. Worse, screening tests often detect abnormalities that would never cause symptoms, leading to unnecessary surgery and other invasive treatments.

been proven to protect women against colorectal cancer (by up to more than 50 percent)," whereas the risk of breast cancer "may possibly increase by 0.6 percent (six in 1,000)." The data reveal that the 50 percent benefit corresponds to an absolute number that is less than six in 1,000—meaning that HRT produces more cases of cancer than it prevents. But according to a 2003 study, 60 of 80 women concluded the exact opposite from the leaflet.

Absolute risks are more informative because they take into account information about background rates. Given the absolute risks, a person can derive the relative risks—but not vice versa. After all, a relative risk reduction of 50 percent could describe either a substantial mortality reduction from 200 to 100 in 10,000 patients or a much smaller one from two to one in 10,000 patients. Randomized trials provide some of the best information in medicine, but unless the results are reported adequately, people will not be able to assess them.

NATURAL FREQUENCIES

Consider a woman who has just received a positive result from a mammogram and asks her doctor: Do I have breast cancer for sure, or what are the chances that I have the disease? In a 2007 continuing education course for gynecologists, Gigerenzer asked 160 of these practitioners to answer that question given the following information about women in the region:

- The probability that a woman has breast cancer (prevalence) is 1 percent.
- If a woman has breast cancer, the probability that she tests positive (sensitivity) is 90 percent.
- If a woman does not have breast cancer, the probability that she nonetheless tests positive (false-positive rate) is 9 percent.

What is the best answer to the patient's query?

A. The probability that she has breast cancer is about 81 percent.

B. Out of 10 women with a positive mammogram, about nine have breast cancer.

C. Out of 10 women with a positive mammogram, about one has breast cancer.

D. The probability that she has breast cancer is about 1 percent.

Gynecologists could derive the answer from the statistics above, or they could simply recall what they should have known anyhow. In either case, the best answer is C; only about one out of every 10 women who test positive in screening actually has breast cancer. The other nine are falsely alarmed. Prior to training, most (60 percent) of the gynecologists answered 90 percent or 81 percent, thus grossly overestimating the probability of cancer. Only 21 percent of physicians picked the best answer—one out of 10.

Many physicians do not know the probabilities that a person has any disease given a positive screening test—that is, the positive predictive value of that test. Nor can they estimate it from conditional probabilities such as the test's sensitivity (the probability of testing positive in the presence of the disease) and the false-positive rate. Such innumeracy causes undue fear. Months after receiving a false-positive mammogram, one in two women reported considerable anxiety about mammograms and breast cancer, and one in four reported that this anxiety affected her daily mood and functioning.

Doctors would more easily be able to derive the correct probabilities if the statistics surrounding the test were presented as natural frequencies. For example:

- Ten out of every 1,000 women have breast cancer.
- Of these 10 women with breast cancer, nine test positive.
- Of the 990 women without cancer, about 89 nonetheless test positive.

Forecasting Infection

If your HIV test is positive and you are a man at low risk of infection, what are the chances that you actually harbor the virus? Conditional probabilities (*left*) leave us with a confusing calculation. Invoking natural frequencies (*right*) leads to an easy answer: out of every 10,000 men, one is expected to be infected with HIV and will test positive; out of the uninfected men, one should also test positive. Thus, two test positive, and one of these is infected. In other words, your chances of infection given a positive result are not 100 percent; instead they are 50 percent.

Source: "Helping Doctors and Patients Make Sense of Health Statistics," By G. Gigerenzer et al., in *Psychological Science in the Public Interest*, vol. 8, No. 2: 2007.

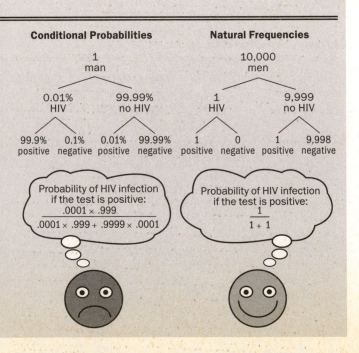

Thus, 98 women test positive, but only nine of those actually have the disease. After learning to translate conditional probabilities into natural frequencies, 87 percent of the gynecologists understood that one in 10 is the best answer. Similarly, psychologist Ros Bramwell of the University of Liverpool in England and his colleagues reported in 2006 that only one out of 21 obstetricians could correctly estimate the probability of an unborn child actually having Down syndrome given a positive test. When they were given the relevant natural frequencies, 13 out of 20 obstetricians arrived at the correct answer.

Physicians need to inform patients that no test is perfect, that every test result needs to be interpreted with care, or that a test needs to be repeated. Every woman who gets a mammogram should be told that many of the suspicious results are false alarms. A similar uncertainty exists with all such tests, even HIV tests. At a 1987 AIDS conference, then Florida senator Lawton Chiles reported that of 22 blood donors in Florida who had been notified that they had tested positive for HIV, seven committed suicide. Although the test for HIV picks up *99.9* percent of true infections, and *99.99* percent of its negative results are accurate, a very low base rate among low-risk heterosexual men means the chance of infection can be as low as 50 percent when a man tests positive in screening [*see box above*]. (When the base rate is higher, however, as it is in the case of homosexual men who have unprotected sex or intravenous drug users who share needles, the chance of true infection with a positive HIV test result is almost certain. So the base rate in a population determines the meaning of a positive test result.)

MORTALITY MATTERS

While running for president, Giuliani claimed that health care in the U.S. was superior to that in England. He apparently used data from the year 2000, when 49 British men in every 100,000 were diagnosed with prostate cancer, of whom 28 died within five years—about 44 percent. Using a similar approach, he cited a corresponding 82 percent five-year survival rate in the U.S., suggesting that Americans with prostate cancer were twice as likely to survive as their British counterparts were. That implication, however, is false because these survival statistics largely reflect diagnostic differences between the two countries rather than better treatment and prolonged survival in the U.S.

To understand why, imagine a group of prostate cancer patients diagnosed (by their symptoms) at age 67 in the U.K., all of whom die at 70. Each survived only three years, so the five-year survival of this group is 0 percent. Now imagine that the same group is diagnosed in the U.S., where doctors detect most prostate cancer by screening for prostate-specific antigens (PSA). (The PSA test is not routinely used in Britain.) These U.S. patients are diagnosed earlier, at age 60, but they all still die at age 70. All have now survived 10 years, and thus their five-year survival rate is 100 percent. Even though the survival rate has changed dramatically, nothing has changed about the time of death. This example shows how setting the

time of diagnosis earlier can boost survival rates (lead-time bias), even if no life is prolonged or saved [*see illustration on opposite page*].

Spuriously high survival rates can also result from overdiagnosis, the detection of abnormalities that are technically cancer but will never progress to cause symptoms in the patient's lifetime. Say 1,000 men with progressive cancer do not undergo screening. After five years 440 are still alive, which results in a survival rate of 44 percent. Meanwhile in another population of men, PSA screening detects 1,000 people with progressive cancer and 2,000 people with nonprogressive cancer (who by definition will not die of cancer in five years). These nonprogressive cases are now added to the 440 who survived progressive cancer, which inflates the survival rate to 81 percent. Although the survival rate changed dramatically, the number of people who die has not changed at all.

In the U.S., screening for prostate cancer using the PSA test in the late 1980s led to an explosion in the number of new prostate cancer diagnoses. In Britain, the effect has been much smaller because of far less use of the PSA test. This diagnostic disparity largely explains why five-year survival for prostate cancer is higher in the U.S. (The most recent figures are 98 percent five-year survival in the U.S. versus 71 percent in Britain.)

Despite the difference in survival rates, mortality rates in the two countries are close to the same: about 26 prostate cancer deaths per 100,000 American men versus 27 per 100,000 in Britain. That fact suggests the PSA test has needlessly flagged prostate cancer in many American men, resulting in a lot of unnecessary surgery and radiation treatment, which often leads to impotence or incontinence.

Because of overdiagnosis and lead-time bias, changes in five-year survival rates have no reliable relation to changes in mortality when patterns of diagnosis differ. And yet many official agencies continue to talk about five-year survival rates. A recent report by the U.K. Office for National Statistics noted that five-year survival for colon cancer was 60 percent in the U.S. as compared with 35 percent in Britain. Experts dubbed this finding "disgraceful" and called for a doubling of government spending on cancer treatment. In fact, the mortality rate for colon cancer in Britain is about the same as that in the U.S. In an even stranger case, an ad for the prestigious University of Texas M. D. Anderson Cancer Center conflated survival rates with mortality rates: "as national *mortality* rates for prostate cancer fluctuated between 1960 and 1990, five-year *survival* rates for prostate cancer among M. D. Anderson patients continued to improve" (emphasis added).

Mortality rates are far more reliable indicators of the value of screening programs than are five-year survival rates, which boost survival because of earlier diagnoses and overdiagnoses. So should a man get a PSA test or a smoker undergo a CT scan to screen for lung cancer? Both exams find more early-stage cancers—but neither has been shown to reduce mortality.

People commonly regard screening as a safeguard for their health, even if an illness is rare. But additional testing may lead to unnecessary medical interventions that can result in harm, which means there is nothing "safe" about this strategy. And for the many overdiagnosed patients, treatment can only cause harm. An epidemic of diagnoses can be as dangerous to our health as disease is.

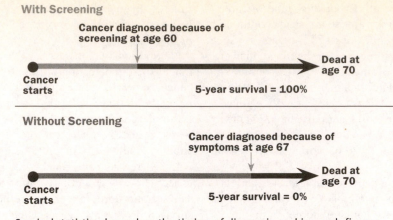

Survival statistics depend on the timing of diagnosis, making such figures misleading. A cancer diagnosis at age 60 (*top*) can dramatically boost five-year survival rates compared with a diagnosis seven years later (*bottom*) without changing the time of death.   *Source:* "Helping Doctors and Patients Make Sense of Health Statistics," By G. Gigerenzer et al., in *Psychological Science in the Public Interest*, vol. 8, No. 2: 2007.

SOLVING PROBLEMS

Statistical misunderstandings would be far less frequent if researchers, doctors and the media used straightforward figures instead of confusing ones: absolute risks instead of relative risks, natural frequencies instead of conditional probabilities, and mortality rates instead of five-year survival rates. In addition to changing the reporting of health statistics, we need to better educate our young people in the science of risk.

Today the U.S. mathematics curriculum centers on the mathematics of certainty—from arithmetic to calculus—and instruction in probability and statistics occurs too late. As H. G. Wells suggested, statistics should be taught as early as reading and writing. Indeed, the U.S. National Council of Teachers of Mathematics has been pushing educators for years to begin instruction in statistics and probability in primary school. If children learned to deal with an uncertain world in a playful way, much of the collective statistical illiteracy would be history.

Furthermore, teachers need to approach statistics differently. Instead of instructing students about how to apply formulas to toy problems involving cards and dice, teachers should show them how to use numbers to solve real-world predicaments. Statistics might even be wrenched away from math educators to create a problem-solving field connected to teaching health in schools. Such a new field might help young people make better decisions about drugs, alcohol use, driving, biotechnology and other relevant health issues.

In an excellent example of this approach, one secondary school textbook tells the real story of a 26-year-old single mother who tested positive in a routine HIV test, lost her job, moved into a halfway house with other HIV-positive residents, had unprotected sex with one of them, eventually developed bronchitis, and was asked by her new doctor to take the HIV test again. She did, and the result was negative, as was her original blood sample when it was retested. The woman had lived through a nightmare because her physicians did not realize that a positive test result is not definitive but that instead, in this woman's case, it means just a 50 percent chance of being infected, because she was in a low-risk group.

Statistical literacy can change lives, helping individuals make better personal choices, recognize misleading advertisements and public service messages, and develop a more relaxed attitude toward their health. The dream of statistical literacy embodies the Enlightenment ideal of people's emergence from their self-imposed immaturity. In Immanuel Kant's words, "Dare to know!"

PART FIVE

Thinking Scientifically About Assessment and Psychotherapy

Two of the most crucial tasks of the practicing clinician are assessment and psychotherapy. Assessment involves the scientifically grounded integration of psychological test data to arrive at a better understanding of clients (Matarazzo, 1990). In turn, the three cornerstones of clinical assessment are reliability, validity, and utility. Reliability asks the question, "Is the measure consistent?"; validity asks the question, "Is the measure assessing what it purports to measure?"; and utility asks the question, "Is the measure clinically useful?"

Reliability is necessary but not sufficient for validity. A measure must be measuring something consistently (reliably) for it to be measuring what it claims to measure. Nevertheless, even an extremely reliable test may be largely or entirely invalid for its intended purpose. Imagine using a measure of hair color (on which different observers would presumably agree highly, a form of reliability called "inter-rater reliability") to assess people's intelligence. The measure in this case would be reliable, but entirely invalid, because hair color is irrelevant to intelligence.

Validity, in turn, is necessary but not sufficient for utility. Even a highly valid measure may display minimal utility for many purposes. For example, if a psychologist is using a valid measure of suicide potential to predict suicide in a sample in which virtually no one commits suicide, the measure will possess little or no utility. Or, if a psychologist gives a client a questionnaire measure of depression that is valid but redundant with other measures of depression the client has received, the questionnaire is unlikely to possess much utility. In the lingo of psychometrics, the science of mental measurement, the questionnaire will probably exhibit little or no *incremental validity* (Meehl, 1959; Sechrest, 1963), that is, the capacity of a measure to contribute information not possessed by existing measures.

Fortunately, over the past several decades, psychologists have developed hundreds of reliable, valid, and useful measures of psychopathology. Nevertheless, some widely used assessment instruments in clinical psychology do not display acceptable psychometric properties. In particular, several projective techniques—those consisting of ambiguous stimuli, like inkblots, that respondents must interpret or make sense of—possess low or at best modest levels of validity. The widely used Rorschach Inkblot Test, for instance, helps to detect conditions marked by thought disorder, like schizophrenia and bipolar disorder (formerly called manic depression), at better than chance levels. But it appears to be largely or entirely invalid for detecting many other conditions, including mood disorders, anxiety disorders, and psychopathic personality (Lilienfeld, Wood, & Garb, 2000; Wood et al., 2010).

Still, when a clinical assessment is conducted properly, it can provide helpful information both for detecting current behaviors—a form of validity that psychologists call *concurrent validity*—and for forecasting

Lilienfeld, S. O., Wood, J. M., & Garb, H. N. (2006). Why questionable psychological tests remain popular. *Scientific Review of Alternative Medicine, 10,* 6–15.

Harkness, A. R., & Lilienfeld, S. O. (1997). Individual differences science for treatment planning: Personality traits. *Psychological Assessment, 9,* 349–360.

Sechrest, L., & Smith, B. (1994). Psychotherapy is the practice of psychology. *Journal of Psychotherapy Integration, 4,* 1–29.

Beyerstein, B. L. (1999). Social and judgmental biases that make inert treatments seem to work. *Scientific Review of Alternative Medicine, 3,* 16–29.

Stuart, R. (2004). Twelve suggestions for developing multicultural competence. *Professional Psychology: Research and Practice, 35,* 3–9.

behaviors—a form of validity that psychologists call *predictive validity*. For example, several measures of psychopathic personality predict future violence and criminal recidivism at better than chance levels (Yang, Wong, & Coid, 2010). In principle, psychological measures can also be helpful in treatment planning and in tracking and enhancing treatment progress. For example, providing psychotherapists with regular feedback about how their clients are scoring on interim measures of psychological symptoms, like depression and anxiety, enhances client outcomes (Lambert et al., 2003). That's probably because such feedback allows therapists to make mid-course corrections when they find out that their clients are not improving as anticipated.

We can define psychotherapy broadly as any psychological procedure designed to help people solve emotional, behavioral, or social problems and to enhance the quality of their lives (Engler & Goleman, 1992). To think scientifically about psychotherapy, we must be able to bring to bear basic knowledge from many domains of psychology, including cognition (thinking), emotion, social psychology, personality, and even perception. For example, because effective psychotherapy involves a certain degree of persuasion, good therapists are aware of the social psychological literature on which techniques are optimal for changing others' minds. The foot-in-the-door technique, for instance, involves asking people to make a small commitment prior to asking them for a larger one (Freedman & Fraser, 1966) and can be a useful way of persuading clients to implement difficult changes in their everyday lives.

Good therapists must also come to appreciate how easily they can be fooled into concluding that useless or even harmful treatments are effective. Many beginning psychology students assume that they can rely merely on their clinical intuition and subjective observations to infer whether a treatment is working. "The client came in very depressed," they may say, "and after five weeks of therapy, he's much better." The student concludes, "So the therapy must have worked." Yet this tempting inference neglects a crucial point: The client might have improved for a plethora of reasons in addition to, or even other than, the therapy itself. For example, the client's improvement may have stemmed from a *placebo effect*, which is improvement resulting from the mere expectation of improvement; *regression to mean*, which is a statistical phenomenon reflecting the tendency of extreme scores to become less extreme after retesting; or *effort justification*, which is the tendency of clients to justify the time, energy, and effort they've expended in therapy by persuading themselves that they've improved. Indeed, this is only a partial listing of artifacts that can fool us into thinking that ineffective therapies are effective (Lilienfeld, Lohr, & Olatunji, 2008).

To think scientifically about psychotherapy, students also need to appreciate its *boundary conditions*—for whom does it work well, and for whom does it not work well? One variable that may place boundary conditions on the effectiveness of psychotherapy is culture. People from certain cultural groups may respond better to certain interventions than those from other cultural groups, and therapists must be alert to this possibility (Cardemil, 2010; O'Donohue & Benuto, 2010). At the same time, it's crucial not to assume reflexively that treatments found to be effective in one culture will generalize to other cultures. In considering the role of culture in therapy, we must walk a fine line. Specifically, we must recognize potential cultural differences in treatment responsiveness while not engaging in stereotyping, which presumes that all individuals within a cultural group will respond similarly to an intervention.

THE READINGS IN PART 5

The five readings in Part 5 address the question of how psychologists can think scientifically about the dual tasks of assessment and psychotherapy, and examine how they can be fooled by techniques that are invalid or ineffective.

Scott Lilienfeld and his colleagues first examine the vexing question of why many psychologists continue to use assessment techniques, like human figure drawings, that possess weak reliability, validity, and utility. As they observe, there are a host of reasons why even entirely invalid measures may superficially appear to be valid. These include illusory correlation and the *P. T. Barnum effect*—the tendency for people to find vague and highly generalized statements to be self-descriptive. Lilienfeld and his coauthors also discuss the role of institutional inertia and clinical tradition in contributing to a reluctance to give up cherished assessment practices that are devoid of convincing evidence. This article is an important reminder that our subjective impressions are rarely trustworthy guides to the validity of psychological measures.

Allan Harkness and Scott Lilienfeld next lay out the basic science of individual differences in personality, and explore how such science can inform treatment planning. They contend that personality traits are real, and that clinical psychologists must distinguish *basic tendencies*—the underlying personality traits themselves—from *characteristic adaptations*—the behavioral expressions of these traits. Harkness and Lilienfeld suggest that psychotherapy should in most cases focus not on altering basic tendencies but on helping clients to find more healthy characteristic adaptations of these tendencies. For example, a therapist treating a client with high levels of sensation seeking who is experiencing legal and marital problems might strive not to reduce the client's level of sensation seeking—which may not even be possible given our current state of knowledge—but rather to encourage the client to find characteristic adaptations that afford more constructive outlets for his sensation seeking. If the client enjoys outdoor activities, the therapist might suggest that he take up hot-air ballooning or rock-climbing, either of which would be more adaptive than breaking the law or fighting with his wife. Harkness and Lilienfeld also discuss ways in which knowledge of clients' personality traits may assist therapists in tailoring their interventions to clients' strengths and weaknesses.

Lee Sechrest and Bradley Smith then argue convincingly that "psychotherapy is the practice of psychology" and that the field of clinical psychology has not relied sufficiently on basic knowledge of memory, learning, perception, emotion, personality, interpersonal processes, and the like in designing effective interventions. They make a persuasive case that good psychotherapists should be drawing continually on basic psychological knowledge to inform everyday practice decisions. For example, if a client with extremely high levels of negative emotionality (a tendency to experience negative emotions of many kinds, like anxiety, guilt, hostility, and mistrust) claims that all of his coworkers dislike him, the therapist should recognize the possibility that the clients' perceptions may be distorted by his negative emotionality, which research has demonstrated to be associated with high levels of criticality toward others (Watson & Clark, 1984). Or, if a therapy client reports that she's suddenly recovered a memory of being sexually abused by her parents at age one and a half, the therapist should be aware that the extensive literature on childhood amnesia prior to age three (Eacott & Crawley, 1998) renders this claim extremely implausible. Effective clinical practice, Sechrest and Smith note, requires more than training in nonspecific skills (e.g., empathy, effective listening) or formal psychotherapy protocols; it requires an ability to capitalize on well-established findings derived from basic psychology.

Barry Beyerstein next examines a variety of biases that can lead practitioners, researchers, and clients to conclude that entirely bogus psychological and medical treatments work. Improvement *following* a treatment is not equivalent to improvement *because of* a treatment. For example, an initial misdiagnosis can lead—or more accurately, mislead—practitioners into concluding that a client has improved *due to* the treatment, when in fact the improvement was merely a naturally occurring remission of a mild or cyclical condition. Placebo effects can fool practitioners into concluding that the treatment itself was effective, when in fact the patient's improvement was due to nonspecific effects stemming from the expectation of improvement. Beyerstein's article reminds us of why observation alone is never sufficient to conclude that a treatment works—because our eyes can deceive us (Ghaemi, 2009; Lilienfeld et al., 2008). Hence the need for controlled research designs, which minimize many or most of the sources of error that Beyerstein identifies.

In the book's final reading, Richard Stuart presents a nuanced and sophisticated perspective on the role of culture in psychotherapy. He provides readers with 12 helpful suggestions for attaining multicultural competence in psychotherapy, including becoming aware of how cultural biases may influence our perception of clients, developing sensitivity to and knowledge of clients' cultural worldviews, placing our assessments in a multicultural context, respecting clients' cultural beliefs but being willing to challenge them when necessary, and being cognizant of cultural differences without succumbing to the error of stereotyping. With regard to the lattermost recommendation, Stuart observes wisely that "the simple fact that clients are identified with one or more ethnic groups does not make it safe to assume that they accept any of the themes that typify these groups" (p. 8). Indeed, research shows that for most psychological traits, differences within groups almost exceed differences between groups (Myers, 2008). As is so often the case in clinical psychology, effective practice requires an acute awareness of how research findings can minimize our risk of errors, and therefore harm, to our clients.

19

Why Questionable Psychological Tests Remain Popular

Scott O. Lilienfeld, James M. Wood, and Howard N. Garb

Many widely used psychological measures, particularly projective techniques, rest on weak scientific footing. We examine five reasons for the continued popularity of questionable psychological tests: (1) illusory correlation, (2) the P. T. Barnum effect, (3) the overperception of psychopathology, (4) the "alchemist's fantasy," and (5) clinical tradition and institutional inertia. We conclude that questionable psychological tests are likely to remain popular unless large-scale changes are made in the education and training of mental-health professionals.

Clinical psychologists and other mental-health professionals have an enormous armamentarium of psychological tests at their disposal. Some of these measures, such as the Minnesota Multiphasic Personality Inventory-2 (MMPI-2)[1] and Personality Assessment Inventory (PAI)[2], have held up reasonably well under research scrutiny (but see Helmes and Redden's 1993 critique of the scientific basis of the MMPI-2[3]). For example, despite the MMPI-2's psychometric shortcomings (e.g., poor content coverage of some important psychological disorders and limited ability to distinguish between certain disorders), its scales are consistently associated with a broad array of psychological disorders, including depression and schizophrenia.[4] In addition, many structured and semi-structured interviews have demonstrated adequate validity for assessing major psychiatric diagnoses.[5] Nevertheless, many other widely used psychological tests rest on extremely feeble scientific footing.[6]

QUESTIONABLE PSYCHOLOGICAL TESTS

Foremost among the popular psychological tests of dubious validity are a number of projective techniques, most of which examine individuals' responses to ambiguous stimuli. The best-known projective technique, the Rorschach Inkblot Test, consists of ten symmetrical inkblots, five of which are in black and white and five of which contain color. Rorschach respondents are asked to look at each inkblot and to say what it resembles. Despite the Rorschach's immense popularity, the substantial majority of clinical uses to which it is put are not supported by scientific evidence. For example, the Rorschach appears to be largely or entirely useless for detecting clinical depression, anxiety disorders, psychopathic personality, violence proneness, oppositionality, emotionality, narcissism, and impulsivity.[7] Nevertheless, the Rorschach is somewhat useful for detecting conditions marked by thought disorder, such as schizophrenia, schizotypal personality disorder, and bipolar disorder (manic depression), for predicting response to psychotherapy, and for assessing normal-range (but perhaps not pathological) interpersonal dependency.[8]

Two other well-known projective techniques are (1) the Thematic Apperception Test (TAT),[9] consisting of 31 cards (most of which depict ambiguous social situations), that requires respondents to tell a story describing the situations portrayed on each card; and (2) human-figure-drawing techniques, such as the Draw-A-Person (DAP) Test,[10] which ask respondents to construct drawings of humans, either alone or in interaction with other people or objects (e.g., houses or trees). Like the Rorschach, the popularity of these measures greatly outstrips their meager base of research support. For example, although the TAT appears to be somewhat useful for assessing achievement motives and individuals' perceptions of others ("object relations"), it has not been found to be helpful for detecting most forms of psychopathology, such as depression.[11] Similarly, human-figure-drawing techniques have not been found to be helpful for detecting specific forms of psychopathology, although they are slightly useful for differentiating global psychopathology from normality.[12–15]

Projective techniques are not the only popular psychological measures of questionable validity. For example, the Myers-Briggs Type Indicator (MBTI), a self-report instrument based on Carl Jung's typological theory of personality, is widely used in counseling, vocational, and industrial/organizational settings. In the lattermost case, it is typically administered for purposes of preemployment screening. The MBTI yields scores on four aspects of personality: extraversion-introversion, thinking-feeling, sensing-intuition, and judgment-perception. Despite its popularity, the MBTI's relations with well-validated measures of vocational preferences and job performance are weak or negligible, as are its relations with well-established models of personality, such as the five-factor model of Extraversion, Neuroticism, Agreeableness, Conscientiousness, and Openness to Experience.[11,16–18]

Despite the weak scientific foundation of the measures we have discussed, they remain widely used in clinical and other applied settings. Watkins, Campbell, Niederding, and Hallmark found that five projective techniques, including the Rorschach and TAT, were among the ten instruments most frequently used by clinical psychologists.[19] For example, 82% of clinical psychologists reported that they administered the Rorschach at least "occasionally" in their test batteries and 43% reported that they "frequently" or "always" administered it. There is some indication, however, that the popularity of projective techniques is waning. Piotrowski, Belter, and Keller reported that several projective techniques, including the Rorschach and TAT, have been abandoned by a nontrivial minority of users.[20] Some authors have attributed the apparent decline in the popularity of projective techniques to the increasing influence of managed care, although at least some of this decline may also stem from the cumulative impact of the criticisms leveled at these techniques over the past several decades.[e.g., 20,21]

This decline notwithstanding, the Rorschach, TAT, and several other projective techniques remain among the most frequently used assessment devices in clinical practice. In contrast to most projective measures, the MBTI actually appears to be increasing in popularity. It was administered to approximately 750 000 people in 1983 and approximately 3 million people in 1993. Moreover, it is administered by 89 companies within the Fortune 100, as well as by thousands of other companies.[6]

Almost certainly, questionable psychological tests remain popular because clinicians sincerely believe that they work. Yet the research evidence typically contradicts many clinicians' intuitions regarding these tests' validity. This striking discrepancy between clinical intuition and research evidence raises an important question: what psychological processes could lead many clinicians to perceive more evidence for the validity of these techniques than is objectively warranted? Although a variety of processes are probably operative, we focus on five here.

ILLUSORY CORRELATION

The first and probably most extensively researched of these processes is illusory correlation. This phenomenon has generally been defined as the perception of (a) a statistical association between variables in its absence or (b) a stronger statistical association between variables than is actually present.[22,23]

In a classic study, Chapman and Chapman first asked practicing clinicians to draw upon their clinical experience to list DAP signs that were most often associated with certain clinical characteristics.[22] They found that clinicians tended to report that certain DAP signs, such as large eyes, were consistently associated with certain psychopathological characteristics, such as suspiciousness, despite the fact that research has revealed scant support for these associations.[13,24] In an ingenious series of studies, Chapman and Chapman then presented undergraduate participants with various DAP drawings that were ostensibly produced by psychiatric patients who suffered from various psychological problems.[23] Each drawing was paired randomly with two of these psychological problems, and participants were asked to carefully inspect a number of these drawings and estimate the extent to which certain DAP signs co-occurred with these problems. Chapman and Chapman found that participants "discovered" the same DAP correlates that had been previously reported by clinicians, despite the fact that the pairing between DAP signs and psychopathological characteristics was entirely random. For example, participants perceived (a) large eyes in drawings as tending to co-occur with suspiciousness and (b) broad shoulders in drawings as tending to co-occur with doubts about manliness, although there was no statistical association between these DAP signs and any psychological problems. These findings suggest, although not do prove, that the invalid DAP signs identified by clinicians stem from the same processes underlying illusory correlation in undergraduate participants.

Chapman and Chapman further found that the illusory-correlation phenomenon was remarkably resistant to efforts to eliminate it.[22] For example, this phenomenon persisted, albeit in attenuated form, even when a significant negative correlation between DAP signs and clinical characteristics was built into the drawings. Moreover, the magnitude of illusory correlation was not significantly reduced even when participants were awarded a $20 prize as inducement for the most accurate judgments of covariation.

Illusory correlation has also been demonstrated with other projective measures. Chapman and Chapman later extended their research design to the Rorschach, demonstrating that illusory correlation can lead individuals to not only perceive invalid Rorschach signs as valid but also impede the processing of valid signs.[23]

Starr and Katkin[25] asked 20 undergraduates, 20 clinical-psychology graduate students, and 20 psychology graduate students in nonclinical areas to read a series of completed sentences (i.e., a stem followed by a response) from the Rotter Incomplete Sentences Blank (ISB).[26] The ISB consists of sentence stems (e.g., "I regret . . .") that participants must complete. The completed sentences (e.g., "I regret nothing I have done") were paired randomly with several presented problems (e.g., "He has difficulty controlling his aggression") that were purportedly solicited from a group of males with psychological difficulties. Despite these random pairings, the three groups of participants tended to perceive substantial levels of covariation between these sentences and certain presented problems. Interestingly, as observed by Chapman and Chapman, the specific correlations perceived by participants corresponded precisely to the associations previously identified by a group of practicing psychologists.[22,23] Analyses of confidence ratings revealed that undergraduate participants tended to produce more extreme ratings (either "sure" or "guessing") than individuals in the other two groups.

More recently, King and Koehler demonstrated that individuals unfamiliar with graphology (handwriting analysis) perceive illusory correlations between certain handwriting features (e.g., large letters) and certain personality traits (e.g., egotism).[27] Their findings may help to account for the persistent popularity of graphology despite overwhelming research evidence contradicting its validity for detecting personality traits or psychopathology.[28]

The findings of the Chapmans and others may actually underestimate the magnitude of illusory correlation in real-world settings. In a study of undergraduate participants, Lueger and Petzel reported that the magnitude of illusory correlation with DAP drawings grew as information-processing load increased.[29] Because we are unaware of similar research with practicing clinicians, the generalizability of this finding to real-world assessment settings requires investigation. Nevertheless, the heavy cognitive demands of clinical settings may promote illusory correlation by decreasing the amount of time that practitioners can effectively process conflicting or counterintuitive assessment information. As a consequence, practitioners may come to rely largely on preexisting beliefs regarding the covariation between projective signs and clinical features.

The phenomenon of illusory correlation does not, by itself, demonstrate that projective measures are of doubtful validity. But this phenomenon offers a plausible explanation for why many clinicians perceive projective techniques as valid even in the absence of compelling data. Moreover, research on illusory correlation clearly implies that the intuitive judgments of clinicians regarding the predictive capacity of psychological instruments should not be accepted without corroborating evidence. Yet some authors appear to misunderstand this point. For example, in defending the clinical use of the TAT, Karon argued that "The reason there is no substitute for a clinical process of inference with the TAT is that variables of interest in personality are literally infinite."[30(94); see also 31] Because of illusory correlation, however, clinicians using the TAT and other measures may come to believe they are drawing accurate clinical inferences when they are not.

In addition, some Rorschach proponents maintain that illusory correlation cannot account for clinicians' erroneous beliefs in the validity of projective techniques. For example, Weiner asked rhetorically:

> How likely is it that so many Rorschach assessors have been using the instrument for so long, in so many places and contexts, solely on the basis of illusory correlation? If this seems unlikely, is it unreasonable to infer that there has been some utility in their work?[32(11)]

Although we agree with Weiner that the continued popularity of the Rorschach among clinicians is not due

"solely" to illusory correlation, we would hasten to point out that astrology, a pseudoscientific belief system that has persisted for approximately 5000 years, probably also derives much of its popularity from illusory correlation.[33] The durability of a belief is a poor barometer of its validity, an error enshrined in the logician's *ad antiquitem* fallacy.[7]

Although the psychological processes underlying illusory correlation are not completely understood, it is likely that one important contributing factor is the availability heuristic, the tendency to judge the frequency of the occurrence of events by the ease with which they can be retrieved from memory.[34,35] Clinicians may selectively attend to and recall cases in which certain projective signs (e.g., large eyes) co-occur with psychopathological characteristics (e.g., suspiciousness), particularly when such co-occurrences confirm their prior beliefs.[cf. 36] In contrast, they may ignore or forget cases in which these signs do not confirm prior beliefs. Another probable contributor to illusory correlation is the representativeness heuristic, the tendency to judge the probability of two events by gauging their superficial similarity ("like goes with like").[37] For example, large eyes are probably representative of suspiciousness in many individuals' minds.[22; see also 5,38]

THE P. T. BARNUM EFFECT

Named after the flamboyant circus entrepreneur who jested that he "liked to give a little something to everyone" in his acts, the P.T. Barnum effect is the tendency of test respondents to accept high base-rate, nonobvious personality descriptors (e.g., "At times you may have difficulty making certain decisions," "You have a great deal of unused potential that you have not yet turned to your advantage;" "At times you are outgoing, whereas at other times you prefer to be alone") as highly self-descriptive.[39; see also 40] The P. T. Barnum effect capitalizes on the fact that most individuals are unaware of the high base rates of minor personality frailties (e.g., indecisiveness). This effect further suggests that individuals may be especially likely to accept Barnum-type descriptions when they are purportedly derived from projective measures, because the interpretation of these measures is opaque to most respondents.

Snyder randomly assigned undergraduates to receive either an inkblot test, a locus-of-control questionnaire, or a ten-minute interview, and then provided them with identical Barnum feedback.[41] Participants rated the accuracy of the feedback most highly when they had previously taken the inkblot test. Similar results were found in a second study in which undergraduates were randomly assigned to administer one of these three measures to a friend and then ask the friend to rate the accuracy of the Barnum feedback. As Snyder noted, "The projective technique may achieve the highest acceptance because people believe they are revealing themselves in ways they do not understand."[41(150)]

Richards and Merrens administered an abbreviated Rorschach, a life-history questionnaire, or a personality questionnaire to samples of undergraduates and provided them with identical Barnum feedback.[42] The Rorschach was rated higher than both self-report measures on accuracy and psychological "depth," although only the difference in depth achieved statistical significance. Although not all researchers have found statistically significant relations between the "face validity" of measures and the acceptance of Barnum descriptions purportedly derived from these measures, these investigators did not directly compare the acceptance of Barnum feedback following projective and structured personality measures.[43,44] (Face validity is the extent to which test respondents can discern what the test is actually measuring.)

Individuals' acceptance of projectively derived Barnum descriptions appears to be robust and resistant to experimental manipulation. Lattal and Lattal administered a widely used figure-drawing technique, the House-Tree-Person Test (H-T-P) to a group of students.[45] Half were later told that the H-T-P was "a relatively invalid and generally questionable personality assessment technique" and half were told nothing about the H-T-P.[45(320)] All students then received the same Barnum feedback. Surprisingly, participants in both groups rated this feedback as highly self-descriptive, with essentially identical ratings in both groups.

The P. T. Barnum effect may account partly for the widespread popularity of projective measures among clinicians.[42] Specifically, high levels of client acceptance of interpretations derived from projective techniques may lead clinicians to overestimate these techniques' predictive powers. The results of these studies demonstrate that personal validation, viz., the extent to which clients express acceptance of assessment feedback, is an untrustworthy foundation on which to base belief in the validity of psychological measures, including projective techniques.[40,46]

THE OVERPERCEPTION OF PSYCHOPATHOLOGY

A third potential reason for the continued popularity of projective techniques among clinicians has, to our knowledge, received little attention. This reason is especially relevant to the Rorschach, although it probably applies to some other projective techniques as well.

Mounting research evidence indicates that the modern norms for the Rorschach, which are derived from the Comprehensive System (CS)[47] tend to overpathologize respondents.[48] (Norms are population baselines that allow test examiners to gauge the extent to which a response is abnormal.) That is, the CS norms tend to make a large number of psychologically normal individuals appear disturbed. For example, Schaffer, Erdberg, and Haroian examined the Rorschach scores of a combined sample of college students and volunteer donors at a California blood bank.[49] Although their MMPI-2 scores were essentially normal, their Rorschach protocols interpreted using the CS norms suggested serious pathology. Approximately one in six scored in the pathological range on the CS Schizophrenia Index, ostensibly an indicator of schizophrenia, and more than one in four produced reflection responses, ostensibly an indicator of narcissism.[a] Combining

findings from 32 studies, Wood et al. reported that CS scores derived from nonpatients were markedly discrepant from the published CS norms and erred consistently in the direction of overpathologizing normal respondents.[48]

Interestingly, the tendency of the Rorschach to overpathologize respondents appears to antedate the CS norms. For example, over a half-century ago, Wittenberg and Sarason noted that the use of the Rorschach sometimes results in identifying normal individuals as severely disordered, even psychotic.[51] Several years later, Grant, Ives, and Ranzoni found that psychologists who used the Rorschach concluded that two thirds of an unselected sample of adolescents in the community were "maladjusted."[52]

Practitioners, who of necessity tend to assess disturbed individuals, may therefore conclude that the Rorschach CS is consistently accurate in identifying pathology. Nevertheless, this apparent accuracy may be largely a function of the tendency of the CS norms to overclassify individuals as pathological. Moreover, for many intact or only mildly affected individuals, the Rorschach CS may indicate pathology when such tests as the MMPI-2 do not. Many proponents of the Rorschach CS[e.g., 53,54] have maintained that this discrepancy demonstrates that the Rorschach can detect subtle or latent signs of psychopathology that the MMPI-2 misses. This is probably an important reason why many clinicians continue to use the test. Yet, this discrepancy may instead be due to the Rorschach's flawed norms.[8]

Paradoxically, the propensity of the Rorschach to overpathologize respondents may contribute to an illusory perception of its validity, because clinicians who use the Rorschach are exposed almost exclusively to pathological individuals. As Wood et al. observed in 2003:

> . . . suppose that a test arbitrarily labels 75 percent of patients as either depressed, troubled in their interpersonal relationships, or both. Such results, though arbitrary, will usually be accurate, because most patients seen by clinicians are depressed or have troubled relationships. The test may seem uncannily sensitive. Of course, if clinicians were to administer the test to a large group of healthy adults, they would find (as Rorschach researchers did in the 1950s) that the test also arbitrarily identifies most normal individuals as maladjusted. But clinicians seldom assess healthy adults as part of their daily work.[7(149)]

The overperception of psychopathology may not be limited to the Rorschach. For example, many common clinical uses of the TAT tend to overpathologize relatively nondisturbed individuals.[55] In addition, clinicians using human-figure-drawing tests have been found to misclassify many normal individuals with poor artistic ability as pathological.[56]

THE ALCHEMIST'S FANTASY

Many advocates of projective techniques subscribe to the belief that a test can perform poorly in research studies yet prove highly informative in clinical practice. Clinicians always

---

[a] See reference 50 for similar findings with children administered the Rorschach.

evaluate a test score in the context of numerous other forms of assessment data, so the argument goes, and intuitively combining multiple sources of information can turn a generally invalid test, such as the Rorschach or TAT, into a wellspring of penetrating clinical insights.[57] We call this notion "the alchemist's fantasy" because advocates seem to believe, like the alchemists of old, that the powers of intuition enable them to transform worthless projective test scores into clinical gold.

The alchemist's fantasy has long encouraged Rorschach users to dismiss negative research findings and to instead emphasize the role of intuition in test interpretation. This fantasy first surfaced in the 1940s, when Rorschach proponents asserted that the intuitive integration of Rorschach scores was so remarkably complicated that it did not lend itself to empirical investigation.[58] This hoary claim has recently been revived by prominent Rorschach proponent Gregory Meyer and his colleagues:

> . . . to the extent that clinicians view all test data in a contextually differentiated fashion, the practical value of tests used in clinical assessment is likely greater than what is suggested by the research on their nomothetic associations.[59(153)]

However:

> . . . trying to document the validity of individualized, contextually embedded references is incredibly complex—and virtually impossible if one hopes to find a relatively large sample of people with the same pattern of test and extratest information (i.e., history, observed behavior, motivational context, etc.). Research cannot hope to approximate such an ideal.[59(153)]

Such arguments rest on the premise that, through intuition and special expertise, Rorschach interpreters can routinely extract important insights by detecting subtle interactions (a) among different scores on a psychological test, (b) among different psychological tests, and (c) between test and non-test information. Nevertheless, this superficially appealing line of reasoning is not supported by research evidence. Studies consistently demonstrate that replicable higher-order interactions in the domain of personality assessment are extremely hard to come by.[60] Instead, in most cases, straightforward additive combinations of variables perform just as well, if not better, than do complex multiplicative interactions among these variables.[61–63] Moreover, there is no compelling evidence that, even if such higher-order interactions were shown to exist, clinicians could routinely capitalize on them.[b]

In addition, claims like those of Meyer and his colleagues assume that "more is always better" in the interpretation of assessment measures.[59] Yet social psychological research on the dilution effect demonstrates that presenting participants with accurate but nondiagnostic information regarding individuals often results in less accurate judgments.[64] Compared with participants presented with relevant information only, participants presented with both relevant and irrelevant information often attend too highly to the irrelevant information, resulting in a dilution of their predictive judgments.

Research on the Rorschach demonstrates the same phenomenon. Numerous studies conducted since the 1940s have found that adding the Rorschach to additional sources of assessment information does not typically enhance the validity of clinical judgments.[5,58,65] To the contrary, in several cases, the addition of the Rorschach to other assessment information has led to a decrease in predictive accuracy. For example, Whitehead gave judges the MMPI alone, the Rorschach (scored using the CS) alone, and both the MMPI and Rorschach, and asked them to perform various diagnostic discriminations (e.g., differentiating bipolar from schizophrenic patients).[66] Whitehead found that adding the MMPI to the Rorschach increased diagnostic hit rates from 58% to 74% but that adding the Rorschach to the MMPI decreased diagnostic hit rates (albeit not significantly) from 76% to 74%.

More is not always better in the domain of assessment information, and it is sometimes worse. Nevertheless, the alchemist's fantasy promotes the illusory impression that valid clinical judgments can emerge from invalid test data.

CLINICAL TRADITION AND EDUCATIONAL INERTIA

Fifth and finally, it is difficult or impossible to quantify precisely the role of clinical tradition and educational inertia in accounting for the widespread popularity of questionable psychological measures. Nevertheless, this role is difficult to ignore.

As noted earlier, projective techniques continue to be used by a large proportion of clinicians in the community,[19] and the MBTI is used by thousands of U.S. companies.[6] This widespread use may provide test users with "communal reinforcement"[67] for administering and interpreting these instruments. The reinforcement that students, clinicians, and employers receive from their colleagues for administering these measures may play a key role in sustaining belief in the utility of these measures, because these students and clinicians may fall prey to the *ad populum* fallacy: the erroneous belief that a technique that is widely used must be valid or effective.

Historically, projective techniques have been highly valued in many graduate psychology programs. Surveys reveal that a large proportion of directors of clinical-psychology programs and internships believe that formal training in projective measures, particularly the Rorschach, TAT, and human-figure-drawing techniques, is of paramount importance in the education of clinical psychologists. For example, Durand, Blanchard, and Mindell reported that 49% of the directors of clinical-psychology graduate programs and 65% of the directors of clinical-psychology internships believed that formal training in projective techniques is important.[68] In a survey of 412 clinical psychologists, Watkins et al. found that 96%, 90%, and 90% of their respondents believed that clinical-psychology students should be competent in the use of projective drawings, the Rorschach, and TAT, respectively.[19] Nevertheless, because no comparable published surveys have appeared over the past decade, it is not known whether these high percentages have remained stable or declined.

---

[b] See reference 63 for a discussion of holistic judgment.

Moreover, a number of recent articles and books on projective techniques continue to portray the research evidence for these techniques in a positive light, ignore or dismiss criticisms of these techniques, or both. These writings may contribute to the mistaken impression that these measures are widely accepted by the clinical science community and foster the notion that skepticism regarding their validity is unwarranted. For example, Rossini and Moretti asserted that "the TAT remains an essential component of the practicing clinical and counseling psychologist's psychodiagnostic repertoire."[69(393); see also 31] Cramer, a prominent TAT researcher, stated that her first step in teaching students about the TAT is to "try to enlist and encourage the development of the students' creative, clinical sensitivity, and to loosen them from the inhibiting skepticism and prejudice regarding projective assessment techniques."[70(247)]

In addition, in a major article prepared by the Psychological Assessment Work Group (PAWG), which was established by the Board of Professional Affairs of the American Psychological Association, Kubisyzn et al. averred that:

> Studies have demonstrated the ability of the Rorschach or the TAT (a) to differentiate among Axis II conditions like borderline, antisocial, narcissistic, and schizotypal personality disorders and Axis I conditions like schizophrenia, major depression, conduct disorder, and panic disorder and (b) to also identify non-DSM conditions, such as differentiating patients who have experienced physical or sexual trauma from those who have not.[71(121)]

Yet with the exception of schizophrenia, borderline personality disorder, and perhaps schizotypal and bipolar disorders, the capacity of either the Rorschach or TAT to make these practically and theoretically important distinctions has not been replicated across independent research teams.[15] For reasons that are unclear, the PAWG cited no negative findings regarding the diagnostic capacities of the Rorschach or TAT, despite the fact that such findings are plentiful.[e.g., 8,72]

Although it is essential that clinicians and researchers maintain open minds concerning the validity of the Rorschach, TAT, and other projective techniques, it is equally essential that they be appropriately circumspect in their claims regarding these measures. Unwarranted assertions may inadvertently encourage practitioners to use projective indexes of questionable validity and to draw unjustified clinical inferences on the basis of dubious evidence. Such assertions may also lead students to draw mistaken inferences regarding the scientific status of projective techniques and other questionable psychological measures.

CONCLUDING THOUGHTS

Although we have identified five factors that we believe contribute to the continued popularity of questionable psychological tests, especially projective techniques, we make no pretense that our list is exhaustive. Other factors, including (a) confirmation bias (the tendency to selectively seek out evidence that supports one's hypotheses and to ignore or minimize evidence that does not),[73] (b) hindsight bias (the "I-knew-it-all-along effect"),[74] (c) overconfidence,[75] and, more broadly, (d) the suboptimal psychometric training and education of graduate students in programs in clinical psychology and allied disciplines[76] may also play significant roles. We strongly encourage researchers to examine the potential influence of each of these factors in producing and sustaining belief in the validity of questionable psychological tests.

It is clear that many of the psychological processes that sustain belief in invalid psychological measures, such as illusory correlation and the P. T. Barnum effect, are understandable errors to which most of us are prone.[63] These processes are in no way unique to clinicians who use questionable psychological tests. To the contrary, individuals who are entirely unfamiliar with these tests readily fall prey to the same errors in judgment.[22,27,42]

How can we combat the continued popularity of psychological tests of doubtful validity? We suspect that the best antidote is systematic education in critical thinking. Regrettably, few graduate programs in clinical psychology and allied areas place a high premium on teaching students basic critical-thinking skills for evaluating evidence.[77] Without such skills, students may be at the mercy of both their fallible intuitions and the often expansive claims of proponents of certain questionable psychological tests.[c,78] Indeed, few graduate training programs require formal exposure to the research literature concerning clinical judgment and prediction, including the heuristics (e.g., representativeness), biases (e.g., hindsight bias), and errors (e.g., illusory correlation) that can lead even highly intelligent individuals to perceive validity in its absence.

Fortunately, promising research on "debiasing" techniques suggests that a number of these cognitive "bad habits"[79] can be reduced by systematic training.[80,81] Moreover, educating students regarding both (a) the psychometric limitations of questionable psychological tests and (b) their intrinsic limitations as information processors can inculcate in them a healthy sense of humility. Such humility may in turn immunize them against uncritically accepting confident claims regarding the validity of psychological tests that rest on a weak scientific foundation.

---

[c] See reference 7 (261–262) for striking examples of overstatements by numerous authors concerning the validity of the Rorschach and TAT.

References

1. Butcher JN, Dahlstrom WG, Graham JR, Tellegen A, Kaemmer B. *MMPI-2: Manual for Administration and Scoring.* Minneapolis, MN: University of Minnesota Press. 1989.

2. Morey LC. *Personality Assessment Inventory: Professional Manual.* Psychological Lutz, FL: Assessment Resources. 1991.

3. Helmes E, Reddon JR. A perspective on developments in assessing psychopathology: A critical review of the MMPI and MMPI-2. *Psychological Bulletin.* 1993; 113: 453–471.

4. Greene RL. *The MMPI-2: An Interpretive Manual* (2nd ed.). Boston: Allyn and Bacon. 2000.

5. Garb, HN. *Studying the Clinician: Judgment Research and Psychological Assessment*. Washington, DC: American Psychological Association. 1998.

6. Paul AM. *Cult of Personality: How Personality Tests Are Leading Us to Miseducate Our Children, Mismanage Our Companies, and Misunderstand Ourselves*. New York: Free Press. 2005.

7. Wood JM, Nezworski MT, Lilienfeld SO, Garb HN. *What's Wrong with the Rorschach? Science Confronts the Controversial Inkblot Test*. San Francisco: Jossey-Bass. 2003.

8. Wood JM, Nezworski MT, Garb HN. What's right with the Rorschach? *Scientific Review of Mental Health Practice*. 2003; 2: 142–146.

9. Morgan CD, Murray HA. A method for investigating fantasies. *Archives of Neurology and Psychiatry*. 1935; 34: 289–304.

10. Machover K. *Personality Projection in the Drawing of the Human Figure*. Springfield, IL: Thomas. 1949.

11. Hunsley J, Lee C, Wood JM. Controversial and questionable assessment techniques. In Lilienfeld SO, Lohr JM, Lynn SJ (eds.), *Science and Pseudoscience in Clinical Psychology* (39–76). New York: Guilford. 2003.

12. Joiner TE, Schmidt KL, Barnett J. Size, detail, and line heaviness in children's drawings as correlates of emotional distress: (More) negative evidence. *Journal of Personality Assessment*. 1996; 67: 127–141.

13. Kahill S. Human figure drawing in adults: An update of the empirical evidence, 1967–1982. *Canadian Psychology*. 1984; 25: 269–292.

14. Lilienfeld SO. Projective measures of personality and psychopathology: How well do they work? *Skeptical Inquirer*. 1999; 23: 32–39.

15. Lilienfeld SO, Wood JM, Garb HN. The scientific status of projective techniques. *Psychological Science in the Public Interest*. 2000; 1: 27–66.

16. Apostal R, Marks, C. Correlations between the Strong-Campbell and Myers-Briggs scales of introversion-extraversion and career interests. *Psychological Reports*. 1990; 66: 811–816.

17. Furnham A. The Big Five versus the Big Four: The relationship between the Myers-Briggs Type Indicator (MBTI) and the NEO-PI five factor model of personality. *Personality and Individual Differences*. 1996; 21: 303–307.

18. Furnham A, Stringfield P. Personality and work performance: Myers-Briggs Type Indicator correlates of managerial performance in two cultures. *Personality and Individual Differences*. 1993; 14: 145–153.

19. Watkins CE, Campbell VL, Nieberding R, Hallmark R. Contemporary practice of psychological assessment by clinical psychologists. *Professional Psychology: Research and Practice*. 1995; 26: 54–60.

20. Piotrowski C, Belter RW, Keller JW. The impact of "managed care" on the practice of psychological testing: Preliminary findings. *Journal of Personality Assessment*. 1998; 70: 441–447.

21. Piotrowski C, Belter RW. Internship training in psychological assessment: Has managed care had an impact? *Assessment*. 1999; 6: 381–385.

22. Chapman LJ, Chapman JP. Genesis of popular but erroneous psychodiagnostic observations. *Journal of Abnormal Psychology*. 1967; 72: 193–204.

23. Chapman LJ, Chapman JP. Illusory correlation as an obstacle to the use of valid psychodiagnostic observations. *Journal of Abnormal Psychology*. 1969; 74: 271–280.

24. Thomas GV, Jolley RP. Drawing conclusions: A reexamination of empirical and conceptual bases for psychological evaluations of children from their drawings. *British Journal of Clinical Psychology*. 1998; 37: 127–139.

25. Starr BJ, Katkin ES. The clinician as an aberrant actuary: Illusory correlation and the Incomplete Sentences Blank. *Journal of Abnormal Psychology*. 1969; 74: 670–675.

26. Rotter JB, Rafferty JE. *Manual: The Rotter Incomplete Sentences Blank College Form*. New York: The Psychological Corporation. 1950.

27. King RN, Koehler DJ. Illusory correlations in graphological inference. *Journal of Experimental Psychology: Applied*. 2000; 5: 336–348.

28. Beyerstein BL, Beyerstein DF. *The Write Stuff: Evaluations of Graphology—The Study of Handwriting Analysis*. Buffalo, NY: Prometheus Books. 1992.

29. Lueger RJ, Petzel TP. Illusory correlation in clinical judgment: Effects of amount of information to be processed. *Journal of Consulting and Clinical Psychology*. 1979; 47: 1120–1121.

30. Karon BP. The Thematic Apperception Test (TAT). In AI Rabin (ed.), *Assessment with Projective Techniques: A Concise Introduction* (85–120). New York: Springer. 1981.

31. Karon BP. The clinical interpretation of the Thematic Apperception Test, Rorschach, and other clinical data: A reexamination of statistical versus clinical prediction. *Professional Psychology: Research and Practice*. 2000; 31: 230–233.

32. Weiner IB. The value of Rorschach assessment. *Harvard Mental Health Letter*. 2001 (Dec.): 4–5.

33. Hines TH. *Pseudoscience and the Paranormal*. Amherst, New York: Prometheus. 2003.

34. Gilovich T. *How We Know What Isn't So: The Fallibility of Human Reason in Everyday Life*. New York: The Free Press. 1991.

35. Tversky A, Kahneman D. Availability: a heuristic for judging frequency and probability. *Cognitive Psychology*. 1973; 5: 207–232.

36. McDonald MG. Illusory correlation: A function of availability or representativeness? *Perceptual and Motor Skills*. 2000; 91: 343–350.

37. Kahneman D, Tversky A. Subjective probability: A judgment of representativeness. *Cognitive Psychology*. 1972; 3: 430–454.

38. Dawes RM, Faust D, Meehl PE. Clinical versus actuarial judgment. *Science*. 1989; 243: 1668–1674.

39. Meehl PE. Wanted: A good cookbook. *American Psychologist*. 1956; 11: 263–272.

40. Forer BR. The fallacy of personal validation: A classroom demonstration of gullibility. *Journal of Abnormal and Social Psychology*. 1949; 44: 118–123.

41. Snyder CR. Acceptance of personality interpretations as a function of assessment procedures. *Journal of Consulting and Clinical Psychology*. 1974; 42: 150.

42. Richards WS, Merrens MR. Student acceptance of generalized personality interpretations as a function of method of assessment. *Journal of Clinical Psychology*. 1971; 25: 457–459.

43. Delprato DJ. Face validity of test and acceptance of generalized personality interpretations. *Journal of Personality Assessment*. 1975; 39: 345–348.

44. Jackson DE, O'Dell JW, Olson D. Acceptance of bogus personality interpretations: Face validity reconsidered. *Journal of Personality Assessment*. 1982; 38: 588–591.

45. Lattal KA, Lattal AD. Student "gullibility": A systematic replication. *Journal of Psychology*. 1967; 67: 319–322.

46. Greene RL, Harris ME, Macon RS. Another look at personal validation. *Journal of Personality Assessment*. 1979; 43: 419–442.

47. Exner JE. *A Rorschach workbook for the Comprehensive System* (5th ed.). Asheville, North Carolina: Rorschach Workshops. 2001.

48. Wood JM, Nezworski MT, Garb HN, Lilienfeld SO. The misperception of psychopathology: Problems with the norms of the

Comprehensive System for the Rorschach. *Clinical Psychology: Science and Practice*. 2001; 8: 350–373.

49. Shaffer TW, Erdberg P, Haroian J. Current nonpatient data for the Rorschach, WAIS-R, and MMPI-2. *Journal of Personality Assessment*. 1999; 73; 305–316.

50. Hamel M, Shaffer TW, Erdberg, P. A study of non-patient preadolescent Rorschach protocols. *Journal of Personality Assessment*. 2000; 75: 280–294.

51. Wittenborn JR, Sarason SB. Exceptions to certain Rorschach criteria of pathology. *Journal of Consulting Psychology*. 1949; 13: 21–27.

52. Grant MQ, Ives V, Ranzoni JH. Reliability and validity of judges' ratings of adjustment on the Rorschach. *Psychological Monographs*. 1952; 66(2).

53. Finn SE. *Using the MMPI-2 as a Therapeutic Intervention*. Minneapolis, MN: University of Minnesota Press. 1996.

54. Weiner IB. Some observations on the Rorschach Inkblot Method. *Psychological Assessment*. 1996; 8: 206–213.

55. Murstein BI, Mathes S. Projection on projective techniques = pathology: The problem that is not being addressed. *Journal of Personality Assessment*. 1996; 66: 337–349.

56. Cressen R. Artistic quality of drawings and judges' evaluations of the DAP. *Journal of Personality Assessment*. 1975; 39: 132–137.

57. Merlo L, Barnett D. All about inkblots. *Scientific American*. 2001(Sept.); 285: 13.

58. Garb HN, Wood JM, Lilienfeld SO, Nezworski MT. Roots of the Rorschach controversy. *Clinical Psychology Review*. 2005; 25: 97–118.

59. Meyer GJ, Finn SE, Eyde LD, Kay GG, Moreland KL, Dies RR, Eisman EJ, Kubiszyn TW, Reed GM. Psychological testing and psychological assessment: A review of evidence and issues. *American Psychologist*. 2001; 56: 128–165.

60. Cronbach LJ. Beyond the two disciplines of scientific psychology. *American Psychologist*. 1975; 30: 116–127.

61. Dawes RM, Corrigan B. Linear models in decision making. *Psychological Bulletin*. 1974; 81: 95–106.

62. Goldberg LR. The search for configural relationships in personality assessment: The diagnosis of psychosis vs. neurosis from the MMPI. *Multivariate Behavioral Research*. 1969; 4: 523–536.

63. Ruscio J. *Clear Thinking with Psychology: Separating Sense from Nonsense*. Pacific Grove, CA: Wadsworth. 2002.

64. Nisbett RE, Zukier H, Lemley RE. The dilution effect: Nondiagnostic information weakens the implications of diagnostic information. *Cognitive Psychology*. 1981; 12: 248–277.

65. Garb HN, Wood JM, Lilienfeld SO, Nezworski T. Roots of the Rorschach controversy. *Clinical Psychology Review*. 2005; 25:97–118.

66. Whitehead WC. Clinical Decision Making on the Basis of Rorschach, MMPI, and Automated MMPI Report Data (unpublished doctoral dissertation). Dallas: University of Texas Health Sciences Center. 1985.

67. Carroll RT. *The Skeptic's Dictionary: A Collection of Strange Beliefs, Amusing Deceptions, and Dangerous Delusions*. New York: John Wiley & Sons. 2003.

68. Durand VM, Blanchard EB, Mindell JA. Training in projective testing: A survey of clinical training directors and internship directors. *Professional Psychology: Research and Practice*. 1988; 19: 236–238.

69. Rossini ED, Moretti RJ. Thematic Apperception Test (TAT) interpretation: Practice recommendations from a survey of clinical psychology doctoral programs accredited by the American Psychological Association. *Professional Psychology: Research and Practice*. 1997; 28: 393–398.

70. Cramer P. Approaching the Thematic Apperception Test. In Handler L and Hilsenroth M (eds.), *Teaching and learning personality assessment* (247–265). Hillsdale, NJ: Lawrence Erlbaum Associates. 1998.

71. Kubiszyn TW, Meyer GJ, Finn SE, Eyde LD, Kay GG, Moreland KL, Dies RR, Eisman EJ. Empirical support for psychological assessment in clinical health care settings. *Professional Psychology: Research and Practice*. 2000; 31: 119–130.

72. Sharkey KJ, Ritzler BA. Comparing diagnostic validity of the TAT and a new picture projection test. *Journal of Personality Assessment*, 1985; 49: 406–412.

73. Davies MF. Confirmation bias in the evaluation of personality descriptions: Positive test strategies and output interference. *Journal of Personality and Social Psychology*. 2003; 85: 736–744.

74. Fischhoff B. Hindsight≠foresight: The effect of outcome knowledge on judgment under uncertainty. *Journal of Experimental Psychology: Human Perception and Performance*. 1975; 1: 288–299.

75. Smith D, Dumont F. Eliminating overconfidence in psychodiagnosis: Strategies for training and practice. *Clinical Psychology: Science and Practice*. 1997; 4: 335–345.

76. Lilienfeld SO, Lynn SJ, Lohr JM. Science and pseudoscience in clinical psychology: Initial thoughts, reflections, and considerations. In Lilienfeld SO, Lohr JM, Lynn SJ (eds.), *Science and pseudoscience in clinical psychology* (1–14). New York: Guilford. 2003.

77. Lilienfeld SO, Lynn SJ, Lohr JM. Science and pseudoscience in clinical psychology: Concluding thoughts and constructive remedies. In Lilienfeld SO, Lohr JM, Lynn SJ (eds.), *Science and Pseudoscience in Clinical Psychology* (461–465). New York: Guilford. 2003.

78. Wood JM, Lilienfeld SO. The Rorschach Inkblot Test: A case of overstatement? *Assessment*. 1999; 6: 341–349.

79. Faust D. Research on human judgment and its application to clinical practice. *Professional Psychology: Research and Practice*. 1986; 17: 420–430.

80. Croskerry P. The importance of cognitive errors in diagnosis and strategies to minimize them. *Academic Medicine*. 2003; 78; 775–780.

81. Renner CH, Renner MJ. But I thought I knew that: Using confidence estimation as a debiasing technique to improve classroom performance. *Applied Cognitive Psychology*. 2001; 15: 2–32.

20

Individual Differences Science for Treatment Planning: Personality Traits

ALLAN R. HARKNESS AND SCOTT O. LILIENFELD

Evolving ethical, legal, and financial demands require a plan before treatment begins. The authors argue that individual differences research requires the inclusion of personality trait assessment for the construction and implementation of any treatment plan that would lay claim to scientific status. A primer of personality individual differences for treatment planning is presented, including an introduction to constructive realism and major research findings from trait psychology and behavior genetics bearing on treatment planning. The authors present 4 important gains for treatment planning that can be realized from the science of individual differences in personality: (a) knowing where to focus change efforts, (b) realistic expectations, (c) matching treatment to personality, and (d) development of the self.

Gone are the days when a therapist could delay planning and simply allow therapy to unfold. Instead, evolving ethical demands (e.g., informed consent), legal demands (e.g., liability management, mandated record keeping), and financial demands (e.g., third-party preapproval) require a plan before treatment begins. In this article, we show that science makes demands as well. The last 40 years of individual differences research require the inclusion of personality trait assessment for the construction and implementation of any treatment plan that would lay claim to scientific status.

SCIENCE SHOULD GUIDE TREATMENT PLANNING

The Fundamental Rule of Treatment Planning

How should a treatment plan be constructed? What information should it use, and what procedures should it prescribe? We offer a simple and perhaps obvious formula and co-opt Freud's terminology to label it. Our *fundamental rule of treatment planning* states that the plan should be based on the best science available.

Ethics and laws provide boundaries for the treatment plan, but within those boundaries, science should determine the treatment. In fact, both ethical and legal guidelines converge in placing science in the driver's seat. The American Psychological Association's (1992) Ethical Standard 1.05 demands that psychologists keep up to date on scientific and professional information, and Standard 1.06 requires that psychologists "rely on scientifically and professionally derived knowledge when making scientific or professional judgments" (p. 1600). For anyone operating in the scientist-practitioner model, no conflict should arise between scientifically and professionally derived knowledge. These guides constitute standards of the profession and are legally essential in determining when practice is adequate and when it falls short. Thus, if treatment planning is to meet or surpass the standards mandated by the field, then the fundamental rule of treatment planning applies: The plan should be based on the best science available.

The fundamental rule imposes a great duty on the therapist. The therapist must be well informed regarding recent scientific findings, even if those findings were not emphasized in the psychologist's schools or practice settings. The necessity of being widely informed is made clear in one of the guides we have for induction: Carnap's (1962) requirement of total evidence.[1]

---

[1] Carnap (1962) explained the requirement: "In the application of inductive logic still another difficulty is involved, which does not concern inductive logic itself. This difficulty consists in the fact that if an observer wants to apply inductive logic to a hypothesis *h*, he has to take as evidence *e* a complete report of all his observational knowledge. Many authors on probability have not given sufficient attention to this *requirement of total evidence*. They often leave aside a great part of the available information as though it were irrelevant. However, cases of strict irrelevance are much more rare than is usually assumed" (p. 208, italics in original). As an example, it is unlikely Gregor Mendel would have correctly induced the dihybrid proportions for unlinked traits if he had been tossing away pea plants from the unlinked experiments; yet his failure to discover linkage has been taken to suggest there may have been some violation of total evidence in the research program.

If relevant facts *X, Y,* and *Z* are available, induction will be flawed if one decides to ignore *Z* and only use one's favorite facts, *X* and *Y.* Use of favorite facts in neglect of the total evidence requirement characterizes much of contemporary treatment planning. In the present article, we seek to remind treatment planners of highly relevant fact *Z:* People powerfully differ from each other in their personality dispositions.

The science of individual differences is an entire branch of psychology. Nevertheless, many psychologists who plan treatments may be relatively unfamiliar with this highly relevant set of facts. In this article, we draw from diverse literature to present an overview of the individual differences science underlying personality trait assessment, and we explore its implications for treatment planning. The assessment of intellectual functioning is another fruit of individual differences science, but discussion of it is beyond the scope of this article. To see how individual differences science has often been neglected in treatment planning, we first examine historical trends in treatment planning.

Treatment Planning Then and Now: A Picture Completion Problem

We briefly sketch treatment planning as it once was and as much of it is now. We argue that an important piece is missing from both eras. In psychotherapies of the 1950s and 1960s, the work was frequently allowed to emerge from the sessions, guided by the emerging dynamics of the sessions. In some schools, planning would have been regarded as a therapeutic error, destined to interfere with, for example, genuineness in a client-centered approach or free association characterizing psychodynamic therapies.

Analysis of the therapies of this era reveals serious epistemological risks in becoming immersed in sessions. With regard to psychoanalysis, for example, Grünbaum (1984) argued that within-session material is suspect as a basis for clinical inferences. Specifically, the client's verbal output may be inadvertently contaminated by subtle therapist suggestions, leading to spurious confirmations of the therapist's predictions. Moreover, therapists may erroneously interpret their clients' consistent verbal responses to suggestion within and across sessions as providing impressive evidence for the corroboration of their predictions.

Without adequate assessment, any planning of this era was especially vulnerable to a problem we label the *clinical hermeneutics error.*[2] Meehl (1973) and Butcher (1990) both noted that in adopting the patient's perspective, the therapist can lose track of the actual degree of pathology and begin to underestimate it. Thus, when the clinician expends effort in high-level depth of processing or in interpreting and explaining the behavior of a patient, there is an attendant loss of normative judgment. Meehl (1973) in his classic paper "Why I Don't Attend Case Conferences," succinctly entitled a section

"Understanding It Makes It Normal." Keddy and Piotrowski (1992), in reviewing the literature on testing in psychotherapy, summarized an appraisal of the Menninger Foundation's Psychotherapy Research Project (a project spanning part of this era) by saying: "The largest source of error was the therapists' tendency to ignore test findings and thereby overestimate the ego-strength of the patients. This resulted in less appropriate interventions and consequently less effective treatments" (p. 33). From the frequent lack of treatment planning of the 1950s, we turn to current practice.

Since the 1980s, with the adoption of Neo-Kraepelinian diagnostic rubrics (see Blashfield's [1984] elegant account of the early stages of this shift), we have experienced a restructuring of much of clinical activity. The Neo-Kraepelinian prescription entails (a) ascertainment of facts to determine the presence or absence of relatively explicit diagnostic criteria, (b) the making of differential and multiaxial diagnoses using the categories and language of the current *Diagnostic and Statistical Manual of Mental Disorders,* now the fourth edition (*DSM–IV;* American Psychiatric Association, 1994), and (c) differential selection of treatment guided by the differential diagnosis. Clinical activity is often reported as having followed this ideal. Coupled with the recent emphasis on empirically validated treatments (Chambless, 1995), it is a process that leaves many psychologists with the feeling that their practice is adequately scientific. We argue that it is not scientific enough.

Our criticism of current practice is that diagnosis, in the absence of a personality individual differences formulation, misses the point that the signs and symptoms that appear under the heading of "presenting complaints" or "targets of treatment plan" may often be manifestations or sequellae of personality traits. That is, the features the diagnostician focuses on may be consequences of (a) extreme levels of personality traits, (b) especially problematic configurations of trait levels (see Grove & Tellegen, 1991), or (c) extreme (i.e., socially or personally maladaptive) adaptations to personality traits or their configural properties (see Clark, Watson, & Mineka, 1994; Eberly, Harkness, & Engdahl, 1991; Watson, Clark, & Harkness, 1994).

As one example, the higher order personality dimension of Negative Affectivity or Negative Emotionality (NE; presented in greater detail later) is associated with a wide variety of psychopathological conditions, including mood, anxiety, and somatoform disorders (Tellegen & Waller, 1994; Watson & Clark, 1984). Although a number of individual differences dimensions are associated with these conditions, many prominent features of these disorders, such as tension, guilt, pessimism, and irritability, are among the core indicators of high NE trait levels and may be thought of as manifestations of this dimension (Clark & Watson, 1991b). The rampant "comorbidities" found when applying the current diagnostic rubrics may in part reflect that many of these phenotypic descriptor categories are saturated with variance from a relatively small number of individual differences variables. Weak discrimination among such categories can be produced by varied but quasi-arbitrary selection of cutting points along these dimensions. Thus, the degree of comorbidity should come as no surprise to clinicians who are aware of individual differences science (Lilienfeld, Waldman, & Israel, 1994).

---

[2] We chose *hermeneutics* to express the psychologist's role as an interpreter, an explainer of the patient's behavior.

In addition, features of disorders that some have considered causal may instead turn out to be simply correlated properties when examined from an individual differences perspective. For example, the cognitive attributional style typical of individuals with major depression, that is, a propensity to make stable, global, and perhaps internal causal attributions for negative life events (Abramson, Seligman, & Teasdale, 1978), may in some cases be a reflection of elevated levels of NE (Clark & Watson, 1991a). Specifically, individuals with high NE tend to focus on the negative aspects of their life situations and to dwell on their inadequacies (Watson & Clark, 1984). As Tellegen (1991) noted (see also Wachtel, 1977), personality traits tend to have an assimilative character in a Piagetian sense in that they influence how individuals interpret and construe life events. Consequently, there is internal consistency in the observation that individuals with high levels of NE, including individuals with depression, often exhibit an attributional style characterized by excessive pessimism and self-blame. Moreover, there is evidence that this attributional style is not specific to depression, but may extend to other conditions characterized by high NE, such as anxiety disorders (Clark & Watson, 1991a). Beck's (1976) well-known *depressive triad*—negative thoughts regarding oneself, the world, and the future—can similarly be seen as consistent with the cognitive processes of high-NE individuals.

The formal distinction between Axis I and Axis II disorders, although well intentioned, has perhaps been an impediment to the integration of personality individual differences with psychopathology. Although this distinction has undoubtedly sensitized a generation of clinicians to the profound clinical relevance of personality, the distinction nevertheless implies that major mental disorders are separate from personality. We argue that this is a perspective not justified by the best science. Both treatment planning and psychopathology research suffer when there is insufficient appreciation of the ubiquitous and intrinsic nature of individual differences. The categories of the *DSM*s are instantiated in people, not identical carbon atoms.

Nevertheless, although critical of certain aspects of current treatment planning based on Neo-Kraepelinian practices, we are not antinosological. For example, taxonicity, in Meehl's (1995) strong sense, is essential to isolating and understanding conditions or forms of individual differences sharing a specific and distinct causal chain. High-quality clinical description, as exemplified in the area of the mental retardations, often consists of both a diagnosis (that truly carries etiological or other important class membership information) and normatively calibrated information on relevant dimensions (e.g., IQ). This reflects the clinical reality that even Meehlian taxons are instantiated within a web of potentiating or compensating individual differences (Meehl, 1972). But much of the current nosological effort is patently antietiological (see Faust & Miner, 1986) to which we object.

We contend that the practices of both eras, the underplnning of the 1950s and 1960s and the current Neo-Kraepelinian diagnose-and-treat formula, violate the fundamental rule. The emerging science of individual differences has been neglected in treatment planning, both then and now.

A PERSONALITY INDIVIDUAL DIFFERENCES PRIMER FOR TREATMENT PLANNERS

Even before Cronbach (1957) spoke of the two disciplines of psychology, Spearman (1930/1961) noted, "Among the worst evils in modern psychology is that its two halves, called 'general' and 'individual,' respectively, have been irrationally and disastrously divorced from each other" (p. 326). The part of psychology that Spearman called individual, or in today's language, individual differences science, is often neglected in the training of clinical psychologists. This bifurcation creates a serious total evidence problem. Therefore, we have attempted to distill the most critical concepts, findings, and implications of personality individual differences science for treatment planning. We present this distillation in this section of the article, calling it a *primer*, although we hope to have educed a novel synthesis and fresh implications.

One Theoretical Viewpoint on Traits: Constructive Realism

Talking about other people and their dispositions, without the discipline of critical scientific analysis, is a ubiquitous human activity. Because of the long history of unexamined habits of lay discourse, some of the helpful basic distinctions and viewpoints that provided great benefits to other fields were slow in coming to individual differences science. Astronomers begin with the falsifiable assumption that the planet under study exists independently of the observer. They automatically separate their theories of the orbit of the planet from the actual orbit, and they further separate the observation measurements from theory, the astronomical object, and its behavior. Such reasonable distinctions have not come easily for personality psychology: Traits, constructs, dimensions, and scales are terms that have been used indiscriminately and imprecisely. Loevinger (1957), however, articulated the elements of a science of human personality that begins with the falsifiable assumption that traits are real, that they exist separately from the observer, and that traits are not to be confused with constructs or measures. Loevinger's approach was then named "constructive realism" by Messick (1981) and was further developed by Tellegen (1988, 1991), Harkness and Hogan (1995), and McCrae and Costa (1995). Here are some of the most critical elements of constructive realism for treatment planners.

Traits are real. Tellegen (1988) defined a trait as "a psychological (therefore organismic) structure underlying a relatively enduring behavioral disposition, i.e., a tendency to respond in certain ways under certain circumstances" (p. 622). According to Tellegen, "In the case of a *personality trait* some of the behaviors expressing the disposition have substantial adaptational implications" (p. 622). Approached in this way, the study of human individual differences is falsifiable and inherently multidisciplinary, involving not only social sciences but biological and medical sciences as well.

Traits are separate from constructs and measures. Constructs are elements in psychologists' theories of traits. As underlying physiological and psychological systems that give rise to dispositions, traits become known through their behavioral implications. Trait inferences are made from such data sources as questionnaire responses, ratings by observers, laboratory data, and the data of life course. From these trait inferences, new predictions of behavior can be made (Tellegen, 1991). But the manifest behaviors are not the traits. Psychologists still wedded to strict operationism will find these distinctions difficult to comprehend. However, most psychologists, following Cronbach and Meehl's (1955) explication of construct validity, have become more comfortable with the scientific respectability of inferred but falsifiable entities and the distinction between them and their observable indicators.

Traits exist in individuals, but traits lead to population concepts. Each person's psychophysical systems give rise to specific dispositions; what Tellegen (1988) called the person's *trait levels.* If people are at different levels of a trait, then across the composite of the population, those individual levels constitute a *trait dimension* (Tellegen, 1988). Just as each person has a specific level of the physical characteristic of height, the dimension of tallness emerges as a population concept. Using populations, one can examine the following question: What are the major dimensions along which people differ? This is a question about the nomothetic structure of trait dimensions, and an answer is offered in the next section.

Some Major Research Findings on Traits

One question that has received considerable attention over the last 30 years has been the following structural question: What are the major dimensions of personality individual differences, and how do those dimensions relate to each other? A general answer is that there are major replicable trait dimensions, and that they are organized hierarchically. Some earlier workers focused either on a few broad trait dimensions or on many narrow trait dimensions. These different levels of generality or specificity, however, are not qualitatively separate phenomena but rather constitute a single hierarchical nomothetic (population) structure in which the covariance of narrower, lower order traits becomes the variance of broader, higher order traits (Eysenck, 1947, 1991; Watson, Clark, & Harkness, 1994).

For the purpose of introducing personality individual differences to treatment planners, we concentrate on three broad-gauge trait dimensions, factors at the Eysenck (1947) and Tellegen (1978/1982) level. As we detail later, much research is available on traits at this level of the hierarchy. However, we are simply using this three-factor level to provide an introduction to findings and concepts necessary for treatment planning; we are not advocating this specific level over other levels of the hierarchy.

We begin with *extroversion* and *neuroticism* (Eysenck, 1947), two dimensions which emerge from factor analyses of virtually all omnibus measures of personality. Tellegen (1978/1982; see also Tellegen & Waller, 1994) and Watson and Clark (1984, 1997) have reinterpreted these two dimensions as the somewhat broader (temperamental, interpersonal) dimensions of Positive Emotionality (PE) and NE, respectively. It is important to note that PE and NE are essentially orthogonal dimensions, rather than opposite poles of a single bipolar dimension (Watson & Clark, 1984).

In addition, we describe findings concerning a third major personality dimension that may bear important implications for treatment planning, a dimension that Tellegen (1978/1982) termed *constraint* (CN; see also Watson & Clark, 1993). This dimension appears to be related to Eysenckian (reversed) psychoticism (Eysenck, 1991) and (reversed) Sensation Seeking (Zuckerman 1979, 1994), In fact, Lykken (1995) concluded that (reversed) Sensation Seeking and CN are "psychometrically equivalent" (p. 105). We agree with Lykken for the most part, but consider Sensation Seeking to be somewhat lower in the personality hierarchy (i.e., narrower) than CN.

Here, then, are three important ways in which individuals differ. Individuals can be predisposed to enjoy life, to become engaged in its activities, to seek and enjoy the company of others, or they may possess low levels of this propensity (i.e., low PE). Another dimension (NE) entails individual differences in the capacity to experience negative emotions of many kinds; to become tense, moody, and irritable; and to perceive life's daily hassles as markedly aversive or even catastrophic. Finally, individuals differ in the extent to which they seek or avoid thrill and adventure, are inhibited or uninhibited, and are traditional or uninfluenced by imposed guidelines of the social order (CN). All three of these individual differences dimensions have substantial genetic influence (e.g., Tellegen et al., 1988) and are associated with a variety of forms of psychopathology (e.g., DiLalla, Gottesman, Carey, & Vogler, 1993; Krueger, Caspi, Moffitt, Silva, & McGee, 1996; Lilienfeld, 1997b), including the personality disorders (Trull, Useda, Costa, & McCrae, 1995).

For each of these three broad personality domains, substantial evidence for convergence between self- and observer reports has accumulated (e.g., Costa & McCrae, 1988, on PE and NE; Harkness, Tellegen, & Waller, 1995). In addition, there is compelling evidence that these personality traits exhibit considerable long-term stability in adulthood (e.g., Costa & McCrae, 1988; Finn, 1986; Harkness, Spiro, Butcher, & Ben-Porath, 1995).

Where Do Personality Traits Come From?

New methods of study have offered the possibility of disentangling features hopelessly confounded in the research designs of classic psychology. By examining people who have different degrees of genetic relatedness and different amounts of shared environmental experience, the relative magnitude of causal contributions of different types of environmental and genetic effects can be estimated. With adequate data and analytic techniques, environmental effects can be subdivided into two sources: *shared* (i.e., environmental factors that increase familial resemblance for a trait) and *unshared* (i.e., environmental factors that do not promote familial resemblance for a trait). Genetic effects can be subdivided as well (see, e.g., Loehlin, 1992).

The research designs of behavior genetics coupled with structural equations modeling (see, e.g., Loehlin, 1992) allow for estimation of the potency of causal sequences that are themselves yet unknown. However, there is nothing more mystical about this than being able to weigh a series of barrels without peering inside them to know their contents. Treatment planners should know about four important issues addressed by the powerful research methods of behavior genetics: (a) the heritability of personality traits, (b) recent initial findings on the source of stability of personality traits, (c) gene-environment correlations, and (d) the apparent impotency of shared family environmental experiences in shaping personality traits. As will be shown later, each of these issues bears critical implications for the planning of efficacious treatments.

Heritability of personality traits. Heritability (h^2) is defined as the proportion of the phenotypic (behavioral, observable) variance in a trait that is attributable to genetic influences. Because it is based on variances, it is a population, not an individual, concept. Heritability does not necessarily imply a lack of malleability. As the example of phenylketonuria (PKU) shows us, a trait may be highly heritable (technically, what is called broad h^2, as PKU involves a Mendelian recessive mechanism), yet it may be modified dramatically by an environmental manipulation (in the case of PKU, early dietary intervention). This is because the *reaction range* (Gottesman, 1963) of many genotypes—the extent to which their phenotypic expression can be modified by environmental factors—is considerable, though probably not unlimited.

Across a large number of twin and adoption studies, the heritabilities of measures of most personality traits have ranged from .30 to .60 (G. Carey & DiLalla, 1994), with .50 being a commonly cited mean figure (Tellegen et al., 1988). The heritabilities derived from twin studies have generally been somewhat higher than those derived from adoption studies, possibly because twin studies include in heritability estimates certain types of genetic effects that adoption studies do not. An alternative explanation of higher h^2 estimates in twin studies is that monozygotic (identical) twins may have more similar trait-relevant environments than dizygotic (fraternal) twins (Loehlin & Rowe, 1992), although the equal-environments assumption[3] has generally been upheld (Kendler, 1983).

Initial findings on the source of personality trait stability. Earlier we cited evidence concerning the stability of personality traits. But from where does this stability in personality derive? Recent research in the field of developmental behavior genetics has yielded provocative answers. Although persons of different degrees of genetic relatedness and degrees of common rearing can be studied at a single point in time, they can also be studied over time (Plomin, 1986). When observations are made at two points in time, genetic and environmental contributions to both stability and change can be examined. To convey a simplified summary of the findings for the dimensions of PE and NE, it appears from initial studies that much of the stability of personality traits stems from genetic factors, whereas change arises primarily from unshared environmental factors (McGue, Bacon, & Lykken, 1993; Viken, Rose, Kaprio, & Koskenvuo, 1994). These initial findings require replication, but if they hold true, the implications for treatment planning are great.

It is important to note that multiple genetic mechanisms underlie the stability of personality traits. These various genetic mechanisms influence behavior through causal chains of differing lengths. Some causal chains are relatively short and some are longer, less direct. That is, some genetic mechanisms have an effect on behavior through relatively direct biological influences of genes on temperamental and personality variables, and some mechanisms influence behavior through less direct causal routes. One important instance of a more indirect mechanism is the case in which individuals with certain genotypes select and create environments that are conducive to the expression of their genotypes. These environments then support and maintain the stability of the traits. This second source of personality stability has been termed *active gene–environment* (g–e) *correlation* by behavior geneticists (Plomin, DeFries, & Loehlin, 1977) and has been referred to as *nature via nurture* by Bouchard, Lykken, McGue, Segal, and Tellegen (1990). Although active g–e correlation contributes to heritability coefficients, Block (1995) complained that it is technically a different source of genetic influence than "direct heritability." However, Block's (1995) dichotomizing into direct versus indirect is too strong: Genes can only affect behavior through causal chains differing in the degree of indirectness. Next, we discuss g–e correlations in more detail, because of their potential importance for treatment planning.

Gene–environment correlations. As noted above, individuals with differing genotypes are not randomly assigned to environments. In the case of active g–e correlation, it is through the agency of the person that environments are selected or created that are consonant with the genotype.

Although the concept of active g–e correlation has only recently received attention from personality psychologists, a number of authors writing from perspectives outside of behavior genetics have proposed that the tendency of individuals to seek and create trait-relevant environments & a major source of personality stability. For example, a cornerstone of Wachtel's (1977) model of *cyclic interactionism* is the propensity of individuals who are exposed to early developmental experiences (e.g., parental rejection) to later select situations (e.g., hostile romantic partners) that maintain and reinforce previously established behavioral propensities.

According to Wachtel (1973), the principal source of cross-situational consistency in personality is precisely this active selection of trait-relevant environments. Of particular relevance to our arguments, Wachtel suggested that psychotherapeutic interventions should be targeted toward the choices of current environmental stimuli, rather than toward the underlying dispositions created, in his view, by early developmental experiences.

Similarly, Snyder and Ickes (1985) argued that the situations in which individuals find themselves are largely a function of preexisting personality dispositions. Such situations, they contended, promote and sustain both the temporal and cross-situational consistency of these dispositions. Snyder and Ickes cited evidence indicating, for example, that extraverts tend to prefer and choose situations that afford opportunities for assertiveness, social intimacy, and achievement (Furnham, 1981); that individuals with an internal locus of control tend to select situations in which they possess considerable personal control (Kahle, 1980); and that high sensation-seekers tend to select leisure-time activities that permit the expression of risk-taking propensities (Zuckerman, 1974).

---

[3] The equal-environments assumption posits that the environmental influences promoting similarity on a given trait are equivalent in monozygotic and dizygotic twins (Plomin, 1986).

Behavior geneticists refer to two other forms of g–e correlation: *passive* and *reactive* (evocative). Passive g–e correlation results when parents provide both genes and environmental influences that contribute to the development of a characteristic in their children. For example, highly impulsive parents may not only pass on their genes to their children but also provide their children with disorganized and poorly structured environments. Reactive g–e correlation occurs when other individuals (not necessarily genetic relatives) respond to behavior produced by the individual's genotype in characteristic ways. For example, a highly sociable child may evoke affectionate reactions from both parents and teachers.

Scarr and McCartney (1983) have placed these three types of g–e correlation within the context of a developmental model of individual differences. According to Scarr and McCartney, passive g–e effects are substantial early in life and decline shortly thereafter, reactive g–e effects persist throughout the life span, and active g–e effects increase from childhood to adulthood. This increase in active g–e correlation, they argued, results from the increase in individuals' capacity to seek out, select, and create niches that are consonant with their genetic predispositions.

The unexpected weakness of shared family influence in shaping personality traits. Perhaps the most surprising finding emerging from recent behavior–genetic studies of personality, and in our view one of the most significant findings in personality and clinical psychology over the past several decades, is the negligible role of shared environmental influences on most or all personality traits in adulthood (Rowe, 1994). For example, the similarity in personality among identical twins reared apart is generally comparable with that among identical twins reared together (Tellegen et al., 1988). suggesting that common environmental experiences do not contribute substantially to personality resemblance. Although shared environmental influences may exert a lasting influence on personality at the extremes of parenting practice (e.g., abuse, neglect; Lykken, 1995), the findings suggest that in the broad range of what Hartmann (1958) called "average expectable environments," sharing family life does not strongly promote personality similarity of family members. If shared environmental effects on personality are observed, they appear to be moderated by age: Shared environment exerts a moderate influence on personality in childhood, but this influence declines or disappears by adulthood (McCartney, Harris, & Bernieri, 1990). Consequently, the primary environmental influences relevant to personality in adulthood appear to be unshared (Plomin & Daniels, 1987), although attempts to pinpoint specific unshared influences on personality traits have met with little success.

The finding that shared environmental influences on most personality traits are negligible bears crucial implications for theories positing a lasting causal role for parental socialization (e.g., Baumrind, 1971). This is particularly important for treatment planners to understand because mechanisms that might have been thought to produce homogenizing influence in families, such as direct parental instruction and role modeling, have been templates in the design of many forms of therapy. Nevertheless, the impact of this counterintuitive finding on contemporary theorizing in personality and clinical

psychology, thus far, appears to have been minimal (Rowe, 1994). Next we turn from behavior genetics to a distinction critical for treatment planners.

Basic Tendencies and Characteristic Adaptations

For any level of an individual difference, there are many potential life adaptations (i.e., the principle of *equipotentiality;* see Pervin, 1994). The thesis that markedly different life adaptations can reflect the same or similar underlying personality dispositions can be traced back at least to Adler (1931). Adler's concept of the *style of life* emphasized that different individuals can fashion dramatically different adaptations as a means of compensating for deep-seated feelings of inferiority. Because psychopathology, according to Adler, can be conceptualized as the adoption of a style of life that interferes with healthy interpersonal relationships (i.e., social interest), the goal of psychotherapy is to assist individuals to find more socially constructive adaptations to their inferiority feelings. Adler's view differs from our own, however, in that it posits only a global state of inferiority as an impetus for life adaptations and does not link different types of life adaptations with specific individual differences in personality.

McCrae and Costa (1995), in a broad model of human nature, distinguished between *basic tendencies* (what would classically have been considered the underlying dispositions, or what Cattell, 1950, called source traits) and *characteristic adaptations,* which are "the concrete habits, attitudes, roles, relationships, and goals that result from the interaction of basic tendencies with the shaping forces of the social environment" (McCrae, 1993, p. 584). So for any level of a basic tendency, there are many potential characteristic adaptations, and these adaptations vary greatly in social cost, personal suffering, and growth or stagnation.

Psychologists have typically focused on adaptation to external circumstances. Individual differences science, however, adds a new perspective. Adaptation involves not only coping with and creating external circumstances but also adaptation to oneself, to one's own basic tendencies. In addition, the very modes of adaptation selected are a function of those basic tendencies. For example, the person high in NE must not only learn how to live in a world providing challenges but also how to successfully live with high NE and accomplish that adaptation with a mind biased to evaluate the world more for its costs than for its opportunities.

A dramatic illustration of this principle can be found in the widely publicized case of Jack and Oscar, a pair of monozygotic twins who were separated shortly after birth and were reunited in their 40s as part of the Minnesota Study of Twins Reared Apart (Begley & Kasindorf, 1979). Jack was raised by a Jewish family in the Caribbean until age 17, when he moved to Israel and joined a Kibbutz. Oscar was raised by his maternal grandmother in the Sudetenland. Although the twins had extremely similar Minnesota Multiphasic Personality Inventories (MMPIs; Holden, 1980), many features of their life histories were strikingly different. Jack was a devoted and deeply religious Jewish person who enjoyed war movies that denigrated Germans. Oscar, in contrast, was an ardent Nazi and antisemite who was prepared to enter the Hitler Youth as World War II ended. The Jack–Oscar case underscores the importance of distinguishing between basic tendencies and characteristic adaptations: Markedly different phenotypic adaptations may reflect similar underlying basic tendencies, in this case, intense loyalty and devotion to sociopolitical causes, religious causes, or both.

As another example, Lykken (1982, 1995) conjectured that the psychopath and the hero are often "twigs from the same branch" (p. 22). Specifically, Lykken argued, low levels of fearfulness (i.e., constraint) can be manifested in either psychopathy or heroism (or, in some cases, both). Lykken (1995) conjectured that explorer Sir Richard Burton, pilot Chuck Yeager, and President Lyndon Johnson were individuals who possessed "the genetic talent" for psychopathy but "because of special talent or opportunity, manage(d) to become tolerably socialized and even . . . achieve great worldly success" (p. 155). Consistent with Lykken's hypotheses, Lilienfeld (1997a) found that in several undergraduate samples, measures of fearlessness were positively and significantly correlated with both indexes of antisocial behavior (e.g., criteria for *DSM–III–R* [American Psychiatric Association, 1987] antisocial personality disorder) and heroic behavior. Because Lilienfeld's findings were derived exclusively from self-report indexes, however, constructive replication (Lykken, 1968) of these results using other modes of assessment is necessary.

Further, Zuckerman (1994) reviewed evidence showing that although criminals have higher average Sensation Seeking scores than students, the average for criminals does not differ from firefighters. Although both crime and firefighting offer sporadic relief from boredom, and perhaps thrills, danger, and adventure, crime and firefighting are utterly different characteristic adaptations when the social cost is counted. Farley (1981) similarly argued that thrill-seeking can predispose to either delinquency or creativity, depending on socioeconomic status and educational methods.

An important implication of the basic tendency versus characteristic adaptation distinction is that one may expect moderate, rather than extremely high, correlations between trait measures and categories of psychopathology. Some diagnostic criteria sets are in fact complex descriptions that mix together basic tendencies and characteristic adaptations. Hence, relatively pure dispositional measures may show only moderate relations with diagnostic categories.

This completes a brief primer on personality individual differences for the treatment planner. In the next section, we examine the direct implications of these concepts and findings for treatment planning.

TRAIT-INFORMED TREATMENT PLANNING: KNOWING WHERE CHANGE IS POSSIBLE, REALISTIC EXPECTATIONS, MATCHING TREATMENT TO PERSONALITY, AND GROWING A SELF

How would treatment planning change if a psychologist followed the total evidence requirement and attended not only to general laws but also to individual difference science by incorporating personality trait assessment? Beyond avoiding

the *clinical hermeneutics error,* we contend that there are four major benefits. First, better information would be available on where to target change efforts; this leads to a second gain, namely, more realistic expectations for change would be generated; third, there is the possibility of matching treatments to personality; and fourth, opportunities for the patient's increased self-knowledge are created.

Knowing Where Change Is Possible

Personality assessment first contributes to treatment planning by helping to decide if problems are intimately linked with a person's broad personality dispositions or whether they are more circumscribed. According to Beutler (1986; see also Beutler & Clarkin, 1990), *simple* problems involve situationally specific and transitory habits mat are primarily products of current environmental contingencies. An example of a simple problem would be a specific phobia of dogs that arises in response to a traumatic conditioning experience and is maintained by current avoidance behavior but is developed in the absence of special dispositional diatheses (e.g., no above average trait-like fearfulness, no unusual conditionability to danger signals). In contrast, *complex* problems involve cross-situationally pervasive signs and symptoms reflecting long-term patterns of adjustment. In this scheme, complex problems, unlike simple problems, can be viewed largely as manifestations or consequences of enduring personality traits. The distinction between simple and complex problems is presumably one of degree rather than of kind, and assessment allows the treatment planner to ascertain where the problem stands on the simple–complex continuum.

Another way in which the individual differences perspective helps to target change efforts involves focusing those efforts on characteristic adaptations rather than on basic tendencies. To illustrate these ideas, we present the following two vignettes.[4,5]

Vignette A. A middle-aged man has a high level of NE. His aptitude for guilt, emotional upset, anxiety, and punitive self-criticism creates powerful negative reinforcement potential for any behavior that produces quick, state-like relief from these feelings. Through trial and error, he learns that cigarettes, fatty foods, alcohol, and the distraction from self-focus provided by television produce brief islands of relief. Strong habits develop. His lifestyle is not shared by his partner, to whom it seems unattractive, causing increasing stress in the relationship.

Vignette B. A young woman in her 20s has a low level of CN, or in Zuckerman's terms, a high level of Sensation Seeking. She might hazard physical risks (and perhaps underestimates risks) rather than endure boredom. She is more spontaneous than planful, seeks the novel, and is not constrained by rules and tradition. In preparation for assessment, a psychologist using Finn's (1996) approach asks her what she might want to learn from an assessment. She asks, "Why do I pick such lousy boyfriends?"

---

[4] Vignette A was constructed from nomothetic findings reported in Harkness et al. (1995).
[5] Vignette B was constructed from a case in the study reported by Harkness, Royer, and Gill (1996).

These vignettes illustrate McCrae and Costa's (1995) distinction between *basic tendencies* and *characteristic adaptations.* Basic tendencies are the trait levels: high NE in Vignette A and low CN or high Sensation Seeking in Vignette B. In contrast, characteristic adaptations are illustrated by smoking, food and leisure choices, and drinking in Vignette A and possibly by the self-reported choice of lousy boyfriends in Vignette B.

A major contribution of individual differences science to the care of human problems comes in focusing interventions on characteristic adaptations rather than on basic tendencies. That is, the main goal is not to change the person in Vignette A to someone low in NE, or to change the person in Vignette B to someone high in CN. Rather, the main goal is to help patients find more promising characteristic adaptations. Another contribution of individual differences science is to remind the treatment planner that these new characteristic adaptations should be constructed with sensitivity to the patient's basic tendencies. Note that we do not deny that change is possible in traits (Eberly, Harkness, & Engdahl, 1991). But in terms of potential yield, characteristic adaptations make better change targets.

What about the patient in Vignette B, who picks boyfriends she describes as lousy? Lykken and Tellegen (1993) showed that although personality does not usually result in likes assorting with likes (e.g., neurotics do not show much tendency to select other neurotics as mates), it was an element of CN that showed the highest spousal correlations. Zuckerman (1994) reviewed studies indicating that Sensation Seeking is one personality variable in which like assorts with like. We can predict that the young woman in Vignette B will be easily bored by sameness and that a predictable, traditional, and cautious man may be unattractive to her. An unpredictable, nontraditional, and perhaps even slightly dangerous man might attract and intrigue her. Thus, she may be initially attracted to those like her (i.e., low CN, high Sensation Seeking). But the initial stages of a relationship are not the whole story. As time goes by, the very features that made the low-CN man attractive (e.g., his unpredictability, his perpetual novelty) may make him a trying, frustrating partner who is unreliable and not sufficiently trustworthy for a lasting relationship. What made him a source of pleasure in the short term may make him a source of pain, frustration, and disappointment in the long term. She may be actively creating a social world of low-CN male partners who are consistent with her traits. The characteristic adaptation, in this case a painful pattern in relationships, may be flowing from a basic tendency. These conjectures would need to be explored; further clinical evidence would be required.

Our emphasis on altering characteristic adaptations is broadly consistent with the approach adopted by some therapists operating within a behavior analytic perspective (M. P. Carey, Flasher, Maisto, & Turkat, 1984). Nevertheless, the individual differences perspective contributes the notion that new adaptations should be designed with attention to the patient's basic tendencies. This naturally requires the guidance of high-quality personality assessment.

Earlier, we noted the finding of weak or nonexistent shared family environmental influence on personality traits. But it is critical for treatment planners to realize that the causal impotence of shared family environmental influence may apply only to basic tendencies, not to characteristic adaptations. For example, although the personality traits that have generally been found to be risk factors for antisocial behavior (e.g., low constraint, aggression) appear to be uninfluenced by shared environmental factors (Tellegen et al., 1988), antisocial behavior itself has been found in several adoption studies to be influenced by shared environmental factors, such as the socioeconomic status of the adoptive parents (Bohman, Cloninger, Sigvards-son, & von Knorring, 1982). Thus, although the underlying dispositions that sometimes lead to antisocial behavior may not be influenced by shared environmental factors, shared influence processes may play an important role in the phenotypic expression of such dispositions.

The concept of active g–e correlations leads to the same targeting of change efforts. As noted earlier, part of the genetic influence counted in a heritability coefficient is of the more indirect type of genetic influence, realized as the person selects and creates environments. Therapists can help patients select and construct social worlds consistent with themselves, but with higher potential for health and growth. The people in these vignettes, and people in general, do not randomly choose adaptations; the adaptations that are created are consonant with their basic tendencies. Finding new adaptations, with less personal and social cost and greater potential for growth, which are also consonant with the patients' basic tendencies, poses an exciting new clinical challenge.

Reactive g–e correlations, realized when the patient's basic tendencies lead to predictable reactions from the social surround, create other opportunities for the treatment planner. Psychoeducation can help sensitize people to the responses they evoke from their environments. Opportunities to interrupt or channel cyclical processes can be explored (see also Wachtel, 1977).

Individual differences science makes available a research-based, comprehensive viewpoint on the transactions creating and maintaining characteristic adaptations of the persons in Vignettes A and B. We contend that this scientifically based viewpoint targets change efforts more rationally than viewpoints of the 1950s or 1960s, when the effort might have been a decade long attempt to restructure basic tendencies. As MacKenzie (1994) put it, "It is somewhat of a culture shock to consider personality as something that someone simply has and must live with, like being tall" (p, 238). We also contend that this research-based viewpoint is more comprehensive and, thus, more observant of the total evidence requirement than current Neo-Kraepelinian diagnostic approaches that focus predominantly on specific phenotypic disorders. More complete science leads to a more complete picture of the person. Further, it leads to more realistic expectations.

Realistic Expectations

A central ethical concern in establishing a negotiated treatment plan with an informed patient involves supplying realistic expectations. If the problem is complex, in Beutler's (1986) terms, then individual differences science is essential for providing realistic prognoses for therapy. A modal personality feature of self-presenting clinical patients is high NE (Miller, 1991; Watson & Clark, 1984). Given this fact, we will hazard a proposal: The single greatest misconception that patients (and perhaps some therapists) hold about therapy is the expectation that a high-NE person can be turned into a low-NE person. Instead, as noted earlier, individual differences science offers the concept of *reaction range* (Gottesman, 1963): Genetically influenced traits may be modified by environmental manipulations, but only within certain limits.

Matching Treatment to Personality

The notion that people actively select and create environments that support, maintain, and perhaps even amplify their personality traits has important implications for treatment selection. Therapy is no different from any other interpersonal situation in its capacity to enthrall, entice, bore, or revolt a patient. If one seeks to have a patient stay in therapy, to remain engaged in the work, and to suffer as little discomfort as possible, then matching treatment to personality offers a strategy. Miller (1991), an eclectic therapist in private practice, provided a scientist-practitioner's account of treatment-matching issues in his sample of 119 private practice patients and family members. He routinely administered personality measures and became a strong advocate of matching therapy to personality. Miller (1991) systematically presented the treatment implications of the structural model he used: the five-factor model. For example, in discussing extroversion (E), in which the rate of verbal production is an issue, he recounted the following:

> I recall one low E client who at first seemed a good candidate for brief psychodynamic therapy. During the first three sessions he became increasingly uncomfortable, as I searched for the aplomb to handle long pauses in our dialog. In the fourth session, I shifted gears and started doing conventional cognitive therapy, a method I did not favor at the time. The client was visibly relieved. Toward the end of this session he said, "Gee, the therapy has finally begun. Did we really have to sit around and stare at each other for 3 weeks?" (p. 424)

Because therapies differ dramatically in degree of structure, directedness, introspective demands, required verbal productivity, emotional precipitation, patient initiative, and depth of interpersonal interaction, rich opportunities exist for matching treatment to personality, or at least for avoiding the type of mismatch Miller (1991) recounted in the above quotation. What is the evidence for the utility of matching?

Relatively few investigators have attempted to examine statistical interactions between personality traits and treatment approaches, and most of these efforts have been unsuccessful (Beutler, 1991). Few studies of personality–treatment matching, however, have been guided by a strong theoretical framework linking structurally informed individual differences to different treatment methods. Nevertheless, not all of the findings have been negative. Spoth (1983), for example, reported that among alcohol abusers, a relatively unstructured treatment that emphasized cognitive control over anxiety tended to reduce anxiety among individuals with an internal locus of control, whereas a more structured treatment that de-emphasized cognitive control over anxiety tended to reduce anxiety among individuals with an external locus of control. Beutler et al. (1991) found that depressed patients with an externalizing coping style tended to respond best to group cognitive therapy, whereas depressed patients with an internalizing coping style tended to respond best to self-directed therapy. We recommend that further studies of personality–treatment interactions within an explicit theoretical framework be undertaken, bearing in mind Cronbach's (1975) caveat that some of these interactions may be moderated by still higher order interactions, thereby rendering generalizations across samples difficult.

Growing a Self

Although to some the construct of self might seem hopelessly vague and unscientific, the topic has been increasingly examined by psychological science. The acceptance of this topic has come as part of the cognitive revolution in psychology. Since Tolman (1948) postulated that rats exploring a maze were developing a cognitive map (the latent learning paradigm), psychology has become increasingly concerned with the internal representation of information. As one example, Rescorla (1988) suggested that one could predict many modern findings in classical conditioning, such as contingency effects, merely by positing that the organism is building an inner mental model of the conditioning events. One such model has been of particular interest to clinical psychology: the inner mental representation of oneself, known simply as the self. From post-Freudian analysts such as Kohut (e.g., Kohut & Wolf, 1978), to cognitive theorists of clinical phenomena such as Beck (e.g., see Beck, Freeman, & Associates, 1990, on self-schemata), to social psychologists (Markus, 1977), there has been increasing interest in the self and its clinical implications.

What are the clinical implications of self? To take one simple example, compare a person who becomes anxious in situations *x, y,* and *z* but is unaware of this tendency, with another person who becomes anxious in situations *x, y,* and *z* but who has an understanding of this tendency, an internal model of self that includes this information. The person with the more comprehensive self has greater resources, options, and capacities than the person with the less comprehensive self.

Consider again Vignette B: the young woman low in CN (high in Sensation Seeking) who wonders why she picks lousy boyfriends. Presumably, her inner representation of self lacks a coherent picture of her status on CN (or Sensation Seeking), including her susceptibility to boredom, and an understanding of how these characteristics lead to attraction to surprising, unpredictable men. Further, she lacks an appreciation of the repeated pattern: initial attraction to an exciting man, only to discover that the initially appealing unpredictability and rule bending makes for poor long-term prospects. Finally, she lacks an integrative understanding of how the cyclical pattern of initial attraction and eventual disappointment flows from her personality. To help her understand this pattern would be to potentiate new perceptions, to provide her with new options, to give her a sense of intellectual power (even if she repeats the pattern), and to open the door to new adaptations. The assertion of self-psychology is that a comprehensive, reality-based model of the self offers new resources for mental health.

We contend that reliable, valid, and well-normed personality assessment—the fruits of psychometric science— in the hands of a talented clinician, offers a basis for empirically grounded, rapid, and accurate increases in self-knowledge. That is, individual differences science can help with a unique goal in the treatment plan: helping the patient grow a self.

Finn's (1996) collaborative therapeutic assessment procedures are ideally suited to this goal. In Finn's procedure, questions are solicited from the patient prior to assessment. Following assessment, the test results are used to answer the patient's questions. This method frames the feedback in terms of the major adaptive challenges facing the patient. It tends to make the results interesting and comprehensible, because answers are worked out in terms of specific problems rather than abstract principles. Most important, Finn and Tonsager (1992), and recently Newman and Greenway (1997), have shown that test feedback, presented in a manner that promotes the growth of self, can itself ameliorate symptomatic distress.

CONCLUSION

Treatment planning should be based on the most complete and best science available. We have provided an overview of individual differences science showing that people differ powerfully from each other in stable basic dispositions called personality traits. The accumulating body of concepts and findings of individual differences science, such as heritabilities, the weakness of shared family influence on personality traits, g–e correlations, and the basic tendency versus characteristic adaptation distinction all bear important implications for treatment planning. We contend that a clinician who understands and applies these concepts is more likely to help patients find

trait-consonant adaptations that will reduce suffering, foster growth, and stand the test of time. Clinicians aware of these concepts can harness psychometric technology to help their patients develop a norm-based and comprehensive sense of the basic tendencies that channel the adaptive struggles of life. To ignore this information is to practice substandard treatment planning.

We have advocated the application of sound scientific principles to treatment planning. Nevertheless, the efficacy of application of even solid science demands testing (Faust, 1997). Although a number of models linking assessment to treatment have been proposed (e.g., a functional analytic strategy, diagnostic strategy), few of these models have been subjected to stringent empirical tests (Nelson, 1988). As noted earlier, Finn and Tonsager (1992) and Newman and Greenway (1997) have demonstrated the positive impact of a thoughtfully designed assessment process on therapeutic goals. Our thesis that explicit consideration of individual differences in personality can aid in treatment planning could be tested by the technique of manipulated assessment (Hayes, Nelson, & Jarrett, 1987; see also Meehl, 1959). This technique treats therapists as participants and randomly assigns them to either receive assessment information or no assessment information. The extent to which the provision of assessment information contributes to treatment efficacy is a direct test of the treatment utility (Hayes et al., 1987) of such information. The use of manipulated assessment designs would provide a stringent test of the hypothesis that the incorporation of personality assessment data within the therapeutic framework we have outlined will produce clinically significant improvements in treatment outcome. However, in realizing these designs, therapists would not merely need assessment information; they would need an adequate understanding of the principles and findings of the individual differences science of personality. Then they could follow the *fundamental rule of treatment planning*.

References

Abramson, L. Y., Seligman, M. E. P., & Teasdale, J. D. (1978). Learned helplessness in humans: Critique and reformulation. *Journal of Abnormal Psychology, 87,* 49–74.

Adler, A. (1931). *What life should mean to you.* Boston: Little, Brown.

American Psychiatric Association. (1987). *Diagnostic and statistical manual of mental disorders* (3rd ed., rev). Washington, DC: Author.

American Psychiatric Association. (1994). *Diagnostic and statistical manual of mental disorders* (4th ed.). Washington, DC: Author.

American Psychological Association. (1992). Ethical principles of psychologists and code of conduct. *American Psychologist, 47,* 1597–1611.

Baumrind, D. (1971). Current patterns of parental authority. *Developmental Psychology Monograph, 4* (Pts. 1 & 2).

Beck, A. T. (1976). *Cognitive therapy and the emotional disorders.* New York: International Universities Press.

Beck, A. T., Freeman. A., & Associates. (1990). *Cognitive therapy of personality disorders.* New York: Guilford Press.

Begley, S., & Kasindorf, M. (1979, December 3). Twins: Nazi and Jew. *Newsweek, 94,* p. 139.

Beutler L. E. (1986). Systematic eclectic psychotherapy. In J. C. Norcross (Ed.), *Handbook of eclectic psychotherapy* (pp. 94–131). New York: Brunner/Mazel.

Beutler, L. E. (1991). Have all won and must all have prizes? Revisiting Luborsky et al.'s verdict. *Journal of Consulting and Clinical Psychology, 59,* 226–232.

Beutler, L. E., & Clarkin, J. F. (1990). *Systematic treatment selection: Toward targeted therapeutic interventions.* New York: Brurmer/Mazel.

Beutler, L. E., Engle, D., Mohr, D., Daldrup, R. J., Bergan, J. Meredith, K., & Merry, W. (1991). Predictors of differential response to cognitive, experiential, and self-directed psychotherapeutic procedures. *Journal of Consulting and Clinical Psychology, 59,* 333–340.

Blashfield, R. K. (1984). *The classification of psychopathology: Neo-Kraepelinian and quantitative approaches.* New York: Plenum.

Block, N. (1995). How heritability misleads about race. *Cognition, 56,* 99–128.

Bohman, M., Cloninger, C. R., Sigvardsson, S., & von Knorring, A. L. (1982). Predisposition to petty criminality in Swedish adoptees: I. Genetic and environmental heterogeneity. *Archives of General Psychiatry. 39.* 1233–1241.

Bouchard, T. J., Lykken, D. T., McGue, M., Segal, N. L., & Tellegen, A. (1990, October 12). Sources of human psychological differences; The Minnesota study of twins reared apart. *Science, 250,* 223–228.

Butcher, J.N. (1990). *The MMPI-2 in psychological treatment.* New York: Oxford University Press.

Carey, G., & DiLalla, D. L. (1994). Personality and psychopathology: Genetic perspectives. *Journal of Abnormal Psychology, 103,* 32–43.

Carey, M. P., Flasher, L. V., Maisto, S. A., & Turkat, I. D. (1984). The a priori approach to psychological assessment. *Professional Psychology: Research and Practice, 15,* 515–527.

Carnap, R. (1962). *Logical foundations of probability* (2nd ed). Chicago: University of Chicago Press.

Cattell, R. B. (1950). *Personality: A systematic, theoretical, and factual study.* New York: McGraw-Hill.

Chambless, D. (1995). Training and dissemination of empirically validated psychological treatment: Report and recommendations. *The Clinical Psychologist, 48,* 3–23.

Clark, L. A., & Watson, D. (1991a). General affective dispositions in physical and psychological health. In C. R. Snyder & D. R. Forsyth (Eds.), *Handbook of social and clinical psychology* (pp. 221–245). New York: Pergamon Press.

Clark, L. A., & Watson, D. (1991b). Tripartite model of anxiety and depression: Psychometric evidence and taxonomic implications. *Journal of Abnormal Psychology, 100,* 316–336.

Clark, L. A., Watson, D., & Mineka, S. (1994). Temperament, personality, and the mood and anxiety disorders. *Journal of Abnormal Psychology, 103,* 103–116.

Costa, P. T., Jr., & McCrae. R. R. (1988). Personality in adulthood: A six-year longitudinal study of self-reports and spouse ratings on the NEO personality inventory. *Journal of Personality and Social Psychology, 54,* 853–863.

Cronbach, L. J. (1957). The two disciplines of scientific psychology. *American Psychologist, 12,* 671–684.

Cronbach, L. J. (1975). Beyond the two disciplines of scientific psychology. *American Psychologist, 30,* 116–127.

Cronbach, L. J., & Meehl, P. E. (1955). Construct validity in psychological tests. *Psychological Bulletin, 52,* 281–302.

DiLalla, D. L., Gottesman, I.I., Carey, G., & Vogler, G. P. (1993). Joint factor structure of the Multidimensional Personality Questionnaire and the MMPI in a psychiatric and high risk sample. *Psychological Assessment, 5,* 207–215.

Eberly, R. E., Harkness. A. R., & Engdahl, B. E. (1991). An adaptational view of trauma response as illustrated by the prisoner of war experience. *Journal of Traumatic Stress, 4,* 363–380.

Eysenck, H. J. (1947). *Dimensions of personality.* New York: Praeger.

Eysenck, H. J. (1991). Dimensions of personality: 16, 5, or 3?— Criteria for a taxonomic paradigm. *Personality and Individual Differences, 12,* 773–790.

Farley, F. H. (1981). Basic process individual differences: A biologically based theory of individualization for cognitive, affective, and creative outcomes. In F. H. Farley & N. J. Gordon (Eds.), *Psychology and education: The state of the union* (pp. 9–31). Berkeley, CA: McCutcbon Publishing.

Faust, D. (1997). Of science, meta-science, and clinical practice: The generalization of a generalization to a particular. *Journal of Personality Assessment, 68.* 331–354.

Faust, D., & Miner, R. A. (1986). The empiricist and his new clothes: *DSM–III* in perspective. *American Journal of Psychiatry, 143,* 962–967.

Finn, S. E. (1986). Stability of personality self-ratings over 30 years: Evidence for an age/cohort interaction. *Journal of Personality and Social Psychology, 50,* 813–818.

Finn, S. E. (1996). *Manual for using the MMPI-2 as a therapeutic intervention.* Minneapolis: University of Minnesota Press.

Finn, S. E., & Tonsager, M. E. (1992). Therapeutic effects of providing MMPI-2 test feedback to college students awaiting therapy. *Psychological Assessment, 4,* 278–287.

Furnham, A. (1981). Personality and activity preference. *British Journal of Social Psychology, 20,* 57–68.

Gottesman, I.I. (1963). Genetic aspects of intelligent behavior. In N. Ellis (Ed.), *Handbook of mental deficiency: Psychological theory and research* (pp. 253–296). New York: McGraw-Hill.

Grove, W. M., & Tellegen, A. (1991). Problems in the classification of personality disorders. *Journal of Personality Disorders, 5,* 31–42.

Grünbaum, A. (1984). *The foundations of psychoanalysis: A philosophical critique.* Berkeley: University of California Press.

Harkness, A. R., & Hogan, R. (1995). Theory and measurement of traits: Two views. In J. N. Butcher (Ed.), *Clinical personality assessment: Practical approaches* (pp. 28–41). New York: Oxford University Press.

Harkness, A. R., Levenson, M. R., Butcher, J. N., Spiro, A., III, Ben-Porath.Y. S., & Crumpler, C. A. (1995, March), *Drinking and personality: MMPI-2 PSY-5 scales in the Boston VA's Normative Aging Study.* Paper presented at the 30th annual MMPI-2 & MMPI-A symposia, St. Petersburg, FL.

Harkness, A. R., Royer, M. J., & Gill, T. P. (1996, June). *Organizing MMPI-2 feedback with psychological constructs: PSY-5 scales and self-adaptation.* Paper presented at the 31st annual MMPI-2 symposium, Minneapolis, MN.

Harkness, A. R., Spiro, A., III, Butcher, J. N., & Ben-Porath, Y. S. (1995, August). *Personality Psychopathology Five (PSY-5) in the Boston VA Normative Aging Study.* Poster presented at the 103rd Annual Convention of the American Psychological Association, New York.

Harkness, A. R., Tellegen, A., & Waller, N. (1995). Differential convergence of self-report and informant data for multidimensional personality questionnaire traits: Implications for the construct of negative emotionality. *Journal of Personality Assessment. 64,* 185–204.

Hartmann, H. (1958). *Ego psychology and the problem of adaptation.* New York: International Universities Press.

Hayes, S. C., Nelson, R. O., & Jarrett, R. B. (1987). The treatment utility of assessment: A functional approach to evaluating assessment quality. *American Psychologist, 42,* 963–974.

Holden, C. (1980, March 21). Identical twins reared apart. *Science, 207,* 1323–1325.

Kahle, L. R. (1980). Stimulus condition self-selection by males in the interaction of locus of control and skill-chance situations. *Journal of Personality and Social Psychology. 38,* 50–56.

Keddy, P., & Piofrowski, C. (1992). Testing in psychotherapy practice: Literature review, survey, and commentary. *Journal of Training & Practice in Professional Psychology. 6,* 30–39.

Kendler, K. S. (1983). Overview: A current perspective on twin studies of schizophrenia. *American Journal of Psychiatry, 140,* 1413–1425.

Kohut, H., & Wolf, E. S. (1978). The disorders of the self and their treatment: An outline. *International Journal of Psychoanalysis, 59,* 413–425.

Krueger, R. F., Caspi, A., Moffitt, T. E., Silva, P. A., & McGee, R. (1996). Personality traits are differentially linked to mental disorders: A multitrait–multidiagnosis study of an adolescent birth cohort. *Journal of Abnormal Psychology, 105,* 299–312.

Lilienfeld, S. O. (1997a). *Fearlessness, antisocial behavior, and heroism.* Manuscript in preparation.

Lilienfeld, S. O. (1997b). The relation of anxiety sensitivity to higher- and lower-order personality dimensions: Implications for the etiology of panic attacks. *Journal of Abnormal Psychology, 106.* 539–544.

Lilienfeld, S. O., Waldman, I.D., & Israel, A. C. (1994). A critical examination of the use of the term and concept of "cormorbidity" in psychopathology research. *Clinical Psychology: Science and Practice, 1,* 71–83.

Loehlin, J. C. (1992). *Genes and environment in personality development.* Newbury Park, CA: Sage.

Loehlin, J. C., & Rowe, D. C. (1992). Genes, environment, and personality. In G. Caprara & G. L, Van Heck (Eds.), *Modern personality psychology: Critical reviews and new directions* (pp. 352–370). New York: Harvester/Wheatsheaf.

Loevinger, J. (1957). Objective tests as instruments of psychological theory [Monograph]. *Psychological Reports, 3,* 635–694.

Lykken, D. T. (1968). Statistical significance in psychological research. *Psychological Bulletin. 70,* 151–159.

Lykken, D. T. (1982, September). Fearlessness: Its carefree charm and deadly risks. *Psychology Today, 16,* 20–28.

Lykken, D. T. (1995). *The antisocial personalities.* Hillsdale, NJ: Erlbaum.

Lykken, D. T., & Tellegen, A. (1993). Is human mating adventitious or the result of lawful choice? A twin study of mate selection. *Journal of Personality and Social Psychology. 65,* 56–68.

MacKenzie, K. R. (1994). Using personality measurements in clinical practice. In P. T. Costa, Jr. & T. A. Widiger (Eds.), *Personality disorders and the five factor model of personality* (pp. 237–250). Washington, DC: American Psychological Association.

Markus, H. (1977). Self-schemata and processing information about the self. *Journal of Personality and Social Psychology, 35,* 63–78.

McCartney, K., Harris, M. J., & Bemieri, F. (1990). Growing up and growing apart: A developmental meta-analysis of twin studies. *Psychological Bulletin. 107,* 226–237.

McCrae, R. R. (1993). Moderated analyses of longitudinal personality stability. *Journal of Personality and Social Psychology, 65,* 577–585.

McCrae, R. R., & Costa, P. T., Jr. (1995). Trait explanations in personality psychology. *European Journal of Personality, 9,* 231–252.

McGue, M., Bacon, S., & Lykken, D. T. (1993). Personality stability and change in early adulthood: A behavior genetic analysis. *Developmental Psychology, 29,* 96–109.

Meehl, P. E. (1959). Some ruminations on the validation of clinical procedures. *Canadian Journal of Psychology, 13,* 102–128.

Meehl, P. E. (1972). Specific genetic etiology, psychodynamics, and therapeutic nihilism. *International Journal of Mental Health, I,* 10–27.

Meehl, P. E. (1973). *Psychodiagnosis: Selected papers.* New York: Norton.

Meehl, P. E. (1995). Bootstraps taxometrics: Solving the classification problem in psychopathology. *American Psychologist, 50,* 266–275.

Messick, S. (1981). Constructs and their vicissitudes in educational and psychological measurement. *Psychological Bulletin, 89,* 575–588.

Miller, T. R. (1991). The psychotherapeutic utility of the five-factor model of personality: A clinician's experience. *Journal of Personality Assessment, 57,* 415–433.

Nelson, R. O. (1988). Relationships between assessment and treatment within a behavioral perspective. *Journal of Psychopathology and Behavioral Assessment, 10,* 155–170.

Newman, M. L., & Greenway, P. (1997). Therapeutic effects of providing MMPI-2 test feedback to clients at a university counseling service: A collaborative approach. *Psychological Assessment,* 9, 122–131.

Pervin, L. A. (1994). A critical analysis of current trait theory. *Psychological Inquiry, 5,* 103–113.

Plomin, R. (1986). *Development, genetics, and psychology.* Hillsdale, NJ: Erlbaum.

Plomin, R., & Daniels, D. (1987). Why are children in the same family so different from one another? *Behavioral and Brain Sciences, 10,* 1–16.

Plomin, R., DeFries, J. C., & Loehlin, J. C. (1977). Genotype–environment interaction and correlation in the analysis of human behavior. *Psychological Bulletin, 84,* 309–322.

Rescorla, R. A. (1988). Pavlovian conditioning: It' s not what you think it is. *American Psychologist, 43,* 151–160.

Rowe, D. C. (1994). *The limits of family influence: Genes, experience, and behavior.* New York: Guilford Press.

Scarr, S., & McCartney, K. (1983). How people make their own environments: A theory of genotype—environment effects. *Child Development, 54,* 424–435.

Snyder, M., & Ickes, M. (1985). Personality and social behavior. In G. Lindzey & E. Aronson (Eds.), *Handbook of social psychology* (3rd ed., pp. 883–947). Reading, MA: Addison-Wesley.

Spearman, C. (1961). C. Spearman. In C. Murchison (Ed.), *A history of psychology in autobiography* (Vol. 1, pp. 299–333). New York: Russell and Russell. (Original work published 1930)

Spoth, R. (1983). Differential stress reduction: Preliminary application to an alcohol-abusing population. *International Journal of the Addictions. 18,* 835–849.

Tellegen, A. (1982). *Brief manual for the Differential Personality Questionnaire.* Unpublished manuscript, University of Minnesota. (Original work created 1978)

Tellegen, A. (1988). The analysis of consistency in personality assessment. *Journal of Personality, 56,* 621–663.

Tellegen, A. (1991). Personality traits: Issues of definition, evidence, and assessment. In D. Cichetti & W. Grove (Eds.), *Thinking clearly about psychology: Essays in honor of Paul Everett Meehl* (pp. 10–35). Minneapolis: University of Minnesota Press.

Tellegen, A., Lykken, D. T., Bouchard, T. J., Wilcox, K. J., Segal, N. L., & Rich, S. (1988). Personality similarity in twins reared apart and together, *Journal of Personality and Social Psychology, 54,* 1031–1039.

Tellegen, A., & Waller, N. (1994). Exploring personality through test construction. In S. R. Briggs & J. M. Cheek (Eds.), *Personality measures: Development and evaluation* (Vol. I, pp. 133–161). Greenwich, CT: JAI Press.

Tolman, E. C. (1948). Cognitive maps in rats and men. *Psychological Review, 55,* 189–208.

Trull, T.J., Useda, J. D., Costa, P. T., Jr., & McCrae, R. R. (1995). Comparison of the MMPI-2 Personality Psychopathology Five (PSY-5), the NEO-PI, and the NEO-PI-R. *Psychological Assessment, 7,* 508–516.

Viken, R. J., Rose, R. R., Kaprio, J., & Koskenvuo, M. (1994). A developmental genetic analysis of adult personality: Extraversion and neurocism from 18 to 59 years of age. *Journal of Personality and Social Psychology, 66,* 722–730.

Wachtel, P. L. (1973). Psychodynamics, behavior therapy, and the implacable experimenter. *Journal of Abnormal Psychology, 82,* 324–334.

Wachtel, P.L. (1977), *Psychoanalysis and behavior therapy: Toward an integration.* New York: Basic Books.

Watson, D., & Clark, L. A. (1984). Negative affectivity: The disposition to experience aversive emotional states. *Psychological Bulletin, 96,* 465–490.

Watson, D., & Clark, L. A. (1993). Behavioral disinhibition versus constraint: A dispositional perspective. In D. M. Wegner & J. W. Pennebaker (Eds.), *Handbook of mental control* (pp. 506–527). New York: Prentice Hall.

Watson, D., & Clark, L. A. (1997). Extraversion and its positive emotional core. In R. Hogan, J. Johnson, & S. Briggs (Eds.), *Handbook of personality psychology* (pp. 767–793). San Diego, CA: Academic Press.

Watson, D., Clark, L. A., & Harkness, A. R. (1994). Structures of personality and their relevance to psychopathology. *Journal of Abnormal Psychology, 103,* 18–31.

Zuckerman, M. (1974). The sensation seeking motive. In B. Maher (Ed.), *Progress in experimental personality research* (pp. 70–148). New York: Academic Press.

Zuckerman, M. (1979). *Sensation seeking: Beyond the optimal level of arousal.* Hillsdale, NJ: Erlbaum.

Zuckerman, M. (1994). *Behavioral expressions and biosocial bases of sensation seeking.* New York: Cambridge University Press.

21

Psychotherapy Is the Practice of Psychology

LEE SECHREST AND BRADLEY SMITH

Theory, research, and practice of psychotherapy would benefit if it came to be generally viewed as the practice of psychology and if it were integrated fully into that discipline. Integration is not an activity, but a fundamental outlook on psychotherapy. Important barriers to integration exist, some quite legitimate, others questionable. Legitimate barriers include our cognitive limitations in apprehending and processing information, real differences between disciplines, the uncertain quality of much of our information, and generally small effects. More questionable barriers are represented by the deliberate separateness of disciplines and even subdisciplines, and overspecialization of scientists and professionals. A truly psychological psychotherapy is not easy to envisage, but it would be firmly grounded in the science of psychology, and with that very large body of knowledge and theory to draw on, flexible and innovative.

INTRODUCTION

Psychology is a diverse field in terms of the phenomena with which it deals, but also in terms of the theories and methods it applies to those phenomena and the empirical findings that result. It has never succeeded in integrating itself across any of its forms of diversity. Currently, for example, cognitive and biopsychological developments appear to be orthogonal, with virtually no constraints on either side to be consistent with the other. Similarly, social psychology largely ignores knowledge about biological influences on behavior and at the same time busies itself with developing its own cognitive psychology, without much relation to anything else called cognitive.

We make a point of the generally fragmented state of the field of psychology because we will in this paper focus on the lack of integration of psychotherapeutic theory and practice into the science of psychology. We do not want it to appear that we are picking on psychotherapy and singling it out for harsh treatment. Our view of the entire field of psychology is not much more favorable with respect to the level of its integration than is our view of psychotherapy. We will refrain from doing more than to mention the almost complete isolation of psychology from other scientific fields.

WHAT IS INTEGRATION?

What do we mean by integration and what is it that is to be integrated? Arkowitz (1989) described three aspects of integration: theoretical integration, search for common factors, and technical eclecticism. What we have in mind is, perhaps, not completely encompassed by his rubric.

We do, however, dismiss the idea of "technical eclecticism" as being an adequate conception with respect to integration in psychotherapy. Lazarus (1989), for example, specifically declares himself a technical eclectic and not an "integrationist." If, as we suspect, many psychodynamic therapists have added relaxation training to their armamentarium of treatment methods, that does not constitute integration unless relaxation itself has been integrated into psychodynamic theory as a construct and as an aim of therapy. Nor do we think that approaches to psychotherapy that try simply to match person and problem to therapist or therapy are integrative in any important sense, a position that Lazarus (1989) appears to endorse. We do not see how it would be helpful to extend the idea of integration to include, for example, the decision that a physician might make in deciding (matching) which antibiotic to use (treatment) for a particular patient's infection (problem). If integration is to mean anything, it must be more than simply "whatever works"—or seems to.

Integration might also be used to refer to the gleaning of useful "findings" from research literature in other than the area of central concern. For example, psychotherapists might encounter the concept of "schema" in their reading and incorporate that idea into their thinking about patients and their problems. Although we do not deprecate the potential value of such incorporations, we do not think they constitute integration, in the sense of making whole, because the process is non-systematic and the outcome is an accretion of information rather than an increment in wisdom. The latter would be implied if the incorporation of information about specific problems in analogous reasoning had ramifications throughout the therapeutic "system," producing a cascade of alterations. The important point is that findings picked unsystematically from the literature, somewhat in the manner of what is often called a "convenience sample," are not likely to be dependable in the long run in any case (Olkin, 1992; Schmidt, 1992).

Nor is what Arkowitz appears to mean by theoretical integration truly what we have in mind. Theoretical integration seems to us too often merely to require the development of some facility in translating the terms of one theory into those of another. Demonstrating that it is possible to translate, let us say, the terms and understandings of Gestalt therapy into those of cognitive behavioral therapy may be a tour de force of reasoning, but it does not necessarily contribute anything new to either domain, just as translating a passage of prose from one language into another makes possible the wider understanding of the passage, but without improving its meaning in any way at all.

Truly useful theoretical integration would occur, we think, only if one or both of the theories involved were somehow cast into an entirely new light and made distinctly more effective. In essence, what would be required would be the development of a new, enhanced theory. We have seen no examples to date. Again, we do not at all wish to suggest that cross-translations between theories are worthless. In some ways, the thinking of Wachtel (1987) about congruencies between psychoanalysis and behavior therapy has been impressive, but in our view, the end result is that both theories and the theoretical integration of them are left outside of psychology.

Predictably, we also do not accord the idea of identifying the common elements in psychotherapy the quality of being adequately integrative. Discovering that two recipes for stew have several ingredients in common does not make the stews the same, nor does it commend the combining of the two recipes. The search for common elements in ostensibly different therapies makes sense to the extent that the two therapies are both effective since, by identifying the common elements, one may have the basis for a synthesis and ultimate integration. Identifying common elements may be helpful in fostering some ultimate integration, but we do not see that identification as itself integrative.

Integration Is Making Whole

We are, admittedly, attempting to capture the use of the term *integration* to be used in its lexical sense of "making whole," of unifying a body of knowledge in a systematic way that is coherent and heuristic. One example may be a new publication,

Nature-Nurture and Psychology (Plomin & McClearn, 1993), which includes chapters by three eminent environmentally oriented researchers who propose new environmental influence theories that encompass genetic influence. Moreover, we also have in mind a much more ambitious view of the integration task than has generally been apparent in thinking about psychotherapy integration, for we intend that psychotherapy should become an *integral part of all of psychology*.

We propose that psychotherapy is the practice of psychology.

To make things as clear as they can be in what is a fairly murky area, we do not mean that psychotherapy is "the practice of psychology and nothing but the practice of psychology," a construction termed "preemptive" by George Kelly (1955). From time to time, psychotherapy may incorporate ideas or research findings from anthropology, sociology, or other social sciences. Psychotherapy may incorporate the use of drugs prescribed by medical doctors for some kinds of problems. Elements of art, theater, or literature may be introduced into psychotherapy processes as they are useful. But we believe that elements introduced from outside psychology are incorporated, into psychotherapy as alien but useful; those elements are not part and parcel of psychology. How people acquire their dispositions, how their brains function, how they are influenced by others, and how they come to believe things or not believe them—those are the substance of psychology, and they are part and parcel of psychotherapy. Making psychotherapy truly psychological would be a great accomplishment, and it would constitute integration of the kind we wish to encourage.

Integration—A Way of Life

Integration is not an activity ("What are you going to do today?" "Well, I have some data to analyze, I need to make some phone calls, and then I want to do some integration"). Integration is a way of thinking, an orientation, perhaps a way of life. The best way by far to achieve satisfactory integration of the science of psychology and the craft of psychotherapy is not to make them separate conceptual compartments in the first place. If psychotherapy is the *practice of psychology,* which it is regularly claimed to be and which we think should be the case, then there is nothing to integrate. One has a case, one applies the best knowledge available about how to assemble relevant information about that case, then one develops a formulation of the case that incorporates a plan for intervention derived from the basic psychological theory and principles that constitute the formulation. What else would a *psychologist* do?

Integration is not a step to be grafted onto some other process. Integration, meaning to make whole, is a way of looking at the field of psychology, its theories and researches, and at one's applications of them (see also Schneider, 1990). One of us (LS) once taught a psychotherapy seminar using a volume of the *Journal of Experimental Psychology* as a text. The task assigned the students was to read and think about the research reported not as "rat study" or "nonsense syllable stuff," but as research on ways of assessing, changing, and maintaining behavior. They were further charged with thinking about how the ideas about assessing, changing, and maintaining behavior might apply to psychotherapy, which is the practice of assessing, changing, and maintaining behavior—or it was then. Perhaps today the framework would have to include ways of assessing, changing, and maintaining cognitions. That is not all of psychology, of course. One might use other bodies of scientific literature to help with ideas about assessing, forming, changing, and maintaining relationships, or achieving influence, or reducing stress, or improving family functioning. But such topics are what psychology is all about, and if psychotherapy is not practice related to such topics, then it is not the practice of psychology. No amount of "integration" will change that.

Barriers to Integration Are Plentiful

Psychotherapy as an enterprise (and as a profession) has developed with scarcely more than a semblance of concern for demonstrating any unity in its enterprise. Such a statement may seem contentiously offensive in a journal devoted to psychotherapy integration, but it appears to be the truth. Meehl (1987), for example, notes that despite the atmosphere of "integrative optimism" he enjoyed early in his career (i.e., the 1940s), "different practioners' clinical impressions have not satisfactorily converged" (p. 11). Occasional attempts have been made to show congruencies between psychodynamic (only Freudian; not, for example, Jungian) and "learning" theories (e.g., most notably by Dollard & Miller, 1950), but those attempts were, in our view, never taken seriously by theorists on either side, let alone by practitioners. Had they been taken seriously, two consequences would have been evident by this time, i.e., after 50 years or so. First, it would be difficult to identify different "schools" of therapy since they would have blended. Second, popular books for practitioners would be a lot more psychological and nearer the mainstream than is the case.

Although the failure of integration might be blamed on ignorance and inertia, barriers to integration are not simply passive obstacles. These barriers have not been worn down by previous pleas for integrative work. In fact, the progressive fragmentation (sometimes called specialization) of the social sciences has probably strengthened most of the barriers to psychotherapy integration. Training psychologists to work and think more and more narrowly about aspects of and practices in the field is not conducive to broad integrative views. Moghaddam (1989) presents a cogent discussion of the fragmentation of the social sciences that strongly supports our view. It is doubtful that education or time alone will reverse this trend.

Biases Underlying Our Position

At this point, we want to make clear our biases if they have not already been guessed or otherwise known. We believe, first, that psychotherapy is properly a *psychological* enterprise. It should be grounded in the fundamental theory and empirical "truths," such as they are, of the field of psychology. That belief has long been held by one of us (Goldstein, Heller, & Sechrest, 1966) and has a firm historical basis for the other. If psychotherapy cannot be so grounded, then it has, in our view, no claim to be recognized as psychotherapy. It could be called almost anything, but it should not be called psychotherapy. Second, we do not admit that any need exists for theories, doctrines, or schools of

psychotherapy independent of the rest of the field of psychology. Psychotherapy is entitled to be "dynamic" exactly to the extent that the rest of the field is dynamic. If the rest of the field of psychology has a place for "archetypes" (hardwired devices?), then so does psychotherapy—but only to the extent justified by the remainder of the field.

A third bias is that both theory and practice in psychotherapy should be empirically justified. We believe the justification should, like the devil, reside in the details and not simply in sweeping generalizations as that "psychotherapy works, as shown by the meta-analysis of Smith, Glass, and Miller (1980)." We should be able to relate what happens in psychotherapy to the more fundamental science of psychology. The objection might easily be raised that the fundamental science of psychology is by no means unified, and we grant that. We also think the entire field should strive toward integration. But the fact that cognitive psychology and neuropsychology are disparate is not a warrant for psychotherapy theorists and researchers to opt out of any attempts at integration. Psychotherapy would be greatly helped by integration with *either* cognitive psychology or neuropsychology.

It follows that we believe that psychotherapy should be firmly grounded in science. If art and intuition play a part, as many practitioners assume, that conviction itself should be scientifically supported. Clearly objections to our position are possible. As luminous a psychological star as Meehl (1992) says that psychotherapy is an art that may not be based in science. This is not the place to get into a discussion of what "science" is, and Mahoney (1991) is wonderfully instructive on that score, but we do mean by that term mainstream, empirical, objective science. We think everyone knows what that means.

When we use the term "clinical psychology," we mean scientific clinical psychology. We do not know what nonscientific clinical psychology is, and we will not try to define what it might be in this paper (see also McFall, 1991). Suffice it to say that even though a nonscientific clinical theory might be interesting, there is no way, other than by scientific test, of demonstrating that any theory is useful. Since clinical psychologists are presumably concerned with knowledge that will lead to demonstrable improvements in applied services, integrators with clinical interests should be encouraged to focus primarily on knowledge that is scientific or scientifically verifiable. Hence, we are not interested in integrating clinical psychology with purely theoretical or "artistic" psychotherapies (whatever they might be).

A fourth bias is that psychological science is not distinct from the rest of science. The theories and principles of psychology should be generally consistent with those from other fields, particularly those better established and more "basic," although we do not subscribe to any reductionist doctrines. For example, no theory of psychopathology is acceptable that is contradictory to what is known about neural transmission in the central nervous system. The observations of psychologists about behavior can be informative to scientists in other fields, e.g., neuroscience, but we do not think that the constructs employed in psychology should be incompatible with what is known in other fields. A case in point is the conception of childhood amnesia and other memory phenomena held by many clinical psychologists involved in treating purported victims of child abuse (Kihlstrom, 1993). Memory has been very well studied by psychologists, and a great deal of quite dependable knowledge is available. Clinical concepts should not be incompatible with that knowledge (see Dickman & Sechrest, 1985).

Finally, we believe that the major responsibility for the failure of integration between psychology and psychotherapy falls on theorists, researchers, and practitioners in psychotherapy. It is true that psychologists generally claim that their theories and research are relevant to problems in human behavior, but except for those few who are specifically engaged in psychotherapy research, psychologists probably do not often claim that their research will be applicable in any specific way to psychotherapy.

Professional psychology, on the other hand, as an aggregate enterprise, routinely claims that the practice of psychology, including therapy, is "scientific," and many individual psychologists make the same claim explicitly, not to say implicitly. Such claims are exaggerated, if not quite untrue, as long as psychotherapy represents only a small, isolated corner of the field. It is the responsibility of psychotherapy to bring itself into the mainstream of the field.

Obviously, the objection might be raised that some modalities of psychotherapy are avowedly derived from basic psychological theory and science. Examples that might be adduced would be cognitive behavior therapy and in vivo desensitization. Our view is that such therapies are only loosely related to the mainstream theories and science of the field, and that they depart from the mainstream ad lib and make only desultory attempts to be fully integrative. For example, the ideas of Tversky and Kahneman (1974) about various cognitive heuristics involved in seeking and processing information are, we think, of great relevance to psychotherapy, to the understanding of both patient and therapist cognitions, but those ideas are not given even short shrift in the cognitive-behavioral psychotherapy literature.

Important areas of knowledge may not easily be integrated because they are separated by large conceptual gaps. For example, knowledge about the operations of the nervous system is separated from knowledge about what a tennis player will do in response to the "Oof!" heard when an opponent serves and the fleeting image of ball and racquet coming together. Nonetheless, it should be possible to link these two areas of knowledge. Psychotherapy theorists may be able to integrate their ideas only to conceptually adjacent areas, but they should have a sense that those areas are, in turn, consistent and integrated with their own neighbors remote from psychotherapy. Our conception of what happens when a pencil lead is drawn across a piece of paper may not be instantly understandable in terms of particle physics, but our conception should, in principle, be linkable to theories in physics.

We do not wish to be thought naive about the difficulties to be met in integrating ideas across the internal boundaries of a more generic theoretical and empirical field. Applications to a specific human problem area are bound to be even harder. Some of the barriers to integration between the broader science of psychology and the narrower application of psychotherapy are quite legitimate. Our aim in this paper is to call attention to legitimate barriers to psychotherapy integration and also to specify barriers that we think are not legitimate. We will refer to the split between clinical psychology and the rest of the field as a more generic problem encompassing psychotherapy.

Do Psychologists Pay Any Attention to Each Other?

The best evidence for the split between clinical psychology and the remainder of psychology, evidence that we find dismaying, is that even though clinical and nonclinical psychologists are often working on complementary and related topics, they rarely cite each other. We suspect that the absence of cross-citations is so widely recognized that it need not even be substantiated. All one need do, for example, is check any issue of the *Journal of Consulting and Clinical Psychology* for citations to any of the literature outside the field of clinical psychology. We happened to peruse *History of Psychotherapy: A Century of Change* (Freedheim, 1992), a 900+ page book purporting to offer "a retrospective investigation of the roots and the development of psychotherapy from four basic perspectives: theory, research, practice, and training" (from the dustjacket). To begin with, the volume has about a 100-page introduction, 200 pages devoted to theory, almost 300 pages on practice, 150 pages on education and training—and 150 pages on research. We suspect that the page allocation probably exaggerates the importance of research in terms of the impact it has had on the psychotherapy enterprise. In the 12 brief chapters (totaling 150 pages) on the research base for psychotherapy, only one reference is made to *any* empirical publication outside the field of psychotherapy research, and it was cited only on a point of ethics and informed consent (for the curious, it was Milgram's, 1974, *Obedience to Authority;* to add insult to the injury, Milgram's name was omitted from the index for the book). A reference to "information processing models" occurs in the chapter on humanistic psychotherapy(!), but only with the assertion that they "hold promise for a reuniting of humanistic approaches with mainstream psychology" (Rice & Greenberg, 1992, p. 218). One may search the index of *History of Psychotherapy* almost in vain for names of psychological scientists other than those working directly in the field of psychotherapy.

We are aware of the arguments that are often made that much of the research appearing in psychological journals is irrelevant to the practice of clinical psychology. Exactly. That is because the practice of clinical psychology, including psychotherapy, is fundamentally not psychological in nature. It is intuitive, it is opportunistic, it is widely, and perhaps wildly, eclectic; it is not psychological. It is probably true that a good bit of what is published in scientific psychological (to us a redundancy) journals is not *immediately* relevant to practice, and some of it may never be relevant to much at all (Bevan, 1986; Miller, 1986). But relevance is in the eye of the beholder, and if an article on attitude change, or identification of some sensory area in the brain, or mental processing time for misspelled words, is not viewed as relevant by a psychotherapist, that is in part because the psychotherapist is not searching for relevance. In passing, we want to say that suggestions occasionally heard that clinical psychologists may not find what is in the journals relevant because they cannot understand what they read is appalling, especially since the reference seems to be to journals such as the *Journal of Consulting and Clinical Psychology*. If scientist/practitioners cannot read *their own* journals, something beyond relevance has gone wrong.

Stricker (1992) takes the position that research and practice in clinical psychology are mutually dependent, and we would not quarrel overly much with that notion. We agree with Stricker and with Arkowitz (1993) that the observations and experiences of practicing clinicians may help identify problems and interesting questions that might well be overlooked by researchers not engaged in clinical activities. We make a distinction, however, between the context of discovery and the context of justification (Popper, 1959), and believe the contributions of practicing clinicians will be largely confined to the context of discovery. Stricker (1992) urges that the boundaries of "research" be expanded to incorporate a wider range of methodologies as "acceptable," but we do not think that is the problem. *All* the scientists we know, at least those interested in clinical and other "real-life" phenomena, already use virtually the entire range of methods. They look about them (observe) to determine what is going on in the world, they read and "deconstruct" texts, they talk to their subjects about what is going on in their heads while they are in experiments, and so on. They do all that, of course, mostly as pilot testing, debriefing, and so on, i.e., in the context of discovery. Justification, however, is another matter. As nearly as we can tell, by calling for an expansion of "acceptable" methodologies, what Stricker is really calling for is an expansion of the acceptable range of uncertainty with respect to justification. Clinical psychology, and psychotherapy as part of it, have enough uncertainty already.

The relative lack of cross-citations, which we take to be an index of disassociation, is, in the short run at least, more damaging to psychotherapy than it is to the remainder of the field. This ignorance, whether willful or not, threatens to diminish the rate and quality of advances in both clinical and general psychology. The vast amount of information that is suitable for exchange between clinical and general psychology exceeds the page allocations for most books, not to mention a journal article (and the authors' expertise). As a result, this paper focuses more on *how* to integrate information (as opposed to listing *what* should be integrated).

LEGITIMATE LIMITS ON INTEGRATION

Practical limitations force all scientists to constrain their intake to narrow bands of the spectrum of available knowledge. If this were not so, then every single effort would be some incomprehensible "Grand Enterprise" too complicated to be of any use. Judgments about the importance or relevance of information makes it possible to create simple and useful theories and bodies of knowledge. Although these judgments are subjective and vary from scientist to scientist, certain exclusion criteria are reasonable and can be justified on a case-by-case basis. In other words, even though no universally agreed upon rules exist for deciding whether to take account of any one bit of information, the process of narrowing one's integrative focus can be systematic and rational.

The Limits of the Human Mind

A very formidable and legitimate constraint on the integration of information is the extent to which one scientist can be familiar with all of the information relevant to a particular topic. This issue has been adeptly addressed by Campbell (1969), and anyone interested in the important enterprise of integrating scientific information is strongly encouraged to read his work. Part of Campbell's argument is that interdisciplinary breadth is highly desirable, but attempting to do too much can reduce accomplishment. He identifies two ideals that may seduce those attempting integration into failure: (a) the "Leonardesque Aspiration" (i.e., the ideal that an integrator should be competent in all of the arts and sciences), and (b) the "Goal of Unidisciplinary Competence" (i.e., the ideal that a scholar should completely master an entire discipline). These ideals may have been viable prior to the 19th or 20th century. However, the current structure of science and the immensity of modern scientific knowledge makes it difficult for anyone to "cover more than one-tenth of a discipline with more than shallow competence" (Campbell, 1969, p. 330). As a result, these ideals could lead either to shallowness or frustration.

A possible solution to these problems is what Campbell calls the "Fish Scale Model of Omniscience." This model exhorts those involved in science to make sure that scientists representing their individual disciplines overlap with each another (like fish scales) in terms of their interests and competencies. The alternative to the Fish Scale model is flurries of independent activity creating multiple, but minimally related, bodies of knowledge that leave gaps in scientific understanding.

Any movement toward integration in psychotherapy may help that part of science progress toward Campbell's ideal, but integration will require team effort or, at the very least, depends on support from integration-minded peers (i.e., others who live the lifestyle of integration). Those who are interested in integration will have to deal with the limits on the extent to which one person can completely understand a subject. As a result, integrators need to expand the horizons of integration beyond the capacity of the individual by becoming members of integrative teams or networks. Achieving omniscience by fish scaling, however, requires that team members be diverse in their competencies; scientists in psychotherapy need to work in close concert with scientists representing other areas of knowledge.

Real Interdisciplinary Differences

Another formidable and legitimate barrier to integration is that scientists from different disciplines, even if committed to working together, may not be able reconcile their interdisciplinary differences. Every discipline develops its own idiosyncratic means of discovering and justifying knowledge, and sometimes one discipline's way of knowing may be incommensurable with another's. As a result, some combinations of disciplines may not readily exchange knowledge in an integrative manner. For example, dramatically different conventions exist for determining what constitutes "good art" and "good science."

Integrative teams must agree on several basic points before their collaboration will be productive: (a) the definition of the problem, (b) measurement methodology, (c) experimental or intervention methodology, and (d) theoretical accounts of the problem (i.e., commensurable explanations of the problem that allow for empirical comparisons). For example, although social biologists are interested in genes, and behaviorists are interested in reinforcement contingencies, both have a common interest in observable behavior and comparable methodologies. As a result, knowledge from behaviorism and social biology can fairly easily be integrated. On the other hand, physiological psychologists who are interested in action potentials may not share a common unit of analysis with family therapists interested in group dynamics. As a consequence, it is unlikely that knowledge from cellular psychology and family therapy can be directly integrated in a useful manner. The integration can be achieved, however, through a comprehensive system of theory and knowledge. Although researchers may agree on a unit of analysis and technical methodology, it is still possible that knowledge may be incommensurable because of different theoretical perspectives. According to Meehl (1986), there are at least three kinds of scientific theories:

> In my terminology, we have *functional-dynamic theories* (e.g., classical mechanics or thermodynamics), whose paradigm is systems of differential equations telling us how certain variables change over time in relation to others. Second, we have what may be called *structural or compositional theories,* which tell us what something is made of, what kinds of substances or parts it includes, and how they are put together. Third, there are *developmental or historical theories* such as the big bang theory, the theory of continental drift in geology, and Darwin's theory of evolution (Meehl, 1986, p. 9).

Psychological research has focused primarily on functional-dynamic theories, which have narrowed the range for psychological integration. Structural or developmental theories might lend themselves more readily to integration across the bounds of psychotherapy.

Incommensurability may stem from real barriers imposed by the structure of science or from the supposition that one area of psychology has little relevance to another. For instance, psycholinguistics (i.e., the study of language processing) seems to have few, if any, common interests with ethology (i.e., the study of animal behavior). However, Noam Chomsky might well disagree with the proposition that ethology and psycholinguistics are theoretically independent since both reflect the basic neural structures with which organisms are provided. Therefore, structural and theoretical boundaries between psychological disciplines are not necessarily absolute and may be breached by new technology, new insight, or a change in scientific values. One person's (or era's) structural or theoretical boundary may be another person's (or era's) arbitrary narrowing of scientific information.

The Quality of Information

Attempts at integration across boundaries of theory and empirical findings should proceed only with due concern for the quality of thinking and information on either side of any boundary. It does the cause of integration no good when bits and pieces of science, perhaps of dubious quality, are seized upon for linking two areas simply because the bits and pieces are handy and happen to fit at the time. Integration that is likely to be useful in the long run requires judgments, perhaps stringent, about the quality of information that is to be used. Of the four general areas of methodological quality control (internal validity, statistical conclusion validity, construct validity, and external validity; Cook & Campbell, 1979), external validity considerations should be of paramount concern to those attempting integration (Brunswick, 1955; Meehl, 1989; Petrinovich, 1989). More specifically, "psychological knowledge" to be integrated should have developed in such a way as to give promise of the generalizability necessary in order to apply it in new ways to new phenomena and in new populations. Ordinarily, that means that effective integration is likely to be limited to established principles or bodies of knowledge; results of single studies are rarely of dependable interest and use. We do not mean to deprecate the heuristic value of single or small collections of studies, for they often serve the purpose of stimulating our thinking in useful ways, perhaps by constituting challenges to standard ways of looking at things. In general, however, we want to avoid adjusting our theories or practices every time a new issue of a journal appears (Schmidt, 1992).

Since clinical psychologists are primarily interested in the behavior and consciousness of psychotherapy clients in their natural environments (e.g., work, home, recreation), integration attempts should be especially attentive to the external validity (Cook & Campbell, 1979) of research that is a focus of integrative effort.

Narrow Knowledge Frustrates Integration

Psychological "knowledge" that is based on narrow operations such as those typical of laboratory investigations, or on narrowly defined populations, such as college students, may not be fully and readily generalizable when attempts are made to extend the coverage of the field. The importance of representative designs in social science research was forcefully put by Brunswick (1955) many years ago, but his arguments have been all but completely ignored in most areas of psychology (see Dawes, 1991; Petrinovich, 1979; Meehl, 1989; Sechrest & Figueredo, in press). As a result of widespread neglect of representative design considerations, much of the psychological data base has been derived from experiments on college students in often bizarre (from any outside perspective) situations. This limitation on the data base is particularly true for much of social psychology (see Dawes, 1991, Sears, 1986), a part of the field of great potential relevance to psychotherapy. These nonrepresentative studies are often characterized by commendable attention to issues of internal validity, thus providing convincing information about what behavior (or associated consciousness) is *possible* in laboratory environments. However, these experiments are not necessarily very informative about the *probable* behavior (or associated consciousness) of subjects in their complex natural environment.

PATTERNS OF RESULTS ARE IMPORTANT   We know by now, or should know, at least, that too much emphasis has been placed on hypothesis testing and outcomes of individual studies (e.g., Cohen, 1990) and too little on the patterning of results across studies. Individual studies, whatever the significance level associated with their results, are rarely unambiguously interpretable and probably even less often provide a basis for course of action. Research findings begin to make sense only when they form part of a "web of evidence." That view of the nature of scientific evidence puts a premium on integration of findings across diverse areas of the field. Olkin (1992) notes that "The search for patterns, rather than for a single number, is the essence of meta-analysis" (p. 36), and that is exactly why integration across the diverse areas of psychology will require increased use of that methodology.

Meehl (1990, 1992) points out that "auxiliary hypotheses," e.g., hypotheses linking specific research operations to scientific constructs, may be as important and critical to the outcome of a study as the hypothesis of focal interest. Auxiliary hypotheses almost invariably require invocation of constructs and other research findings from areas remote to the one of interest. The importance and functioning of auxiliary hypotheses may also become more evident with application of the more sophisticated methodology available in meta-analytic studies.

SOUND METHODS ARE REQUIRED   Of course, we do not want to be taken as suggesting that considerations of the internal (and construct, and statistical conclusion) validity are not of great importance. The quality of scientific information (evidence) characterizing a field must be examined carefully. It does us little good to expand our attention to problems or areas plagued by poor quality research and, consequently, evidence of questionable dependability. Careless or opportunistic reliance on whatever findings happen to be available is poor practice. That a researcher claims in an article that something has been "found" or that a "hypothesis is supported" should not be taken as a warrant to adopt that finding as one's own.

Consideration of methodological quality will often put research on difficult-to-measure psychological variables (e.g., emotion and quality of life) at a disadvantage compared to relatively easier-to-measure variables (e.g., choice behavior and reaction time). Many of the important, critical problems in psychology are difficult, and unassailable methods are hard to come by. Obviously, information about difficult problems may pose some serious problems, but if integration is to be achieved, the difficult problems cannot be avoided. Tukey has been quoted as saying, "It is better to have an approximate answer to the right problem than to have an exact solution to the wrong one" (Tukey, 1988, p. 144). Mitroff and Featheringham (1974) have called this latter sort of answer the "Type III error" (see Mahoney, 1978, who refers to it as theoretical validity), which is to be avoided at all costs. An artful aspect of integration is to learn to spin the web of evidence while communicating quite exactly the variations in the strength of the web.

Treatment Effect Sizes

Even if a high-quality, representative study generates results that are statistically significant, this information may not be of consequence if it only accounts for a small amount of variance. We are aware of arguments favoring the position that "significant" findings are important whatever their size (e.g., Chow, 1988). Those arguments may border on the absurd, however, when one considers that the null hypothesis is never likely to be true (e.g., see Meehl, 1978; Schmidt, 1992). That is particularly the case when one is involved in an area of applied theory in which one intends to have an important (i.e., not simply significant) effect.

Calculating measures of effect size is a fairly objective enterprise, but choosing between alternative measures of effect size requires some subjective reasoning. For example, deciding whether to use the statistical effect size d (e.g., Smith *et al.,* 1980) or a measure of clinically significant change (e.g., Jacobson & Truax, 1991) depends on practical and theoretical considerations that may not be entirely objective. Interpretation of effect size estimates is further complicated by the fact that not all of them should necessarily be calculated from a base of zero. Meehl (1991) has described the "crud factor" in psychological research, the ubiquitous correlation of about .30 that seems to characterize relationships between variables, whether a correlation makes sense or not. Incremental validity (Sechrest, 1963) might also be considered, i.e., the added contribution of any variable to understanding (or prediction) based on what we already know. Insistence on multivariate analyses such as hierarchical regression would do a great deal to establish whether claims of "new" knowledge are justified.

As implied, theories often can be simplified by eliminating variables with trivial influence. However, when variables uniquely explain a large amount of variance, whether we like it or not, those variables almost certainly must be taken into account in our theories and models. For example, McClosky and Figueredo (1992) recently found that 56% of the variance in Child Behavior Checklist Scores is explained by the level of violence in the family. An effect of that magnitude virtually demands that, regardless of the importance that a theorist accords to family violence, theories of child psychopathology need to deal with the fact that child psychopathology is strongly related to family violence.

QUESTIONABLE BARRIERS TO INTEGRATION

We have suggested that the task of integration is not likely to be easy and that some of the barriers are understandable. Some barriers, though, are, in our view, arbitrary, and even self-erected. Those barriers are not legitimate, and steps should be taken to eliminate them as rapidly as possible.

An initial, helpful distinction should be made between topical and disciplinary specialization. Topical specialization is consistent with Campbell's recommendations for interdisciplinary science and legitimately narrows integrative focus to a workable level. For example, juvenile delinquency is a topic, or problem, worthy of specialization by theorists and researchers of great diversity. Although any one scientist could not know everything there is to be known about delinquency, knowledge could, nonetheless, be extensive. That body of knowledge might, however, make only passing contact with areas such as adult psychopathology or cognition and memory. A specialist in juvenile delinquency ought to be able to talk with just about anyone else working on that problem, no matter what the disciplinary background of that person. On the other hand, disciplinary specialization often scatters knowledge into isolated clusters that compete rather than communicate with each other. For example, there are biological, psychological, and sociological accounts of juvenile delinquency that, taken by themselves, are simplistic conceptualizations of a shared topic of interest. Nevertheless, proponents of these three ethnocentric disciplines compete with each other for preeminence, rather than trying to learn from each other in an integrative manner.

Blind allegiance to arbitrary boundaries between areas of psychology is widespread and automatic. As noted earlier, clinical psychologists rarely cite nonclinical psychologists, and general psychologists rarely cite clinical works. This intellectual apartheid is destructive and completely unwarranted. We see no valid reason that clinical and cognitive psychologists who have a shared interest in retrospective recall (Dickman & Sechrest, 1985) should routinely ignore each other's work. At best, this type of segregation will lead to incomplete or redundant theories. At worst, competition and alienation between potentially complementary lines of research will lead to politically motivated decisions that terminate promising lines of research (Campbell, 1969).

Failures to integrate theoretically relevant knowledge within the broad field of psychology might be attributed to the relative immaturity of the science of psychology. For instance, factors such as differential rates of technological advancements within psychological disciplines can make it difficult to integrate information (Cronbach, 1975). Thus, as psychological disciplines mature and reach technological parity, one might optimistically expect that some major barriers to integration will disappear. Likewise, the intellectual climate (Zeitgeist, ruling paradigm) can shift as technical advances are made in a discipline. As opinions about the commensurability of knowledge change as a discipline develops, integration may encounter less interference.

Unfortunately for those who would appreciate the full-scale integration of psychological knowledge, the decline of developmental barriers between disciplines may be the exception rather than the rule. Two major threats to the integration movement are the ethnocentrism of disciplines (Campbell, 1969) and the specialization movement within psychology (Moghaddam, 1989).

Disciplinary Apartheid

Campbell (1969) argues that harmful gaps between disciplines develop when arbitrarily defined groups (e.g., university departments) develop their own bureaucracies (e.g., unidisciplinary funding structures, exclusive societies, and specialty journals). These bureaucracies passively interfere with integration by segregating scientists. To quote Campbell, "The departmental grouping of communicators allows unstable language to drift into unintelligibility across departments. A basic law is that speakers of the same language, once isolated into separate communities, drift into local idiosyncrasies and eventually unintelligibility, once the common conversation is removed"

(Campbell, 1969, p. 337). Arbitrary groupings of disciplines interfere with common conversation when scientists with similar interests (e.g., social psychologists and sociologists) are housed in different buildings, attend different conferences, and publish in different journals. Moreover, crossing disciplinary boundaries is rarely rewarded and often punished (e.g., interdisciplinary work may be difficult to publish and devalued by bureaucrats leaning toward arbitrarily defined department cores). Furthermore, administrators may actively interfere with integration by neglecting subdisciplines distant from the arbitrarily defined core disciplines (Campbell, 1969). Thus, institutional factors affecting communication, collaboration, publication, funding, and promotion can passively and actively create illegitimate barriers to integration.

We find it discouraging that psychotherapy seems to be so completely isolated not only from the remainder of the field of psychology, but from so much of the rest of the world. Howard and Orlinsky (1992), commenting on concerns for outcome research on psychotherapy, commented:

> Researchers were preoccupied by their need to respond to Eysenck's challenge concerning the effects of psychotherapy: to demonstrate whether or not therapy "worked." If it "worked," then patients should have improved by the end of treatment—never mind how. Moreover, if it "really worked," then patients should have maintained their gains intact against the passage of time—never mind what their lives were like. (p. 410)

The latter sentence represents precisely a failure of integration, a failure to integrate knowledge about the effects of real-life circumstances on people's fates, with knowledge about the limited effects of psychotherapy. A surgeon, for example, does not boast of the "success" of a gallbladder removal if the patient dies immediately of a heart attack. What *is* the value of psychotherapy for persons whose life circumstances are so desperate that relief from intrapsychic pain is only temporary and outweighed by the outrageous slings of fortune? Psychotherapists are often proud to claim that they "treat the whole person," but treating the whole person means helping him or her to deal with the whole of his or her lot of troubles. Strange it is that in the 900-page book on psychotherapy and its development, including its theories and its research base, in which the Howard and Orlinsky passage appears, no apparent mention is made of any real-life problems such as poverty, abuse, discrimination, divorce, child custody, and so on. Psychotherapy needs to get a life!

Overspecialization

Moghaddam (1989) raises concerns about the fact that psychology is becoming increasingly specialized, and as a result, the number of divisions within psychology is increasing rather than decreasing as psychology matures. Moghaddam acknowledges that increased specialization will inevitably lead to more research; however, he astutely observes that a simple increase in the number of studies does not necessarily lead to a better understanding of the topic under study. On the contrary, because psychology is a contextual rather than atomistic science, information from overly narrow psychological research cannot be summed to form a comprehensive theory. As a result, specialization can ruin integrative efforts by creating a fragmented data base filled with useless disjointed parts.

It is important to make a clear distinction between Moghaddam's and Campbell's conceptions of specialization. Moghaddam is referring to the proliferation of specialties for largely nonscientific reasons. This type of specialization is rampant in clinical psychology, and is driven primarily by economic, psychological, and social factors. More specifically, there are at least 400 so-called different approaches to psychotherapy, but there is very little evidence that these approaches are differentially effective (Arkowitz, 1992). Indeed, it is virtually impossible that all of these approaches are truly different. For one thing, psychology certainly does not have enough concepts, let alone theories, nor anywhere near a large enough body of data, to support the simultaneous flourishing of 400 different therapies. As a matter of simple logic, it should be apparent that there cannot be 400 different approaches to alleviating the psychic ills of people. Most of any 400 proposed could differ from others only at the margin, most likely only in name. Finally, if 400 different therapies really exist, in the same way that 400 different drugs exist, then it follows that each therapy will have to be validated separately, and they should not be allowed to be "free riders" on some sort of generic outcome studies (e.g., Smith *et al.,* 1980).

In any case, as a result of this ideational profligacy, the proliferation of labels rather than knowledge draws attention away from integrative thinking about common factors and the common core of knowledge in which they *must* be based. At least they must be based in that common core of knowledge *if* they have any base *and* if they lay claim to the imprimatur of psychology. Clinical psychology should obliterate the boundaries of so-called different schools of psychotherapy because they tend to be illegitimate barriers to integration.

In contrast to Moghaddam, when Campbell refers to the need for specialization for scientific reasons, he is referring to *topical specialization* as opposed to *disciplinary specialization.* For example, it may be possible for a psychologist to achieve a reasonably complete and comprehensive understanding of psychological approaches to depression. As a result of recognizing their own limitations, specialists in the psychology of depression should seek out other scientists, such as physicians and social workers, who have a comprehensive biological and sociological understanding of depression (respectively). Teamwork between cooperative groups of topical specialists from different disciplines can result in a truly comprehensive understanding of depression.

As noted by both Campbell and Moghaddam, in an ideal world, topical specialists should never be constrained by arbitrary disciplinary barriers.

BEHAVIOR THERAPY: AN INSTANCE OF NEARLY SUCCESSFUL INTEGRATION

Although clinical and nonclinical psychologists tend to ignore each others' work, some fruitful exchanges of information and ideas have, at times, taken place between these two groups. A good example is provided by the development of behavior therapy as a mode of psychotherapy. Even though much of what is generally regarded as behavior therapy is only loosely based on formal learning theory, and even more loosely based on research related to that theory, this clinical enterprise was clearly inspired by the work of Thorndike, Watson, Skinner, Hull, and other basic behavioral scientists. Its scientific origins may be one of the major reasons for the rise and fairly ready acceptance of behavior therapy. From its origins, behavior therapy derived the theoretical and empirical clout to rival what once was the reigning psychotherapeutic approach, i.e., psychodynamic psychotherapy.

In what sense was behavior therapy integrative? First, and particularly in its Skinnerian branches, concepts and practices were transferred directly from mainstream psychology into therapeutic settings. Those settings were, however, regarded not as isolated sites for applications, but they, themselves, constituted settings in which experimentation constituted the treatment modality. Goldstein (1968) once suggested that research on psychotherapy and the doing of psychotherapy are, or should be, equivalent, and that idea was applicable at least to Skinnerian behavior therapists. No separate "treatment" journals were required by the behavior modifiers. Perhaps the integration was not as complete for other approaches to behavior therapy, but modalities such as systematic desensitization and *in vivo* desensitization, relaxation training, and cognitive behavioral therapy could all claim a reasonably close affinity to a more general body of psychological theory and research.

Even though this paper is directed primarily toward clinical psychologists, we do insist that nonclinical psychologists will benefit from attending to clinical research. It can be plausibly argued that the cognitive revolution in psychology owes a great deal to clinical psychology. For example, the very idea of unconscious processing of information was kept alive over the years, and near the forefront of attention, by the insistent interests of clinical psychologists. Although we do not take seriously the claim, not infrequent, that Freud has been vindicated by recent acceptance of the idea that under some circumstances some unconscious processing of information may occur, the fact is that without continuing pressures from clinical psychologists, concern for that processing might have been reduced or even absent from cognitive psychology.

BIOPHOBIA: A PATHOLOGICAL CONDITION IN CLINICAL PSYCHOLOGY

No area of psychology offers more substance for integration by psychotherapy theorists and researchers than biopsychology. Nor is any area of psychology more fraught with import for psychotherapy. Biopsychology is diverse, and many of its aspects could be delineated specifically for their implications for psychotherapy theory, research, and ultimately, practice. Of special interest, however, should be work done over the past 20 years or so in behavior genetics. This work compels the conclusion that many behaviors and problems of central concern to psychotherapy have a large biological component that cannot, or at least should not, be ignored. Surely, for example, it should matter in the treatment of panic disorder, alcoholism, or social anxiety that these conditions appear to reflect the operations of genetic dispositions. Recently the National Institute on Alcohol Abuse and Alcoholism (1992) thought the need for attention to genetic factors sufficiently serious to cause them to put out an "Alcohol Alert" bulletin on the topic. Theories of psychotherapy very often stem from etiological notions, and to the extent that etiological propositions have to be shared across alternative or complementary explanations, they are diluted, thereby vitiating to some extent the rationale for the therapeutic approach. The image (or metaphor) of "the child within" expresses a rather specific proposition about adult psychopathology. That image is dimmed somewhat if it must accommodate the additional knowledge that the adult psychopathology is an expression of a small set of genes.

Clinical psychology generally, and psychotherapy most specifically, seem to have manifested such a negative reaction to any ideas about the biological basis for behavior that it can be labeled as phobic. The predominant response to biopsychology is avoidance. An example is the book *From Research to Clinical Practice* (Stricker and Keisner, 1985), a book meant to explore the implications of basic scientific research in psychology for psychotherapy. The book is subtitled *The Implications of Social and Developmental Research for Psychotherapy,* and it contains no explicit references at all to biological bases for behavior, an area of coursework required of all clinical psychologists. A chapter in the book is devoted to aggression, but not even a hint occurs that people might differ biologically in their disposition to aggression. Infant development is discussed, including a variety of apparently inborn, hardwired behaviors, without any mention of the implications of the existence of such hardwiring for either psychopathology or psychotherapy. In past years (prior to 1970 or so), articles frequently appeared in journals alleging some version or other of psychogenic bases for such problems as autism, peptic ulcers, stuttering, migraine headache, etc. All of these, and many other conditions, medical and behavioral, have been shown to have a strong, although perhaps not exclusive, biological basis. We asked a friend not long ago, a prominent psychoanalytically oriented psychologist, what the reaction of psychoanalysts has been to the discovery that so many of the problems they once laid claim to have now been shown to have a genetic or other biological basis. He responded, "They just don't write about those problems anymore." In other words, they have not made any effort to integrate biopsychological thinking into their positions; they simply avoid dealing with the issues.

Stating that learning has unique effects on behavior above and beyond the effects of heredity is not an integrative hypothesis. This limited approach involves the sequential partitioning of variance such that the "nuisance" effects of heredity are removed so that the "pure" effects of learning can be studied. Unfortunately, this limits generalization of "pure" environmental effects to conditions in which everyone is genetically identical. Likewise, speculating that heredity places constraints or boundaries on learning is not an integrative hypothesis. The simple-minded assumption that genetic factors can be ignored within certain arbitrarily defined boundaries is not helpful. Both the confound and boundary condition "solution" to genetic issues fail to consider heredity by environment

interactions, which can arise from truly integrative thinking (Wahlsten, 1991).

We are mystified. Acceptance of the fact that a behavior has a biological substrate or that a condition has a genetic component does not seem to us representative of a threat to psychotherapy as an element in treatment, perhaps not even as the primary element. Acceptance that there are biological bases for behavior, which seems implicitly requisite in the APA educational requirement, may, and should, alter some aspects of psychotherapeutic intervention. For example, understanding that most issues in psychotherapy have at least some biological basis may alter expectations about the difficulties to be surmounted in some cases and the outcomes to be expected. Acceptance of the reality of biology does not negate the legitimacy of clinical psychology nor of psychotherapy. Just as a high level of emotional arousal produced by an external physical stimulus (e.g., an auto accident) may be quelled by a biological intervention (e.g., a tranquilizer), so may a problem of biological origin be reduced by a psychological intervention, e.g., pain may be reduced by hypnosis. Psychotherapy as an enterprise, however, is going to seem increasingly foolish and irrelevant over the years if it cannot come to terms with the biological side of the human condition (see also Schneider, 1990). We all ought to start watching the tables of contents, bibliographies, and indexes of books on psychotherapy for evidence that some level of integration is beginning to occur. If we do not soon encounter that evidence, it will be to the detriment of psychotherapy and not the science of psychology.

What difference might it make in what psychotherapists do whether or not they try to take into account biological and genetic bases for behavior? That is an interesting and difficult question since so little thought has been given to it that one does not know very well just where an integrative view might matter. We do think, however, that awareness of a biological or genetic basis for problems being dealt with in psychotherapy might cause the reflective therapist to focus more on factors that reinforce and maintain the pattern of behavior of concern and less on psychodynamics. We also believe knowing that a genetic basis is strongly implicated in a case, e.g., alcoholism, might cause the therapist to adjust his or her expectancies about positive outcomes and prospects for achieving them, perhaps resulting in less optimism but greater determination. Understanding the biological basis for anxiety might cause a therapist to focus more on such interventions as relaxation as a way of controlling anxiety episodes before trying to get at psychic factors involved in them.

PAST, PRESENT, AND FUTURE OF INTEGRATION

The kind of integration that is being proposed in this paper is by no means unprecedented; it has simply been uncommon. Nearly 30 years ago, Goldstein *et al.* (1966) showed how mainstream psychological research might be made relevant to psychotherapy research, if not directly to practice. On the premise that psychotherapy involves a social relationship between patient and therapist, many propositions about psychotherapy practice were deduced from social psychological research. Research on transfer of training was examined for ideas about how the generalization of experiences in psychotherapy to the patient's "real life" might be enhanced. Hamilton, Greenberg. Pyszczynski, and Cather (1993) have recently shown how their work on self-regulation, squarely in social psychology, helps in understanding both psychopathology and psychotherapy. Goldstein *et al.* never imagined that ideas from mainstream psychological research could be translated directly into psychotherapeutic practice, but they did contend that those ideas would be well worth testing in a psychotherapeutic context.

Subsequent volumes (Higgenbotham, West, & Donnelson, 1988; Stricker & Keisner, 1985) have taken similar approaches, although the degree of integration achieved in all these works has to be considered carefully. As noted earlier, integration that does not go beyond simply reinterpreting psychotherapy or some aspect of it in terms of another set of constructs is not fully integrative, nor is a very high level of integration represented by simply showing that research in some area of psychology is relevant to psychotherapy. It is our impression that integration of psychotherapy and the rest of the field will require, at every turn, the collaborative efforts of both active researchers and active psychotherapists.

Full integration can be claimed only when the concepts and their structure are identical in two areas of thought or endeavor. For example, in medicine there is no "medical biochemistry" or "medical physiology." Physicians trying to make sense out of an unusual response of a patient to some drug do not invoke a special theory of calcium devised for the clinical setting. Psychology has a plethora of terms for describing interpersonal affairs, and it is not obvious that a specialized term like "transference" adds anything other than confusion and jargon. The term "stimulus generalization" is even more fundamental and suffices to encompass much of what appears to be meant by transference (Sechrest, 1962). If "transference" is merely shorthand for two or more basic psychological constructs related to interpersonal relations, then its use, although perhaps unnecessary, at least admits of direct translation. If transference means something more than can be described in mainstream psychological constructs, then that should be made clear, and that excess meaning could then be opened to investigation. The objection might be raised that transference is, after all, the older term, but that objection may be resisted on two grounds. One is that transference, even if older, is not really a psychological construct. The second is that older terms are regularly replaced as they are shown to be either inadequate or easily assimilable into the more systematic vocabulary. No one, for example, uses the term "animal magnetism" today.

The cause of integration across all of psychology, and from psychology to psychotherapy, would be helped greatly were a more satisfactory integrative structure or viewpoint available. Schneider (1990), and probably others, has proposed "life-span development" as such an integrative structure. All of psychology relates in one way or another to the processes or consequences of development. From such a standpoint, the province of psychotherapy would involve those activities or interventions meant to restore aberrant processes or states to their expected functioning or level. It is also possible that a more integrative view would make clear the distinctions between psychotherapy and other restorative interventions, such as counseling by a parent or "the purchase of friendship" (Schofield, 1964).

CONCLUDING REMARKS

Our position is that integration across psychology and science in general is simply a matter of good scientific thinking practiced on a day-to-day basis. We have used scientific and methodological reasoning to identify several legitimate and questionable barriers to integration. Ideally, all psychologists would become topical specialists who disregard prefixes such as "psycho" or "socio" (as in psychobiology or sociobiology). At the very least, psychologists need to make some major changes in clinical training and practice to bring these enterprises into the mainstream of contemporary psychological science. More than anything, though, successful integration of psychotherapy into the broader field of psychology would make available a much greater range of theoretical constructs and a much stronger and deeper scientific data base. Psychotherapy should become an applied area of *psychology*. Psychology generally, psychotherapists widely, and patients most specifically would all benefit.

If integration of psychology and psychotherapy is to be successful, however, integration must be integral in the scientific and professional activities of psychotherapists. Integration must be at the center of one's thinking about psychotherapy anytime and all the time. One cannot achieve the seamless theory and practice of psychotherapy that we advocate, and that we think is singularly appropriate to our field, by thinking of integration as something that one tries every now and again to do a bit of. Psychotherapy *is* psychology in action.

An integrated psychotherapy will require psychotherapists to read and otherwise inform themselves much more widely in psychology than now appears to be the case. Since it is unrealistic to think of any psychologist reading more than a small fraction of all the articles published in psychological journals, more review articles will be needed, e.g., along the lines of Goldstein *et al.* (1966), Dickman and Sechrest (1985), and Higgenbotham, West, and Forsyth (1988). A change in outlook of psychotherapists will also be required, however, for instead of dismissing most of psychology as irrelevant, psychotherapists will have to learn to think hard about the content—and methods—of psychology, and how it may be specifically applied in their work.

A psychological psychotherapy will provide a basis for the comprehensive understanding of each client, and how the full range of biological, social, and situational influences have converged to produce the distress that led to the need for treatment. It will also provide an understanding of the full array of factors operating to maintain the person's difficulties, including biological processes that may constitute feedback loops keeping distress at high levels even when ostensible reasons for it are not operative, how the person's cognitive processes may block or facilitate various avenues of change, what outside forces may be affecting the client favorably or adversely, and where the greatest leverage for change may lie. An integrated psychological therapy will help identify the widest range of opportunities to bring about changes in the client's condition and life in order to alleviate the symptoms that brought him or her into therapy, but also to produce change that will be lasting and that will have maximum impact on quality of life. An integrated psychological psychotherapy will not be able to be characterized according to school. There will not be any cognitive-behavior therapy, any psychodynamic therapy, any supportive therapy. But there will be cognitive-behavioral interventions for those aspects of problem complexes that seem amenable to those approaches, and there will be psychodynamic interventions for other aspects of problems. Psychotherapists will become more active participants in the attempts of their clients to solve their problems and achieve more satisfying lives.

A psychologically integrated psychotherapy will not be merely eclectic, for it will be guided by both the scientific theory and evidence available at any one time. Psychotherapy will be coherent, although broadly based and not doctrinaire. At least it will be coherent if the field of psychology is coherent. In our view, though, psychology is making great strides in knowledge about many aspects of behavior, e.g., in the workings of the brain, in the genetic bases for behavior, in cognitive functions, in the course of human development over the life span, and so on. These gains in knowledge provide a large, sound data base rich with implications for psychotherapy. It will be a shame if psychotherapy continues as a fragmented enterprise on the borders of psychology, limited both conceptually and scientifically by self-imposed insulation from what by its origins is its birthright.

References

Arkowitz, H. (1989). The role of theory in psychotherapy integration. *Journal of Integrative and Eclectic Psychotherapy, 8,* 8–16.

Arkowitz, H. (1992). Integrative theories of therapy. In D. Freedheim (Ed.), *History of psychotherapy: A century of change* (pp. 261–303). Washington, DC: American Psychological Association.

Arkowitz, H. (1993). *The art and science of clinical research.* Address to Department of Psychology, Dalhousie University, Halifax, Nova Scotia, Canada.

Brunswick, E. (1955). Representative design and probabilistic theory in a functional psychology. *Psychological Review, 62,* 193–217.

Campbell, D. T. (1969). Ethnocentrism of disciplines and the fishscale model of omniscience. In M. Sherif & C. W. Sherif (Eds.), *Interdisciplinary relationships in the social sciences* (pp. 328–348). Chicago: Aldine.

Campbell, D. T., & Fiske, D. W. (1959). Convergent and discriminant validation by the multitrait-multimethod matrix. *Psychological Bulletin, 56,* 81–104.

Chow, S. L. (1988). Significance test or effect size? *Psychological Bulletin, 103,* 105–110.

Cohen, J. (1990). Things I have learned so far. *American Psychologist, 45,* 1304–1312.

Cook, T. D., & Campbell, D. T. (1979). *Quasi-experimentation: Design and analysis in field settings.* Boston: Houghton-Miffin.

Cronbach, L. J. (1957). The two disciplines of scientific psychology. *American Psychologist, 12,* 671–684.

Cronbach, L. J. (1975). Beyond the two disciplines of scientific psychology. *American Psychologist, 30,* 116–126.

Cronbach, L. J., & Snow, R. E. (1977). *Aptitudes and instructional methods: A handbook for research on interactions.* New York: Irvington.

Dawes, R. M. (1991). *Discovering human nature versus discovering how people cope with the task of getting through college: An extension of Sear's argument.* Presented at the Third Annual Convention of the American Psychological Society, Washington, DC.

Dickman, S., & Sechrest, L. (1985). Research on memory and clinical practice. In G. Stricker & R. H. Keisner (Eds.), *From research to clinical practice: The implications of social and developmental research for psychotherapy* (pp. 15–44). New York: Plenum Press.

Dollard, J., & Miller, N. E. (1950). *Personality and psychotherapy: An analysis in terms of learning thinking and culture.* New York: McGraw-Hill.

Freedheim, D. K. (1992). *History of psychotherapy: A century of change.* Washington, DC: American Psychological Association.

Goldstein, A. P. (1968). Psychotherapy research and psychotherapy practice: Independent or equivalent? In S. Lesse (Ed.), *An evaluation of the results of the psychotherapies* (pp. 5–17). Springfield, IL: C. C. Thomas.

Goldstein, A. P., Heller, K., & Sechrest, L. (1966). *Psychotherapy and the psychology of behavior change.* New York: John Wiley.

Hamilton, J. C., Greenberg, J., Pyszczynski, T., & Cather, C. (1993). A self-regulatory perspective on psychopathology and psychotherapy. *Journal of Psychotherapy Integration 3,* 205–248.

Higgenbotham, H. N., West, S. G., and Forsyth, D. R. (1988). *Psychotherapy and behavior change.* New York: Pergamon Press.

Howard, K. I., and Orlinsky, D. E. (1992). The Chicago Northwestern studies. In D. K. Freedheim (Ed.) *History of Psychotherapy: A century of change* (pp. 408–413). Washington, DC: American Psychological Association.

Jacobson, N. S., & Truax, P. (1991). Clinical significance: A statistical approach to defining meaningful change in psychotherapy research. *Journal of Consulting and Clinical Psychology, 59,* 12–19.

Kelly, G. A. (1955). *The psychology of personal constructs.* New York: W. W. Norton.

Kihlstrom, J. F. (1993, April). *The recovery of memory in the laboratory and the clinic.* Invited address presented at the joint annual meeting of the Rocky Mountain Psychological Association and the Western Psychological Association, Phoenix.

Lazarus, A. A. (1989). Why I am an eclectic (not an integrationist). *British Journal of Guidance and Counseling, 17,* 248–258.

McCloskey, L., & Figueredo, A. J. (1992). *A causal model of the relationship between family violence and psychopathology.* Presentation at the University of Arizona.

McFall, R. M. (1991). Manifesto for a science of clinical psychology. *The Clinical Psychologist, 44,* 75–88.

Mahoney, M. J. (1978). Experimental methods and outcome evaluation. *Journal of Consulting and Clinical Psychology, 46,* 660–672.

Meehl, P. E. (1987). Theory and practice: Reflections of an academic clinician. In E. F. Bourg, R. J. Bent, J. E. Callen, N. F. Jones, J. McHolland, and G. Stricker (Eds). *Standards and evaluation in the education and training of professional psychologists* (pp. 7–23). Norman, OK: Transcript Press.

Meehl, P. E. (1989). Law and the fireside inductions (with postscript): Some reflections of a clinical psychologist. *Behavioral Sciences and the Law, 7,* 521–550.

Meehl, P. E. (1990). Why summaries of the research on psychological theories are often uninterpretable. *Psychological Reports, 66,* 195–244.

Meehl, P. E. (1992). Cliometric metatheory: The actuarial approach to empirical, history-based philosophy of science. *Psychological Reports, Monograph Supplement, 71,* 339–467.

Mitroff, I. I., & Featheringham, T. R. (1974). On systematic problem solving and the error of the third kind. *Behavioral Science, 19,* 383–393.

Moghaddam, F. M. (1989). Specialization and despecialization in psychology: Divergent processes in the three worlds. *International Journal of Psychology, 24,* 103–116.

National Institute on Alcohol Abuse and Alcoholism. (1992). *Alcohol alert: The genetics of alcoholism.* No. 18, PH 328, 1–6.

Olkin, I. (1992, July/August). Reconcilable differences. *The Sciences,* pp. 30–36.

Petrinovich, L. (1979). Probabilistic functionalism: A research conception of research method. *American Psychologist, 34,* 373–390.

Platt, J. R. (1965). Strong inference. *Science, 146,* 347–353.

Plomin, R., & McClearn, G. E. (1993). *Nature-nurture and psychology.* Washington, DC: American Psychological Association.

Popper, K. R. (1959). *The logic of scientific discovery.* New York: Basic Books.

Rice, L. N., & Greenberg, L. S. (1992). Humanistic approaches to psychotherapy. In D. K. Freedheim (Ed.), *History of psychotherapy: A century of change* (pp. 197–224). Washington, DC: American Psychological Association.

Schmidt, F. L. (1992). What do data really mean? Research findings, meta-analysis, and cumulative knowledge in psychology. *American Psychologist, 47,* 1173–1181.

Schneider, S. F. (1990). Psychology at a crossroads. *American Psychologist, 45,* 521–529.

Schofield, W. (1964). *Psychotherapy: The purchase of friendship.* Englewood Cliffs, NJ: Prentice-Hall.

Sears, D. O. (1986). College sophomores in the laboratory: Influences of narrow data base on psychology's view of human nature. *Journal of Personality and Social Psychology, 51,* 515–539.

Sechrest, L. (1962). Stimulus equivalents of the psychotherapist. *Journal of Consulting Psychology, 18,* 172–176.

Sechrest, L., & Figueredo, A. J. (in press). Approaches used in conducting outcome and effectiveness research. *Evaluation and Program Planning.*

Shavelson, R. J., Webb, N. J., & Rowley, G. L. (1989). Generalizability theory. *American Psychologist, 44,* 922–932.

Shoham-Salomon, V., & Hannah, M. T. (1991). Client-treatment interactions in the study of differential change processes. *Journal of Consulting and Clinical Psychology, 59,* 217–255.

Smith, M. L., Glass, G. V., & Miller, T. I. (1980). *The benefits of psychotherapy.* Baltimore, MD: Johns Hopkins University Press.

Smith, B. H., & Sechrest, L. B. (1991). Treatment of aptitude X treatment interactions. *Journal of Consulting and Clinical Psychology, 59,* 233–244.

Stricker, G. (1992). The relationship of research to clinical practice. *American Psychologist, 47,* 543–549.

Stricker, G., & Keisner, R. H. (1985). *From research to clinical practice: The implications of social and developmental research for psychotherapy.* New York: Plenum Press.

Tukey, J. W. (1988). A conversation with Frederick Mosteller and John W. Tukey. *Statistical Science, 3,* 136–144.

Tversky, A., & Kahneman, D. (1974). Judgement under uncertainty: Heuristics and biases. *Science, 165,* 1124–1131.

Wahlsten, D. (1990). Insensitivity of the analysis of variance to the heredity-environment interaction. *Behavior and Brain Sciences, 13,* 109–161.

22

Social and Judgmental Biases that Make Inert Treatments Seem to Work

Barry L. Beyerstein

What we call public opinion is generally public sentiment.

Benjamin Disraeli

If only ignorant and gullible people accepted farfetched ideas, little else would be needed to explain the abundance of folly in modern society. But, as James Alcock discusses elsewhere in this issue of Scientific Review of Alternative Medicine (SRAM), many people who are neither foolish nor ill-educated still cling fervently to beliefs that fly in the face of well-established research. Trust in the further reaches of complementary and alternative medicine (CAM) is a case in point. Paradoxically, surveys find that users of unscientific treatments tend to have slightly more, rather than less, formal education, compared to nonusers.[1] How are we to account for the fact that college graduates, and even some physicians, can accept therapeutic touch, iridology, ear candling, and homeopathy? Experts in the psychology of human error have long been aware that even highly trained experts are easily misled when they rely on personal experience and informal decision rules to infer the causes of complex events.[2,3,4,5] This is especially true if these conclusions concern beliefs to which they have an emotional, doctrinal, or monetary attachment. Indeed, it was the realization that shortcomings of perception, reasoning, and memory will often lead us to comforting rather than true conclusions that led the pioneers of modern science to substitute controlled, interpersonal observations and formal logic for the anecdotes and surmise that can so easily lead us astray. This lesson seems to have been largely lost on proponents of CAM. Some, such as Andrew Weil, reject it explicitly, advocating instead what he calls "stoned thinking," a mélange of mystical intuition and emotional satisfaction, for deciding which therapies are valid.[6]

CAM remains, for the most part, "alternative" because its practitioners depend on subjective reckoning and user testimonials rather than scientific research to support what they do. They remain outside the scientific fold because most of their hypothesized mechanisms contradict well-established principles of biology, chemistry, or physics. If CAM proponents could produce acceptable evidence to back up their methods, they would no longer be alternative—they would be absorbed by mainstream medicine. It is my purpose in this article to draw attention to a number of social, psychological, and cognitive factors that can convince honest, intelligent, and well-educated people that scientifically-discredited treatments have merit.

Those who sell therapies of any kind have an obligation to prove, first, that their products are safe and, second, that they are effective. The latter is often the more difficult task because there are many subtle ways that honest and intelligent people (both patients and therapists) can be led to think that a treatment has cured someone when it has not. This is true whether we are assessing new treatments in scientific medicine, old nostrums in folk medicine, fringe practices in CAM, or the frankly magical panaceas of faith healers.

To distinguish treatment-induced changes in some underlying pathology from various kinds of symptomatic relief that might follow any sort of intervention, there has evolved a set of objective procedures for testing the effectiveness of putative remedies. It is reliance on these procedures that distinguishes so-called "evidence based medicine" from all the rest. Unless a ritual, technique, drug, or surgical procedure can be shown to have met these logical and evidential requirements, it is ethically questionable to offer it to the public, except on an admittedly experimental basis—especially if money is to change hands. Since most "alternative," "complementary," or "integrative" therapies lack this kind of support, one must ask why so many otherwise savvy consumers—many of whom would not purchase a toaster without turning to Consumer Reports for unbiased ratings from financially disinterested experts—trustingly shell out considerable sums for unproven, possibly dangerous, health products. We must also wonder why claims of alternative practitioners should remain so refractory to contrary data that are so readily available.

So, if an unorthodox therapy:

a. is implausible on a priori grounds (because its implied mechanisms or putative effects contradict wellestablished laws, principles, or empirical findings in physics, chemistry, or biology);

b. lacks a scientifically-acceptable rationale of its own;

c. has insufficient supporting evidence derived from adequately controlled outcome research;

d. has failed in well-controlled clinical studies done by impartial evaluators and has been unable to rule out competing explanations for why it might seem to work in uncontrolled settings; and

e. should seem improbable, even to the lay person, on "common sense" grounds,

why would so many well-educated people continue to sell and purchase such a treatment?

Users of unscientific treatments fall broadly into one of two camps. Once a user of either stripe decides to try an unconventional treatment, and believes that his or her personal experience alone is adequate to decide if it has worked or not, the judgmental biases and errors discussed below have a strong tendency to make even the most worthless interventions seem valid. As Alcock points out in his article in this issue, users of the first type try unconventional therapies because they assume, erroneously, that someone else has put them to the test. I.e., they place misplaced trust in the usual authorities on whom they rely. They see an uncritical news item, receive a testimonial from a friend, or see a dubious product displayed alongside the proven ones in their local pharmacy. They may also overgeneralize from the occasional news report of an "alternative" treatment that has actually passed scientific scrutiny and been adopted by orthodox medicine.

The other sort of user chooses his or her alternative treatments out of a broader philosophical commitment. For users who choose CAM on ideological grounds, their fondness for these practices is rooted in a much larger network of social and metaphysical assumptions. Needless to say, their cosmological outlook differs substantially from the rationalist-empiricist worldview that underlies scientific biomedicine. Because these adversaries enter the fray with so few shared axioms and rules of evidence, it is not surprising that a consensus is rarely reached. Proponents of CAM disagree with their detractors, not only about the basic constituents of the universe and the nature of the forces that govern them, but also, at the epistemological level—i.e., they cannot even agree about what are valid methods for settling such disputes.[7] Health being such a basic human concern, it is to be expected that differing opinions about the causes and remedies for disease would form an integral part of these two incommensurate worldviews—one objective, materialistic and mechanistic, the other subjective, animistic and morally-driven. Because our views on health and disease are

so enmeshed with our beliefs about the nature and meaning of life itself, not to mention the underpinnings of our moral precepts and our fundamental conceptions of reality, to attack someone's belief in unorthodox healing is to threaten this entire, mutually-supportive system of bedrock beliefs. Not surprisingly, such attacks will be resisted with strong emotion.

The ability to defend one's basic worldview is abetted by a number of cognitive biases that filter and distort contrary information. I shall return to these psychological processes that incline supporters to misconstrue their experiences to support their belief in CAM. But first let us examine the cultural milieu that has fostered a widespread desire to espouse such practices.

SOCIAL AND CULTURAL REASONS FOR THE POPULARITY OF UNPROVEN THERAPIES

As the 21st century approaches, several social trends have coalesced that enhance the popularity of CAM, in spite of (and to some degree, because of) its rejection by mainstream science. Today's resurgence of folk medicine can be traced, in part, to nostalgic holdovers from the neo-romantic search for simplicity and spirituality that permeated the "counterculture" that attracted so many youthful converts during the 1960's and '70's.[8] The aging flower children of the '60's and '70's now form the backbone of the "New Age" movement wherein unorthodox healing forms a central thrust.[9] Many of the "baby boomers" who spearheaded the earlier movement now find that CAM satisfies the mystical longings, desire for simpler times, and naive trust in the beneficence of "Nature" they absorbed during those tumultuous times. CAM also resonates with that era's mix of iconoclasm, reliance on feeling over reason, mistrust of science, and promotion of consumer advocacy. Let us examine how some of these features have promoted belief in non-scientific medicine among its clientele.

1. The low level of scientific literacy among the public at large. Surveys consistently report that, despite our overwhelming dependence on technology for our safety, nutrition, health, shelter, transportation, entertainment, and economic well-being, the average citizen of the industrialized world is shockingly ignorant when it comes to even the rudiments of science.[10,11] In a recent survey, only 52% of Canadians who were polled could say how long it takes the earth to orbit the sun! These days, it is quite possible to make it through college and even graduate school with virtually no exposure to science courses at all. Consequently, most people lack the basic knowledge and critical thinking skills to make an informed choice when they must decide whether a highly-touted healthcare product is a sensible buy or not. When consumers haven't the foggiest idea how bacteria, viruses, prions, oncogenes, carcinogens, and environmental toxins wreak havoc on bodily tissues, shark cartilage, healing crystals, and pulverized tiger penis seem no more magical than the latest breakthrough from the biochemistry lab.

2. An increase in anti-intellectualism and anti-scientific attitudes riding on the coattails of New Age mysticism.   As a major plank in the New Age platform, CAM is permeated with the movement's magical and subjective view of the universe, epitomized in its catchphrase, "You create your own reality."[9] In advocating emotional over empirical and logical criteria for deciding what to believe, New Age medical gurus such as Andrew Weil and Deepak Chopra have fostered the attitude that "anything goes."[6] Even in elite academic institutions, there are strong proponents of the notion that objectivity is an illusion and how you feel about something determines its truth value.[12,13] To the extent that this has led many people to devalue the need for empirical verification in general, it has enlarged the potential following for those who sell magical and pseudoscientific health products.[14,15,16,17,18]

Mind-body dualism permeates New Age thought, not least of all in its alternative medicine wing. Ironically, though, it is the New Age supporters of CAM who accuse their scientific critics of being dualists.[19,20] However, it is the CAM aficionados who are the real dualists, as evidenced by their constant appeal to undetectable spiritual interveners in matters of health. They need this obfuscation in order to support the oft-heard canard that scientific medicine undervalues the effects of mental processes on health.[7] The confusion this has spread in the public mind has paved the way for a resurgence of many variants of "the mind cure" so popular in past centuries; i.e., the belief that the real causes and cures for almost all disease lie in the mind, conceived by New Agers as coextensive with the immaterial soul.[21] It is easy to understand the appeal of such beliefs among those who have elevated wishful thinking to a virtue. Wouldn't it be nice if laughter and thinking optimistic thoughts would keep us healthy, prayer could rid us of diseases, or imagining little Samurais in the bloodstream attacking malignant cells would purge the body of cancer? Admittedly, there is evidence for psychological effects on one's health, but the size of these effects has been blown out of all proportion by CAM promoters such as Herbert Benson.[22] Several good critiques of the errors, experimental confounds and artifacts that permeate the literature on spiritual beliefs and health have appeared recently.[23,24,25]

A related and troubling supposition common to New Age health propaganda is that one's moral standing can alter how forces in the natural world will affect us. In accepting this anthropocentric and animistic worldview, alternative healers are reverting to the pre-scientific notion that health and disease are tied to one's personal worthiness, rather than to naturalistic causes. This has fostered the return of an endless variety of long since discredited practices that purport to make patients "deserve wellness," rather than attacking the cellular bases of their diseases. Often, this merely leads to blaming the victim, for, implicitly, the patient must have done something despicable to "deserve" his or her affliction. And if the treatment fails, as it so often does, sufferers feel worse yet, for they must have been undeserving of a cure.

3. Vigorous marketing of extravagant claims by the "alternative" medical community.   Strong profit motives have led alternative healers to promote themselves through aggressive marketing and intense legislative lobbying.[26] Routinely, promises are made that no ethical scientifically-trained practitioner could or would make. In addition, new diseases of dubious scientific status are invented—and treated.[7,27] Unfortunately, facing this slick promotional barrage is a citizenry poorly equipped, in general, with the skills or information for evaluating this hyperbole.[11]

4. Inadequate media scrutiny and attacking critics. With some notable exceptions, the electronic and print media have tended to give CAM a free ride. The enthusiastic claims of the "alternatives," typically supported by nothing but anecdotes and testimonials, make uplifting stories that are all too rarely challenged by journalists who know that audience satisfaction cashes out in the rush for ratings.

Another disturbing trend that has had a chilling effect on some who would criticize unscientific treatments stems from the fact that many of these procedures have been imported from non-European cultures and championed by female practitioners. A rhetorical tactic that allows self-promoters to sidestep the substance of fair criticisms is to hurl accusations of racism and sexism at anyone who dares to express doubts. E.g., some practices, such as "therapeutic touch," that have been rejected by scientific medicine are being embraced by an increasing number of nursing schools. Because these are still predominantly female institutions, looking to enhance the autonomy, scope, and earning power of their graduates by monopolizing new, sometimes dubious, spheres of practice, critics of practices salvaged from the trashbin of scientific medicine often find themselves accused of sexism. Similarly, when a colleague and I published a critique of several unsupported aspects of Traditional Chinese Medicine (TCM),[26] we were accused of cultural insensitivity and racism.[28] We were chided for presuming to criticise the effectiveness of TCM when we were not steeped in the philosophy of the culture that spawned it. To accept this absurd argument would be to agree that no one but a gourmet cook could tell when she's been served a bad meal. My rejoinder is, of course, that the truly racist and sexist attitude would be to hold empirically testable claims from other cultures or female proponents to a lower standard of proof than any others—this would amount to an assertion that their defenders are intellectually inferior. In the final analysis, appeals such as these to "other ways of knowing" amount to nothing more than tacit admission that these treatments cannot pass the standard procedures for vetting would-be therapies. Fortunately, since good science is practised in the same way by all ethnic groups and both sexes, there are many strong opponents from within these communities who find ancient, unproven practices just as dubious as do white male critics.[29,30]

5. Increasing social malaise and mistrust of traditional authority figures—the anti-doctor backlash.   Growing disillusionment with the conventional wisdom and apprehensiveness about the future has fostered a certain crankiness in Western societies. This has intensified the willingness of many people to believe that our social, economic, and political shortcomings must be due to active connivance on the part of powerful, secretive cabals, rather than the cumulative mistakes of well-intentioned planners muddling through as best they can. Consequently, there is a growing desire to espouse grand conspiracy theories and to attack the institutions or interest groups that are suspected of plotting against the common good.[31] In this climate of suspicion, government is increasingly seen as a party to the plot and the scientific and medical professions have also begun to bear the brunt of what Richard Hofstadter identified decades ago as the "paranoid streak" in American politics.

These conspiratorial musings have coincided with two other, not entirely unjustified, undercurrents to promote an anti-doctor backlash that CAM proponents have been quick to exploit. One is a sense of disappointment arising from the failure of certain overly-optimistic predictions of medical breakthroughs to materialize. The other is the realization that medicine, as a self-regulating profession, has not always held the public good at the top of its political agenda.[32] This has added fuel to the social envy many people feel regarding the status, political clout, and earning power of the medical profession. As Ambrose Bierce once wrote, a physician is "one upon whom we set our hopes when ill and our dogs when well."

The inability of many people to separate in their minds certain self-serving actions of medical associations in the economic/political arena from the debate over whether scientific medicine's treatments are genuinely better than those of CAM has been a boon to the latter. In this fractious climate, the "alternatives" have also benefitted by painting themselves as defenders of the democratic ideal of "choice." This would be commendable if consumers had the wherewithal to make an informed choice.

6. Dislike of the delivery methods of scientific biomedicine.   There exists a widespread but exaggerated fear that modern medicine has become excessively technocratic, bureaucratic, and impersonal. The narrowing of medical specialties, the need to maximize the cost-efficient utilization of expensive facilities, the advent of third-party payment and managed care, and the staggering workloads of medical personnel have led some patients to long nostalgically for the simpler days of the kindly country doctor with ample time and a soothing bedside manner. They tend to forget, however, that this was often all a doctor of that era had to offer. Nonetheless, medical schools are coming to a renewed appreciation for the tangible benefits of interpersonal relationships in healthcare delivery and have begun, in their admission procedures, to look more closely at applicants' social skills in addition to their academic and technical excellence. The "alternatives" can rightly claim some credit for moving this up the agenda.

7. Safety and Side Effects.   A quaint bit of romanticism that draws converts to New Age, "holistic" healthcare is the assertion that "natural" remedies are necessarily safer, gentler, and more efficacious, than those of technological origin.[7] One hears frequently, for instance, the ludicrous claim that herbal concoctions have no side effects. If the ingredients in a natural product are potent enough to affect one's physiology in an advantageous way, they are certainly powerful enough to cause side effects as well. To say otherwise is to admit that one is administering an inert substance. In fact, some popular herbal concoctions are far from benign—a growing number of reports show allergic, toxic, even lethal, reactions among users of certain herbal remedies.[30,33,34,35,36,37] Numerous examples of mislabeling and serious contaminations of popular herbal products have also been reported. As usage rates rise, interactions with prescribed medications are also becoming more prevalent, since patients rarely know what is in the concoctions they are self-prescribing or receiving from herbalist. This danger is compounded by the fact that users are often reluctant to admit such indulgences to their physicians. Public awareness of the possible adverse effects of herbal concoctions has tended to be sparse because, unlike prescription drugs, there is no requirement that ill effects of supplements and herbal medications be reported to central registries. Unfortunately, under current U.S. law, the reverse onus exists, requiring the government to show that a supplement or herb is unsafe before manufacturers and vendors can be forced to remove it from the market.[37]

Among purveyors and users of herbs and supplements, even when adverse effects do occur, they are likely to be ignored or attributed to other causes. That is because there is a touching belief in these quarters that beneficent Nature would never pull such dirty tricks. In the same naive fashion, health food devotees staunchly maintain that "natural" Vitamin C from plants is more effective than the identical molecule manufactured in the chemistry lab, an idea equivalent to saying that bricks recycled from a cathedral will produce a better house than bricks salvaged from a brothel. Boosters of "natural" products should also be reminded that tobacco, bacteria, viruses, and prions are quite natural too, and that some of the most deadly poisons known (e.g., belladonna, strychnine, cytisine, aflatoxin, and mycotoxins) are found in wholly natural plants. On the other hand, over a third of all drugs routinely used in scientific biomedicine were derived from herbal sources, including many of the most widely used drugs in cancer chemotherapy.[37] The difference, of course, is that the active ingredients in these products, though originally from nature, are now known and have passed rigorous tests of safety and efficacy. This allows their purity and dosages to be accurately controlled, something that cannot be said of herbalists' products whose active ingredients have been shown in lab assays to vary, in different samples, by a factor of as much as 10,000.[37]

Possible adverse consequences of other branches of alternative medicine have also been slow in being compiled, for similar socio-political reasons.[7] Fortunately, the Internet is beginning to provide some valuable sources of such cautionary information, though warnings are in danger of being swamped by the torrent of hype and self-promotion on the net. A number of websites containing scientifically reliable data about herbal remedies and supplements are listed in reference number 37, below. Similar listings regarding other aspects of CAM can be found at "www.quackwatch.com" and "www.healthwatcher.net," the websites maintained, respectively, by Drs. Stephen Barrett and Terry Polevoy. Dr. George Lundberg, the new editor of the online medical journal, Medscape, (www.medscape.com) has also announced that this electronic journal will be expanding its coverage of the possible harms of alternative treatments.

PSYCHOLOGICAL REASONS FOR THE POPULARITY OF ALTERNATIVE THERAPIES

Psychologists have long been aware that people generally strive to make their attitudes, beliefs, knowledge, and behaviors conform to a harmonious whole. When disquieting information intrudes and cannot easily be ignored, it is fascinating to observe the extent to which we can distort or sequester it to reduce the inevitable friction. It is to these mental gyrations that we now turn.

1. The Will to Believe. We all exhibit a willingness to endorse comforting beliefs and to accept, uncritically, information that reinforces our core attitudes and self-esteem.[40] Since it would be nice if many of the hopeful shibboleths of alternative medicine were true, it is not surprising that they are often seized upon with little demand for proof. Once adopted, such beliefs are remarkably resistant to contrary arguments. As Zusne and Jones[41] have emphasized, magical and pseudoscientific beliefs are typically parts of more fundamental systems of belief, ones that define to the holder's basic concept of reality. Anything this central to one's cosmology and social outlook will be defended strongly, by filtering or misconstruing contrary input if need be.[42]

2. Logical Errors and Lack of a Control Group. One of the most prevalent pitfalls in everyday decision-making is to mistake correlation for causation. Logicians refer to this error as the Post Hoc, Ergo Propter Hoc fallacy ("After this, therefore because of this"). It is the basis of most superstitious beliefs, including many of the underpinnings of CAM. We all have a tendency to assume that things which occur together must be causally connected, although, obviously, they needn't be. E.g., there is a high correlation between the consumption of diet soft drinks and obesity. Does this mean that artificial sweeteners cause people to become overweight?

When we count on personal experience to test the worth of medical treatments, we necessarily do so in situations where we lack complete information. The task of determining cause and effect is made even more difficult in the case of healthcare by the fact that many relevant factors are varying simultaneously—something casual observation cannot accurately track. This, plus the fact that the outcome of any single case could always have been a fluke, makes it virtually impossible to isolate actual causes when we base our decisions on personal experience in a single instance. Personal endorsements supply the bulk of the support for unorthodox health products, but they are an extremely weak currency because of what Gilovich[43] has called the "Compared to What?" problem. Without comparison to a similar group of sufferers, treated identically except that the allegedly curative element is withheld, any individual recipient can never know whether he or she would have recovered just as well without the vaunted treatment. Probably the single biggest failing of the CAM movement is its inability to see the need for the simple control group.

3. Judgmental Shortcomings. Those who cast doubt on fringe treatments are frequently dismissed with the rejoinder, "I don't care what your research studies say; I know it worked for me." It is well established, however, that this kind of intuitive judgement often leads to seriously flawed conclusions.[4,44] Unfortunately, the typical purveyor and purchaser of unproven therapies is insufficiently aware of the many perceptual and cognitive biases that can lead to faulty decisions when we depend on personal experience to decide what has caused a disease or whether a therapy "has worked" or not. Redelmeier

and Tversky[45] showed how people are prone to perceive illusory correlations in random sequences of events. They then demonstrated how these intuitive feelings of association have led to the false but widespread belief that arthritis pain is influenced by the weather. Proponents of CAM, who take many folk beliefs like this at face value, seem oblivious to how easy it is to be misled by uncontrolled observations and misrecollections such as these.

The pioneers of the scientific revolution were aware of the large potential for error when informal reasoning joins forces with our penchant for jumping to congenial conclusions. By systematizing observations, studying large groups rather than a few isolated individuals, instituting control groups, and trying to eliminate confounding variables, these innovative thinkers hoped to reduce the impact of the frailties of reasoning that lead to false beliefs about how the world works. None of these safeguards exists when we base our decisions merely on a few satisfied customers' personal anecdotes—unfortunately, these stories are the "alternative" practitioner's stock in trade. Psychologists interested in judgmental biases have repeatedly demonstrated that human inference is especially vulnerable in complex situations, such as that of evaluating therapeutic outcomes, which contain a mix of interacting variables and a number of strong social pressures. Add a pecuniary interest in a particular outcome, and the scope for self-delusion is immense.

The job of distinguishing real from spurious causes in everyday situations requires not only controlled observations, but also systematized abstractions from large bodies of data. Dean and his colleagues[46] showed, using examples from another popular pseudoscience, handwriting analysis, that without large, sophisticated databases and statistical aids, human cognitive abilities are simply not up to the task of sifting valid relationships out of huge masses of interacting data. Similar difficulties would have confronted the elders of pre-scientific medicine, and for that reason, we cannot accept their, or their descendants', anecdotal reports as sufficient support for their methods.

Noticing interesting correlations in one's surroundings is a reasonable starting point for a systematic, controlled analysis that could actually reveal the underlying causal structure that might be exploited. Observing such a correlation, however, should never be the end point in a search for a relationship that could eventually be put to therapeutic use.

In defending their enterprise, proponents of CAM generally ignore these cautions and encourage instead another unfortunate human tendency, that of placing more faith in personal experience and intuition than on controlled, statistical studies. The "alternatives" encourage this in their followers by calling it independence of thought, which, of course, can sometimes be a good thing. They should know, however, that it can also lead the appraiser astray in many situations in which personal experience is not a good guide to the actual state of affairs.

4. Psychological distortion of reality. Distortion of perceived reality in the service of strong belief is a common occurrence (see Alcock[40] and his article in this issue of SRAM). Even when they derive no objective benefits, devotees who have a strong psychological investment in alternative medicine can convince themselves that they have been helped.

According to cognitive dissonance theory[47], when new information contradicts existing attitudes, feelings, or knowledge, mental distress is produced. We tend to alleviate this mental discord by reinterpreting, i.e., distorting, the offending input. To have received no relief after committing time, money, and "face" to an alternate course of treatment (and most likely to the cosmology of which it is a part) would be likely to create this kind of internal dissonance. Because it would be too disconcerting, psychologically, to admit to one's self or to others that it had all been a waste, there would be strong psychological pressure to find some redeeming value in the treatment.

5. Self-serving biases and demand characteristics. There are many self-serving biases that help maintain self-esteem and promote harmonious social functioning.[42] None of us wishes to admit to ourselves or others that we believe foolish things or that we are accepting people's trust and money under false pretenses. Because these core beliefs in our own virtue and intelligence tend to be vigorously defended—by warping perception and memory if need be—fringe practitioners, as well as their clients, are prone to misinterpret cues and remember things as they wish they had happened, rather than as they really occurred. In this way, therapists who don't keep good records and apply proper statistics (as is generally the case in CAM) can be selective in what they recall, thereby overestimating their apparent success rates while ignoring, downplaying, or explaining away their failures.

An illusory feeling that one's symptoms have improved could also be due to a number of so-called "demand characteristics" found in any therapeutic setting. In all societies there exists a "norm of reciprocity," an implicit rule that obliges people to respond in kind when someone does them a good turn. Therapists, for the most part, sincerely believe they are helping their patients and it is only natural that patients would want to please them in return. Without clients necessarily realizing it, such obligations (in the form of implicit social demands) are sufficient to inflate their perception of how much benefit they have received. Thus controls for this kind of compliance effect must also be built into properly conducted clinical trials.[48] Again, proponents of CAM downplay the need for such controls, possibly a form of self-delusion in itself.

WHY MIGHT THERAPISTS AND THEIR CLIENTS WHO RELY ON ANECDOTAL EVIDENCE AND UNCONTROLLED OBSERVATIONS ERRONEOUSLY CONCLUDE THAT INERT THERAPIES WORK?

Although the terms "disease" and "illness" are often used interchangeably, for present purposes, it is worth distinguishing between the two. In what follows, I shall use "disease" to refer to a pathological state of the organism arising from infection, tissue degeneration, trauma, toxic exposure, carcinogenesis, etc. By the term "illness" I will mean the feelings of malaise, pain, disorientation, dysfunctionality, or other subjective complaints that might accompany a disease state. Our subjective reaction to the raw sensations we call symptoms is, like all other perceptions, a complex cognitive construction. As such, it is molded by factors such as beliefs, suggestions, expectations, demand characteristics, self-serving biases, and self-deception. The experience of illness is also affected (often unconsciously) by a host of social, monetary, and psychological payoffs that accrue to those admitted to the "sick role" by society's gatekeepers (i.e., health professionals). For certain individuals, the privileges and benefits of the sick role are sufficient to perpetuate the experience of illness after a disease has healed, or even to create feelings of illness in the absence of disease.[27,49] Awareness of these dynamics can be quite minimal in the non-diseased patient who has learned, through subtle psychological mechanisms, to feel ill. A conscious intent to deceive is definitely not required.

Unless we can tease apart the many factors that contribute to the perception of being ill, or being improved, personal testimonials offer no basis on which to judge whether a putative therapy has, in fact, cured anyone's disease. That is why blinded placebo-controlled clinical trials, with objective physical measures if possible, are absolutely essential in evaluating therapies of any kind. Bearing this in mind, then, why might someone mistakenly believe that they had been helped by an inert treatment?

1. The disease may have run its natural course. Many diseases respond well to "the tincture of time." In other words, they are self-limiting. Providing the condition is not chronic or fatal, the body's own recuperative processes will restore the sufferer to health. Thus, before the curative powers of a putative therapy can be acknowledged, its proponents must show that the percentage of patients who improve following treatment exceeds the proportion expected to recover without any intervention at all (or that they recover reliably faster than if left untreated). Unless an unconventional therapist releases detailed records of successes and failures over a sufficiently large number of patients with the same complaint, she cannot claim to have exceeded the norms for unaided recovery. As noted above, without an adequate control group, any given practitioner will never know how his clients would have fared without his ministrations.

To be fair, the "alternatives" are correct that many effective treatments in conventional medicine are also aimed at symptomatic relief or strengthening the body's own recuperative mechanisms, rather than attacking the disease process itself. It's just that proponents of CAM offer little convincing evidence that their own unique efforts along these lines are particularly effective. Nonetheless, the "alternatives" can take some satisfaction in the fact that the debate they have provoked has spurred conventional biomedical researchers to seek more effective ways of stimulating natural recovery processes, such as enhancing certain immune reactions. Unfortunately, their disinterest in research means that the "alternatives" will contribute little to the understanding that will eventually lead to therapeutic improvements.

2. Many diseases are cyclical. Arthritis, multiple sclerosis, allergies, and gastrointestinal complaints are examples of diseases that normally "have their ups and downs." Not surprisingly, sufferers tend to seek therapy during the downturn of any given cycle. In this way, a bogus treatment will have repeated opportunities to coincide with upturns that would have happened anyway. Again, in the absence of appropriate control groups, consumers and vendors alike are prone to misinterpret improvement due to normal cyclical variation as a valid therapeutic effect.

3. Spontaneous remission.   Any anecdotally reported cure could have been due to a rare but possible "spontaneous remission." Even with certain cancers that are nearly always lethal, tumors occasionally disappear without further treatment. One experienced oncologist reports that he has seen 12 such events in about 6000 cases he has treated.[50] Alternative therapists can receive unearned acclaim for such remissions because many desperate patients turn to them out of a feeling that they have nothing left to lose. When the "alternatives" assert that they have snatched many hopeless individuals from death's door, they rarely reveal what percentage of their apparently terminal clientele such happy exceptions represent. What is needed is statistical evidence that their "cure rates" exceed the known spontaneous remission rate and the placebo response rate (see below) for the conditions they treat.

The exact mechanisms responsible for spontaneous remissions are not well understood at present, but much research is being devoted to revealing and possibly harnessing processes in the immune system or elsewhere that are responsible for these unexpected turnarounds. Some researchers think that spontaneous remissions are less the result of immune surveillance than due to the fact that certain biochemical reactions necessary for growth in malignant masses can, on occasion, reach a self-limiting stage before the accumulated tumor mass kills the patient. Whatever the mechanism, the documented existence of spontaneous remissions in a variety of diseases, in people who do not avail themselves of alternative treatments, means that an occasional dramatic, unexpected turnaround cannot be used to validate the power of prayer or a fringe therapy.

4. The placebo effect and the need for randomized, double blind assessments.   A major reason why bogus remedies are credited with subjective, and occasionally objective, improvements is the ubiquitous placebo effect[18,50,51] (see also Jittler, Beyerstein, and Beyerstein, this issue of SRAM). The history of medicine is strewn with examples of what, with hindsight, seem like crackpot procedures that were once enthusiastically endorsed by physicians and patients alike.[16,52,53] Misconceptions of this sort arise from the false assumption that a change in symptoms following a treatment must have been a specific consequence of that procedure. Through a combination of suggestion, belief, expectancy, cognitive reinterpretation, and attentional diversion, patients given biologically useless treatments can often experience measurable relief nonetheless. Some placebo responses produce actual changes in physical symptoms; others are subjective changes that make patients feel better although there has been no measurable change in their underlying pathology.

Through repeated contact with valid therapeutic procedures, we all develop, much like Pavlov's dogs, conditioned responses in various physiological systems. Later, these responses can be triggered by the setting, rituals, paraphernalia, and verbal cues that signal the act of "being treated." Among other things, placebos can cause release of the body's own morphine-like pain killers, the endorphins.[18] Because these learned responses can be palliative, even when a treatment itself is irrelevant to the source of the complaint, it is necessary that putative therapies be tested against a placebo control group—i.e., similar patients who receive a sham treatment that resembles the "real" one, except that the suspected active ingredient is withheld.

It is essential that the patients in such tests be randomly assigned to their respective treatment groups. Otherwise, sicker or more compliant people could end up in one group or another, or people with harmful or helpful lifestyles or certain habits, industrial exposures, etc., could be disproportionately allocated. These group differences could produce effects that might be spuriously attributed to the experimental manipulation— something researchers call an "experimental confound." Good examples of the mischief such confounds can wreak are discussed in a recent critique of studies purporting to show that various religious practices enhance health.[25] Indeed, practicing members of certain faiths do seem to enjoy certain medical benefits. The question, however, is whether faith itself is responsible, i.e., a benevolent deity looks out for the pious, or simply that observant believers also tend to smoke and drink less, engage in fewer risky activities, live in less toxic environments, enjoy better social support networks, come from certain ethnic backgrounds, and so on. And, of course, given that stress can have adverse health consequences, belief in a supernatural protector could be health-promoting via its ability to alleviate anxiety, regardless of whether the belief is true or not. Once again we see the perils of assuming that correlation implies causation.

In addition, adequately controlled research requires that all recipients must be "blind" with respect to whether they are receiving the active versus the placebo treatment. Because the power of what psychologists call expectancy and compliance effects is so strong, the therapists must also be blind as to the group membership of individual patients.[48] Hence the term "double blind"—the gold standard of outcome research. Such precautions are required because barely perceptible cues, unintentionally conveyed by treatment providers who are not blinded, can bias test results. Likewise, those who assess the treatment's effects must also be blind, for there is a large literature on "experimenter bias" showing that honest and welltrained professionals can unconsciously "read in" the outcomes they expect when they attempt to assess complex events.[54,55] If one's professional advancement or net worth depends on validation of a putative treatment, there is all the more need for blind assessments. Ideally, the end points being measured will be objective, and if the measurements can be mechanized and automated to reduce the effects of observer subjectivity, so much the better. It is odd that CAM supporters who would not think much of a wine tasting that failed to obscure the labels on the bottles still downplay the need for blinded assessments when it comes to their own stock in trade.

When the clinical trial is completed, the blinds can then be broken to allow statistical comparison of active, placebo, and no-treatment groups. Only if the improvements observed in the active treatment group exceed those in the other two groups by a statistically significant amount can the therapy claim legitimacy.

Defenders of CAM often complain that conventional medicine itself continues to use many treatments that have not been adequately vetted in placebo-controlled, double-blind trials. This may be so in some instances, but the percentage of such holdovers is grossly exaggerated by the "alternatives."[56] At any rate, this does nothing to enhance the credibility of CAM, for merely arguing that "they're as bad as we are" offers no positive evidence in favor one's own pet belief. The crucial difference between scientific biomedicine and alternative medicine is that the former is institutionally committed to finding empirical support for its treatments and eventually weeds out those that fail to pass muster. And, unlike the "alternatives," biomedicine does not cling to procedures that contradict well-established principles in the basic sciences. Scientifically-based therapies change because new research accumulates; alternative medicine is mired in the past and changes rarely, if ever. This is because the latter has no serious commitment to testing its rationales and procedures under controlled conditions. Alternative medicine clings to the belief that its procedures must be valid because they have stood the test of time. But the longevity of racism, sexism, and the belief in demonic possession belies the assertion that ability to survive implies validity.

5. Some allegedly cured symptoms were probably psychosomatic to begin with.   The pioneering neurologist Joseph Babinski (1857–1932) coined the term "pithiatism" to refer to conditions he concluded were "caused by suggestion, cured by persuasion." A constant difficulty in trying to measure therapeutic effectiveness is that there are many such complaints that can both arise from psychosocial distress and be alleviated by support and reassurance. At first glance, these symptoms (at various times called "psychosomatic," "hysterical," or "neurasthenic") resemble those of recognized medical syndromes.[27,57] Although there are many "secondary gains" (i.e., psychological, social, and economic payoffs) that accrue to those who slip into "the sick role" in this way, we need not accuse them of conscious malingering to point out that their symptoms are nonetheless maintained by subtle psychosocial processes.[49]

Alternative healers cater to these members of the "worried well" who are mistakenly convinced that they have organic diseases or morbidly fearful that they may lose their good health. Their complaints are instances of somatization, the tendency to express psychological concerns in a language of symptoms like those of organic diseases.[27,58,59] The "alternatives" offer comfort to these individuals who need to believe their symptoms have medical rather than psychological causes. Often with the aid of pseudoscientific diagnostic devices, fringe practitioners reinforce the somatizer's conviction that the cold-hearted, narrow-minded medical establishment, who can find nothing physically amiss, is both incompetent and unfair in refusing to acknowledge a very real organic condition. A large proportion of those diagnosed with "chronic fatigue," "environmental sensitivity syndrome," irritable bowel syndrome, fibromyalgia, and post-traumatic stress disorders (not to mention many suing manufacturers because of the allegedly harmful effects of silicone breast implants[61]) look very much like classic somatizers.[59,60] Similar dynamics seem to underlie reports of a more recent variant of what Stewart[59] has called this family of "fashionable diseases," i.e., "Gulf War Syndrome."[62]

If a patient's symptoms were psychologically caused to begin with, he or she is likely to respond favorably to an acceptable blend of suggestion, reassurance, psychological support and reaffirmation. Often this is what (probably unknowingly) these patients are really seeking though their illness behavior. In rejecting this interpretation, CAM practitioners ask why, if the malaise is really of psychological origin, wouldn't relief have been achieved already from any of the typically long list of abandoned conventional physicians? One answer is that the patient-doctor rapport necessary for such reassurance to be effective is likely to become strained as soon as the doctor says she cannot find any physical cause for the illness. If a physician even hints at a psychosomatic diagnosis, the relationship is likely to be poisoned irrevocably—for, sad to say, even in this supposedly enlightened age, psychological diagnoses still carry a social stigma for many. Thereafter, no amount of support and reassurance is likely to bridge the gap that has been opened. Curiously, though, when the alternative healer gives the sought-after physical diagnosis and then, in the next breath, reverts to the New Age line that all diseases are caused by mental/spiritual shortcomings, the same patient may well accept this about-face with enthusiasm. To the extent that alternative healers are often charismatic personalities, who are willing to spend extensive amounts of time reassuring their clients and catering to their existential concerns, this heightens their ability to capitalize on patient suggestibility.[63] It also stands to reason that suggestions arising from someone who buys into the patient's metaphysical outlook might be more effective in countering psychosomatic complaints than those following from a philosophically skeptical point of view.

When, through the role-governed rituals of "delivering treatment," fringe therapists supply the reassurance, sense of belonging, and existential support that their clients are seeking, this is obviously worthwhile, but all this need not be foreign to scientific practitioners who have much more to offer besides. The downside is that catering to the desire for medical diagnoses for psychological complaints promotes pseudoscience and magical thinking while unduly inflating the success rates of medical quacks. Saddest of all, it perpetuates the prejudicial anachronism that there is something shameful or illegitimate about psychological problems.

6. Symptomatic relief versus cure.   Short of an outright cure, alleviating pain and discomfort is what sick people value most. Many allegedly curative treatments offered by alternative practitioners, while unable to affect the disease process itself, do make the illness more bearable, but for psychological reasons. Pain is one example. Much research shows that pain is partly a sensation like seeing or hearing and partly an emotion.[64,65] Researchers have found repeatedly that anything that successfully reduces the emotional component of pain leaves the purely sensory portion surprisingly tolerable. Thus, suffering can often be reduced by psychological means, even if the underlying pathology is untouched. Anything that can allay anxiety, redirect attention, reduce arousal, foster a sense of control, or lead to cognitive re-interpretation of symptoms can alleviate the agony component of pain. Modern multi-disciplinary pain clinics put these strategies to good use every day.[65] Whenever patients suffer less, this is all to the good, but we must be careful that purely symptomatic relief does not divert people from proven remedies for the underlying condition until it is too late for them to be effective.

7. Many consumers of alternative therapies hedge their bets.   In an attempt to appeal to a wider clientele, many unorthodox healers have begun to refer to themselves as "complementary" or "integrative," rather than "alternative." Instead of ministering primarily to the ideologically committed or those who have been told there is nothing more that conventional medicine can do for them, the "alternatives" have begun to advertise that they can enhance conventional biomedical treatments. They accept that orthodox practitioners can alleviate specific symptoms but contend that alternative medicine treats the real causes of disease—dubious dietary imbalances or environmental sensitivities, disrupted energy fields, or even unresolved conflicts from previous incarnations.[7] If improvement follows the combined delivery of "complementary" and scientifically-based treatments, the fringe practice often gets a disproportionate share of the credit.

8. Misdiagnosis (by self or by a physician).   In this era of media obsession with health, many people can be induced to think they suffer from diseases they do not have. When these healthy folk receive the oddly unwelcome news from orthodox physicians that they have no organic signs of disease, they often gravitate to alternative practitioners who can always find some kind of "energy imbalance," nutritional deficit, or dubious "sensitivity" to treat. If "recovery" should follow, another convert is born.

Scientifically trained physicians do not claim infallibility, and a mistaken diagnosis, followed by a trip to a shrine, alternative healer, or herb counter can lead to a glowing testimonial for having cured a grave condition that never existed. Other times, the diagnosis may have been correct but the time course, which is inherently hard to predict, might have proved inaccurate. If a patient with a terminal condition undergoes alternative treatments and succumbs later than the conventional doctor predicted, the alternative procedure may receive credit for prolonging life when, in fact, the discrepancy was merely due to an unduly pessimistic prognosis. I.e., survival was longer than the expected norm, but within the range of normal statistical variation for the disease in question.

9. Derivative benefits.   Alternative healers often have forceful, charismatic personalities.[62,67,68] To the extent that patients are swept up by the messianic aspects of CAM, a psychological uplift may ensue which can have both short and longer term spinoffs. If an enthusiastic, upbeat healer manages to elevate the patient's mood and bolster his expectations, this enhanced optimism can lead to greater compliance with, and hence effectiveness of, any orthodox treatments he or she may also be receiving. This expectant attitude can also motivate people to improve their eating and sleeping habits and to exercise and socialize more. These changes, by themselves, could help speed natural recovery, or at the very least, make the recuperative interval easier to tolerate.

Psychological spinoffs of this kind can also reduce stress, which has been shown to have deleterious effects on the immune system.[69,70] Removing this added burden may speed healing, even if it is not a specific effect of the therapy. As with purely symptomatic relief, this is far from a bad thing, unless it diverts the patient from more effective treatments, or the charges are exorbitant.

CONCLUSION

Before anyone should agree to accept an unconventional treatment, he or she should ask whether it has been subjected to the sort of controlled clinical trials described above. As should be obvious by now, personal endorsements are essentially worthless in deciding the value of any therapy. Instead, supporters of unorthodox therapies should be able to supply empirical evidence, based on large groups of patients and published in refereed scientific journals. Only by this process of peer-review can we be assured that the supporting research has been checked for the sources of error and bias described above. For example, reviewers look to see that the sample sizes were sufficiently large, the experimental design and statistical analyses were appropriate, and that obvious confounding variables were controlled for. The peer review process will determine that the participants were randomly assigned to treatment groups and that they were treated and assessed under double-blind conditions. It will also ensure that the condition of each patient was accurately assessed and documented before and after the intervention and, ideally, that the participants were followed up for a reasonable interval thereafter to gauge the duration of any beneficial changes. And, of course, because any single positive outcome could always have been a statistical fluke, replication by independent researchers with converging methodologies is the ultimate assurance. A single experimental result practically never settles an important scientific issue. It is the long-term track record that counts. And even with published papers that pass on the foregoing criteria, one should always look to see how large the reported treatment effects are. Beware of the "true but trivial effect." There are many statistically-significant outcomes in research articles that are real but too small to be of any clinical use.

Any practitioner who cannot supply this kind of backing for his or her procedures is immediately suspect. One should be even more wary if, instead of peer-reviewed research, the "evidence" comes solely in the form of anecdotes, testimonials or self-published pamphlets or books. To be credible, supporting research articles should come from impartial journals in the appropriate scientific fields, rather than from journals owned by associations promoting the questionable practice, or from the "vanity press" which accepts virtually all submissions and charges the authors for publication of their work.

If the practitioner is ignorant of, or openly hostile to, mainstream science and cannot supply a reasonable scientific rationale for his methods, the would-be buyer should proceed with caution. If the "doctor's" promotional patter is laced with allusions to spiritual forces or vital energies or to vague planes, vibrations, imbalances, and sensitivities, suspicions should also be aroused. Likewise, if the treatment provider claims secret ingredients or processes (especially if they are named after him- or herself), extols ancient wisdom and "other ways of knowing," or claims to "treat the whole person, not diseases," there is also good reason to question his or her legitimacy. If the therapist claims to be persecuted by the medical establishment, encourages political action on his or her behalf, and is prone to attack or even sue critics rather than answering their criticisms with valid research, alarm bells should begin to ring. Practitioners who sell their own supplements and other proprietary concoctions in their offices and stress the need for frequent return visits by healthy people, "in order to stay healthy," are also a cause for concern. The presence of any pseudoscientific or conspiracy-laden literature in the waiting room ought to set a clear thinker looking for the nearest exit. And above all, if the promised results go well beyond those offered by conventional therapists, the probability is that one is dealing with a quack. In short, if it sounds too good to be true, it probably is.

When people become sick, any promise of a cure is especially beguiling. As a result, common sense and the willingness to demand evidence are easily supplanted by false hope. In this vulnerable state, the need for critical appraisal of treatment options is all the more necessary, rather than less. Potential clients of alternative therapists would do well to heed the admonition of St. Paul: "Test all things; hold fast to what is good" (I Th. 5:12). Those who still think they can afford to take a chance on the hawkers of untested remedies should bear in mind Goethe's wise advice: "Nothing is more dangerous than active ignorance."

References

1. Millar, W. J. Use of alternative heath care practitioners by Canadians. Canadian Journal of Public Health. 1997; 88(3): 154–158.
2. Nisbett R, Ross L. Human Inference: Strategies and Shortcomings of Social Judgment. Engelwood Cliffs, NJ; Prentice-Hall; 1980.
3. Schick T, Vaughn L. How to Think About Weird Things: Critical Thinking for a New Age. Mountain View, CA: Mayfield Publishing; 1995.
4. Gilovich T. How We Know What Isn't So: The Fallibility of Human Reason in Everyday Life. NY: Free Press/Macmillan; 1991.
5. Levy D. Tools of Critical Thinking. Needam Heights, MA: Allyn and Bacon; 1997.
6. Relman A. A trip to Stonesville. The New Republic. 1998.
7. Beyerstein B, Downie S. Naturopathy. The Scientific Review of Alternative Medicine. 1998; 2(1): 20–28.
8. Frankel C. The nature and sources of irrationalism. Science. 1973; 180: 927–931.
9. Basil R., ed. Not Necessarily the New Age. Amherst, NY: Prometheus Books; 1988.
10. Kiernan V. Survey plumbs the depths of international ignorance. The New Scientist. April 29 1995, p. 7.
11. Beyerstein, B. The sorry state of scientific literacy in the industrialized democracies. The Learning Quarterly. June 1998, Vol. 2, No. 2., pp. 5–11.
12. Gross P, Levitt N. Higher Superstition. Baltimore, MD: Johns Hopkins University Press; 1994.
13. Sokal A, Bricmont J. Intellectual Impostures. London: Profile Books; 1998.
14. Stalker D, Glymour, C., eds. Examining Holistic Medicine. Amherst, NY: Prometheus Books; 1985.
15. Barrett S. Health Schemes, Scams, and Frauds. Mt. Vernon, NY: Consumer Reports Books; 1990.
16. Barrett S, Jarvis W. The Health Robbers: A Close Look at Quackery in America. Amherst, NY: Prometheus Books; 1993.
17. Pantanowitz D. Alternative Medicine: A Doctor's Perspective. Cape Town, South Africa: Southern Book Publishers; 1994.
18. Ulett GA. Alternative Medicine or Magical Healing. St. Louis: Warren H. Green; 1996.
19. Beyerstein B. The brain and consciousness-Implications for psi phenomena. The Skeptical Inquirer.1987; 12: 163–173.
20. Beyerstein B. Pseudoscience and the brain: Tuners and tonics for aspiring superhumans. In S. Della Sala, ed. Mind Myths: Exploring Popular Misconceptions About the Mind and Brain. Chichester, UK: J. Wiley and Sons. pp. 59–82; 1999.
21. Meyer D. The Positive Thinkers: A Study of the American Quest for Health, Wealth, and Personal Power from Mary Baker Eddy to Norman Vincent Peele. New York, NY: Doubleday-Anchor; 1965.
22. Benson H. Timeless Healing: The Power and Biology of Belief. New York, NY: Simon and Schuster; 1996.
23. Tessman I, Tessman J. Mind and body. Science. 1997; 276: 369–370.
24. Tessman I, Tessman J. Troubling matters. Science. 1997; 278: 561.
25. Sloan RP, Bagiella E, Powell T. Religion, spirituality and medicine. Lancet. 1999; 353: 664–667.
26. Beyerstein B, Sampson W. Traditional medicine and pseudoscience in China (Part 1). The Skeptical Inquirer. 1996; 20(4): 18–26. Sampson W, Beyerstein B. Traditional medicine and pseudoscience in China (Part 2). The Skeptical Inquirer, 1996; 20(5): 27–34.
27. Shorter E. From Paralysis to Fatigue: A History of Psychosomatic Medicine in the Modern Era. New York, NY: Free Press/Macmillan; 1992.
28. Hui KK. Is there a role for Traditional Chinese Medicine? JAMA. 1997; 277(9): 714. (a reply by W. Sampson and B. Beyerstein follows)
29. Knauer D. Therapeutic touch on the hot-seat. The Canadian Nurse. 1997; X: 10.
30. Thadani M. Herbal Remedies: Weeding Fact from Fiction. Winnipeg, Manitoba: Context Publications; 1999.
31. Robins R, Post J. Political Paranoia: The Psychopathology of Hatred. New Haven, CT: Yale University Press; 1997.
32. Starr P. The Social Transformation of American Medicine. New York, NY: Basic Books; 1982.
33. Ernst E. Harmless herbs? A review of the recent literature. American Journal of Medicine. 1998; 104: 170–178.
34. Tyler VE. The Honest Herbal, 3rd ed. New York, NY: Pharmaceutical Products Press; 1993.
35. Sutter MC. Therapeutic effectiveness and adverse effects of herbs and herbal extracts. The British Columbia Medical Journal. 1995; 37(11): 766–770.
36. Carter, R. 1996. Holistic hazards. The New Scientist. 13 July, 1996, pp.12–13.
37. Winslow L, Kroll D. Herbs as medicines. Arch. Internal Med. 1998; 158: 2192–2199.
38. Ko RJ. Adulterants in Asian patent medicines. New Engl. J. Med., 1998: 339(12):
39. Betz W. Herbal crisis in Europe. In press, The Scientific Review of Alternative Medicine.
40. Alcock J. The belief engine. The Skeptical Inquirer. 1995; 19(3): 14–18.
41. Zusne L, Jones W. Anomalistic Psychology: A Study of Magical Thinking. 2nd ed. Hillsdale, NJ: Lawrence Erlbaum Associates; 1989.

42. Beyerstein B, Hadaway P. On avoiding folly. Journal of Drug Issues. 1991; 20(4): 689–700.

43. Gilovich T. Some systematic biases of everyday judgment. Skeptical Inquirer. 1997; 21(2): 31–35.

44. Tversky A, Kahneman, D. Judgement under uncertainty: Heuristics and biases. Science. 1974; 185: 1124–1131.

45. Redelmeier D, Tversky A. On the belief that arthritis pain is related to the weather. Proc. Natl. Acad. Sci. USA. 1996; 93: 2895–2896.

46. Dean G, Kelly I, Saklofske D, Furnham A. Graphology and human judgement. In B. and D. Beyerstein, eds., The Write Stuff. Amherst, NY: Prometheus Books, 1992; pp. 342–396.

47. Festinger L. A Theory of Cognitive Dissonance. Stanford, CA: Stanford University Press; 1957.

48. Adair J. The Human Subject. Boston, Ma: Little, Brown and Co.; 1973.

49. Alcock J. Chronic pain and the injured worker. Canadian Psychology. 1986; 27(2): 196–203.

50. Roberts A, Kewman D, Hovell L. The power of nonspecific effects in healing: Implications for psychosocial and biological treatments. Clinical Psychology Review. 1993; 13: 375–391.

51. Ernst E, Abbot NC. I shall please: The mysterious power of placebos. In S. Della Sala, ed. Mind Myths: Exploring Popular Assumptions About the Mind and Brain. Chichester, UK: J. Wiley & Sons, 1999; pp. 209–213.

52. Hamilton D. The Monkey Gland Affair. London, UK: Chatto and Windus; 1986.

53. Skrabanek P, McCormick. J. Follies and Fallacies in Medicine. Amherst, NY: Prometheus Books; 1990.

54. Rosenthal R. Experimenter Effects in Behavioral Research. New York, NY: Appleton-Century-Crofts; 1966.

55. Chapman L, Chapman J. Genesis of popular but erroneous diagnostic observations. Journal of Abnormal Psychology. 1967; 72: 193–204.

56. Ellis J, Mulligan I, Rowe J, Sackett D. Inpatient general medicine is evidence based. Lancet. 1995; 346: 407–410.

57. Merskey H. The Analysis of Hysteria: Understanding Conversion and Dissociation, 2nd ed. London, UK: Royal College of Psychiatrists; 1995.

58. Stewart D. Emotional disorders misdiagnosed as physical illness: Environmental hypersensitivity, candidiasis hypersensitivity, and chronic fatigue syndrome. Int. J. Mental Health. 1990; 19(3): 56–68.

59. McWhinney IR, Epstein RM, Freeman TR. Rethinking somatization. Ann. Int. Med.; 1997; 126: 747–75.

60. Huber P. Galileo's Revenge: Junk Science in the Courtroom. New York, NY: Basic Books; 1991.

61. Angell, M Science on Trial: The Clash of Medical Evidence and the Law in the Breast Implant Case. New York, NY: Norton; 1997.

62. Joseph SC. A comprehensive clinical evaluation of 20,000 Persian Gulf War veterans. Military Medicine. 1997; 162(3): 149–155.

63. O'Connor G. Confidence trick. The Medical Journal of Australia. 1987; 147:456–459.

64. Melzack R. Pain: Past, present and future. Canadian J. Psychol. 1993; 47: 615–629.

65. Brose WG, Spiegel D. Neuropsychiatric aspects of pain management. In The American Psychiatric Press Textbook of Neuropsychiatry. Washington, DC: American Psychiatric Press Inc.; 1992; pp. 245–275.

66. Smith W, Merskey H, Gross S, eds. Pain: Meaning and Management. New York, NY: SP Medical and Scientific Books; 1980.

67. Nolen WA. Healing: A Doctor in Search of a Miracle. New York, NY: Fawcett Crest; 1974.

68. Randi J. The Faith Healers. Amherst, NY: Prometheus Books.1989.

69. Ader R, Cohen N. Psychoneuroimmunology: Conditioning and stress. Annual Review of Psychology. 44: 53–85; 1993.

70. Mestel, R. Let mind talk unto body. New Scientist. July 23, 1994; pp. 26–31.

23

Twelve Practical Suggestions for Achieving Multicultural Competence

Richard B. Stuart

Multicultural competence can be defined as the ability to understand and constructively relate to the uniqueness of each client in light of the diverse cultures that influence each person's perspective. Because the complexity of culture is often overlooked, multicultural research often inadvertently strengthens the stereotypes that it is intended to thwart. To avoid stereotypic thinking, clinicians must critically evaluate cross-cultural research and be thoughtfully creative in applying it to clinical practice. Twelve suggestions are offered for the use of multicultural research as a source of questions that enhance respect for clients' cultural identities rather than as answers that foreclose it.

Although it is easy to endorse the principle of culturally sensitive practice, it is often much harder to make it a reality. The mandate is clear: Psychologists should be "aware of and respect cultural, individual, and role differences . . . [must practice] only within the boundaries of their competence . . . [and must] make a reasonable effort to obtain the competence required by using relevant research, training, consultation, or study" (American Psychological Association, 2002, pp. 1063–1064). This is no small task because "we are prisoners caught in the framework of our theories; our expectations; our past experience; our language" (Popper, 1970, p. 52). We tend to believe that others see the world as we do. And when we do acknowledge different perspectives, we normally form convenient notions about the differences that create little more than the illusion of understanding. To achieve true multicultural understanding, psychologists need to learn how to find and use resources that will allow them to "approach clients with sensitivity to their diversity while avoiding the trap of pan-ethnic labels . . . that dilute and obscure the moderating effects of national origin, immigration history, religion and tradition" (Fisher et al., 2002, p. 1026), not to mention individual differences.

Because of the rapidly changing composition of the American population, psychologists are confronted by such challenges with ever increasing frequency. More than 1 in 10 Americans are now foreign born, and 1 in 3 belong to groups identified as minorities. Paradoxically a *majority* of the population in three states (California, Hawaii, and New Mexico) as well as the District of Columbia are "minorities." These new populations fill neighborhoods and clinic waiting rooms as well. It is now so widely accepted in government, business, and human services that culture influences every aspect of human endeavor (Surgeon General, 2001) that Glazer (1997) recently entitled his book, *We Are All Multiculturalists Now.* This is a remarkable achievement for a term that did not appear in the *Oxford English Dictionary* until 1989.

Despite innovative efforts to teach cultural competence (e.g., Dana, 2002), stereotypic thinking still clouds many evaluation and intervention efforts. The roots of this problem can be found in the inherent complexity and instability of culture, the difficulty of defining target groups, flaws in the design or interpretation of data on cultural differences, and uncertainty about how to use the growing body of knowledge about culture and its influence. After a reminder of past missteps with equally laudable goals, the current problem is defined, and 12 guidelines are offered as aids to gaining the necessary cross-cultural understanding.

SOCIOECONOMIC STATUS (SES): A PREQUEL TO MULTICULTURALISM?

Multiculturalists might benefit from considering the fate of a past effort to enhance the effectiveness of mental health services on the basis of sociological data. Shortly after the end of World War II, mental health professionals accepted the notion that society could be divided into distinct classes, each of which was associated with a variety of adaptive or abnormal personality characteristics. The poor were generally believed to be both morally and functionally different from the more prosperous (Gilens, 1999). For example, Hollingshead and Redlich (1958) presented evidence that "the differential distribution of neurotic and psychotic patients by class is significant beyond the .001 level of probability" (p. 222), with the former more prevalent among the more affluent and the latter more prevalent among the poor.

These results were taken as confirmation of the social Darwinist belief that lower SES individuals were anomic, depraved, incapable of deferring gratification, and so class conscious that they suffered from frustrated upper-class mobility strivings (Miller & Reissman, 1961). They were also deemed to be kin-bound and therefore lacking in individual responsibility, lacking in rationality, and suffering from a "relatively limited range of perception of the world around them (i.e. the middle class world)" (Simmons, 1958, p. 24).

Although a half-century of research has yet to demonstrate a clear trend in treatment outcome related to SES (Lam & Sue, 2001), preferred forms of mental health services were withheld from those in the lower strata of society on the assumption that they lacked the capacity to benefit from the treatment methods available at the time. By the time these service changes were materializing, sociologists had found considerable behavioral variability within socioeconomic strata, many behavioral similarities across classes, and many demographic factors including age, family size, education, and ethnicity that covaried with SES. Therefore, rather than providing a valid database for improving mental health services, findings related to SES were used to introduce biases and invalid beliefs that compromised the quality of programs they were intended to enhance (Stuart, 1964).

This is not to say that income and economic well-being are unrelated to mental and physical health. Strong negative correlations have been found between varied measures of income and various forms of mental and physical morbidity (McLoyd, 1998) as well as the willingness to seek and continue in treatment (Edlund et al., 2002). Nevertheless, the within-group heterogeneity in these studies weakens generalizations about what might be called the *culture of social class.* In its *Resolution on Poverty and Socioeconomic Status,* the American Psychological Association (2000) stressed the need for continued study of the impact of poverty and its effects, but nowhere does it mention the culture of SES or status-linked personality ascriptions that previously led to negative stereotyping and victimization of the poor. Instead, poverty is understood to be a stressor to which individuals adapt in individual ways. As the following review will show, the current approach to multiculturalism runs a similar risk of erroneously labeling people in an effort to understand them.

COMPLEXITIES IN THE NATURE OF CULTURE

It would be easier to navigate through the sociocultural complexities of the world if people fell into neatly defined categories. Unfortunately, cultures are subjective, have fuzzy boundaries, change constantly, and are highly heterogeneous. Even when people have strong ethnic identities, no one culture is likely to monopolize their outlooks.

The word *culture* was first used in its anthropological and sociological context by E. B. T. Taylor (1871/1924) to mean "that complex whole which includes knowledge, belief, art, morals, law, custom, and any other capabilities and habits acquired by man as a member of society" (p. 1). Kleinman (1996) described Taylor's concept as essentially supporting "the biological basis of racial differences . . . and of higher and lower levels of civilization" (p. 16), pinpointing the risk of its being used to support prejudice. Over time, cultural theorists split their emphases between a code of conduct embedded in social life and the symbolic products of these activities. The latest thinking combines both traditions, defining *culture* as the source of ties that bind members of societies through an elusive "socially constructed constellation consisting of such things as practices, competencies, ideas, schemas, symbols, values, norms, institutions, goals, constitutive rules, artifacts, and modifications of the physical environment" (Fiske, 2002, p. 85).

These internalized rules create traditions that go deeper than reason. For example, Kroeber (1963) observed that as a sign of respect when entering a holy place, Muslims take off their shoes and Jews their hats, but neither group could explain the observance beyond saying that this is how things had always been done. In Kelly's (1955) terms, cultural orientation might be construed as the master plan behind superordinating constructs that covertly influence manifest cognitive content. Because much of the strength of cultural influences stems from the fact that they operate in the background of behavior at the value, linguistic, and construct levels, people often have difficulty defining their cultural influences, and social scientists have difficulty measuring them.

In addition to being subjective, cultures also have fuzzy boundaries. Owing to the influence of mass media, global Internet communities, tourism, intermarriage, education, and mass migrations, the boundaries of every culture are fluid to some extent. We live in "an increasingly interconnected world society, [so] the conception of independent, coherent, and stable cultures becomes increasingly irrelevant" (Hermans & Kempen, 1998, p. 1111). Ideas therefore diffuse across groups, and so certain beliefs and attitudes may have more stability than the groups that originate or espouse them.

Because of this diffusion of influences and the need to adapt to new challenges, once stable cultures are ever changing. Adjustments to external stresses that are necessary to the survival of cultures typically affect behavior before they are recognized and codified. The challenges are often sensed first by only certain group members, who then promote adaptations that are often resisted by others. As a personally witnessed example, when a group of young adults returned to the Taos Pueblo from service during World War II, some resumed their traditional lives but others took jobs in Los Alamos and the surrounding area. While respectful of tribal traditions, the returnees also wanted changes, ranging from the way the community made decisions to more tangible matters, such as adding plumbing and side-entry doors in pueblo living units. Their new ideas caused divisions along generational lines in the once homogeneous community and challenged the unity of its culture.

Culture is transmitted through enculturation, that is, environmental influences that operate to promote unconscious introjection and conscious learning (Tseng, 2003). Families play key roles as arbiters of the dominant culture and creators of their own microcultures. Parenting is the ultimate form of socialization, through which children learn how to function in society. But parents vary in their ability and desire to transmit cultural beliefs to their children, and children are not passive recipients of their parents' values and practices. This explains the fact that the culture with which young adults leave their families of origin is rarely a carbon copy of parental beliefs, making for a diversity of characters at every family reunion.

Immigration also influences cultural outlooks by challenging the ethnic identities with which newcomers arrive. *Ethnicity* refers to "social groups that distinguish themselves from other groups by sharing a common historical path, behavioral norms, and their own group identity" (Tseng, 2003, p. 7). Immigrants may assimilate by moving away from their ethnic heritage and immersing themselves in the mainstream, integrating the two sets of views, separating by withdrawing from the mainstream and accepting only heritage beliefs, or marginalizing by failing to accept or integrate either set of beliefs (Berry & Sam, 1997). Multiple factors influence acculturation, including the receptivity of the host culture to immigrants, the extent to which the immigrants' characteristics are distinctive, and the extent to which members of the native culture are willing to accept those who assimilate. The winner of these internal culture conflicts will be determined by such factors as the strength with which heritage beliefs were held prior to migration, the amount of contact immigrants have with others who adhere to heritage beliefs, and the nature and duration of socializing contact with host society.

The complexity of the acculturation process is revealed by countless biographies of immigrants who excelled in the "new country." For example, Harmetz (2002) described the socialization of Billy Wilder, a German Jew who came to the United States to escape Hitler in 1933:

> As quickly as possible, Mr. Wilder made himself an American. He avoided the cafes and living rooms where refugees met to drink coffee and speak German. Instead he lay on the bed in his rented room and listened to the radio and learned 20 new English words every day. (p. A21)

Within 5 years, he wrote the first of his 25 film scripts in English, a remarkable achievement for a man who did not speak English when he arrived in this country. It is also noteworthy that along with many other newcomers, he may have affected the host culture almost as much as he was affected by it.

Although it might be assumed that having an internally consistent, single cultural identity is essential for positive mental health, in reality no individual is a repository of a "pure" culture. Everyone belongs to multiple groups—nation, region, gender, religion, age cohort, and occupation to name a few—each of which exerts a different cultural influence that may be congruent, complementary, or in conflict with any of the others. Every influence is interpreted by each person, who decides whether and, if so, how personal beliefs should respond to each of these influences. Therefore, every individual is a unique blend of many influences. Whereas culture helps to regulate

social life, specific beliefs are products of individuals' minds. Because of this complexity, it is *never* safe to infer a person's cultural orientation from knowledge of any group to which he or she is believed to belong.

CULTURAL SENSITIVITY OR CULTURAL STEREOTYPES?

For more than a century, scholars have studied most of the world's cultures with invaluable results, defining culture as "the unique behavior and lifestyle shared by a *group* [italics added] of people" (Tseng, 2003, p. 1). Deep insights have been gained into the ways in which groups of people evolve different approaches to dealing with the existential and pragmatic issues in human existence. However, when psychologists make inferences about individual clients from assumptions about the cultures that influence them, in effect they commit the logical flaw of basing ideographic predictions on nomothetic data sets. The problem thus lies less in the original studies than in the ways in which they are applied, often resulting in stereotypic thinking.

While cautioning against stereotyping, Sue (1999) promoted use of the term *Asian American*. This implies commonalities among the 3.6 billion people who live in Asia, divided among many nations as different as Afghanistan, China, India, Syria, and Japan. Ethnic differences within and between these nations are at least as great as those between nations in the eastern and western hemispheres. If the within-group differences among Asians are great, they may be even greater for Asian Americans. Recent census data revealed that 10.2 million people identified themselves as having pure Asian backgrounds, and another 1.7 million identified themselves as having mixed backgrounds. Asian Americans include new immigrants and those whose families have lived in the United States for many generations, those living in urban ethnic concentrations that support use of the native language and traditions as well as those who live in totally integrated communities in which their group is a small minority. And they may embrace Buddhist, Hindu, Islamic, Shiite, Shinto, Christian, and other doctrines, followed by some with fundamentalist fervor and others in name only.

Attempts to categorize other large populations are vulnerable to similar criticism. For example, the phrase *African American* can be misleading. It implies that 33.9 million people share certain salient characteristics because of their ties with some of the 797 million people of Africa, who live in 50 different countries and speak more than 1,000 different languages, unless, of course, their forebears came from the West Indies, South America, Australia, or New Zealand. Confirming the existence of many different varieties of African American identity (Cross, 1991), Shipler (1997) described the contrasts between southern Black identity, with its greens and black-eyed peas, and urban black identity, with its rap, and from working to middle-class status. He noted that the definition of *Black* is undergoing rapid change, with iterations of the culture closely held by different groups at the same time. Therefore, it is entirely misleading to speak about a monolithic African American culture.

The same problem prevails in efforts to generalize about the 2.5 million Native Americans who range from being full blooded to only fractional members of any of more than 500 different tribes (Sutton & Broken Nose, 1996). They may live and work on tribal lands, live on tribal lands and work elsewhere, or spend no time on tribal lands. And they may adhere to tribal culture in every aspect of daily life, primarily during ceremonies, or not at all. Perhaps what they have in common is being classified as "Indians," a term given by Spanish explorers to all of the cultures they found in North America, defined by the fact that as non-Christians they were considered to be uncivilized and without culture (Berkenhoffer, 1978).

Finally, in the 2000 census, 36 million Americans were identified as "Hispanic." Hardly a homogeneous group, two thirds were from Mexico, 14% were from Central or South America, 11% were from Puerto Rico, 4% were from Cuba, and 7.3% were from other Spanish (and Portuguese!) speaking regions of the world, with their national origin being the identity that they preferred over the homogenizing term (Kaiser Family Foundation, 2002). And Rodriguez (2002) eloquently bemoaned the inaccuracy of assuming homogeneity even among those who have roots in the same country. One need only reflect on the huge heterogeneity among Caucasians in the United States to grasp the true meaning of his concerns.

When psychologists attempt to apply the conclusions of studies that aggregate so much diversity under a single label, they fall victim to the *myth of uniformity*, the naive belief that all members of a group will have the same characteristics. Given that even identical twins raised together are not exactly alike, people who simply share a cultural or racial background can hardly be considered birds of a feather. Epidemiologists refer to this as an "ecological fallacy [that] arises when an attempt is made to ascribe to individuals the average properties of large groups of population" (Lawson, 2001, p. 207). Equally erroneous is the "atomistic fallacy [that] arises when an individual's . . . experience is used to impute average characteristics for a population group" (Lawson, 2001, p. 207). Making either of these errors leads to the acceptance of a stereotype in which the conclusion goes far beyond the data on which it is based.

Stereotypes can be convenient: Like emotions, they store a considerable amount of information in quickly accessible form. They may be positive or negative and may help or harm the targeted group, but they always operate as prejudices that bias what is perceived and the way it is interpreted (Crandall, Eshleman, & O'Brien, 2002).

There is a very fine line between sensitivity to the implications of a person's membership in a particular group and losing sight of that person's individuality. Linguistic convenience can easily give rise to stereotyped thinking that undermines respect for the uniqueness of individuals, the avowed goal of multiculturalism. Awareness of different cultures does provide hypotheses about what the majority of some groups *may* believe, but it offers scant information about any given individual. Oddly, psychologists who realize the foolishness of assuming that men and women always conform to the Mars–Venus distinction are generally much more willing to classify people according to their ethnicity.

A PLAN OF ACTION

Multicultural competence is defined as the ability to understand and constructively relate to the uniqueness of each client in light of the diverse cultures that influence each person's perspectives. To achieve this competence, it is necessary to avoid stereotypes and identify the multiple cultural influences that often operate unconsciously in the mixed identities of most clients. The 12 suggestions in Table 1 can help in acquiring the necessary skills.

1. *Develop skill in discovering each person's unique cultural outlook.* Good therapy involves both acceptance and change. Change is easier and more meaningful when grounded in acceptance because new ideas are better comprehended when delivered in the client's literal and figurative languages. The multicultural literature (e.g., American Psychiatric Association, 1994, Appendix 1) identifies areas of culture that are *potentially* relevant to clients. Open-ended questions derived from this literature can be used to determine the psycho-logic of clients' responses, their weltanschauung. Thomas (1999) referred to these as "preferred thematic gestalts . . . [i.e.,] that which feels 'right', how it explains or justifies their life, and how it defines what they think to be their 'true' selves and leaves out what doesn't fit" (p. 142). Ethnographic interviewing can be used to help clients articulate the meaning of their words and actions.

2. *Acknowledge and control personal biases by articulating your own worldview and evaluating its sources and validity.* Multicultural sensitivity begins at home. When a clinician's biases go unchecked, any perceptions of clients reveal more about the therapist than the client. For example,

---

TABLE 1   Twelve Suggestions That Facilitate Multicultural Competence

1. Develop skill in discovering each person's unique cultural outlook.
2. Acknowledge and control personal biases by articulating your worldview and evaluating its sources and validity.
3. Develop sensitivity to cultural differences without overemphasizing them.
4. Uncouple theory from culture.
5. Develop a sufficiently complex set of cultural categories.
6. Critically evaluate the methods used to collect culturally relevant data before applying the findings in psychological services.
7. Develop a means of determining a person's acceptance of relevant cultural themes.
8. Develop a means of determining the salience of ethnic identity for each client.
9. Match any psychological tests to client characteristics.
10. Contextualize all assessments.
11. Consider clients' ethnic and world views in selecting therapists, intervention goals, and methods.
12. Respect clients' beliefs, but attempt to change them when necessary.

Eisenberg (1996) recounted the way in which Charcot influenced a female patient to act in conformity with his expectations of how hysterics act and then accepted her responses as proof of the validity of his assumptions. From Freud through modern behaviorism, ideas that began as thoughtful observations of individuals were recast as universal laws of human behavior (Dowd, 2003). In every instance, such overeager projections have resulted in "cultural parochialism" (Hughes, 1985, p. 21) that has led to the unwarranted imposition of the beliefs of some people upon many. To guard against this, psychologists can benefit by periodically rearticulating their beliefs about human behavior and its management, using the model proposed by Kleinman (1996) to uncover the value assumptions in the fourth edition of the *Diagnostic and Statistical Manual of Mental Disorders* (*DSM–IV*; American Psychiatric Association, 1994). Some of these beliefs pertain to predictions about the behavior of identified groups. Those that originate in the research literature should be evaluated in light of therapists' own experiences. Those that are derived from experience should be crosschecked against the literature. A bidirectional flow between the evolving knowledge base of psychology and clinicians' practice wisdom is the only way to achieve responsible operational theories.

3. *Develop sensitivity to cultural differences without overemphasizing them.* Even when differences between cultures are prominent, it is important to realize that other aspects of group beliefs and behavior may be common across cultures. This is hardly surprising, given the fact that cultures evolve as groups attempt to deal with the universal challenges of human existence. For example, through a 50-nation study, Schwartz and Bardi (2001) found a "surprisingly widespread consensus regarding the hierarchical order of values" (p. 268). In light of this and similar evidence, the observation of one difference should not be the basis for assuming that everything else must be different as well. This is as true for individuals, and so clinicians must avoid the trap of overgeneralizing from observations of one or more anomalies. The failure to do so introduces "cultural red herrings" into clinical assessment (Stein, 1985).

4. *Uncouple theory from culture.* Researchers have identified meaningful differences in thought processes, such as the holistic versus analytic traditions (Nisbett, Peng, Choi, & Norenzayan, 2001) and the Confucian and Socratic reasoning styles (Tweed & Lehman, 2002). Although these patterns have been attributed to broad cultural groups, they are not necessarily the province of any particular group and can be found in people with very diverse characteristics. Moreover, these cognitive styles may be relevant to intervention whether or not the client belongs to the group most associated with them. Rather than coupling cognitive styles with ethnic background, it would be more helpful to offer detailed descriptions of the cognitive orientations and allow clinicians to determine their relevance to a planned intervention. As an example, Perry (1971) described nine "positions" in adult cognitive development. Many spouse abusers have the dualistic orientation found at the low end of Perry's continuum. But some abusers are capable of higher order, relativistic thinking. Rather than offering a standardized treatment to overcome dualism to all abusers, it is wiser to first determine whether the classification applies, trying to change it

only when it does. Bond and Tedeschi (2001) term this "unpackaging" culture at the individual level, through which "the empty, categorical variable of 'culture' is replaced by a measurable, psychological variable as the causal agent. Culture now enters the model as a 'positioning' factor, a set of influences that affect the typical level of that psychological variable" (p. 311). In this way, the focus is on the individual, and culture is introduced as a mediator or moderator when relevant.

5. *Develop a sufficiently complex set of cultural categories.* People have far more diversity than is reflected in the language used by many multiculturalists. Two comparisons illustrate the utility of creating many categories. A Ugandan tribe that permits sex and marriage among family members under prescribed conditions has words for 68 different kinds of relatives so that the rules can be understood and obeyed. And the *DSM–IV* was increased to 312 diagnostic entities from the 106 categories in the first edition of the *DSM* to improve precision in describing psychopathology, with additional categories under consideration. In comparison, a vocabulary limited to such terms as *first-* or *second-generation Asian American* or *on-* or *off-reservation Native American* hardly supports precise clinical assessment. Until a more complex vocabulary is available, it is better to describe rather than categorize clients' identities.

6. *Critically evaluate the methods used to collect culturally relevant data before applying the findings in psychological services.* Unfortunately, because of the complexity of cultures, crosscultural research often suffers from methodological flaws. For example, the *invalidity of measurement* is a problem well illustrated by Freeman's (1999) account of errors in Margaret Mead's influential but essentially inaccurate conclusions about sexual behavior in the Samoan Islands. In addition to controlling interpretive errors like those that beset Mead, one must also determine that the questions and expected answers have equivalent meanings in all cultures in which the measures are used (Cheung & Leung, 1998). Not even back-translation guarantees shared meaning. *Subject selection* is one of two sampling problems in cross-cultural studies. Survey researchers must define the population to which they plan to generalize their results and then draw a sample that is projectable to the larger group (van de Vijver, 2001). Unfortunately, adherence to this standard is a rarity in cross-cultural research, as illustrated in Hofstede's (1980) attempt to extrapolate data from IBM employees to portray the cultures of the 66 countries in which they were employed. This explains the failure of efforts to replicate these results (Fiske, 2002). *Sample size* problems are seen in the use of small convenience samples as a basis for descriptions of huge nations (e.g., Arbisi, Ben-Porath, & McNulty, 2002; Cheung & Ho, 1997). Such studies may provide interesting ideas, but their results cannot be taken at face value. For tests to be used cross-culturally without qualification, the validation sample in the new population must be comparable in size and characteristics to the group used in developing the instrument, *and* the norms for this group must be statistically and clinically similar to those in the original normative sample.

7. *Develop a means of determining a person's acceptance of relevant cultural themes.* It can be useful to learn about a person's acceptance of peer-group and cultural beliefs, and many instruments have been developed for this purpose. At one extreme are simplistic three-item inventories that ask, for example, how closely people identify with their ethnic or racial group, whether they prefer to associate with people like them, and how many of their close friends are indeed like them. Answers to these questions yield crude indications of respondents' ethnicity. At the other extreme are more comprehensive, multi-item inventories that address a range of values, knowledge, and behaviors related to specific cultures (e.g., Cuellar, Arnold, & Maldonado, 1995; Van, Cross, Worrell, & Fhagen-Smith, 2002). Although psychometrically strong instruments like these measure respondents' expressed identification with a particular ethnic group, they do not reveal which specific beliefs and practices are accepted, how strongly each is accepted, or whether acceptance of particular beliefs is situation specific. Test results may be useful sources of general information that can then be validated and refined through sensitive, nondirective interviewing.

8. *Develop a means of determining the salience of ethnic identity for each client.* Ethnicity certainly contributes to identity. However, it may not be the component that is most salient for any given person or situation. Decisions are affected by the interaction among many factors, such as developmental stage, gender, sexual orientation, religion, nationality (as opposed to ethnicity), disability, and occupation (Hays, 2001). Ethnicity may dominate, influence, or be inconsequential with respect to any of these variables. For example, the decision of whether to stay in an abusive relationship by an African American Catholic mother recently diagnosed with breast cancer is not likely to be guided by ethnicity alone, or even primarily. Therefore, sensitive assessment involves asking clients to articulate the sources of their perspectives rather than arbitrarily overweighting any one of them solely on the basis of demographics.

9. *Match psychological tests to client characteristics.* As with every other aspect of developing multicultural sensitivity, test selection and interpretation is far more complex than it first appears. Test data are meaningful when the test has been derived from and normed in the culture of the respondents (Merenda, 1994). But because few such measures exist, psychologists often must use instruments developed in one culture to evaluate clients identified with another. This always carries the risk of finding too little or too much pathology. The temptation to normalize deviant responses to compensate for ethnic influences should be avoided, because it distorts findings (Kehoe & Tenopyr, 1994). It has been suggested that subsets of norms for specific beliefs and behaviors should be developed for cohorts of clients (Okazaki & Sue, 2000). This helps to guard against overpathologizing, but it carries the risk of collecting measurement data that are irrelevant to the client or are not comparable with the groups with which the test was originally developed. Great care must be taken to evaluate the appropriateness of each instrument, and reports must acknowledge that cultural bias may impact findings. It is also prudent to give the examinee the benefit of the doubt in interpreting any abnormal or substandard responses and to consider alternative explanations for such data.

10. *Contextualize all assessments.* It is easy to find commonalities in the behavior of subsets of members of identifiable populations and to attribute these to culturally mediated traits believed to typify these groups. But these same patterns can often be more parsimoniously explained by identifying the similar challenges faced by group members, in which case they are better explained as adaptive reactions to the environment. Whaley (2001) insightfully reframed the "paranoia" attributed to many African Americans as "cultural mistrust" born of decades of negative experience with Caucasians. Rather than ascribing traits to racial or other cultural groups, much as was done in the past to members of certain SES strata, it is prudent to first identify any common environmental stresses and then consider whether "traits" could be relabeled as coping responses.

11. *Consider clients' ethnic and world views in selecting therapists, intervention goals, and methods.* It is often difficult to help people make changes necessary for attaining their goals. Intervention is not likely to succeed when it is offered by providers who do not earn clients' trust, use language or concepts that are not understood, or require behavioral or cognitive skills that the clients lack. An example of a bad match is asking an elderly Korean woman who is haunted by memories of her slavery in a Japanese "comfort station" during World War II to accept service from a Japanese male. So, too, is asking a client whose tradition sees helpers as very active to accept the services of a nondirective therapist. Intelligent matching of providers and methods to clients' preferences and expectations not only removes unnecessary obstacles to effective therapy but also enhances outcome (Morris, 2001).

12. *Respect clients' beliefs, but attempt to change them when necessary.* To be sensitive to another person's culture is to understand the unique way in which specific values, beliefs, and practices help to create meaning. Therapists who are insensitive to clients' beliefs will have great difficulty in establishing the rapport needed to motivate them to make sustainable changes. Empathic therapists see the world from the client's perspective, but they do not necessarily accept everything in the client's view as healthy. Indeed, it may be appropriate for therapists to attempt to change selected beliefs (Rogler, Malgady, Constantino, & Blumenthal, 1987). For example, if a husband believes that his culture permits him to beat his wife when she does not submit to his will, psychologists have an obligation to attempt to change this belief, even if the man's wife accepts the doctrine. In instances such as these, knowledge of the belief system shared by the couple helps to contextualize the abuse, but the professional obligation to prevent harm takes precedence over the mandate to respect diversity.

CONCLUSION

Psychological assessment requires far more than a social history, clinical diagnosis, treatment recommendations, and prognosis. Culturally sensitive assessment requires therapists to respond appropriately to the unique perspectives of each client. To be open to their clients' messages, therapists must be aware of, and control, their own perceptual and interpretative biases. Therapists must recognize and control their own perceptual biases in order to understand the major influences on each client. Acknowledgement of ethnicity is important. But the simple fact that clients are identified with one or more ethnic groups does not make it safe to assume that they accept any of the themes that typify these groups. The cross-cultural literature is a useful guide for generating a list of *hypotheses*, each of

which should take the form of a question rather than a set of assumptions that are routinely accepted. Furthermore, actual clinical experience with ethnic groups can be a source of information to verify and expand the literature. In summary, culturally competent psychological services require self-reflection, a critically evaluative use of the literature, thoughtful accumulation of personal practice wisdom, and above all, a great sensitivity to the uniqueness of each client.

References

American Psychiatric Association. (1994). *Diagnostic and statistical manual of mental disorders* (4th ed.). Washington, DC: Author.

American Psychological Association. (2000). *Resolution on poverty and socioeconomic status.* Washington, DC: Author.

American Psychological Association. (2002). Ethical principles of psychologists and code of conduct. *American Psychologist, 57,* 1060–1073.

Arbisi, P. A., Ben-Porath, Y. S., & McNulty, J. (2002). A comparison of MMPI-2 validity in African American and Caucasian psychiatric inpatients. *Psychological Assessment, 14,* 3–15.

Berkenhoffer, R. (1978). *The White man's Indians: Images of the American Indian from Columbus to the present.* New York: Vantage Press.

Berry, J. W., & Sam, D. (1997). Acculturation and adaptation. In J. W. Berry, M. H. Segall, & C. Kagitcibasi (Eds.), *Handbook of cross-cultural psychology: Social behavior and applications* (pp. 291–326). Boston: Allyn & Bacon.

Bond, M. H., & Tedeschi, J. T. (2001). Polishing the jade: A modest proposal for improving the study of social psychology across cultures. In D. Matsumoto (Ed.), *The handbook of culture and psychology* (pp. 309–324). New York: Oxford University Press.

Cheung, F. M., & Ho, R. M. (1997). Standardization of the Chinese MMPI-A in Hong Kong: A preliminary study. *Psychological Assessment, 9,* 499–502.

Cheung, F. M., & Leung, K. (1998). Indigenous personality measures: Chinese examples. *Journal of Cross-Cultural Psychology, 29,* 233–248.

Crandall, C. S., Eshleman, A., & O'Brien, L. (2002). Social norms and the expression and suppression of prejudice: The struggle for internalization. *Journal of Personality and Social Psychology, 82,* 359–378.

Cross, W. E., Jr. (1991). *Shades of Black: Diversity in African-American identity.* Philadelphia: Temple University.

Cuellar, I., Arnold, B., & Maldonado, R. (1995). Acculturation Rating Scale for Mexican-Americans–II: A revision of the original ARSMA scale. *Hispanic Journal of Behavioral Sciences, 17,* 275–304.

Dana, R. H. (2002). Introduction to special series: Multicultural assessment: Teaching methods and competence evaluation. *Journal of Personality Assessment, 79,* 194–199.

Dowd, E. T. (2003). Cultural differences in cognitive therapy. *Behavior Therapist, 26,* 247–249.

Edlund, M. J., Wang, P. S., Berglund, P. A., Katz, S. J., Lin, E., & Kessler, R. C. (2002). Dropping out of mental health treatment: Patterns and predictors among epidemiological survey respondents in the United States and Ontario. *American Journal of Psychiatry, 159,* 845–851.

Eisenberg, L. (1996). Foreword. In J. E. Mezzich, A. Kleinman, H. Fabrega Jr., & D. L. Parron (Eds.), *Culture and psychiatric diagnosis: A DSM–IV perspective* (pp. xii–xv). Washington, DC: American Psychiatric Press.

Fisher, C. B., Hoagwood, K., Boyce, C., Duster, T., Frank, D. A., Grisso, T., et al. (2002). Research ethics for mental health science involving ethnic minority children and youths. *American Psychologist, 57,* 1024–1040.

Fiske, A. P. (2002). Using individualism and collectivism to compare cultures—A critique of the validity and measurement of the constructs: Comment on Oyserman et al. (2002). *Psychological Bulletin, 128,* 78–88.

Freeman, D. (1999). *The fateful hoaxing of Margaret Mead: A historical analysis of her Samoan research.* Boulder, CO: Westview Press.

Gilens, M. (1999). *Why Americans hate welfare.* Chicago: University of Chicago Press.

Glazer, N. (1997). *We are all multiculturalists now.* Cambridge, MA: Harvard University Press.

Harmetz, A. (2002, March 29). Billy Wilder, master of caustic films, dies at 95. *New York Times,* pp. A1 & A21.

Hays, P. A. (2001). *Assessing cultural complexities in practice: A framework for clinicians and counselors.* Washington DC: American Psychological Association.

Hermans, H. J. M., & Kempen, H. J. G. (1998). Moving cultures: The perilous problems of cultural dichotomies in a globalizing society. *American Psychologist, 10,* 1111–1120.

Hofstede, G. (1980). *Culture's consequences: International differences in work-related values.* Beverly Hills, CA: Sage.

Hollingshead, A. B., & Redlich, F. C. (1958). *Social class and mental illness.* New York: Wiley.

Hughes, C. C. (1985). Culture-bound or construct-bound? The syndromes and *DSM–III.* In R. C. Simons & C. C. Hughes (Eds.), *The culture-bound syndromes: Folk illnesses of psychiatric and anthropological interest* (pp. 3–24). Dordrecht, the Netherlands: D. Reidel.

Kaiser Family Foundation. (2002). *News release: Latinos share distinctive views and attachment to heritage, but attitudes differ by language and place of birth, assimilation at work across generations.* Retrieved January 14, 2003, from www.kff.org

Kehoe, J. F., & Tenopyr, M. L. (1994). Adjustment in assessment scores and their usage: A taxonomy and evaluation of methods. *Psychological Assessment, 6,* 291–303.

Kelly, G. A. (1955). *The psychology of personal construct.* New York: Norton.

Kleinman, A. (1996). How is culture important for *DSM–IV?* In J. E. Mezzich, A. Kleinman, H. Fabrega Jr., & D. L. Parron (Eds.), *Culture and psychiatric diagnosis: A* DSM–IV *perspective* (pp. 15–25). Washington, DC: American Psychiatric Press.

Kroeber, A. L. (1963). *Anthropology: Culture, patterns, and processes.* New York: Harcourt, Brace, Jovanovich.

Lam, A. G., & Sue, S. (2001). Client diversity. *Psychotherapy, 38,* 479–486.

Lawson, A. B. (2001). *Statistical methods in spatial epidemiology.* Chichester, England: Wiley.

McLoyd, V. C. (1998). Socioeconomic disadvantage and child development. *American Psychologist, 53,* 185–204.

Merenda, P. F. (1994). Cross-cultural testing: Borrowing from one culture and applying it to another. In L. L. Adler & U. P. Gielen (Eds.), *Cross-cultural psychology* (pp. 53–58). Westport, CT: Praeger.

Miller, S. M., & Reissman, F. (1961). The working class subculture: A new view. *Social Problems, 9,* 81–96.

Morris, E. F. (2001). Clinical practices with African Americans: Juxtaposition of standard clinical practices and Africentricism. *Professional Psychology: Research and Practice, 32,* 563–572.

Nisbett, R. E., Peng, K., Choi, I., & Norenzayan, A. (2001). Culture and systems of thought: Holistic versus analytic cognition. *Psychological Review, 108,* 291–310.

Okazaki, S., & Sue, S. (2000). Implications of test revisions for assessment with Asian Americans. *Psychological Assessment, 12,* 272–280.

Perry, W. G., Jr. (1971). *Forms of intellectual and ethical development in the college years: A scheme.* New York: Holt, Rinehart & Winston.

Popper, K. R. (1970). Normal science and its dangers. In I. Lakatos & A. Musgrave (Eds.), *Criticism and the growth of knowledge* (pp. 51–58). Cambridge, England: Cambridge University Press.

Rodriguez, R. (2002). *Brown: The last discovery of America.* New York: Viking Press.

Rogler, L. H., Malgady, R. G., Constantino, G., & Blumenthal, R. (1987). What do culturally sensitive mental services mean? The case of Hispanics. *American Psychologist, 42,* 565–570.

Schwartz, S. H., & Bardi, A. (2001). Value hierarchies across cultures: Taking a similarities perspective. *Journal of Cross-Cultural Psychology, 32,* 268–290.

Shipler, D. K. (1997). *A country of strangers.* New York: Knopf.

Simmons, O. G. (1958). *Social status and public health. Pamphlet 13.* New York: Social Science Research Council.

Stein, H. F. (1985). The culture of the patient as a red herring in clinical decision making: A case study. *Medical Anthropology, 17,* 2–5.

Stuart, R. B. (1964). Promise and paradox of socioeconomic status conceptions. *Smith College Studies in Social Work, 35,* 110–124.

Sue, S. (1999). Science, ethnicity, and bias: Where have we gone wrong? *American Psychologist, 54,* 1070–1077.

Surgeon General. (2001). *Mental health: Culture, race, and ethnicity.* Rockville, MD: U.S. Department of Health and Human Services.

Sutton, C. T., & Broken Nose, M. E. (1996). American Indian families: An overview. In M. McGoldrick, J. Giodano, & J. K. Pearce (Eds.), *Ethnicity and family therapy* (pp. 31–44). New York: Guilford Press.

Taylor, E. B. T. (1924). *Primitive culture.* Gloucester, MA: Smith. (Original work published 1871)

Thomas, B. (1999). Reflections on the role of psychological theory in psychotherapy. *Gestalt Review, 3,* 130–146.

Tseng, W.-S. (2003). *Clinicians' guide to cultural psychiatry.* New York: Academic Press.

Tweed, R. G., & Lehman, D. R. (2002). Learning considered within a cultural context: Confucian and Socratic approaches. *American Psychologist, 57,* 89–99.

Whaley, A. L. (2001). Cultural mistrust: An important psychological construct for diagnosis and treatment of African Americans. *Professional Psychology: Research and Practice, 32,* 555–562.

van de Vijver, F. J. R. (2001). The evolution of cross-cultural research methods. In D. Matsumoto (Ed.), *The handbook of culture and psychology* (pp. 77–97). New York: Oxford University Press.

Vandiver, B. J., Cross, W. E., Jr., Worrell, F. C., & Fhagen-Smith, P. E. (2002). Validating the Cross Racial Identity Scale. *Journal of Counseling Psychology, 49,* 71–85.

REFERENCES

American Psychological Association (2002). Ethical principles of psychologists and code of conduct. *American Psychologist, 57,* 1060–1073.

Baker, T. B., McFall, R. M., & Shoham, V. (2009). Current status and future prospects of clinical psychology: Toward a scientifically principled approach to mental and behavioral health care. *Psychological Science in the Public Interest, 9,* 67–103.

Bartley, W. W. (1984). *The retreat to commitment* (2nd ed). New York: Knopf.

Blair, J., Mitchell, D., & Blair, K. (2005). *The psychopath: Emotion and the brain.* Malden, MA: Blackwell.

Bunge, M. (1984). What is pseudoscience? *Skeptical Inquirer, 9*(1), 36–46.

Cardemil, E. V. (2010). Cultural adaptations to empirically supported treatments: A research agenda. *Scientific Review of Mental Health Practice, 8,* 8–21.

Chambless, D. L., & Hollon, S. (1998). Defining empirically supported therapies. *Journal of Consulting and Clinical Psychology, 66,* 7–18.

Chapman, L. J., & Chapman, J. P. (1967). Genesis of popular but erroneous diagnostic observations. *Journal of Abnormal Psychology, 72,* 193–204.

Clancy, S. A. (2005). *Abducted: How people come to believe they were kidnapped by aliens.* Cambridge, MA: Harvard University Press.

Dawes, R. M. (1994). *House of cards: Psychology and psychotherapy built on myth.* New York: Free Press.

Eacott, M. J., & Crawley, R. A. (1998). The offset of childhood amnesia: Memory for events that occurred before age 3. *Journal of Experimental Psychology: General, 127,* 22–33.

Engler, J., & Goleman, D. (1992). *The consumer's guide to psychotherapy.* New York: Simon & Schuster.

Freedman, J., & Fraser, S. (1966). Compliance without pressure: The foot-in-the-door technique. *Journal of Personality and Social Psychology, 4,* 195–202.

Frick, P. J., & White, S. F. (2008). The importance of callous-unemotional traits for the development of aggressive and antisocial behavior. *Journal of Child Psychology and Psychiatry, 49,* 359–375.

Garb, H. N. (1998). *Studying the clinician: Judgment research and psychological assessment.* Washington, DC: American Psychological Association.

Ghaemi, N. (2009). *A clinician's guide to statistics and epidemiology in mental health: Measuring truth and uncertainty.* New York: Cambridge University Press.

Gottesman, I. I. (1991). *Schizophrenia genesis: The origins of madness.* New York: W.H. Freeman.

Hempel, C. R. (1970). *Aspects of scientific explanation.* New York: The Free Press.

Hunsley, J., Lee, C. M., & Wood, J. M. (2003). Controversial and questionable assessment techniques. In S. O. Lilienfeld, S. J. Lynn, & J. M. Lohr (Eds.), *Science and pseudoscience in clinical psychology* (pp. 39–76). New York: Guilford.

Hurley, D. (2005, April 19). The divorce rate: It's not as high as you think. *New York Times.* Retrieved from http://www.nytimes.com/2005/04/19/health/19divo.html on October 2, 2010.

Institute of Medicine (2001). *Crossing the quality chasm.* Washington, DC: National Academies Press.

Kuhn, T. (2009). *The structure of scientific revolutions.* New York: Books, LLC.

Lambert, M. J., Whipple, J. L., Hawkins, E. J., Vermeersch, D. A., Nielsen, S. L., & Smart, D. W. (2003). Is it time for clinicians to routinely track patient outcome?: A meta-analysis. *Clinical Psychology: Science and Practice, 10,* 288–301.

Lilienfeld, S. O. (2007). Cognitive neuroscience and depression: Legitimate versus illegitimate reductionism and five challenges. *Cognitive Therapy and Research, 31,* 263–272.

Lilienfeld, S. O. (2010). Can psychology become a science? *Personality and Individual Differences, 49,* 281–288.

Lilienfeld, S. O., Lohr, J. M., & Olatunji, B. O. (2008). Encouraging students to think critically about psychotherapy: Overcoming naive realism. In D. S. Dunn, J. S. Halonen, & R. A. Smith (Eds.), *Teaching critical thinking in psychology: A handbook of best practices* (pp. 267–271). Boston, MA: Blackwell Publishers.

Lilienfeld, S. O., Lynn, S. J., & Lohr, J. M. (2003). *Science and pseudoscience in clinical psychology.* New York: Guilford.

Lilienfeld, S. O., Lynn, S. J., Ruscio, J., & Beyerstein, B. L. (2010). *50 great myths of popular psychology: Shattering widespread misconceptions about human behavior.* Malden, MA: Wiley-Blackwell.

Lilienfeld, S. O., & O'Donohue, W. T. (Eds.). (2007). *The great ideas of clinical science: The 17 principles that all mental health professionals should understand.* New York: Routledge.

Lilienfeld, S. O., Wood, J. M., & Garb, H. N. (2000). The scientific status of projective techniques. *Psychological Science in the Public Interest, 1,* 27–66.

Loftus, E. F. (1993). The reality of repressed memories. *American Psychologist, 48,* 518–537.

Lykken, D. T. (1995). *The antisocial personalities.* Hillsdale, NJ: Erlbaum.

Mahoney, M. J. (1977). Publication prejudices: An experimental study of confirmatory bias in the peer review system. *Cognitive Therapy and Research, 1,* 161–175.

Matarazzo, J. D. (1990). Psychological assessment versus psychological testing: Validation from Binet to the school, clinic, and courtroom. *American Psychologist, 25,* 999–1017.

McFall, R. M. (1991). Manifesto for a science of clinical psychology. *The Clinical Psychologist, 44,* 75–88.

McFall, R. M. (1996). Making psychology incorruptible. *Applied and Preventive Psychology, 5,* 9–16.

McNally, R. M. (2010). *What is mental illness?* Cambridge, MA: Harvard University Press.

Meehl, P. E. (1959). Some ruminations on the validation of clinical procedures. *Canadian Journal of Psychology, 13*, 106–128.

Meehl, P. E. (1977). Specific etiology and other forms of strong influence: Some quantitative meanings. *Journal of Medicine and Philosophy, 2*, 33–53.

Mischel, W. (2009). Editorial: Connecting clinical practice to scientific progress. *Psychological Science in the Public Interest, 9*(2), i–ii.

Myers, D. (2002). *Intuition: Its promises and perils.* New Haven, CT: Yale University Press.

Myers, D. (2008). *Psychology.* New York: Worth.

Nickerson, R. S. (1998). Confirmation bias: A ubiquitous phenomenon in many guises. *Review of General Psychology, 2*, 175–220.

O'Donohue, W. T., Ammirati, R., & Lilienfeld, S. O. (2011). Quality improvement: Using science to reduce error. In N. Cummings & W. T. O'Donohue (Eds.), *21st century behavioral healthcare reforms* (pp. 203–226). New York: Routledge.

O'Donohue, W. T., & Benutto, L. (2010). The many problems of cultural sensitivity. *Scientific Review of Mental Health Practice, 8*, 34–37.

O'Donohue, W. T., & Lilienfeld, S. O. (2007). Science is an essential safeguard against human error. In S. O. Lilienfeld & W. T. O'Donohue (Eds.), *The great ideas of clinical science: 17 principles that every mental health professional should understand* (pp. 3–27). New York: Routledge.

Patterson, G. (1995). Coercion theory. In W. T. O'Donohue & L. Krasner (Eds.), *Theories of behavior therapy* (pp. 313–348). Washington, DC: American Psychological Association.

Paulos, J. A. (1989). *Innumeracy: Mathematical illiteracy and its consequences.* New York: Hill and Wang.

Pirsig, R. (1974). *Zen and the art of motorcycle maintenance: An inquiry into values.* New York: Harper.

Popper, K. (1959). *The logic of scientific discovery.* New York: Basic Books.

Quine, W. V. O., & Ullian, J. S. (1978). *The web of belief.* New York: Random House.

Ruscio, J. (2006). *Critical thinking in psychology: Separating sense from nonsense.* Pacific Grove, CA: Thomson-Wadsworth.

Sechrest, L. (1963). Incremental validity: A recommendation. *Educational and Psychological Measurement, 23*, 153–158.

Seife, C. (2010). *Proofiness: The dark arts of mathematical deception.* New York: Viking.

Spiegler, M. D., & Guevremont, D. C. (2009). *Contemporary behavior therapy.* Belmont, CA: Wadsworth.

Tversky, A., & Kahneman, D. (1974). Judgment under uncertainty: Heuristics and biases. *Science, 185*, 1124–1130.

Watson, D., & Clark, L. A. (1984). Negative affectivity: The disposition to experience aversive emotional states. *Psychological Bulletin, 96*, 465–490.

Wood, J. M., Lilienfeld, S. O., Nezworski, M. T., Garb, H. N., Allen, K. H., & Wildermuth, J. L. (2010). Validity of Rorschach inkblot scores for discriminating psychopaths from nonpsychopaths in forensic populations: A meta-analysis. *Psychological Assessment, 22*, 336–349.

Yang, M., Wong, S. C. P., & Coid, J. (2010). The efficacy of violence prediction: A meta-analytic comparison of nine risk assessment tools. *Psychological Bulletin, 136*, 740–767.